DR. PITCAIRN'S
COMPLETE GUIDE TO
NATURAL HEALTH
FOR DOGS & CATS

RODALE
LIVE YOUR WHOLE LIFE™

Every day our brands connect with and inspire millions of
people to live a life of the mind, body, spirit — a whole life.

DR. PITCAIRN'S
COMPLETE GUIDE TO
NATURAL HEALTH
FOR DOGS & CATS

RICHARD H. PITCAIRN, DVM, PhD,
AND SUSAN HUBBLE PITCAIRN

RODALE

© 2005 by Richard H. Pitcairn and Susan H. Pitcairn
Cover photograph © by Tsi Pictures/Getty Images

Printed in the United States of America
Rodale Inc. makes every effort to use acid-free ♾, recycled paper ♻.

The lists of natural cleaning methods that appear on pages 142 and 143 are used with the permission of Creative Homeowner © 1998.

Illustrations by Lizzie Harper
Book design by Tara Long

Library of Congress Cataloging-in-Publication Data

Pitcairn, Richard H.
    Dr. Pitcairn's complete guide to natural health for dogs & cats / Richard H. Pitcairn and Susan
Hubble Pitcairn.— 3rd ed., rev. and updated.
       p.   cm.
    Includes index.
    ISBN-13 978–1–57954–973–2 paperback
    ISBN-10 1–57954–973–X paperback
    1. Dogs. 2. Cats. 3. Dogs—Health. 4. Cats—Health. 5. Dogs—Diseases. 6. Cats—Diseases.
I. Pitcairn, Susan Hubble. II. Title.
SF427.P63 2005
636.7'089—dc22   2005013905

Distributed to the trade by Holtzbrinck Publishers

2 4 6 8 10 9 7 5 3 1   paperback

We inspire and enable people to improve their lives and the world around them

For more of our products visit **rodalestore.com** or call 800-848-4735

CONTENTS

FOREWORD

I first heard of Richard Pitcairn twenty years ago. I had been practicing veterinary medicine six years and had developed confidence in my veterinary skills—at least I no longer felt that I was a "new graduate" with only book learning and limited experience. Alongside that confidence, however, I was beginning to see that my new skills often lacked answers for many of my patients' illnesses. I could offer temporary relief, but little else for so many animals with skin disease and other chronic illnesses, who constituted a large portion of my patients.

I began to seek other healing methods and attended a conventional veterinary conference that offered a one-day overview of holistic medicine by Carvel Tiekert, the founder of the American Holistic Veterinary Medical Association. Dr. Tiekert's lecture covered many modalities, including acupuncture, nutrition, and homeopathy. After the presentation, I asked him where he recommended I begin my journey into holistic medicine. He spoke three words: "Get Richard's book." I pressed him a bit further, wondering about courses or other classes, but he merely reemphasized, "Get Richard's book!"

I followed his advice and immediately, as I began perusing the book, I understood why he tendered such a simple recommendation. I found Dr. Pitcairn's (and Susan Pitcairn's) book chock full of advice ranging from nutrition to homeopathic and herbal recommendations for quite a range of common ailments in cats and dogs. Additionally, the Pitcairns offered advice on how lifestyle, emotional support, and toxins affected animal health. While I was not unaware of these factors, I had certainly not learned anything of significance in veterinary school about how central such conditions are in creating healthy animals. My copy quickly became dog-eared, as I referred as often to it as to my texts from veterinary school.

I also ordered several copies to sell in my veterinary hospital, as I believe my primary role as a doctor is to educate my clients in animal care. I feel that I have done my best when my clients no longer need to call me, and Dr. Pitcairn's book helps me lessen my clients' dependence upon me.

A few years later I studied homeopathy with Dr. Pitcairn, and I was immediately impressed with his dedication, his scholarship, and his concern regarding the inadequate education we had received in veterinary school on nutrition and other methods to improve animal health. I also understood why his book was so thorough, well rounded, and clear, as he brought the same qualities to his seminars.

When the second edition of the Pitcairns' book came out, I again purchased a copy for myself as well as copies for my clients, though I had by then sold my veterinary hospital so I could focus on homeopathy, for I also developed (in part through Dr. Pitcairn's teaching and friendship) a love of this unusual branch of medicine.

Now, as I read this third edition, coming twenty years after I first saw the book and twenty-three years after its initial publication, I continue to be impressed with both the evolution of many aspects of the book as well as with the fact that its core information remains as useful and accurate as when it was first written. Additionally, this new edition has the benefit of those extra two and a half decades of Dr. Pitcairn's experience. I especially value the updates and continual emphasis upon nutrition and lifestyle, factors that I also see as paramount in healing. I see in my own practice that feeding animals well and maintaining a healthy, stress-free home (emotionally healthy as well as toxin-free) remain the most important factors in keeping animals and people healthy. And as an ecologist, I deeply appreciate Dr. Pitcairn's guidance in limiting our impact upon nature, offering less toxic options for parasite control and health care.

The treatment sections, of course, contain excellent guidance for what to do when an animal does become sick, with herbal and homeopathic suggestions. You will often be able to treat your animals at home, avoiding the stress of driving them to a veterinary clinic, hospitalization, injections, and the like, all of which can impede healing because of the stress. A rather unexpected (to me, anyway) benefit of holistic medicine is its gentle approach to health. For, while veterinarians all wish to help their patients, those patients tremble at the idea of visiting veterinarians. This was one of my biggest disappointments as a veterinarian. I wanted my patients to like me, but they all feared me— until I began using non-painful, holistic methods like those in this book.

I still refer occasionally to the book for

ideas when I need help with my patients, as there are a lot of gems within its pages. And it remains in my "short list" of recommended reading for my clients. I remain grateful for those like Dr. Tiekert and Dr. Pitcairn, who have guided so many veterinarians and non-veterinarians toward a better understanding of how to heal those animals with whom we share our lives. I believe you will feel the same once you spend a little time with *Dr. Pitcairn's Complete Guide to Natural Health for Dogs and Cats.*

Your animal companions will be grateful as well, not only for helping them stay healthier, but also, more importantly, for keeping them at home, out of those dreaded veterinary hospitals!

—Don Hamilton, DVM
Author, *Homeopathic Care for Cats and Dogs: Small Doses for Small Animals*

PREFACE

I am a very lucky man.

There are few of us that have the good fortune to have their dreams come true. One of my dreams, from an early age, was to be able to relieve the suffering of disease, and even cure (in the true sense of the word) the terrible diseases that afflict our animal friends. Twenty-seven years ago, I "discovered" homeopathic medicine. Along with nutrition, this wonderful method of treatment became the tool that I needed to bring this dream to fruition.

Since converting my practice to the use of homeopathy and nutrition, my experience of being a veterinarian has been transformed. I am really, truly seeing animals get well from conditions that are simply considered incurable or hopeless from the conventional perspective. Not all patients can be helped, of course. It depends on how much damage has been done. However, a much larger percentage of chronically ill animals can be brought to health than one would ever expect from our experience with the dominant school of medicine.

To me, this has been a most illuminating experience. I never thought that there was a system of medicine that could do a better job than what I was taught in veterinary school. How could I have gone through all those years of training and not have heard of it? I now realize that this is the situation for many veterinarians who are looking for a better answer. Responding to this need, in the last few years I have turned my attention to the training of other veterinarians in this system of healing. As I put this third edition of this book "to bed," we are in the middle of the twelfth Professional Course in Veterinary Homeopathy, a post-graduate training program for veterinarians. We have well over 400 veterinarians that have taken this training and are using homeopathic medicine in their practices. In 1995, the Academy of Veterinary Homeopathy was established and serves as the guiding organization for training and research. This is the first veterinary homeopathic professional organization in the United States.

These are very exciting developments for those of us in alternative medicine. I am very grateful for my good fortune in seeing these things come to fruition. I am also very thankful for the wonderful acceptance our book has had among both the public and the veterinary profession, so my final thanks is to you, the reader, for your interest and for your support.

—Richard H. Pitcairn

Everything connects to everything, which connects to everything else. You can't understand life in fragments. That has been a guiding principle behind this book and, I believe, the key to its success and endurance.

From a wider perspective, the topic of natural care for dogs and cats offers an enormous opportunity to show the value of taking a holistic approach to any aspect of life. That has been the real joy in creating it, as a kind of tribute to the sacred wholeness of creation.

Now, even more than the second time

around, I see this book as our admission that, despite our specialized scientific knowledge, we simply cannot grasp the wholeness of life from the details of its workings. So, ultimately, the best we can do in caring for a living creature is to approximate the natural conditions under which it thrived for millions of years, and, where we can, to gently stimulate the natural vital force to right itself when it has become unbalanced. From this perspective, one can meaningfully look anew at every detail of how we care for animals: their diet, their living quarters, their social interactions with other animals and with us, the ways they are affected by the environment, and the use of natural remedies.

From this larger perspective, we are also freed, indeed impelled, to explore past the limits of old assumptions: Perhaps "pet food" is not the only thing that pets can eat; perhaps animals are affected by our thoughts and feelings; perhaps there is a system of healing that trusts and goes with the body's intelligence rather than tinkering with its expression; perhaps we have come to the point that, for our mutual survival, we must consider the ecological impact of our choices.

If this book serves to communicate a healthy respect for the intelligence behind creation and a sense that we would do well to interfere with natural processes as little as possible, then I would know that its deeper purpose, and mine, has been fulfilled.

—Susan Hubble Pitcairn

ACKNOWLEDGMENTS

Producing a book is a lot like making a film. It's a team effort. Yet the authors' or actors' names and faces appear so prominently that we can easily overlook the tremendous contributions made by those working behind the scenes.

Though this is the third edition of this book, we want to repeat our thanks to the editor of the first edition, who helped make it accessible and helpful to so many pet owners. Carol Keough lovingly coached us through the original edition. She carved away the excess, sanded the rough spots and polished the surface until the whole thing began to shine. To her we owe tremendous thanks for the success that this book has become. Special thanks also to my ever-supportive co-workers during that time, Tootie Truesdell and Dottie Warner.

For the updated, revised, and much expanded second edition, Charlie Gerras offered patient, encouraging support and helped us stay at least somewhat on schedule as we struggled to meet the deadlines. Special thanks go to my associate Jana Rygas, DVM, for her detailed contributions to behavioral issues in chapter 11 and to Deborah Kearns and Sheya Rondeau, my dedicated assistants, for years of positive, intelligent service on behalf of natural medicine.

Our appreciation extends no less to the many dedicated people at Rodale Press who worked on both editions, particularly to John Feltman and Mark Bricklin, whose faith and encouragement originally convinced us that we should put our earlier understanding to pen and typewriter, and to Sharon Faelten and Rob Sayre, who urged us to put our increased experience to scanner and keyboard, which resulted in edition two.

This third edition had the gentle guidance of Jennifer Kushnier, my editor at Rodale, who patiently allowed my many absences from "the project" as I traveled for teaching purposes. Thanks also to Jan McLeod for careful fact-checking and the volunteers at Rodale Press for trying out the "new, revised" recipes. Through all the editions there have been many contributors at Rodale and we thank each and every one.

A very special contribution was made by Patti Howard of Washington, D.C., a client and friend who very graciously proof-read each page and made very helpful suggestions as to animal welfare that corrected some of my simplistic understanding. I aspire to her sensitivity.

To Dr. Carvel Tiekert of Bel Air, Maryland, founder of the American Holistic Medical Association, and a good friend, much gratitude for the thoughtful suggestions that enhanced the Quick Reference Section and brought it up to date.

Dr. Lynn Peck, a lecturer at the University of Florida, did a careful reading of the manuscript and helped bring clarity and accuracy at several places. Her assistance is much appreciated.

For the development of our ideas and experience, we are very grateful to the many wonderful clients, readers, and colleagues whose shared commitment to natural healing for animals has made all the difference. In the wider circle of our lives, we are very blessed to have some of the finest clients and colleagues that any veterinarian could ever hope for. You are too many to name, but we treasure the difference you have made in our lives and in this work.

I am especially grateful for those clients that "stayed the course" when the challenge was great—who did not give up or lose hope. It allowed all of us to celebrate the victory of recovery of health and gave me the opportunity to learn in the most difficult of situations.

To Anitra Frazier, author of *The New Natural Cat*, heartfelt thanks for years of support and encouragement. Special gratitude to Jessica Higgs, my assistant, for her cheery and generous self.

When it comes to the heart of this book, and the ideas within it, it is graced by hundreds of pioneers whose commitment to healing and understanding has inspired, informed, challenged, taught and healed us and many others. I am deeply grateful to Dr. Samuel Hahnemann who devoted his entire life to the development of homeopathy, a medicine of gentleness and beauty.

Lastly, to all the animals of the world, both domestic and wild, who feel, who suffer too much, yet show delight and forgiveness to us, who share with us the fate of this increasingly fragile planet—we offer our appreciation and the hope that this work will be of benefit.

To them, and to all the human members of the "crew," we dedicate this book.

—Richard H. Pitcairn, DVM, PhD
—Susan Hubble Pitcairn, MS

PART ONE

NATURAL HEALTH FOR PETS

"SENSITIVE ASSAYS HAVE DETECTED RESIDUES OF OVER A HUNDRED DIFFERENT FOREIGN CHEMICALS AND METALS IN OUR TISSUES—COMPOUNDS AND SUBSTANCES THAT WERE VIRTUALLY ABSENT FROM THE ENVIRONMENTS OF OUR PREDECESSORS."

—MARC LAPPÉ

CHAPTER 1

WE NEED A NEW APPROACH TO PET HEALTH CARE

"Why don't you take care of this one?" my colleague asked me, with the look of someone about to unload an unwelcome problem. He pointed through the door to a little middle-aged dog sitting forlornly on the examining table. If his coat had ever been sleek, soft, and healthy, it was no more. Obviously, his hair had been falling out for some time, revealing large greasy patches that had an unpleasant odor. Even his spirits were low. Unfortunately, I'd seen cases like his all too often.

Waiting nearby were the dog's equally dejected guardians, an aging couple who had "tried it all" and still cared enough about their little companion to try once more. The dog's hospital record showed a long history of treatments—cortisone shots, medicated soaps, ointments, more shots, more salves—none of which brought any noticeable improvement.

"The poor little guy is just *so miserable*, doctor," began Mrs. Wilson anxiously. "We would do anything if we thought it would help."

It didn't take me long to decide that it was finally time to step off the beaten path and try out a new nutritional approach to this kind of case, an idea that had been brewing in my mind for some time. We were at a medical dead end and there was nothing to lose. But more importantly, I knew there was a good chance that what I had in mind might work. As I examined Tiny, I explained to the Wilsons why I thought an improved diet was their animal's best chance for recovery.

"Skin problems like his are probably the most common and frustrating of the conditions we try to deal with," I told them. "Because the skin is such a visible area of the body, it can show the first signs of underlying problems, particularly those caused by inadequate diet. The skin grows very rapidly, making a whole new crop of cells about every three weeks. It needs a lot of nourishment, so when the diet lacks what's really needed, the skin is one of the first tissues to break down and show abnormalities like the kind we see here in Tiny."

As we went on talking about the effects of diet and the shortcomings of highly processed pet foods based on low-quality food by-products, the Wilsons saw that a change could make a big difference. So we worked out a suitable feeding program for Tiny, emphasizing fresh natural foods.

Starting now, Tiny would eat meat, whole grains, and fresh vegetables. In addition, the Wilsons would give him several supplements rich in nutrients important to the health of the skin as well as to the rest of the body—brewer's yeast, vegetable oil, cod-liver oil, kelp, bonemeal, vitamin E, and zinc. I also recommended that they bathe Tiny occasionally with a mild, non-medicated shampoo to help remove irritating, toxic secretions from his skin without burdening his body with harsh chemicals.

During the next weeks, my thoughts often went to Tiny, wondering how he was doing on this new treatment. A month after their first visit, the Wilsons returned to show the results of the treatment. Tiny was like a new dog.

"You wouldn't believe the difference!" Mrs. Wilson exclaimed. "He runs around and plays like he's a puppy again." Tiny was indeed full of life, jumping around excitedly on the examining table. His coat was much healthier, and hair was rapidly filling in the previously bare spots.

It was very rewarding to all of us, but most of all to Tiny. For the Wilsons, there was the added benefit of realizing that their dog's health was now in their control and that keeping him well did not require monthly injections of cortisone or other medications.

A NEW SENSE OF PURPOSE TAKES HOLD

Tiny's case was one of my first clinical attempts to apply the results of a long learning process concerning the vital role of nutrition in health. Now, after 27 years of seeing successes such as this with improved diet, the essential importance of nutrition in restoring health is obvious to me.

I did not, however, always approach cases in such a manner. My veterinary school training in nutrition had included little more than the admonition: "Tell your clients to feed their animals a good commercial pet food and to avoid table scraps." Beyond that, nutrition just wasn't considered an important part of our education. I accepted this attitude at face value, and after graduation I set out to conquer disease, armed with the usual arsenal of drugs and surgical techniques gleaned from my years of schooling.

Faced with the day-to-day challenges of my first job in a busy mixed practice (small and large animals), I soon learned that many diseases simply did not respond to treatments as I had been told they would. In fact, it often seemed that what I did to help mattered very little. I was like a bystander at the battle for recovery—doing a lot of cheering and occasionally making a contribution of sorts, but often feeling ineffectual.

So I tried to make sense of what I saw, and gradually several basic questions arose: Why do some animals recover easily, while others never seem to do well, regardless of which drugs are used? Why do some animals in a group seem to have all the fleas and catch all the diseases going around, while others are never affected? I knew there must be some basic understanding that I just didn't grasp about the ability of an animal's body to defend and heal itself.

When you ask a question long enough and deeply enough, life seems to provide the opportunity to find an answer. Soon a job offer as an instructor at a veterinary school was dropped in my lap. Always eager to be in a climate of learning, I immediately accepted.

Once I was back in academia, I decided to take a course or two myself. The next thing I knew, I was a full-time graduate student in veterinary immunology, virology, and biochemistry. Surely here, I thought, I can learn the real secrets of the body's defense systems. And so I set about studying and researching various problems, particularly the body's immune response to cancer.

Some five years and a PhD degree later, I found that the answers to my questions still eluded me. Though I had acquired an even greater wealth of factual information about the mechanisms of immunology and metabolism, I still did not feel a sense of real insight about the issues that concerned me.

THE BIG PICTURE: THE HOLISTIC APPROACH

I had begun to realize what was causing me to feel baffled by conventional veterinary medicine. Knowledge was fragmented, and specialists clung to narrow academic disciplines. For example, one group of immunologists would hold a particular viewpoint on disease mechanisms and a second group, a different view. It seemed that no effort was being made to reconcile the opposing positions. And then there were the microbiologists, the virologists, the biochemists, the pathologists, and a host of others, all of whom tended to see things through different sets of filters! Our research aims had become so narrowly defined and carried out that we were missing the whole picture. I didn't fully realize it at the time, but I felt, somehow, that what we really needed was a holistic approach to the problem of disease.

As a result, I started doing two things that were decisive and have continued to define my style of operation ever since. One was to read broadly in many fields and from many sources to get a larger scope of concepts and ideas. The other was to experiment with new ideas that made sense to me by trying them out on myself.

I made it a first priority to learn more about nutrition. After some self-directed study, I was convinced that nutrition was a very significant factor in maintaining health and treating disease. Therefore, it amazed me to find that the indifference to nutrition that prevailed when I was a student in veterinary school was still in place. There was a wealth of research, for example, showing that a number of specific vitamins are essential to the normal functioning of the im-

mune system—though they were never mentioned throughout my years of graduate study. Most surprising to me was the fact that proper nutrition could boost the body's natural resistance to disease. Here was an incredible truth—unique in that it meant the body need not rely on drugs for better health. With this information, people could take charge of their own health. At last I was beginning to find some answers to my questions.

PERSONAL DIVIDENDS FROM A DIET CHANGE

I decided to change my own diet. I began to use whole grains, to cut out sugars and other junk foods, to eat less meat, and to take supplements like nutritional yeast, wheat germ, and various vitamins. Before long I was feeling better than I had in years.

I also started exercising regularly, using herbs, and exploring my inner life. All these measures eventually played a part in removing some things from my life that I didn't need—like a potbelly I was developing, plus colitis, ear infections, excess tension, susceptibility to colds and flu, and a number of negative psychological habits.

Though these personal experiments didn't constitute so-called statistically significant studies, they were tremendously valuable to me. There is nothing more convincing about the value of a treatment than feeling better after using it. You don't need the interpretation or opinion of any authority to acknowledge positive changes in your own body and mind.

After helping myself, I began to apply my newfound knowledge to animals—first my own pets and then, as I returned to clinical practice, to some "hopeless" cases like Tiny. At one point, I adopted a stray kitten half-starved and ragged from life in the woods. We named her Sparrow because she looked like a small bird made up mostly of feathers and fluff. At first, I fed her a conventional kibble and she did all right. But when she became pregnant a year or two later, I decided to boost her strength. I faithfully added fresh, raw beef liver, raw eggs, bonemeal, fresh chicken, brewer's yeast, and other nutritious foods to her daily fare.

Unlike many cats I've seen, she never lost any weight or hair during pregnancy, and her delivery was exceptionally fast, easy, and calm. She always had plenty of milk to nurse her three large, thriving kittens, and all of them grew up to be much larger than their mother. I kept one of these kittens and continued adding supplements to the diets of both mother and offspring, who became very chubby and happy. I was always amazed at how remarkably healthy they were. I never needed to use any flea control on them. And if one of these cats got scratched or bitten in a fight, the injury healed quickly and never developed into an infection or abscess. Sparrow lived to the ripe age of 18 years and never needed veterinary care for any of the common cat problems.

One thing led to another, and soon I be-

came deeply interested in using herbs as a treatment. A particular occasion convinced me that these natural remedies could bring about almost miraculous cures. It was late one Sunday night and my son, Clark (then about six), was besieged by a high fever, flushed face, swollen throat glands, and incipient bronchitis (to which he was prone). He was very restless and cried with extreme discomfort and pain. I had nothing in the house to give him except some aspirin, which neither reduced his fever nor enabled him to get to sleep.

I felt stuck, and I thrashed about in my mind, desperately searching for some way to help Clark. Then all at once I remembered I had some goldenseal (*Hydrastis canadensis*) capsules in the house. Goldenseal has been found very useful for reducing inflammation of the lining of the bronchial tubes, the nose, and the eustachian tubes (which drain the ears to the throat), especially when the inflammation is accompanied by a harsh, dry cough and fever. I gave him one capsule with a little water. Five to ten minutes later, Clark suddenly got up and, for the first time in hours, went to the bathroom and voided a large quantity of urine. Afterward, he lay down, relaxed, and fell asleep. Clark's fever dropped rapidly, and by the next morning he was normal.

As you can imagine, this experience was very encouraging to me. Looking back, I realize how fortunate I was to have hit it so perfectly. Goldenseal was quite appropriate for the symptoms my son showed. This remarkable experience inspired me to pursue many fruitful directions later on, such as herbology, naturopathy, and, especially, homeopathy. This last has completely changed my understanding of the nature of disease and its cure.

Though I eventually branched out in other directions, I have found over the years that proper nutrition is the essential foundation of a holistic approach to health and healing. Without it, there is little to work with in helping an animal to recover. And I feel certain that many of the chronic and degenerative diseases we see today are caused by or complicated by inadequate diet.

After all, the physical body requires certain substances it cannot make internally. As with any complicated and delicate machinery, one missing element in the fuel that powers the body can bring the whole mechanism to a standstill. For example, it appears that the immune system, with its production of specialized white blood cells and antibodies, is particularly susceptible to nutritional imbalance. Perhaps, because of the fast growth of these specialized cells and their complex function, deficiencies show up sooner here than in, say, the skeletal system.

That said, let's take a closer look at what your animal friend is actually eating. What is and isn't provided by the diet can make a big difference in your pet's health.

CHAPTER 2

WHAT'S REALLY IN PET FOOD

As I present this chapter, I realize that you could read it and just become discouraged and depressed about the whole challenge of feeding your pet properly. I don't want that to happen. I think it necessary to inform you about pet foods so you can understand how important this issue is. It is true that I am not going to have good things to say about most commercial pet foods, and because the advertising for these products is so frequently encountered and so convincing, it is not enough for me to say "Don't use them." Instead, I am going to go into some detail about what is in pet food, the problems associated with processed and packaged products, and also the lack of quality control that is typical of the industry.

After we're done with this chapter we'll look at nutritional solutions available to you—how you can prepare food yourself with simple recipes that are superior to most of what is out there. The encouraging news is that these recipes have been used for more than 20 years by my clients and by readers of the previous editions of this book with great success. So do not despair.

I find that animals respond very quickly and positively to a nutritious diet. In fact, it is the *major tool* you need to eliminate many of the chronic diseases your animal encounters in these times. If you follow the guidelines in this book, it is almost certain that your animal will become more healthy. I assure you that it is entirely possible to overcome the effects of prior feeding of poor quality foods, even if such a feeding practice spans years. It is actually surprising how quickly health will improve thanks to such a simple change. So screw up your courage and come with me into the little-explored world of pet foods.

LABELS CAN BE MISLEADING

The consumer is often told to "look at labels" as the way to identify which foods are best. It sounds good. Unfortunately, the way labeling is used does not really help us understand the quality of the food. For example, one of the important ingredients, one we are cautioned especially to check, is protein. But if we just look at total protein, as indicated on the label, we have not considered two important factors: *biological value* and *digestibility*. Let's see if we can understand these terms.

A protein's *biological value* (which has also been called the nitrogen balance index) depends on each protein's unique composition of the amino acids that make it up. These amino acids are building blocks from which the body constructs its own tissues. Eggs are given an ideal value of 100, which means they are the most useful form of protein known. On this relative scale, fish meal is ranked 92, beef and milk 78, rice 75, soybeans 68, yeast 63, and wheat gluten 40.

The *digestibility* of a protein (or any food) is simply the extent to which the gastrointestinal tract (stomach and intestines) can actually absorb it. For example, one source might be 70 percent digestible, whereas another is 90 percent. Some proteins—like those in hair—are less digestible because they are harder or impossible for the body to break down, even though they are still proteins.

Interestingly, the prolonged high temperatures used to sterilize some pet foods can destroy much of the usefulness of even those proteins that start with a high biological value. That's because the heat causes proteins to combine with certain sugars, naturally occurring in the food, to form compounds that can't be broken down by the body's digestive enzymes. After all, these foods that are heat-processed at these high temperatures have never been encountered by the digestive systems of animals before. How could evolution have prepared them to break them down?

Because manufacturers are required to list only the amount of *crude protein*, rather than the amount that your pet can actually digest and use, they can and do include inexpensive sources that may supply your pet with much less usable protein than you would imagine. Most people don't realize that terms like "meat by-products" can actually mean poultry feather meal, connective tissues (gristle), leather meal (yes, leather, like that used to make belts or shoes), fecal waste from poultry and other animals, and horse and cattle hair. Robert Abady, founder of the Robert Abady Dog Food Company, describes meat and bone meal as "generally comprised of ground bone, gristle, and tendons, and is the cheapest and least nutritious of the by-product meals." The same is true of lamb meal, poultry or chicken meal, or fish meal.

All of these are widely used in pet foods. Such ingredients would certainly boost the *crude* protein content, but provide relatively little nourishment. (It's surely not *my* idea of a good meal for an animal.)

Because of the addition of tough, fibrous ingredients, dogs are typically able to utilize only about 75 percent of the protein in meat meal. And all meat meal is made even less digestible by the high cooking temperatures required to sterilize it. Dried blood meal, another cheap ingredient, contains even less usable protein.

As with protein, other basic ingredients can vary widely in both quality and digestibility.

Carbohydrates can be an excellent source of nutrients. In many products, however, as in a soft-moist dog food, they usually come from such empty-calorie sources as sugar (sucrose), propylene glycol, and corn syrup. I have also been told that leftover donuts from the fast-food industry have been used as carbohydrates in pet food, as well as moldy and rancid grains unacceptable for human consumption. Higher quality products, on the other hand, will contain complex carbohydrates from whole grains—which are much more nutritious. Except for the sugars, it is difficult to tell by reading the label just what you are getting in your pet food.

Other examples of carbohydrate sources are:

❖ Rice flour—finely powdered, usually the end process of milling and of very low nutritional value.

❖ Beet sugar—the dried residue from the sugar beet.

❖ Corn gluten meal—dried residue from corn after the removal of starch, germ, and bran. Little, if any, nutritional value.

❖ Brewer's rice—rice sections that have been discarded from the manufacturing of beer, which contain pulverized, dried, spent hops. Little, if any, nutritional value.

❖ Rancid or moldy grains—unacceptable for human use.

Fats most often come from animal fats rejected for human consumption. Such fats may be rancid, a state that makes the fats actually toxic to the body. Rancidity also robs fats of essential vitamins.

Fiber may simply come from whole grains and vegetables, or it can mean that extra filler fiber has been added from sources like peanut hulls, hair, or even newspapers.

As you see, by itself the chemical analysis on the label does not mean a whole lot. To underscore this point, one veterinarian concocted a product containing the same composition of the basic proteins, fats, and carbohydrates as a common brand of dog food by using old leather shoes, crankcase oil, and wood shavings. My point is that labels don't always tell us enough. Be especially wary of pet food that lists its ingredients in generic categorical terms like these:

❖ Meal and bone meal

❖ Meat by-products

❖ Dried animal digest

❖ Poultry by-product meal

❖ Poultry by-products

❖ Digest of poultry by-products

❖ Liver glandular meal

❖ Chicken by-products

❖ Dried liver digest

❖ Fish meal

❖ Fish by-products

The Pet Food Institute, which represents the industry, has repeatedly sought permission from the Food and Drug Administration (FDA) to use more of these collective ingredient terms. The industry members argue that it allows them to choose a "least cost mix" from each class of ingredients. Some of the sought-after terms have included "processed animal and marine protein products," "vegetable products," and "plant fiber products." Can you see how a term like "vegetable products" doesn't really tell us anything about what is in the food? After all, a vegetable product can mean any part of any plant or the residue of any plant after manufacturing. They want these labels to be used because they are so vague and ill-defined, and it gives them much latitude in choosing what to put in the food under the same label term.

Can you imagine "poultry by-products" or "dried animal digest" used by less reputable manufacturers to include such waste ingredients as feathers or hair in your pet's dinner? The supposition isn't farfetched. I remember reading a news story some years back of a large commercial bakery using wood pulp as a fiber source in one of its bread products for *humans.*

The second factor that complicates comparisons among pet food labels is varying moisture content. To compensate for its effect on the nutritional analysis, you would have to do a little math.

For instance, the label on a can of dog food may say that the protein content is 6 percent. Yet the label on a box of inexpensive kibble may say the contents are 20 percent protein. Sounds like a lot more, doesn't it? Well, that comparison can easily mislead you.

To compare percentages of any nutrient in pet foods accurately, you must first level the playing field by converting each food to a percentage of the total dry weight. It is only fair that we compare fresh, canned, or kibbled foods after we take the water factor out, isn't it? The more water present in the food to start with, the less concentrated the different ingredients are.

Imagine squeezing every single drop of water out of the canned food or the kibble and *then* measuring the proportion of protein in the solids that remain. That figure is the percentage of protein by *dry weight*. If that is done with each food we are going to compare, then we are able to make direct and accurate estimations of the content of each nutrient. And it is usually the case that, with the water removed, canned foods actually have a higher proportion of protein than dry foods.

But remember, there's no easy way to determine what percentage of protein is actually usable by the animal, and this is where you can be fooled again by the labeling.

WHAT ABOUT VITAMINS AND MINERALS?

While various vitamins, minerals, and amino acids are usually added to pet foods to make up for what is lost in processing, the exact amount is not stated. Additionally, some of the vitamins present in the original ingredients, or added by the manufacturer and therefore listed on the label, may be lost before your animal ever eats the food. They can be destroyed by heat processing, especially in the presence of oxygen, and by interactions with other substances, like chemical contaminants, or by exposure to air during the shelf storage of the product.

Vitamins A, E, and B_1, all important in fighting disease, are particularly susceptible to such loss. For example, researchers report that a number of cat foods are so low in vitamin B_1 that they create deficiencies after only a few weeks of feeding them to your cat. Another study shows that the processing method used in a certain cat food altered its vitamin B_6 in a way that made it useless to cats' bodies, and deficiency symptoms followed. Furthermore, cats fed low-fat diets absorb vitamin A rather poorly. This problem is of most concern for cats on dry food, which is, by necessity, fairly low in fat. Vitamin A is essential to health, important in resistance to infections, repair of tissues, and for maintenance of good vision. Deficiency can result in loss of appetite, loss of smell, soft teeth that decay easily, and several other unpleasant outcomes.

Minerals added to a product may be chemically complete in their basic chemical form, but can lack the associated complex organic structures found in natural foods. These naturally formed complexes in which minerals are stored in the body are often referred to as chelates. Sometimes this association is created artificially and sold as "chelated minerals" in natural food stores, but, of course, the best form is that available in whole foods.

Undoubtedly there is a great deal we still don't understand about the way nutrients act and interact within the body. Manufacturers might add a number of synthetic or isolated vitamins and minerals and still not fully replace those natural forms lost in processing or insufficiently supplied in the first place. As I see it, this also means that trying to provide a natural diet that is as nutritious as possible is safer and more beneficial than using denatured or low-quality food and then trying to compensate by adding in a few isolated nutrients. Through our ignorance, we may be leaving out crucial but little-understood ingredients.

INSTA-MEAL

In spite of our discussion thus far on the inadequacies of labeling, let's imagine that somebody actually put together a packaged food that has all the nutrients that have been discovered as necessary so far. It is marketed as a "complete" diet for human beings called "Insta-Meal." At last science and business have combined their know-how to provide you with a simpler, cheaper way to handle the daily chore of planning and preparing meals.

The label looks good. It says this product contains all the recommended daily requirements for fats, carbohydrates, proteins, vitamins, and minerals needed to keep you

ticking. To compensate for any loss of natural nutrients in processing, the manufacturer has added an array of synthetic vitamin and mineral compounds bearing such impressive names as pyridoxine hydrochloride, calcium pantothenate, iron carbonate, potassium chloride, and manganous oxide—everything that nutritionists have found necessary.

To make Insta-Meal look more appetizing, the manufacturer has added a sprinkling of FD&C Red No. 40 and seasoned the mixture with a dash of disodium guanylate (a flavoring commonly used in instant soups and processed Chinese foods). And to give the product a long shelf life, the makers have tucked in a little butylated hydroxy-anisole (a common preservative known as BHA).

The least expensive version of this revolution in eating is blended, extruded, and cut into bite-size chunks about the size of croutons, then baked until crunchy. According to the ads, you can now have a complete diet for less than half the cost of eating the old-fashioned way. And all you need to do is shake some of the bits into a bowl and serve a little tap water on the side. What could be simpler?

Worried about variety? You might try these exciting variations:

❖ To every three cups of Insta-Meal, add one cup of hot water. Mix and let stand a couple of minutes. New Insta-Meal makes its own tasty sauce.

❖ Mix two cups of Insta-Meal with two cups of milk, broth, or water in your blender. Pour into a greased loaf pan and bake at 350°F for 20 minutes. Presto! InstaCasserole!

❖ Prefer a hearty, meaty style? Try our five canned flavors—Tuna Twist, Chunky Chicken, Mulligan Stew, Turkey Dressing, or, for vegetarians, Savory Soylinks.

❖ For that occasional sweet tooth, try new soft-moist Insta-Patties, preserved with sugar. This item comes in four fruity flavors.

The whole concept of Insta-Meal for humans is repulsive. Who would want to eat this same food over and over again? It is obvious that the "variations" are a joke. Yet, somehow, we have accepted the idea that such a diet is right for our pets. Perhaps the thought of eating kibbles for the rest of your own life helps make the point that pets forced to do so are being shortchanged.

OKAY FOR YOUR PET, NOT OKAY FOR YOU?

According to the manufacturer and several authorities on nutrition, the insta-system is much better than the old haphazard way of eating. In fact, you'd do best to eat only Insta-Meal the rest of your life.

But *would* you? Certainly you'd refuse such a diet, even if there were a "natural" variety, free of artificial additives. Not only would you long for the taste of a varied and natural diet, but your body would know something was missing.

Most people would soon be climbing the walls in frustration, desperate for a salad or some fruit—anything whole and fresh. Or just different! And while lying awake at night, you might wonder about the true meaning of some common Insta-Meal label ingredient terms like bakery by-products, poultry meal, and (shudder) sterilized restaurant by-products.

I have nothing personal against the makers of processed foods for pets, nor do I seek to put them out of business. They're probably doing their best to provide nutritionally balanced products at reasonable prices, making use of materials that might otherwise go to waste or just be used as fertilizer. It's just that I don't believe *any* version of completely cooked, dried, canned, or frozen prepared food constitutes an optimal diet for the good health of either human or beast. I believe all of us—humans and animals—should have a variety of fresh, wholesome, unprocessed food included in our daily diets.

At first many Americans are surprised at the idea of feeding pets what they call people food. It doesn't seem proper. However, Europeans feed their dogs much more naturally, minimizing the use of commercial foods. Many breeders have commented to me that such European dogs are far healthier than American dogs. No diet that we can formulate from least-cost products and process for convenience and long storage can ever rival those mysteriously complex fresh-food diets offered for eons by Nature herself.

OBJECTIONS TO COMMERCIAL PET FOODS

The many objections we can make about the nutritional quality of animal convenience foods fit into two categories. First, they *don't* contain some things we wish they *did*: adequate quantities and qualities of proteins, fats, vitamins, and minerals, as well as the more intangible qualities unique to live, fresh foods. Second, they *do* contain other things we wish they *didn't*:

- ❖ Slaughterhouse wastes
- ❖ Toxic products from spoiled foodstuffs
- ❖ Non-nutritive fillers
- ❖ Heavy-metal contaminants
- ❖ Sugar
- ❖ Pesticides and herbicides
- ❖ Drug residues
- ❖ Artificial colors, flavors, and preservatives
- ❖ Bacteria and fungi contaminants

When you feed your pet convenience foods, you unknowingly help to create another problem: The presence of various toxins and pollutants actually *increases* the body's need for high-quality nutrients necessary for combating or eliminating these same contaminants. When the overall nutrition is already lower than it should be, we are inviting trouble.

"But wait," you say, "my cat loves this dry food and won't eat anything else!" I have heard this statement many times. But here's the thing to understand: Animals don't know

any better. When a food has the right smell and taste, like those they have become used to over the last several millennia, they will eat it. Have you ever heard an ad for pet food in which the statement is made about all the research that has gone into the making of the food? Have you every wondered about how much of that "research" was discovering that irresistible flavor?

So far, we have considered a couple of important factors: the issue of how commercial pet foods are labeled and how misleading that can be in determining their value, as well as how feeding the same processed food over and over again clearly cannot support the same level of health that follows a natural diet. Now let's turn to the quality of commercial pet foods.

THE QUALITY OF PET FOODS

Pet food makers make a big effort to produce competitive, consistent products manufactured from a fluctuating market of least-cost ingredients. Using computerized analyses, they draw from these constituents to presumably make a product that meets or exceeds minimal nutritional standards for dogs and cats. Two questions concern us now: What are these standards, and are they enforced?

The usual standard is that set by the Association of American Feed Control Officials (AAFCO) which "is a private advisory body whose members are representatives of individual state and government agencies, the U.S. Food and Drug Administration and other federal and foreign agencies that share responsibilities in the regulation of animal feed."

Like me, you likely assumed that pet food is regulated as to *quality* by organizations like this, right? AAFCO, however, has no input as to the ingredients actually used in pet foods, as it has no enforcement authority and does no analytical testing on pet food or the sources of protein, fiber, or fats used. Feeding trials, which are done for some (not all) of the foods are "either run by the company itself or by a contracted facility, and the company then attests to the results."

Even more disappointing, as Ann Martin reports in her book *Food Pets Die For*, acceptance of even the AAFCO standard of quality is not universal. She sent a letter to each state asking, "Could you please advise if your state adheres to the AAFCO guidelines regarding pet food ingredients?" Ann had replies from only 20 states. Of these 20, just 13 stated that they adhere to AAFCO guidelines. Some officially have no guidelines at all.

Some of the food you buy might say "USDA inspected." But the point to realize is that the inspection was to determine if the food was suitable *for human consumption*. What was not edible goes into pet food. So it is incorrect to think that because the food is inspected, what your pet is eating is of high quality. It actually means the opposite—that *because* it is inspected, your dog or cat is eating the discarded remnants. An even

more shocking fact, to me, is that the standard for human beings, which is higher than that for animal food, is so low.

Prevention magazine once published a letter from a reader who offered an inside glimpse of the pet food industry:

I once worked in a chicken butchering factory in Maine. Our average daily output was 100,000 chickens. . . . Directly ahead of me on the conveyor line were the USDA inspectors and their trimmers. The trimmers cut the damaged and diseased parts off the chickens and dropped them in garbage cans, which were emptied periodically. These parts were sent to a pet food factory.

So the next time you hear a pet food commercial talk about the fine ingredients they use in their product, don't you believe it.

Similarly, a story appeared in our local paper revealing that dead animals found on the highway are sent to rendering plants, where they are used in pet food. The reporter actually talked to the Road Department, which led him to Animal Control, which then led him to Eugene Chemical & Rendering Works, where he was told the rendered material was sold to companies that make pet (and livestock) feed. Similar reports have surfaced, so I don't think this is just a local phenomenon. Ann Martin offers considerable evidence in her book that pets are routinely rendered by veterinary hospitals or shelters and recycled into pet food.

It is very difficult to determine exactly what pet food makers are using as ingredients. It can change on any day, and they don't volunteer information like this. It takes some insider information or good detective work to find these things out. There are no federal regulations against using what are called 4-D sources—that is, tissues from animals that are dead, dying, disabled, or diseased when they arrive at the slaughterhouse.

HEALTH EFFECTS?

What effect might these wastes be having on animals? After all, maybe it is entirely acceptable to feed these by-products to animals. Don't they eat all sorts of stuff off the ground, even digging up dead animals to eat at times? This statement is generally true for canines, but not wild cats, that eat only freshly killed prey. Wolves and dogs seem to be able to eat meat that is not fresh, even partly decayed, without becoming ill. But here is the difference—in nature, the animals captured and eaten are not chronically ill or filled with drugs or hormones. Having worked with livestock medicine in my early years, I know that a significant percent of the animals sent to slaughter, but not suitable for human consumption, have first been extensively treated with drugs. Since veterinary treatment failed, they are then processed for whatever monetary value can be captured by turning them into food—even pet food.

It is a similar situation for the animals killed on the highway. Yes, it is possible that a deer was healthy when hit by a car and killed. This meat would be considered appropriate to use. But think of the many agricultural fields sprayed with insecticides or herbicides. Animals caught in these fields or that enter them after they are sprayed can become sick and disoriented, wandering into a road where they are easily killed.

The pets recycled from veterinary hospitals or shelters can have high levels of antibiotics and various other drugs (in the last attempt to keep them alive), or perhaps the final euthanasia solution. Most of these drugs end up in the food. That is why animals that have had drug therapy are not used in human food. It would make people sick.

From his experience as a veterinarian and federal meat inspector, P. F. McGargle, DVM, has concluded that feeding slaughterhouse wastes to animals increases their chance of getting cancer and other degenerative diseases. This practice has also been related to mad cow disease, which is discussed in chapter 3. Those wastes, he reported, can include moldy, rancid, or spoiled processed meats, as well as tissues riddled with cancer.

These meat scraps can also contain hormone levels comparable to amounts that have produced cancer in laboratory animals. Dr. McGargle attributed these high levels to two causes: synthetic hormones routinely fed to livestock to stimulate rapid growth, and meat meal, often produced from glandular wastes and fetal tissues from pregnant cows. Both are naturally high in hormones. When this material is processed, even by high heat, the hormones remain active. Ironic, isn't it, that the high heat destroys nutrients but retains the harmful drugs? High hormone levels have the most severe effect on cats, who are extremely sensitive to them. The hormone implants that are used to fatten steers and caponize male chickens, for example, are considered toxic to cats, even in *very low* levels.

WHY SOME PET FOOD SMELLS THAT WAY

Although USDA inspectors are only allowed a few seconds to examine each carcass, there are many animals with obvious signs of disease or abnormality, according to Deborah Lynn Dadd, author of *The Non-Toxic Home and Office.* Dadd's research shows that:

"Each year about 116,000 mammals and nearly 15 million birds are condemned before slaughter. After killing, another 325,000 carcasses are discarded and more than 5.5 million major parts are cut away because they are determined to be diseased. Shockingly, 140,000 tons of poultry are condemned annually, mainly due to cancer. The diseased animals that cannot be sold are processed into . . . animal feed."

It's no wonder that so many pet foods have such an awful smell and appearance, despite the heavy use of artificial flavors and colors to make them more appealing. According to breeder Lee Edwards Benning, author of *The Pet Profiteers*, one marketing study showed that some kids found the smell of dog food so obnoxious they refused to feed their own pets—poor Mom got stuck with the job. The same study showed that even Mom had qualms. She said she hesi-

tated to use the family's knives, forks, and spoons to dig the glop out of the cans.

Perhaps consumer turn-off was one factor that led to the development of ever more "convenient" pet foods. Since they were first introduced, the popularity of "burgers," soft-moist chunks, and dry kibble has grown, while the popularity of canned foods has diminished. Unfortunately, this trend means the average pet is eating more "junk food," because these new foods are full of sugar and preservatives to keep them fresh without canning or refrigeration.

ANOTHER MISSING INGREDIENT: LIFE

All processed pet foods—whether sold in cans, bags or frozen packages, in either giant supermarket chains or local health food stores—are missing something that seems to me to be the most important "nutrient" of all. This key ingredient is practically ignored by nutritional scientists, but we can sense when it's there. It is a quality found only in freshly grown, uncooked whole foods: *Life energy!*

To those accustomed to mechanistic explanations of the universe, this statement might sound a bit farfetched. Yet in recent years, some researchers have been confirming through laboratory tests a phenomenon that's been described by many people around the world for centuries. It is a subtle force field that permeates and surrounds all living things. What exactly this field is, and how it operates, is still largely a mystery. There are, however, a number of successful therapies, such as acupuncture, homeopathy, and various Eastern disciplines (see chapter 14), which address healing at this energetic level.

Through a special medium of photography developed in Russia by a husband and wife team, the Kirlians, a number of investigators are now discovering a whole new world of colorful and complex emissions and "auras" of energies given off by living organisms. They seem to vary, especially according to the individual's emotional state, health, and use of drugs.

The Kirlians were the first to discover that the energy field around "a withered leaf (shows) almost no flares. . . . As the leaf gradually dies, its self-emissions also decrease correspondingly until there is no emission from the dead leaf." What are the implications of this finding for animals (or people) who never or rarely eat anything still fresh or raw enough to retain this mysterious energy?

PROVING THE POTENCY OF RAW FOODS

Raw food contains more vitamins and minerals than cooked food, because cooking destroys many nutrients. When nutritional standards were originally set up for dogs and cats, it was presumed that raw foods, not cooked, would be used to feed these animals. Yet, most of the foods available commercially are very thoroughly cooked, more than would be done in a home kitchen, and none

of these are nutritionally equivalent to what was established by these original standards.

Let's talk about using raw foods for animals. By this I mean feeding uncooked food as much as possible. Some things, like grains and some vegetables, will have to be cooked to be digestible, but meat, poultry, fish, dairy, eggs, soft vegetables, and fruits can all be fed raw with great benefit.

The living testimony exemplified in the many people and animals who thrive on diets that include plenty of fresh raw vegetables, fruits, dairy products, and other foods is enough to convince me that a diet of cooked foods alone will not maintain your pets in top-notch condition. Moreover, my clinical experience over the last 27 years confirms this. The difference in many animals given a home-prepared, raw food diet after eating processed foods most of their lives is nothing short of amazing.

One illustration of this point concerns a remarkable experiment run by Sir Robert McCarrison, a doctor stationed in India some years ago. Impressed by the enviable degree of health enjoyed by the Hunza, Pathan, and Sikh peoples, he wondered if a diet similar to theirs could produce comparable physique and health in experimental rats.

For a period of 27 months, Dr. McCarrison fed over 1,000 rats a variety of live foods, including sprouted beans, fresh raw carrots and cabbage, and raw whole milk, along with whole wheat flatbread and a bit of meat and bones once a week. He also provided the rats with good air, sunlight, and clean living quarters. At the close of the experiment, when the rats had reached an age equivalent to about 55 years in human terms, he sacrificed and autopsied them thoroughly for signs of disease. To his amazement he could find none. The only deaths that *had* occurred among those rats were from accidents.

Later, Dr. McCarrison fed two other diets to groups of rats—one that was typical of poor people from England and the other typical of poor people in parts of India. Rats who lived on the poor Indian diet of rice had disease in every organ they possessed! Those who lived on the boiled, sweetened, and canned foods commonly eaten by the English poor grew so high-strung that they ate each other, the weaker rats succumbing first.

THE POTTENGER CAT STUDIES

One of the most fascinating sources of information about the importance of raw foods has come from what is now known as the Pottenger Cat Studies. Dr. Pottenger did not set out to study cat nutrition, but he became intrigued by differences in the health of cats he was using in experimental studies. Turning his attention to this topic, he did a series of nutritional comparisons. For several generations, one group of cats was fed completely raw food (meat, bones, milk, and cod liver oil). Other groups of cats were fed the same foods either partially or completely cooked. What he found is of definite impor-

tance to anyone who wants to raise a truly healthy pet:

❖ Cats on the entirely raw food diet were completely healthy, never needing veterinary attention.

❖ The more the food was cooked, the less healthy were the cats that ate it.

❖ The health problems evident in the experimental cats on the cooked diet were remarkably like those commonly seen in cats today—mouth and gum problems, bladder inflammation, skin disorders, and the like.

❖ Over a period of three generations, the cats on the cooked food diet continued to deteriorate until they could no longer reproduce.

❖ When the cats were put back on a raw food diet, it took *three generations* for the animals to *totally* recover from the effects of the cooked diet.

Why is this? Foods are so complex that there is still much we don't understand about them. Researchers have discovered, for example, that cats require a dietary source of taurine, an amino acid that many mammals, including humans, can make in their own bodies from the food protein they eat. Cats cannot do this and so must obtain it, already made by other animals, in their food. Taurine, found only in animal tissues, is largely destroyed by cooking. One study found that an average of 52 percent of the taurine in raw meats was lost through baking and an average of 79 percent through boiling. As a result of processing, many commercial cat foods once had low levels of taurine. Now it is added to cat foods and supplements. (When meat is fed raw as we recommend, by the way, calculations show that our recipes for cats contain taurine in amounts comparable to that found in the wild diet.)

In caring for our own cats, my wife and I came to the conclusion that we would rather not wait for more discoveries. Instead, we would rather be cautious, choosing to feed our cats a diet that most closely resembles that of their evolutionary history.

THE ADDITIVES IN YOUR PET'S FOOD

Since graduating from veterinary school in 1965, I've noticed a general and steady deterioration in pet health. We are now seeing very young animals with the same kinds of diseases that we used to see only in older animals. It is clear to me that there is an accumulation of poor health being passed on from generation to generation; this accumulation increases with each step. Without the perspective of several decades, veterinarians just coming out of veterinary school think that these degenerative conditions in younger animals are "normal." They do not realize what has happened over the passage of time.

I believe that, along with poor quality nutrients, the *chemical additives* in pet food have played a major part in that decline. Just look at the label of a typical burger product for dogs. The ingredients are listed in order of

their prominence. (For example, if water is the first ingredient, the product contains more water than anything else.) A popular soft-moist burger lists corn syrup as its third major ingredient. But what is this common sweetener doing in a burger? It's providing the soft-moistness! The FDA approved the use of corn syrup in its hydrogenated form as a "humectant and plasticizer"—that is, an ingredient that can give the product dampness and flexibility, as well as preserving the food against decay. If this does not seem familiar to you, here is a product you will recognize that uses the same method of preserving food: jam! Food scientists trying to develop similar products for people have acknowledged that despite the American sweet tooth, soft-moist dog food is so sweet that "humans just wouldn't like it."

Chemically derived from cornstarch, corn syrup produces the same energy highs and lows as table sugar and causes the same stress on the pancreas and adrenals, a condition that may result in diabetes. It's easy to see that corn syrup is an undesirable ingredient, especially when you consider the other shortcomings of such an isolated refined sugar. Not only does it dilute other nutrients in the food by providing "empty calories" devoid of vitamins, minerals, proteins, or fats, but it also can over-stimulate the production of insulin and acidic digestive juices. These interfere with a dog's ability to absorb the proteins, calcium, and other minerals that *are* in the food. Moreover, it can inhibit the growth of useful intestinal bacteria.

The following common ingredients have appeared in soft-moist and other pet foods.

Propylene glycol. This compound, known to cause illness in dogs, is also used to maintain the right texture and moisture and to tie up the water content, thus inhibiting bacterial growth. Of the commonly used preservatives, it is considered to cause the most health problems in dogs—dry itching skin, hair loss, dehydration, excessive thirst, and tooth and gum problems.

Potassium sorbate. A commonly used preservative, chemically similar to fat.

Ammoniated glycyrrhizin. Add this to the list of sweeteners. It is also considered a potent drug that should be tested further for safety.

Sucrose. Simply table sugar.

Propyl gallate. Manufacturers add this chemical to retard spoilage, but it is suspected of causing liver damage.

Ethoxyquin. Originally developed for use in the production of rubber and as an herbicide, this common preservative is among the compounds most suspect as causes of severe health problems in dogs. It has been found to cause liver tumors in newborn mice. The Food & Drug Administration, Center for Veterinary Medicine (FDA/CVM), has received reports that "include allergic reactions, skin problems, major organ failure, behavior problems and cancer." This organization, however, did not consider the evidence sufficient to make any changes in the regulation of the substance. A feeding test in dogs commissioned by Monsanto, the manufacturer of ethoxyquin, showed a change in liver color and increased liver enzymes in the dogs fed the chemical, but these changes were not considered significant because the dogs were not observably ill. Ethoxyquin continues to be used as a preservative.

Butylated hydroxytoluene (BHT). This poorly tested preservative is implicated by some scientists as a cause of liver damage, metabolic stress, fetal abnormalities, and serum cholesterol increase.

Sodium nitrite. This compound is widely used as both a preservative and a red coloring agent. Sodium nitrite used in food can produce powerful carcinogenic substances known as nitrosamines.

Many dogs are allergic to foods containing chemical preservatives, enduring symptoms such as excessive scratching, chronic diarrhea, or just not feeling well—problems that will continue as long as the chemicals are fed.

COLOR ME SICK

Another class of common additives usually listed simply as *artificial coloring* does not require specific labeling. In pet food, the class typically includes the following coal tar derivative dyes, all allowed without adequate lifetime feeding studies and put in the food to make the food look acceptable to the human consumer.

❖ Red No. 3
❖ Red No. 40 (a possible carcinogen)
❖ Yellow No. 5 (not fully tested)
❖ Yellow No. 6

- Blue No. 1
- Blue No. 2 (shown in studies to increase dogs' sensitivities to fatal viruses)

Similar dyes that were banned from both pet and human foods in the mid-1970s included Red No. 2 (which appeared to increase cancer and birth defects) and Violet No. 1 (a suspected carcinogen that can also cause skin lesions).

Although concerned citizens have tried to get the FDA to ban the inclusion of artificial colors in pet foods, their use continues unabated. In 1979, a petition to bar color additives from pet food was submitted to the FDA. The petition said that adding artificial color to the foods covered up the true appearance of the product and was a deceptive practice. The consumer could not tell the ingredients apart—they were all colored alike, and one could not tell what was meat, what was vegetable, or what were the other ingredients.

How did the FDA respond to this request? They said that by their definition this practice was not deceptive because it was only deception if, by adding color, you were trying to make the food look better than it really was. But (go slowly because the next part does not make sense), because the term "artificial colors" was listed on the label, then it couldn't really be deception because the consumer could read on the label that colors had been added and therefore they couldn't be fooled. Does this make sense to you?

In a crowded marketplace where all the major competitors use these colorings to make their food look more like fresh red meat, a company that tries to sell a product in its true colors—various unattractive shades of gray—could put itself at a serious disadvantage. Since dogs and cats don't see colors like we do, the inclusion of these dyes is for *human* eyes, not to make the foods more attractive to animals. You can, however, find some pet food products in health food stores that *don't* use artificial colors, preservatives, and flavors.

FLAVOR ME FOOLED

Even more lax are the controls governing the largest class of food additives used in the United States—*artificial flavorings.* Largely due to a powerful lobby, the manufacturers of these delights can synthesize new flavorings, call them safe with little or no testing, and then use them without the need for FDA permission under the general term "artificial flavorings." Since we have no way at all of trusting or assessing the safety of what is used, anyone seriously concerned about health would be wise to completely avoid using products—for themselves or their pets—that contain this mysterious group of ingredients.

INADVERTENT CHEMICAL CONTAMINATION

Besides those chemicals intentionally added to pet food, there are others that sneak in on their own. *Chemical contamination* of the food chain is an increasing problem that is becoming a major factor in chronic disease, particularly for animals. It is difficult for us to comprehend just how frequently these chemicals appear in food. The process starts with the herbicides, insecticides, and fungicides used to grow crops. Despite Rachel Carson's landmark warning about the dangers of pesticides, today we use produce pesticides at a rate 13,000 times greater than we did in 1962, the year that her book *Silent Spring* first appeared. The process continues with antibiotics, growth stimulants, hormones, tranquilizers, and other drugs fed to livestock consuming grains.

Heavy Metals

Another important class of contaminants is heavy metals (arsenic, cadmium, and especially mercury), which are increasingly finding their way into our food chain. It was a major shock to many of us to find that the EPA has been allowing the recycling of industry waste—material loaded with heavy metals—into commercial fertilizers. We read how industry is cleaning up their act by putting "scrubbers" onto smokestacks of factories to collect all this nasty stuff so it doesn't get into the air. But once collected, where does it go? We didn't think it would be used in fertilizer and end up in our food.

The problem is this: Heavy metals, like many contaminants, are not destroyed over time. In the soil, plants take them up into their tissues, where they remain for the life of the plant. When this plant is eaten by an animal, the metals enter the animal's body and collect there. The more plant that is eaten, the more heavy metal collects in the tissues. If that animal is eaten by another animal, that additional accumulation, more concentrated, is passed on. The contaminants in the soil become more concentrated in plants, then more concentrated in the grazing animals that eat plants, because they eat so many plants. Then the carnivores that eat these grazing animals consume a greater load. Each step results in more accumulation. The problem for carnivorous animals, those that eat other creatures, is that the buck stops with them.

If these elements were neutral, having no effect, it wouldn't matter. But they are not neutral—they are very toxic. Every year, more and more of these metals are spewed into our biosphere, and the effects on people and animals are staggering.

For example, according to a study published in the *New England Journal of Medicine*, the average chemical pollution of breast milk in American women compared to that of American women who are complete vegetarians was *35 times* higher! Yet less than one out of every quarter million animals slaughtered in the U.S. is tested for toxic chemical residues.

Lead, the Most Common Hazardous Metal

In one study, a sampling of canned pet foods revealed lead contamination levels ranging from 0.9 to 7.0 parts per million (ppm) in cat foods and 1.0 to 5.6 ppm in dog foods. Daily intake of only six ounces of such foods would exceed the dose of lead considered potentially toxic for children.

Much of this contamination comes from the use of bone meal in pet foods. Though they are otherwise an excellent source of calcium and other minerals, the bones of American cattle contain high levels of lead, owing to our prolonged usage of leaded gasoline over several decades. The only safe bone meal nowadays is from cattle raised in South America, Ethiopia, or some other country with few automobiles. A complication is that poisoning by these contaminants is very difficult to recognize. They come on gradually and are not very distinctive in their symptoms. Lead poisoning can appear as a type of anemia that is recognizable, but not all animals poisoned with lead will exhibit this. Some will be hyperactive, have seizures, become hysterical, go blind, have stomach cramps and diarrhea, constipation, or develop thickened and itchy skin. Not all these symptoms occur—there may be just one.

This wide range of possible symptoms is typical of these environmental poisons and makes recognizing them very difficult. Think of a common problem, like a cold. Not hard to recognize when someone has a cold, is it? Runny nose, sneezing, stuffed up. These contaminants don't show up like that. One animal can have anemia, another seizures. How would you even know they are caused by the same thing?

If your pet has accumulated lead, for example, and was sick from just this one thing (for the sake of discussion, ignore all the other factors we have been considering), and you took your pet to a veterinarian for help, I think it is very, very unlikely that lead poisoning would be recognized. I posed that question to a number of vets that I know, ones I have trained in the use of homeopathic medicine. The anemia I mentioned would be a give-away, so I asked them, "If there was no obvious anemia, would you be likely to make the diagnosis of lead poisoning in an animal suffering from it?" Out of 13 that answered, 10 said they did not think they would recognize it. The three that said they might had prior experience with lead-poisoned animals and were therefore on the lookout. A lot of these environmental contaminant problems just come in under our radar.

EFFECTS OF CHEMICAL CONTAMINATION ON THE BODY

The problem of ingesting all these chemicals is three-fold. First, because the body must eliminate toxic substances, it uses up energy and nutrients that could be put to constructive use. Second, anything that the body cannot get rid of accumulates in the tissues. Third, those accumulated substances in the tissues can interact with each other in unexpected ways. Let's look at each of these in turn.

Depletion of energy and nutrients. The body uses several natural mechanisms to detoxify and eliminate harmful substances. Primarily, these processes occur in the liver (detoxification), kidneys (elimination), skin (additional elimination, especially through deposits in the hair), and immune system (reactions against harmful substances). Certain enzymes and their associated vitamins assist this process. The more toxic the chemical, the harder the body must work to get rid of it—and the more these enzymes and vitamins are used up. This strain by itself would be significant enough in a polluted world—but there is more.

Toxic accumulation. The second problem is that the body cannot detoxify *all* substances. That's because for thousands and thousands of years, animal detoxification mechanisms were fine-tuned to deal with the *natural* poisons encountered throughout their lifetime. The last few decades, however, have seen the introduction of unbelievable quantities of substances and chemicals never before encountered in a natural setting. As of 1989, some 70,000 different chemicals were in use in our society, with nearly 3,000 *new* chemicals introduced annually.

When you consider the huge numbers of these substances that are in use and being produced each year, it becomes obvious why this nation's ability to adequately test for harmful effects is compromised. As of 1990, only about 2,000 (approximately 3 percent) of all these chemicals in everyday use had been tested in animals for their ability to cause cancer (and half were found to be carcinogenic). So is it any wonder that some of these chemicals cannot be processed by the body? Most have never been encountered before.

When the body is incapable of detoxifying chemicals, it must store them in tissues, where they can interfere with normal function. The degree of interference depends upon the concentration. The more there is, the more significant the effect. And unfortunately, there is a third factor to consider.

Interactions between stored chemicals. Imagine two different synthetic chemicals—substance A and substance B—that are stored in the same body tissue. They have four "choices":

- They can "ignore" each other, having no interaction.
- A can act on B, possibly making B more toxic.
- B can act on A, possibly making B more toxic.
- Each can act on the other, possibly increasing the other's effects.

Now, if we consider *three* substances, A, B and C, there are *nine* possible interactions, according to the rule that the number of possible interactions is the square of the number of substances present. (There's that math again—the square is a number multiplied by itself.) Reflect back to the quote at the beginning of this section—that assays have detected over 100 chemical contaminants in our tissues. Now you can begin to understand the complexity of all their interactions, which can follow 10,000 possible pathways.

When scientists study any *single* chemical and tell us that it is not harmful at a certain level, this may be true. But they have no idea how it will interact with *other* contaminants in the body. Furthermore, it is *not possible* for them ever to know. If the best that scientists have been able to accomplish so far is to test only about 2,000 of our industries' 70,000 chemical substances for their cancer-causing potential, then there is no reasonable way that they will ever be able to decipher all their other interactions.

WHAT IS THE ALTERNATIVE?

What does all this mean? What can we do in the face of this situation? First, on the larger scale, it is clearly time for each of us to begin to do what we can to reduce our society's use of untested, potentially dangerous synthetic chemicals, not only for our animals, but for all who live on the earth and for all who are yet to come. This will surely mean many changes in our patterns of consumption.

One of the most important changes we can make is in the daily choices about what we feed our pets, as well as ourselves. We just can't expect to maintain good health on over-processed, denatured, contaminated foods. We are going to have to make some changes.

That's the bad news. The good news is that when it comes to how you feed your pet, there are practical, affordable ways to make those kinds of healthy changes. In the next few chapters we will show you, step by step, practical and affordable ways to introduce fresh, even organically grown foods into your dog's or cat's diet.

First we share some stories about animals that found a new lease on life when their diet was switched to fresh, natural diets. Then we will show you how to do the same—how to select the best ingredients and how to put them together in a variety of carefully for-mulated, nutritionally balanced recipes for various needs. For those not quite willing or able to switch completely, we also provide formulas for fresh foods and supplements that can be added to higher-quality kibbles, the "alternative" products increasingly avail-able that are made with more care and with better ingredients. Throughout, we will in-clude time- and money-saving tips. Most ani-mals will love the new food. But for those who are stuck in their habits (like a few cats we all know!), we'll show you how to help your pet make the transition to a new way of eating that's as old as the hills.

CHAPTER 3

TRY A BASIC NATURAL DIET— WITH SUPPLEMENTS

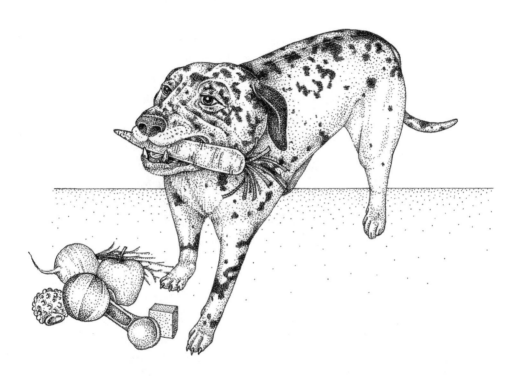

Feeding your pet a fresher, more natural diet takes a little more time and effort. It's certainly not as easy as opening a bag of kibble. You are building health one day at a time, and though it is an extra effort, it is much easier than continual health problems with your pet. Imagine avoiding those visits to the vet for treatments that never really solve the problem, of sparing your loved companion the suffering that goes with illness. Isn't it worth extra exertion to have improved quality of life together?

Countless clients, along with readers of this book's earlier editions, have switched their pets to more wholesome diets and have rejoiced at the results. For example, this letter from a grateful New Jersey woman gives you an idea of what can be accomplished with such a little change:

My little dog Noel was going downhill very fast two years ago. She was eight. Her coat was dull and smelled awful. Her breath had a foul odor. Her eyes were dull and she slept all day under a chair. She had always been friendly, but her temperament changed. She would try to bite me and growled if I tried to get her to come outside and play. I bought pet vitamins and they stimulated her appetite but she was still so sick-looking.

Well, thanks to your wonderful book there's been a big change. Noel's on a natural diet now. No more dry and canned food. What a difference! Her coat and her breath don't have an odor. At 10 years of age, her eyes shine and she's prancing around like a puppy. Noel loves whole grains, tofu, beans, eggs, cheese, and all vegetables. (I also give her the supplements you recommend.) Another change: her muzzle was turning gray but now the hair is coming in black again, the color it was when she was a puppy. Thank you so much for saving Noel's life.

Another woman reported a similar turnaround in her daughter's cat:

Some months ago my daughter's 9-year-old cat had numerous ailments and she was sorrowfully considering putting it to sleep. I dug out an article you wrote some time ago on diet and since she had nothing to lose, she

tried it. Her cat didn't eat for two days but then, lo and behold, he started to eat and like it. But the amazing thing is the change in that cat. The personality even changed. He is more playful than he ever was, comes when called and is simply a nicer cat. She will never go back to commercial food again.

Isn't this simply amazing? But it is not simply that nutrition will help those animals that are ill. One of the greatest benefits is avoiding a life of ill health altogether. Look at a letter I recently received that demonstrates this very well. It was entitled, "Thank you, my dog is 14 today."

Just had to find some way to say thank you. My dog Ivy is fourteen years old today and I have been feeding her from your book since she was about four weeks old. It started because I was broke and couldn't afford quality dog food and was working in a health food store where one of my customers was a phone client of yours and recommended your book.

I have never had a vet bill for an illness and at fourteen, she is amazing. She is still active and vital, a little stiffness in the back legs, but will still leap for a Frisbee. Her eyes and mind are clear, her hearing is fine and she even has good breath.

No one believes her age, including the vet—she is a joy. Her sister died two years ago of cancer and she ate [a commercial food] all her life. I know her incredible health is due to her healthy diet and on her birthday I wanted to express my gratitude.

HOW TO USE
A HOMEMADE DIET

Results like these speak for themselves. Yet we've all heard some veterinarian or pet food manufacturer warn against feeding pets table scraps or homemade diets. Such foods, they contend, have not been scientifically formulated to meet animals' needs and may ruin a pet's health. So why this discrepancy between the excellent results with home-prepared food and these dire warnings? For one thing, it depends on what you are actually feeding. If we just scraped junk-food leftovers into a pet's bowl it wouldn't be so healthy, would it? Even if you're more conscientious than that, it's still easy to be misguided by your own tastes and needs, not realizing that what's good for you may not be good for your pet. (For example, because they are carnivores, dogs and cats need far more protein and calcium on a pound-for-pound basis than humans require.)

Nonetheless, do-it-yourself animal feeding has been with us since the first dog and person crossed paths at least 10,000 years ago. And generation after generation of animals got by just fine on the scraps and extras of our ancestors. The problem today is that we don't have the same scraps and extras as our ancestors, but a lot of artificial foods high in sugar, fat, and chemicals. So, let's choose our ingredients with care and all will be fine.

We also have the benefit of modern dietary analysis and research, so I believe it

makes sense to use that information and adhere to it in formulating a pet's diet. Why do I say that, when few of us bother to calculate the exact nutrients in our own meals? The reason is that, unlike humans or wild animals with free access to natural and varied food supplies, our pets have little choice about what they eat. Rarely, if ever, do they get to follow their instincts in selecting individual foods; usually, a number of ingredients are mixed together and it's a matter of eating all or nothing. Moreover, the instincts of homebound pets are not as finely tuned as the instincts of wild animals. Like us, pets can easily develop a taste for the strong flavors of junk food.

The recipes in this book are palatable, easy to make, and nutritious. Using a computer, we have been able to analyze the contents of each recipe and its suggested variations. Relying on standard data for the most important food constituents (given in the *USDA Handbook on the Composition of Foods*), we adjusted the recipes to make sure the amount of each nutrient met or exceeded the minimal amounts recommended for dog and cat foods as provided by the guidelines from the Committee on Animal Nutrition, Board on Agriculture, and the National Research Council.

Sounds very exact, doesn't it? Realize, however, that even though foods have been analyzed for their constituents, what actually is present in what you buy can vary considerably. The wheat or oats of today may not be the same as what you used a month ago. This is because crops (and livestock) are products of their environment, and how they are raised determines what nutrition they ultimately provide. It is well known that there can be considerable variation in protein content, vitamins, and minerals, for example, depending on the soil, the amount of irrigation, the time of harvesting, and the storage period. This is why I recommend not using the same recipe all the time and also varying the ingredients in the recipes (substituting the ones suggested as possible alternatives). This way you compensate for these inevitable differences in food values.

But first, let's talk about the best basic foods to use, along with some nutritional supplements that should be added as a necessary part of the diet.

THE FOUNDATION PRINCIPLES

The first important principle in this do-it-yourself way of feeding animals is, as we said above, to aim for variety, because that helps to ensure the best balance of nutrients. Soon you will identify several combinations that are best suited to your lifestyle and your animal's preferences.

Another worthwhile principle is to stick to the recipes fairly closely. They've been carefully formulated to provide the best combinations. Sometimes people try to take shortcuts by omitting the calcium supplement, for example, but that will cause a deficiency problem if done regularly.

Third, I strongly encourage you to use or-

ganically raised and minimally processed foods whenever possible. It's best for the immediate health of your pet, and it's best for the long-term health of the Earth and everything on it. Fortunately, it's possible for people throughout most of the United States to find organically raised grains. Organically produced food costs more than conventionally produced food, at least at the check-out. Part of the reason that conventionally raised food costs less is because some of the costs are hidden in government subsidies and the heavy use of chemicals, which reduces the time needed to care for the crops. They are hidden costs that we will pay for some day. Organic foods, however, are less expensive if purchased in bulk in natural food stores. (See "Best Ingredient Choices for Feeding Your Pet," on pages 46–47, which will also help you find the best protein buys.) It may be difficult to find or afford organic meat, and it often can be obtained only in a frozen form. Just do what you can, and try to use the best whole, fresh ingredients you can afford. When these are made into balanced recipes, they are still a big improvement over commercial pet food products, which we know can be laced with everything from cancerous tissue to sugar, dyes, and moldy grains (see chapter 2).

The fourth general principle is to be patient yet persistent as you gradually introduce these new foods to your animal friend. Most people find their pets love these foods, but some animals hesitate to eat them at first, simply because the foods are unfamiliar.

Also, any change of diet—even a switch from one commercial brand of food to another—means the pet's digestive system has to adapt. So take time to introduce the new foods, certainly a few days and maybe a period of weeks in some animals with digestive weakness, substituting ever-greater proportions of natural foods for commercial foods. (See chapter 6 for more discussion on making the switch.)

THE BASIC FOOD GROUPS

Now let's consider each of the basic food groups used in our recipes—and how best to buy, store, and prepare them.

MEATS

Meat is the food with the most chemical contamination and is also produced at a great cost to the environment and with considerable suffering by the livestock raised according to modern farming methods (see the discussion in chapter 5). Still, it remains that meat is the most natural food for carnivores. It contains much protein and is rich in many other nutrients needed by dogs and cats. In our recipes we try to balance these issues—using meat as a major ingredient, but bringing in other nutritious food sources as well. That's why most of the recipes in this book include some fresh meat combined with high-protein grains, legumes, or dairy products to produce a total amount of protein that exceeds the recommended standards. The resulting protein levels are comparable to (usually greater than) the protein levels found in commercial foods, which use a similar process of combining plant and animal proteins. In chapter 5, we also include some meatless recipes that are suitable for feeding dogs.

It has become popular of late to feed a diet made up almost entirely of raw meat and bones. While this way of feeding is closer to the natural diet, it has some disadvantages, primarily in being too rich for inactive animals and being so high in chemical contaminants (less so for organic bones and meat).

Regarding the suitability of such a high protein and fat diet for pet dogs, consider that wolves, for example, will spend much of their time hunting and traveling long distances—as much as 50 or 100 miles in a day. Extreme physical activity and a high-meat diet go hand in hand. Their lifestyle requires that level of food, which in turn is only obtained by great effort. Our pet dogs, on the other hand, are mostly inactive; their food is brought to them. Feeding them such a rich diet compares with the couch potato who eats steak and fries while watching the tube; the most strenuous activity is going into the kitchen to get more food. It is out of balance for the amount of activity that pet dogs experience.

Yes, many animals will have improved health on a mostly meat and bones diet, but much of that comes from getting away from commercial foods and avoiding the cooked and depleted foods commonly used in commercial products.

The other consideration is the added load of environmental contaminants that is inevitably picked up. Unless meat is organic, the more that is eaten, the more chemicals are absorbed. As just one example, the use of synthetic estrogen (DES), a female hormone used to fatten cattle, is carried over into the meat and thus into your dog, gradually having effects over time. The potential effects are not completely known, but since the hormone is used to make cattle gain weight, we can certainly expect at least that much to happen. Estrogen has also been implicated in cancer development in laboratory animals.

Bones present their own problems. Lead is one of the biggest concerns, as noted in chapter 2, because lead is deposited in bones and does not break down. It is interesting that bone meal meant for human consumption (sold in natural food stores) cannot be derived from U.S. cattle, because there is excess lead in their bones. These same bones, however, are used in pet food, and the more fed, the more lead exposure there is.

I once attended a presentation by a veterinarian who promoted this type of diet and brought up the question about the contaminants in meat, especially lead in bones. The response was that they did not have that problem in Australia (where he was from). When I again described the problem with contamination in U.S. cattle and other livestock, he did not have a solution.

Our Solution

Considering how subtle the effects of lead poisoning and that of other chemicals in food can be, I am still advising my clients to use the balanced recipes in this book, using "human-grade" foods as much as possible. I think it is safer in the long run. We have tried to achieve a balance in our recipes between using raw meat as well as grains and vegetables to provide an optimum amount of protein and other ingredients.

Another criterion we used when choosing meats was convenience. That's why our recipes use meats that are widely available, usually ground up, which makes it easier to mix them in with the recipe and harder for finicky eaters to pick them out. (This is more an issue with cats than with dogs, who enjoy all types of foods.) If your dog or cat will eat all the ingredients in the recipes, then using meat in chunks is better for the health of the gums and teeth.

Most of the recipes in this book call for lean meats, which are considerably higher in protein and lower in fat. The following meats are roughly interchangeable within each group. This means that you can, on occasion, substitute one meat for another in a recipe, pound for pound or cup for cup. The meats are also listed in approximate order of best values, with the first ones representing the most protein for the typical price paid.

Lean meats (interchangeable): Turkey and/or giblets, liver (beef, chicken, or turkey), mackerel, most chicken and/or giblets, tuna, heart (beef, chicken, or turkey), lean hamburger, lean chuck, duck (without skin), rabbit, or various fishes.

Fatty meats (interchangeable): Roaster chicken (with skin), fatty beef heart, brains, regular hamburger, fatty chuck, sirloin steak, lamb, or pork.

Occasionally, you can substitute any of these fatty meats where the recipe calls for a lean meat. When you do, reduce the amount of oil in the recipe by about a tablespoon for every cup of meat. Cuts of meat vary, so use your best judgment in evaluating the degree of fat in a meat.

Note: If you would like more detailed information as to the amount of fat in various meats and fish, then check the table "Fat Content of Meats," page 449.

Also note: One pound of ground meat equals about 2 cups.

Guidelines for Selecting and Preparing Meats

Use variety. Feed more than one kind of meat in a meal, using different cuts. Include some muscle or flesh meats, such as hamburger, chicken, and turkey, as well as some organ meats, such as heart, liver or kidneys, or giblets.

Note: Some people have seen great health benefits in their animals from regularly feeding them small amounts of raw liver. Just be sure that you don't go overboard with liver. Limit it to less than 10 percent of the meat you feed overall. Not only does the liver concentrate and store many pollutants, but it

could overdose your pet with vitamin A, which is one of the few vitamins known to cause problems if consumed in excess.

In the years since the first edition of this book came out, fresh raw liver, beef heart, and other parts (other than muscle) have become increasingly difficult to obtain. I asked at a major supermarket chain about the availability of either liver or heart and was told it is simply no longer available to them. They can't order it. I did, however, find frozen liver in the freezer section. In some communities it is possible to find a butcher that makes this available—we have one in ours.

Emphasize purer sources. One veterinarian I know who worked as a meat inspector has observed that turkeys, ducks, and sheep have lower cancer rates than chickens, cattle, and hogs. He attributes this difference to the amount of meat meal fed each species. So you would probably do well to emphasize turkey and lamb, for example, unless you can obtain quality-raised chicken or beef. Some natural food stores carry meats described as organically raised or chemical-free (meaning that no drugs, hormones, or the like were used in the livestock feed). Also, it's a good idea to look for free-range chickens, rather than those stressed by being raised in the intensely crowded confines of the typical little cages in factory farms.

Try ground meats. This is especially good for cats, because you can readily blend in other ingredients, and the cats can't pick out the meat and leave the rest. If you have a food processor, you can grind chunks of meat along with the other ingredients to make a nice texture; otherwise, buy it already ground or ask the butcher to grind it for you. (Chunks of meat have benefits, too, because chewing them exercises an animal's jaws, which helps condition the gums.)

Feed meat raw whenever possible if the animal will accept it. I make this recommendation on the basis of research, clinical practice, and the natural habits of predators since the beginning of time. My clients have been feeding their pets this way successfully for more than 25 years. All the meats listed in the recipes in this book may be fed raw. If, however, you substitute by using a little fish, rabbit, or pork now and then, you should cook them first to kill parasites like tapeworms or trichinosis organisms, which these foods can carry.

You should be aware that most veterinarians oppose feeding raw meat because of concern about diseases like salmonella or *Escherichia coli*. After more than 25 years of experience in recommending this practice, I can attest to seeing no problem with infections from these diseases. On the contrary, I've observed an improved level of health. This is not to say that animals can never become ill from eating raw meat, but they certainly seem to be less susceptible to it than people are. Perhaps this is because dogs and cats are natural carnivores and raw meat is their natural food. They have much stronger stomach acids than people, and this likely protects them from a multitude of these

problems. If you are uncomfortable about feeding raw meat to your pet, feel free to cook it, of course, but remember, the nutritional values (given for raw meats) will be compromised to an unknown degree.

Tip: If your time is really limited, or you're very concerned about feeding raw meat, you might substitute tofu, which is also easier for your pet to digest. It does, however, cost about the same per gram of protein as most commercial meats. With a little flavoring like low-sodium soy sauce or meat drippings, most dogs will accept tofu.

The Threat of Mad Cow Disease

"What about Mad Cow Disease?" you may ask. A 1992 English study of 444 dogs that showed symptoms suggesting this disease found brain abnormalities similar to those discovered in cattle and people. A consultant microbiologist said it was "absolutely certain that the presence of scrapie- (the name for the "mad cow" disease in sheep) associated fibrils shows these dogs had the disease." In 2000, in Norway, an 11-year-old golden retriever died from spongiform encephalopathy (Mad Cow), and a link was established to pet food brought in from England. Cats are also affected by this disease, and at least 75 of them have already died from the feline version of the disease in England.

Spongiform encephalopathy (Mad Cow Disease) originally became a problem because of the practice of feeding lamb meal— rendered tissues coming from sheep—to cattle. Yes, strange as it is, these animals that live on grasses and plants are being fed tissue from their own kind. No wonder these strange illnesses pop up. In hindsight we can see this was a completely avoidable problem, and the only reason for this cannibalistic way of feeding livestock was to reduce costs and to find a way to use rendered animal parts.

Cattle in the United States are fed the same way. "For years," reported the *New York Times* in 2004, "calves have been fed cow's blood instead of milk, and cattle feed has been allowed to contain composted wastes from chicken coops, including feathers, spilled feed and even feces." These rendered animal materials are especially likely to be fed to dairy cows because intensive milk production requires more protein and fat in the diet. According to Tom Cook, president of the National Renderers Association, most of the meat and bone meal produced in the 240 plants in the United States and Canada, which process about 50 billion pounds of animal remains a year, is used in feed supplements for animals. As he was quoted in the *Times* article, 43 percent goes to poultry, 23 percent to pet food, 13 percent to swine, 10 percent to cattle, and 11 percent to other uses, such as feed for farmed fish.

Though Europe tests 25 percent of their cattle for this disease and Japan 100 percent, in the United States only five or six in a million cattle are tested. Even so, Mad Cow Disease was found in Canada in May 2003 (7 percent of the beef consumed by Americans comes from Canada) and in cattle in Washington state in early 2004. We can see the pos-

sibility of this becoming a significant problem in our future, and there is no indication that the feeding of animal tissue to cattle and sheep will be curtailed. Even if it is, cooking meat does not kill the disease. The only way to avoid this with any certainty is to not eat meat—not a choice for obligate carnivores like cats. It might be prudent to avoid beef and lamb, which are the major sources right now, though this restricts the choices considerably. We don't know whether chickens, turkeys, or farmed fish will be susceptible to this disease. They are fed the same kind of material that has spread it in livestock, so the risk is certainly there. There are also many other animals that have developed similar diseases, such as antelope, mink, and ostrich.

I think the best defense against such diseases is a healthy body, which is an additional reason for feeding your animals the most natural and nutritious diet in the first place.

Storage

We have tried to formulate the recipes in this book for convenient quantities of meats, as purchased in pounds. If you're feeding a large dog or several animals, you will probably use up all the meat you buy before it spoils. But if you have one small animal, you will need to take a different tack: Either divide the meat into recipe-size portions and freeze them for future preparation, or make up the whole recipe at once and freeze any part of the mixture that your pet won't eat in the next two to three days. This will also reduce the time spent in preparing your pet's diet.

Undoubtedly, freezing the meat destroys some of its fresh qualities, but defrosted raw meat is still better than cooked meat and far superior to the meat by-products in commercial food.

You will probably need to freeze extra meat more often for cats than for dogs. Because dogs are natural scavengers, they can tolerate, and even relish, meat that is too gamy for human consumption. Cats, however, are truer carnivores. That's why they are very selective about the freshness of their meat and will readily let you know when their daily fare has aged beyond its time.

Tip: Reuse your soft plastic dairy and deli containers to freeze extra portions when you make up a recipe. Thaw each container in the refrigerator 24 hours before you want to serve it. If the food is not completely thawed, simply add a little hot water and use a fork to break it up in the serving bowl. Hot water also increases the palatability of any food just removed from the refrigerator. Try to use up frozen meat within three to four months.

If you are going to use the microwave to heat up the food or to thaw it, then remove it first from plastic containers and don't cover it with plastic wrap. Studies have shown that microwave heating of food releases toxic material from the plastic into the food. Warming food taken from the refrigerator needs only about 10 seconds time.

EGGS AND DAIRY PRODUCTS

Besides meat, dairy products are good sources of protein. We recommend raw eggs and cottage cheese in the diets because they are economical, convenient sources of dairy protein. Yogurt and cheese are relatively expensive and less-concentrated protein sources than eggs. They are fairly balanced foods, however, so feel free to feed them (and milk, too) on the side.

About eggs: Eggs are a complete protein and are a good source of preformed vitamin A. I recommend the no-hormone, no-drug, free-range eggs often sold in natural food stores. The extra cost is worth it. Eggs are such a good protein source that the cost for the "natural" variety is about the same per gram of protein as that of most factory-farm-raised meat in supermarkets, in some cases even cheaper.

Opinions are divided about whether adult dogs and cats can digest raw eggs properly. For example, one study concluded that raw egg whites can cause a biotin deficiency. But this condition has only been seen in experiments in which egg whites were fed to rats in great excess, making up almost their entire diet. Personally, I have never seen the biotin problem. I think it's important to remember that predators in the wild rely on raw eggs as part of their fare. As a change, you can lightly scramble or boil the eggs occasionally. It also works well to add eggs to freshly cooked grains; the heat sets the egg just enough to improve food texture.

The threat of salmonella poisoning is also a common worry where raw eggs are concerned. In all my years of practice, however, I have not seen a dog or cat affected by this organism in connection with eating raw eggs. If it were to happen, it would affect those animals that are weak from illness and have digestive problems; if this is your situation, then cooking eggs may be the smart thing to do.

Digestion of milk products: Some people believe raw milk and raw cheeses should form the bulk of a cat's diet. Others say that cats, especially Siamese, do not digest lactose (milk sugar) properly, and that drinking milk causes gas and diarrhea in cats. Based on the feedback from my clients, I do not find that milk causes such problems in the great majority of cats. (In addition, my experience is that if cats are sensitive to milk, proper treatment can eliminate the sensitivity.) So I suggest feeding milk to cats unless it is obvious it does not agree with them.

Pasteurization, however, does alter the chemical structure of protein and can destroy beneficial enzymes and bacteria found in milk, making it less digestible. So if your animal has a problem, try feeding it fresh, raw milk. Ordinarily, cottage cheese, yogurt, and goat's milk are also easily digested. But if your cat still has difficulty, omit milk products from the diet.

Please do not presume that feeding your pet milk with every meal means you can omit the bone meal or other calcium supplements in the recipes. To be used properly in the body, calcium must be provided in a specific ratio to phosphorus. Cats and dogs require such high amounts of calcium that the amount in milk is just about enough to balance the phosphorus in the milk itself. But that level of calcium is not enough to balance the high phosphorus levels in meats and grains. Bones provide much more extra calcium, and they are the natural way that predators achieve this balance.

GRAINS

Whole grains are a very cost-effective and environmentally sensitive way to provide the mainstay of your pet's diet. Not only do grains supply carbohydrates and an array of vitamins and minerals, they are inexpensive sources of protein as well. When one type of grain is combined with other grains, the biological effectiveness of its protein is greatly enhanced because the balance of amino acids is more complete. According to official standards, carbohydrates may properly supply over half of the diet for dogs and cats, on a dry weight basis.

Grains are one group of foods that definitely should be cooked. Because the intestinal tracts of dogs and cats are much shorter than those of cereal-eating animals ,like cows and horses, grains fed to dogs and cats need some pre-digestion (in the form of cooking). Once prepared this way, they are completely utilizable by the body. Usually, wild carnivores eat these foods only if they appear in the stomach of their prey, thus the grains are partially digested already.

To save both time and energy, we emphasize quick-cooking and economical grains—oatmeal, cornmeal, millet, and bulgur. They are well-accepted by most dogs and cats and are high in nutrition. Oats and bulgur, for

RECOMMENDED GRAINS

This table contains cooking directions for recommended grains, including the amount of water to use per cup of dry grain. It also indicates yields and caloric and protein contents.

GRAIN (1 C. DRY)	WATER (C.)	COOKED YIELD (C.)	COOKING TIME (MIN.)	CALORIES	PROTEIN AMOUNT (G.)
Barley	2–3	2$\frac{1}{2}$–3	30–60	696	19
Brown rice	2	2$\frac{1}{2}$	30–45	720	15
Buckwheat	2–3	2$\frac{1}{2}$–3	20–30	570	20
Bulgur	2	2–2$\frac{1}{2}$	10–20	602	19
Cornmeal	4	3$\frac{1}{2}$–4	10–30	462	12
Millet	3	3	20–30	641	19
Rolled oats	2	2	10	312	11
Wheat berries	3$\frac{1}{2}$	2$\frac{1}{2}$	60	652	20
Whole-wheat couscous	1$\frac{1}{2}$	2$\frac{1}{2}$	3–5	602	19

Note: Another good source of grain protein is whole-wheat bread. Two slices provide 122 calories and three grams of protein. Crumble up the bread before mixing it in the recipes.

example, are loaded with protein, and millet is rich in iron. Larger grains like rice and whole wheat berries or barley are best used with dogs; unless these larger grains are mashed, cats tend to pick them out. Crumbled whole-wheat bread is a quick and convenient ingredient when preparing food for a cat or small dog, but it's too expensive to use regularly for feeding large dogs. Amaranth, whole-wheat couscous, buckwheat, quinoa, and spelt—all highly nutritious grains—are beginning to make their way into the American diet. They are usually costlier, but use them if you wish, substituting

them in amounts similar to those for bulgur.

Each recipe in the next chapter suggests several grain substitutions that provide comparable or greater nutritional value. Amounts are provided, but you might need to refer to the "Recommended Grains" table above for cooking instructions.

LEGUMES

Beans and other legumes are emphasized in several of our recipes for dogs. That's because they provide a great deal of protein at less cost than any other food, allowing you to reduce your dog's meat consumption if you wish. It takes more time to prepare legumes, but when you fix large quantities of food, a little planning about including legumes will be well worth it. Here are some tips for saving time and/or energy when cooking legumes.

Use quick-cooking legumes such as split peas and lentils. Lentils are high in protein and because of their thin skins, they require no soaking. There's also no need to soak split peas, which makes both these legumes good choices on a compressed schedule.

Presoak longer-cooking beans overnight. Soaking beans at least three hours—and changing the water at least once, if soaked longer—helps reduce intestinal gas after they're consumed. It also helps to boil the soaked beans for 30 minutes, discard the cooking water, and finish cooking with fresh water. (Beans are done when you can easily lift off the outer "skin" of the bean.)

Use a pressure cooker. If you have one of these appliances, you can cook beans in 35 to 45 minutes.

Precook a large quantity of beans and freeze them in recipe-size portions for future use. For this reason, the recipes list amounts for both dry and cooked beans.

Suggested legume-for-legume substitutions that provide adequate nutritional value are given with the recipes in the next chapter. Amounts are provided, but you may need to refer to the "Recommended Legumes" table below for cooking instructions.

RECOMMENDED LEGUMES

This table contains cooking directions for our recommended legumes, including the amount of water to use per cup of dry legume. It also shows yields and caloric and protein content.

LEGUME (1 C. DRY)	WATER (C.)	COOKED YIELD (C.)	COOKING TIME (MIN.)	CALORIES	PROTEIN AMOUNT (G.)
Kidney, red beans	3	$2^1/_2$	90	645	42
Lentils	4	$2^3/_4$	30	578	42
Pinto beans	2	$2^1/_2$	90	628	41
Soybeans	5	$2^3/_4$	180	806	68
Split peas	4	$2^1/_2$	30	696	48
White or black beans	4	$2^1/_2$	45–60	629	41

Note: Tofu, which is made from soybeans and doesn't need cooking, is also very high in protein. One pound of tofu has 35 grams of protein and 654 calories.

Vegetables

Despite their image as exclusive meat-eaters, the wild cousins of dogs and cats do consume plant foods—sometimes these are found in the stomach contents of their plant-eating prey (often the first part of a kill a wolf eats). Sometimes wild animals eat plant foods directly. Dogs especially like vegetables, which are valuable for adding vitamins, minerals, and roughage to the diet. Most vegetables are so low-calorie that you can add them to the recipes in modest quantities with little effect on the proportions of the major nutrients. Some vegetables must be cooked to help carnivores digest them properly, but others may be fed raw, much like the grasses they sometimes nibble in the back yard.

These are the best-liked veggies that can be fed raw to dogs:

- Chopped parsley
- Alfalfa sprouts
- Finely grated carrots with peel
- Finely grated zucchini and other soft squash with peel
- Lettuce and mixed greens
- Green, red, orange, yellow, or purple bell peppers
- Fresh corn (especially if chopped up, but dogs can gnaw on cobs)
- Finely grated beets (don't be alarmed when urine or stool turns pink!)

These vegetable favorites should be cooked before being fed to both dogs and cats:

- Corn
- Peas
- Green beans
- Broccoli
- Cauliflower
- Potatoes
- Hard winter squash
- Any hard vegetable that cannot be grated or pulverized

Though they may also be cooked, whole raw carrots are favored by many dogs who enjoy chewing on them much as they do bones. Such foods help exercise and clean teeth and gums.

Cats generally do not like vegetables, though you will find the occasional cat that will kill for a cucumber. You can add veggies into the cat diet, but they have to be well mixed or they will be studiously picked out and left in the dish in favor of the meat and fat.

Avoid feeding pets vegetables high in oxalic acid, a compound that interferes with calcium absorption. These include spinach, Swiss chard, and rhubarb.

In contrast to most vegetables, potatoes provide plenty of calories in the form of both carbohydrates and protein. Fortunately, they are also well-liked by many pets. So it's okay to use leftover cooked or mashed potatoes occasionally in place of some lower-protein grains such as rice, cornmeal, and barley. Some people think their animals have trouble digesting potatoes, but others find that their pets relish spuds. Try using potatoes and judge your animal's reaction for yourself. (Be sure to cut out all green or sprouting parts, which contain solanine, a somewhat toxic substance.)

A word of caution about fresh produce: Most likely, many vegetables and fruits have been sprayed at some point during production. (This is another reason to select organically grown vegetables whenever possible. With organically grown vegetables, you are also sure that the produce has not been dyed, waxed, or irradiated.) Be sure to wash non-organic produce thoroughly. If you think it's appropriate, use a bit of dishwashing detergent (a way to reduce pesticide residues significantly) and rinse thoroughly.

Grow Your Own!

Organic produce may be hard to come by in your area, but you can always grow your own. Even apartment-dwellers can raise high-nutrition vegetables in the form of sprouts and potted greens.

Here's how to grow fresh, nutritious sprouts. First, buy one or two sprouting jars, or make your own by putting a piece of screen or cheesecloth inside a canning jar ring on a one-quart jar. Add two tablespoons alfalfa seeds or ½ cup lentils or mung beans (all available at natural food stores). Cover with water and soak for eight hours or overnight.

Afterward, drain off the water onto some thirsty houseplants. Rinse the sprouting seeds three or four times a day and place the jar mouth angled slightly down so the water can drain into a bowl or sink. After a couple

of days, flood the jar and wash off excess seed coats through a coarser screen, if desired. In three to five days the sprouts will be ready to eat. If your pet won't eat the sprouts at first, you might try chopping them up and mixing them in the food.

Many dogs and cats also relish wheat grass. They'll even "graze" directly from the pots, if allowed, in the same way they go for lawn grass. This is part of a natural cleansing instinct, so you shouldn't try to discourage it. If herbicides and synthetic fertilizers have been applied to your lawn or if your pet is housebound, growing wheat grass can provide your animal with a safe, healthy source of greens.

Here's how to grow wheat grass. Soak one to two tablespoons of wheat berries (available at natural food stores) overnight. Drain the water onto some thirsty houseplants. Almost fill a flower pot or tray with potting soil and sprinkle the seeds evenly on top, spacing them about one berry apart. Cover with ¼ inch of potting soil. Water daily, just enough to keep the soil slightly moist.

When the shoots are about four inches high, offer them to your animal friend for grazing or "mow" some of the grass down to about an inch with a pair of scissors. Chop the trimmings and mix them into a meal occasionally.

Herbs are special plants. In addition to being excellent sources of minerals, they also possess mild medicinal qualities. Occasionally, add a pinch of dried or a greater amount of fresh of any of the following herbs to your pet's food: alfalfa, parsley, thyme, dandelion, red clover, raspberry or blackberry leaves, basil, comfrey, linden flowers, or fenugreek.

PUTTING IT ALL TOGETHER

Now that we have considered the major food groups that make up the bulk of the recipes, let's take a moment to put them in perspective.

"Best Ingredient Choices for Feeding Your Pet," found on pages 46–47, gives you a quick way to compare the major ingredients, considering the following factors: cost per gram of protein, cooking time, and best nutrients.

The foods are grouped by basic categories: grains, legumes, meats, and dairy products. Based on a price survey of our local natural food store and a major supermarket, we sorted the various choices within each category of food into price groups. Where I was able, I chose to list the organic foods, as you will want to use them when possible. This is important. The price groups start with the least expensive—foods that cost less than a penny per gram of protein; next, foods that cost about a penny per gram of protein; then, foods costing three cents and four cents per gram of protein and so on.

What we find here locally is typical in my experience for the West Coast. Generally these natural and organic foods are fairly easily obtained on the West and East coasts of the United States. In other parts of the country, it might take more tracking down, and sometimes ordering long distance, but they can still be obtained.

Where the organic choice was not available, I listed the conventional sources. Also, where possible, I used bulk prices, from the bins where you can package it yourself. So if you buy packaged grains at a supermarket (where grains and legumes are seldom offered in bulk), figure a little more for the price.

Chicken, hamburger, and turkey are the best protein buys in meats. Processed foods such as tofu, bread, cheese, and yogurt are relatively expensive.

Now let's look at some of the secondary foods—snacks, flavorings, and nutritional supplements that are part of a recommended pet diet.

SNACKS AND FLAVORINGS

Healthful natural snacks, flavorings, and supplements help to round out a pet's diet, adding both appeal and nutrition. A good general rule for feeding snacks is to allow your animal fairly ample amounts of any healthful food it really likes, up to 20 percent of the diet. The following snacks, which can also be used as training rewards, are healthy alternatives to the kinds of human junk food that pets sometimes get hooked on.

Bones

Both cats and dogs, but especially dogs, have a high calcium requirement. That's why bone meal or other calcium supplementation is an important component in my recipes. You may also let your pet gnaw on bones occasionally as a snack, not as a major part of the diet. It's the animal's most natural way to get calcium, and many pets relish bones.

Be careful about feeding chicken, turkey, fish, or pork bones to your dog, however, because they splinter easily and can cause injury. Cats can manage much smaller bones quite well (it is really just matching bones to mouth size—we want them too large to swallow whole). They do well with chicken, game hen, quail, and other bones similar in size. I have noticed that if cats are started young in life with the experience of getting raw bones, then they will accept them as part of the diet. Older cats, without this experience, look at them the way you look at the things they drag in from the yard.

Dogs do better with large, meaty bones, again large enough that they can't break them up and swallow big pieces. We want them to *gnaw* on the bones, which is what exercises the teeth and gums.

Feed your pet raw bones only, because cooked bones can splinter into sharp fragments. Also be careful of frozen bones, which are rock hard and can break teeth. It seems to me that bones once frozen are also more brittle, so I prefer that any bones used are raw and not frozen.

Save the bones you can't give directly to your animal and simmer them in water to make a mineral-rich stock that you can then use for cooking your pet's grains. Adding a little vinegar and salt to the brew helps to extract the minerals.

One word of caution: If your dog is not used to eating bones, he may go crazy with delight when he is introduced to one. As a result, he may eat too much bone at one time, irritating his digestive tract. The result can be either constipation or diarrhea. Also, if your animal's health is not the greatest, digesting bones may be difficult at first. I believe this problem is related to weak stomach acid that develops because of a nutritional deficiency. So go easy at first and limit the time you allow your pet to gnaw on bones. Watch them at first to make sure they are not swallowing big pieces—a 15-minute trial period is a good start. As your pet's health improves, digesting bones will be easier. Also note that it is not unusual for a dog's stool to be hard and white after eating a lot of bones.

Both dogs and cats benefit from an occasional bone fast (one or two days a month in which they are given nothing but water and raw bones). These regular, short fasts mimic natural conditions in which predators have both lean and fat times. They offer the animal's digestive tract an opportunity to put aside regular duties and get at some overlooked "housecleaning." The practice of fasting also has the added benefit of keeping your pet's teeth and gums strong and healthy.

A similar idea is to occasionally feed your cat nothing all day but a small whole Cornish game hen, uncooked, or a piece of raw chicken with the bone in.

continued on page 48

BEST INGREDIENT CHOICES FOR FEEDING YOUR PET

Use the table below as a confidence builder when you begin to prepare healthful homemade food for your pet. At a glance you have all the information you need for choosing the most desirable ingredients—the least costly, quickest to prepare, most additive-free, and richest in nutrients vital to cats and dogs. Because protein is basic in planning a meal for these pets (much more important than for humans), cost counts. Check the first column on the left for the approximate price per gram of protein in various foods. Where possible, I used the price for organic food. You can assume less cost for conventional food, about a third or half less.

APPROX. COST PER GRAM OF PROTEIN	GRAINS	FEATURES	LEGUMES	FEATURES
Less than 1 cent	Wheat, whole grain	O, I, P	Soybeans	O, A, Ca, I, P
	Rye, whole grain	C	Split peas	O, **A,** P
	—	—	Pinto beans	O, Ca, P
	—	—	Red kidney beans	O, I, P
1 cent	Oats, rolled	O, Ca, I, P, S	White beans	O, I, P
	Corn meal	O, **A,** S	Lentils	O, A, I, P
	Barley	O	—	—
	Millet	O, B, I, S	—	—
2 cents	Bulgur	O, I	—	—
	—	—	—	—
3 cents	Buckwheat	O, **Ca,** P	—	—
	Brown rice	O	—	—
	Yeast, brewer's	**B, I, P**	—	—
4 cents	Whole-wheat bread	O, I, P	—	—
	—	—	—	—
	—	—	—	—
5 cents	—	—	Tofu	O, **Ca, I, P**
6 cents	—	—	—	—
	—	—	—	—
	—	—	—	—
7 cents	—	—	—	—
8 cents	—	—	—	—
9 cents	—	—	—	—
10 cents	—	—	—	—
11 cents	Potatoes	B	—	—
15 cents	—	—	Soy yogurt	O, **Ca, I, P**

Boldface signifies remarkable values of unusually nutritious ingredients in their category.

KEY

O = available organically grown
A = high in vitamin A
B = high in B vitamins
Ca = high in calcium
I = high in iron
P = high in protein
S = short cooking time (saves time, money, natural resources)

MEATS	FEATURES	DAIRY PRODUCTS	FEATURES
—	—	—	—
—	—	—	—
—	—	—	—
—	—	—	—
Mackerel, canned	**Ca**, P	—	—
Beef liver, frozen	**A, B, I**, P	—	—
—	—	—	—
—	—	—	—
Turkey, ground, frozen	**P**	Eggs	**A, I**, P
Chicken, whole	**P**	Eggs (free range)	**A, I**, P
Tuna, canned, oil	**A, P**	Cottage cheese	A, Ca, **P**
Tuna, canned, water	**A, P**	Cottage cheese	O, A, Ca, **P**
Hamburger, 80% lean	P, A, I	—	—
Hamburger, 93% lean	P, A, I	Eggs, free range	O, A, I, P
Salmon, canned	A, **Ca**, P	Milk, 2%	A
—	—	Swiss cheese	Ca
Turkey, ground, fresh	**P**	Cheddar cheese	O, Ca
Lamb, ground	P	Milk, fat free	A
Chuck roast steak	P	Milk, whole	A
—	—	Yogurt, plain, nonfat	**B, Ca**
—	—	Yogurt, nonfat	O, **B, Ca**
—	—	Milk, soy	O
—	—	Milk, 2%	O, A
—	—	Milk, nonfat	O, A
—	—	Milk, whole	O, A

Biscuits

Homemade biscuits are another great treat for pets. (See recipes in "Additional Recipes" on page 444.) If you don't have the time to make your own, look for the additive-free commercially made biscuits that are found in many health food stores. Read the labels carefully and watch out for meat meal and meat by-products, sugar (sucrose), and any artificial colors, flavorings, and preservatives.

By including some hard foods in the diet, such as biscuits, bones, or even whole carrots, you provide your pet with a good way to exercise and clean its teeth and gums.

Fruit

Many dogs have a sweet tooth, and they enjoy an occasional piece of fruit as a snack. They like dried fruits such as figs, dates, prunes, and apricots, as well as fresh fruits like apples, bananas, and berries. Like vegetables, fruits are great storehouses of vitamins, minerals, and vital energy. (There have been a few reports of grapes and raisins making some dogs sick, so avoid them.) For best digestion, feed such foods apart from the regular mealtime. Dried fruits are especially good natural sources of potassium, an important mineral that can sometimes be in short supply; other good sources are bananas, peanuts, potatoes, and tomato sauce. Dates are extremely rich in folic acid, an important B vitamin.

Nuts and Seeds

We don't include nuts and seeds in our recipes because they are often expensive and contain more fat than protein. I have, however, heard a few reports of healthy dogs that have eaten no form of concentrated protein other than nuts for many years. One of my clients gives his dog peanut butter sandwiches as a snack when they go on picnics. If you do use peanut butter, *make sure it is organic.* Peanuts are very heavily treated with chemicals, more than other crops.

Nuts and seeds are best digested raw, either when made into a nut butter or when finely ground. Now and then, you can include some in your pet's diet in place of fatty meats, if you like.

Veggie Burgers

Have you ever tried any of the meat-substitute burgers made especially for vegetarians? Many of them are quite delicious, and we've found that a lot of pets think so too. We discovered this one day when our cat was going through a period of "finicky-ness," turning up his nose at what seemed to us like a perfectly acceptable rendition of what he usually eats. (Maybe "usual" was the problem and he just wanted a little more variety.)

In any case, when we decided to share a little of the veggie "burger" we were eating, he snarfed it up in nothing flat. We pulled another one out of the freezer, popped it in the toaster, and he demolished it as well. We knew we were on to something, and since then, we've found these make excellent taste-tempters, both for mixing in with his usual fare and for an occasional meal in itself.

Not all meatless burgers are created equal, however. The tastiest ones seem to be those that incorporate some dairy products and that aren't too heavy on the soybeans or tempeh (a soybean product).

If your cat or small dog relishes them, you may even be tempted to feed meatless burgers as a major part of its diet; they are convenient and often use organic ingredients. However, we wouldn't recommend using them for more than, say, a third of the diet. We don't have any way to know how well their nutritional content meets the special needs of dogs and cats. Nor do we know how much calcium, vitamin A, taurine, and so on to add to make any needed adjustments. Cats especially need meat in their diet, and it is difficult to supply what they need if vegetable sources make up much of the diet. We'd advise ⅛- to ¼-teaspoon bone meal per burger when you do serve it. Crumble up the burger and mix in the powder.

Flavorings

Nutritional yeast and other items in our recommended nutritional supplements section (see "Supplements," page 50) also serve to add flavor to food. In addition, you can experiment with moderate amounts of the following flavorings: tamari (naturally brewed soy sauce), miso, tomato sauce, butter, garlic, mild chili powder, natural broth powders, and herbed sea salt mixtures. Broken-up corn chips (saltless and organic, if you can get them) coated with brewer's yeast are also a hit with many pets. Just don't get carried away!

Look to your animal for preferences. It's interesting that dogs, given a choice, usually prefer unsalted food. It appears that they have some natural good food sense, doesn't it?

Garlic

Not only is garlic tasty to many pets, it also helps to tone up the digestive tract and discourage worms and other parasites, including fleas. Garlic is particularly potent when it's added fresh. Besides crushing a clove or two directly into a recipe, there's a tasty condiment you can add to your pet's daily fare as you serve it. Simply crush a clove of garlic into a small amount of tamari soy sauce. Let it sit about ten minutes, then remove the garlic. Use about ⅛ teaspoon to each cup of food.

Yeast Sprinkle

Besides the yeast that is included in the Healthy Powder supplement (see page 52), many animals love to have a little yeast sprinkled on top of their meals, much the way we enjoy a little parmesan cheese on top of pasta. Large-flake torula (nutritional) yeast is one of the best flavored, though it is increasingly difficult to find. If you cannot locate some, then use brewer's yeast, which is almost the same. If you use yeast often, mix some up in a jar with a little powdered calcium supplement for optimal calcium/phosphorus balance. If your pet likes garlic, you can also add a little in powdered form.

Here's the formula: one cup nutritional yeast plus 3,000 mg elemental calcium (such as provided by Animal Essentials Calcium Supplement). Add to this one to four teaspoons unsalted garlic powder (optional). Mix well and sprinkle on top of the food to be served. It will entice many finicky animals, especially cats.

If this is too much trouble, you can use yeast alone as a flavoring agent. As long as only a small amount is used, the balance of minerals will not be significantly affected.

A note on yeast and allergies: Some people say that yeast should not be used as food for animals because it may cause allergies. I can only report that my experience is to the contrary. I find that yeast is an excellent food without any side effects. Granted, an occasional animal may be allergic to yeast, as to any commonly used food, but it does not *cause* allergies. I find that pets are most often allergic to foods like beef, chicken, corn, and soy. These foods are not causing the allergies; rather, it is the allergic animal that becomes sensitive to what it usually eats. That is why it often helps to change a diet from beef to lamb, for example, which relieves the symptoms—at least until they become sensitive to the new ingredients!

SUPPLEMENTS

In addition to the basic natural food groups mentioned earlier, I always recommend including several nutrition-packed food supplements—such as bone meal, nutritional or brewer's yeast, lecithin, kelp, vegetable oil, and several vitamins—in the diet. The pur-

pose of these supplements is to fortify the diet with plenty of important vitamins and minerals. Unfortunately, these nutrients are often inadequately represented even in fresh foods today because of loss during storage and cooking, soil depletion, and forced-growing methods.

Even the complication of acid rain has been causing a decrease in the ability of plants to take up essential minerals from the soil. The problem is this: minerals are slowly released from the rocks and clays that make up soil. Then the plants take up the minerals, dependent on how acid or alkaline the soil is. If the soil is too acidic, the plants can't "grab" it. Thus, the long-term effect of acid rain is lowered mineral content of plant foods.

Another factor is that even under the best of conditions, it takes time for the plant to absorb the minerals. Under modern conditions, in which artificial fertilizers are used to accelerate the growth of plants, the time for mineral absorption is less, which leads to low mineral levels. Of course these two factors work together, and the net result is less mineral content with time. The Earth Summit Report of 1992 revealed that North American farm and range soils had been depleted of over 85 percent of their minerals.

For animals that are not in the best of health, mineral supplements are an essential part of the diet. Another reason I recommend supplements is to balance the ingredients of the recipes given in this book so that they meet the nutritional standards for dogs and cats for such important nutrients as calcium, iron, linoleic acid, vitamin A, and the B vitamins set by the Association of American Feed Control Officials. So don't think of supplements as something optional. They are an integral part of each recipe (unless noted otherwise).

The basic supplements described below are usually included in each recipe. Following is a summary of the purpose of each supplement, as well as various supply sources, and instructions for preparing the supplement for inclusion in the diet.

CALCIUM SUPPLEMENT

Some supplemental source of calcium is an essential ingredient in every recipe. Also, every recipe should have a proper calcium/phosphorus ratio. Though there is a wide range of what can support health, it is optimal if the ratio of calcium/phosphorus for dogs is between 1.2 and 1.4 parts calcium to 1 part phosphorus—thus, a little more calcium than phosphorus in the diet. Cats do better with a ratio of 1 part calcium to 1 part phosphorus.

I hasten to add that there is considerable flexibility in this. Most animals will do just fine with a wide range from 1 to 2 parts calcium to 1 part phosphorus. The actual amounts in food prepared is difficult to determine exactly. Generally, the minerals from bones or pure calcium sources are readily absorbed by the body, while those from plant sources may be less digestible. For example, only about 30 percent of the phosphorus in grains is available to the body. The recipes in the next chapter are calculated to include the minerals in the foodstuffs as well as what is added from bone meal, with the assumption that most will be absorbable.

Here are some ways to add this calcium.

Bone Meal

Buy the powdered bone meal that is sold for supplementation of animals. You can use that sold in natural food stores for human use but it will be less convenient and more expensive. The quality is the same—that is, not from U.S. livestock—and the advantage of the animal products is the availability in powder form to add to the food. These products come from purer sources than the bone meal sold in garden-supply departments—which is never to be used as a food.

Bone meal is the most natural calcium source for carnivores and provides many trace minerals. It is also a convenient, easy to use, and very concentrated form of calcium. It contains phosphorus as well as calcium, but in the recommended amounts there is plenty of extra calcium to balance out the phosphorus. Bone meal is the best choice when feeding large dogs, especially those with bone problems or signs of hip dysplasia. There are several brands available, and they vary somewhat in calcium concentration. See the "Table of Calcium Supplementation Products" on page 67.

Seaweed

Animal Essentials has provided a form of calcium derived from seaweed growing off the coast of Ireland. It is a very pure form of calcium and has the advantage of not coming from an animal source. It also provides many excellent trace minerals.

Di-calcium Phosphate

For those people who prefer not to use animal products but who want a higher combined amount of calcium and phosphorus in the diet than provided by a calcium product alone, substitute di-calcium phosphate for bone meal. This product is sometimes available in pet stores or in natural food stores. You should use about two-thirds the amount stated for bone meal in any recipe.

Calcium Tablets or Powder

Each recipe gives a suggested dose of calcium, expressed in milligrams. Unlike bone meal, this choice provides no additional phosphorus, which means less total calcium is needed to balance the total amount of phosphorus already available in the recipe.

You can supply "plain" calcium as calcium carbonate, chelated calcium, calcium gluconate, or calcium lactate. Except for the calcium carbonate, these are also considered the most assimilated forms of calcium. Avoid products that also contain phosphorus or magnesium.

Look on the label to see how much powder or how many tablets you must use to equal the milligrams of calcium called for in a recipe. If you buy tablets, use a blender, mortar and pestle, or pill crusher to grind them to a powder before mixing into the food. The easiest form to use is the

pure powder from Animal Essentials (see page 51).

Eggshell Powder

This is the cheapest route, because you can make the supplement yourself from egg shells, which are very high in calcium carbonate. Here's how to make eggshell powder. Wash the eggshells right after cracking and let them dry until you have accumulated a dozen or so. (Each whole eggshell makes about a teaspoon of powder, which equals about 1,800 milligrams of calcium.) Then bake at 300°F for about ten minutes. This removes a mineral-oil coating sometimes added to keep eggs from drying out. It also makes the shells dry and brittle enough to grind to a fine powder with a nut and seed grinder, blender, or mortar and pestle. Grind well enough to eliminate sharp, gritty pieces.

HEALTHY POWDER

This rich mixture of nutrients is used in all the recipes. The recipes, by themselves, provide necessary protein, fat, and carbohydrate, but to make sure there is adequate vitamin and mineral content as well, we use this mixture of several important food elements, which are available at most natural food stores: nutritional or brewer's yeast (rich in B vitamins, iron, and other nutrients); lecithin (for linoleic acid, choline, and inositol, which help your animal emulsify and absorb fats, improving the condition of its coat and digestion); powdered kelp (for iodine and trace minerals); enough calcium to balance the high phosphorus levels in yeast and lecithin (enabling you to add this powder in any reasonable quantity to any recipe or other diet); and vitamin C (not officially required for dogs or cats because they synthesize their own, but clinical experiences suggest its value).

We prefer the use of nutritional (or torula) yeast in the formula but, as I noted earlier, it has become difficult to find the last few years. I don't know why, but often all you can find is brewer's yeast, which is very similar. The difference is that nutritional yeast is grown to be used as a food supplement, while brewer's yeast is left over from brewing beer. Nutritionally they are basically the same, except that brewer's yeast is higher in chromium, a trace mineral important in the use of sugar by the body. You can substitute brewer's yeast in place of nutritional if it cannot be found.

HEALTHY POWDER

2	cups nutritional or brewer's yeast
1	cup lecithin granules
1/4	cup kelp powder
4	tablespoons Group I bone meal powder*
1,000	milligrams vitamin C (ground) or 1/4 teaspoon sodium ascorbate (optional)

* Calcium and phosphorus in bone meal products varies. See the "Table of Calcium Supplementation Products" in chapter 4,

page 67, to compare brands. I have grouped bone meal products into Group I, Group II, and Group III as a way of working with them in the recipes. In the recipes I am assuming the use of Group I bone meal sources, so adjust amounts if you are using a different brand. If you use a brand from Group II in this recipe, then double the amount of bone meal indicated. If you are using a non-bone-meal source (like eggshells or Animal Essentials calcium), then instead of bone meal, add 3 slightly rounded tablespoons of Animal Essentials calcium or 2 level tablespoons of powdered eggshell. These other sources will result in the Healthy Powder being a little on the low side for calcium, but adequate.

Mix all ingredients together in a 1-quart container and refrigerate.

Add to each recipe as instructed. You may also add this mixture to commercial food as follows: 1 to 2 teaspoons per day for cats or small dogs; 2 to 3 teaspoons per day for medium-size dogs; 1 to 2 tablespoons per day for large dogs.

VARIATIONS:

Yeast substitution: The yeast is optional, and if you prefer not to use it, then reduce the calcium in the Healthy Powder formula to 3,200 milligrams calcium or 1¾ teaspoons eggshell powder. Then use half the usual amount of Healthy Powder specified in each recipe. To replace the lost nutrients, add a complete multi-vitamin-mineral supplement for animals to the daily food, using the amount recommended on the label. Do not add vitamin A, C, or E, because they should be adequately supplied by the pet vitamin.

Kelp substitution: If your animal doesn't like the flavor of kelp or you can't find it, you can substitute ¼ cup of alfalfa powder. Kelp has wonderful trace minerals in it, but we also value alfalfa, also very high in trace minerals, as an adequate substitute. If neither of these works out, then obtain a trace mineral supplement at a natural food store. Look at the label and see what the dose is for a human being. Assume that human to weigh 150 pounds and reduce the recommended dose for the weight of your animal. For example, if your dog weighs 20 pounds, then the amount to use is 20 divided by 150 = 13 percent of the recommended amount. Use this as a guide as to how much of the tablet or capsule to give.

I am always a little nervous when concentrated supplements are given because it is possible to give too much. Using natural food sources for trace minerals is definitely my preference.

OILS

Fats and oils provide, spoonful to spoonful, more than twice as much energy as other food sources. A certain amount of fat in the diet is natural and necessary. Cats especially enjoy and consume large quantities in their natural diet. Fats are also required for the maintenance and growth of many tissues in the body. Of special importance, however, are the fatty acids, smaller components of fats that are necessary for good health. Many of them can be produced in the body from other foods, but some are acquired from the food eaten. An example is the fatty acid called linoleic acid (omega-6), which is a requirement for dogs and cats. It is found in fresh foods, in the natural diet; if available in the diet, a dog can produce whatever other fatty acid is required from this one fatty acid.

ANALYSIS OF THE HEALTHY POWDER INGREDIENTS

INGREDIENTS	CALORIES (KCAL.)	PROTEIN (G.)	FAT (G.)	CARBOHYDRATES (G.)	FIBER (G.)	ASH (G.)
Nutritional yeast, 2 cups	886.4	123.5	3.2	118.4	10.56	24.64
Lecithin granules, 1 cup	800.4	2	96	15.96	0	0
Kelp, ¼ cup	124.28	0	0.57	30.64	3.86	12.48
Bone meal, approx. 9 gms	25.92	3.18	0.69	3.51	0	28.48
Vitamin C, ¼ tsp powder	0	1.38	0	0	0	0
Totals	1,837	128.0	100.46	168.5	14.42	65.6
% of 4 food groups	—	27.7%	21.7%	36.4%	3.1%	14.2%

Cats need linoleic acid and another one called arachidonic acid, so they have additional fatty acid requirements.

Do these matter? Yes. Without adequate quantities come many health problems, including significant skin eruptions, loss of hair, skin that won't heal from wounds, liver and kidney degeneration, increased susceptibility to infections, heart and circulatory problems, weakness, retarded growth, spontaneous abortions, sterility, impairment of vision, loss of ability to learn, symptoms similar to arthritis, and more. We can see from this list that these nutritional components are aptly named *essential* fatty acids.

Deficiencies are common, and most animals suffer a *mild* deficiency that results in less severe symptoms. The usual symptoms of deficiency appear as a dull, dry coat, excessive loss of hair, greasy skin, accompanying itching and scratching, and a greater likelihood to develop skin infections or conditions like abscesses or ringworm. Deficiencies are common, because the fatty acids are the most fragile of all the food ingredients and the ones that break down first during processing and storage. This is a chief reason that food preservatives are used—in an attempt to protect them. Without preservatives, the contained fats become rancid, their use lost to the body, and also become toxic and poisonous (of course we prefer natural, nontoxic preservatives). Rancid fats have a very definite odor, rather acrid. You have likely smelled them yourself in fatty food that has sat around too long.

Essential fatty acids also tend to naturally reduce inflammation in the body. When deficient in animals prone to inflammation (such as with allergies or immune diseases), these conditions become worse than would otherwise be the case on an adequate diet. It is difficult to overemphasize the importance of these essential nutrients.

CALCIUM (MG.)	PHOS. (MG.)	IRON (MG.)	SODIUM (MG.)	POTASSIUM (MG.)	VIT. A	THIAMINE	RIBOFLAVIN	NIACIN	VIT. C
1,356.8	5,481.6	61.76	48	6,547.2	0	44.8	16	142.0	0
960	3,598.8	5.76	1,714.42	0	0	0	0	8	0
623.12	137.06	0.07	1,714.42	3,009.45	0	0	0	0	0
9,215.77	4,607.88	6.91	0	0	0	0	0	3.13	0
0	0	0	124	0	0	0	0	0	1,000
12,155.6	13,825.3	74.5	1,886.42	9,556.65	0	44.8	16	145.2	1,000
2.63%	2.99%	.02%	.41%	2.07%	—	<1%	<1%	<1%	<1%

Sources of Essential Fatty Acids

❖ Linoleic acid (omega-6) is found in safflower, sunflower, corn, evening primrose, and borage oils. It is also found in poultry fat and pork fat (not much in beef or butter).

❖ Linolenic acid (omega-3) include fish oils (especially cold-water fish such as salmon, mackerel, halibut, and herring). They are also found in canola and flax oils, flax seeds, walnuts, soybeans, and freshly ground wheat germ. It is thought that dogs and cats can make omega-3 from linoleic acid (above), and the need for this is not clear at this time. I advise people to include some omega-3 because I think it may be helpful and certainly spares the body having to convert it from the limited amount of linoleic acid present in most diets.

❖ Dried beans (great northern, kidney, navy, and soybeans) are inexpensive sources of both omega-6 and omega-3 essential fatty acids.

❖ Certain fish are very high in omega-6 and omega-3, and the body can usually convert the fatty acids from fish more easily than from other sources. Good choices, in addition to those mentioned above, are sardines, herring, lake trout, and albacore tuna.

❖ Arachidonic acid, a requirement for cats only (or in dogs with very little linoleic acid in their diets), is present in some fish oils (like cod liver oil), pork fat, and poultry fat. All the functions of this nutrient in the cat are not known, but substances derived from arachidonic acid have important roles in the control of blood clotting, pain, inflammation, and contraction of the muscles of the intestines and bladder. Arachidonic acid is especially important for normal cat reproduction.

Use the cold-pressed oils; because they have not been heated excessively, they retain more of the essential fatty acids. At home, refrigerate them in a well-sealed container, and never heat them. Oxygen (from exposure to air) destroys them rapidly. If you like, you can premix vitamin E (see page 58) into the oil. Use 1,600 to 2,000 IU per cup. (Don't pre-mix vitamin A into it, however, as this could create excesses in some recipes.) An excellent source of omega-3 is freshly prepared flax oil, which is available in the refrigerated section of natural food stores. Udo's Choice, also refrigerated, is a brand that blends several oils together for a broader spectrum, with an optimal ratio of omega-3 and omega-6. It doesn't have arachidonic acid in it, so that will need to be added separately. A convenient source of arachidonic acid is cod liver oil, available in natural food stores. Add 2–3 drops to the food each day.

These products are convenient, especially an oil blend like Udo's oil, because the work has been done for you already. You can have very fresh and biologically active material in your refrigerator ready to use when you are preparing a meal or to supplement a commercial food. Realize that it is very, very difficult for a processed food to contain adequate quantities, so it is excellent insurance to get in the practice of adding these fragile nutrients to food before serving.

Note: You may substitute butter, beef fat, pork fat, or poultry fat (preferably the last two, which contain arachidonic acid) for up to 50 percent of the oil in the cat recipes (do not substitute butter in dog recipes). Cats normally have high levels of animal fat in their diets and do well with it. Cats also do better with an animal source of unsaturated fatty acids, like cod liver oil.

VITAMINS

Vitamin A

This important vitamin is included in many of the recipes, especially for cats. Most of the dog food recipes don't call for it because dogs can make their own vitamin A from carotene, found in vegetables. (But if you omit vegetables from your dog's diet, add about 1,000 IU of vitamin A for every cup omitted.) Cats, on the other hand, require a pre-formed animal source of vitamin A. They are also sensitive to either too little or too much in their diets, so adhere to the amount listed in each recipe. There are four ways to provide the vitamin A in each recipe:

❖ **Cod liver oil.** Because it is also an excellent source of unsaturated fatty acids, cod liver oil is highly recommended, if your pet accepts it. Seal well and refrigerate it to prevent rancidity. Read the label to see how many teaspoons provide the amount of vitamin A called for in the recipe.

❖ **Vitamin A and D capsules.** Buy the lowest potency. This will probably be 10,000 IU of vitamin A per capsule. Break open or pierce the capsule to use.

❖ **Liquid vitamin A and D.** These drops are more convenient than capsules, if you can find them. Get the variety sold for humans in health food stores. The typical potency is about 1,600 IU per drop. Use the number of drops closest to the total amount called for.

❖ **Pet vitamins.** These tablets will also add extra vitamins and minerals to the diet. If you use pet vitamins, you may omit both vitamins A and E from the recipes. Instead, simply add the pet vitamins directly to each meal as suggested on the product label.

Note: Some pet supplements supply large amounts of calcium without phosphorus, as you'll discover from the label. If this is the case, decrease the calcium supplement in the recipe a bit. Further, it is important to avoid any pet supplements containing the preservative sodium benzoate, especially for cats, because this preservative is an accumulative poison.

Vitamin B

B vitamins are essential for normal body functioning and therefore for a healthy body. The term "B vitamins" refers to a family of vitamins, including thiamine, riboflavin, pantothenic acid, niacin, B_6 (pyridoxine), biotin, choline, folic acid, and vitamin B_{12}. When you use a B vitamin supplement, be sure each of these are included in the formula. Deficiency of these vitamins is common—mostly due to the fragility of these chemical substances to the conditions of processing and storage. Even with a home-prepared diet, it is a good idea to supplement with a B-complex formula. Food purchased from a market is not necessarily fresh and, unless organic, may have undergone forced growth and be subsequently low in natural vitamins.

The amount to use varies with the size of the animal. If you are using a formula made for human beings (which is perfectly fine as long as there is no sodium benzoate preservative in it), a good rule to follow is to adjust the dose proportionately for the size of your animal. For example, let's assume you have a 50-pound dog and your B vitamin is recommended at two capsules a day (for the average human). Assume that the human dose is for a 150-pound person; since your dog weighs one-third of the human weight, give only ⅓ of that dose to your dog.

What if the animal is really, really small, like a cat or little dog? Give about 5 mg of the B-complex formula to ensure correct proportions of the major (thiamine, riboflavin, and niacin) and minor B vitamins.

Vitamin E

I include extra vitamin E, an antioxidant, in the diet for several reasons. Not only does it aid important body functions, such as fighting disease, but it also helps minimize the effects of pollution. Vitamin E helps to preserve and protect the vitamin A and fatty acids in other supplements and in foods. There are two ways that this supplement can be provided:

❖ **Natural-source vitamin E capsules.** Look for products containing the d-alpha tocopherols, which are the natural form. (The dl-alpha tocopherols, with a lower-case "l" after the "d," are a synthetic, and generally less expensive, form.) The gelatin capsule variety provides a good "storage container." Open a fresh capsule for the recipe or premix it into the vegetable oil (see page 56). It's okay to use more vitamin E than the amount called for, if that's more convenient.

❖ **Wheat-germ oil.** This is a good way to provide vitamin E in a natural complex. But be careful not to feed your animal rancid wheat-germ oil, which is detectable by a slightly bitter or burning aftertaste—taste it yourself. Buy wheat-germ oil in capsule form. Read the label to determine the appropriate amount to use.

Taurine (optional)

When preparing cat food, pet food manufacturers have been adding taurine, a component of protein. Unlike most animals, cats cannot synthesize this amino acid themselves, so they have to get it from their diets—which basically means from meat.

Taurine is necessary, because a deficiency is known to cause degeneration of the retina and possible blindness, as well as cardiac problems. Apparently, shortages in taurine levels in pet foods occur as a result of processing procedures. Studies have shown that up to 80 percent of the taurine that occurs naturally in meat can be lost from the cooking temperatures in commercial food production.

Investigating further, however, I learned that the daily taurine content of the wild feline diet is about 25 to 50 milligrams and that this amount has been found adequate in most experimental studies. In the wild, of course, the cat would consume the heart, brain, and other high-taurine organs, so maybe muscle meat is actually deficient by the standards of the overall prey. Commercial food manufacturers now supplement with taurine to bring the levels up. You can do the same thing with these recipes. I am not concerned about the taurine content of my cat diet if the meat is fed raw. If, however, you feed the meat cooked (e.g., from your own leftovers), use a partly vegetarian diet (see chapter 5). To err on the safe side, there are three ways to address this shortage:

❖ Add capsule(s) or tablet(s) of taurine in the amount stated in the recipes as an optional ingredient. Pills or powdered capsules of taurine can be purchased at many stores that specialize in nutritional products. Also, many vitamin-mineral supplements for cats now contain taurine. Read the label to see how many units are needed to provide the amount of taurine indicated in the recipe, rounding the figure upward if necessary. Be sure to add heat-sensitive taurine to the recipe only after the cooked grain has cooled down, or the heat might destroy it.

❖ Use Vegecat, a supplement for vegetarian cats that provides the taurine that is missing in a meatless diet.

❖ Include tuna, mackerel, clams, and heart in the diet. All are naturally high in taurine. (Maybe that's why most cats love them!)

There are two other amino acids, cousins to taurine, which cats require. They are arginine and cysteine, both of which are readily found in meat, eggs, and a variety of other foods. Most diets are adequate in these. If you follow the diet guidelines we have discussed here, there will be no problem supplying adequate amounts.

Now that you have a good understanding of what goes into a fresh, natural diet for your pet, learn how to put it together in practical, tasty, balanced recipes! That's our next chapter.

CHAPTER 4

EASY-TO-MAKE RECIPES
FOR PET FOOD

Now it's time to really talk turkey—to show you a variety of delicious, well-balanced recipes for feeding your animals. Fixing fresh, nutritious meals for pets is very little trouble once you get the hang of it. Many people even find it fun, especially when the concoction meets with the enthusiastic approval of an eager eater.

To ensure the best nutritional content, I again remind you to follow the recipes fairly closely. Do, however, use a variety of grains, meats, and vegetables rather than sticking to the same formula every time.

Follow these tips for easier preparation of your pet's meals, preserving extras and adding appetizing touches when serving.

Keep recipes and supplies handy. Once you work out a basic routine, copy the recipes onto cards or durable cardstock, adding notes if you care to. Store them with your pet's supplements in a cupboard or some other spot convenient to your food preparation area. That way they'll always be right at hand while you're mixing the chow.

Use quick-cooking grains. These include rolled oats, bulgur, cornmeal, whole-wheat couscous, and quinoa. For a small pet it sometimes makes sense to use crumbled whole-wheat bread.

Coordinate pet food preparation with cooking your own food. Unless you're fixing very large quantities of animal food, it's often convenient to prepare it while waiting for your own food to cook. Better yet, coordinate both meal plans, using the same basic grains—maybe rice or cornmeal—and other ingredients, such as tuna or lean hamburger.

Freeze extras. For small animals, make up one to two weeks' worth of food at a time, freezing extras in plastic dairy and deli containers. Thaw the frozen meals in the refrigerator 24 hours in advance of feeding time.

Warm up prepared food. Since you will probably make enough chow to last for several days at a time and refrigerate the extras, here's how to warm up cold food to make it more palatable for your pet and easier to digest. Rinse your pet's bowl with warm water. Dish the food into the bowl and pour a little hot water over it. Use a fork or shake the bowl to lightly mix the food in the water without making it mushy. Sprinkle a little yeast or other flavoring on top, if you wish. I don't recommend microwave cooking because it would defeat the purpose of using raw meat. Warming the food, however, for 10–15 seconds is fine. Take it out of the plastic first.

Where possible, the recipes very much exceed the minimal requirements usually recommended for feeding animals. It is my opinion that "minimum" is not the same as "optimal," and I prefer that both dogs and cats have more protein and fat than available in commercial foods. For example, the minimum recommended requirement for dogs is 18 percent protein and 5 percent fat—yet the natural diet of wolves is around 54 percent protein and 43 percent fat (as fed at the San Diego Zoo). Big difference.

A frequent question I've tried to resolve over the years is how much to feed. The difficulty in giving specific amounts is that food quantity is extremely variable depending on what the food makeup is (especially fat content), the size and age of the animal, and its level of activity. Just consider the difference between the small Yorkie weighing 12 pounds and having almost no exercise and the 65-pound sled dog that is pulling heavy loads all day.

What I have found to be the most reliable approach is to feed what seems to be a reasonable amount, enough to satisfy the dog or cat in 20 minutes or so (not leaving food out during the day), and then monitor body weight.

A simple indicator: You should be able to feel your pet's ribs easily as you slide your hand over his sides; if you can't, he's probably too heavy, so begin to feed a smaller quantity. Visible ribs usually mean the opposite, and you need to feed more. In cases of obesity, use the weight-loss recipes in the next chapter.

If you have a number of animals, you will, of course, need to multiply the recipe amounts accordingly.

BOOSTER MIXES FOR DOG KIBBLE

Let's start with something simple: three fresh food combos that you can add to a good-quality dog kibble, such as those sold at natural food stores. If you're not ready to jump whole hog into the home-prepared diet, or if you have several large dogs, these shortcuts offer a convenient way to provide many of the benefits of fresh foods and nutritious supplements and still maintain nutritional balance. By adding fresh meat, dairy products, vegetable oil, and food supplements, you boost your dog's intake of quality protein, fatty acids, lecithin, B vitamins and minerals—all helpful for skin and coat problems.

Resist any temptation to simplify these additions by just throwing a slab of meat or a dash of oil on the kibble rather than following the recipes as given. Meat is dramatically low in calcium as compared with its phosphorus content, so using meat alone could result in a net dietary calcium deficiency. That's why a calcium supplement is added to the recipes. Extra oil by itself is also counterproductive, as it will lower the overall percentage of protein and every other nutrient in the kibble, which may already contain a marginal amount of the essentials.

As with other recipes, you can always premix larger amounts of these supplements and freeze extras, thawing and using them as needed.

Here is the idea behind these supplements. I start with the likely minimum values present in many dog kibbles, e.g., 18 percent protein, 9 percent fat (or less), and about 67 percent carbohydrate (grains and vegetable products). Then I add in the good things I want you to add—fresh meat, vegetable oil, and vitamins—then balance for calcium and phosphorus. Of course a better quality, higher protein product will bump up the amounts, but likely not significantly (most commercial foods are not very high in protein or fat).

Here's the first one.

FRESH MEAT SUPPLEMENT FOR DOG KIBBLE

3	pounds (6 cups) chopped or ground raw turkey*, chicken, lean hamburger, lean chuck, or lean beef heart
1/4	cup vegetable oil (cold pressed, organic)
1	tablespoon Healthy Powder (page 53)
1½	teaspoons Group I** bone meal
1	tablespoon Animal Essentials calcium (or Group III† equivalent for 3,000 mg calcium)
50–200	IU vitamin E
5,000	IU vitamin A with 200 IU vitamin D (or alternate regularly with Fresh Egg Supplement, page 64)

Mix the oil, powder, bone meal, and vitamins together. Then combine the mixture with the meat, coating it well.

At mealtime, feed about 6 tablespoons of this mixture for every cup of dog kibble served. You can either mix the meat supplement and kibble together or serve each separately.

Yield: *Slightly more than 6 cups.*

* I assumed using whole turkey for my calculations in this recipe. Once mixed with kibble, it yields at least 30 percent protein, 20 percent fat, and 50 percent carbohydrate.

Look at "Protein, Fat, and Carbohydate Content of Various Meats" on page 86, to see how proteins in various meats compare. Notice that the protein in whole turkey is half that of lean hamburger. You can, however, substitute meats without concern in this recipe supplement—if you prefer to keep the protein lower, then use correspondingly less of the higher-protein meats.

** Calcium and phosphorus in bone meal products vary. See the "Table of Calcium Supplementation Products" on page 67 to compare brands. I have grouped bone meal products into Group I, Group II, and Group III as a way of working with them in the recipes. If you use a brand from Group II in this recipe, then double the amount of bone meal indicated.

† If you are using the pure calcium from Animal Essentials instead of bone meal, use 2 teaspoons of Animal Essentials and add 2 tablespoons of brewer's yeast to the recipe. If you are using one of the other sources of calcium from Group III, then adjust the amounts accordingly. If you are using another calcium source than is listed here, the total amount of calcium added in this recipe = 5,500 mg (5.5 grams).

COTTAGE CHEESE SUPPLEMENT FOR DOG KIBBLE

Cottage cheese is an inexpensive, convenient, and palatable source of protein that can boost the nutritional value of kibble.

2	teaspoons vegetable oil
1¹/₂	teaspoons Healthy Powder (page 53)
1	teaspoon Group I bone meal*
5,000	IU vitamin A with 200 IU vitamin D
2	cups creamed cottage cheese
¹/₂	cup vegetables (optional)

* See "Table of Calcium Supplementation Products" on page 67. If Group II bone meals are used, double the recipe amount. You can also skip the bone meal and instead use 1 teaspoon Animal Essentials calcium. If you are using another calcium source than is listed here, the total amount of calcium added in this recipe = 2,000 mg (2 grams).

Mix the oil in the kibble. Toss in the powder and bone meal, coating the kibble; add the vitamin A. Serve the cottage cheese and vegetables together on the side, or mix them into the kibble.

Add about 4 tablespoons per cup of kibble.

Yield: About 2³/₄ cups

Mixed with kibble, it results in a combined food of at least 20 percent protein, 10 percent fat, and 60 percent carbohydrate. This is considerably lower in protein and fat than the meat supplement in the preceding recipe and is more suitable for the dog or cat that needs a lower protein diet or does not react well to a food that is too rich.

FRESH EGG SUPPLEMENT FOR DOG KIBBLE

1	teaspoon vegetable oil
1	teaspoon Healthy Powder (page 53)
1¹/₂	teaspoons Group I bone meal*
50–200	IU vitamin E
4	large eggs

* See "Table of Calcium Supplementation Products" on page 67. If Group II bone meals are used, double the recipe amount. If you wish to avoid using bone meal, skip that ingredient and instead add 1 teaspoon of Animal Essentials calcium. If you are using another calcium source (from Group III calcium supplements), the total amount of calcium added in this recipe = 2,500 mg (2.5 grams).

Mix ingredients together. At mealtime, add about 2 tablespoons per cup of kibble. Use the eggs raw.

Yield: 1¹/₂ cups

Once mixed with kibble, this boosts the values to at least 20 percent protein, 10 percent fat, and 70 percent carbohydrate.

BASIC RECIPES
FOR DOGS

The following recipes are meant to form the mainstay of the fresh, home-prepared diet for dogs. See "Nutritional Composition of Recipes for Dogs" on page 68 for nutritional data on each recipe. Each recipe indicates how many cups to feed adult dogs of different breed sizes. The weight range for each group is defined as follows:

- ❖ Toy: up to 15 pounds
- ❖ Small: 15 to 30 pounds
- ❖ Medium: 30 to 60 pounds
- ❖ Large: 60 to 90 pounds
- ❖ Giant: over 90 pounds

Amounts to feed will vary according to activity level, ingredient substitutions, weather, and so on. Let your dog's appetite and weight be the ultimate gauge.

DOGGIE OATS

Oats are a good choice of grain for pets. Not only are oats quick-cooking, but they contain more protein per calorie than any other common grain. It's best, though, to add some variety by substituting other grains at times (as recommended), because each grain varies in its amino acid composition and its vitamin and mineral levels. This versatile maintenance recipe for adult dogs provides a protein level of 33 percent (using turkey with the oats) and 30 percent fat. Substituting tofu for turkey lowers the protein and fat content considerably.

5	cups raw rolled oats (about 11 cups cooked)
3	pounds (6 cups) raw whole, ground, or chopped turkey
1/4	cup vegetable oil
1	cup cooked vegetables (or less if raw and grated—may be omitted occasionally)
6	tablespoons (rounded 1/3 cup) Healthy Powder (page 53)
4	teaspoons Group I bone meal*

10,000	IU vitamin A (optional if using carrots)
400	IU vitamin E
1	teaspoon tamari soy sauce or 1/4 teaspoon iodized salt (optional)
1–2	cloves garlic, crushed or minced (optional)

* See "Table of Calcium Supplementation Products" on page 67. If Group II bone meals are used, double the recipe amount. The amount of calcium contributed by bone meal = 5,600 mg (5.6 grams).

Bring about 10 cups of water to a boil. Add the oats, cover, and turn off the heat, letting the oats cook for 10 to 15 minutes, or until soft. Don't stir while cooking or the oats will become mushy. Then combine with the remaining ingredients and serve.

Yield: About 18–19 cups, with about 230 kilocalories per cup.

Daily ration (in cups): Toy—1 to 2; small—about 4; medium—6 to 7; large—about 8; giant—9+.

You can make substitutions in this recipe by using a different grain or meat (or both). See "Food Ingredient Substitutions" on page 74, for guidance. Varying the recipe to include different ingredients insures you have not overlooked some important nutrient and prevents deficiencies.

If you use oats or bulgur, you may occasionally substitute either of the following for each pound of meat: 1 pint cottage cheese plus 4 eggs, or 16 ounces of tofu plus 4 eggs. Add the eggs while the grain is still hot so they'll set slightly for the best texture. See the next chapter for more vegetarian recipes suitable for dogs.

MINI DOGGIE OATS

For your convenience, here is the previous recipe, divided by ¼.

1¼	cups raw rolled oats
¾	pound (1½ cups) raw whole, ground, or chopped turkey
1	tablespoon vegetable oil
¼	cup cooked vegetables (or less if raw and grated—may be omitted occasionally)
1½	tablespoons Healthy Powder (page 53)
1	teaspoon Group I bone meal (see previous recipe)
2,500	IU vitamin A (optional if using carrots)
100	IU vitamin E
¼	teaspoon tamari soy sauce or a pinch of iodized salt (optional)
½	clove garlic, crushed or minced (optional)

Yield: About 5 cups, with 230 kilocalories per cup.

Daily ration: Same as for Doggie Oats (above).

TABLE OF CALCIUM SUPPLEMENTATION PRODUCTS

GROUP I

PRODUCT	CALCIUM & PHOSPHORUS (PER TSP.)
KAL, Inc. Bone Meal	Calcium = 1,500 mg Phosphorus = 750 mg
Solid Gold	Calcium = 1,369 mg Phosphorus = 684 mg
Group I average amounts	Calcium = 1,435 mg Phosphorus = 717 mg

GROUP II*

PRODUCT	CALCIUM & PHOSPHORUS (PER TSP.)
NaturVet Bone Meal	Calcium = 860 mg Phosphorus = 430 mg
Now Bone Meal Powder	Calcium = 500 mg Phosphorus = 250 mg
Solgar Bone-All	Calcium = 714 mg Phosphorus = 336 mg
Group II average amounts	Calcium = 691 mg Phosphorus = 339 mg

  * Note that the Group II values are approximately 1/2 that of Group I, so if you use one of these supplements, double the amount of bone meal called for in the recipe.

GROUP III**

PRODUCT	CALCIUM & PHOSPHORUS (PER TSP.)
Animal Essentials Calcium	Calcium = 1,000 mg Phosphorus = 2 mg
Eggshells (dried & powdered)	Calcium = 1,800 mg Phosphorus = 6 mg
Calcium carbonate powder†	Calcium = 1,775 mg Phosphorus = 0
Calcium gluconate†	Calcium = 188 mg Phosphorus = 0
Calcium lactate†	Calcium = 317 mg Phosphorus = 0

  ** Note: These products are almost entirely calcium with very little phosphorus. Excessive use of them can alter the ratio of calcium to phosphorus. Generally use about 25 percent less than Group I bone meal. It is easier to balance the recipes using bone meal and, unless specified otherwise, the recipe calculations are based on using Group I bone meal.

  † These supplements are often available in health food stores or pet supply stores. What I have listed is from brands I could find locally. Don't assume calcium content of all brands is the same. Check labels.

SUPPLIER CONTACT:

KAL, Inc. Bone Meal	Many sources.	Search for "KAL bone meal" on the Web.
Solid Gold	(800) 364-4863	www.solidgoldhealth.com
NaturVet Bone Meal	(888) 628-8783	www.naturvet.com
Now Bone Meal Powder	(877) 342-5217	www.nowcatalog.com
Solgar Bone-All	(877) SOLGAR-4	http://solgar.com
Animal Essentials Calcium	(888) 463-7748	www.animalessentials.com

NUTRITIONAL COMPOSITION OF RECIPES FOR DOGS

RECIPE	TOTAL KCAL.	DRY WEIGHT (G.)	PROTEIN (%)	FAT (%)	CARB (%)
KIBBLE SUPPLEMENTS					
Meat Kibble Supplement	8,296	1,725	30	20	50
Egg Kibble Supplement	5,983	1,376	20	10	70
Cottage Cheese Kibble Supplement	6,188	1,425	20	10	60
BASIC RECIPES					
Doggie Oats	4,426	820	33	30	36
Dog Loaf	1,091	224	29	25	42
One-on-One	1,114	236	32	17	47
FAST & FRESH					
Quick Canine Oats & Eggs	698	140	29	23	44
Quick Canine Oatmeal	1,100	244	23	15	58
Quick Canine Hash	1,163	252	29	17	50
THERAPEUTIC DIETS (FROM QUICK REFERENCE SECTION)					
Dog Allergy Diet 1	5,648	1,092	27	24	47
Dog Allergy Diet 2	5,898	1,273	23	18	57
Canine Kidney Diet	1,343	256	17***	25	55
Dog Weight Loss Diet 1	1,559	367	31	12	53
Dog Weight Loss Diet 2	1,683	400	26	15	56
Standard Recommendations†	See chart on page 87	—	≥ 18	≥ 5	≤67
Wild Diets††	—	—	54	42	1

* *Some of these entries are shown as zero but more accurately have trace amounts of these ingredients in the calculations. I have rounded up or down and have entered zero when the amounts are less than 0.5 percent.*

** *For this calculation I have assumed the vitamin supplement provides 10,000 IU of vitamin A for the entire recipe.*

*** *In the Canine Kidney Diet, we are deliberately making the amount of protein low to spare the kidneys. The recipe is also kept low in phosphorus because of the tendency for this mineral to build up in the bloodstream. Thus the ratio of calcium to phosphorus is unusually high in the recipe.*

**** *The amount of vitamin A in this diet appears extremely high. This comes from the carrots, which contain large amounts of beta-carotene, which can be converted to Vitamin A if needed. There is, however, no problem of overdose with beta-carotene as there is with pre-formed vitamin A.*

FIBER (%)	ASH (%)	CALCIUM (%)	PHOSPH. (%)	CALC:PHOS RATIO	VIT. A ($^{IU}/_{KG}$)
0*	0	.80	.60	1.5:1	~ 3,000
0	0	.80	.70	1.2:1	~ 2,000
0	0	.80	.70	1:1	~ 4,000
1	1.6	.96	.76	1.3:1	~ 13,000
1	4	.82	.59	1.4:1	~ 7,500
2	4	.81	.83	1:1	~ 21,000
1	4	1.30	.95	1.4:1	~ 17,000
1	4	.89	.69	1.3:1	~ 6,000
1	4	.90	.68	1.3:1	~ 20,000
1	2	1.02	.83	1.2:1	~ 9,000**
2	2	.86	.66	1.3:1	~ 8,000**
0	4	.93	.31	3:1	~ 20,000
3	3	.84	.62	1.3:1	~ 149,000***
4	4	.68	.48	1.4:1	~ 25,000**
—	—	≥ .60	≥.50	1:1—2:1	5,000—50,000
—	—	—	—	—	—

† Standard Recommendations are based on the guidelines for producing commercial foods. The amounts in our recipes are meant to exceed these minimums in most categories.

†† The ingredient percentages for the typical wild diet are also included in the table, for comparison purposes. Not all categories are known and therefore some are left empty.

Note: Except where noted for wild dogs, standard recommendations are percentage total dry weight and are for maintenance of adult dogs under normal conditions. Sources: AAFCO Nutrient Profiles for Dog Foods—Report of the Canine Nutrition Expert Subcommittee, 1992; the Merck Veterinary Manual, 6th Edition, 1986; and the Committee on Animal Nutrition, Board on Agriculture, National Research Council revised 1985 edition of Nutrient Requirements of Dogs. Note: The symbol "≥" is to read as "amount listed equal or greater than." Thus, the notation "≥ 5,000 IU" reads "the amount should be equal to or greater than 5,000 IU." The symbol "≤" reads the opposite, meaning "equal to, or less than."

DOG LOAF

This recipe uses egg as a binder; you can either serve it raw or bake it like a meat loaf, with bread crumbs or other grains. As presented here, with these ingredients, it is about 30 percent protein, 25 percent fat, and 42 percent carbohydrates. Depending on which meat and grain you use, the amounts of each ingredient will vary within acceptable ranges. The egg provides adequate vitamin A, plus there is vitamin A in the vegetables.

$^1/_2$	pound (1 cup) fairly lean beef chuck (low fat)
6	slices whole-wheat bread, crumbled (about 3 cups)
1	cup whole milk
2	large eggs
$^1/_4$	cup cooked corn or other vegetables (can be omitted occasionally)
1	tablespoon Healthy Powder (page 53)
1	teaspoon of Animal Essentials calcium (or a generous $^1/_2$ teaspoon of powdered egg shell)*
1	tablespoon vegetable oil
100	IU vitamin E
$^1/_4$	teaspoon tamari soy sauce or dash of iodized salt (optional)
1	small clove garlic, crushed or minced (optional)

* These provide 1000 mg calcium from the Group III calcium supplements. See information on calcium supplements in "Table of Calcium Supplementation Products" on page 67. If you use one of the other sources of calcium from the Group III calcium supplements, provide 1000 mg.

Combine all ingredients, adding water, if needed, to make a nice texture. Serve raw. Or press the mixture into a casserole dish so it's 1 to 2 inches thick and bake at 350°F for 20 to 30 minutes, or until set and lightly browned.

If you use a moist grain and don't bake the mixture, you may choose to serve the milk separately rather than combine it in the mix. Another alternative is to mix ¼ cup powdered milk right into the recipe.

Yield: About 5½ cups, at 200 kilocalories per cup.

Daily ration: About the same (or slightly more) as amounts for Doggie Oats (page 65).

Beef substitutes: Try ground or chopped chicken, turkey, medium chuck, or hamburger instead of the beef in this recipe. Beef or chicken liver may be used once in a while, but not on a regular basis.

ONE-ON-ONE

Here's a truly inspired recipe, easy to remember and easy to multiply because it uses exactly one unit of each ingredient! It is also economical and ecologically sound, deriving part of its protein from beans. This recipe, using hamburger, contains 32 percent protein, 17 percent fat, and 47 percent carbohydrates. The amounts will vary somewhat depending on what meats are used. For example, the protein will be about 15 percent less with turkey or chicken, but, significantly, those meats will be about 70 percent lower in fat. To make up the difference, add extra fat in the form of lard, butter, or vegetable oil. (See the table "Protein, Fat, and Carbohydrate Content of Various Meats" on page 86 for more information on meat contents.)

The calcium to phosphorus ratio is acceptable, though a tad on the low side, so use other recipes occasionally to balance this out.

The key to convenience in this recipe is to cook large quantities of beans in advance. Follow the cooking directions on the package. Freeze extra quantities in 1-cup containers (or appropriate multiples if you increase the recipe) and thaw as needed. The main version uses rice because it's a grain many people use in their own menus, but the other grain choices listed are higher protein and, for the most part, faster cooking.

1	cup brown rice (or 2¼ cups cooked)
1	cup (½ pound) lean hamburger (or turkey, chicken, lean heart, or lean chuck)
1	cup cooked kidney beans (about half of a 15-ounce can)
1	tablespoon Healthy Powder (page 53)
1	tablespoon vegetable oil
1	teaspoon Group I bone meal (or 2 teaspoons Group II bone meals)*
1	10,000 IU vitamin A and D capsule
1	400–800 IU vitamin E capsule
1	teaspoon tamari soy sauce or dash of iodized salt (optional)
1	small clove garlic, crushed or minced (optional)

* See information on calcium supplements in "Table of Calcium Supplementation Products" on page 67. The amount of calcium added from the bone meal sources is 1,500 mg (1.5 grams).

Bring 2 cups of water to a boil. Add the rice and simmer for 35 to 45 minutes. Mix in the other ingredients and serve.

Yield: About 4½ cups, at 250 kilocalories per cup.

Daily ration (in cups): Toy—a little less than 2 cups; small—about 4 cups; medium—6 to 7 cups; large—about 8 cups; giant—9 to 10 cups.

If you want to boost the protein content a little, add one large egg or 1 tablespoon of nutritional yeast.

Grain substitutes: Instead of rice, you may use (with the highest protein versions listed first) 2 cups rolled oats (+ 4 cups water = 4 cups cooked); 1 cup bulgur (+ 2 cups water = 2½ cups cooked); 1 cup millet (+ 3 cups water = 3 cups cooked); 1½ cups cornmeal (+ 4 cups water = 4 cups cooked); or 1 cup barley (+ 2 to 3 cups water = 2½ to 3 cups cooked).

Bean substitutes: You may use one cup, of cooked soybeans, pintos, black beans, or white (navy) beans instead of kidney beans. Soybeans have the most protein.

FAST AND FRESH: DOGS

Here are three really simple recipes for those inevitable occasions when you have an eager eater nudging you, and you suddenly discover that you're all out of dog food, both home-prepared and commercial. These recipes are not meant to serve as regular fare, but they do provide a fairly complete meal made of basic items you're likely to have on hand. You can feed them to your pooch up to two or three times a week.

Note: You may also feed any of the basic cat recipes (page 75) to dogs. They contain more protein than dogs require, but that's no problem unless your dog is on a low-protein diet because of kidney troubles.

QUICK CANINE OATS AND EGGS

1   cup raw rolled oats (or 2 cups cooked oatmeal)

4   large eggs

2   tablespoons Healthy Powder (page 53)

1   teaspoon Animal Essentials calcium (or a slightly rounded ½ teaspoon of powdered eggshell or 1,000 mg of calcium from another Group III calcium supplement)*

* See information on calcium supplements in "Table of Calcium Supplementation Products" on page 67.

Bring 2 cups of water to a boil. Add the oats, cover, and turn off the heat, letting the oats cook in the hot water for about 10 minutes, or until soft. (Use extra oatmeal from your own breakfast or else make some up.) Then stir in the eggs, Healthy Powder, and calcium. Let the eggs set slightly from the heat, then cool for a few minutes before serving.

Yield: About 3 cups, at 230 kilocalories per cup.

Daily ration: Same as for Doggie Oats (page 65). (Makes one meal, or a half-day's ration, for a medium size dog. Double the recipe to make breakfast for a giant size dog.)

Grain substitutes: Instead of oats, you may use ½ cup bulgur (+ 1 cup water = 1¼ cups cooked) or ½ cup whole-wheat couscous (+ ¾ cup water = 1¼ cups cooked).

QUICK CANINE OATMEAL

Here's another simple recipe that uses only two eggs and may resemble your own breakfast.

2	cups raw rolled oats (or about 4½ cups cooked oatmeal)
2	cups 2 percent milk
2	large eggs
1	tablespoon Healthy Powder (page 53)
1	teaspoon Animal Essentials calcium (or a slightly rounded ½ teaspoon of powdered eggshell or 1,000 mg of calcium from another Group III calcium supplement)*

* See information on calcium supplements in "Table of Calcium Supplementation Products" on page 67.

Bring 4 cups of water to a boil. Add the oats, cover, and turn off the heat, letting the oats cook in the hot water for about 10 minutes, or until soft.

Put the oatmeal into your pet's food bowl. Mix in the Healthy Powder and calcium and top with the milk. In a separate small bowl, stir the egg slightly to blend the yolk and white, and give both to the dog. Or, you may certainly mix it with the oatmeal.

Yield: A little less than 7 cups, with about 160 kilocalories per cup.

Daily ration (in cups): Toy—2 to 3; small— about 6; medium—9 to 10; large—11 to 12; giant—14+.

QUICK CANINE HASH

1	cup bulgur or whole-wheat couscous (or 2¹/₂ cups cooked)
1	cup (¹/₂ pound) chuck, hamburger, turkey, or chicken
1	tablespoon vegetable oil
2	tablespoons Healthy Powder (page 53) or substitute nutritional yeast
5,000	IU vitamin A
1¹/₂	teaspoons Animal Essentials calcium (or a scant teaspoon of powdered eggshell or 1,500 mg of calcium from another Group III calcium supplement)*

* See information on calcium supplements in "Table of Calcium Supplementation Products" on page 67.

Bring 4 cups of water to a boil, add the bulgur, cover, and simmer 10 to 20 minutes. For couscous, use 3 cups water and cook 3 to 5 minutes. Add the meat or poultry, Healthy Powder, and calcium and serve.

Rotate this recipe with those that contain bone meal, to make sure all micro-nutrients are included.

Yield: About 3¾ cups, with about 310 kilocalories per cup.

Daily ration (in cups): Toy—1½; small—3 to 3½; medium—5; large—6 to 6½; giant—7 to 8.

Grain substitutes: Instead of bulgur or couscous, use 1½ cups rolled oats (= 3¼ cups cooked). With poultry or other lean meats only: 1 cup millet (+ 3 cups water = 3 cups cooked); or 1 cup brown rice (+ 2 cups water = 2½ cups cooked).

FOOD INGREDIENT SUBSTITUTIONS

You can make substitutions in these recipes. It will change the amounts of protein, fat, carbohydrates, and total calories some, but not significantly. It is a good idea to rotate foods periodically to make sure that there is sufficient variety.

For cooking instructions (grain to water) look at "Recommended Grains" on page 40 in chapter 3.

Grain Substitutes: 1 cup rolled oats = ¹/₂ cup bulgur, millet, corn meal, or barley; scant ¹/₂ cup of rice; 2¹/₂ cups potatoes.

Meat Substitutes: These meats are equivalent in amount: turkey, chicken, hamburger, chuck, beef heart.

One pound of meat = 1 pint cottage cheese + 4 eggs, or 16 ounces tofu + 4 eggs.

BASIC RECIPES FOR CATS

Now let's look at some recipes for cats, starting with basic maintenance recipes that you can use as the foundation of your cat's new diet. See "Nutritional Composition of Recipes for Cats" on pages 76–77 for information about the nutritional composition of these recipes.

Daily rations are given after each recipe for small (4 to 6 pounds), medium (7 to 9 pounds) and large (10 to 15 pounds) adult cats. Increase amounts for more active cats. Many factors can affect the quantity needed, so the best guide is your cat's appetite and whether the food maintains the cat at a normal weight.

The next two recipes are the most economical and ecologically sound ways to feed your cat a fresh diet and still provide very generous protein and fat, well exceeding what is available in commercial foods. As prepared, the recipes provide 40 percent protein, 28 percent fat, and 29 percent carbohydrate.

BEEFY OATS

3	cups raw rolled oats (or 4½ cups cooked oatmeal)
2	large eggs
2	pounds (4 cups) ground lean beef heart (or lean chuck, lean hamburger, liver, kidney, or other lean red meats)
4	tablespoons Healthy Powder (page 53)
1	tablespoon Animal Essentials calcium (or a slightly rounded 1½ teaspoon of powdered eggshell or 3,000 mg of calcium from another Group III calcium supplement)*
2	tablespoons vegetable oil or butter (or 1 tablespoon each)
10,000	IU vitamin A
100–200	IU vitamin E
1	tablespoon fresh vegetable with each meal—finely grated if cooked (optional)
500	milligrams taurine supplement (optional)

* See information on calcium supplements in "Table of Calcium Supplementation Products" on page 67.

Bring 6 cups (1.5 quarts) of water to a boil. Add the oats, cover, and turn off the heat, letting the oats cook in the hot water for about 10 minutes, or until soft. Then stir in the eggs, letting them set slightly for a few minutes. Mix in the remaining ingredients.

Yield: About 9–10 cups, with around 337 kilocalories per cup. Immediately freeze whatever cannot be eaten in the next 2 to 3 days.

Daily ration (in cups): Small—about ½ cup; medium—a scant cup; large—about 1 ⅓ cups.

Grain substitutes: 1½ cups millet (+ 3 cups water = 4½ cups cooked millet) or 1½ cups bulgur (+ 3 cups water = 4½ cups cooked bulgur).

NUTRITIONAL COMPOSITION OF RECIPES FOR CATS

RECIPE	TOTAL KCAL.	DRY WEIGHT (G.)	PROTEIN (%)	FAT (%)	CARB (%)
BASIC RECIPES					
Beefy Oats	3,203	603	40	28	29
Poultry Delight	2,228	458	48	21	27
Feline Feast	2,412	417	50	36	11
Mackerel Loaf	3,031	574	43	30	21
Fatty Feline Fare	3,434	570	32	43	22
FAST & FRESH					
Quick Feline Eggfest	163	27	48	44	4
Quick Feline Meatfest	453	79	58	38	1
Quick Feline Meatfest (without Healthy Powder)	443	76	59	38	0
THERAPEUTIC DIETS (FROM QUICK REFERENCE SECTION)					
Cat Allergy Diet	3,492	646	30	30	40
Feline Kidney Diet	2,268	435	25*	24	46
Cat Weight Loss	1,026	200	39	28	32
Standard Recommendations†	~350	—	$\geq$ 26	$\geq$ 9	—
Wild Diets††	—	—	46	33	16

   In the Feline Kidney Diet, we are deliberately making the amount of protein low to spare the kidneys. This recipe is also kept low in phosphorus because of the tendency for this mineral to build up in the bloodstream. Thus, the ratio of calcium to phosphorus is unusually high in the recipe.

   **A ratio of one part calcium to one part phosphorus is an ideal ratio for cats. There is, however, considerable latitude among acceptable ratios, because the body has the ability to select and conserve low nutrients and eliminate excess. Optimal ratios are considered to be between 0.9 to 1 and 1.1 to 1.*

   ***The 5,000 IU of vitamin A per kilogram of food is a minimum standard. The recipes are designed to have considerably greater amounts of vitamin A for the maintenance of good health.*

   † Standard Recommendations are based on the guidelines for producing commercial foods. The amounts in our recipes are meant to exceed these minimums in most categories.

FIBER (%)	ASH (%)	CALCIUM (%)	PHOSPH. (%)	CALC:PHOS RATIO	VIT. A ($^{IU}/_{KG}$)
1	3	.77	.68	1:1	~ 18,000
1	3	.77	.65	1.2:1	~ 26,000
>1	3	.84	.76	1.1:1	~ 27,000
1	6	.83	.83	1:1	~ 15,000
1	2	.90	.85	1:1	~ 19,000
0	4	.94	.76	1.2:1	~ 7,000
0	3	.81	.67	1.2:1	~ 2,000
0	3	.69	.57	1.2:1	~ 2,000
0	0	.70	.70	1:1	~ 18,000
0	4	.74	.30	2.5:1	~ 20,000
3	2	.74	.61	1.2:1	~ 10,000
—	—	≥.80	≥ .60	1:1**	≥ 5,000***
—	3	–	–	–	–

†† The ingredient percentages for the typical wild diet are also included in the table, for comparison purposes. Not all categories are known and therefore some are left empty.

Note: Except where noted for wild felines, standard recommendations are percentage total dry weight and are for maintenance of adult cats under normal conditions. Sources: AAFCO Nutrient Profiles for Cat Foods—Report of the Feline Nutrition Expert Subcommittee, 1992; the Merck Veterinary Manual, 6th Edition, 1986; and the Committee on Animal Nutrition, Board on Agriculture, National Research Council revised 1986 edition of Nutrient Requirements of Cats.

Note: The symbol "≥" is to read as "equal to or greater than amount listed." Thus, the notation "≥ 5,000 IU" reads "the amount should be equal to or greater than 5,000 IU." The symbol "≤" reads the opposite, meaning "equal to, or less than."

FELINE FEAST

Corn is the grain of choice for many cats, so that's the grain I used in the main version of this recipe. For the best texture, try polenta, which is more coarsely ground than the flourlike meal usually called cornmeal. Polenta is commonly sold in natural food stores. Yummied up with extra yeast for even more flavor, this high-protein formula is a sure winner. It's excellent for pregnant or nursing cats and their growing kittens.

Since this recipe contains a higher proportion of meat than the others, you can substitute many kinds of grains and meats, both low- and high-protein types, because there is plenty of protein to spare. If you use lean meats, the dry weight percentage of protein ranges from a low of 41 percent (lean beef heart with rice or potatoes) to a high of 52 percent (turkey with oats). If you use fattier meats, the protein value ranges from a low of 30 percent (fatty beef heart with rice or potatoes) to a high of 40 percent (regular hamburger with oats). Alternate the use of poultry and red meats, or combine both in the same recipe to ensure plenty of iron and other nutrients that vary in different cuts. Using lean beef chuck as the meat and cornmeal as the grain, the recipe provides 50 percent protein, 36 percent fat, and 11 percent carbohydrates.

1	cup cornmeal or polenta (about 4 cups cooked)
2	large eggs
2	tablespoons vegetable oil or butter (or 1 tablespoon each)
2	pounds (4 cups) ground turkey or chicken (or lean chuck, lean heart, lean hamburger, liver, giblets, fish, or other lean meats)
4	tablespoons Healthy Powder (page 53)
2	teaspoons Animal Essentials calcium (or a slightly rounded teaspoon of powdered eggshell or 2,000 mg of calcium from another Group III calcium supplement)*
10,000	IU vitamin A
100–200	IU vitamin E
1	tablespoon fresh vegetables with each meal (optional)
500	milligrams taurine supplement (optional)

* See information on calcium supplements in "Table of Calcium Supplementation Products" on page 67.

Bring 4 cups of water to a boil. Add the cornmeal or polenta, stirring rapidly with a fork or whisk to keep it from getting lumpy. (It's easier to avoid lumping if you use polenta.) When it is thoroughly blended, cover and simmer on low 10 to 15 minutes. When the cornmeal or polenta is creamy, stir in the eggs and oil or butter. Mix in the remaining ingredients.

Yield: About 9 cups, with 268 kilocalories per cup. Immediately freeze whatever cannot be eaten in the next 2 to 3 days.

Daily ration (in cups): Small—about ¾; medium—1+; large—1¾ to 2 cups.

Meat substitutes: It's a good idea to use fattier grades of meat occasionally, but eliminate the oil or butter from the recipe when you do. You can substitute 2 pounds of beef heart with fat showing, regular hamburger, poultry with skin, or choice chuck roast.

Grain substitutes: 2 cups raw rolled oats (+ 4 cups water = 4 cups cooked); or 10 slices whole-wheat bread; or 4 cups cooked and mashed potatoes; or 1 cup (dry volume) of any of the following: bulgur, millet, buckwheat, barley, brown rice, couscous, amaranth, spelt, or quinoa.

POULTRY DELIGHT

This recipe is similar to the preceding one, except that here poultry is combined with millet. The two ingredients complement each other because poultry is lower in iron than red meats, but millet is high in iron compared with other grains. The two also balance each other in relative protein levels: Poultry is high in protein and millet is low. This recipe has a higher proportion of meat, which some cats prefer. The recipe provides 48 percent protein, 21 percent fat, and 27 percent carbohydrate if you use a low-fat meat (such as turkey or chicken without the skin). When beef is used, the fat content is much higher, into the high 30 percent range.

1	cup millet (3 cups cooked)
2	large eggs
2	pounds (4 cups) ground turkey or chicken (or lean chuck, lean heart, lean hamburger, liver, giblets, fish, or other lean meats)
1	tablespoon Healthy Powder (page 53)
1	tablespoon Animal Essentials calcium (or a slightly rounded 1$^1/_2$ teaspoon of powdered eggshell or 3,000 mg of calcium from another Group III calcium supplement)*
4	tablespoons vegetable oil or butter (or 1 tablespoon each). Some cats will prefer the taste of lard, either beef or pork.
10,000	IU vitamin A
100–200	IU vitamin E
1	teaspoon fresh vegetable with each meal (optional)
500	milligrams taurine supplement (optional)

* See information on calcium supplements in "Table of Calcium Supplementation Products" on page 67.

Bring 2 cups of water to a boil. Add the millet, cover, and simmer 20 to 30 minutes or until the water is absorbed. You may need to add a bit more water during cooking. When the millet is soft, stir in the eggs to let them set a bit from the heat. Then mix in the remaining ingredients.

Yield: About 8 cups, with 280 kilocalories per cup. Immediately freeze whatever cannot be eaten in the next 2 to 3 days.

Daily ration (in cups): Small—about ²⁄₃; medium—1; large—1²⁄₃.

Grain substitutes: 2 cups rolled oats (+ 4 cups water = about 4½ cups cooked) or 1 cup bulgur (+ 2 cups water = 2½ cups cooked).

MACKEREL LOAF

Canned mackerel makes a good seafood to use for cats occasionally. Not only is it an economical protein source, but it comes from deep waters and is less likely to be polluted than those fishes from areas closer to the coast. Cats can sometimes get addicted to seafood. If yours shows signs of addiction, hold firm; it's important to keep feeding a variety of foods. This recipe provides 43 percent protein, 30 percent fat, and 21 percent carbohydrates.

4	large eggs
3	cups whole milk (or less, as needed for moisture)
3	tablespoons Healthy Powder (page 53)
1½	teaspoons Animal Essentials calcium (or a scant teaspoon of powdered eggshell or 1,500 mg of calcium from another Group III calcium supplement)*
100–200	IU vitamin E
1	tablespoon fresh vegetables with each meal (optional)
500	milligrams taurine supplement (optional)
2	tablespoons vegetable oil (or a mixture of vegetable and fish oils)
2	15-ounce cans of mackerel, undrained (or 3 6-ounce cans tuna in oil or ½ pound cooked cod or other whitefish)
6	slices whole-wheat bread, crumbled

* See information on calcium supplements in "Table of Calcium Supplementation Products" on page 67.

Blend the eggs, milk, supplements, vegetables, and oil together. Add the mackerel and bread and mix well. Serve raw or bake in a shallow dish at 350°F for about 20 minutes.

Yield: About 11 cups, with 275 kilocalories per cup. Immediately freeze whatever cannot be eaten in the next 2 to 3 days.

Daily ration: *Same as for Poultry Delight.*

Grain substitutes: 1½ cups rolled oats (+ 3 cups water = 3 cups cooked); or about 1 cup cornmeal or polenta (+ 4 cups water = 4 cups cooked); or 1 cup whole-wheat bulgur (+ 2 cups water = 2½ cups cooked).

FATTY FELINE FARE

This dense, satisfying formula is rich in animal fat—at a level comparable to the fat in the wild feline diet. Stick to the suggested grains and use only bone meal for the calcium source to ensure adequate total amounts of protein, phosphorus, and calcium. If you are lucky enough to live by a butcher or a small market that processes meat themselves, you can ask them to grind fatty beef heart for you—an excellent alternative to the usual muscle meat.

1	cup millet (or 3 cups cooked)
1	large egg
2	pounds (4 cups) raw chuck roast (or the regular, fattier grades of beef heart or hamburger, or roaster chicken with skin)
2	tablespoons Healthy Powder (page 53)
1	tablespoon Group I bone meal*
10,000	IU vitamin A
100–200	IU vitamin E
1	tablespoon fresh vegetable with each meal (optional)
500	milligrams taurine supplement (optional)

* See "Table of Calcium Supplementation Products" on page 67. If Group II bone meals are used, double the recipe amount.

Bring 3 cups of water to a boil. Add the millet, cover, and simmer 20 to 30 minutes or until the water is absorbed. You may need to add a bit more water during cooking. When the millet is soft, stir in the egg to let it set a bit from the heat. Then mix in the remaining ingredients.

Yield: About 7½ cups, with 457 kilocalories per cup. Immediately freeze whatever cannot be eaten in the next 2 to 3 days.

Daily ration (in cups): Small—⅓ to ½; medium—½ to ⅔; large about 1 cup.

Grain substitutes: 2 cups rolled oats (+ 4 cups water = 4 cups cooked) or 1 cup bulgur (+ 2 cups water = 2½ cups cooked).

FAST AND FRESH: CATS

Here are two quick and easy recipes for those occasional times when you suddenly realize you forgot to thaw out the regular cat fare, or you just plain ran out of it—and there's a hungry feline standing at your feet who won't take wait-a-while for an answer. These recipes are not intended for regular use, but they do provide a fairly complete meal using items you probably have on hand. As noted previously, you may also occasionally use these recipes for dogs that don't require a low-protein diet. In fact, all these mixtures are higher in protein than required for either dogs or cats, but they won't complain.

QUICK FELINE EGGFEST

This mix is among the simplest I know and is a very natural food for small predator types of cats. It is high in protein, vitamin A, and iron as well as B vitamins. The recipe provides 48 percent protein, 44 percent fat, and 4 percent carbohydrates.

2	large eggs
scant ¼	teaspoon Animal Essentials calcium (or a pinch of powdered eggshell or 200 mg of calcium from another Group III calcium supplement)*
pinch	of nutritional yeast (optional, for flavoring)

* See information on calcium supplements in "Table of Calcium Supplementation Products" on page 67.

Use a fork to mix the egg yolks and whites, stirring in the calcium at the same time. Sprinkle the yeast on top and serve raw. Or, if the recipe is too "gooey," you may scramble this egg mix lightly.

Yield: One meal, or about half a day's rations, for a 10-pound cat (or dog), with about 163 kilocalories for the entire recipe. A smaller cat might eat only one egg at a meal.

I apologize for measurements like "pinch," but the amounts are so small that it would not make sense to be specific. For example, the amount of calcium needed from eggshells would be ⅛th of a teaspoon. You will have to take my word for it that a pinch (the amount held between the finger and thumb) will be about right.

QUICK FELINE MEATFEST

Along with ease of preparation, this recipe boasts a calcium-balanced way to feed your cat chunks of meat, which help exercise his or her teeth and gums. (If you were to mix chunks of meat with grains for your cat, he'd probably pick out the chunks and leave the grains.) This recipe provides 58 percent protein, 38 percent fat, and 1 percent carbohydrates.

1	cup raw or cooked chicken or turkey with skin (or chuck, hamburger, or heart)
1	teaspoon Healthy Powder (page 53)
¹⁄₂	teaspoon Animal Essentials calcium (or a ¹⁄₄ teaspoon of powdered eggshell or 500 mg of calcium from another Group III calcium supplement)*

* See information on calcium supplements in "Table of Calcium Supplementation Products" on page 67.

Chunk the poultry or meat just enough so you can mix in the calcium and so your cat can manage it.

Yield: 1 cup, with about 450 kilocalories.

Daily ration (in cups): Small—¼ to ½; medium—½ to ⅔; large—about 1 cup.

If you're feeding dogs this meal, each cup of meat provides about half a day's needs for a 40-pound dog or one-third a day's needs for an 80-pound dog.

If your cat does not like the taste of the added Healthy Powder, you can make the recipe without using it and the balance will still be adequate.

THE ROLE OF NUTRITIONAL STANDARDS IN OUR RECIPES

In formulating our recipes, we took several nutritional guidelines into consideration, drawing upon the recommendations of the Association of American Feed Control Officials (AAFCO), the *Merck Veterinary Manual*, the Committee on Animal Nutrition, Board on Agriculture, the National Research Council revised 1985 edition of *Nutrient Requirements of Dogs*, the revised 1986 edition of *Nutrient Requirements of Cats*, and several other sources from the research literature.

We calculated the nutritional content of the recipes based upon information in the *United States Department of Agriculture Handbook of Nutritional Composition of Foods* and other sources (see the nutritional composition charts on pages 68–69 and 76–77). Be aware, however, that the nutritional contents of foods can vary considerably, depending on how it is raised, stored, and prepared. Generally, organically raised food is much more nutritious and closer to the values on which we based our calculations.

In most cases our formulations exceed the official standards, which represent the bare minimum considered necessary for adult maintenance. We tried to strike a balance between those minimal standards and the natural wild diet.

IDEAL CAT FOOD

For adult cats, the AAFCO industry standards currently advise a minimum of 26 percent protein and 9 percent fat (commercial cat foods usually contain between 8 and 12 percent fat). The 1986 edition of *Nutrient Requirements of Cats* suggests that about 15 percent protein and 10 percent fat can be adequate, but it is clear that cats prefer a higher protein food and 25 percent fat or more when given a choice. The source of fat also makes a difference in acceptability; kittens, for example, prefer beef tallow over chicken fat.

In the wild, cats consume about 47 percent protein and 33 percent fat. I consider these levels to be our goal. Though you need not be exact, if you can stay around these amounts you will be much closer to duplicating the natural diet. Weighing these factors, some of our basic cat recipes fall between the minimal and the "wild" standards, but much closer to the natural levels than the minimal ones; others are higher in some areas.

Protein in our recipes ranges from 32 to 59 percent, averaging about 47 percent—close to that of the natural diet. The fat levels vary from 21 to 44 percent, averaging about 35 percent. For healthy adult cats you can feel confident in emphasizing recipes at either end of the continuum, as you choose.

IDEAL DOG FOOD

For dogs, the current AAFCO standards advise a minimum of only 18 percent protein for adult maintenance and 22 percent for reproduction and growth (previous recommendations have been as high as 28 percent for lactation). The minimal level for fat is 5 percent (8 percent for reproduction and growth), although feeding studies have shown dogs can tolerate rations up to 50 percent fat if otherwise adequately nourished.

There is a direct relationship between fat and protein in the diet. The more fat in the

PROTEIN, FAT, AND CARBOHYDRATE CONTENT OF VARIOUS MEATS

MEAT (1 LB.)	PROTEIN (G.)*	FAT (G.)	CARBS (G.)
Hamburger, lean (cooked)	125	51	0
Chicken, roaster, flesh & skin (cooked)	123	67	0
Hamburger, regular (cooked)	110	92	0
Venison, lean (raw)	95	2	0
Turkey, ground, dark (raw)	95	20	0
Chicken breast (raw)	94	11	0
Beef chuck, lean (raw)	92	53	0
Chicken, light meat & skin (raw)	90	18	0
Beef liver (raw)	90	17	24
Chicken liver (raw)	89	17	13
Beef chuck, roast (raw)	85	89	0
Chicken heart (raw)	84	27	0.5
Chicken, ground, dark (raw)	82	17	0
Lamb leg (raw)	81	74	0
Beef chuck, fatty (raw)	79	115	0
Beef heart, lean (raw)	78	16	3
Beef heart, some fat (raw)	70	94	0.5
Lamb shoulder (raw)	69	109	0
Turkey, total edible (raw)	67	49	0

Sorted by grams of protein per pound of meat, from high to low.

AVERAGE CALORIC NEEDS FOR ADULT DOGS

WEIGHT (LB.)	KCAL./DAY
10	410
15	550
25	840
40	1,150
50	1,380
60	1,555
70	1,690
80	1,890
100	2,270

Note: Increase values for working dogs or during cold weather.

AVERAGE CALORIC NEEDS FOR ADULT CATS

WEIGHT (LB.)	KCAL./DAY (ACTIVE CAT)	KCAL./DAY (INACTIVE CAT)
6	191	218
7	223	254
8	255	290
9	286	327
10	319	363
12	383	463

diet, the more protein is needed. There are metabolic interactions between the two, and when a diet is fattier, an animal will eat less to assuage its hunger. That's why a dog can become undernourished if you add oil or meat drippings to its food without increasing the protein, vitamin, and mineral content accordingly.

Dr. Ben E. Sheffy of Cornell University in Ithaca, New York, has developed detailed minimum protein standards for dogs that range from 13 to 37 percent, depending on how much fat is in the diet and upon special needs, such as those described in the next chapter. All of our dog food recipes meet or exceed whichever of the standards is higher—Dr. Sheffy's or AAFCO's.

How Much to Feed?

I believe that your animal's appetite is generally a good guideline for how much to feed. Here's some information, however, that will help you gauge quantities to prepare based on average caloric needs for dogs and cats and the caloric content (kcal.) stated in the caloric needs charts above.

In nature, a cat eats on a 28-hour cycle, and it is normal for them to decline food occasionally when we feed them according to our schedules instead of theirs.

CHAPTER 5

SPECIAL DIETS
FOR SPECIAL PETS

The guidelines used for the production of commercial pet foods are those that will be adequate for maintenance. "Adequate for maintenance" means just what it says. Such food provides enough to *maintain* a healthy animal. I am sure there are animals living very peaceful and calm lives that meet this criteria, but many of those I meet could use a little extra nutritional help. What minimum nutrition does not guarantee is a beneficial surplus for the animal that is under stress—either physically or emotionally.

We designed our recipes in chapter 4 to not only maintain health in the adult animal, but also to provide for special needs situations. As we've noted, our recipes provide amounts of protein and fat that are much closer to those available in the natural, "wild" diet, though we cannot duplicate them exactly without feeding live prey. As they are, the levels are more than adequate for maintenance and also suitable for animals needing more calories, more protein, and more fat.

Such animals include:

Puppies and kittens. Extra protein and calories are needed for new tissue growth and youthful activity.

Breeding, pregnant, and lactating females. Conceiving, carrying, birthing, and nursing offspring call for unusually high protein intake to grow new tissue.

Animals undergoing strenuous exercise or stress. Such conditions signal the body to consume high amounts of energy as well as protein, which is needed for activity and tissue repair.

Animals that need to regain strength after surgery, injury, illness, or malnourishment. Higher-than-usual amounts of protein and energy are vital for healing.

Animals exposed to extreme temperatures. Very hot weather calls for diets high in protein to compensate for decreased food intake caused by a sluggish appetite. Cold weather exposure demands more calories to keep the animal warm; these calories are best supplied by a high-fat diet.

Another special category is the pet of vegetarian families. Ethical, ecological, or health considerations lead some people to eliminate meat from their diets. If they reduce their pet's meat intake as well, they must replace certain nutrients meat would provide.

Let's look at ways to satisfy each of these special dietary needs in turn. (See the Quick Reference section beginning on page 287 for diets created specifically to meet the needs of dogs and cats with disease problems, such as kidney and urinary disorders.)

GUIDELINES FOR FEEDING IN SPECIAL CONDITIONS

It is not surprising that the need for food increases when there is either increased growth or increased repair or replacement of body tissues.

Growth occurs during:

❖ Maturing from puppyhood or kittenhood to adulthood

❖ Pregnancy

Increased repair and replacement occurs during:

❖ Production of milk while nursing

❖ Hard exercise

❖ Cold weather

❖ Hot weather

❖ Emotional stress

❖ Recovering from an illness

Growing puppies need twice as much energy per pound of body weight as does the adult dog. When they get to be about 40 percent of the final adult weight, the ratio changes to 1.6 times adult energy needs. For example, if an adult 25-pound dog needs 840 Kcal per day, that works out to about 34 Kcal per pound of body weight (840 divided by 25 = 33.6). The young, just-weaned puppy of the same breed, weighing only 2 pounds, will need 68 Kcal per pound (twice that of the adult) to be able to grow larger.

When he develops to 40 percent of the adult weight (10 pounds), then the requirement drops to 54 Kcal per pound (34 × 1.6 = 54.4). At 80 percent adult weight, it drops further to 1.2 times maintenance (34 × 1.2 = 40.8, or 41, Kcal/lb). (See the chart, opposite, "How to Predict Your Puppy's Adult Size," for guidance.)

Have all of these calculations scared you? Don't worry about it. Just understand that the little puppies are going to eat about twice as much per pound of body weight as the adult dog. Then as they get older quantities drop gradually until they are mature (about 14 months).

Some dogs never seem to get to the point of "maintenance," acting hungry all the time and scavenging for food whenever they can. This, however, is an aberration, a symptom of imbalanced metabolism, and needs treatment beyond nutritional adjustment.

We can rank conditions in order—those needing concentrated food at the top, gradually decreasing in that requirement as we go down the list. We can also match conditions with recipes from chapter 4, so you know which ones are most suitable.

HIGH-ENERGY RECIPES FOR DOGS

In our recipe development, we followed guidelines proposed by Ben E. Sheffy, PhD, of Cornell University, that boost recommended levels of protein beyond the usual standards as the energy density (or fattiness) of a diet increases. Extra protein is necessary because a dog eats less total food in a fattier, higher-calorie diet. So, in order to receive the same amount of protein, a dog must eat a diet in which protein constitutes a higher proportion of the total.

In a lower-fat diet with a caloric density of just 3.5 kilocalories per kilogram of dry weight, Dr. Sheffy suggests a minimum of 23 percent protein for proper growth. In fattier diets (5 kilocalories per kilogram), however, he recommends at least 30 to 33 percent protein. Most of our recipes tend toward the upper end of this range, with caloric densities of around 4.5 to 5 and protein levels close to 30 percent. (Caloric densities means that a lot of calories are packed in a small amount of food.)

HOW MUCH SHOULD YOU FEED YOUR DOG?

There is no specific answer to this question. The general guide as to "how much" is

HOW TO PREDICT YOUR PUPPY'S ADULT SIZE

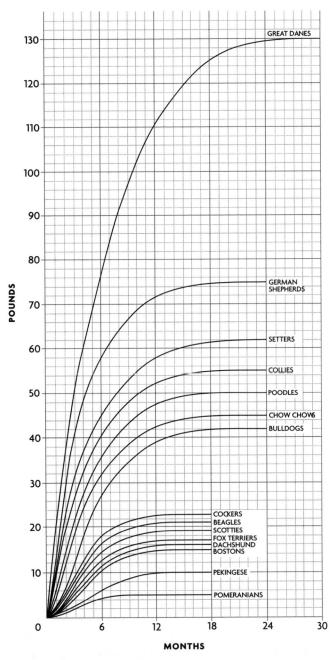

SOURCE: Adapted from *Current Veterinary Therapy V: Small Animal Practice*, ed. Robert W. Kirk (Philadelphia: W. B. Saunders, 1974).

FEEDING DOGS WITH EXTRA NEEDS

SPECIAL CONDITION	RECIPES*	ENERGY DENSITY**	NOTES
Pregnant female (last trimester)			
Nursing (need increases with size of the litter)	Dog Oats	5.4	The nutritional requirement with exercise and weather is
	Dog Loaf	4.9	related to how much exer-
Puppy, weaned & growing	Quick Canine Oats	5.0	cise and how extreme the temperature. The more heat
Hard exercise			or cold, the greater the need.
Cold weather exposure			
Hot weather exposure			
Puppy, about half grown			
Nursing (past peak)	One-on-One	4.7	In this group, the energy need is less. The nursing fe-
Exercise (moderate)	Quick Canine Oatmeal	4.5	male is "winding down" and
Stress	Quick Canine Hash	4.6	the exercise is not as ex-
Malnourishment			treme as above.
Pregnant female, first two trimesters			
Exercise (mild)	One-on-One***	4.7	Energy needs here are less than the group above but
Convalescence	Quick Canine Oatmeal	4.5	slightly above the usual adult
	Quick Canine Hash	4.6	maintenance level.

* The recipes listed here are a general recommendation, to give you some idea of which ones are most concentrated in energy and therefore most useful for these conditions. Nonetheless, all the recipes are suitable, and it is likely that any of them would serve adequately. Remember too that the energy provided in the recipe will vary somewhat depending on what food substitutions you have made. Leaner meat provides less energy than fatty; chicken meat provides less than chicken with the skin included.

** The energy density number tells us the amount of energy per cup of food. The higher the number, the more energy in the food.

*** These are the same recipes as in the second category. However, expect that the amount eaten will be less. Realize too that any of the recipes in the first category can be used as well. I am indicating here what will be sufficient.

offered with each recipe in chapter 4, but there is so much variation among individual animals that a "general guide" is about as close as we can get. A healthy dog will eat just enough food to maintain its adult weight. If the food is low in energy content, then more quantity will be eaten. The higher energy foods, as in our recipes, require less quantity for the same result.

Let your dog's appetite and weight be your guide. A good plan is to feed an adult dog either once or twice a day, leaving the food down for 20 minutes. If it is not eaten, take it up until next time, covering and refrigerating it in the meantime. If your dog loses weight, then you need to increase the amount given. A normal, healthy dog eating these recipes should not lose weight.

If your dog gains weight, then she is either eating too much or not getting enough exercise—or both. Cut down the quantity, or feed only once a day. If the problem persists, then there is likely a thyroid imbalance that may need correction with holistic treatment. There are recipes in the Quick Reference section that will help with the dog determined to be overweight.

Feed half-grown pups and adult dogs with extra needs two or three times a day, allowing them to eat as much as they want at one meal (take it up, cover, and refrigerate it until next time).

Younger puppies should be fed three or four times a day.

Note: Larger dogs require fewer calories per pound of body weight than smaller dogs.

That's why a 55-pound dog isn't fed 11 times more than a 5-pounder.

CATS WITH SPECIAL NEEDS

For cats, special needs conditions are the same as for dogs—growth, pregnancy, etc. The recipes for cats in chapter 4 provide enough protein and fat for felines with special needs. All recipes are very generous with both protein and fat and can be used for growing kittens as well as pregnant and lactating cats. The recipe for Poultry Delight (page 80) is a little lower in fat than the rest but still quite adequate for most needs.

FEEDING ORPHANED OR REJECTED KITTENS AND PUPPIES

Mother's milk is the best food there is, so use these recipes as a last resort. Sometimes a female cannot or will not nurse all her young adequately, and sometimes, unfortunately, the mother dies. In such cases you can keep the babies alive with a formula designed to mimic as closely as possible the natural constituents of the nursing cat's or dog's milk. You can buy commercial products that do this, but if you want to give your young charges the benefits of raw fresh foods, use the formulas that follow.

To boost the protein content of cow's or goat's milk to the level found in cat's and dog's milk, add protein powder. Buy an unflavored powder that contains at least 80 percent protein (dry weight basis) and lists its proteins from animal sources: casein, lactalbumin, and egg albumin. Unlike powders based on soy proteins, animal protein powders will meet the special amino acid requirements of your young orphans. These powders are sold in many health food stores.

Supplement these formulas with vitamins made especially for adult dogs or cats. Select a powdered formula or crush the tablet and mix it into the milk. If the formula contains calcium but not phosphorus, cut back a bit on the bone meal or calcium supplement in the recipe.

If you use a calcium source other than bone meal, it's safest to use one based on calcium lactate or calcium gluconate. These are better absorbed than calcium carbonate, a common source that is also the basis of eggshell powder.

KITTEN FORMULA

This formula closely replicates the constituents of cat's milk, which is 42.2 percent protein, 25 percent fat, 26.1 percent carbohydrates, and 6.7 percent ash. This formula contains 44 percent protein, 25 percent fat, 26 percent carbohydrates, and 4 percent ash. The calcium to phosphorus ratio is ideal at 1.2 to 1. Energy density is 5, meaning it is a concentrated food.

2	cups whole milk (goat milk preferred)
2	large eggs
5	teaspoons protein powder (from animal protein sources)
$\frac{1}{4}$	teaspoon of Group I bone meal (or $\frac{1}{2}$ tsp of Group II bone meal or about 350 mg calcium from a Group III source or $\frac{1}{8}$ teaspoon eggshell powder)*
1–2	days' worth of cat vitamins (adult dosage), powdered or crushed
100	milligrams taurine supplement (if not in cat vitamins)

*See information on calcium supplements in "Table of Calcium Supplementation Products" on page 67.

Mix the ingredients well. Warm just to body temperature and feed with a pet nurser or doll bottle. It is important that the milk continue to be warm, so you may have to reheat it occasionally by placing it in a pan of hot water. Make sure it is body temperature—not too hot! Check it on your wrist or with a thermometer (101°F).

Yield: About 3 cups of formula, around 190 kilocalories per cup.

Give each kitten just enough at each feeding to enlarge the abdomen slightly without distending it (usually 8 cc, which is about 1½ teaspoons). Don't overfeed. Stop before the kitten does. Feed according to "Kitten Feeding Schedule," opposite.

After each feeding, gently massage the kitten's belly to stimulate a bowel movement, and swab the genital and anal areas with a tissue moistened slightly with warm water. Mama cats lick the same areas to stimulate proper urination and defecation.

After two weeks of age, you can begin to

KITTEN FEEDING SCHEDULE

AGE (WK.)	WEIGHT	HOW OFTEN TO FEED	TOTAL AMOUNT/DAY (TBSP.)
0–2	4–8 oz.	every 2 hours	2–4
3	8–10 oz.	every 3 hours	4–6
4–5	10–24 oz.	every 4 hours	6–10
6	2+ lbs.	3 times a day	8–12

add a high-protein dry cereal, such as baby cereal or oats, to the formula, or ground up liver or kidney. Start introducing solids (cat recipes mentioned above or high-quality canned food) when the kittens are 3 to 4 weeks old. Mix them with the formula to make a thin mush. Begin weaning the kittens from the bottle at about 4 to 6 weeks. By 6 weeks of age the kittens will likely be able to eat all of their food from a bowl.

PUPPY FORMULA

Comparable in formulation to a dog's natural milk (33.2 percent protein, 44.1 percent fat, 15.8 percent carbohydrate, and 6.9 percent ash), this mixture contains 33 percent protein, 43 percent fat, 21 percent carbohydrates, and 3 percent ash. It has a calcium-to-phosphorus ratio of 1.3 to 1 and provides about 250 Kcal per cup.

³⁄₄	cup half-and-half (milk and cream)
1	cup whole milk (goat milk preferred)
2	large eggs
¹⁄₂	tablespoon protein powder
¹⁄₂	teaspoon of Group I bone meal (or 1 tsp of Group II bone meal, or about 700 mg calcium from a Group III source, or ¹⁄₃ teaspoon eggshell powder)*
1–2	days' worth of dog vitamins (adult dosage), powdered or crushed

*See information on calcium supplements in "Table of Calcium Supplementation Products" on page 67.

Mix ingredients well and warm to body temperature. Using a pet nurser or doll's bottle, feed enough to slightly enlarge the abdomen but not distend it. (Amount varies according to age and breed size. If in doubt, consult recommendations for the commercial formula.) Feed on the same schedule described for kittens. Clean each puppy after the feeding, as described for kittens. When the puppies are 2 to 3 weeks old, introduce solids (mixed with formula to make a gruel) and ground liver; wean them from the bottle at 4 to 5 weeks.

Feeding large litters can require a great

deal of time, and some find it easier to tube-feed puppies when they are very small and need feeding every 2 hours. There are some excellent books on care of newborn puppies that can guide you with this technique.

ORPHAN PROBLEMS

The biggest challenge to health in young kittens and puppies is diarrhea that results from inappropriate formulas or overfeeding. Be especially cautious about giving too much milk formula until you gain some experience. If diarrhea does develop, stop feeding the formula until it stops and instead give electrolyte fluid, such as Rebound to replenish lost fluid.

Here's a very useful herbal formula for treating diarrhea in the very young. Prepare a chamomile "tea" by adding 1 pint boiling water to 2 teaspoons of dried chamomile herb. Let steep for 10 minutes, pour off liquid through a sieve or cheesecloth and add ½ teaspoon of sea salt for each pint of recovered liquid. You can use this as a temporary remedy to stop many diarrheas. Give a "dose" (a couple of minutes of nursing) three times a day. In between, administer electrolyte solution by mouth (or injection if your veterinarian is helping you). Consult the Quick Reference section, page 329, for further advice on treating persistent diarrhea.

The other major problem is constipation. This can be a result of not enough formula or perhaps inadequate stimulation to produce a bowel movement after nursing (your job). Puppies or kittens will have rounded bellies (like they are full), but become listless. (Such behavior, or if a puppy crawls away from its nest and feels cold to the touch, is a sign of illness.) The easiest thing to do is to give an enema with warm water (see chapter 15 for instructions). For kittens, use an eye dropper; for puppies that are larger, you might need a plastic syringe.

If this is not sufficient, the remedy *Nux vomica* 6C or 30C given once will usually suffice. With such little mouths, it is easiest administered by dissolving the pellet in some pure water and dripping a few drops into the mouth. (See the discussion of homeopathy in chapter 14.)

THE VEGETARIAN DIET: CAN WE CUT MEAT USE FOR PETS?

Now let's consider a special diet for normal, healthy dogs and cats whose vegetarian owners have qualms about feeding meat to their pets. Even if this is not a direct concern for you, I urge you to read this section because it raises important issues that affect everyone. The possibility of no-meat diets for dogs and cats doesn't even occur to most of us because we have all been deeply conditioned by our culture to think that even we humans *must* eat meat.

Actually, that concept is relatively new in our country, and it results from an era of prosperity. In 2002, for example, Americans each consumed 23 pounds more meat than they did in 1970. Poultry consumption alone increased by 37 pounds in that same period. Meanwhile, grain and potato consumption fell. Furthermore, about half of us keep predators as pets, far more than the number nature would support in the wild. These cultural patterns are taken for granted, and most of us live our lives without realizing what this high level of meat consumption actually means.

So let's discuss some reasons why more and more people are cutting down on meat and perhaps dairy products in their own diets and why they are interested in feeding their dogs or cats in the same way. The first group of reasons stems from health concerns, the second from global, ethical, and environmental issues.

VEGETARIANS ARE HEALTHIER

Many of the people throughout history who chose a vegetarian diet did so because they believed it was a healthier way to eat. Now there is a body of scientific research that supports their views. Consider these facts, compiled by John Robbins, author of *Diet for a New America.*

❖ Women who eat eggs or meat daily face a breast cancer risk that averages more than three times higher than those who eat these foods once a week. Consuming butter and cheese just two to four times a week multiplies the risk by the same degree.

❖ Fatal ovarian cancer risk is three times higher for women who eat eggs frequently (three or more times a week, rather than once or less).

❖ Men who eat meat, dairy products, and eggs daily triple their risk of fatal prostate cancer over those who eat these foods sparingly.

❖ While the average American man has a 50 percent chance of dying from a heart attack, that risk is only 15 percent for those who consume no meat and just 4 percent for men who eat no animal products at all.

❖ Americans who drop consumption of meat, dairy products, and eggs by half reduce their heart attack risk by 45 percent.

❖ At age 65, the average measurable bone loss of female vegetarians is only about half that of female meat-eaters.

❖ Diseases that can be prevented, relieved, and sometimes even cured by a low-fat diet that is free of animal products include: strokes, hypertension, diabetes, asthma, gallstones, osteoporosis, irritable colon syndrome, and prostate, breast, colon, and endometrial cancers.

Why these differences? For one thing, research indicates that meat fat favors the production of certain carcinogens in the intestines. But perhaps even more critical are the toxins that accumulate in animal tissues. The chemical pollution of breast milk in American women averages *35 times* higher than that of complete vegetarians.

Some of these differences might originate with the fact that we humans evolved to eat a largely meatless diet. Most other primates are basically vegetarians. Our teeth and digestive tracts seem best suited to such foods.

Just as I write this today, a report has come out from a study sponsored by the American Cancer Society (in the *Journal of the American Medical Association,* January 2005) that eating red meat or processed meat increases the incidence of colon cancer. In a very large study of 150,000 people, those eating red meat had a 35 percent greater likelihood, and those eating processed meats (bacon, hot dogs, lunch meats) had a 50 percent higher chance of developing this problem.

IS LESS MEAT BETTER FOR DOGS AND CATS, TOO?

For our pets, that part of the equation is somewhat different. The cat is considered a true carnivore and clearly requires nutrients adequately supplied only by meat and animal products. Although the dog prefers meat, both its physiology and behavior indicate that it is better classed as an opportunistic omnivore—an animal that can meet its needs from a wide variety of sources. Wild coyotes and wolves, for example, consume vegetable matter, including grasses, berries, and other fresh material, plus predigested food from the digestive tracts of their vegetarian prey. In fact, a three-generation test found that dogs fed meat as a sole source of protein, along with other essential elements, had difficulties producing adequate milk for their young, as compared with dogs fed a diet that included milk and vegetables.

Strictly from a health viewpoint, it seems that the most natural diet for a dog or cat would be primarily fresh raw meat, eggs, and bones (or bone meal), supplemented with vegetables and fruits for dogs. Yet, such a diet may not be best for today's domesticated pets. Their needs may differ from those of their hunting ancestors who got more exercise, lived in purer environments, and often, by necessity, fasted between large meals. Thus their bodies could cleanse themselves more easily, eliminating uric acid and other waste products of meat metabolism.

Our primary concern about feeding meat to dogs and cats, however, is that meat is now the most polluted food source in the market. Even the highest-quality cuts approved for human consumption contain residues of antibiotics, synthetic hormones, and toxic materials such as lead, arsenic, mercury, DDT, and dioxin. There are also more pesticide residues in meat than in dairy products, grains, vegetables, and fruits.

The long-term effect of all this toxic material—particularly the pesticides and heavy metals—may be increased cancer rates, allergies, infections, kidney and liver problems, irritability, and hyperactivity for our pets.

Looking beyond the immediate personal health issues, what about the big picture? What about the impact of meat production on the environment, on the world's hungry, and on factory-farm animals?

GLOBAL, ETHICAL, AND ENVIRONMENTAL CONCERNS

"A reduction in meat consumption is the most potent single act you can take to halt the destruction of our environment and preserve our precious natural resources," contends Robbins. And he makes the following points:

❖ If Americans were to adopt a meatless diet and stop exporting livestock feed, we could return 204,000,000 acres to forests—almost an acre for every American who would become vegetarian.

❖ Over two-thirds of the topsoil in the United States has been lost, with 85 percent of this loss associated with livestock production.

❖ It takes 78 calories of fossil fuel to produce 1 calorie of protein from beef. Only 2 calories will produce the same amount of protein from soybeans.

❖ The 5,215 gallons of water California uses to produce only *one* edible pound of beef would grow 209 edible pounds of wheat, or 10 pounds of eggs, or provide 300 five-minute showers.

It's clear that we can't continue with this pattern of inefficient consumption. For the sake of future generations, it would be wise for us to begin to rely more on plant sources for our daily food.

Even as we waste resources needed for the future, we contribute to the present world hunger problem. Some 20 million people a year die from malnutrition. Yet 15 vegetarians can be fed on the amount of land needed to feed 1 person eating a meat-centered diet. If Americans would reduce their intake of meat by only 10 percent, 100 million people could be adequately nourished using the same amount of land, water, and energy no longer devoted to livestock feed. That's five times the number of people who now die of malnutrition.

Finally, let's consider the impact of meat production on the animals involved. When all we see is a neatly wrapped package in the supermarket and maybe a few cows out in the countryside, we may imagine that the meat came from animals who spent long, peaceful lives lazily scratching for bugs in a barnyard or grazing in sunny pastures. At the end of their idyllic lives, we imagine, they are slaughtered quickly and humanely. Unfortunately, the reality is usually quite different.

I used to work with livestock and was often appalled at the crowded, stressful, and uncomfortable conditions under which most chickens, pigs, and cows actually live and die. Farming has become big business, and most animals are treated more like profit-making units than creatures capable of feeling pain and distress. To minimize costs and maximize profits, most of them are packed into crowded quarters like items in a production line, deprived of normal environments and relationships. They may never even see daylight or stand on the ground.

Those who enjoy the companionship of dogs and cats often have a special appreciation and caring for all sorts of animals. Knowing something about the realities of modern meat production understandably causes many to wonder whether they can reduce or eliminate meat from their pets' diets. *Animal Liberation*, by philosopher Peter Singer, is an excellent book on the ethics of how we treat animals, with many graphic details about factory farming.

For these reasons, I recommend prioritizing the recipes in chapter 4 that use the least amounts of meat. While all of the basic dog recipes are tailored to require fairly low amounts of meat, the minimal-meat choices for dogs are (in this order): Quick Canine Oatmeal (page 73), Quick Canine Oats and Eggs (page 72), Dog Loaf (page 70), and One-on-One (page 71). The best choices for cats are Quick Feline Eggfest (page 83) and Mackerel Loaf (page 81).

In general, use more poultry, eggs, and dairy products than beef, since their production consumes fewer resources. And whenever you have the choice, select turkey over chicken. Turkeys are often raised more humanely and with a more vegetarian feed. They also produce the most protein. (They are, however, less fatty, and you should add some extra fat in the recipe to compensate.)

For dogs, consider a predominantly lacto-ovo vegetarian diet (one that includes milk and eggs along with plant-based foods); for cats, a partial one. Vegetarian clients have often asked if you can safely exclude meat from a pet's diet. For dogs, the answer is yes, if you are careful in what you feed. Controlled research shows that dogs fed soy protein grow as well as those fed meat, and

several meatless pet foods are now marketed through health food stores. For cats, the answer is "Yes, with special supplements, maybe, but a diet that excludes meat is not the best for the cat."

The Vegetarian Society of the United Kingdom reports that meatless diets are successfully fed to both dogs and cats throughout Great Britain. Dogs do well, they say, on a breakfast of whole-grain cereal and milk and a dinner of high-protein food like cheese, eggs, ground nuts, and textured vegetable proteins or legumes mixed with raw and/or cooked vegetables. They also suggest including whole-wheat bread, brown rice, sprouts, fruit, and some hard foods, such as whole carrots and hard, whole-grain biscuits, for exercising the teeth and gums.

The same British group reports that vegetarian cats thrive on a varied diet of high-protein sources that include textured vegetable proteins, wheat germ, oats, beans, yeast, milk, cheese, eggs, ground nuts, legumes, and canned meat substitutes marketed for vegetarians. They also advise some vegetables (cucumbers, carrots, and the like), as well as the occasional melon.

In my own experience, however, I must say that I see some vegetarian animals that *aren't* so healthy. (Of course, it's the sick animals that people tend to bring to veterinarians!) My observation is that problems arise mostly when owners exclude *all* animal foods, including milk products and eggs, from their pets' diets. While people can do well on a carefully planned pure vegetarian (vegan) diet, I would not impose it on dogs—and certainly not on cats.

Cats have certain needs that can only be supplied from animal tissues. Unlike both humans and dogs, they cannot convert the beta-carotene found in vegetables to vitamin A—they require an animal source of vitamin A such as cod-liver oil, cheese, or eggs. They also need a preformed source of arachidonic acid (also found in cod-liver oil) and ample levels of taurine, an amino acid not present in plant foods. Taurine is found in the highest concentrations in heart tissue and seafoods and to a lesser extent in meats and dairy products. And even in a meat-centered diet, up to 80 percent of the taurine in the ingredients can be lost through cooking. (Perhaps this is why so many cats on processed foods crave seafoods!)

Studies show that a taurine-deficient diet causes cats to suffer degeneration of the retina, leading to blindness and problems with their hearts (cardiomyopathy) and other functions. These changes can be prevented or reversed by using lactalbumin (from milk) or egg albumin as the dietary protein source.

Some vegetarians have experimented with a meatless or even a near-vegan diet supplemented with taurine for cats; there is also a product called Vegecat that is formulated to provide taurine and the other components needed to compensate for a meatless diet. Many people report success with this approach, though I have no experience with it personally.

My thought is that we just don't know all there is to know about the nutrients cats normally obtain from meat. Aside from the uncertainty of a meatless diet's health effects, there is also a palatability issue. Cats often turn down vegetarian recipes! Like the little carnivores they are, they crave animal protein and fat.

You can, however, reduce your cat's meat consumption by alternating the following polenta recipe with at least three or four feedings a week of Mackerel Loaf (page 81) or Beefy Oats (page 75). Use beef or poultry heart, which are both high in taurine, for at least half of the meat in these two recipes. Also, it's wise to add one to two teaspoons of unflavored protein powder derived from lactalbumin or egg albumin to any vegetarian recipe, along with a taurine supplement equaling 50 or more milligrams a day.

It's a good idea to include some hard foods for vegetarian dogs to chew on to keep their teeth and gums in top shape. Instead of bones, you can offer raw carrots, apples, or biscuits made from one of the recipes in "Additional Recipes" on page 444.

Even if you are not trying to feed a meatless diet to your animal, you can still use these vegetarian recipes now and then to decrease the level of pesticides and other toxic residues in your pet's diet and lower your costs. Besides, it's good to know that you can lighten your load on the planet by using less meat and reduce suffering for both humans and animals at the same time.

POLENTA FOR CATS

This recipe derives its protein from meatless animal sources yet still manages to provide 32 percent protein, 24 percent fat, 39 percent carbohydrate, and a high energy density of 5.2.

By comparison, the feline diets in chapter 4 derive much of their protein from meat, so be sure to add the taurine in this recipe to make up the difference.

½	cup cornmeal or polenta (about 2 cups cooked)
4	large eggs, beaten
½	cup grated natural cheese such as Swiss or cheddar
½	tablespoon Healthy Powder (page 53)
½	tablespoon brewer's (or nutritional) yeast
½	teaspoon Animal Essentials calcium (or ¼ teaspoon of powdered eggshell, or 500 mg of calcium from another Group III calcium supplement)*
50–100	IU vitamin E
200	milligrams taurine supplement (found in many cat vitamins, Vegecat, or as a separate supplement)
2	teaspoons protein powder—from lactalbumin or egg albumin
1	tablespoon vegetables (such as cooked or very finely grated squash) with each meal (optional)

*See information on calcium supplements in "Table of Calcium Supplementation Products" on page 67.

Bring 2 cups of water to a boil. Add the cornmeal or polenta, stirring briskly with a fork or whisk. (Or, mix the meal in ½ cup cold water first and add this to 1½ cups boiling water.) When blended, cover and simmer about 10 minutes or until the cornmeal is a smooth mush. While it is still hot, stir in the eggs and cheese. After the mixture has cooled, stir in the remaining ingredients.

Yield: About 3¾ cups, with about 240 kilocalories per cup. Feed 1 to 1½ cups a day; more if your cat is very active.

Grain substitutes: ½ cup millet (+ 1½ cups water = 1½ cups cooked); ½ cup whole-wheat couscous (+ ¾ cup water = 1¼ cups cooked); 1 cup raw oats (+ 2 cups water = 2 cups oatmeal).

POLENTA FOR DOGS

The following recipe for polenta is suitable for a "veggie" dog, and it is followed by three other canine vegetarian recipes. In these meatless recipes, it is probably best to include an iron supplement, because dairy products and legumes contain less iron than meats do. To help counterbalance this deficiency, use plenty of millet, which is high in iron. Eggs, especially if naturally raised, are also well-supplied with this mineral.

$^1/_2$	cup powdered milk + 4 cups water (or 4 cups low-fat milk)
1	cup cornmeal (uncooked)
2	large eggs, beaten
$^1/_2$	cup grated cheese
$^1/_2$	teaspoon Animal Essentials calcium (or $^1/_4$ teaspoon of powdered eggshell, or 500 mg of calcium from another Group III calcium supplement)*
$^1/_2$	tablespoon Healthy Powder (page 53)
1	teaspoon vegetable oil
100–200	IU vitamin E
15	milligrams iron supplement
$^1/_2$	cup vegetables (optional—finely grated or cooked)

*See information on calcium supplements in "Table of Calcium Supplementation Products" on page 67.

Bring powdered milk and water to a boil. (If using only milk, scald and stir to avoid burning.) Add the cornmeal quickly with a whisk and blend until smooth. Cover and turn down to simmer until the cornmeal is soft and mushy, about 10 minutes. While the cornmeal is still hot, blend in the eggs and cheese. After some cooling, stir in the remaining ingredients. Provides 23 percent protein, 14 percent fat, and 59 percent carbohydrates.

Yield: About 5½ cups, with 230 kilocalories per cup.

Daily ration (in cups): Toy—about 1½ to 2; small—3½ to 4½; medium—6 to 7; large—about 8; giant—about 10 cups.

Grain substitutes: 1 cup millet (+ 3 cups water = 3 cups cooked); 1 cup whole-wheat couscous (+ 1½ cups water = 2½ cups cooked); 2 cups raw oats (+ 4 cups water = 4 cups oatmeal).

MEXI-DOG CASSEROLE

Adapted from a delicious recipe for people, here's another bean-based dish. This one is topped with a cheesy layer of cornmeal. It makes a large quantity, so you might want to reserve some for yourself (minus the supplements) when you make it for your pet.

4	cups pinto beans (or 10 cups cooked or canned)
3	cups whole milk
1	cup yellow cornmeal
2	cups grated cheddar cheese
4	large eggs
2	tablespoons vegetable oil
$\frac{1}{4}$	cup Healthy Powder (page 53)
5	teaspoons Animal Essentials calcium, approximately $1\frac{1}{2}$ tablespoons (or $2\frac{3}{4}$ teaspoons of powdered eggshell, or 5,000 mg of calcium from another Group III calcium supplement)*
10,000	IU vitamin A
200–400	IU vitamin E
20	milligrams iron supplement
1–2	cups vegetables (optional)

*See information on calcium supplements in "Table of Calcium Supplementation Products" on page 67.

Soak the beans overnight. Drain, rinse, and pick out any broken or damaged beans. Bring beans to a boil in 8 to 10 cups of water. Simmer, covered, for 1½ hours or until you can blow the skin off a bean. (To reduce gas—from your dog, not the beans—discard cooking water after the first half-hour and start over with fresh water for the final hour.)

Meanwhile, make the cornmeal topping. Scald the milk. Gradually add the cornmeal, stirring with a whisk or fork. Cover and steam until soft, about 10 minutes. Remove from heat and add the cheese and eggs. After the mixture has cooled, add the remaining ingredients and serve. Freeze anything that can't be eaten in 3 days. Provides 24 percent protein, 11 percent fat, and 61 percent carbohydrates.

Yield: 17 to 18 cups, with about 387 kilocalories per cup.

Daily ration (in cups): Toy—½ to 1¼; small—around 2½; medium—about 4; large—about 5 to 6; giant—more than 6 cups.

Bean substitutes: You may use equal amounts (before cooking) of kidney, white, or black beans.

Variation: You can omit the beans and serve the corn topping by itself. If you do, change amounts as follows: reduce the calcium to 1 teaspoon of Animal Essentials calcium, ½ teaspoon of eggshell powder, or 1,000 mg calcium from some other source. The resulting food (5.2 Kcal/kg.) is good for active dogs.

EASY EGGS AND GRAIN

This simple-to-make dish relies on eggs for its main protein source. Eggs provide an economical protein and are generous in both fat and lecithin, an essential nutrient for nerve function. Look in a natural food store for an unflavored powder that includes some of its protein from lactalbumin and egg albumin.

1	cup bulgur (uncooked)
4	eggs
1	tablespoon chopped parsley or sprouts or ½ cup cooked vegetables
3	tablespoons protein powder
2	tablespoons Healthy Powder (page 53)
3	tablespoons vegetable oil (flax oil is excellent)
1½	teaspoons Animal Essentials calcium (or a scant teaspoon of powdered eggshell, or 1,500 mg of calcium from another Group III calcium supplement)*
100–200	IU vitamin E
5	milligrams iron supplement (optional)
1	clove garlic, minced (optional)
½	teaspoon tamari soy sauce (or a dash of salt)

*See information on calcium supplements in "Table of Calcium Supplementation Products" on page 67.

Bring 2 cups of water to a boil. Add the bulgur, cover, and turn down to simmer until the grain is soft, 10 to 20 minutes. Stir in the eggs while the bulgur is still hot. After it cools a bit, add the remaining ingredients and serve. Provides 28 percent protein, 21 percent fat, and 47 percent carbohydrates.

Yield: About 5 cups, with about 320 kilocalories per cup.

Daily ration (in cups): About the same as Mexi-Dog Casserole (opposite).

Grain substitutes: 1 cup millet (+ 3 cups water = 3 cups cooked); 1 cup whole-wheat couscous (+ 1½ cups water = 2½ cups cooked); or 2 cups raw oats (+ 4 cups water = 4 cups oatmeal).

NUTRITIONAL COMPOSITION OF RECIPES
FOR NEWBORN FORMULAS & VEGETARIAN DIETS

RECIPE	TOTAL KCAL.	DRY WEIGHT (G.)	PROTEIN (%)	FAT (%)	CARB (%)
FORMULAS FOR NEWBORNS					
Puppy Formula	588	102	33	43	21
Kitten Formula	565	114	44	25	26
VEGETARIAN RECIPES					
Polenta for Cats	903	175	32	24	39
Polenta for Dogs	1,260	274	23	14	59
Mexi-Dog Casserole	6,771	1,558	24	11	61
Mexi-Dog Casserole, without beans	3,141	601	23	26	47
Easy Eggs & Grain	1,598	333	28	21	47
Beans & Millet	4,718	1,077	26	14	57
Standard Recommendations (cats)†	-350	–	≥ 26	≥ 9	–
Standard Recommendations (dogs)†	See chart on page 87	–	≥ 18	≥ 5	≤ 67
Wild Diets (cats)††	–	–	46	33	16
Wild Diets (dogs)††	–	–	54	42	1

* Some of these entries are shown in zero but more accurately have trace amounts of these ingredients in the calculations. I have rounded up or down and have entered zero when the amounts are less than 0.5 percent.

** The high amount of vitamin A comes mostly from the egg yolks.

*** The 5,000 IU of vitamin A per kilogram of food is a minimum standard. The recipes are designed to have considerably greater amounts of vitamin A for the maintenance of good health.

† Standard Recommendations are based on the guidelines for producing commercial foods. The amounts in our recipes are meant to exceed these minimums in most categories.

†† The percentages of ingredient of nutrient types encountered in a natural, wild animal diet is included for comparison purposes. Not all categories are known and therefore some are left empty.

FIBER (%)	ASH (%)	CALCIUM (%)	PHOSPH. (%)	CALC:PHOS RATIO	VIT. A ($^{IU}/_{KG}$)
0*	3	1.2	.91	1.3:1	~ 24,000**
0	5	.93	.76	1.2:1	~ 25,000**
0	5	.69	.57	1.2:1	~ 20,000
0	4	.73	.53	1.4:1	~ 10,000
3	4	.67	.54	1.2:1	~ 12,000
1	3	.84	.61	1.4:1	~ 30,000
1	4	.71	.55	1.3:1	~ 8,000
3	4	.73	.53	1.4:1	~ 12,000
–	–	≥ .80	≥ .60	1:1**	≥ 5,000***
–	–	≥ .60	≥ .50	1:1–2:1	5,000–50,000
–	3	–	–	–	–
–	–	–	–	–	–

Note: *Except where noted for wild dogs or cats, standard recommendations are percentage total dry weight and are for maintenance of adult dogs and cats under normal conditions. Sources: AAFCO Nutrient Profiles—Report of the Canine Nutrition Expert Subcommittee, 1992; Report of the Feline Nutrition Expert Subcommittee, 1992; the Merck Veterinary Manual, 6th Edition, 1986; the Committee on Animal Nutrition, Board on Agriculture, National Research Council revised 1986 edition of* Nutrient Requirements of Cats; *and the Committee on Animal Nutrition, Board on Agriculture, National Research Council revised 1985 edition of* Nutrient Requirements of Dogs.

Note: *The symbol "≥" is to read as "equal to or greater than amount listed." Thus, the notation "≥ 5,000 IU" reads "the amount should be equal to or greater than 5,000 IU." The symbol "≤" reads the opposite, meaning "equal to, or less than."*

BEANS 'N' MILLET

Here's a well-balanced meatless recipe for dogs that makes use of beans and cottage cheese, both of which are high in protein and economical.

2	cups kidney beans (or 5 cups cooked or about 38 ounces canned)
2	cups millet (or 6 cups cooked)
4	cups low-fat cottage cheese
6	tablespoons (a little more than $^1/_3$ cup) vegetable oil
4	tablespoons Healthy Powder (page 53)
5	teaspoons (a little less than 2 tablespoons) Animal Essentials calcium (or a scant 3 teaspoons of powdered eggshell or 5,000 mg of calcium from another Group III calcium supplement)*
$^1/_2$	cup cooked carrots, broccoli, or peas (optional)
2	teaspoons tamari soy sauce (or $^1/_2$ teaspoon salt)
1–2	cloves garlic, crushed or minced (optional)
5,000	IU vitamin A
50–200	IU vitamin E
10	milligrams iron supplement (optional with millet; recommended with other grains)

*See information on calcium supplements in "Table of Calcium Supplementation Products" on page 67.

Soak the beans overnight. Drain, rinse, and pick out any broken or damaged beans. Bring the beans to a boil in 6 to 8 cups of water. Simmer, covered, for 1½ hours or until you can blow the skin off a bean. (To reduce intestinal gas, discard cooking water after first half-hour and start over with fresh water for the final hour). Meanwhile, prepare the millet. Bring 6 cups of water to a boil. Add the millet, cover, and simmer on low for 20 to 30 minutes, or until soft. Combine when both are done; then add the remaining ingredients and serve.

Yield: About 14 cups, with about 337 kilocalories per cup.

Daily ration (in cups): Toy—½ to 1; small—about 3; medium—4 to 5; large—5½ to 6; giant—about 7 cups+.

Grain substitutes: You may use 2 cups (before cooking) of bulgur, brown rice, or barley.

Bean substitutes: You may use equal amounts (before cooking) of lentils, pintos, soybeans, or white or black beans. Or to save time, you may use a 16-ounce package of tofu. In this case, it's okay to use creamed cottage cheese instead of low-fat, and you'll still have plenty of protein.

CHAPTER 6

HELPING YOUR PET MAKE THE SWITCH

Most pets love their new diets. But some may run into a few snags along the way—snags that can be prevented or remedied. Here are some examples of the common problems I've encountered over the years.

One reader phoned to tell me that her cats would not eat the foods in the diet I suggested.

"What have you given them?" I inquired.

"You name it! I've tried adding supplements like bone meal, nutritional yeast, and wheat germ. I've offered them meats, dairy products, grains, vegetables, everything you can think of!

But practically all they will touch, especially the older cat, is just canned tuna and chicken. Not only that, but it has to be one *certain* brand, if you can believe that!"

Similarly, a client reported back after following a course of natural foods and remedies for her dog's chronic problem: "Henry was doing okay and then suddenly he just stopped eating and began acting like he was sick. He just lay around and didn't seem to have any energy."

Another owner who had started to feed the natural diet called for reassurance and advice: "My dog liked the new food, and he's been on it a few weeks. But yesterday he just passed a whole bunch of worms! What do I do?"

In the first instance—a cat who turns up its nose at new foods—we are dealing with the fussy feline, star of cat food commercials. Many cats have become habituated ("addicted") to the particular foods they were given as kittens or foods they've been fed over a long period of time. Under such circumstances, the body's natural instinct for selecting a healthy, balanced diet diminishes considerably. Similarly, among humans, narrow food preferences that were learned early in life often become deeply entrenched habits.

In cases like the last two—the dog that stopped eating and the dog that passed worms—I am actually happy to hear about these responses to the switch. I know from experience that such signs can be favorable omens in terms of natural healing. After a brief period on a higher-quality diet, it is fairly common for an animal in sub-optimal health to discharge accumulated toxic material or to undergo a brief aggravation of its symptoms (often called a healing crisis). These apparent setbacks are normal, often necessary, bumps on the road to well-being.

Nearly all the snags your pet might encounter in a change of diet will be of these two types—getting a finicky eater to like nutritious food or helping an animal through the sometimes uncomfortable stages of a natural cleansing process.

THREE WAYS TO INTRODUCE THE NEW FOODS

When you have a finicky eater on your hands, first make sure you serve the food in an appealing manner. Rather than serving refrigerated food cold, warm it up a bit, which greatly increases aroma and appeal. Also, be sure to serve the food in a safe place, not in the middle of your path of movement around the kitchen. Beyond that, you can choose one of three strategies: Introduce new foods gradually until they're accepted, let your animal go without eating until it's hungry enough to try the new fare, or compromise with a combination of the natural diet and your pet's old favorites.

The gradual transition. This not only helps your pet get used to the taste of new foods but also gives the animal's digestive system time to adjust. Whenever the diet is changed abruptly, even from one commercial brand to another, temporary diarrhea or loss of appetite might occur. That's because the bacterial flora in the digestive tract is still adjusting to the new material. By switching over gradually, you can reduce or avoid acceptance problems and the possibility of discomfort for your pet. If the gradual method doesn't work, you probably have a food addict on your hands, and more drastic measures will be necessary.

Fasting for a few days. This stimulates a lagging appetite, helps cleanse the body, and deconditions old taste habits all at the same time.

To fast, your pet needs a healthful setting—plenty of fresh air, quiet, access to the outdoors, and some moderate exercise.

Here's the process.

1. Begin the fast with a break-in period of one to two days. Feed a smaller quantity of the usual food during this first phase, perhaps adding a little meat, cooked grain, and/or vegetables.

2. Move to a liquid fast for the next two to three days. During that time give your animal only liquids, such as pure water, vegetable juices, and broths.

3. To break the fast, add some solid foods to the liquid regime over a day or two, perhaps vegetables (for dogs) or eggs, yogurt, or small amounts of fresh meat (for dogs and cats).

4. After a day or so, increase the amount of meat and add a grain, gradually adding other ingredients until the recipe

is approximated; then add the supplements (often the least-accepted part of the diet, except for nutritional yeast, which many animals love).

In stubborn cases, it often pays to continue fasting the animal a few more days. One client reported worriedly that her cat wouldn't eat any of the natural foods offered in the "breaking-out" period. I advised her to keep the cat on liquids for a while longer. She did, and in a few days she called back enthused to say that her formerly finicky cat was now eating all kinds of things it would never touch before—like vegetables, grains, meats, nutritional yeast, and even soy grits! In addition to the longer fast, she found it helped to mix a little bit of fish (an old favorite) into the new diet.

Some people are frightened by the idea of fasting their pet. At first it does seem that some animals would rather starve to death than eat anything but the food to which they're addicted. But the instinct for survival is very strong. Sooner or later, the pet comes around. Somehow we have convinced ourselves that a day or two without food will take a cat or dog close to death's door. Not true. Cats, being true carnivores, actually prefer a 28-hour eating cycle. In fact, healthy cats trapped in moving vans and such have been known to survive without any food or water for periods of up to six weeks. Because they live with people, they have adapted to eating two or even three times a day. This eating schedule, however, is not natural to them, or even desirable.

Obese dogs have been known to fast on just water and vitamins for as long as six to eight weeks without ill effect. Wild carnivores fast naturally, since the prey they live on may elude them for days at a time. So don't worry about trying the fast on your pet for a few days.

How long should you let your animal go hungry before giving up and returning to the old diet? With dogs, two days should be enough. Cats are different, however, and going without food for a while seems to be no big deal for them. Many of my client's cats do not really become hungry and willing to try a new food until 5 days of fasting have gone by. I have not seen healthy animals go longer than that before they become truly hungry.

Your veterinarian may have told you that cats must eat every day or run the risk of liver disease and jaundice. This does happen, but only in those cats that already are not well. These animals will often be overweight, have a finicky appetite, and a history of other problems. If you have a young, vigorous cat of normal weight, it should be fine to fast them for a while. If you are not sure or your cat is older or has a history of other health problems, then run it by your veterinarian first. Many holistically minded veterinarians have experience with fasting animals and can guide you.

Some cats or dogs, however, simply do not develop a normal hunger even after several days of not eating. A weak appetite like this is often a symptom of chronic illness. I do not mean that these animals are necessarily ill with symptoms or a defined disease.

Rather, they are in a sub-optimal or low-grade state of health. In such cases I use individualized homeopathic treatment to improve the animal's overall level of health. Afterward, the animal begins to eat more normally. If your pet won't eat and you don't have access to a vet who practices homeopathy, you may want to try the third approach.

"The compromise." Suppose you've tried a gradual transition and your pet just won't convert to a new diet. Or perhaps fasting just doesn't work for you. It is difficult for some people to let their animals get hungry. They can't handle the agitation that the animal shows in asking for food. And in other cases, the cat or dog is not healthy enough to undertake a fast. In such situations, it is best to compromise by mixing the new food into the old.

Sometimes even a small bit of the pet's familiar fare makes a difference. One woman I know finds that mixing just a spoonful of her pets' favorite canned cat food into the natural recipe does the trick. "There seems to be something about the sight and sound of the old familiar can-opening process that gets them excited," she told me. Another trick you might try is to pulverize some of the usual dry kibble in a food processor or blender and then sprinkle it over the natural food recipe, perhaps mixing some in as well. This is just the kind of catalyst that some finicky felines need to get them started eating a natural diet. Then nature takes over.

It's likely that after eating a compromise mixture of both natural and commercial foods for a while, your pet will become so used to the new foods that the old ones will be forgotten. Eventually, many pets turn up their noses at their old favorite canned food or kibbles.

TAKING CHARGE

Don't allow your animal's habits to run your life. Remember, for the average healthy animal, the most important factor in accepting a new food is hunger. Many animals will not accept a change in diet simply because they are not really that hungry. They lack the motivation to try something new. Cats, in particular, are well-adapted to cycles of feast and famine, and it often takes several days for them to reach a state of true hunger. When food is available several times a day, they learn to just nibble, but seldom develop a decent appetite.

Ideally, cats should be fed once a day. Most people, however, prefer feeding them twice daily. This can work out fine as long as the food is available for no more than 20 minutes at each feeding, morning and evening. Practitioners find that cats fed frequently during the day and those with constant self-feeding access to kibble are not in tip-top health, have a poor hair coat, and tend to form "gravel" in the bladder, with resultant cystitis (bladder inflammation). Carnivores need a certain interval between meals so that the body can digest food properly and eliminate the many toxins associated with a meat-based diet.

With dogs, things are simpler. By nature, the dog is a partial scavenger, so it is adapted to eat whenever the opportunity arises. It's okay to feed a healthy dog once or twice a day, or even more often.

CLEANSING REACTIONS

Some animals, particularly those in marginal health, may experience some physical difficulties even if the transition to a natural diet is gradual. They may seem out of sorts for a few days or even throw up hair balls or pass worms. Often, these are transient cleansing reactions. But not always. If you suspect that your pet is having excessive difficulty, a checkup, as described in "How to Give Your Pet a Quick Checkup" on page 114, will let you know if your pet has an underlying health problem that is being aggravated by a change of diet.

If your animal really does not look healthy to you, it is time to get some help. Ask your local veterinarian to work with you on the diet switch. Explain what you are trying to do and why, perhaps sharing the recipes and analyses. Ask your veterinarian to examine your pet periodically to make sure that there are no health problems of which you are unaware and to see that your pet responds to the diet as expected and does not lose weight or weaken.

If your veterinarian does not want to help as you switch your pet to a fresh foods diet, don't hesitate to seek help elsewhere. Veterinarians interested in nutrition and a holistic approach to medicine are growing in number. Most states have a few; some will consult by phone, which can be quite helpful.

Your animal might be in poor health without your realizing it. Perform this brief exam to get a much better idea of your pet's actual state. If any of the exam symptoms are apparent, then resolve any concerns that arise by consulting your vet.

1. Does the hair coat feel greasy? Is the skin color a normal gray-white or is it pink or red with inflammation? Do you see dandruff-like scales of dead skin among the hairs?

2. Use your fingers to brush the hair against the grain. Do you see numerous little black specks? These are the excreta of fleas.

3. Now smell your fingers. If the odor they picked up is rancid, rank, or fishy, it's a sign of poor health.

4. As you examine the eyes, check for matter in the corners. Pull down the lower eyelids so you can see the underside. Are the lids red inside or irritated on the edges?

5. Look into the ear holes. Do you see a lot of wax? Do the insides look oily? Sniff to check for an offensive odor.

6. Inspect the gums for a red line along the roots of the teeth. To check the back teeth for that red line, raise the upper lip and push back the corners of the lips at the same time (it is not necessary to open the mouth).

7. Now check the teeth themselves, including the back ones. Are they gleaming white or coated with a brown deposit? Does the breath smell okay or are you overcome by it?

8. Last, feel the backbone in the middle of the back and run your fingers back and forth (sideways) over it. Do you feel definite bones there? Is there a prominent ridge sticking up in the middle? If your answers to these questions are yes, your animal is much too thin.

THE BODY RESPONDS

By examining your pet regularly, you can easily monitor its overall health. No matter what you've heard, it's *not* normal for a dog to have a "doggy odor" or a cat to have foul breath. Pets that have an unpleasant smell about them show signs of a chronic low health level. If your pet is in mediocre condition or it has a particular disease, starting the new diet may trigger a cleansing process.

What happens? For years your animal has been eating over-processed food that was probably loaded with the harmful ingredients discussed in chapter 2. No doubt it has also been exposed to environmental pollutants and, perhaps, some strong drugs. So when your pet finally eats really fresh, nutritious food that is minimally polluted, strange things begin to happen. The body responds!

Your animal usually feels better at first. Energy and nutrients are flowing through the tissues. The quality of the blood and its oxygen-carrying capacity improves, so the animal starts to be more active. The added exercise in turn helps recharge lazy tissues.

After two to three weeks, the animal may feel perky enough to tackle some long-neglected interior housecleaning by throwing off debris it's been accumulating. For example, a mass of worms that, until now, have been existing comfortably may be swept out, leaving behind a clean intestine.

More often, the cleansing results in a lot of discharge from the kidneys, colon, or skin, all important excretory organs. Thus, the urine might become dark and strong-smelling, the feces dark, temporarily containing mucus or blood, or the skin might erupt with sores or develop a lot of dandruff. Sometimes a lot of dead hair falls out as the skin becomes more active, getting ready to grow a new crop of fresh, healthy hair (much like a plant dropping dead foliage before putting out new leaves).

THE HEALING CRISIS

Appearances can be deceiving. In spite of what you see, your pet's body is getting *cleaner*. I know that's hard to grasp. Most of us expect that when a physical problem is being treated effectively, the condition will steadily improve until the disturbance just disappears. (Certainly, we don't expect it to look worse!) That's how antibiotics and other familiar drugs often work—at least for a while. Unfortunately, such drugs sometimes simply suppress the symptoms, leaving the underlying disorder that led to the illness unchanged, so the same problems or related ones may crop up again. One long-term effect of using drugs to control diseases is that the body tends to become lazy about attempting to keep itself healthy. That's when an animal gets the kind of symptoms described in "How to Give Your Pet a Quick Checkup."

In bygone times, people more clearly recognized the stages of healing—one of which was a period of crisis that might show up as a fever, inflammation, or temporary exaggeration of symptoms. At such a point the patient either began to recover or died. This healing crisis, as it has been called, represents the point at which the body's defenses are mobilized to their maximum capabilities. It's an all-out effort.

When we interfere with this process by injecting antibiotics or cortisone, for example, the defense system is not utilized. That means it can't address the underlying weakness that gave rise to the disease in the first place. Like an underused muscle, the defense system gets weak. Soon resistance to any new disease is weakened, and the body needs more drugs to cope with new problems. Poor nutrition lowers disease resistance even further, which then leads to the use of still more drugs. Weakened by infections and the toxic elements of drugs, the body demands more of the available nutrition, which overtaxes the supply and creates a deficit. Before we know it, we are caught in a vicious circle.

What will break this cycle? A good diet, for one thing. By supplying optimum nutrients, we can increase disease resistance and help the body to eliminate the toxic effects of drugs. So don't be discouraged by these signs of detoxification when you improve your pet's diet. You have things moving.

INTERPRETING REACTIONS

"But," you might ask, "how can I tell whether my pet's in the process of detoxification or is suffering from some serious disease?" This is a sticky point, of course. If you feel uncertain, consult your veterinarian. And if you favor a conservative approach (minimum drugs, maximum wait-and-see), tell the vet so. But here are some general clues to help you interpret what is happening.

 ❖ If your pet has a high-energy level and has a good appetite, temporary symptoms such as passing worms, mucus, or a little blood are probably insignificant. And bear in mind that it is also common for an animal switching from all-commercial to all-fresh food to undergo a lethargic period of a day or two, usually within two to four weeks of the diet change. This is a cleansing period that may result in a temporary energy drop and appetite loss, plus more time spent sleeping.

 ❖ Returning symptoms of problems previously suppressed by drugs—such as skin eruptions, bladder irritation in cats, and ear problems in dogs—mean the body is rallying its increased energies to try to heal underlying chronic disturbances that should have been dealt with long ago. If these problems persist or become intense, you will need help from a veterinarian who knows how to work with the body to bring this process to healthy completion. I use homeopathy, but there are other natural treatment methods that support the body in this process, including acupuncture and herbology. Refer to chapter 14 for more information on these valuable tools for good health.

 ❖ If your pet's energy level decreases steadily for more than a few days or if you see mental/emotional changes such as depression, irritability, or forgetfulness *that were not present before*, your pet may have serious problems that should be checked out by a vet.

 ❖ If any symptoms—such as loss of appetite, abnormal stools, or other problems of elimination—continue despite your precautions, food allergy is a likely possibility. Stop using the new foods. If the problem clears up, reintroduce vegetables, grains, meats, dairy products, brewer's yeast, and legumes one at a time until you find out which one is causing the problem. When you identify the culprit, eliminate it from the diet permanently. Foods commonly known to cause allergic reactions in pets are described along with a special diet in the "Allergies" section on page 296.

Cats sometimes find it harder to metabolize unsaturated oils than saturated ones (animal fats). Choosing olive oil as your cat's oil source and adding ample vitamin E to the diet should allay this problem. Or else stick to animal fats like lard, butter, or meat trimmings and drippings.

In summary, a natural healing process is not always simply "getting better." There may be ups and downs and evidence of discharge. It is highly recommended that you work with a veterinarian that is able to interpret these changes accurately, which is usually one trained in homeopathy, Chinese medicine, herbology, or other systems of natural healing.

HERBS TO EASE THE PROCESS

Should your pet have some moderate distress in changing to a fresh diet, you can smooth the way (or try to prevent problems from the start) with some herbs that help cleanse the body and rebuild tissue. Use only one herb, rather than a combination. Pick the one that best matches the problems listed in the brief descriptions that follow. See the Schedule for Herbal Treatment on

page 438 for amounts relative to your pet's size.

Alfalfa (*Medicago sativa*) is an excellent tonic that stimulates digestion and appetite. It helps animals gain weight and improves physical and mental vigor. Alfalfa is best used for animals that are underweight, nervous, or high-strung. It can also help those with muscle or joint pains or animals with urinary problems—especially where there is crystal formation and bladder irritation. Depending on your dog's body size, add from 1 teaspoon to 3 tablespoons of ground or dry-blended alfalfa to the daily ration. Or make a tea by steeping 3 tablespoons of the herb in 1 cup of water for 20 minutes. Mix it with food or administer it orally with a bulb syringe (or turkey baster), using the "Dog Sizes" table on page 118 as a guideline for how much to give. Cats can be given 1 teaspoon (dry) per day.

Burdock (*Arctium lappa*) cleanses the blood and helps the body detoxify. It's particularly good for easing skin disorders. Soak 1 teaspoon of the root in 1 cup of spring or distilled water in a glass or enamel pan for 5 hours. Then bring to a boil, remove from heat and let cool. Check "Dog Sizes" on page 118 for how much to give. Cats can be given ½ teaspoon per day.

Garlic (*Allium sativum*) helps to eliminate worms, strengthen digestion, and beneficially stimulate the intestinal tract. Use it to promote intestinal health. It is also indicated for animals that have been on a high meat or fish diet, and those that tend to be overweight or suffer hip pain from arthritis or dysplasia. Include fresh, grated garlic with each meal, using ½ to 3 cloves, depending on the animal's size (see the table below). Cats can be given ¼ clove per day.

Oats (*Avena sativa*) are also a tonic, particularly for the animal whose main weakness is in the nervous system, as in epilepsy, tremors, twitching, and paralysis. Oats also counter the weakening and exhaustive effects of heavy drugging and diseases. They help to cleanse the body and nourish new tissue growth. Use oatmeal as the chief grain in the diet.

Also, you can use oat straw to provide a healing bath: Boil 1 to 2 pounds of the straw in 3 quarts of water for 30 minutes. Add this to the bathwater or sponge on repeatedly as an after-bath rinse by standing the animal in a tub and reusing the solution. Such treatment is useful for skin problems, muscle and joint pain, paralysis, and liver and kidney problems. Dogs enjoy it more than cats.

One of these herbs along with the benefits of the new diet should make the road to good health smoother and shorter. After a month or two, give your pet another exam (see "How to Give Your Pet a Quick Checkup" on page 114), and I bet you'll see a difference.

Above all, don't be discouraged from trying a change of diet. Remember, most animals that switch to natural foods do not experience the problems I have described in this chapter. The majority enjoy the new diet and digest it well. And if you follow the advice here about easing the transition period, in all probability your pet will simply be happier and healthier than ever before.

DOG SIZES

Use this table as an approximate guide in determining how much herb to give your dog. If your dog falls into a size between those listed, then use the next higher group.

DOG SIZE	ALFALFA DRY (TSP.)*	ALFALFA LIQUID (C.)	BURDOCK LIQUID (TSP.)	GARLIC CLOVES
Toy = 10–15 lbs	1	$^1/_8$ (2 Tbsp)	1	$^1/_2$
Small = 20–40 lbs	3	$^1/_3$ (5 Tbsp)	2	1
Medium = 45–70 lbs	5	$^1/_2$ (9 Tbsp)	3 (1 Tbsp)	2
Large = 75–90 lbs	7	$^3/_4$ (13 Tbsp)	5	$2^1/_2$
Giant = 100 lbs & over	9 (3 Tbsp)*	1 (16 Tbsp)	6 (2 Tbsp)	3

* tsp = teaspoons (there are 3 teaspoons in a tablespoon)

** Tbsp = tablespoons (there are 16 tablespoons in a cup)

CHAPTER 7

EXERCISE, REST, AND NATURAL GROOMING

You can't expect to keep your car in top shape by merely filling the gas tank. You also have to change the oil, lube the joints, replace parts that wear, and get an occasional tune-up. Without this kind of attention, even the best car eventually becomes a junker.

Certainly, animals can't be equated with machines. But like machines, they need more than just the right fuel (food). Besides a healthy diet, animals need pure water, fresh air, sunlight, regular exercise, grooming, space of their own, and much more.

So while good nutrition is essential for maintaining or improving your pet's health, you can't stop there. Many additional factors, both obvious and subtle, affect well-being. What we must do is develop a broad view that allows us to see the many diverse elements as a whole—a whole that can enhance your pet's life or threaten it.

Consider for a moment the difference between the lifestyle of our pets and the ways of their wild ancestors. A typical city dog, for example, eats highly processed foods nearly all the time and never spends a fresh, sunny day investigating the path of a stream or running hard through sweetly scented woods on the trail of prey. Instead, she devotes most of her life to sleeping or pacing indoors on vinyl floors and carpets made from synthetic fibers. Her time "outdoors" is often spent in a stuffy parked car waiting while her owner does an errand.

She doesn't socialize much with her own kind, but does have an intense mutual attachment with one or more humans, who often display complex and confusing emotions. But mostly the humans are at work or at school, and she is alone in the confines of an apartment, house, or yard.

If she is lucky, every week or two she's treated to one of her great delights—a walk through the fields. But her fun is somewhat marred by painful foxtails that lodge easily in the abnormally long, curly hairs of her coat. When she gets home, she quenches her thirst with tap water that smells of chlorine. Sometimes, largely because of these condi-

tions, she's a bit irritable and snappish, or depressed and bored. But overall she's good-natured and takes each day as it comes.

Do our animal friends really have to lead lives lacking in so many basics? Let's examine an animal's real needs and see what we can do to meet them.

The circumstances that affect a pet's health are complex, of course, but we can understand them better if we remember one basic principle: The less we interfere with nature, the more life's processes flow healthfully. Not all of us are able to let our dogs run free in natural settings, even occasionally, but we can control many other important factors that affect the quality of a pet's life. Among these are exercise, grooming, and exposure to environmental pollutants.

THE IMPORTANCE OF EXERCISE

For the wild cousins of domestic dogs and cats, regular exercise is an integral and necessary part of daily life. They *must* keep on the move because they *must* hunt for food. A walk to the food bowl is the only exercise many house pets ever get.

Yet regular exercise is essential for optimal health. Sustained, vigorous use of the muscles stimulates all tissues and increases circulation. Blood vessels dilate and blood pressure rises. As a result, tissues become oxygenated, which helps to clean the cells of toxins. Digestive glands secrete their fluids better and the bowels move more easily.

Join your pet in jogging, taking a walk, playing ball, or chasing sticks and Frisbees. Nearly all dogs benefit from half an hour or more of daily vigorous exercise. If your pet is old and weak or has a bad heart, settle for slow walks around the block.

Cats, on the other hand, are not inclined to chase balls or jog, but they usually get enough exercise if they are allowed outside part of the time and have a suitable place to "scratch." The practice of removing claws (equivalent to cutting off the last joint of each of your own fingers) is not only cruel and painful, but it also eliminates the important feline exercise pattern of using the claws to knead and stretch, which benefits the muscles of the forelegs, backbone, and shoulders. A cat that can't perform this ritual is likely to become weaker and thus more susceptible to illness and degeneration.

Most cats also love to play "thing-on-a-string," chasing and batting at a piece of string with a loop or mouse toy attached to one end. Pet stores sell many such toys for both cats and dogs. When playing games with a pet, however, do not use your bare hand as the "bait" or the object of teasing. This can teach your animal that it's all right to scratch or bite your hands, a lesson you will want him to "unlearn" in the future.

Make sure the toys you give your pet are safe for biting and chewing. Some of the best toys are those made of leather, rawhide, and similar natural materials. Another word of caution: Don't leave your animal alone with a ball of yarn or string. Your pet might swallow some of the string or become dangerously entangled in it.

If your dog is temporarily unable to walk because of a sore foot or a partial paralysis, encourage him to swim in place in a bathtub, large trough, swimming pool, or natural body of water to get exercise. Swimming strengthens the body in the same way running does. If your pet tends to sink, place a towel or cloth as a sling under the body for support. This exercise is especially good for dogs with back problems.

QUIET AND REST

Every creature needs a clean, quiet, private place to sleep and rest, a place where it will be warm in the winter and cool in the summer. Even if your pet sleeps in your bed some of the time, provide a suitable place or two of its own. A lot of animals—especially big dogs—are denied these havens. Many are left out in the elements, but unlike their wild cousins who have a cozy den to hide in, they must make do with a patch of dirt next to a noisy street or perhaps a drafty slab of cement beneath a porch roof. The difference is an important one.

Cats and smaller dogs are happy with a padded basket or even just a clean folded blanket or towel in a corner or on a chair. Large dogs don't necessarily require a bed such as a basket, but they do need some kind of secure, clean place that is comfortable in both winter and summer—such as a carpeted corner in a room or dog house, an old chair, or a special rug of its own in a quiet spot.

Use natural fabrics and stuffings for the bedding, such as cotton, wool, feathers, and kapok. Woven wool fleece (called Sherpa Wool or Flokati) resembles sheepskin and makes a warm, soft, washable natural cover for a pet to sleep on. Sold by the yard in many fabric stores, it provides the same healthy sleeping benefits as more costly sheepskin mattress pads sold for human use. Buy enough to cut two sheets a little larger than your pet's body. No sewing is needed. Pets love them and, besides, they look so cozy curled up on them!

Study your pet's preferences and try to provide several quiet sleeping spots, given the circumstances of your home and climate. Your pet might like one quiet, out-of-the-way place and another that's closer to the center of activity, where it's easy to keep an eye on things. Cats instinctively gravitate to small, defined areas with a little elevation, which makes them feel safer. Commercially made window perches or carpeted shelves affixed to windows give cats a front-row seat on all their favorite shows on "cat TV." You might also consider carpeted cat houses on posts, sold at many pet stores.

Are you worried that your pet sleeps too much? It's normal for a pet that is left alone most of the day to sleep a lot during that time. But if your companion animal does not greet you on arrival or goes back to sleep soon after you come home, it could mean the pet's low on energy. This is especially true with dogs. Cats naturally sleep more than dogs and often take frequent naps throughout the day and night. My way of deciding if a cat sleeps too much is to learn if there are several active periods during the day and if the cat grooms himself several times a day. The healthy cat will alternate sleep with activity—looking out the window, going outside, exploring, and grooming. If this activity is rare, there may be a problem.

CLEANLINESS IS NEXT TO HEALTHFULNESS

A clean animal is a beautiful animal, and, more importantly, a healthy one. Every living organism is constantly breaking down and eliminating natural metabolic products and old cells. Ordinarily, about a third of the body's cells are dying at any one time. Each of these cells must be broken down and replaced. In today's world, the body must work even harder to counteract the heavy load of synthetic chemicals in the air, soil, water, and food chain.

These accumulated toxins, as well as external dirt and secretions, can encourage the growth of germs and parasites. They also sap general vitality by overburdening normal organ and glandular functions. A buildup of toxins may not cause a specific disease by itself, but it can make a pet more susceptible and set the stage for worse conditions—infectious disease, acute inflammation, or gradual organ degeneration punctuated by occasional flare-ups. For example, an animal with chronically inflamed skin may develop a sudden moist eczema ("hot spots"); another may get an attack of nephritis (kidney inflammation) arising from a silent degeneration and loss of kidney tissue over years.

If you doubt that this load of toxins our pets face every day is a heavy one, take a closer look at some animals you know. Give them the checkup described in "How to Give Your Pet a Quick Checkup" on page 114. I see a lot of animals that show low-level signs of chronic excessive toxicity. Oily or smelly secretions on the skin, ears, or eyes or deposits on the teeth are signs that the body is struggling to eliminate toxins.

Here are three natural ways you can assist the hard-working organs—the skin, liver, kidneys, digestive tract, and lungs—that carry wastes out of your pet's body.

❖ Daily exercise stimulates waste removal through improved metabolism and circulation.

❖ An occasional day of fasting relieves the digestive tract of its usual duties and frees the organs to break down toxins stored in the liver, fats, and other tissues. During a fast, the organs can also consume excess baggage, such as cysts, scars, and growths. The process and the therapeutic uses of fasting are described more fully in chapter 15.

❖ Regular grooming not only removes dirt and secretions directly, but stimulates the skin's natural elimination processes as well. Let's take a closer look at this important aspect of pet care.

NATURAL GROOMING AND SKIN CARE

Nobody ever gives a wolf or a bobcat a bath and those animals seem to do just fine, so why should we have to groom our pets? For one thing, a wild animal moves from place to place, which means it can get away from a colony of parasites such as fleas. A pet, on the other hand, keeps getting re-infested with these critters from the eggs dropped in its quarters.

Furthermore, a lot of domestic animals are bred to have abnormally long, or curly, or very fine hair, which can be too great a challenge for their limited self-grooming tools—tongue, paws, and teeth. As a result, mats, plant debris, and dirt build up, predisposing the skin to irritation. Also, dust and debris on your pet's fur can contain various toxic and unhealthful contaminants, such as lint from synthetic fibers, tiny flakes of paint, or debris from automobiles (including asbestos fibers from brake linings).

Of course, it's better for the pet's health if you remove this debris from his coat than if the animal licks it off and swallows it. Because we humans have intervened in the natural order and changed the physical structure and environment of our animals, it's up to us to help care for the skin and coat of those pets that need it.

Long-haired pets need daily brushing with a special "slicker" pet brush made for picking up hair. Short-haired animals may need brushing less often. Another excellent tool for regular grooming is a flea comb (described on page 128). Frequent brushing and combing stimulate hair and skin health, bringing normal secretions from oil glands onto the skin and discouraging fleas. It also keeps mats from building up and helps to remove burrs and other plant debris.

Make regular checks of the feet, ears, eyes, and vagina or penis sheath to detect and remove foxtails and other plant stickers before they penetrate the skin's surface and cause harm, requiring removal by your veterinarian. If you live in a hot climate, it's also a good idea to have your dog's coat thinned by a professional groomer.

Bathing also plays a major role in pet grooming. It is one of the safest and most effective ways to control fleas, which are killed by the soap and water. But don't bathe your pets too often, because bathing can dry the skin. Unless your adult dog is unusually dirty, a bath every month or two is plenty. In the case of a bad flea infestation, skin problems, or discharges, however, you may want to bathe the animal every week. If you do, be sure to use a gentle shampoo that will not strip all the natural oils from the hair.

Cats don't need frequent bathing since they generally do a good job of it by themselves. But if your cat has problems with bad skin or fleas, you can bathe it monthly; otherwise, once or twice a year is adequate.

Select a good-quality castile soap or a natural shampoo. Don't use hair conditioners, sulphur-tar shampoos, shampoos containing dandruff suppressors, or any other chemical medication. Avoid pet shampoos that contain synthetic insecticides (see "Common Ingredients in Flea-Control Products" on page 130), unless the safer approaches described below have not been successful. If fleas are a problem, look for a natural pet shampoo containing flea- and insect-repellent herbs. Some contain d-limonene, a natural extract from citrus fruits that will kill fleas with minimal side effects and are suitable for use with dogs. Or you can make your own insect-repellent shampoo by adding a few drops of essential oil of pennyroyal or eucalyptus to a bottle of natural shampoo or castile soap. (Do not apply these oils directly to the skin. They are too irritating.)

Some pets resist bathing. If yours is one of these, be gentle and speak in soft, reassuring tones throughout the experience. Remove the collar and lower your pet into a laundry tub, bathtub, or sink as you gradually fill it with comfortably lukewarm water. Wet and lather up your pet's neck first, to trap any fleas that might try to escape toward your pet's head. Shampoo the entire body and rinse lightly, using either a spray attachment or a container of lukewarm water. Then shampoo a second time, working the lather well into the skin and letting it stay on for five minutes or as long as your friend will allow. This assures the most complete treatment of fleas. Meanwhile, you can comb out and drown any critters making their way toward high ground.

Then rinse your animal thoroughly. It's nice to follow this plain-water rinse with a vinegar-water rinse (1 tablespoon white vinegar to 1 pint warm water). It removes soap residue and helps prevent dandruff. Pour on the solution, rubbing throughout the fur. Then rinse again with plain water.

At this point you might like to try this homemade herbal rinse.

ROSEMARY CONDITIONER

Rosemary tea, used by Anitra Frazier, author of *The New Natural Cat*, makes an excellent conditioner that promotes a glossy coat and helps to repel fleas.

1	teaspoon dried rosemary (or 1 tablespoon fresh)
1	pint boiling water

Combine and steep for 10 minutes, covered. Strain and cool to body temperature. Pour it over your pet after the final rinse. Rub in and towel dry without further rinsing.

When you're finished with the bath, use several towels to blot off excess water. Then let your pet do what comes naturally, shaking and licking off more of the water. Make sure she has a warm place to dry off.

For pets that just won't put up with water baths, try this simple dry shampoo.

Place ½ to 1-cup bran, oatmeal, or cornmeal on a cookie sheet. Put the oven on low for 5 minutes to warm the grain. Removing a little at a time, so that the rest stays warm but not too hot, rub the grain into the fur with a towel. Concentrate on the greasy, dirty areas. Then brush these areas thoroughly to get the grain out.

Finally, here's a spot remover that will help you get rid of grease spots in your pet's fur between baths, especially those spots that cats get on their heads from prowling under cars. Rub a few drops of Murphy Oil Soap and a small amount of warm water onto the greasy spots. Then rinse thoroughly with warm water.

FLEA CONTROL: BEYOND TOXIC CHEMICALS

Now we come to fleas, the bane of many a beast. Fortunately, there are safe alternatives to the toxic chemicals often used for controlling these pesky little creatures on your pet and in your home. And that's important, because the worst environmental pollutants that threaten pets are surely the poisons that well-meaning owners regularly dip, spray, powder, collar, and shampoo directly onto and into their flea-bitten companions.

The labels of most flea products bear such odd cautions as "Avoid contact with skin." (I've never been able to figure out why it's all right to thoroughly drench a pet with something that's too nasty for humans to touch briefly and then wash off afterward. Skin is skin, after all.) In any case, animals and veterinary technicians alike are often poisoned from the application of insecticides and even from the "inert" ingredients in flea-control products, both of which are absorbed through the skin and by inhalation. In addition, pets may lick these compounds off while grooming, and we may pick them up while stroking our animals. Some flea collars and powders are so potent that they produce extreme skin irritations and permanent hair loss on pets.

The net effect of all this poisoning is to make the fleas stronger and ourselves weaker. Because fleas reproduce so rapidly, those that survive flea-control products are the ones that have developed resistance to insecticides. This is especially a problem in places like California and Florida, where warm winters facilitate year-round flea breeding.

It is a common observation among veterinarians that the animals in poorest health attract the most fleas. So the problem is not just the presence of fleas. It's that we have weakened our pets to the point where fleas can take advantage of them. Moreover, our excessive use of vaccines, antibiotics, and cortisone-like drugs has created severe allergy problems so that many pets cannot tolerate fleas at all.

What's in all these flea-control products, anyway? Pet, house, and garden products all contain one or more classes of insecticides, many of which are nerve poisons. "Common Ingredients in Flea-Control Products" on page 130 lists some of the more common pet insecticides, both synthetic and natural. Most of these, especially the organophosphates and carbamates, have caused poisonings as the result of misuse or overdose, particularly

in young or sick dogs and in cats. These symptoms are noted in the chart; however, I think that there are also more subtle delayed effects that we do not yet fully understand. For example, some studies show that organophosphates can cause permanent nerve damage to humans, including burning, tingling, and weakness in the legs and arms, starting 8 to 14 days after exposure.

Other dangerous chemicals sometimes found in pet products include: *sodium arsenite, boric acid, benzethonium chloride, napthalene* (used in mothballs), *oil of anise, para-cymene (xylene), pine tar* and *sodium cresylate*. Others considered less toxic but still dangerous include: *benzene hexacholoride, chlo-*

LABELS REVEAL
LETHAL LEVELS

Individual labels are a guide to the product's relative danger. The terms below signify the ingested amount that would kill an adult human.

Label Term	Lethal Amount for Adults
Danger— Poison	Just a pinch
Warning	About a teaspoon
Caution	Two tablespoons to two cups
No label	Considered nontoxic

ranil, DDD, dimethyl phthalate, depentene, and *menthols.*

SAFE, EFFECTIVE FLEA CONTROL

The best approach to controlling fleas is to start with the least toxic and most natural choices, resorting to stronger measures only if reasonable control is not achieved. As a prerequisite to any flea-control program, I recommend building up your animal's health and resistance as much as possible through a healthy diet and lifestyle. Along with that, it's important to practice thorough sanitation and cleaning.

Understanding the life cycle of the flea makes it clear why cleaning is so important. Adult fleas live about three to four months. During that time they are steadily laying tiny white eggs on your pet that look like dandruff or salt crystals. Flea eggs hatch out into larvae that live in the cracks and crevices of rugs, upholstery, blankets, floors, sand, earth, and the like.

Because these tiny larvae cannot jump or travel very far (less than an inch), they feed on the black specks of dried blood ("flea dirt") that fall off along with the eggs during grooming and scratching. After one to two weeks, the larvae go through a cocoon stage (pupa). A week or two later, they hatch out as small fleas that hop onto the nearest warm body passing by (usually your pet—sometimes you!), bite it for a meal of blood, and then start the whole process all over again. This cycle takes anywhere from 2 to 20

weeks, depending on the temperature of the house or environment. During summer—flea season—the entire cycle is usually just 2 weeks long. That's why fleas increase so rapidly at that time.

The bad news is that, no matter how many adult fleas you manage to kill, numerous future fleas are developing in the environment simultaneously. The good news is that these eggs, larvae, pupa, and the flea dirt they feed upon can be sucked up by a vacuum cleaner or washed away in the laundry. And because the developing fleas are so immobile, they are most concentrated wherever your pet sleeps, so you know where to focus your efforts.

Your important ally in the battle against fleas is cleanliness, both for your pet and your home, particularly in your pet's sleeping areas. Regular cleaning interrupts the life cycles of the fleas and greatly cuts down on the number of adult fleas that end up on your pet, especially if you act before flea season begins. So start your program with these nontoxic steps.

Steam clean your carpets at the onset of flea season (or whenever you begin your flea-control program). Though it is somewhat expensive, steam cleaning is effective in killing flea eggs.

Thoroughly vacuum and clean floors and furniture at least once a week to pick up flea eggs, larvae, and pupae. Concentrate on areas where your pet sleeps and use an attachment to reach into crevices and corners and under heavy furniture. If there is a heavy infestation, you may want to put a flea collar (or part of a flea collar) in the vacuum bag to kill any adult fleas that get sucked up and might crawl away. Or else immediately dispose of the bag or its contents because it can provide a warm, moist, food-filled environment for developing eggs and larvae. Mop vinyl floors.

Launder your pet's bedding in hot, soapy water at least once a week. Dry on maximum heat. Heat will kill all stages of flea life, including the eggs. Remember that flea eggs are very slippery and easily fall off bedding or blankets. So carefully roll bedclothes up to keep all the flea eggs contained on the way to the washing machine.

Bathe the animal with a natural flea-control shampoo. Use a nontoxic shampoo as recommended above, such as one containing d-limonene (dogs only).

Use a flea comb to trap and kill fleas that are on your pet. Most pet stores carry special fine-toothed combs that trap fleas for easy disposal. Make a regular habit of flea-combing your pet while you watch TV or talk on the phone. Depending on the degree of infestation and the time of year, this might be daily (at the onset of the flea season), weekly, or monthly.

Gently but thoroughly comb as many areas as your pet will allow, especially around the head, neck, back, and hindquarters. As you trap the little buggers, pull them off the comb and plunge them into a container of hot, soapy water (or dip the comb and pull the flea off underwater). Cover your lap with an old towel to catch extra clumps of hair and flea dirt and to wipe the comb off as you work.

When you're finished, flush the soapy water and fleas down the toilet.

If your pet goes outdoors, follow these steps as well.

Mow and water your lawn regularly. Short grass allows sunlight to penetrate and warm the soil, which kills larvae. Watering drowns the developing fleas.

Encourage ants. Perhaps I should say "do not discourage ants." They love to eat flea eggs and larvae. This is another reason not to use pesticides that kill all the insects in your yard.

"Sterilize" bare-earth sleeping spots. If your pet likes to sleep or hang out in a certain bare or sandy area, occasionally cover the spot with a heavy black plastic sheet on a hot, sunny day. Rake up any dead leaves and other debris first. The heat that builds up under the plastic does an excellent job of killing fleas and larvae. Of course, this is not appropriate to use where you want to preserve live grass or plants.

Apply agricultural lime on grassy or moist areas. This helps to dry out the fleas. Rake up any dead leaves and grassy debris first.

Along with the above steps, you might try these methods to repel fleas that may try to jump back on your pet, especially those harder-to-kill ones hanging out in the backyard.

Use an herbal flea powder. You'll find them in pet stores and natural food stores, or you can make your own. Combine one part each of as many of these powdered herbs as you can find: eucalyptus, rosemary, fennel, yellow dock, wormwood, and rue. Put this mixture in a shaker-top jar, such as a jar for parsley flakes.

Apply the flea powder sparingly to your pet's coat by brushing backward with your hand or the comb and sprinkling it into the base of the hairs, especially on the neck, back, and belly. To combat severe infestations, use several times a week. Afterward, put your animal friend outside for a while so the disgruntled tenants vacate in the yard and not in your house. Some herbal flea powders also contain natural pyrethrins, which are not strong flea-killers but do seem to greatly discourage them.

Use an herbal flea collar. These are impregnated with insect-repellent herbal oils. Some are made to be "recharged" with the oils and used again. Buy them at natural food stores.

Try a natural skin tonic. The animal herbalist Juliette de Bairacli-Levy recommends this lemon skin tonic, which many of my clients successfully use on their pets for a general skin toner, parasite repellent, and treatment for mange.

Thinly slice a whole lemon, including the peel. Add it to 1 pint of near-boiling water and let it steep overnight. The next day, sponge the solution onto the animal's skin and let it dry. You can use this daily for severe skin problems involving fleas. It is a source of natural flea-killing substances such as d-limonene and other healing ingredients found in the whole lemon.

Add ample nutritional or brewer's yeast and garlic to the diet. Some studies show yeast supplementation significantly reduces flea numbers, though others indicate no effect. My experience with using yeast is that it has some favorable effect, particularly if the animal's health is good. You can also rub it directly into the animal's hair. Many people also praise the value of garlic as a flea repellent, though so far studies do not support this.

If these methods do not control the fleas sufficiently, take the following steps.

Get your carpets treated with a special anti-flea mineral salt. There have been some developments in safe flea control. My clients report success with a service that applies or sells relatively nontoxic mineral salts for treating carpets. (Fleabusters is the company recommended.) Effective for up to a year, the products safely kill fleas and their developing forms over a few week's time.

Once or twice a year, sprinkle natural, unrefined diatomaceous earth along walls, under furniture, and in cracks and crevices that you cannot access with a vacuum. This product, which resembles chalky rock, is really the fossilized remains of one-celled algae. Though direct skin contact is harmless to pets and people, it is bad news for many insects and their larvae, including fleas. The fine particles in the earth kill insects by attacking the waxy coating that covers their external skeletons. The insects then dry out and die.

(continued on page 134)

COMMON INGREDIENTS IN FLEA-CONTROL PRODUCTS

INSECTICIDES	EFFECTS OF OVERDOSE AND POSSIBLE LONG-TERM EFFECTS	NOTES
ORGANOPHOSPHATES Chlorpyrifos, Cythioate, DDVP, Diazinon, Dichlorvos, Dursban, Endothion, Fenthion, Korlan, Malathion, Naled, Neguvon, Parathion, Phosmet, Propetamphos, Ronnel, Trichlorfon, and Vapona.	*Initially:* salivation, involuntary defecation, urination, vomiting, wide stance. *Progresses to:* difficulty standing, weakness, convulsions, tremors, constricted pupils, teary eyes, slow heartbeat, labored breathing. May also cause dermatitis, aggravate heart and respiratory disease. Fenthion may cause chronic appetite and weight loss, depression, mild head and neck tremors. Vapona (DDVP, Dichlorvos), widely used since 1950s, may pose significant leukemia hazard.	Among the most common pet insecticides, found in all types of products. Some are used systemically (kill fleas through pet's blood). Can be extremely toxic. Considered responsible for most pet poisonings. Most are readily absorbed through the skin, eyes, stomach, and lungs. Act by decreasing cholinesterase activity, which sends nerve signals, in effect paralyzing the nerves. Being studied for delayed neurotoxic effects. Fenthion and Cythioate should not be used for cats, puppies, or sick dogs. Malathion and Ronnel are among the least toxic in this group.
CARBAMATES Aldicarb, Baygon, Bendiocarb, Bufencarb (BUX), Carbaryl, Carbofuran, Ficam, various Methylcarbamate compounds, Moban, Maneb, Propoxur, Sevin, Zectran, Zineb, and Ziram.	*Initially:* salivation, involuntary defecation, urination, vomiting, wobbliness, wide stance. *Progresses to:* difficulty standing, weakness, convulsions, tremors, constricted pupils, teary eyes, slow heartbeat, labored breathing. Can cause depression of bone marrow, degeneration of the brain.	Based on carbamic acid, found in all types of pet products. Like organophosphates, toxic effect is immediate, but carbamates are generally less severe. Sevin and Carbaryl do not accumulate in tissues and are said to be much less toxic than, for example, Parathion.

INSECTICIDES	EFFECTS OF OVERDOSE AND POSSIBLE LONG-TERM EFFECTS	NOTES
ORGANOCHLORINES		
Dichlorophene, DMC, Endosulphan, Endrin, Heptachlor, Isobenzan, Lindane (Gamma BHC), Methoxy-chlor, Paradichlorobenzene, Toxaphene, TDE. Banned or restricted: DDT, DDE, Aldrin, Dieldrin, and Chlordane.	Exaggerated responses to touch, light, and sound. Spasms or tremors appear (usually first in the face), progressing to epilepsy-like seizures, often followed by death. No known antidote. Many members of this group have been shown to cause cancer in experimental animals. Because of concern about carcinogenic potential, Lindane was banned as an indoor fumigant in 1986.	Less immediately toxic than carbamates, which have largely replaced them. But they accumulate in tissues and persist for years in the environment (e.g., DDT was banned in 1972, but it's still found in 55 percent of Americans). Insects have developed resistance to many. Cats are particularly vulnerable to this group, especially to Lindane, DDT, and Chlordane. Dogs are susceptible to Toxaphene and DDE.
SPOT-ON TYPE INSECTICIDES		
Fipronil, Imidacloprid, Permethrin, Pyriproxyfen.	New neurotoxins, the active ingredients of products to be applied to the skin and absorbed into the body. When fleas jump on and bite the poison kills them.	Many toxic effects. Has caused cancer in animals, altered thyroid hormone levels, caused seizures and severe skin disease in some animals, with parts of the skin coming off, difficult breathing, enlarged livers, miscarriages, and many other effects.
Methoprene	Considered nontoxic, but usually combined with toxic chemicals to kill adult fleas.	A growth regulator used in foggers or commercial sprays to inhibit fleas from hatching from the pupal stage. Only effective indoors. Implicated in killing aquatic life in streams and creeks as it washes off treated animals.

(continued)

INSECTICIDES	EFFECTS OF OVERDOSE AND POSSIBLE LONG-TERM EFFECTS	NOTES
SPOT-ON TYPE INSECTICIDES (CONT.)		
Rotenone and other cube resins	Skin irritation. Overdose can cause death through paralysis of respiration. Chronic exposure may injure liver and kidneys.	Derived from a poisonous tropical legume. Considered fairly toxic to mammals. Loses much potency in presence of light and oxygen; has little residual action. Slower-acting but more potent than Pyrethrin. Found in shampoos, dips, and powders.
D-Limonene	Toxic signs in cats: excess salivation, weakness, muscle tremors. No toxic effects reported in dogs.	Natural citrus extract. Dissolves flea's waxy coating, causing dehydration and death. Kills 99 percent of fleas if shampoo lather left on for ten minutes.
Natural Pyrethrins and Synthetic Pyrethroids Allethrin, Resmethrin, and Permethrin.	Can cause allergic dermatitis and systemic allergic reactions. Large amounts may cause nausea, vomiting, ringing in the ears, headaches, and other central nervous system disturbances, but rapidly detoxified in the intestines. Prolonged use may cause slight liver damage. Permethrin may be a slight carcinogen (according to mice studies).	Labeled nontoxic. Considered least toxic to mammals of all insecticides. Derived from chrysanthemums. Mostly in aerosol sprays, sometimes in flea shampoos and sprays. Causes rapid paralysis of insect nervous system (many die, but many also recover in a few hours, so repeat applications are necessary). Synergists may be added to inhibit flea's detoxification process and increase residual effect.

INSECTICIDES	EFFECTS OF OVERDOSE AND POSSIBLE LONG-TERM EFFECTS	NOTES
Arecoline Hydrobromide	Vomiting, unconsciousness, diarrhea, and depression. Though natural, it must be considered a potentially toxic substance.	The active compound found in the areca nut, an Oriental folk remedy for worms, it has long been used in tapeworm control. Considered unsafe for cats. Can cause undesirable responses in dogs also.
Benzyl Benzoate	Nausea, vomiting, diarrhea, and a slowing of the heartbeat and breathing rate.	Often used for mange control. Can be toxic if applied over too large an area or too often. Cats more susceptible, but dogs occasionally die from excessive use.
Piperonyl Butoxide, N-octylbi-cycloheptene dicarosimide E	Large doses cause vomiting and diarrhea.	Not true insecticides. Added to other ingredients to block flea's detoxification process and increase effectiveness.
Boric acid derivatives (Flea-busters Rx for Fleas)	Ingestion may cause nausea, vomiting, diarrhea, rash, dizziness.	Mineral salts applied to carpets to kill developing fleas. Low toxicity. Reported to be very effective for up to a year.
Micro-encapsulation Process	Reduces toxicity of insecticides to pets and people because the tiny capsules pass through intestines before all their contents are absorbed.	Use of thin nylon or urea shell around minute bits of insecticide, used for sustained release and longer action. Less effective if used with flea repellents.

I do not recommend using diatomaceous earth frequently or directly on your animal—mostly because of the irritating dust that can be breathed in by both of you. It is also messy. Be careful about breathing it in. Wear a dust mask when applying. It is not toxic, but inhaling even the natural, unrefined form of this dust can irritate the nasal passages.

Important: Do not use the type of diatomaceous earth that is sold for swimming pool filters. It has been very finely ground, and the tiny particles can be breathed into the lungs and cause chronic inflammation.

Use a spray or powder containing pyrethrins or natural pyrethrum. These are the least toxic of all the insecticides used on pets, and they are found in both conventional and natural flea-control products. For a more lasting effect, use a microencapsulated product, which is perhaps labeled "slow release." Repeat the applications as you simultaneously use the carpet treatment system or diatomaceous earth. This will help kill both adult fleas and developing fleas at the same time.

For more information concerning both external and internal parasites, as well as skin problems in general, see "Skin Parasites" on page 382, "Worms" on page 422, and "Skin Problems" on page 388.

CHAPTER 8

CREATING A HEALTHIER ENVIRONMENT

No matter where we have lived, Richard and I (Susan) have always made sure to have a beautiful garden, filled with flowering shrubs and perennials and edibles. Caring for our piece of paradise often fills the better part of a weekend. We enjoy it, of course, or we wouldn't do it.

Yet sometimes we get so busy snipping off branches or pulling up weeds that we lose touch with the slower pace of life's mysteries constantly unfolding before us. When we get too wrapped up in our activity, it helps to take a lesson from our cat. Like all cats, he's quite adept at just sitting and looking.

Today was one of those times. Putting aside my projects, I went out to the yard to just sit and look. Settling down in an out-of-the-way spot under a wisteria, I gazed down a seldom-used path. It was teeming with ants among the small, leafy weeds that thrive in shady places that are hard to hoe.

At first, a glimmer of gardener thoughts passed through my mind. Were these carpenter ants? Should I destroy them so they don't destroy our home? Should I pull up some of those weeds before they go to seed? But letting these thoughts pass on by, I calmed down and returned to just looking.

No longer filtering the scene through gardener eyes, I began to see more deeply. The weeds had a beauty of their own, as lush and diverse as a forest floor. Even the ants were admirable, so energetic and so enduring. They had crawled over this land long before we humans appeared. And despite all the wars we wage upon them, ants still thrive and will probably outlive us. It felt good to just let them be.

I felt humbled at how little I understood about the thousands of backyard plants and animals whose lives were affected by my actions.

A small moment. But without such moments in our busy lives we might gradually detach ourselves from nature and unwittingly accept the idea that we are free to tamper with the web of life.

With each passing year, we humans dump innumerable tons of toxins into the web of life, destroy millions of forest acres, and hasten the extinction of many species, some that we don't even know about. We further weaken the thin layer of ozone that protects us from the sun's radiation. We jam the airwaves with millions of electronic signals whose effects on our bioelectric fields we barely understand. Surely, we wouldn't tolerate these actions if we realized how profoundly they affect the fate of every living thing, including ourselves, our children, and our animals.

A shocking national survey by the Public Health Service showed that Americans have hundreds of toxic chemicals stored in our fatty tissues. Nearly all of us have such harmful substances as dioxin, benzene, styrene, and ethyl phenol. A significant majority have PCBs, radioactive isotopes, creosote, lead and other heavy metals, asbestos, and numerous pesticides.

Surely, these are also contained in the bodies of our pets, perhaps in greater proportions because of their smaller sizes.

DIRT IS DIRTIER NOW

In evaluating the special impact of chemical pollution on our pets, it's essential to realize that dogs and cats live in close contact with the ground. They sit, play, and sleep on it. Even indoors, pets are exposed to plenty of dust. A six-room urban house may accumulate as much as 40 pounds of dust in a year. And when our pets lick all this dust off their fur, they actually consume it. That used to be fairly safe—"you'll eat a peck of dirt before you die," moms used to say. But dirt is a lot "dirtier" nowadays. We need to take special precautions to protect children and pets from possible harm.

A scientific team of "dust busters" found that 25 out of 29 typical homes they studied in Seattle had rugs with excessive levels of toxins and mutagens. They also found that toddlers ingest more than twice as much dust as adults. And contaminated dust is probably more risky for pets than it is for children. Pets wear no protective clothes or shoes and, like a shag rug, their fur attracts dirt (till they lick it off).

LEAD

Because they settle to the ground, heavy metals are a particular hazard in dust. Lead is among the most widespread of these and enters the environment primarily from flaking layers of lead-based paint and from power plants. Because lead was used as a pigment and drying agent in "alkyd" oil-based paint, about two-thirds of the homes built before 1960 contain heavily leaded paint (as well as some homes, though fewer, built after 1960). Lead paint may be on any interior or exterior surface, but particularly on woodwork, doors, and windows. Cats, especially, will start licking walls as a symptom of digestive trouble and swallow paint flakes in this way.

In 1978, the Consumer Product Safety Commission lowered the legal maximum lead content in most kinds of paints to 0.06 percent (considered a trace amount). You can have your home tested for this common contaminant, and there are several do-it-yourself kits available at paint stores and home centers (note they are not sensitive enough to pick up low levels, which can still affect pregnant women).

Other sources of lead are auto exhaust, lead water pipes, batteries, colored newsprint, and smelters. At typical levels, lead primarily affects the blood and nervous systems. Symptoms can be vague, often including listlessness, loss of appetite, irritability, stupor, uncoordination, vomiting, constipation, and abdominal pain. Not surprisingly, lead poisoning has caused seizures in small, urban dogs. Other dangerous metals polluting the environment include cadmium, mercury, and arsenic.

ASBESTOS

Another common ingredient in urban dust, asbestos produces particles that have been found in the lungs of virtually every city dweller who had an autopsy. In homes it comes from hot-water pipe coverings, furnace insulation materials, asbestos roof shingles, millboard, textured paints, vinyl floor tiles and tile adhesive, ceiling texturing, and other ceiling coating materials.

The greatest danger is inhaling the small microscopic fibers that settle in the lungs and never come out. The body can't get rid of these fibers, and the subsequent inflammation causes serious lung disease. Some contaminated lungs develop cancer, as well.

GENERAL PRECAUTIONS

So what's a caring person to do? Here are some simple suggestions supported by the Seattle study.

❖ Use entrance mats and remove or clean shoes at the front door.

❖ Houseclean thoroughly and often.

❖ Keep the entryway swept or hosed off to minimize sources of outdoor dirt. If possible, pave dirt or gravel driveways or entryways.

❖ Avoid shags and deep-pile carpets when you decorate. Consider a natural wood or tile floor with washable rugs instead.

❖ Brush and bathe your pet regularly.

Follow these suggestions when remodeling or repainting.

❖ Be especially careful about sanding or cutting into paint layers of homes built before 1978, because most of them contain lead paints.

❖ Wear a dust mask while working on painted areas and keep pets and children away.

❖ Clean up thoroughly after each workday.

❖ If intact, old lead paint layers can be painted over or covered with drywall. Consider replacing old wood doors and windows, because simply operating them can create lead dust.

❖ Wipe the work area frequently with a solution of trisodium phosphate (sold at hardware stores). Be sure to wear gloves.

INDOOR AIR POLLUTION

Besides toxic dust, air can also carry unhealthy gases and vapors, such as formaldehyde, ozone, chloroform, and radon. These waft into the atmosphere from household products, furniture, and many other common sources. A New Jersey study testing 20 common air pollutants showed that indoor levels were actually much worse than outdoor levels, in some cases 100 times greater.

FORMALDEHYDE

Formaldehyde is a very common contaminant because it is used in so many products and is also a by-product of combustion. The usual sources are general household products, unvented fuel burning appliances such as gas stoves or kerosene gas heaters, some carpets, pressed wood products, particleboard used as subflooring, shelving, cabinetry, and furniture, and also hardwood plywood paneling. Medium density fiberboard (MDF) releases the most formaldehyde of any of the wood products and is commonly used for drawer fronts, cabinet doors, furniture tops, and closet shelving. Softwood plywood and flake or oriented strandboard—typical products used for external construction—release much lower amounts of formaldehyde than those we have already mentioned.

Reactions to indoor air pollution may appear as chronic headaches, fatigue, itchy or watering eyes, nasal or throat infections, or dryness, depression, dizziness, nausea, colds, asthma, bronchitis, and allergies. If any of these show up in your pets or family members who are usually indoors, note whether the symptoms have appeared after moving, remodeling, or purchasing new furniture or carpets. Are the symptoms worse when the house is tightly sealed? If so, it makes sense to set about reducing the indoor pollution in your home. In any case, it's good preventive medicine for the whole family and your pets to take these steps.

Ventilate your home. If you're in an area of low air pollution, just open your windows as often as possible to ventilate. If outdoor air is smoggy or temperatures are too extreme, on the other hand, try using an electronic fiber or charcoal air filter, or HEPA filter. A great solution is to install a whole house fan or heat recovery ventilator (which brings in outside air but without losing the heat in the house).

Further, scientists have learned that certain houseplants reduce pollutants, especially philodendrons (formaldehyde, benzene, and carbon monoxide), spider plants (carbon monoxide), aloe veras (formaldehyde), and gerbera daisies and chrysanthemums (benzene).

Radon

Radon is an odorless, colorless, tasteless radioactive gas that occurs naturally and is found in the soil and well water in low levels everywhere. It is produced naturally by the breakdown of uranium in the soil and gradually percolates up into the atmosphere. It can be trapped in buildings with confined spaces and build up to higher levels. That it is the second leading cause of lung cancer in the United States makes this common conta-

minant an important issue. It gets into homes by entering through small cracks in the flooring or around the holes for pipes and wiring in the walls. Houses with basements or slab-on-grade can be protected by some mechanism of suctioning air from the soil with piping (and usually a fan) to release it into outside air. Crawlspace houses use crawlspace ventilation (passive, or active with a fan) and perhaps a heavy plastic sheet over the earth with a vent pipe under the sheet to draw radon outside.

Visit the Environmental Protection Agency's Web site at www.epa.gov to find out if you live in a radon "hot spot." Activated charcoal screening tests, available through the mail, can help you find out if you should take further action. For more information or to order a test kit, call the National Safety Council at (800) 557-2366 or the National Radon Hotline at (800) 767-7236. For an updated list of approved testing companies in your state, either call one of the above 800 numbers or visit the EPA's Web site.

OUTDOOR POLLUTION

In the great outdoors, pollution is something to seriously consider. We are used to many products that contain chemicals, and we forget that they give off sometimes harmful substances.

Pressure-Treated Wood

Because wood sunk in the ground or exposed to water outside can quickly rot or be eaten by bugs, it is treated with a poison that does not allow any of these things to attack it. The usual substance is a combination of copper and arsenic. The wood is soaked in a liquid preservative under high pressure so that it penetrates the wood. This process allows the wood to survive 10 or 20 times longer than untreated wood, so it has a definite advantage. The drawback is that the chemicals remain on the surface as well as inside the wood and can run off with water and contaminate the soil around the post or structure built with it.

One of my clients traced behavioral and health problems of her cats to a new enclosure built with such wood. After she covered the wood with a nontoxic sealer to prevent the fumes from reaching the animals, the cats returned to normal.

It helps, therefore, to seal pressure-treated wood posts used to build a cattery or dog pen. Realize, however, that if your animal chews on this wood, it is poisonous. Be watchful.

HOUSE AND GARDEN PESTICIDES

Besides the insecticides used in flea and tick products, pets may also be exposed to high levels of other household pesticides. The National Academy of Sciences reports that homeowners use four to eight times as many chemical pesticides per acre as farmers do. Many home and garden insecticides are the same as those used on pets. Additional risks come from herbicides, fungicides, and rodent poisons. Because of their contact with the ground, pets are more likely to pick up residues. In 1991, the National Cancer Institute found that dogs who lived where the homeowner used 2,4-D, a common broadleaf weed killer, had twice the rate of lymphoma (a cancer of the lymph glands) as dogs who lived where it was not used.

Even if you don't use pesticides, they may drift onto your property from neighbors' yards or from heavily sprayed areas such as nearby parks, campuses, power line corridors, and orchards. Ask people to call you when they plan to spray so you can close your windows, since pesticides have a longer lifespan indoors.

TERMITE CONTROL

Poisonous residues may persist in your house from previous occupants. The termite insecticide chlordane, for instance, has been detected in the air of some homes 14 years after application. It's also been found in soil after 30 years.

AUTOMOTIVE PRODUCTS

Though we must consider the possible danger to animals from what is stored in the garage, it is easy to overlook what might drip or leak from automobiles. One is antifreeze fluid. Sometimes when cars overheat, some antifreeze runs out on the ground. Apparently it tastes good (I have never tried it), and animals will lick it up, causing serious poisoning that often ends in death. Less toxic but still harmful are transmission fluids, used oils, even batteries left out on the ground. The battery posts are lead and the insides contain acid.

Store all of these things inside the garage in sealed containers, within locked cabinets at least 4 feet off the ground. It's not a bad idea to install child-proof safety latches on the cabinet doors, either.

If you spill any of these hazardous materials, don't wash it away. Sprinkle with sawdust, vermiculite, or cat litter to absorb it, then sweep it up and put it in a plastic bag to dispose of as hazardous waste.

CONSIDER SAFER ALTERNATIVES

There are several excellent books that detail safer alternatives to dangerous pesticides and other household products (see drpitcairn.com). If you must use a pesticide, seek a knowledgeable nursery salesperson to help you choose the least-toxic products. Some products seem to be relatively harmless to animals if used as recommended—though often what we think of as "safe" is simply lack of sufficient experience. There are also nontoxic and organic products available. Follow label directions carefully, which often means keeping pets off areas that have been recently treated. Should you suspect a possible poisoning, call the Environmental Protection Agency's National Pesticide Telecommunications Network, a toll-free service available 24 hours a day, at (800) 858-7378.

WHAT TO DO

Remove pollutants wherever possible. Inventory all the household products tucked away in your kitchen, bathroom, laundry room, and garage that contain poisonous and sensitizing chemicals. Clear out any products that are more than a few years old and that you no longer use (they may contain chemicals that have since been banned) and those with rusting or leaking containers. Safer substitutes may be available.

For disposal, call your local trash collection service to ask about special household hazardous waste collections. Where we live, there are certain days you can take these things to the landfill and we make an appointment to do so. If this kind of service is not available, tighten any loose containers, wrap them in several layers of newspaper, seal them in a heavy plastic bag, and put them in the trash. Do not pour such substances down the drain or on the soil.

For those products you keep, tighten lids and update fading labels. If possible, store them in a well-ventilated area away from living space. Even well-sealed containers can emit fumes, so don't confine your pet in the same space—a garage, for example.

Make sure that all gas, oil, or wood furnaces and appliances are properly serviced and ventilated. This reduces levels of carbon monoxide and other combustion by-products. You can buy carbon monoxide detection units for about $30. They plug into an electrical outlet and warn you if there is a leakage of this dangerous gas.

Seal boiler rooms from the rest of the house. When you replace units, buy electric models or choose gas furnaces with sealed combustion chambers and pilotless gas appliances.

ALTERNATIVES TO CHEMICAL WARFARE ON YOUR PETS

There are many very effective, natural, and inexpensive ways to clean your home and its contents. Here are just a few ideas from the Center for Hazardous Materials Research:

ALL-PURPOSE CLEANERS

❖ Oven cleaner: scrub with a paste of baking soda, salt, and water. Then leave ¼ cup lemon juice in the oven overnight and wipe away any remaining grease the next morning. Ventilate the kitchen and avoid breathing fumes.

❖ Oven spill remover: sprinkle salt on the spill immediately. Let the oven cool a few minutes, then scrape the spill away and wash the area clean with water.

❖ Window and glass cleaner: measure 3 tablespoons lime juice, 1 tablespoon white vinegar, and ¾ cup water into a clean spray bottle, which you can then spray on windows. Wipe clean and dry with a cotton cloth or paper towel.

❖ Scouring powder: use a solution of vinegar, salt, and water, or use baking soda and water. Apply with a sponge and wipe clean.

❖ Toilet bowl cleaner: pour ½ cup white vinegar and 3 tablespoons of baking soda into the toilet bowl, let stand for 30 minutes, then scrub and flush.

❖ Ceramic tile cleaner: mix ¼ cup white vinegar into a gallon of warm water. Apply with a sponge.

❖ Disinfectants: use ½ cup borax dissolved in hot water and apply with a sponge (store borax in a safe place; can be toxic if eaten). Use sodium carbonate (washing soda) in clothes washer in place of commercial detergents.

POLISHES

❖ Furniture polish: mix 2 parts vegetable or olive oil with one part lemon juice. Apply this mixture to the furniture with a soft cloth and wipe dry.

❖ Brass polish: polish with Worcestershire sauce.

❖ Copper polish: soak in vinegar and salt solution and wipe clean.

❖ Silver polish: soak in a quart of warm water containing 1 teaspoon baking soda, 1 teaspoon salt, and a piece of aluminum foil. Use a soft bristle toothbrush to remove stains.

SPOT REMOVERS

❖ Set-stain removal: dab with white vinegar.

❖ Non-set stains: sponge up or scrape off as much as possible immediately. Rub with club soda followed by cold water.

❖ Butter, gravy, chocolate, or urine stains: dab with a cloth dampened with a solution of 1 teaspoon white vinegar and 1 quart cold water.

❖ Grease stains: rub with a damp cloth dipped in borax, or apply a paste of cornstarch and water. Let it dry and brush the mixture off.

❖ Ink stains: wet the fabric with cold water and apply a cream of tartar and lemon juice mix. Let it sit for an hour and then wash in the usual manner.

❖ Red wine stains: clean immediately with club soda, or dab out excess moisture with an absorbent cloth and sprinkle salt on the stain. Let stand seven hours, then brush or vacuum away.

DEODORIZERS

❖ Air freshener and deodorizers: sprinkle baking soda in odor-producing areas. Set vinegar out in an open dish. Sprinkle borax in corners of the room (do not allow pets or children to eat the borax). Place an open box of baking soda in the refrigerator to absorb food odors. Pour baking soda down garbage disposal for drain odors. Sprinkle baking soda over entire carpet and vacuum after 30 minutes.

DRAIN AND GARBAGE DISPOSAL CLEANING

❖ Drain cleaners: pour boiling water down your drain weekly. To unclog drains, pour in ½ cup baking soda followed by ½ cup vinegar. Cover and wait for several minutes. Then flush with boiling water.

FLOOR, RUG, AND UPHOLSTERY CLEANING

❖ Floor wax strippers and polishers: Mix laundry starch with water to make it thick, then bring it to a boil. Mix 1 part of this thick-boiled starch and 1 part soap suds; rub the mixture on the floor and polish with a dry cloth. To remove, pour a little club soda on the area, scrub well, let soak for 5 minutes, and wipe.

❖ Rug and upholstery cleaner: mix ½ cup mild dishwashing detergent with 1 pint boiling water. Let cool. Whip into a paste with mixer. Apply with a damp sponge. Wipe the suds. Rinse with 1 cup vinegar in 1 gallon of lukewarm water and let dry. Another rug cleaner is a shampoo made of 6 tablespoons soap flakes, 2 tablespoons borax, and 1 pint of boiling water. Let cool before applying.

ALTERNATIVE PESTICIDES

❖ Ants: remove accessible food and water (removing a water source not always easy). Pour a line of cream of tartar or chili powder where the ants enter the house. They won't cross it. Outside, pour boiling water over their nests.

❖ Roaches: clean up food. Place bay leaves near cracks or caulk all cracks where accessible. Use sticky traps of boric acid powder and very little water. Set out a dish containing equal parts of oatmeal and plaster of Paris.

❖ Fleas and ticks: feed pets brewer's yeast and garlic. Vacuum pet's bedding regularly. Place eucalyptus seeds, leaves, and cedar chips near bedding.

❖ Moths: set cedar chips, cedar blocks, newspapers, or lavender flowers around closets. After it's cleaned, wrap wool clothing in plastic bags during warm weather. A cedar closet is ideal for storing wool clothing.

PET POISONINGS

A lot of the chemicals that are bad for pets, including pesticides, enter through an eager mouth attached to a curious nose. Poisonings account for 1 to 2 percent of veterinary cases, with a greater risk for dogs. A prime danger is antifreeze poisoning, which we have already mentioned. Another risk is the consumption—usually by dogs—of poisons put out for snails, slugs, and rodents. Cats sometimes eat a poisoned mouse that is too sick to run away. The other frequent source of poisoning is insecticides and herbicides used in a yard. Realize that if you have sprayed chemicals in your garden or on the lawn that your animals should not walk there until those chemicals are no longer active. Think how sick we would be if we walked through a chemically treated lawn and then licked our feet when we got in the house.

Though it is rare, small animals have also been poisoned by eating parts of certain plants, including oleander, castor bean, dumb cane (dieffenbachia), chokecherry, jimsonweed, morning glory, and others. Provide your pet with fresh greens such as sprouts, parsley, or wheat grass to cut the temptation to nibble on toxic plants. Cats especially will eat plant material when they have digestive illness. In my experience, this is also a common symptom of chronic illness, which leads to eating both houseplants and outdoor plants that are not so good for them. If your cat does this, it does not suffice just to restrict them from getting to the plant—you have to correct the underlying disorder. Often, feeding a fresh food diet will take care of it.

OTHER CHEMICALS TO BE CAREFUL WITH

Paradichorobenzene, a big word for the chemical that is commonly the active ingredient in moth repellents. It is known to cause cancer in animals. This chemical is also the key ingredient in many air fresheners.

Perchloroethylene is widely used in dry cleaning. Again, studies have shown it causes cancer in animals. So if there is any odor in your dry cleaned goods, remove them from their plastic bags and let them air outside for a few hours until the odor disappears. Don't put them right in the closet in the plastic bag. Guess where the vapors leak to? A good dry cleaning service will return your clothes to you with very little odor.

Phenol and cresol are found in many products that are used to disinfect, sanitize, and deodorize. Both are toxic, especially to cats that are particularly sensitive to any phenol compound and become terribly ill with any exposure.

Aluminum chlorhydrate and zirconium are found in some deodorants and can cause skin inflammation and, if inhaled, cancer. The aluminum compound is considered a possible factor in Alzheimer's disease. Be careful where you leave these.

Diethanolamine, selenium sulfide, and coal tar are harmful chemicals found in many dandruff shampoos and hair conditioners. All three chemicals are suspected carcinogens. Keep containers up high where your dog can't chew on them.

TOXIC CHEMICALS IN FOOD

Animals can develop subtler forms of poisoning just from eating what they're supposed to eat. One survey showed that canned cat foods contain high amounts of lead, from 0.9 to 7.0 parts per million (ppm). A daily intake of six ounces of these foods (about what a cat or small dog eats) could contain as much as four times the amount of lead considered potentially toxic for children. (Read more about how unlikely your vet would be able to recognize this subtle poisoning in your pets in chapter 2.)

Pet foods containing fish and fish by-products may contain high levels of mercury, a risk for cats addicted to seafood. Excessive mercury intake can damage the nervous system, causing tremors, irritability, anxiety, loss of appetite, inflammation of gums and looseness of the teeth, and difficulty sleeping. It can also damage the kidneys.

Commonly added to public water supplies to prevent tooth decay, fluoride is considered safe at the level of 4 ppm in water or a maximum of 2.5 milligrams daily for children. But because of its accumulation in the food chain, 11 to 193 ppm have been found in leading pet foods (canned foods are worst). That means that a large dog could be consuming a whopping 21 to 368 milligrams daily.

Excessive exposure to fluoride may cause tiredness, mottling of the teeth, kidney and bladder disorders, arthritis, pain and crippling in the joints, stomach problems, hair loss, skin disorders, bronchitis, asthma, and numerous other conditions. It can also reduce blood vitamin C levels, weaken the immune system, and cause birth defects and genetic damage. Ten European countries have banned fluoridation of water.

Hundreds of other toxic chemicals accumulate in the food chain, and it is very difficult to protect yourself and your pets from such unseen dangers. You can, however, reduce the risks by feeding a fresh, un-processed diet that contains relatively little meat, especially liver and kidneys, which concentrate toxins. Many contaminants are stored in fats, so it's better to go with low-fat dairy products or lean meats. Corn oil is preferable to either soy or cottonseed oil because it's generally lower in pesticide content. When possible and practical, use organically grown foods and organic, non-genetically modified oils.

You can also help your pet cope with pollutants by including certain vitamins and minerals in the diet. Calcium, for instance, helps protect against some heavy metals and radiation. Vitamin A and selenium also help combat radiation. Vitamin E counters the effects of many smog pollutants, and kelp helps the body resist radioactive strontium. Lecithin is also useful. These nutrients are included in our recommended diet.

If you live in a particularly polluted area, give your pet vitamin C (for pollutants in general and especially for cadmium, lead, copper, and DDT) and zinc (for cadmium, lead, and copper). Depending on your pet's size, use 100 milligrams for the small animal, up to 500 milligrams of vitamin C for the larger dogs. Vitamin C is safe to use, so don't worry about being precise with the dose. In the same way, you can add zinc in the range of 5 to 20 milligrams. (For these vitamins, you can use regular supplements intended for human use; zinc tablets will have larger amounts than these and need to be cut down.)

CLEANING UP THE WATER

Fluoride is only one of the questionable ingredients in many public water supplies. All told, more than 2,100 toxic chemicals have been detected in U.S. water. Some of the most common contaminants are lead, cadmium, arsenic, insecticides, nitrates, fungicides, herbicides, benzene, toluene, and dioxin. Many of these pollutants are known to cause cancer or damage the kidneys, liver, brain, and cardiovascular system. Communities with particularly polluted sources of water have unusually high cancer rates of the gastrointestinal and urinary organs.

In spite of these hazards, most utilities test for less than 30 chemicals, and only a tiny fraction use modern technologies to remove them. That's because most treatment plants were built decades ago simply to kill bacteria and reduce sediment. Though it has served well as a disinfectant, the chlorine added to most municipal water also combines with organic debris to create a number of carcinogenic compounds, such as chloroform. Also, chlorine itself can be irritating to the mucous membranes of the eyes, nose, throat, airways, and lungs, especially in sensitive individuals. As a result, lifetime users of chlorinated water have an increased rate of bladder cancer and possibly of colon and rectal cancers. Scientists are currently investigating alternative means of disinfecting water.

Since pure water is so important for your family, including your pets, we strongly recommend use of a good quality water purifier. Though initially costlier than bottled water, it is much cheaper in the long run, costing only pennies a gallon. Take your time to select a good-quality purifier that will do the job well. If you'd like further information, *Nontoxic, Natural and Earthwise*, by Debra Lynn Dadd, has an excellent discussion of the topic.

Also, change your pet's water daily. Keep the bowl clean and in a place protected from dust and debris. Most of all, make it available, so that your pet will not be as tempted to drink from a contaminated puddle, creek, or pond.

ELECTROMAGNETIC EFFECTS ON HEALTH

Let's look now at some less familiar but potentially important environmental influences on health. All plants and animals operate by tiny electrochemical pulses that beat at about the same rate as the low frequency energy field of the Earth. Similarly, life has adapted over eons to a spectrum of other natural electromagnetic energies—light from the sun, background radioactivity from the Earth's crust, and charged air molecules (positive and negative ions). In just a few decades, however, we have blanketed ourselves with an electronic smog of new frequencies created by our house wiring, power lines, appliances—radio, TV, microwave, and cellular phone broadcasts—and radioactive nuclear blasts and leakages. Unaware, we have initiated a dangerous thinning of the ozone layer that shields us from destructive levels of ultraviolet radiation. And at the same time, we have retreated to a more indoor lifestyle, with reduced exposure to beneficial levels of sunlight and ionized air.

How do all these changes affect us? It is difficult to evaluate these effects. Studies have been contradictory; some studies identify subtle damage to immune systems and brain function, while others report they cannot find these effects. It has been suggested that increased childhood leukemia and brain cancer have been observed in those living near high-tension power lines, which emit large fields of Extremely Low Frequency (ELF) energies. Other studies have denied such a correlation. It is known that ELF generated by house wiring and appliances can trigger high blood pressure, nervousness, allergies, and impaired sleep. They alter the heartbeats, blood chemistry, and behaviors of lab animals.

Here are some of the effects that have been reported by investigators.

❖ Proximity to video display terminals on computers is connected to miscarriages among female workers.

❖ Lab studies tie microwave exposure to fatigue, headaches, cataracts, tumors, birth defects, and changes in blood cells, hormones, and signals to the heart.

❖ Increased ultraviolet radiation from the thinning ozone layer is blamed for doubling the world-wide rate of melanoma, a deadly form of skin cancer.

❖ Lab animals raised indoors under pink lights had smaller litters and developed behavioral problems, calcium deposits in the heart, and increased tumor rates, plus inflammation and dead tissue on the skin of their tails. Ordinary incandescent light bulbs have more pink rays in them than natural sunlight—a potential effect on housebound pets.

❖ Many people become depressed, tired, and prone to gain weight when deprived of sunlight in winter. Full-spectrum lights provide relief for many who suffer from this Seasonal Affective Disorder (SAD).

❖ Urban dwellers and their pets often experience depleted levels of negative ions in favor of positive ions. This phenomenon can be traced to such factors as paving, smog, synthetic fabrics, and building ductwork. Shortages and imbalances of ions can trigger insomnia, anxiety, depression, headaches, dizziness, tremors, and heart palpitations. Lab animals deprived of all ions died young.

It is difficult to know what to do about all this "electronic smog," especially considering how extensive it is and how unlikely that it will go away.

As best I can tell, radiations that might have the most significant health effects (other than from radioactive material) are mi-crowave transmissions, which come from towers installed in many neighborhoods. Stay attentive to plans for installing these near where you live and get involved in the decision. If your pet has become ill with behavioral disorders, immune problems, or anemia, check the possibility that a new tower has been installed close to your home and note if that period corresponds to when your pet became ill. We can't know for sure that this is the cause, but it might make sense to board your pet with a friend or family member some distance away to see if that helps. I know this isn't a permanent solution, but it may help to determine whether these effects contribute to the problem you are dealing with.

WHAT CAN WE DO ABOUT ENVIRONMENTAL CAUSES OF ILL HEALTH?

It is unfortunate that we don't have more information and guidance with these issues. It is also unfortunate that many of the studies are paid for by the same companies that produce the products. Perhaps they are conducted in a fair and neutral way, but who can say? We know that unfavorable reports are often "buried," while those that are liked hit the journals.

On a personal, rather than societal, level, I think there may be too much investment in the use of chemicals in our homes, yards, and farms to really alter the practice in a serious, life-changing way. It has truly become a way of life.

Modern electronic devices are wonderful as well, and I quite understand their usefulness. I too use a computer with wireless access, a cell phone, microwave, television—all the modern technologies—and quite enjoy them. Still, there is this nagging thought: What if they are causing harm? I wish we could know for sure.

Determining whether any of these environmental hazards are causing chronic health problems for your pet takes some careful detective work and is difficult to confirm. All I can suggest is that you consider it as a possibility. Think about when the problem began and when it's better or worse to see if there is a relationship to some identifiable environmental factor. Also consider any potential hazards in your home, neighborhood, or region that may be linked with your pet's symptoms. Test kits and environmental consultants might be able to help you pinpoint dangerous conditions (which may threaten your whole family) and lead you to take corrective actions. Take obvious precautions like not letting your cat sit on the TV while it is on to avoid x-ray exposure from the flyback transformer.

You pretty much have to consider all this on your own. Realize that very few veterinarians will think of these environmental factors in treating health problems in your animal. There is a very strong veterinary bias towards assuming "infections" and therefore treating health problems with antibiotics—or if that is not effective, suppressing symptoms with anti-inflammatory drugs. Think of your own experiences. Has your veterinarian ever inquired about the possibility of exposure to formaldehyde in your home (was new furniture brought in?), exposure to pressure-treated wood (new fence or dog kennel, arsenic poisoning?), or perhaps fluoride poisoning from the high levels in processed foods? I am not saying this to criticize the veterinary profession. They do the best they can. The problem is that the *training* received in school does not consider these factors as significant—and if your veterinarian has never been informed, how could he or she even know about the possibility?

Meanwhile, the best medicine is prevention. Do what you can to follow the "Do's" and "Don'ts" on page 150. A great deal of the contamination in our homes comes from what we deliberately bring into them. Think about this the next time you are at the store.

Environmental pollution and disturbances are a fact of modern life. Perhaps we will adapt to many of them eventually. Meanwhile, it's wise to use the many sensible ways available to make our homes healthier for both our pets and ourselves. Along the way, we can take a lesson from the animals. They can teach us how to feel our connection with nature and do what we can to care for our larger home, the Earth.

HOW TO PROTECT YOUR PET FROM ENVIRONMENTAL POLLUTION: A CHECKLIST OF DO'S AND DON'TS

DO

• Brush and bathe your animal frequently to remove toxic particles from its fur.

• Use natural and least toxic methods of flea control instead of dangerous insecticides.

• Feed a fresh diet featuring organic foods whenever possible.

• Reduce pollutants by using low-meat recipes and minimizing liver, tuna, and animal fats in the diet.

• Include these pollution protectors in the diet: Vitamins A, E and C, calcium and zinc.

• Use a water filter or bottled water for your pet's (and your own) drinking water. Change the water daily and keep the bowl away from dusty areas.

• Use natural fibers for pet bedding (organic cotton, wool, kapok, and so forth).

• Vacuum and dust frequently.

• Remove shoes at the door, especially in homes that are near dusty industrial, high-traffic, or farm areas.

• Avoid shag and deep-pile rugs; if you already have them, vacuum and steam clean often.

• Ventilate your house well to reduce indoor air pollution or install whole-house ventilation.

• Let your pet outdoors in moderation or provide sunny, open windows with screens; otherwise, purchase a full-spectrum light for the animal's usual daytime rest area.

• Close your windows and keep your pet inside on smoggy days or when pesticides are being sprayed nearby. Use air filters if you live in a polluted area.

• Reduce indoor air pollution by removing outdated and unwanted toxic chemicals, and store others in ventilated areas away from pets and living space. Use nontoxic alternative products.

• Grow houseplants that filter the air, such as philodendrons, spider plants, aloe vera, chrysanthemums, and gerbera daisies.

• Keep pets from chewing on poisonous plants and their fruits.

• Guard against pets encountering solvents, paints, drugs and other chemicals, and the dust from remodeling projects.

• Test your home and take recommended actions if radon gas is a risk in your area.

• Consider using a negative ion generator if you live in a large building with central heating ducts, in a heavily paved city, or in an area often subject to hot, dry winds or smog.

DON'T

• Pet your animal with dirty hands.

• Confine your pet to a garage, basement, or shed that contains household chemicals or lacks natural light.

• Keep your pet outside if you live by a busy roadway.

• Exercise your pet on smoggy days or along busy streets.

• Carry your pet in the back of a pickup truck.

• Allow your pet to roam near a toxic dump, old landfill, or industrial/commercial area.

• Let your pet drink from or play in puddles or other contaminated waters.

• Apply or dump anything in your yard that you would not want to enter the water, food, or air you consume—motor oil or paint, for example.

• Allow smoking inside your home.

• Let your pet sleep near or under house foundations that may have been treated with poison for termites.

• Use pesticides unless absolutely necessary.

• Let your pet sleep on or near an operating TV, microwave, computer monitor, electric blanket or heater, clock-radio, or plug-in electric clock.

• Use medical x-rays unless needed.

• Overexpose your animal to the sun, especially if you live in an ozone-depleted area.

CHAPTER 9

CHOOSING A HEALTHY ANIMAL

Selecting a pet with good genetic characteristics is one of the most important steps you can take to increase the chances that your animal will have a healthy, happy life. For one thing, that means overriding the temptation to decide on a particular breed just because you like its looks—or to pick out the most pitiful-looking pup in the litter because it elicits your sympathy. But it's not quite as simple as picking out the liveliest, friendliest, and most inquisitive one you find, either.

Every type of dog or cat (pure or mixed breed) has physical characteristics—face, build, relative body proportions—that invite predictions about its potential well-being. Different breed types also have different behavioral tendencies. In this chapter you'll learn more about these indicators and how to use them to select a quality companion animal. If you plan to breed a dog or cat, you'll also learn how to help prevent congenital problems and birth defects.

My work as a veterinarian has often led me to ponder these issues. For instance, one day someone brought a lost miniature poodle to a clinic where I used to work. The poor dog was covered from head to foot with burrs, foxtails, and tangled hair. One eye was closed and discharging pus, and the areas between his toes were red and swollen. Clearly, he was a victim of the "foxtail season."

Foxtails, or plant awns, are those stickery little things that attach to your socks when you walk across a field. They latch onto dogs, too. And because of their pointed ends, these burrs work their way not only into the coat but sometimes right through the skin, burrowing also into the eyes, ears, nose, mouth, vagina, rectum, and between the toes.

Because our patient was so badly affected, we had to give him a general anesthetic before beginning the long process of removing the stickers. First we pulled and clipped the burrs out of his coat, then we worked them from between his toes. While my assistant, Dottie, attended to the feet, I found and removed two or three foxtails from deep in the ear canal. Careful examination revealed another lodged in the eye—the cause of the inflammation and discharge.

As we worked, Dottie and I began talking about how pets get into such a state after even a short trek in the fields.

"Here is the cause of the problem," I said, holding up some of the matted hair we had clipped off. "An animal with this kind of curly coat is like walking Velcro. Once the stickers brush against it, there's almost no place else for them to go but deeper in."

I pondered the matter for a moment. "You know," I went on, "people have unwittingly created this type of problem by deliberately breeding dogs to have such hair, as well as floppy ears like these. Both are perfect traps for foxtails. Wild animals don't have anywhere near this difficulty with stickers."

Situations like this have led me to reflect on the many ways we have interfered with the natural reproductive patterns of domestic animals. In the process of selective breeding, we have created a host of abnormal body structures that increase the likelihood of health problems. In addition, drugs, synthetic chemicals, radiation, and certain infectious diseases can damage a fetus and further increase the incidence of birth defects.

Animals born with defects can face lifelong health troubles despite excellent care and feeding. That's why it's so important to understand how these malformations are caused and what can be done to prevent or minimize them. First let's look at problems that have developed because of inbreeding and unwise selection.

THE EFFECTS OF BREEDING

When we humans began to domesticate animals, we took over many of nature's decisions about which animals were best suited to carry on the line. No doubt we made many good choices, often picking the strongest and the healthiest. But often animals were chosen for a unique appearance or some unusual behavior that pleased us or suited a particular need—horses with thick, beefy legs for pulling heavy loads; toy versions of dogs for lap companions; no-tail novelty cats. The inbreeding created new lines that had never before existed.

Consider the dog. As the first animal to be domesticated (some 10,000 to 20,000 years ago from wolves that began to associate with humans), the dog has probably been bred more than any other animal. Over thousands of generations, we developed dogs of every size and purpose. With a social structure and instinct similar to our own, they have served us well as hunters, herders, sled dogs, watch dogs, guide dogs, religious symbols, personal companions, and even as a source of food.

Cats, by contrast, were the last animal to share the home life of humans. They were lured by the many mice in the granaries of ancient Egypt and stayed to become a religious symbol of that culture. Not easily trained, the cat was not bred for any further duties except companionship. Their natural talent as mousers made cats welcome in households all over the world.

Just page through a picture book on breeds and you'll see the different breeding histories of dogs and cats. Dogs show much more variety in size, shape, and hair texture than cats. The difference in appearance between certain modern breeds of dogs and their wild ancestors is particularly striking in comparison with the relatively minor changes in cats.

Surely this greater interference with natural selection explains why a clinical study of birth defects in cats, cows, dogs, and horses showed that dogs had the most congenital malformations at birth and cats the fewest, despite the fact that cats are generally more sensitive to chemicals and other agents known to cause birth defects.

How does selective breeding lead to defects and malfunctions? An important factor in the creation of many breeds is *neoteny*, or a return to more primitive or undeveloped characteristics—either those that occurred early in the species' existence or those common to immature puppies or kittens: short legs and muzzles, silky hair, floppy ears, and the tendency to bark (adult wolves rarely bark).

So, many of the features we find appealing in purebred animals are actually the products of arrested development—either physical or psychological. A desired trait is often a trade-off for a defect or loss of function. For instance, breeding dogs for a short muzzle (upper jaw) has spelled trouble for breeds like bulldogs, boxers, and terriers. That's because separate genes determine other features that are closely related, such as the teeth and the soft palate (which separates the mouth and throat), and the genes continue to size them for a normal muzzle. So the crowded teeth are forced to grow in crooked and sideways, and the soft palate hangs so far back into the animal's throat that the threat of suffocation is ever present.

Inbreeding adds to the problem. To fix a given characteristic into a breed (so that it will breed *true*, that is, reappear consistently), selected brothers and sisters must be mated, or a parent crossed with its offspring. Such intensive inbreeding might ensure the desired trait, but it might also perpetuate basic weaknesses in the line, such as poor resistance to disease, low stamina, low intelligence, birth defects, and inherited diseases that include hemophilia or deafness.

Breeding to meet market demand can also lead to disaster. During the 1920s, for example, the recently imported Siamese cat became so popular that breeders mated siblings as well as parents and offspring to meet the demand. The kittens born of these matings so weakened the breed that it almost died out entirely. Sobered by this experience, breeders began to make wiser selections. Many breeds of dogs—such as the collie, the cocker spaniel, the beagle, and the German shepherd—have also suffered as a result of surges in popularity.

The problem of genetic disease is particularly sad. Animals undergo much unnecessary suffering because they're often bred for financial gain or for some trait considered "cute," unusual (such as squat faces, long faces, curly or silky hair, hairlessness, wrinkly skin, floppy ears, or missing tails), or useful (such as short legs for access to dens in hunting or massive size for fighting or guarding). The question of whether the animal will have a comfortable, well-adapted, potentially healthy body rarely comes up. And we don't seem troubled by the high rate of defective pets. People rightly get alarmed at a human birth defect rate of one in a thousand, but many pet breeders simply accept statistics that predict 10 to 25 percent of their litters may be born defective. Generally, the largest and smallest breeds tend to suffer the most from genetic weaknesses.

Some other examples of problems created in breeding "un-wolfly" shapes and sizes of dogs include the bulldog, Chihuahua, and others bred to have a small pelvis. Many of these animals require cesarean deliveries. Giant breeds such as Saint Bernards and Great Danes are known for their bone problems and their short lives. Breeds that have abnormally short noses and jaws (bulldogs, Pekinese, boxers, and Boston terriers) generally suffer from breathing problems. As might be expected, dogs bred to have short legs (dachshunds and basset hounds) also tend to have deformed spines. Among cats, breeding for tailless cats (the Manx breed) has also led to litters with severe malformation of the urinary tract and genitals.

Another ethical issue involves producing countless litters to satisfy the demands of people who insist on purebreds. At the same time, millions of mixed-breed animals that would make equally good pets go begging. Up to 75 percent of the dogs and cats born each year face death by accidents, starvation, or euthanasia because they can't find permanent homes. Selecting a mongrel from the local animal shelter, however, won't necessarily reduce the risk of acquiring a pet with congenital problems. Often an adopter chooses an animal that especially arouses pity, perhaps one with strangely colored eyes, or drooping ears and eyes that look sad, or a short, pushed-in, childlike face.

Sometimes pets just find their way into our homes and hearts (such as the deaf white cat that came to us as a stray), and we accept them as is. But at least we can decide not to breed an unhealthy animal or one with characteristics that interfere with normal functioning.

ENVIRONMENTAL INFLUENCES ON BIRTH DEFECTS

Environmental poisons and stresses also contribute to congenital problems. Some of these hazards (mutagens) can cause a change in one or more genes that can be passed on to future generations. The result could be a sad legacy of genetic defects and diseases, as well as spontaneous abortion, lowered disease resistance, decreased life span, infertility, or unnatural behavior. Add unwise breeding practices to the mix, such as mating affected parents and their offspring, and the effects can be even worse.

Other hazards (teratogens) attack the embryo but are not passed on. Depending on the timing and the amount of exposure during pregnancy, such factors can cause deformed bodies, miscarriages, retarded growth, congenital tumors, and various disabilities or abnormalities that surface.

If you are planning to breed an animal, it is very wise to take special care to minimize certain risk factors suspected of damaging genes and/or fetuses. The following are the most important to avoid because they can pose a threat both before and during pregnancy.

❖ Radiation (the worst threat; use filtered water and avoid unnecessary diagnostic x-rays and radioisotopes)

❖ Lead, mercury, and cadmium (see chapter 8)

❖ Chlorpromazine, phenobarbital and urethane (veterinary sedatives and anesthetics)

❖ The insecticides carbaryl, dichlorvos, dieldrin, fipronil, Imidacloprid, Permethrin, Pyriproxyfen, and lindane (some are banned, yet they persist in the environment and accumulate in animal fat, so emphasize diets with lean meats; also minimize use of any chemical insecticides)

❖ Aflaxtoxin (may be in moldy or spoiled foods)

❖ Fungicides (especially captan and griseofulvin)

❖ Anti-cancer drugs (not a good idea to breed an animal that has had cancer anyway)

In addition, do your best to protect your pet from the following:

Before breeding: the antibiotics Actinomycin D, erythromycin, and streptomycin; the antiseptics hexachlorophene, mercury chloride, and hydrogen peroxide; the drugs Butazolidin (phenylbutazone), EDTA, methylene blue, and ethidium bromide; canine distemper (or the live vaccine); the herbicides 2,4-D and 2,4,5-T; chemical soil sterilants; formaldehyde (see chapter 8); and benzene (found in cigarette smoke and car exhaust; don't keep your pet in a garage).

During pregnancy: overheating (from being in a hot car or exercising in hot weather); lack of oxygen (from anesthesia, high altitude, anemia, air pollution, or chemical exposure); traumatic injury; most veterinary antibiotics, corticosteroids and sedatives; aspirin; feline leukemia virus (or vaccine); microwave ovens; herbicides, especially paraquat and MCPA; many chemicals, especially complex organic hydrocarbons (follow advice in chapter 8); general underfeeding

and malnourishment; insufficient levels of vitamins A, D, or B complex, iron, magnesium, zinc, copper, iodine, or manganese; excessive amounts of calcium, vitamin A, iodine, or salt; certain poisonous plants (jimsonweed, locoweed, skunk cabbage, and wild pea).

Some of these factors are known to cause reproductive problems only when given in high doses to experimental animals. For that reason they may not be an issue under ordinary exposures. Their safety, however, is questionable, and it is best to err on the side of caution.

The harm caused by these agents can show up in everyday veterinary practice, not only in laboratory experiments. For instance, pups born of a mother given corticosteroid therapy during pregnancy have been born grossly swollen with fluid. Also, extreme leg and leg joint deformities occurred in an entire litter of cocker spaniel puppies born to a mother treated with the corticosteroid dexamethasone during the second half of pregnancy.

COMMON CONGENITAL PROBLEMS IN DOGS

The parts of the dog's body most frequently affected by birth defects are the central nervous system, eyes, muscles and bones. For example, the German shepherd, collie, beagle, miniature poodle, and Keeshond can inherit epilepsy. A variety of other nervous system disorders are sometimes passed on within certain breeds. These include paralysis of the front and back legs (Irish setter), a failure of muscle coordination (fox terrier), idiocy (German shorthaired pointer and English setter), and abnormal swelling of the brain (Chihuahua, cocker spaniel, and English bulldog).

Congenital eye abnormalities, including cataracts, glaucoma, and blindness, are found in *most* of the common breeds.

Hernia is a typical muscular problem. The basset hound, basenji, cairn terrier, Pekinese and Lhasa apso all have a high risk for inguinal hernias (the gut protrudes into the groin). Umbilical hernias (gut protrudes through the navel) are inherited defects in the cocker spaniel, bull terrier, collie, basenji, Airedale terrier, Pekinese, pointer, and Weimaraner.

Besides bone-related problems like those mentioned in very small, large or short-legged dogs, many canines suffer lameness from abnormal hip formation (dysplasia), probably the most common inherited defect among dogs (see "Hip Dysplasia" on page 359). It is seen in most purebreds, particularly cocker spaniels, Shetland sheep dogs, German shepherds, and many large breeds.

For more specific information on particular breeds, see "Behavioral Patterns and Congenital Defects in Dogs" on page 164.

COMMON CONGENITAL PROBLEMS IN CATS

While there have been very few thorough studies of birth defects in cats, the most common problems occur in the nervous system, including the brain, spinal cord, and skeletal tissues. (This is true of all domestic animals and humans.) In alphabetical order, the special congenital problems that affect cats follow.

Brachycephalic head (Peke face): Marked by an unusually short and wide head, the deformity is exemplified by long-haired Persians and newer strains of Burmese. Cats from these lines produce lethal birth defects involving the eyes, nasal tissue, and jaws in nearly one out of four kittens. Also, a brachycephalic head is associated with an increased incidence of cleft palate.

Brain and skull problems: Cats that have an undersized cerebellum in the brain may have poor coordination, tremors, excessive tension in the limb muscles, and slowed reflexes. Swelling of the brain (hydrocephalus) can be inherited in the Siamese. In some cats, the roof of the skull does not close, causing abnormal expansion of the brain. In others the brain degenerates even before birth (a condition that's usually fatal).

Cancer of the ear: White-haired cats are the prime victims of this ailment because of repeated sunburn of their sensitive ears.

Cardiovascular defects: Key malformations include a narrowing of the aorta, the heart's main artery, or nonclosure of the aortic duct. Both conditions are common causes of heart murmurs. Cats may also have other kinds of heart and aorta malformations.

Cleft palate: In some Siamese, a cleft palate seems to be hereditary, but it can also be caused by various drugs ingested during pregnancy.

Cryptorchidism: The phenomenon of undescended testicles is not unusual among male cats.

Deafness: Many blue-eyed white cats are deaf from birth and often have poor resistance to disease, reduced fertility, and impaired night vision.

Eye and eyelid defects: The absence of the outer half of one or both upper lids (seen in Persians, Angoras, and the domestic shorthair) is included here, along with an albino or a multicolored iris (which is sometimes associated with deafness on the same side, sensitivity to light, and eye incoordination), degeneration of the retina (particularly in Siamese and Persians), strabismus (an inward rotation of one eye when the other is fixed on an object, common in Siamese), and nystagmus (involuntary movements of the eye).

Hair abnormalities: Some cats are born with (or bred for) hairlessness or curly, short, plushlike hair, such as the "Rex" mutant, which has missing or abnormal guard hairs.

Hair balls (frequent): It's well known that this is a chronic problem in longhairs.

Kidney missing: This abnormality occurs most often in males, and usually the right kidney is missing.

Limb defects: Kittens sometimes show missing or extra toes or legs at birth.

Mammary gland abnormalities: This occurs in the formation of the ducts that supply milk.

Spina bifida: The vertebrae fail to close normally around the spinal cord, leading to motor and sensory problems in areas fed by affected nerves. The Manx, in particular, suffers from this problem because it is associated with the gene for taillessness. Symptoms can also include a hopping gait and incontinence.

Tail defects: A missing tail is typical of the Manx but rare in others. Associated defects include spina bifida with hindquarter deformities and an abnormally small anus. Other cats can be born with a kinked tail.

Umbilical hernias: Part of the intestines or some fat protrudes through the navel in this commonplace defect. Hernias of the diaphragm are also frequent.

PREVENTING CONGENITAL PROBLEMS

You can't always help an animal that is born with a congenital problem. Sometimes surgery can correct a structural defect, and proper grooming, veterinary care, and feeding can control certain other problems. But the very best treatment for congenital defects is prevention. That means:

Never breed unhealthy animals. Avoid breeding those pets with obvious birth defects or behavior difficulties. Even though the animal may not have a specific genetic problem, its overall support system is under par for developing healthy offspring. Also, avoid acquiring such animals unless you are willing to provide them with the special care they need.

Don't breed or select animals with family health problems. If their close relatives have congenital defects or inheritable behavioral or physical troubles, stay away. The tables beginning on page 164 can help alert you to particular problems that may plague the breed(s) you are considering. Try to check on the medical histories of both parents and research what percentage of related puppies or kittens have had defects. It should be less than 5 percent.

Do not breed close relatives. Mating two animals of the same family (such as parents, siblings, aunts and uncles, and grandparents) tends to "fix" latent defects into their offspring.

Don't select or breed inbred animals. Be particularly careful with breeds that are currently popular in your area, because it's likely they have been weakened by intensive inbreeding.

Favor breeds that best resemble canine or feline ancestors. Look for size, face shape, ear shape, color, coat length and texture, tail shape, and limb proportions that most closely match that of wolves, coyotes, and wild cats. (Try to match at least four or five of these characteristics.) Canine examples include most of the retrievers, sled dog breeds, basenjis, shepherds, pointers, and spitzs. Feline examples include most shorthairs, especially those with more natural colors such as tabbies, silvers, and ancient breeds such as Korats and Abyssinians. If a given characteristic differs, consider the potential effect. A curly coat, for instance, will attract stickers. A pushed-in face will cause breathing problems. Long, floppy ears may harbor mites.

Occasionally, I have had the opportunity to examine and treat injured coyotes or foxes, and never have I found one with a foxtail in its ears or anywhere else on its body! Every inch of their bodies reflects the intelligence of millions of years of natural evolution and adaptation. I have been quite impressed with how perfectly their teeth fit together and with their fine hair coats, fastidious cleanliness, natural grace, and high intelligence. (Don't try to adopt a truly wild animal: The place for them is in the wild, and they do not make good pets.)

Protect fertile and litter-bearing females. If you plan to breed your female pet, avoid use of potentially damaging flea powders, cortisone, vaccinations, sedatives, anesthetics, and x-rays, unless natural aids fail and circumstances demand this kind of medical treatment. Feed her an optimal diet (see chapter 5) and make sure she does not consume food additives, moldy foods, poisonous household chemicals, or lawn grass or other plants treated with toxic herbicides, insecticides, or fungicides. This rule applies before and during pregnancy and during lactation.

Also, see that she does not become overheated. Excess heat can retard fetal brain growth. Don't leave her locked in a hot car

with the windows closed (a good piece of advice concerning any animal) or overexercise her in hot weather (likewise). Nor should you take her on an arduous trek into high country or transport her in the baggage compartment of an airplane, because the lack of oxygen at high altitudes can induce a variety of fetal abnormalities.

SELECTING A HEALTHY ANIMAL

The tables that follow will alert you to potential problems in various breeds and mixed breeds. But how can you tell if a particular animal is healthy? Here is a "checkup" list you can use to pinpoint any congenital defects present. It also helps assess the likelihood of chronic health problems to come.

❖ What color is the coat? White animals, beautiful as they are, often fall victim to extra problems, such as skin cancers or deafness in white, blue-eyed cats. (Test for deafness by clapping your hands behind the animal's head.) Gray collies sometimes have a blood immune problem, with increased susceptibility to infection.

❖ Check the nose and jaws. Are they unusually long and pointed or unusually short and pushed in? Odd shapes here should act as a warning against trouble with teeth and gums, in addition to potential respiratory problems.

❖ Are the upper and lower jaws the same size? Do the teeth fit together well? (This particularly applies to dogs.) Are the gums pale or inflamed? Is there a red line at the edge of the gums next to the teeth?

❖ Are the eyes normal-looking? Are they both the same color? Be cautious about eye trouble if the eyes are unusually small or large compared to other canines or felines. Discharges from the eyes signal plugged tear ducts, because tears and liquids would ordinarily be discharged through the nasal cavity.

❖ Does the animal move normally? Or does it swing its hips from side to side as it walks—a warning sign of possible canine hip dysplasia? Are the legs a normal length, and are the front and back legs in the right proportion relative to each other?

❖ Does the pigmentation over the nose look normal? If not, the animal may be subject to sunburn and skin cancer.

❖ Observe the animal carefully for normal temperament. Be wary of animals that seem unusually aggressive, clinging, jealous, fearful, suspicious, hyperactive, noisy, or unaware. Whether because of inheritance or environment, such problems may be difficult to live with and even harder to correct. If you want a playful or affectionate animal, choose the one that responds to your overtures. Roll a dog on its back and hold him there. If he fights to get up, he may be difficult to train and aggressive. A dog that keeps its tail low or acts submissive will be the most devoted and easiest to train.

Once you have the trust of the animal (and with the owner's assistance, if necessary), take a closer look for problem signs.

❖ Is the coat attractive? Does it look and smell healthy and clean, or is it slightly greasy or thin? Are there reddish patches? Is the skin light pink or off-white in color, pliant and firm, or are some areas unusually thin, thick, dry, dark, red, or crusty? Is the skin covered with fleas?

❖ Does the animal breathe quietly and easily? Raspy, heavy sounds, especially after a little exertion, are not good signs.

❖ Look inside the ears. Check for any signs of inflammation or dark, waxy discharge. This could signal a chronic tendency toward ear trouble.

❖ Feel around the navel. You're looking for a lump, which could be a sign of a hernia.

❖ Check the scrotum in an adult male for the presence of both testicles.

In spite of the many problems inappropriate breeding has caused, it is still possible to find a genetically healthy animal or one with only minor problems. If you don't plan to breed the animal and don't mind the extra work of caring for an animal with inherited prob-lems, you can select from a wider variety. Although you cannot always foresee or control potential congenital problems, with just a bit of common sense you can actually do a great deal to minimize the risks. In the process, you will be doing a big favor not only for your own animals and yourself, but also for those whose time is yet to come.

CHOOSING THE BEST PET FOR YOU

When choosing a dog or cat, pick a breed that suits your lifestyle and preferences. Both dogs and cats vary widely in their temperaments and their needs, often along breed lines. Every day humane societies must euthanize healthy animals turned in because their unhappy owners did not anticipate certain issues. For instance, a mild-mannered person would be unwise to select a large dog from a breed that tends to dominate the owner. Similarly, a family with toddlers in the house should choose a breed less likely to snap at children. Those who live in an apartment with no yard should pick an animal suited to smaller confines, such as the Korat cat.

It is also important to consider size variations when you are selecting a dog. Clusters of traits tend to accompany size. Small dogs, for example, may be especially active and have a high demand for affection. Large dogs tend to be quieter and more patient with children. Dogs that are unusually large or unusually small tend to have the most genetic problems, especially structural ones. Larger and more active dogs require the most space and consume the most food, which involves economic and ecological considerations. For example, a 70- to 80-pound dog needs as many calories every day as an adult woman. So if you plan to feed your dog a natural diet, as recommended in this book, it will be easier to deal with a smaller dog. Many people find it too expensive or too much work to prepare food for a larger dog. Such dogs almost always end up on a diet of commercial food, with the accompanying lower level of health.

BEHAVIORAL PATTERNS AND CONGENITAL DEFECTS IN DOGS

BREED	WEIGHT (LB.)	PHYSICAL NEEDS	TRAINING	COMPANIONSHIP
TOY AND SMALL DOGS				
Basenji	23	Should sleep indoors.	—	—
Beagle	20–35	Should sleep indoors.	More difficult.	Very active.
Boston terrier	15–25	Should sleep indoors.	—	Very affectionate, active, needs attention.
Brittany spaniel	25–40	Regular grooming. Should sleep indoors.	Easy. Submissive.	Patient with toddlers.
Chihuahua	2–6	Lots of exercise. Should sleep indoors. Sensitive to cold.	Difficult. Dominant. Nondestructive.	Very affectionate, active, needs attention. Not very playful. May snap at toddlers.
Cocker spaniel	20–30	Regular grooming. Should sleep indoors.	—	Very affectionate, but may snap at children.
Dachshund	15–25	Should sleep indoors.	Destructive (chews, digs).	—

WATCHDOG AND AGGRESSION	POSSIBLE CONGENITAL DEFECTS*	NOTES
Quiet.	Anemia. Hernias. Opaque cornea. Enteritis (diarrhea).	Clean, no odor. Doesn't bark. Natural size, shape and coat. Patient.
Barks excessively.	Cataracts, glaucoma and other eye problems. Epilepsy. Hemophilia. Cleft lip and palate. Spinal deformities. Short or missing tail. Skin allergies.	—
More likely to bark at intruders. Barks excessively.	Cataracts. Obstructed breathing.† Pituitary cysts.‡ Deformed spine, knees. Tumors. Excess or missing teeth. Hernias.	—
Less likely to bark at intruders. Nonaggressive.	—	Sweet, well-mannered. Good swimmer.
More likely to bark at intruders. Barks excessively.	Deformed spine, knees. Dislocated shoulder. Heart and breathing problems.† Hemophilia. Swelling of brain.	—
Less likely to bark at intruders.	Cataracts, gradual blindness, glaucoma and other eye problems. Kidney disease. Hemophilia. Cleft lip and palate. Misshapen jaw, tail. Deformed spine, knees. Dislocated shoulder. Swelling of the brain. Hernias.	—
Strongly defends territory.	Bladder stones. Pituitary cysts.‡ Deafness. Diabetes. Circulatory problems. Disk disease. Incomplete kidney. Cleft lip and palate. Malformed jaw, spine, limbs.	Long-haired dachshund more tranquil, barks less.

(continued)

BREED	WEIGHT (LB.)	PHYSICAL NEEDS	TRAINING	COMPANIONSHIP
TOY AND SMALL DOGS (CONT.)				
Fox terrier	17	Regular grooming. Should sleep indoors.	Difficult. Dominant. Destructive (chews, digs).	Not so playful. May snap at toddlers. Very active.
Lhasa apso	10–15	Regular grooming. Should sleep indoors.	Dominant.	Very affectionate, needs attention. Not so playful.
Maltese	6	Regular grooming. Should sleep indoors. Sensitive to cold.	—	Very affectionate, needs attention. May snap at toddlers.
Pekinese	10–14	Regular grooming. Should sleep indoors.	Difficult. Nondestructive.	Very affectionate, but not so playful. May snap at toddlers.
Pomeranian	5	Regular grooming. Should sleep indoors.	Difficult.	Not so playful. May snap at toddlers.
Poodle (miniature)	12–25	Regular grooming. Should sleep indoors.	Easy.	Very affectionate, active, playful, needs attention.
Poodle (toy)	8–12	Regular grooming. Should sleep indoors.	—	Very affectionate, needs attention. May snap at toddlers.
Pug	16	Should sleep indoors. Sensitive to heat.	—	—

WATCHDOG AND AGGRESSION	POSSIBLE CONGENITAL DEFECTS*	NOTES
Barks excessively. Strongly defends territory. Aggressive.	Glaucoma. Deafness. Nervous and cardiovascular defects. Excess or missing teeth. Dislocated shoulder. Skin allergies. Muscular incoordination. Goiter.	Very excitable, may try to dominate owner.
Barks excessively.	Inguinal hernias. Kidney defects.	Can be stubborn.
Barks excessively. Nonaggressive.	—	Less aggressive than most small dogs. Long-lived.
Barks excessively.	Eye abnormalities. Obstructed breathing.† Pituitary cysts.‡ Deformed spine. Hernia.	Classic apartment dog. Ancient breed.
Barks excessively.	Dislocated shoulder. Deformed knees. Collapsed trachea. Heart defects. Underdeveloped teeth.	Usually excitable but some are calm. Most natural size, shape, and coat. Seasonal shedding. Related to spitz.
Barks excessively. Nonaggressive.	Gradual blindness, eye problems. Epilepsy, nerve and heart defects. Hemophilia. Bladder stones. Collapsed trachea, obstructed breathing.† Diabetes. Deformed spine, limbs. Dislocated shoulder.	—
Barks excessively.	Gradual blindness. Knee problems. Collapsed trachea. Heart defects. Muscle problems in lower rear legs.	More likely than other poodles to snap at children.
More likely to bark at intruders. Nonaggressive.	Male pseudohermaphroditism. Ingrown hairs in tissue.	Less aggressive, excitable, and snappish than other small dogs.

(continued)

BREED	WEIGHT (LB.)	PHYSICAL NEEDS	TRAINING	COMPANIONSHIP
TOY AND SMALL DOGS (CONT.)				
Schnauzer (miniature)	12–15	Regular grooming. Should sleep indoors.	Dominant.	Very affectionate, playful, active, needs attention. May snap at toddlers.
Scottish terrier	20	Regular grooming. Needs lots of exercise. Should sleep indoors.	Difficult. Dominant. Destructive (chews, digs).	May snap at toddlers. Very active.
Shetland sheepdog	16	Should sleep indoors.	Easy. Submissive.	Very playful.
Shih Tzu	12	Regular grooming. Should sleep indoors.	—	Very affectionate, active. Needs attention.
Welsh corgi, Pembroke	27	Should sleep indoors.	Easy. Submissive. Nondestructive.	Very playful.
West Highland white terrier	16	Regular grooming. Needs lots of exercise. Should sleep indoors.	Difficult. Destructive (chews, digs).	Very affectionate, playful, active, needs attention. May snap at toddlers.
Yorkshire terrier	4–7	Regular grooming. Should sleep indoors. Sensitive to cold.	Difficult.	Very affectionate, active, playful, needs attention. May snap at toddlers.
MEDIUM DOGS				
Airedale	50	Regular grooming. Needs lots of exercise. Should sleep indoors.	Dominant. Destructive (chews, digs).	Very playful, active.
Australian shepherd	40	May sleep outdoors in a doghouse.	Easy.	Very affectionate, playful, active, needs attention. Patient with toddlers.

WATCHDOG AND AGGRESSION	POSSIBLE CONGENITAL DEFECTS*	NOTES
More likely to bark at intruders. Barks excessively. Strongly defends territory. Aggressive.	Cataracts. Hemophilia.	—
More likely to bark at intruders. Strongly defends territory.	Nerve defects. Deafness. Bladder stones. Short limbs. Skin allergies. Tumors.	Needs regular, long walks. Barks less than many small dogs.
Barks excessively. Nonaggressive.	Eye and cardiovascular problems. Hemophilia. Nasal sunburn. Bladder cancer.	Seasonal shedding. Sometimes stubborn, suspicious of strangers.
Nonaggressive.	Cleft lip and palate. Kidney defects.	Less aggressive than many small dogs.
Strongly defends territory.	Bladder stones. Gradual blindness. Difficult births.	Good combination family pet/watchdog.
More likely to bark at intruders. Barks excessively. Strongly defends territory. Aggressive.	Skin allergies. Diseased jaw. Central nervous system problems. Inguinal hernias.	Very active, excitable and aggressive. Needs patio or yard.
More likely to bark at intruders. Barks excessively.	Knee problems. Displaced retina. Underdeveloped teeth. Birth problems.	Excitable.
More likely to bark at intruders. Strongly defends territory. Aggressive.	Small cerebellum. Trembling of hind quarters, nerve problems. Hernias.	Regular clipping customary. Needs affection.
Quiet. Nonaggressive.	Small eyes and other eye problems.	Benign watchdog. Energetic yet not high-strung.

(continued)

BREED	WEIGHT (LB.)	PHYSICAL NEEDS	TRAINING	COMPANIONSHIP
MEDIUM DOGS (CONT.)				
Basset hound	40–55	Should sleep indoors. Difficult. Submissive.	Nondestructive.	Not so playful or affectionate. Patient with toddlers.
Dalmation	45	Should sleep indoors	Dominant. Destructive (chews, digs).	May snap at toddlers. Needs attention.
English bulldog	50	Should sleep indoors.	Difficult. Nondestructive.	Not so playful or affectionate.
English springer spaniel	50	Regular grooming. Should sleep indoors.	Easy. Submissive. Sometimes destructive.	Very affectionate, playful, needs attention. Patient with toddlers.
Great spitz	40	Regular grooming. Should sleep indoors.	—	—
Keeshond	40	Regular grooming. May sleep outdoors in a doghouse.	Easy. Submissive. Nondestructive.	Patient with toddlers.
Norwegian elkhound	50	May sleep outdoors in a doghouse.	—	Not so affectionate. Patient with toddlers.
Poodle (standard)	35–50	Regular grooming. Should sleep indoors.	Easy. Submissive.	Very affectionate, playful, needs attention.

WATCHDOG AND AGGRESSION	POSSIBLE CONGENITAL DEFECTS*	NOTES
Less likely to bark at intruders. Quiet. Nonaggressive.	Spinal deformities. Short limbs. Glaucoma. Hernias.	Mild. Descended from blood-hound.
—	Skin allergies. Deafness. Uric acid problems. Nerve system problems.	Can be melancholy if alone.
Less likely to bark at intruders. Quiet, nonaggressive.	Obstructed breathing. Heart problems. Cleft lip and palate, excess or missing teeth. Birth, fertility problems. Pituitary cysts.‡ Deformed spine. Tumors. Swelling of brain.	—
—	Weakened skin. Hemophilia. Displaced retina. Some lines have abnormal aggression (attack people), so check lineage.	Playful family pet, safe with children, but can be destructive.
Less likely to bark at intruders. Strongly defends territory.	—	Natural size, shape, and coat. Seasonal shedding. Considered ancestor of all breeds. Suspicious of strangers.
—	Epilepsy. Heart defects.	Natural size, shape, and coat. Odorless. Seasonal shedding. Some lines may be more active, aggressive.
More likely to bark at intruders.	Gradual blindness. Tumors. In-complete kidneys.	Natural size, shape, and coat. Seasonal shedding.
More likely to bark at intruders. Strongly defends territory. Nonaggressive.	Cataracts and other eye problems. Bladder stones. Hemophilia. Skin allergies. Behavior problems.	Intelligent, good family dog. Can learn words.

(continued)

BREED	WEIGHT (LB.)	PHYSICAL NEEDS	TRAINING	COMPANIONSHIP
MEDIUM DOGS (CONT.)				
Samoyed	45–65	Regular grooming. May sleep outdoors in a doghouse.	Difficult. Dominant. Destructive (chews, digs).	Not so affectionate or playful. May snap at toddlers.
Siberian husky	35–60	Needs lots of exercise. May sleep outdoors in a doghouse.	Destructive (chews, digs).	Not so affectionate. May snap at toddlers. Very active.
LARGE AND GIANT DOGS				
Afghan hound	60	Regular grooming and exercise. May sleep outdoors in a doghouse.	Difficult. Dominant. Destructive (chews, digs).	Not so affectionate or playful. May snap at toddlers.
Akita	85	Regular grooming. Needs lots of exercise. Should sleep indoors.	Easy. Nondestructive.	Not so affectionate or playful. Patient with toddlers. Calm
Alaskan malamute	85	May sleep outdoors in a doghouse.	Can be destructive.	—
Bloodhound	90	May sleep outdoors in a doghouse.	Submissive. Nondestructive.	Not so affectionate or playful. Patient with toddlers. Calm.
Boxer	50–70	Needs lots of exercise. Should sleep indoors. Sensitive to cold.	Dominant.	Patient with toddlers.
Chesapeake Bay	55–75	—	Easy. Submissive. Destructive (chews, digs).	Very affectionate, needs attention. Patient with toddlers. Calm.

WATCHDOG AND AGGRESSION	POSSIBLE CONGENITAL DEFECTS*	NOTES
Strongly defends territory. Aggressive.	Heart defects. Diabetes. Hemophilia.	Natural size, shape. and coat. Seasonal shedding. Best watchdog of all the sled dog breeds. Odorless.
Less likely to bark at intruders. Strongly defends territory. Aggressive.	Different-colored irises.	Natural size, shape, and coat. Seasonal shedding. More playful than other sled dogs. Hardy.
Less likely to bark at intruders. Strongly defends territory. Aggressive.	Cataracts. Malformed elbow. Decaying spinal cord.	Require good training. Hardy to weather.
More likely to bark at intruders. Strongly defends territory. Quiet. Aggressive.	—	Natural size, shape, and coat. One of best watchdogs without dominating owner. Odorless.
Quiet.	Eye abnormalities. Hemophilia. Anemia with malformed bones. Dwarfism. Day blindness. Incomplete kidneys. Hemorrhaging.	Natural size, shape, and coat. Clean, odorless. Does not bark. Okay in apartment with daily walks.
Less likely to bark at intruders. Quiet. Nonaggressive.	Susceptibility to distemper.	Very calm, quiet, polite. Excellent tracker.
Quiet. Strongly defends territory.	Cardiovascular defects. Obstructed breathing.† Extra teeth. Subject to rheumatism.	Short-lived. Good family dog/watchdog. Less destructive than most guard dogs.
—	—	Good family dog, swimmer.

(continued)

BREED	WEIGHT (LB.)	PHYSICAL NEEDS	TRAINING	COMPANIONSHIP
LARGE AND GIANT DOGS (CONT.)				
Chow Chow	60	Regular grooming. May sleep outdoors in a doghouse.	Difficult. Dominant. Nondestructive.	Not so affectionate or playful. May snap at toddlers. Calm.
Collie	40–65	Regular grooming. Should sleep indoors. Sensitive to heat.	Easy. Submissive. Nondestructive.	Not so affectionate. Patient with toddlers. Calm.
Doberman pinscher	70	Needs lots of exercise. May sleep outdoors in a doghouse.	Easy.	—
German shepherd	60–85	Regular grooming. Needs lots of exercise. May sleep outdoors in a doghouse.	Easy. Dominant. Destructive (chews, digs).	Not so affectionate. Very playful.
German shorthaired pointer	45–70	Needs lots of exercise. May sleep outside in a doghouse.	Destructive (chews, digs).	Very playful, active. Patient with toddlers.
Golden retriever	55–75	Regular grooming.	Easy. Submissive. Nondestructive.	Very affectionate, playful, needs attention. Patient with toddlers.
Great Dane	100–150	Should sleep indoors.	—	Not so affectionate or playful. Patient with toddlers. Calm.

WATCHDOG AND AGGRESSION	POSSIBLE CONGENITAL DEFECTS*	NOTES
Strongly defends territory. Nonaggressive.	—	Natural size, shape, and coat. Seasonal shedding. Aggressive, but good guard dog with training. Loyal. Best with quiet owner.
Nonaggressive.	Retinal atrophy. Deafness. Epilepsy. Hemophilia. Hernia. Nasal sunburn. Bladder cancer. Eye problems. Cyclic neutropenia. Heart defects. Dwarfism.	Seasonal shedding. Good family pet, nonaggressive yet fairly good watch and guard dog.
More likely to bark at intruders. Quiet. Strongly defends territory. Aggressive.	Incomplete kidneys. Spinal deformities. Heart degeneration. Bone problems. Liver problems. Eye problems.	Long-lived. One of best watchdogs, easiest to train.
More likely to bark at intruders. Strongly defends territory. Aggressive.	Cataracts. Epilepsy. Kidney and bladder disease. Heart defects. Cleft lip and palate. Behavior problems.	Natural size, shape, and coat. One of best watch and guard dogs. Genetic lines vary a lot (check them out).
Less likely to bark at intruders. Nonaggressive.	Cataracts. Cardiovascular defects. Hernias. Behavior problems, idiocy. Cancer of connective tissue. Out-turned eye membrane. Swelling caused by obstructed lymphs. Decaying spinal cord. Skin cancer (melanoma).	Fine temperament, but can be destructive. Not for apartments.
Less likely to bark at intruders. Quiet. Nonaggressive.	Cataracts, gradual blindness. Generally a healthy, hardy dog.	One of best family dogs. Good swimmer.
Quiet. Strongly defends territory.	Heart defects. Bladder stones. Deformed spine. Out-turned eye membrane. Paralysis.	Bred as a guard dog. Size requires commitment to training.

(continued)

BREED	WEIGHT (LB.)	PHYSICAL NEEDS	TRAINING	COMPANIONSHIP
LARGE AND GIANT DOGS (CONT.)				
Irish setter	45–70	Needs lots of exercise. Should sleep indoors.	Difficult. Destructive (chews, digs).	Very affectionate, playful, active, needs attention.
Labrador retriever	55–75	May sleep outdoors in a doghouse.	Easy. Submissive. Nondestructive.	Very playful. Patient with toddlers.
Newfoundland	140	Regular grooming. May sleep outdoors in a doghouse.	Submissive. Nondestructive.	Not so playful. Patient with toddlers. Calm.
Old English sheepdog	95	Regular grooming. May sleep outdoors in a doghouse.	Difficult.	Calm.
Rottweiler	110	May sleep outdoors in a doghouse.	Easy. Dominant. Nondestructive.	Not so affectionate or playful. Calm.
St. Bernard	100–200	Regular grooming. Needs lots of exercise. May sleep outdoors in a doghouse.	Difficult. Dominant. Nondestructive.	Not so affectionate or playful. Calm.
Vizsla	65	Should sleep indoors	Easy. Submissive. Nondestructive.	Very playful. Patient with toddlers.
Weimaraner	75	Should sleep indoors.	Destructive (chews, digs).	—

SOURCE: *"A Catalogue of Congenital and Hereditary Disorders of Dogs,"* in Current Veterinary Therapy IX: Small Animal Practice, ed. Robert Kirk, 1986, pp. 1281–1285.

Miniature breeds: Tend to have collapsed tracheas, knee problems, difficult births, and abnormal carbohydrate metabolism.

WATCHDOG AND AGGRESSION	POSSIBLE CONGENITAL DEFECTS*	NOTES
Barks excessively. Nonaggressive.	Gradual blindness. Heart and nerve defects. Hemophilia. Paralysis of legs. Joint problems in forelegs. Degeneration of kidneys.	Very playful, lively. Long-lived.
Quiet. Nonaggressive.	Cataracts, gradual blindness. Bladder stones. Hemophilia.	Natural size, shape, and coat. Good swimmer. Good family dog, safe with children. Hardy, healthy.
Less likely to bark at intruders. Quiet, nonaggressive.	Out-turned eyelids. Heart defects.	Natural size, shape and coat. Seasonal shedding. Excellent temperament. Good swimmer. Quietest, least aggressive of large dogs.
Less likely to bark at intruders. Quiet. Nonaggressive.	Cataracts.	Much grooming required.
More likely to bark at intruders. Quiet. Strongly defends territory. Aggressive.	Diabetes.	One of best, calmest guard dogs and bodyguards, though may dominate owner.
Less likely to bark at intruders. Strongly defends territory.	Out-turned eye membrane. Missing eye lens. Hemophilia. Paralysis.	Calm, but may dominate owner, snap at children. Not for indoor life.
Less likely to bark at intruders. Quiet. Nonaggressive.	Hemophilia.	Good family dog, safe with children.
—	Nerve defects. Hemophilia. Hernias.	Moderate in most characteristics. Fairly lively, affectionate. Can be stubborn.

Giant breeds: Hip and elbow dysplasia (joints improperly joined, causing lameness) and bone cancer are common.
†Caused by small nostrils and overly long, soft palate, predisposing to collapse of larynx.
‡Can result in diabetes, genital atrophy, and obesity.

BEHAVIORAL PATTERNS AND CONGENITAL DEFECTS IN CATS

BREED	NEEDS	COMPANIONSHIP
SHORT-HAIRED CATS		
Abyssinian	Clean coat with a wet mitt or glove. Prefers outdoors.	Affectionate, likes attention. Cautious. Active, inquisitive. Bonds to one person. Can learn simple tricks.
American shorthair	Regular brushing. Prefers outdoors.	Affectionate, likes attention.
American wirehair	Regular brushing. Prefers outdoors.	Affectionate, likes attention.
Bombay	Clean coat with a wet mitt or glove. Prefers indoors.	Affectionate, likes attention. Sedate.
British shorthair	Likes indoors or outdoors. Adapts to cold.	Affectionate, likes attention.
Burmese and Malayans	Clean coat with a wet mitt or glove. Likes indoors or outdoors.	Affectionate, likes attention. Enjoys travel. Vocal, "talkative."
Egyptian Mau	Likes indoors.	Sedate.
European shorthair	Likes indoors or outdoors. Adapts to cold.	Active, inquisitive.
Exotic shorthair	Regular brushing. Likes indoors.	Affectionate, likes attention. Sedate.

HUNTING AND AGGRESSION	POSSIBLE CONGENITAL DEFECTS*	NOTES
—	—	Natural shape and coat. Needs special attention from owner (petting, playing) or becomes sad, may run away.
Good mouser.	Abnormal or short tail, indented nose, extra toes. Thin or obese. Eyelid defects. Deafness in white, blue-eyed cats.	Fur adapts to cold, wet, thorns. Needs occasional brushing after outdoor excursions. Accepts baths well if started young.
Good mouser. Aggressive with other cats.	Crooked tail.	Wiry coat a mutation. May dominate other cats.
—	Curly hair, abnormally short tail.	Tranquil, good indoors.
Good mouser.	—	Natural shape and coat. Fur adapts to cold, wet, thorns, etc. Large, strong.
Good mouser.	—	Natural shape and coat. Long-lived, healthy. Requires affection, quiet. Good indoors.
Good mouser.	—	Natural shape and coat. Okay indoors. Delicate to changes of weather.
Good mouser.	Deafness in blue-eyed, white cats.	Natural shape and coat. Long-lived. Resists cold. Strong, adapts to many environments.
Good mouser.	Short or abnormal tail.	Tranquil, good indoors (Persian-American shorthair cross).

(continued)

BREED	NEEDS	COMPANIONSHIP
SHORT-HAIRED CATS (CONT.)		
Japanese bobtail	Regular brushing. Likes indoors or outdoors.	Affectionate, likes attention. Active, inquisitive.
Korat	Clean coat with a wet mitt or glove. Likes indoors.	Can learn simple tricks.
Manx	Regular brushing.	Active, inquisitive, playful.
Rex	Clean coat with a wet mitt or glove. Prefers indoors.	Sedate.
Russian blue	Regular brushing. Prefers indoors.	Affectionate, likes attention. Sedate.
Scottish fold	Regular brushing. Likes indoors or outdoors. Adapts to cold.	Affectionate, likes attention. Bonds to one person.
Siamese (also Colorpoint shorthairs, Oriental shorthairs)	Regular brushing. Likes indoors or outdoors.	Active, inquisitive. Bonds to one person. Enjoys travel. Accepts a leash. Vocal, "talkative."
Sphynx	Prefers indoors. Sensitive to cold.	Affectionate, likes attention. Sedate.

HUNTING AND AGGRESSION	POSSIBLE CONGENITAL DEFECTS*	NOTES
Good mouser.	—	Loves fish.
Aggressive with other cats. Good mouser.	Tends to get respiratory infections.	Natural shape and coat. Dislikes street noise.
Good mouser.	Taillessness compromises balance. Hopping gait. Incontinence. Still-births. Lack of undercoat. Small head. Spina bifida, hind limb, and pelvic deformities, small anus.	Muscular, playful. Friendly to all. Likes to climb.
—	Kinked tail.	Likes indoors. Very inquisitive.
—	Obesity.	Natural shape and coat. Good indoors, likes quiet. Especially affectionate.
Good mouser.	Folded ears may harbor ear mites, impair hearing.	Content indoors with occasional escape. Resists cold weather.
Aggressive with other cats.	More susceptible to disease than other breeds. Nasal obstruction, chin malformation, cleft palate. Retinal degeneration. Weak legs.	Natural shape and coat. Long-lived. Sensitive, unpredictable. Jealous. Needs space. Can be walked on a leash.
—	A hairless mutation. Susceptible to catching colds. May have overly wrinkled skin.	Must live indoors in temperate climate.

(continued)

BREED	NEEDS	COMPANIONSHIP
LONG-HAIRED CATS		
Balinese and Javanese	Extra grooming to avoid hair balls. Likes indoors or outdoors.	Active, inquisitive. Bonds to one person. Vocal, "talkative."
Birman	Extra grooming to avoid hair balls.	Sedate.
Himalayan (Color-point longhair) and Kashmirs)	Extra grooming to avoid hair balls.	Active, inquisitive. Bonds to one person.
Maine coon cat	Extra grooming to avoid hair balls. Likes outdoors. Adapts to cold.	Affectionate, likes attention. Bonds to one person.
Persian/Longhair	Extra grooming to avoid hair balls. Prefers indoors.	Affectionate, likes attention. Sedate.
Ragdoll	Extra grooming to avoid hair balls. Prefers indoors.	Sedate.
Somali	Extra grooming to avoid hair balls. Prefers outdoors. Sensitive to cold.	Active, inquisitive. Somewhat standoffish.
Turkish Angora	Extra grooming to avoid hair balls. Prefers indoors.	Affectionate, likes attention. Bonds to one person. Sedate.

HUNTING AND AGGRESSION	POSSIBLE CONGENITAL DEFECTS*	NOTES
Good mouser.	Weak hind legs. Can be sickly. Crossed eyes.	Affectionate, but mostly with one person. Similar to Siamese.
—	Crossed eyes, kinked tail.	Tranquil, devoted.
Good mouser.	Crossed eyes.	Adapts to indoors, but likes a lot of space. Affectionate, does not fight with other cats.
Good mouser.	Generally healthy, can with-stand cold.	Natural shape and coat. Prefers a yard, but okay indoors. Likes fish. Muscular. Friendly, but bonds to one person.
Good mouser.	Must be brushed daily to avoid hair ball problems. Eyelid de-fects. Retinal degeneration. Peke face.	Tranquil, home-loving. Muscular. Sociable even to other cats. Affectionate. Classic indoor cat.
—	Crossed eyes, deformed tail.	Soft body, mild character. Requires quiet owner, best indoors.
Good mouser.	Excessive shyness.	A long-haired Abyssinian. Sometimes mistrustful. Needs some outdoor space.
—	Short tail.	Progenitors of Persian/Long-hairs. Easier to brush than Persian. Almost shorthaired in summer. Sweet, well-behaved. Best indoors.

SOURCE: *Siegal, Mordecai (ed.) and Gino Pugnetti,* Simon and Schuster's Guide to Cats *(New York: Fireside, 1983).*

All long-haired cats tend to get hair balls.

CHAPTER 10

EMOTIONAL CONNECTIONS AND YOUR PET'S HEALTH

While the big hulk of a dog glared at me suspiciously, I carefully examined the foul-smelling, hairless patches that oozed bloody discharges on his back, underside, legs, and muzzle. As if to demonstrate just how bad it was, he jerked around and chewed violently on the base of his tail.

"Stop that, Bandy!" my client yelled sharply. Calming down, he explained, "The biting and chewing only makes things worse, so I always make a point of scolding him."

"There are some particularly bad spots under his tail," the

184

man's wife pointed out. Slowly, I started to raise the big dog's tail to take a look.

Hurling around, he snapped at me angrily, barely missing my hand. Pronouncing the exam complete, I sat down with the distraught couple to find out more about how this problem began.

"It happened pretty quickly," the woman began. "He had just a slight mange on his face when I got him as a puppy three years ago, but the real problem—chewing and licking all over himself—has gone on for about six months. The vet called it a flea allergy but didn't offer much for it. We ended up taking the dog to several vets, one of whom said it was 'hot spots.'"

The woman described how the veterinarian shaved the areas and gave Bandy antibiotics and cortisone. But, she said, nothing really helped. Finally, the veterinarian told the couple that they would either have to put Bandy to sleep or do a bunch of expensive treatments that still might not work.

"Do you have any idea why it got bad six months ago? Anything special happen around that time?" I inquired.

"Well, all I can think of was that our baby was born a couple of months before it started. I didn't want Bandy to be around the baby—you know, worms and all that—and the dog was acting jealous because he wasn't 'Number One' anymore, so we started keeping him outside all the time. Maybe that affected him. I don't know. I've had itchy skin myself for years, and I've never been able to find out the cause."

As we went on to discuss the dog's irritability, the woman mentioned that she *preferred* an aggressive dog. That way she felt safer living in the country. Occasionally, the man would interject something. As he did, I sensed an underlying tension between the couple.

This case came to me soon after I first began to look at medicine in a new way, exploring a wide variety of factors that might affect an animal's health. It prompted me to pay closer attention to the emotional factors in pet illnesses. Through the years I have repeatedly observed several patterns that I first noticed in Bandy's case, as well as some others. In summary, the patterns go like this:

❖ Pets may develop health problems soon after an upsetting change in the household, usually involving a loss of attention, a relationship, or territory.

❖ The health of a pet can be affected by recurrent feelings of tension, anxiety, depression, anger, and other emotional upsets in the home.

❖ Attitudes and expectations about the illness or disturbance can have a pronounced effect on the outcome.

❖ Pet illnesses often mirror those of the primary person with whom the pets are bonded.

I have noticed these connections particularly in pets with emotional and behavioral problems, but such patterns often seem to affect chronic physical problems as well.

By paying special attention to emotional issues in the home, it's possible to foster the kind of positive emotional climate that helps a pet maximize its ability to restore and maintain health.

PROBLEMS THAT START AFTER LOSSES

Many animals suffer a loss of attention and/or territory when a baby or a new pet arrives in the home. The same may occur when the family moves (perhaps to a small apartment or to an area with unfriendly neighboring pets). It can happen when someone dies or leaves the home, or when a person takes a time-consuming job, goes on a long vacation, or just loses interest. Or perhaps the house has just been redecorated and the animal is no longer welcome inside.

This loss may soon be followed by a decline in the pet's health. In cases like Bandy's (banished to the outside after the baby was born), boredom and frustration may combine with a pre-existing tendency for skin irritations and lead to excessive licking, scratching, and chewing. This, in turn, may aggravate what was only a slight weakness, creating more inflammation and irritation. Before long, a vicious cycle is well underway, with the skin increasingly inflamed and itchy.

Quieter types of pets may react by becoming more lethargic and apathetic. This inactivity and disinterest, in turn, lowers the strength of the immune system, and the pet may become susceptible to an infectious disease.

In yet another scenario, some pets may become stressed by territorial conflicts caused by a new animal's presence in the family or even in the neighborhood. If the disputes are not resolved, the constant stress can wreak havoc on the first animal's well-being, once more setting up fertile ground for germinating new health problems.

Problems like these may even be reinforced unintentionally by an innocent reaction. Say your dog is feeling lonely because you went back to work and just don't have as much time for him as you used to. Before long, he develops a minor symptom—a cough—that worries you. Every time he coughs you rush over, pet him, and murmur comforting words. (This sounds a little bit like dog training, doesn't it?) Pretty soon the dog gets the idea that every time he coughs he gets what he wants—your loving attention. What incentive is there for him to get well and stop coughing?

Even if you were to scold the dog (as Bandy's person did for scratching), he could perceive the scolding as a reinforcement of sorts. Receiving even such negative attention when he is usually ignored is preferable to feeling completely neglected.

Such scenarios are most likely to develop with symptoms such as coughing, limping, or scratching that involve some action over which the animal has some control. Veterinarian Herbert Tanzer, author of *Your Pet*

Isn't Sick (He Just Wants You to Think So), has found that teaching people to stop coddling pets in response to a symptom and to coddle them more at other times has resolved many irksome cases that seemed to have no physical cause.

What to do: Watch for any changes in your pet's psyche that might be the result of new household schedules or a family crisis. Animals are individuals just as people are. Some require more attention, social bonding, territory, and routine than others. Try to see altered situations at home from your animal's perspective and use your common sense in trying to make adjustments that will ease the situation. Perhaps you simply need to spend some special one-on-one "together" time with each animal; or you might have to construct a solid fence to keep out intruding neighborhood dogs. Maybe one person's German shepherd needs daily walks, but just holding and petting a Siamese more often could be all that's required to calm her.

Sometimes the answer lies in confining a new pet to limited space until the "senior" pet accepts the newcomer. With animals that are particularly hostile or territorial toward other animals (especially cats), you might have to remain a one-pet family. However, with highly sociable animals, especially dogs that have just lost an animal companion, you might do well to get a new pet, particularly one of the opposite sex, one that seems to have a friendly attitude.

It could be as difficult as deciding that your animal needs a more suitable home than the one you are able to provide. But then, it could also be as easy as allowing Rover back on his favorite chair and protecting your new upholstery with a towel or blanket.

Resist the temptation to baby your pet or to fuss over him whenever he limps, coughs, or scratches. Instead, pet him and play with him more at the times when he's behaving normally. And, of course, take him to the vet for a professional evaluation and give him whatever care he needs.

HUMAN EMOTIONS AND ANIMAL PSYCHES

The well-being of our pets is also affected by our feelings. Most dogs and cats form strong bonds with the people they depend on for food, shelter, safety, and affection. That's why it's especially important for them to tune into our emotional cues. Except perhaps for a few brief verbal commands or names, pets rely completely on the emotional messages communicated by our posture, tone of voice, facial expressions, and, well, just plain feelings in the air.

As a result of this connection, pets often seem to soak up angry, sad, or fearful feelings from family members who are experiencing tension or conflict over issues that have nothing to do with the animal. Frequent arguments in the home are especially stressful for a pet, which may react with irritability or fear. Emotional tensions in particular may affect health problems that have either a behavioral component (such as increased aggressiveness, destructiveness, or extreme restlessness) or a nervous component (such as irritated skin, ears, bladder, and the like). Just as a pet might react to losses, an emotionally stressed animal with a predisposition to skin or bladder problems, for example, might scratch or urinate still more, further irritating the tissues and setting up the conditions for a vicious circle.

Other times, a person's anxious emotions and expectations can aggravate a pet's existing health problem. Most commonly, one becomes upset on first noticing that a family pet is not feeling well. Deeply worried that the condition may worsen or even become fatal, it is common to be afraid of doing something wrong in treatment and losing a dear friend as a result. The animal senses this anxiety. Something must be wrong! The uncertainty only increases the pet's anxiety, which may already be heightened by the discomfort of illness. The animal may even begin to hide. When fearful and stressed, your pet may have a diminished capacity to heal.

Conversely, your calm, positive response to a pet's first symptoms relaxes and reassures the animal, helping to strengthen its immune response. All else being equal, I have observed time and time again that the animals likeliest to recover from chronic and difficult illnesses are those that live with people that manage to be calm and maintain a positive outlook. While it may be difficult to find calm in the face of suffering, it's the best thing you can do for your animal.

Besides sending a danger signal to your pet, your anxiety could also hinder treatment. Clients have often told me that acting from fear or a sense of urgency, they made decisions that they later regretted. When animals get tumors or cancers, clients often feel under tremendous pressure to have the growths immediately removed, as though every passing hour were critical. But there is no evidence to support such urgency. In fact, the stress of the surgery can make the animal even more difficult to treat when using less drastic methods. Similarly, the intense scratching that accompanies skin allergies sometimes drives clients to get corticosteroids, which can undo several weeks of progress resulting from nutritional and homeopathic treatment. True healing of chronic disease requires, above all, patience. The desire for immediate relief is very seductive. That's the appeal of using strong drugs to control symptoms. But since they don't actually cure the underlying ailment, the illness recurs, gradually worsening over time or taking a different and more difficult form.

Over-anxiety can also push people to jump from one veterinarian or treatment to the next, whether conventional or holistic. This can overwhelm and confuse your pet's body, never allowing any one method a chance to work. On the flip side, worry and discouragement can lead people to give up on medical treatment without really trying.

One final way our psyches may impact our pet's health is something of a mystery. Veterinarians see many cases in which pets develop the same problems as the people they live with, seemingly beyond coincidence. This could be caused by a common toxin or other agent in the environment. But it's also possible that the strong bond between some pets and people can create a kind of sympathetic resonance, akin to "catching" a yawn or the urge to scratch from someone nearby. Many experiments and anecdotes attest to a mysterious, seemingly extrasensory connection between animals and people. This could be a factor when it seems that the same health problem is shared between a person and an animal.

What to do: First, don't worry about whether your emotions have affected your pet's health. Even if they may have, it was never intentional. In any case, the best thing from this point forward is to be as relaxed, confident, and calm as you can. Whenever you are in an upset state, it is best not to engage in too much interaction with your pet or other family members. Taking a break can give you a fresh perspective.

Don't let yourself be hurried into medical decisions. Give treatments a chance to work and make any changes purposefully and carefully, in cooperation with your veterinarian.

Finally, learn to have faith in the power of healing. Life always seeks to right itself—to close a wound, to lift up our spirits. Try also to accept the fact of death, for it is part of a larger cycle of eternal renewal. After the winters of our lives—all the disappointments, the lows, the losses—spring will always come again.

CHAPTER 11

NEIGHBORLY RELATIONS: RESPONSIBLE PET MANAGEMENT

Living with animals can be a wonderful experience, especially if we choose to learn the valuable lessons animals teach through their natural enthusiasm, grace, resourcefulness, affection, and forgiveness. In that same spirit, a kind person is very dear to an animal. But when it comes to living habits, the natural tendencies of people and animals often widely differ. To some of us, the joys of an animal's company are well worth the little extra mess or noise that may be part of the package. Our neighbors, however, may not be as tolerant of muddy paw prints on the car, loud barking in the early morning, dug-up flowerbeds or extra "watering" of the bushes.

That's why taking responsibility for the impact our dogs and cats have on the rest of the community is one of the most important aspects of our responsibility of caring for an animal. Whether it's someone else's pet or our own, we all know the unpleasantness of dealing with animals that have not been well-taught or restrained. In fact, a nationwide survey revealed that the number-one citizen complaint made to city governments concerned "dog and other pet control problems."

I recall a neighborhood Doberman who used to bound into my front yard, relieve himself, then run up to my window and bark angrily at me as I sat in my own living room. And how many times have you walked through a parking lot when a big dog suddenly thrust its head through an open car window and barked ferociously, its huge jaws just inches from your face? I think of a veterinarian friend whose hand was painfully mauled by an aggressive dog. And I remember a town I used to live in where packs of roaming dogs used to chase down joggers and bicyclists as though they were prey. I always had to keep an eye on all the "ambush" spots when I jogged.

Recently we moved into a new home. Our next door neighbor's deck abuts our side yard and often contains several dogs excitedly barking and growling viciously inches from us as we work in our flower beds or mow the lawn. It is surprising to me that there is not more consideration in these situations. They can't possibly think we enjoy it.

If you have built a bird feeder in your yard only to see the neighbor's cat catch and eat the little songsters, it can be an upsetting experience. Such situations often pit neighbor against neighbor, with pets caught in the middle. And yet if animals could speak, they would probably complain about us humans—about being tied up or locked up too much, for example. Some might growl softly as they reflect on life with a rock 'n' roll fan addicted to top-volume stereo. Pets injured by cars might demand to know why we have to rush around so dangerously. And the millions of pets dropped off at animal shelters by the people that have been caring for them might tell how it feels to be abandoned. (Over half of these were given up because of unresolved behavioral problems.)

How can we, if we wish to be caring and responsible, address the inevitable conflicts between animals and people? I say start by considering the viewpoints and needs of all concerned—both humans and animals. Often a pet problem results from conflicting views on how animals should behave. For example, the person that loves his dog might think it's most natural, and therefore best, for his dog to roam freely; the neighbors, however, think the dog should be confined because it causes problems when allowed to do so. In other cases, a person has definite ideas about how his pet should act—but the *animal's* ideas are different, and the expected behavior is highly unnatural.

First let's look at various ideas about how companion animals can best fit into human communities. Once we are clear on our basic standards, we can work out our differences with our pets.

WHAT IS APPROPRIATE BEHAVIOR FOR PETS?

Certain rules for pet behavior are pretty clear. That's because we apply the same standards to ourselves. We do not permit:

- Jumping on, biting, scratching, chasing, attacking, or other aggression (except in defense against real threats).
- Excessive noise.
- Messes or destruction (especially inside the house or on someone else's property).
- Trespassing onto another's territory.

I list these because I've often seen people stand by as their dogs barked threateningly at harmless strangers or relieved themselves on a neighbor's lawn. To excuse such behavior by saying, "Well, dogs will be dogs," is not acceptable. Of course, we can't expect dogs to be just like us, but we can expect they will be controlled by those responsible for them and, at the very least, that owners will clean up after them. After all, they are living in a human community—not the other way around.

Numerous towns have laws that require dogs to be on a leash when not on their own property. But many people resent such interference with their pets' freedom. Well-intended as this attitude toward animals' rights might be, it overlooks the very real problems created by large numbers of dogs and cats on the loose in an environment quite unlike a natural habitat. Completely dependent on humans, these animals exist in our communities in numbers far greater than a natural ecosystem could support. As a result, these animals endanger both the community and themselves in several ways.

- More than a million dogs and cats are killed by cars in the United States annually. Unconfined pets also *cause* thousands of car accidents every year when people swerve or brake to avoid hitting them.
- Every year at least a million people are bitten by dogs in the United States, making dog bites our second most commonly reported public health problem. A survey revealed that people in some areas of Pittsburgh feared being bitten by roaming packs of dogs as much as they feared being mugged. Dogs harass elderly people carrying groceries as well as young children with lunch bags.
- Free-roaming dogs kill or injure wildlife, livestock, and other pets. I've treated my share of small dogs and cats chewed up by such packs. The people responsible for the attacking dogs usually have no idea what the family dog really does on an afternoon romp. Too many

cats prowling through a neighborhood can also be a menace to birds, small wildlife, and each other.

✧ Pets excrete a huge amount of body waste into the environment, much of it deposited in public places and on neighbors' lawns. These wastes can transmit harmful organisms to humans through sandbox play and gardening. They can also ruin a good lawn.

✧ Wandering pets may fall victim to poisons, sometimes intentionally placed. More often they become victims when their scavenging instincts unavoidably merge with our toxic world—ingesting antifreeze, pesticides, decaying road kills, and bait for wildlife control.

✧ Others may be kidnapped. Every year in the United States hundreds of thousands of dogs and cats are nabbed and sold to research labs, where they may be subjected to painful experiments and used as bait to train dogs for illegal dogfighting. Millions of other lost pets are impounded by animal control agencies. Usually, they are held for several days so that they may be claimed. But if a pet is frequently allowed to roam for long periods of time, then that pet's absences (especially cats) may not be noticed until it is too late and the animal has been euthanized.

✧ On the loose, unaltered pets freely follow their mating instincts. Competing males may engage in bloody and occa-sionally fatal fights. Multiplying far beyond the carrying capacity of either the natural ecosystem or our society, only about one in six of the millions of puppies and kittens born yearly in this country will find a home.

Government attempts to cope with animal control problems are a significant public expense, costing taxpayers many millions of dollars a year—in addition to untold private expenses for injuries, damaged property, and protective measures.

Let's look at how to get our animals to understand and agree to some basic behaviors that will enable them to live successfully in the human community. The issues and the solutions differ a bit for dogs and cats, so let's take up each in turn. I'll start with dogs, who are much more apt to cause problems for our neighbors than cats are.

CONTROLLING YOUR DOG

Responsible care of a dog starts with confining him to your property at all times, unless he's under your direct control and supervision. This doesn't mean to just lock him in the house or garage or tie him up outside. Your neighbor's desire for privacy might be satisfied, but your dog's natural needs for attention and exercise would be frustrated. This plan might even backfire, because frustrated and unhappy pets are the ones most likely to develop behavioral problems, such as destructiveness or excessive barking. (Some people have their dogs "de-barked"—an operation that removes the vocal cords, one which I personally will not perform, since dogs can be trained not to bark excessively.)

My parents lived for years next to a poor dog that was chained to a post in the back yard all year round and who spent most of his time barking and yowling at the top of his lungs—day after day after day. Talking to the neighbors did no good, and my dad often took food over to the dog out of pity for him. It is hard to realize that nothing could be done about a situation like this. As it stands now, this is not illegal and the neighbors were not breaking any laws. Dogs are considered property and they can be treated like this with impunity.

When your pet is in your yard, be sure to provide a snug shelter or install a pet door that allows him to go in and out of the house at will. Ideally, you should have a securely fenced yard to keep your dog from roaming when he's outdoors. If you tie him to a stake, the chain can tangle, limiting your pet's range and possibly endangering him. Barking and aggression are likely to result—as with the situation my parents faced. If fencing is impractical, clip his leash to a metal ring that slides along a clothesline or suspended cable. This allows greater freedom of movement with less likelihood of tangling. Or you could construct a large pen. Some people install Invisible Fence or other electric systems that train a dog to stay within its boundaries. Aggressive dogs, how-ever, have been known to overstep the boundary in response to strong temptations. Another limitation of invisible electric fences compared to physical ones is that they don't keep other dogs or people out, so your dog is still at risk of being stolen or attacked by another dog.

Such electronic fencing systems rely on a wire buried around the perimeter of the yard; if the dog tries to go past the wire, it triggers a mild electric shock in a special collar. It does not harm the dog but is un-comfortable, and they soon learn not to do it. I knew of one dog, however, that so de-sired to get out that he would endure the discomfort anyway. Knowing the shock was coming, he would start making crying sounds at the point he decided he was going to "go for it"—well before he could feel any-thing. That didn't stop him from making the run and getting away, though. He would start crying as he started his run, getting louder as he approached the barrier, and with a final yelp would leap out of the yard and on to freedom. My client tried two electronic collars on him at the same time, both to no avail.

If you don't have a yard, choose one of the breeds that are relatively sedate or small and adapt well to a life spent largely indoors. But many dogs are more naturally active, ex-ploratory, and hardy and strongly desire to be outdoors. With such a dog, you need to make a commitment to regular, vigorous walks and lots of attention. All dogs do best with daily walks—which are good for you, too! So you must be sure to teach your dog how to behave on an outing. This includes his walking on a leash without pulling you and without jumping on, barking at, or chasing any humans or animals encountered on the way. If he is well behaved, you may be able to let your dog loose under your supervision in some areas. (Be sure to bring a scooper and a bag to clean up after him wherever you go.) Many communities provide "dog parks" just for that purpose, where your dog can run freely and socialize with other dogs.

Make sure your dog always wears a current license and identification in case he should get loose. If he were to get lost and impounded, a license would be the key to his safe return. Always include a current phone number and address on the tag. People are more willing to help return a lost pet if you can be reached easily. A tagged animal also stands a better chance of receiving necessary medical care.

A new way of identifying animals is the injectable "micro-chip." These are small electronic circuits that can be put under the skin with a needle (they are that small—about the size of an uncooked grain of rice). They sit under the skin permanently and when the proper scanner is used, a code will identify the animal. A phone call will unite the lost pet with its person. As far as I can determine, there is no harmful effect from using them.

When you're home together, give your pup lots of affection. Most important, build a relationship together that allows you to leave him relaxed and comfortable when you must part. In fact, to have a wonderfully well-behaved dog, you need only to understand a few basic principles about what it takes for him to feel secure and to cooperate fully. From that foundation, you can teach your dog all he needs to know. While a comprehensive training program is beyond the scope of this book, I can present an overview.

WHY WE NEED A WIDE-ANGLE VIEW OF CANINE CULTURE

It's essential to understand the deeper emotional makeup of your pet as a species. Of course, our pets have much in common with us emotionally (one reason we share our lives with them), but each understands the world through its own very different dog or cat senses. Unless we interact with them with these inborn traits in mind, we achieve limited results, or even trigger behavior problems.

With our pets, we share a need for affection and for rewarding interactions with other creatures and our environment. In the same way that a healthy diet is the foundation for your animal's physical health, a steady "diet" of positive interactions with you and with the world is essential for your pet's psychological health, and the key to a peaceful relationship for both of you. These emotional needs are just as continual and demanding as physical needs. We wouldn't consider letting our pets go unfed for several days at a time, but an animal's desire for attention often goes unmet for that long.

Social needs are especially important for dogs. Just as some species need a particularly high level of protein in order to thrive, the dog must have a steady diet of happy social encounters. He also needs a clear, trustworthy leader in his immediate family. These two traits evolved strongly in wolves, enabling them to hunt and live together cooperatively, which enhanced their chances of survival. Dogs are not wolves, but they are likely descended from them and are very, very similar in their behavior. They have inherited this need for social order from their ancestors.

Most people have heard about the importance of playing the role of "alpha wolf" in the "pack" that now includes you, your dog, and your family. The concept is that every pack of wolves or dogs must have one established leader that looks out for the whole group.

Unfortunately, this useful idea is sometimes misunderstood. The alpha-wolf role is misinterpreted as a macho, tough guy in a heavy-handed boss/servant relationship. Few of us had this in mind when we decided to get a dog. We wanted a companion, not a slave. You don't have to dominate your dog (in fact, domination is both unnecessary and possibly even dangerous), but you do have to be a responsible leader.

If you neglect this role of leader or don't make it clear on a consistent basis, you're being unfair to your dog. That's because he will feel compelled to fill the leadership va-

cancy himself. Since he's a dog living in a human world, it is impossible for him to do this successfully. The normal behaviors of a dog doing his best to lead will get him in all kinds of serious trouble in our society. He may become aggressive to visitors, children, other dogs, and even to you. He may bark excessively, run away, not come when called, or be overprotective of food, toys, or the family car. He may pull on the leash or jump on people. If we try to correct these behaviors, the dog will get irritated with us because, for subordinates, we are acting way out of line. Then he tries to correct us, and we get more upset—which gets him more upset.

Dogs have a strong desire for stability. So when we accidentally signal to a dog that he is to act as a leader, then later reprimand him for doing so, we can upset his mental stability and derail his predictability. Unfortunately, this situation exists in many caring households. Unless we understand the dog's point of view and adapt our efforts to it, things won't improve.

Eternal vigilance is the leader's primary responsibility. He must be concerned with every sound, every stimulus, every change in the environment. When it's clear that someone else is in charge, a dog is apt to go sleep in a corner. But if he's trying to take care of his pack, he notices everything. He'd like to react, to investigate, but he can do very little because he's confined.

Inadequate human leadership can make the family dog more vulnerable to "separation anxiety." This is a discomfort some dogs experience when left alone, and they show it by whining, barking, chewing, digging, pacing, escaping, and urinating or defecating in inappropriate places. The dog is not "getting even" for being left alone. He's just trying to relieve his internal anxiety about being left with the only activities available to him. They give him a temporary respite from tension, but, unfortunately, they can easily become habits. Lack of exercise and stimulation, bad diet, poor health, breed characteristics, and emotional changes in the family can all contribute to this type of anxiety as well, but a key factor often overlooked is that the dog is confused about leadership roles in the family.

BECOME A POSITIVE LEADER FOR YOUR DOG

So how do you become the reliable leader your dog needs? Wolf packs succeed when their members are happy, healthy, and in relative harmony with each other. If they were constantly squabbling over their ranks, they'd be at a disadvantage for rounding up food. So, to maintain social stability, wolves use ongoing nonviolent signals to remind each other of their standing in the pack.

The need to train your dog provides a perfect context to mimic this repeated posturing and to make your leadership clear to your dog again and again. The idea is to convey to your dog that *he gets what he wants in life when he listens to you first.* You make this work by applying it dozens of times daily, in little ways.

First, make it fun for your dog to watch you for signals. Whenever he sustains eye contact with you, constantly reinforce him with treats, affection, and whatever he loves to do (playing ball, going for a walk, and so on). Associate it with a command like, "Rover, watch!" Make it fun, and soon the command itself will be enough to get your pet's attention. Once you can get his attention in this way, you're ready to proceed to other lessons.

Next, show the dog in lots of little ways that he must look to you first to get what he wants. If your pet wants to go outdoors, you tell him to wait. You walk out first. Then he gets to go out. If the dog wants to eat, first tell him to sit. When he sits, you feed him. If the animal wants affection, first tell him to lie down and have him stay for 30 seconds. Then release him with a code word like "okay" and play together. Once the routine gets established and your pet knows a few simple commands and learns that getting it right earns him lots of praise *plus* the thing he wants, he'll love it.

Every time you tell your dog what to do and he listens, it gently reinforces the idea that you're in charge, so he doesn't need to be concerned. It constantly signals to the dog that you're the leader, and it provides an ongoing supply of the attention he loves. Some dogs will accept this at once; others will put up a struggle about who's top dog. But consistent, daily, enjoyable reminders of your roles will lead to a more relaxed and confident pet.

Make praise and reward the cornerstone of your relationship. A basic command is "watch," meaning for him or her to pay attention to you—and wait for the next direction. Once this is accomplished, by simply applying the central command to be attentive, you will soon be past the struggling stage in teaching your dog the basics. Learning itself will become an enjoyable game for him. Your pet will eagerly try to figure out what you want so he can do it.

MAKE LEARNING FUN

When you need to correct a misbehavior, always praise your dog as soon as he does the right thing. Show him, if necessary. For example, suppose your puppy jumps up on you when you come home. The limited approach is that you put your knee in his chest or pull down on his collar, saying "Off." With repetition, he'll learn to stop jumping up on you. But if you also praise the animal enthusiastically as soon as his front feet hit the ground, then give a treat, he will be even more interested in playing the learning game. He may jump up on you again, just to get the treat once more. Again, quickly correct the dog and praise him the instant he's back on the floor. After a few times, praise him even when he is "off," but hold back the treat. Tell him to "Sit." Show him how to do it if he doesn't know or is too excited, then give him the treat as soon as he even comes close to getting it right.

Now your dog is really eager to figure this thing out. As he keeps trying, you keep showing him which action has bad consequences and which action has good consequences. If your pet starts to think he's supposed to run up, jump on you, and then sit, you'll have to modify the correction to get the "jump up" part out. Eventually the concept will click: "Maximum pleasure comes if I run up and sit." By the time the situation arises again, he may have forgotten how it works, but it will soon come back to him.

It takes many repetitions to teach a dog certain behaviors. That's why showing him what to do and rewarding him when he does it works so much better than merely correcting the pup for misbehavior. When a dog just gets a correction, he usually tries to figure it out for just a short while, and then he goes elsewhere. If he's forced to stay, he'll stop paying attention. Your dog will stick with you in learning if you make the instruction fun, so that every misbehavior becomes an enjoyable opportunity to learn what is expected. Not only will the pup get it right, but it will be ingrained.

Responses to certain commands are fairly easy to teach once you get into the right mode: Watch, Sit, Stay, Down, Off (no jumping), Wait, Let's Go (walking on a loose leash), Gentle (no biting), and simple tricks like Roll Over.

For example, to teach a dog how to walk on a leash without pulling you, first teach him to place his primary attention on you (the "Watch" game described above—that puts the focus of attention on you). Put him on a leash. Using a pleasant tone, tell the dog, "Rover, watch!" Then say, "Let's go" or "Close" and start walking. Whenever he steps in front of you, focuses his attention elsewhere, or pulls away on the leash, repeat the command "Stay close" or "Let's go." As soon as he moves toward you and slacks up on the leash, offer profuse praise and/or a treat. Head off again promptly. If he doesn't respond to the command, give a quick correction with the leash and change the direction you're walking to get his attention. Repeat these steps each time he pulls on the leash. He'll soon learn that a loose leash when walking is a great idea. It can take some high energy and quick reactions on your part to promote this response at first, but future years of relaxed walks with your dog are well worth it.

Similarly, you can use a reward to train your dog to come when called. Holding a treat that he loves in your hand, tell him, "Look, here's a treat!" While the pup is running to get it, tell him, "Come!" Reward him with the treat and plenty of praise. After several weeks of repetition, he'll associate the word "come" with good things, and you'll need to use the reward only occasionally to keep his interest up. Don't, however, be too eager to test out his understanding of "come" in challenging situations. It may take months of practice before he knows "come" well enough to come when there are strong temptations close by (like another dog to investigate).

There are many resources available to help you with additional specifics of training certain behaviors. Visit www.drpitcairn.com for several resources I recommend.

ADDITIONAL TIPS FOR TRAINING

Bearing in mind what I have already said, here are some related tips to help you get started or to get a fresh start with the pet you already have. Most of these apply to cats as well as to dogs.

Remember that all animals learn by association. In attempting to understand the world around them, dogs build associations. Jumping on the couch is followed closely by a feeling of soft comfort, so an association is built between jumping on the couch and feeling good.

Your animal is constantly learning. The couch consistently rewards his jumping on it with softness and comfort, which encourages more jumping (unless you give another message even more consistently). If your dog runs toward an open door and gets bumped on the nose as it closes, he'll be less likely to try that again.

Be careful about what you teach your animal unintentionally. Our pets learn from all their interactions with us, not just the ones we think of as training. When your nervous dog barks fearfully at something and you pet him to calm him down, you have just unintentionally told him, "Good dog, that was a good response to that situation." Do you want your dog to respond that way all the time? If not, you must tell him so in some other way.

Be the Teacher

Teach your pet that you're worth learning from. At first your dog will listen to you because your voice is new and interesting. But if you don't capitalize on that initial interest and consistently reinforce his paying attention to you, don't be surprised if your dog starts to tune you out unless you raise your voice or take strong action.

Make it real. Take pleasure in your dog and your role as his teacher and leader. You can't fake it for long. Your dog provides an excellent excuse for you to be enthusiastic, silly, playful, and creative. Using treats helps to pique a dog's interest in new things, but unless you link your praise and enthusiasm with this initial motivation, he'll end up responding to food but not to you.

Be clear about what you want and show him exactly what it takes to be a "good dog" in your eyes. You don't want your dog to rush up to visitors and bark at them, but what do you want him to do? A dog will find it much easier to learn "When the doorbell rings, I go and sit quietly on my bed" than the vague concept "I can do anything but rush up at people and bark too many times." The simpler and more consistent the association, the more likely it is to build. Doorbell-bed-sit is much easier than "Anything but . . ."

Put a beginning and an end on your requests. Called a "release," this important dog training idea is often neglected in practice. When you teach your dog to stay, watch, or heel, teach him that your command continues till you say it's over by using a releasing word like "okay." This signals that he now may get up or look away or stop heeling. If you let a command end without a release, he learns that you're in charge of when things start, but he can decide when they end.

Have high expectations of your dog, but be sure they're reasonable ones. Do expect your pet to listen to you the first time you make a request that he has learned thoroughly. Correct, don't punish, if he doesn't. But don't expect him to make judgment calls. If he's allowed on the couch at home, don't get mad at him if he jumps on the couch at your in-laws'.

Use gentle training aids. There are new halters for dogs that can be especially helpful for gently gaining control. Individualize your training to suit your dog's temperament. Breeds and individual dogs differ widely in their interest in and responses to training and handling. Is your dog a timid Sheltie or a gregarious Lab? Adapt the intensity and timing of your corrections and praise accordingly. Terriers require lightening-quick responses. Hounds welcome extra enthusiasm. Notice what kind of activity your dog especially loves, such as playing ball or going for a walk, and use that as a reward.

Use repeated cues to help get your point across. To praise your dog, speak in a varied and interesting voice, petting him and showing your affection. To discourage undesired behavior, give timely corrections with a leash and use a no-nonsense tone of voice.

Use proper timing. Always correct your dog *while* he is misbehaving, never after the fact, while he is partially behaving well. He will associate your correction or your praise with what he did a half-second ago, not with what he did or thought before that. For instance, if you scold him as he's taking his sweet time ambling over to you after you've called him, he won't know that you're unhappy about his slowness, he'll just think it's a bad idea to come at all.

Think of training your pet as an exercise in cross-cultural communication. We are a highly verbal species, but dogs are not. You are helping your pet understand the language of the dominant culture (human). To do so, you must try to become at least a little bilingual, taking the time to learn dog (or cat) culture. You may sometimes feel more comfortable interpreting your pet's behavior in human terms than in trying to grasp the perspective of another species. But it will be easier to get past that obstacle if you embrace the challenge of showing your pet how to fit into this world successfully.

Be patient with yourself. You're learning something new, too. Building a solid relationship with your pet is a great investment, and it does take plenty of time and energy. You may feel awkward as you ease into the task. It can be emotionally challenging at times to be firm, patient, and clear, or to keep from venting your anger at your pet's mistakes.

Hold on to the deeper parts of your connection with your pet. Don't let your leader role be an obstacle to your companionship. You're not dominating or taking advantage of your dog; you're showing you care enough about him to learn a way to interact that makes his life happier and more successful.

PROBLEM BEHAVIORS IN DOGS: BARKING

Many canine problem behaviors—such as excessive barking, biting, destructiveness, chasing, and other aggressive actions—are beyond simple training techniques. Here's where the whole-relationship, whole-environment approach outlined earlier in this chapter is really crucial. Sometimes a simple change will solve a problem. Bringing your dog inside at night may stop his barking. But often, undesirable behaviors are a normal canine response to a confusing environment. Are you giving mixed or unintended messages? Are your pet's important emotional needs being met? Deal with the problem head on as soon as you can. Otherwise, it can become a time bomb that explodes into serious consequences.

A barking dog is one of the most common neighbor complaints. Just as a considerate person will not play music at full volume or subject the sensitive ears of a pet to loud noise, a pet should not be allowed to make noise that bothers people. Constant barking can drive anyone mad.

If a dog is not well-trained and is barking from aggression or anxiety, it's hard to get him to stop. It's even more difficult as the intensity and emotion of the barking escalates. Remember, yelling at a barking dog is like barking back at him. You may stop him that way for the moment by intimidating him, but the barking problem will persist.

Many people have found that a loud but *different* sound will stop dogs from barking. Examples are rattling a can with small stones or marbles in it, or shaking a ring of keys or throwing it on the floor. The shock of this different sound will stop the dog, breaking his concentration. It is a good training aid. Once he is quiet, reward the dog with praise.

You probably want your dog to bark when visitors or possible intruders arrive on your property, and then to stop barking when assured that things are fine. Dogs can learn to do this, but you'll need to start the training for this early. When unusual noises occur or when strangers approach the house, you can praise your dog for giving two or three warning barks. However, he will also need to know a command like "Quiet," so when you tell him to stop barking, he understands what you expect. You can't wait until the problem situation arises to work on this if you expect results. You must lay the groundwork by setting up situations that allow your dog to learn "Bark" and "Quiet" under relaxed circumstances, not under pressure when a real visitor arrives. If your dog is accustomed to learning from you, this is not difficult. Even if he has already learned to bark nonstop, you can teach him to replace it with something better by commanding,

"Chew on your bone" or, "Go find your toy." Only when he knows you're in charge is he likely to let you handle the situation. If he's barking because he thinks that's what you want, and he has learned a command for "that's enough," then he'll probably stop when you tell him to be quiet.

It is an important point to make that some people actually approve of their dogs barking at *anyone* coming near—this reflects their own insecurity. Do you think your dog would know this? You bet he does. I can see, from my experience and hearing clients talk, that this is an aspect perhaps not adequately appreciated. There is no way that your dog is going to stop barking if you, internally, really approve of it. If you are having a lot of trouble getting your dog to stop barking, it is worth a little introspection to see if you *really* want this to stop. A change at this level may be needed.

ARE YOU THE BARKEE?

What if you are the victim of a barker? It does happen that you may have a neighbor that simply doesn't care, sad to say. If you can't work out this problem, one solution is an electronic device that is used to control the barking of a nuisance dog. They work like this: the sound of the dog bark triggers a loud ultrasonic sound back, loud enough to be uncomfortable to the dog but inaudible to human beings. They can be set to go off after a certain number of barks, so if your limit is 4 barks, then you set it that way and mount it on your home or fence in the direction of the barker. It doesn't take long for the dog to get tired of being out-shouted.

It's too bad we have to do things like this, but living close together brings these problems, when they occur, to the forefront of neighbor disagreements.

PREVENTING DOG BITES

Dog bites can be serious business. Every year a handful of Americans, mostly small children, are killed by family pets or neighbors' dogs. United States medical personnel treat at least a million dog bite cases annually, ranging from nips on the ankle to mutilation requiring stitches or reconstructive surgery. It's true that vicious bites come mostly from guard dogs and roaming dog packs; the majority of dog bites, however, come from animals known to their victims, dogs that have a reputation for being "nice." Your own child could be the victim of such a dog, perhaps even your own pet.

In my first year of practice, two of my patients were the cause of a child being killed. We knew these dogs to be trouble because of their behavior in our clinic, usually biting whoever would hold them, but the client did not take any action that we knew of to control her dogs. One morning, while she was babysitting and carrying someone else's child, she went out to stop her dogs from digging holes in the back yard. I will spare you the details, but it was unfortunate that she was carrying the child in her arms when she went out. It was a shock to all of us and

brought home to me the real dangers of the uncontrolled aggressive animal.

There are many causes of canine aggression. Problems can often be traced to an inconsistent leadership or an overly emotional home. Other factors that can lead a dog to bite are: too little exercise, violent treatment, teasing, failure to correct dogs that nip you in play, too much confinement, physical discomfort from aging or injury, poor breeding, and minimal human contact during puppyhood (more likely for dogs from "puppy mills").

THE VACCINE FACTOR

Chronic encephalitis underlies many canine behavior problems, including aggression. This condition is an inflammation of the brain and central nervous system in reaction to vaccines or due to an auto-immune disease (see "Vaccinations" on page 411). Over the years, I began to associate some of this aggressive behavior with bad results from rabies vaccinations, specifically. Dogs that were formerly pleasant would become suspicious, aggressive, impulsive, and destructive, often breaking out of their yards to wander—in a word, dangerous animals. These are symptoms of rabies disease, and though these dogs did not have rabies, it did appear that the vaccine had set off some of the same behaviors as the disease. I always cautioned people with dogs like this not to vaccinate them again, but the legal requirement for rabies can make this a difficult accomplishment. Many veterinarians now offer to take a blood sample to test for immunity to rabies (rabies titer), but not all counties will recognize this as legitimate.

PREVENTING AGGRESSION

You should prevent your dog from endangering strangers by keeping him inside or secured behind a fence, or else under your control on a leash. If your dog is left alone in a yard with a fence that a neighbor child can reach through, talk to local parents, urging them to make sure their children understand possible dangers. (If necessary, put up a BEWARE OF DOG sign.)

Watch for subtle warning signs of a problem and take them very seriously. Many people mistakenly deny that their dog poses a potential danger, either because they see it as an insult to the dog or themselves or because they don't know how to solve the problem. Their dog might have actually snarled or bit at someone, but they make excuses—he was startled or had his tail stepped on, for example. Such aggressive reactions tend to get worse, not better, especially in older pets. Take my word for it and correct this now before it causes some real harm. Think how you'd feel if you ignored the problem and a child was bitten.

Play it safe. The guidelines that follow should reduce the risk of dog bites from your own dog, as well as someone else's. Make sure your children understand and follow them.

First, learn these tips on how to avoid provoking a dog:

Don't disturb a dog while it's eating or sleeping. If your leadership with your own dog is clear, you should be able to take his food. But if there is any doubt, don't try.

Do not intrude upon the private territory of a restrained or confined dog. Neutral territory, like a park, is usually much safer for any interaction.

Never tease a dog by dangling food or toys over its head. A playful nip can easily get out of control.

Stop hugging or holding a pet that wants to be free. He may feel he has to fight (bite) to get away.

Teach children to avoid stray dogs completely. Also, it's dangerous to pet a strange dog on a leash unless you ask if it's safe. The dog might be a watchdog trained to attack— or just in a bad mood.

Do not scream and wave your hands around dogs. Children who do this when scared or excited can unintentionally provoke aggressive dogs.

Once you know how to avoid provoking a dog, it's also helpful to know how to mollify a dog that approaches you in a threatening manner. You can tell from a dog's body language whether he means serious business or just wants to engage in some rough-and-tumble play.

A friendly dog avoids direct eye contact, looks to the side, perhaps exposes his throat and even grins. He keeps his ears flat, tail tucked down, and body low. If his head is lower than his tail (think of bowing), but he is crouching, pouncing, or thrusting about, he's probably just playing and is not a threat.

Be on the lookout for these signs of a potentially dangerous dog: ears raised up and forward, teeth bared in a snarl, and hair raised on the shoulders and rump. Even more threatening signs: becoming stiff-legged, raising a front leg, urinating, growling, staring you in the eye, and slowly waving a high, arched tail. An animal that bites out of fear may send mixed messages, so read the whole animal carefully and avoid threatening any dog that acts wary of you. Unfortunately, some dogs attack without any of these warning signs. Some Shar-Peis, pit bulls, and Chows are especially notorious in this way, endangering even experienced animal handlers.

If a dog runs at you, stay calm. Turn partially sideways and speak in a soothing voice. Keep your head slightly lowered and your hands down. This conveys peaceable intentions. Do not face the dog head-on or stare it in the eye. Do not turn and run unless you are certain of reaching safety. The dog tends to see a running creature as escaping prey. Some veterinarians and animal handlers confound threatening animals they must approach by whistling softly (while turned away) or calling in a friendly tone.

If a dog chases you on your bike, slow down and speak soothingly. Get off your bike if you can, on the side away from the dog. Walk at an unhurried pace, without turning your back to the dog.

If a dog should bite you, stay calm. A scream may provoke the attacker further. Try to put an object (like a purse, newspaper, book, or jacket) near his mouth to give him something besides you to bite. Wash the wound with soap and water. Call your doctor for advice. Report the incident right away to the public health department and establish the dog's identity if you can.

When two dogs fight, get out of the way. I have seen many clients receive terrible injuries from trying to intervene in a dog fight. If you feel safe at a distance or behind a barrier, the best way to break up a fight is to turn a hose on both dogs.

"CONTROLLING" CATS

There's general agreement that dogs should not be allowed to wander (it's the law in many cities). But the attitude toward cats is somewhat different, leading some people to keep their cats indoors and others to let them out. Here are some of the main things to consider in making your decision.

Cats cause less harm to people or property outdoors. They mostly endanger themselves, each other (from accidents, dogs, cat fights, transmission of feline leukemia virus), and small wildlife. Most people welcome their natural tendency to kill mice, rats, and gophers.

If allowed outdoors, cats can't be confined by a fence and most cannot be walked on a leash. Unlike dogs, cats resist training. They come "as is." Their natural behavior is pretty much what you get.

They use gardens and children's sandboxes as litter boxes. This can be a considerable nuisance and even a public health problem. A cat afflicted with toxoplasmosis can pose a risk to a gardener who is pregnant and who could become infected with the organism via buried feces (see below).

Indoor life generally suits cats better than dogs. That's because cats are less active, less social, normally sleep more, and take readily to using a litter box. Some cats actually seem to prefer living indoors.

Many people who live in apartments, in congested urban areas, near busy roads, or in areas frequented by packs of dogs or coyotes keep their cats inside as a safety measure. With proper care, many cats live indoors contentedly, especially the more home-loving breeds—Korats, Persians, Bombays, Angoras, and Ragdolls. Be sure to offer an indoor cat plenty of attention, toys, and a nice shelf by a sunny, screened window. If you're away a lot, consider getting a second cat as company for the first. Persians, Himalayans, and Kashmirs tend to be most sociable and are least apt to fight with other cats.

Some cats have an instinctive love of the outdoors. As a group, outdoor cats are hardier, better hunters, and more active. These include shorthairs, Abyssinians, Somalis, and Maine Coon cats. While they can adapt to indoor life, especially with a good window spot or screened porch, they really prefer an occasional romp in a garden. If you live in a fairly safe neighborhood (low traffic, no aggressive animals on the loose, no neighboring houses full of sickly cats), I feel it's often wise to allow a cat some freedom. This choice may mean a shorter life (there is always the risk of injuries from traffic or from other animals), but it may be a more satisfying one for the cat.

If it seems too dangerous to let your cat roam outdoors, there are a couple of safer ways to give your cat a taste of nature. The first is to build a fully enclosed pen (called a cattery), which could be constructed to connect with a window that opens onto your backyard. (Avoid the use of preservative-treated wood, which can make cats sick.) The other option, which works for a few cats (especially the Siamese-type breeds), is to take your cat for an occasional walk on a leash and harness.

If you do allow your cat to wander outside at times, here are some guidelines:

❖ Spay or neuter your cat. This will reduce fights and spraying and address the pet overpopulation problem as well.

❖ Confine your cat at any sign of disease. It's especially important to keep your cat indoors and separate from other cats if it has a contagious disease.

❖ Teach your cat to come when called. Repeat her name often when you are playing together or feeding her. Ring a bell or whistle just before feeding her dinner. Call her frequently, offering a tidbit of her favorite food. Praise her and give her lots of affection when she responds. Soon she will associate pleasant things with coming when she's called, and she may begin to associate the bell or whistle with feeding time.

❖ Be sure your cat is wearing a collar and identification tag with your name and phone number on it. Soft leather or nylon collars are the most comfortable. To avoid the danger that she'll get her collar caught on something, fit your cat with the special quick-release type that automatically opens with sufficient pressure on the collar. Attach a bell to the collar to warn birds—the birds will thank you!

❖ It is safest for your cat to keep her in after the evening feeding. Cats are more apt to get into fights or get hit by cars at night.

❖ Invite your neighbors to let you know if your cat is causing problems for them. If you get such reports, take responsibility for your cat's behavior and do what's needed to rectify the situation.

❖ Be prepared to break up occasional cat fights. If you catch two felines staring each other down, a loud clap of the hands will usually cause one or both to back off. If the fur is already flying, splash water on the combatants.

CAT BEHAVIOR PROBLEMS

What's called good behavior in a cat varies greatly from household to household. If you allow your cat to sleep on your neck, wake you up at 4:00 A.M. for breakfast, and walk on the countertops, that's pretty much your business. It won't affect your neighbors.

It could, however, take its toll on you and your home. Most cat behavior problems veterinarians see involve inappropriate urination and defecation (for example, spraying or not using the litter box). Others involve aggression, usually toward other cats, but sometimes even to family members, excessive fearfulness or fussiness, and scratching furniture. Let's look at some of these.

Bear in mind how life looks from your cat's point of view. Like humans and dogs, most cats enjoy affection and attention, but their primary focus in life really revolves around having a comfortable, safe environment with food and a sunny place to sleep. Cats want to secure these things for themselves, and since you're the source of food, that means you, too.

In nature, most cats are loners and must fend for themselves in adult life. They must keep constant tabs on their world and make sure other cats don't intrude on their hunting range, which can only provide limited support of carnivores. They spend much of their lives watching and waiting, dozing, but keeping an eye out for passing prey (or predators). Cats need to know their territory well and all that's going on there. They like predictability. And they like cleanliness (smells are dead giveaways to prey).

THE GREAT LITTER BOX PROBLEM

Some of the most troublesome cat problems can be resolved if you take on a feline attitude. For example, when cats urinate and defecate outside the litter box, it can mean they are unhappy about something in the environment. It's a cat's way of expressing agitation, not a personal message to you. Inappropriate elimination may mean the litter box is not clean enough or the particular litter that's used is not to their liking. Some longhaired cats get upset because the dirty litter gets in their fur. Sometimes the cat is just reacting to a change of litter box location, which is best done in a gradual manner. Certain cats just seem to want a more vertical surface, a problem that may be solved by propping a second litter box on its side, inside the main horizontal one. One of my clients has solved this problem by setting up a piece of plexiglass at one side of the litter box (any rigid washable material would do). She then drapes a small terrycloth towel over it, which her cat seems to prefer to urinate on, and washes it frequently.

The other major cause of urinating or having bowel movements outside a box is that there may be something wrong physically. The cat can sense there is something not right and doesn't want to put the urine or stool where other cats can smell it and realize they are not well. Once the problem is corrected, the behavior returns to normal. It is always a good idea to look closely at the urine to see if there is a hint of blood or perhaps some gritty, gravelly stuff in it. Yes, you have to use your fingers to feel it. To see blood in urine, put a white paper on the bottom of the litter pan and just a little litter over it. You may be able to see the pinkish tinge contrasting with the white paper by

shaking the litter aside. Inappropriate elimination may signal chronic health problems, such as allergies.

If there are bowel movements outside the box, look to see if the stool is normally formed or has mucus or blood around it. Some stools are hard at the beginning and soft at the end, which is not quite normal. Any of these things can indicate intestinal irritation, possibly from worms, allergies, infection, or immune problems.

If your cat is spraying (the way cats mark territory), it can mean that he is disturbed by recent adjustments in his life and surroundings—a new person in the household, a more anxious attitude from you because of stress, or a move to a new home. A very common cause of agitation can be the presence of a new cat, even if it's just in the neighborhood.

Once a cat has sprayed in a particular spot, he tends to keep doing it. Thoroughly cleaning the area will help, but often cats can smell the urine scent through any scrubbing you might do. It may help to finish off by applying mint tea or something that smells minty, as cats generally don't like that smell. Another thing you can do is to tape aluminum foil over the area for a while. That will prevent smelling the old urine and if they do spray again, it tends to splash the urine back at them.

Many other problems are a matter of proper training, and you can apply similar principles to those discussed for dogs. If you don't want your cat to jump on your counter, scratch your couch, get on your lap when you're at a table or a desk, bat at you when she's hungry, or wake you early in the morning, you can usually head off these problems if you nip them in the bud. It's best to decide on your limits from the beginning, then enforce them consistently. Say "No" and gently but firmly push her away, shove her off, or put her out for a while. Never yell at, scold, or strike your cat; it will frighten her and she will avoid you or your touch. If a situation seems to require serious discouragement, try a spray bottle. Cats can become afraid of the spray bottle, but not generally the one who holds it. Draping plastic over a couch or chair leg for a time will reduce its appeal, especially if you place a scratching post nearby.

"TRAINING" CATS

Act when she first starts the behavior, and, if you're consistent, the behavior will not build. If you let things slide, it can be very difficult to retrain a cat out of a bad habit. Unlike dogs, cats don't get as involved with you and your enthusiasm and praise, which makes cats much less interested in the training game.

It also helps to remember that both cats and dogs are gamblers. Research shows that if they are positively rewarded for a behavior as few as one time in 20 tries, they may continue the behavior. They're willing to gamble on the reward despite the long odds. This is what you're up against in trying to get a cat

to change its behavior. If you don't want kitty on the counter, but every once in a while when she gets up there she finds food, that jackpot will motivate her to try again at least another 15 or 20 times. On the other hand, negative consequences (being pushed away, told "No," squirted, finding an uncomfortable piece of plastic) often have to be much more consistent to condition a cat.

Because of this, your training efforts are even better spent in making sure your animal is never rewarded for undesirable behaviors. Keep food off the countertop. Don't pick your cat up to remove her from the counter, admonishing her sweetly and scratching her affectionately in the process. Avoid the temptation to say "Yes" now and then when you really should say "No."

Another effective technique is to channel your animal's behavior into a rewarding direction. Give her a treat whenever she earns it. Or consistently greet her with affection when she jumps on your lap in appropriate times and places, like when you're stretched out in your easy chair in the evening. Provide her with an appealing scratching post (see below) and some toys for pouncing. Most cats behave much better if you create suitable outlets for their energy.

Sometimes a cat trains itself into a bad habit and the "untraining" job falls to you. Be ready to call on any tool available to you—psychology and physiology included—to get the job done. One common problem that can take months to untrain is the cat who wakes you early in the morning to be fed. If you respond, the cat is likely to waken you earlier and earlier. The next thing you know, it's happening in the middle of the night.

You can thwart this problem early on if you start a new habit of feeding your cat later in the morning and you stick to it. Her body clock, however, is still used to the early habit, and even if you stop feeding your cat until later, she'll be restless and anxious from hunger. To reverse the trend, you'll have to move the feeding time, gradually later and later, over a period of weeks or even months, until you reach the time that works best for you.

SCRATCHING AND BITING: WHAT TO DO

A common training problem with cats is teaching them not to scratch your carpets, drapes, and furniture. The best solution is to "reward" your cat for appropriate behavior by providing a scratching post that surpasses anything else. Pet stores carry scratching posts or you can order an excellent one by mail. The best ones are covered in natural sisal rope, which many cats enjoy scratching. Rub a little powdered catnip into it occasionally to make it irresistible.

To make your own post, nail an untreated 4 × 4 (2 to 3 feet tall) to a base of half-inch plywood about 16 inches square. Then wrap the post with sisal rope or a piece of carpeting turned inside out to expose the rough side (posts with soft coverings are not sufficiently attractive to most cats). For maximum

stability, lean the post up against the corner of a room or tilt it on its side. Make sure the post is secure. If it falls over and frightens your kitty even once, it may be enough to make her avoid the post altogether.

If your cat needs instructions on the use of a scratching post, simply lay it sideways and place her on top of the post. Scratch the post yourself with one hand and use the other to firmly stroke her neck and back (that will stimulate the urge to scratch). Don't try to push your cat's feet against the post, as cats will resist force. If your pet is still inclined to scratch at the furniture or drapes at times, move the drapes or the chair slightly and put the post in that spot. Move the post gradually and put the furniture back when the cat is actually using the post instead. You may need to cover a corner of the couch or roll up the drapes temporarily until your cat makes the transition. It's often good to position the scratching post near the spot where your cat sleeps, since many cats like to stretch and scratch on waking from a nap.

Declawing your cat is *not* a suitable solution to scratching problems. It is a painful and difficult operation that many veterinarians refuse to do. In fact, it's the equivalent of removing the first joint of all your fingers. It can impair a cat's balance, weaken it (from muscular disuse), and cause a cat to feel nervous and defenseless. The resulting stress can lower your pet's immunity to disease and make it more likely to be a biter.

It is helpful to trim your cat's claws. Because they are shaped like a scythe, their very tip is the part that does the most damage. A cat will slide that curved tip behind a loop of upholstery fabric and pull its foot straight back—snapping the loop. If the cat makes a practice of this, your sofa will soon look like it needs a shave.

The nail tip is also the part that so easily punctures the skin. It can be removed with ordinary nail clippers. (Be sure to clip only the *very tip*, or you might hurt the cat.) Wait until your cat is relaxed, perhaps taking a nap in your lap. To extend a claw for clipping, press your index finger on the bottom of her foot while pressing with your thumb just behind the base of the nail at the top of the foot. Press *gently*. The claw will slide from its sheath so that you can get at it with the clippers you're holding in your other hand. You may get to cut only two or three claws in a single sitting, but you can try again later.

Here's another piece of advice about claws. Never let a cat or kitten scratch your bare hands—even in play. If you do, the animal will think it's okay to bite and scratch you and won't understand that he can hurt you. So when playing games like "pounce on the prey," use a toy or a piece of cord. Save your hands for stroking and holding.

If your cat has developed a habit of clawing or biting at you, you can break it fairly easily by consistently following a method described by Anitra Frazier in her book *The New Natural Cat*. If the claws are in you, relax and calmly disengage them by first pushing the feet a bit forward. To get out of a bite grip, relax and press your arm or hand

toward the teeth (which confuses the cat). Then put the cat away from you with a gentle but firm message of disapproval and disappointment. To underline the message, ignore her for several minutes. Don't even look at her. A few repetitions are usually all that is needed for a cat to learn that if she wants to play with you, it's not acceptable to claw and bite. Thereafter, she will respect your wishes.

To avoid more serious contact with cat teeth and claws, which are quite sharp, never try to hold on to a cat that wants to be free (unless you are trained in handling cats properly). Teach children this point, too. If

THE FIRST VET VISIT

Regardless of whether you let your cat outdoors or keep it inside, you need to teach it to accept a carrier. A few days before your cat's first visit to the veterinarian, place an open carrier out in the house. Encourage the cat to view it as a fun place to explore. To entice him further, place a tidbit inside. Without this familiarity, you could have a battle on your hands trying to shove a resistant cat into a cage on your way out the door to the vet's.

you must restrain a cat to give it medicine, wrap it firmly in a towel or blanket. To transport it, use an animal carrier. (I know of more than one serious accident caused by a frightened cat bounding loose in a moving car.)

CAT AGGRESSION

A few cats have a more deep-seated problem with aggression. I'm talking about cats that are completely, violently intolerant of all other cats, even their own adult offspring. And once in a while, I've treated cats that are pretty nasty to their caretakers, too. Over the years I've come to the conclusion that many of these problems are more rooted in the constitutional makeup of certain cats than in situations.

Chronic disease can also play a role in such behavior problems. In many cases, careful, individualized homeopathic treatment has helped. Cats that are unusually timid or aloof for no apparent reason have also responded to this treatment.

GOOD SANITATION: A BASIC NECESSITY

Sanitation is an important issue for both dogs and cats; it's right at the top of the initial training agenda.

For puppies, the most painless housebreaking takes advantage of two things: a pup's natural cleanliness and the regularity of his bowels. Well-socialized pups go outside of their own den to soil. It's not reasonable to expect a young puppy to understand that your whole house is his den.

When mistakes are made in the house, a pup has usually run into another room (outside the den to him) to go. So set your pup up for success. For his first few weeks, confine him to a crate or very small room in the house at all times when you're not directly involved in playing with or watching him. Feed him on a regular schedule and take him outside a few minutes after each meal and nap. When you put him outside to relieve himself, go with him to make sure that he goes. Praise him when he does. Afterward, let him run around a bit indoors. Then put him back in his crate or room to sleep. Gradually, expand the size of the area you designate as his den—include uncarpeted areas first, just in case he makes a mistake. If he does, don't scare him and don't punish him, just take him outside. Then back up your training a day or two and shrink the size of the area he can roam in until he's doing well again.

If you have to work all day, you may need to have someone else come in to let him out, or else train him to use papers when he's young and then switch to outside only as he becomes able to hold his bowels longer. Don't expect a young pup to be able to go more than four to six hours at most without a pit stop. Do keep him confined to a small area while you're gone. For a young pup, this space should be at least the size of a large dog's kennel and no bigger than a very small kitchen.

Animals instinctively seek to relieve

themselves away from their own living area, which is why the neighbor's yard is often a favorite bathroom. You can wean a dog away from this habit and save a major part of your own lawn, too, by teaching him to use just a certain portion of your yard, such as behind the garage or near certain shrubs. Place some of his stool there and take him to that spot when it's time for him to answer nature's call. When he uses the spot, praise him enthusiastically. Placing some kind of low border around the area can help to make its limits clear to him and to friends and family.

When you're walking your dog on stormy days or in cold weather, you naturally want him to do his business A.S.A.P. Some people choose to associate command words like "hurry up" with the act of defecating or urinating. This may sound funny, but it can be very useful. On cold or rainy days, this command can actually encourage your dog to go.

To discourage defecation in certain areas of the yard or garden, promptly remove droppings from areas you don't want the dog to soil. If necessary, spray those areas with a dog-repelling deodorant made with natural ingredients like citron, lemon oil, eucalyptol, geranium oil, capsicum, and oil of lavender.

Dispose of accumulated pet wastes regularly. Though I don't recommend composting them because temperatures may not be high enough (140°F) to kill harmful organisms, you might consider using a small mechanism made especially for dog and cat wastes, known as the Doggie Dooley. Buried in the ground, it works like a small septic tank.

Both the danger of spreading disease and simple common decency dictate that you clean up any solid wastes your dog may deposit on someone's lawn or in public places. Various types of scoop gadgets make it convenient to pick up and dispose of droppings. Though it may not be the most pleasing chore in the world, it certainly won't be any better for the person down the street. If you think of animal wastes in the same category as human wastes, it makes your responsibility for cleanup much clearer.

For cats it's usually a simpler matter. Just provide a full, clean box of litter. Cats prefer litter of a sandy, granular type. Keep it clean and keep it in the same place. Too much odor or too much change could put your cat off. Keep a clean litter box in your yard as well as in your house, and the cat will have something else to use besides Mrs. Jones's flowerbed. Keep the boxes out of reach of toddlers and clean them regularly. Wash your hands well afterward, because cat feces can carry potentially harmful organisms. (This is a good practice to follow after a dog cleanup, too.)

UNDERSTANDING AND PREVENTING ANIMAL/HUMAN DISEASES

A vital aspect of responsible pet care is working to prevent the spread of disease from pets to humans. Many public health authorities see these diseases as a serious problem. The most effective measure is prevention—through careful sanitation practices, avoiding bites and scratches, and keeping your pet healthy. Reasonable precautions will minimize the spread of disease.

Most diseases picked up from cats and dogs fall into three groups, depending on their means of transmission—through feces or urine, skin and hair contact, or bites and scratches.. Let's consider each group individually.

DISEASES TRANSMITTED IN WASTES

Roundworms (*Toxocara canis, Toxocara cati*): The infectious form of these worms is their eggs, which can incubate for several weeks in the ground where an animal has defecated. If a child plays there and puts his dirty hands in his mouth, he can swallow the eggs and become infected. Thus, migrating animal roundworms are most often seen in toddlers. The disease is only rarely fatal. More commonly, it is mild and hardly noticeable at all in adults. Children are more likely to be contaminated and will have more problems than adults. When children swallow these common parasites carried by dogs and cats, the parasites often migrate through the body tissues and cause damage, including liver enlargement and fever. These symptoms may last as long as a year. In some

children the larvae may enter the eye and cause inflammation. This is serious business, since surgeons have been known to mistake the eye lesions for early cancer and unnecessarily remove an eye. There is also some research that suggests that some children may become allergic to the migrating parasites, which complicates the situation.

Hookworms (*Cutaneous larva migrans*): These parasites are similar to roundworms, but they enter the body differently. Instead of being swallowed, the hookworm larvae directly penetrate the skin where it comes in contact with feces-contaminated soil or sand—usually the bare feet. Though the parasites try their best, they are not really suited to living in people and eventually die after moving several inches under the skin. The inflammation is called creeping eruption and eventually ends after several weeks or months. In the United States, it is most often seen in the South.

Leptospirosis: Swimming in or otherwise coming in contact with water contaminated with animal urine is the way this serious bacterial disease is usually acquired. Many animals can carry it, particularly rats. Pets can catch it by drinking contaminated surface water (or licking it off their fur) or by eating food on which rats have urinated. In humans the disease is similar to flu, with fever, headache, chills, tiredness, vomiting, and muscular aches. In addition, the eyes and the membranes covering the brain and spinal cord can be inflamed. In some cases, the liver and the kidneys are damaged. Few die from this condition, but it can make you miserably sick for two or three weeks.

Tapeworms (*Dipylidium caninum*): Tapeworms are a different type of worm, in that they cannot directly infect people with their eggs. Rather they go into some other creature first, end up in the muscle tissue, and then infect the human intestines when these animals are eaten.

Pets can pick up the common tapeworm by biting at and swallowing fleas or eating gophers, which can carry the infectious form. Children can get tapeworms either by ingesting fleas while nuzzling the pet's fur or being licked on the mouth by an animal with a flea on its tongue. Human infestation is rare, however, compared with infestations of other types of tapeworms we can get from eating undercooked, infected beef or pork.

Toxoplasmosis: Many people are exposed to this infectious disease through ordinary activity and develop a natural resistance to it. On rare occasions, however, it has killed adults. More often, it causes birth deformities in children born to women who were infected during pregnancy and had not previously developed immunity. It can be picked up by contact with feces from an infected cat or contact with contaminated soil. Also, the disease can come from eating raw or undercooked meat. Because the fetus of a pregnant woman can be very vulnerable, this problem is covered in detail under "Toxoplasmosis" on page 405.

Prevention of Diseases Transmitted in Wastes

Besides cleaning up your pet's droppings, there are a few simple precautions you should take and should teach to your children.

❖ Wash your hands after contact with soil where an animal may have relieved itself.

❖ Avoid going barefoot in areas where an animal may have relieved itself, particularly in warm climates, where hookworms flourish.

❖ Remind children to wash their hands before eating and not to put their hands in their mouths while playing with animals or on potentially contaminated grounds. Teach them all other precautions as well.

❖ If your dog has gone swimming or wading in a pond or creek that could be harboring leptospirosis, give it a bath.

DISEASES FROM SKIN AND HAIR CONTACT

Fleas: Though fleas prefer feasting on pets, they will make a meal of people if the opportunity appears. Flea infestation is often at its worst in a house that was formerly occupied by an animal and then left vacant. Many young fleas, recently hatched, will be eager to eat.

Ringworm (*Microsporum canis*): Caused by a fungus that eats skin and hair, ringworm often shows up in humans as scaly, red areas.

As the organism grows, it spreads outward in a circle, much as a ripple forms when a stone is dropped into a pond. In dogs, affected areas tend to be hairless, thickened, scabby, and irritated. They are typically disk-shaped and about an inch or more in diameter. But most ringworm transmitted by pets comes from cats, who tend to show very few observable symptoms (dogs can also carry the spores without showing visible signs). An infected cat may have hairless gray areas without inflammation or scabbing. Generally, the animal doesn't itch either.

Children are more susceptible to ringworm than adults, though humans can get it at any age. The disease is on the rise and is now the most common fungal disease reported.

Rocky Mountain spotted fever (*Rickettsia rickettsii*): While usually not fatal to humans (it is commonly treated with antibiotics), this infectious disease can still make a person mighty sick. Starting suddenly with fever, headache, chills, and reddening of the eyes, it may last several weeks. In the eastern and central United States the responsible organisms are carried by the dog tick (*Dermacentor variabilis*). In the west they are borne by the wood tick (*Dermacentor andersoni*). Incidence of the disease has risen sharply in North America in recent times.

The most common means of contracting spotted fever is from a direct bite by an infected tick. Pets can readily transport these infected ticks into a house or yard, where people can later be bitten. (All the tick's young will carry the infection, too.) It also is possible to become infected while pulling a tick off your animal if the tick's body is crushed or its feces released. So it's safest to wear gloves when you remove ticks.

Scabies (*Sarcoptic mange*): In dogs, this form of mange is less common than the demodectic ("red") mange. It does, however, occur in both dogs and cats and causes itching, irritation, and thickening of the skin. People can be infected by contact—usually from holding an afflicted animal close. The result is intense itching, especially at night, and in those areas that were most in contact with the animal (like the inside of the arm, the waist, chest, hands, and wrists). Though the animal mange mite can live in human skin, it cannot reproduce there. So eventually the problem ends on its own—lasting just a few weeks at most. If, however, reinfection occurs, then of course it can keep happening. Note that we humans have our own brand of scabies mites, which can cause us prolonged aggravation and is not self-limited like the dog scabies.

Prevention of Diseases from Skin and Hair Contact

A healthy animal is less likely to harbor parasites like fleas, ringworm, and mange mites. Therefore, proper nutrition and overall care are important preventive measures for both of you. In addition, frequent grooming and inspection, along with herbal repellents, will catch most of these problems early. Be especially attentive when your animal has been in contact with other pets or is under stress from disease, emotional upset, or a stay in a kennel.

Nuzzling and hugging animals can be great fun, but if you like to do a lot of this, you take your chances whether your animal may carry these diseases. Wash your hands after prolonged contact. Minimize contact with animals that may have ringworm. Also, since stray hairs can carry active ringworm spores, too, keep the house clear of hairs if your animal is infected (or keep your pet confined outside in a pen or fenced yard until the problem is cured).

Avoid or minimize bodily contact with an animal with mange and do not let it sleep on your bedding, clothes, or towels.

DISEASES CAUSED BY BITES AND SCRATCHES

Cat scratch fever: After being scratched by a cat, some people develop a fever, malaise, and enlarged lymph nodes near the area of the scratch or bite. These symptoms usually occur one to two weeks after the injury. The condition is not serious or fatal, but it is uncomfortable and may be followed by complications. Nobody knows what causes it. A cat bite infected with the bacteria *Pasteurella multocida* looks similar and should be differentiated from cat scratch fever by your doctor.

Rabies: Everyone has heard of this disease and of its high fatality rate (close to 100 percent once the clinical signs appear). Caused by a virus transmitted through the saliva of a biting animal, it travels from the bite area to the brain in a matter of days or weeks. There it causes severe tissue inflammation, with symptoms such as convulsions, hysteria, and frothing at the mouth. The most common sources of human exposure are skunks, foxes, raccoons, bats, and dogs, though theoretically almost any warm-blooded creature can acquire the disease and transmit it.

The animal with clinical signs of rabies shows peculiar or erratic behavior. For instance, a wild animal may uncharacteristically approach humans or be sluggish and unable to dodge a speeding car. A dog may show evidence of a personality change—acting friendlier than usual or hiding in dark places. Eventually, a staggering, glazed-eyed, aggressive condition may develop—the stereotype of the rabid dog.

Prevention of Diseases Caused by Bites and Scratches

The best way to prevent cat scratch fever is to be cautious when handling cats, as suggested earlier. Cats, however, are not always predictable and might turn on you suddenly if they become frightened or ill. After a scratch or bite, encourage the wound to bleed for a minute or two to help flush it out. Then wash the wound well with soap and water and soak it in a hot Epsom salts solution.

Alternate the hot soak with a soak in some cold (not ice) tap water, going back and forth several times to stimulate blood flow and immune response. Do your final soak in the cool water.

Stray dogs or wild animals should never be handled unless you have special training or equipment to do so safely. If you see a dog or wild animal with symptoms resembling rabies, get away from it and phone an animal control agency or the police as soon as possible. One complication is that a dog can transmit rabies through a bite (or saliva-contaminated scratch) three days *before* any clinical signs appear. So if you're bitten by any stray or wild animal, get help, and try to follow the animal to learn where it lives so it can be caught and tested. The testing procedure for dogs begins by putting a live animal in quarantine for ten days, during which time it is observed by a veterinarian. If rabies symptoms develop, the animal is killed and the brain sent to a lab for verification. If necessary, you might try to catch a small creature like a bat or a skunk, using a bucket, tub, or dog carrier. If you must kill it, don't injure the head.

If you are bitten by an animal that's a stranger to you or by one you suspect might be rabid, follow the same procedure as for cat scratches and bites. Also, report to your doctor as soon as possible. Your chances of getting rabies are really very low. About 35,000 Americans require rabies post-exposure treatment annually. Only about 30 percent of untreated people bitten by animals known to be rabid actually get the disease. Dog bites account for less than 5 percent of the rabies cases in North America.

THE PET POPULATION PROBLEM

Finally, one of the most important ways to be a responsible pet caretaker is to ensure that your animal does not add to the burgeoning pet overpopulation problem.

Spaying your female pet will keep packs of males from invading your property every time she comes into heat, and neutering a male will reduce his desire to roam and fight, which your neighbors will appreciate. Moreover, that one simple procedure in a cat will spare you years of trying to remove the offensive odor of tomcat urine from your house.

Why do people allow their pets to breed when there are already too many being born? They believe:

❖ Their children should witness the process.
❖ They can find homes for the litter, or they assume the local humane society will do the job.
❖ A spay or neuter operation costs money, can be painful, and holds possible adverse health effects if all does not go smoothly.
❖ Neutering a pet is unnatural and takes away a pet's true self.
❖ It's easy and fun to make a little extra cash selling purebred offspring.

Yet when you consider the vast suffering that befalls unwanted, homeless dogs and cats, these reasons have little merit. For example, it is surely more important to teach children responsibility to animals in general than it is to bring more surplus pets into the world as "an experience" for the children. Humane societies cannot find homes for most of the animals they receive. And even if you could find homes for the animals you breed, how many pets will be kept? And how many offspring will *they* produce? If she and her descendants are allowed to breed freely, one female dog can be the source of thousands of animals in just five or six years. Cats are even more prolific. And assuming you are able to find good, responsible people to care for each puppy or kitten, consider that these people might otherwise have adopted animals that were destroyed for want of homes.

Anyone who can afford to provide decent care for a pet can also afford a spay or neuter operation. Many towns and cities have low-cost clinics. Ask your local humane society for information about these. The operation is painless, performed under anesthesia by skilled veterinarians, and involves very little risk. It not only prevents unwanted births and discourages straying and fighting among the animals, but it prevents health problems like cancers of the reproductive organs, stress and complications from breeding, and abscesses and injuries from mating. Contrary to popular belief, neutered pets do not automatically get fat. Because they may be less active, they may burn less energy. So the solution is just to feed less.

If you are extremely conscientious, the old-fashioned methods of animal birth control, the door and the leash, may work for a female dog. Lock her up securely inside your house during the two- to three-week period of her heat. Be prepared for the fact that male dogs for miles around are likely to gather on your doorstep.

Confinement does not work for cats. They come into heat more often than dogs, they can be very vocal, and they are very persistent in trying to get out. They almost inevitably succeed at some point. You should also know that an unspayed female cat prevented from mating may develop hormonal imbalances from complications, cystic ovaries, or uterine problems caused by not completing the reproductive cycle.

The idea that keeping pets reproductively intact is best because it's "more natural" is very short-sighted. We don't live in a natural world. These are not animals out in the woods hunting for their food and being hunted, falling victim to disease and hardship, living as an integral part of a balanced ecosystem and being governed by a complex interplay of hormones, social systems, and territories that regulate their breeding. These are descendants of wild animals living in close company with us and with thousands of other animals in an entirely unnatural and overpopulated environment. A male wolf in the wild is exposed to the scent of females in heat only a few weeks out of the year. An intact male dog is bombarded by the same scent much more frequently. That's a long way from being natural or fair.

As for the profit incentive behind breeding pets, not only do such ventures often yield little financial return, but repeated breeding can cost you money if the female's health breaks down. Most puppy mills, which add 2.5 million puppies to the glut of dogs born annually in this country, are actually small home businesses run by amateurs whose ignorance and carelessness in breeding is a direct cause of much of the rise in congenital and health problems in many breeds. Surely there must be a better way to earn a buck.

I can understand and appreciate people's desire to see their pets bear young. But, unlike most people, I have had direct exposure to the scope and everyday reality of the pet overpopulation problem. I worked for sev-eral years at a humane society clinic associated with an animal shelter, where I saw first-hand the tragic results of uncontrolled breeding. One walk into the refrigerator containing barrels of euthanized animals is enough to convince anyone of the needless suffering involved in uncontrolled animal reproduction.

The sheer numbers are staggering. Estimates are that 5 to 12 million animals are euthanized each year in U.S. shelters. The reality—in flesh and blood and not just as abstract statistics—is devastating. Each one looks at you, and each is capable of much love and potential. And most never leave that shelter alive. When everyone takes responsibility for pet overpopulation, we'll see an end to the suffering it causes. It's best for society and best for the animals.

CHAPTER 12

LIFESTYLES: TIPS
FOR SPECIAL SITUATIONS

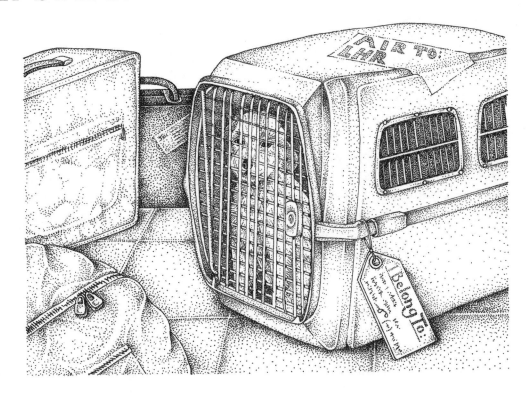

Every now and then you read the true-life story of a remarkable pet. Perhaps it's about a cat that survives without food or water for a month after being trapped accidentally in a transcontinental delivery truck. Or a tale of the family dog that gets lost during a cross-country move and somehow tracks down its home hundreds of miles away. Such stories of resourcefulness and devotion are both inspiring and amazing.

But all too often such incidents end badly. Everyday life poses special challenges for animals living in a human world. For example, there is the emotional stress of travel and moving, the ease with which an animal can get lost in our busy cities, the dangers common household gadgets hold for our four-footed housemates. With a little planning, we can make the going smoother for all involved.

VACATIONS AND TRAVEL

For many of us, travel is part of day-to-day living. Sometimes it's just an overnight business or a weekend fun trip; sometimes it's a month-long vacation. Whether your four-legged friend travels with you or stays at home, you need to give some thought to your pet's special needs at such times.

If you and your pet have a close bond, the animal could grieve during an absence that lasts several days or more, unaware that you plan to return soon. A long absence can sometimes lead to such an emotional upset—particularly for a dog—that your pet remains depressed for weeks after your return. In fact, it could spell the beginning of the end for a weak animal.

A deeply concerned woman wrote me this letter.

My dog, Lassie, will soon be 18. We've had family troubles including several deaths in these last two years, and now my husband and I are planning a ten-day cruise which we believe is necessary for our own health. But we will have to leave Lassie in a kennel. I read in a book that if you leave an old dog in a kennel, it might not last until you return. This has troubled us terribly, as Lassie

is so accustomed to our care. Do you have any suggestions on how to care for our wonderful mutt, who has served us so well?

I sympathize with their plight. Not only would Lassie miss her human companions at a kennel, but she would be confined in a strange and perhaps uncomfortable run or cage, surrounded by barking and whining animals that might disturb her rest. She might not accept the unfamiliar food offered her; while in that stressed and weakened state, she could be susceptible to such diseases as "kennel cough," a contagious respiratory ailment (common where groups of dogs are housed). Even some younger animals do poorly during kennel stays. On the other hand, people do need to get away sometimes, and they can't always take a pet along.

Though it would not be my first choice, many an animal may be successfully placed in a kennel, if it is responsibly run and if the stay is not too long. You should definitely check out the facility in person before committing your animal to it. Look for such things as the degree of privacy provided (each animal should have a place to rest quietly), the sanitation, the noise level, and the availability of sunlight, exercise space, fresh air, water, decent food, and medical care, should the need arise.

One of the greatest drawbacks of a kennel stay is the standard requirement that the dog or cat be vaccinated beforehand. Vaccines are often over-used and can cause persistent health problems, especially in older animals. If your dog was vaccinated when young, there is no need to vaccinate again for the life of your animal (the exception is the schedule for rabies vaccination which, though likely not necessary that it be repeated so often, is controlled by community laws). Even though there is no scientific justification for vaccinating before going into a kennel, and some studies have even shown increased susceptibility to kennel cough in those dogs that have been vaccinated, many operators of kennels still make it a requirement. In my opinion, they should leave this decision to the veterinarian and not have a policy that applies to all.

If your animal is weak, old, or sickly, it is even more important that vaccines be avoided. One alternative is to try in-home care. This is also a good choice if you are planning a long absence or if you simply want to provide a better alternative to the kennel experience. We have used a house sitter—either a friend or a family member—with success. We have been fortunate in finding someone that needs a place to stay and trading the use of our home for them taking care of our pets and plants. No such person in your life? Ask a veterinarian, breeder, or local pet store staff to recommend a professional pet-sitter who will stop by once or twice a day to feed, groom, pet, and exercise your animal, and bring in the mail and water the plants, too. Twice a day is better for your pet (and we have used that schedule ourselves), but I realize cost is a factor. In our area, this service presently costs about $10 per visit. It is more in some areas of the country. In Washington, D.C., for instance, it is $20/day for cats and $35/day for dogs. If they are coming to your home, make sure they are insured and bonded as well. Most are. I have had very good luck with this type of service.

If you can't get any leads from professionals, you might seek out teenagers who want a summer job, students in an animal health technician program, or humane society volunteers. A close friend, neighbor, or relative who already knows and likes the animal might even take pleasure in providing the care you want for your pet while you're away. In such cases it might also work out for a friendly and well-behaved dog to stay at the sitter's residence. In contrast to dogs, cats are generally less stressed by being left alone, as long as they're on their own turf.

Here are some pointers on how to make the whole process go smoothly.

Introduce the sitter to your pet before you leave. Professional pet-sitters like to meet the pet before you leave and make sure they understand its routine. Do what you can to encourage your pet to be friendly with this new person. You could even arrange for the sitter to spend some time with your animal—perhaps going for a walk, playing, or holding it quietly for a while. Such preparations alleviate much of the stress and concern for you and are particularly good for an old or easily excitable pet.

Make certain the sitter you hire can and

will provide adequate food, water, exercise, and attention. If you are using a home-prepared diet, make some up ahead of time and, if it's a long trip, freeze it in convenient packages for the sitter to thaw and use. The feeding of your home-prepared food is very important to clarify with your sitter. The most common complaint I have heard is that the sitter, while doing a good job in most respects, does not follow directions on feeding, so that people arrive home to find all their carefully planned meals still in the freezer. I don't know why this is, but it is something you should emphasize in your instructions.

Leave money and necessary instructions for taking the animal to the vet in case of an illness or an emergency. Provide phone numbers where you or a close relative can be reached during your trip.

Add anti-stress supplements to your pet's diet. If your pet tends to be excitable or seems likely to be upset at your absence, you can help him cope with emotional stress through nutrition. Starting about a week before the trip, add a complete B-complex tablet (including vitamins B_2, B_6, and pantothenic acid at the level of 5 to 15 milligrams, depending on the pet's size) and/or a liberal amount of nutritional yeast to its food. Also, give one to two grams of vitamin C, particularly after any stressful period. If possible, space the vitamin C dosage throughout the day. The sitter should feed the vitamins while you're gone, and you should continue to give the supplements for about a week after your return, unless your animal seems fine. If you know your pet is likely to be upset during this time it may help to add Bach's Rescue Remedy to the water dish—four drops each time the bowl is filled.

Pay the sitter adequately. The fee or barter should be sufficient to convey a sense of your animal's value to you.

When you say good-bye to your pet, do so with a calm demeanor and untroubled mind. Since animals readily pick up people's feelings, you might start things off on the wrong note if you are nervous or upset when you leave. It may even help to look the animal in the eye and visualize a happy reunion scene. Once you are gone, don't cause yourself needless worry and anxiety. You did what you could.

Occasional absences, if thoughtfully handled, should not be a problem. Some animals, however, do develop physical or psychological ailments after being passed around from one temporary home to another. Any person with wanderlust or other out-of-town pursuits that cannot include a pet should consider placing her dog or cat in a permanent and supportive home where the pet will be better off.

TIPS FOR TRAVEL

What about taking a pet along on a vacation?

People find that many dogs and some cats (primarily the Siamese and Siamese-related breeds) can be excellent traveling companions if they are basically well-behaved and psychologically and physically healthy. However, certain precautions and considerations are basic.

Make sure your pet is wearing a current I.D. Should you get parted, you need some way for the finder to reach you. The best type are waterproof identification "barrel" tags in which you can enclose a small piece of paper that says "If lost, please call—collect." Give your cell phone number, the phone number of a friend or relative who is willing to take messages, or else provide the number of the place where you are staying. These tags are difficult to find, but very practical.

On long road trips, give your pet daily exercise. For traveling dogs, at least half an hour of a vigorous game of fetch or a jog with you is important. If you like to let your dog run loose, do so only in a safe and appropriate area and, even then, only if the dog is well-trained to return on command.

Cats should wear a harness attached to a leash. Car rides and strange places are more upsetting to a cat than to a dog, and felines might bolt. Cats do well in a comfortably sized crate that can also hold a little litter pan. You can put a disposable diaper under the pan in case of any "spills" during the ride.

Never leave your pet in a sealed car on a hot day. Heat can build up very fast in a closed car, which acts like a solar oven, causing an animal to go into heat prostration. This may lead to serious brain injury and even death. See "Handling Emergencies and Giving First Aid" on page 429 for first-aid treatment, should this problem ever occur.

Take familiar items with you. A basket or piece of bedding from home can make any animal feel safer and more at ease. You could also take favorite toys to give your pet something to do.

Use commercial pet health foods for convenience, if necessary. But add vitamin C and vitamin B-complex (as suggested above) to help traveling animals deal with stress.

Anticipate nature's calls. For a cat, a litter box is basic gear for a road trip. Pre-filled disposable ones for traveling are now available at pet supply stores. Take a dog on a short stroll on a leash at least twice a day. Carry disposable bags and a scooper to use in public parks, cities, motel properties, and beaches.

Prepare for health problems that are common to most travelers. *Constipation* can plague traveling pets. It can be caused by lack of exercise or water, infrequent stops, or anxiety about strange new territories. Temporary constipation is not a serious problem and will usually clear up before long. For a dog, you can prepare a useful preventive with figs, prunes, and raisins as well as fresh berries or other fruits in season. Bran or psyllium husks are also helpful.

Nausea grips some animals when they ride in a car or plane, and they will either vomit or salivate excessively. The B-complex supplementation mentioned above will help prevent nausea. Also, encourage your pet to lie down on the floor of the car as a preventive. If motion sickness does occur, give your dog some peppermint tea or peppermint capsules to help settle her stomach (not so well tolerated by cats). An alternative to using peppermint tea is a formula made from the 38 flower preparations discovered by Dr. Edward Bach (see chapter 14 for more information). Mix together Aspen, Elm, Scleranthus, and Vervain and give two drops of this formula every two hours to relieve the emotional upset and subsequent nausea.

It may be wise to fast a susceptible pet the day before departure or on the first day of the trip. For an animal going by public transit in a carrier, a 12- to 24-hour fast before the trip will generally prevent it from eliminating during the journey.

The homeopathic remedy *Aconitum napellus* 30C is very useful for minimizing fear and upset before traveling. Give one pellet of this medicine an hour before leaving home; give another pellet just a few minutes before actually leaving the house. This usually is enough for most animals and most trips. If nervousness returns, give your pet another dose (one pellet) during the trip itself. Rarely will this remedy be needed more than three or four times; in fact, most animals travel well with just the two doses given before leaving home. This medicine is very safe to use and often functions better than a tranquilizer.

Eye irritation may occur in a dog that likes to ride with its head out the window, testing all the interesting scents it passes. Sometimes dust and debris enter the dog's eyes at high speeds, scratching the cornea and irritating sensitive membranes. For a minor irritation,

I suggest washing the eyes out with this mild salt (saline) solution quite similar to tears: Add a level ¼ teaspoon of sea salt to one cup of pure water and stir. Keep the solution at room temperature; pour a small amount into a cup or dish and apply it by dripping it from a saturated cotton ball into the eye or by using a glass or plastic dropper. Administer the liquid until it runs out of the eye to flush out irritating substances.

For more serious irritations, use a cup of the same saline solution and add five drops only of tincture (or alcoholic extract) of the herb *Euphrasia officinalis*, or eyebright. Use this solution in the eye four times a day.

If your pet has a serious corneal injury, the animal will keep its eye shut most of the time. In such a case, seek veterinary help. (See also "Corneal Ulcers" on page 344.)

AIRLINE TRAVEL

Do not take an unhealthy pet on an airline. If you do take a pet on a flight, make sure that the animal won't be exposed to extreme temperatures or possible suffocation while in the cargo compartment. Shorter flights generally pose less of a problem.

Many airlines, however, allow you to take a small dog with you in the passenger compartment. Your dog must weigh less than 15 pounds (or it will have to go cargo). If small enough, however, it can be put in a carrier that will fit under the seat in front of you. You will be responsible for hand carrying your dog into the plane.

The airlines have strict rules about the size

and type of carrier to use with your small dog:

- ❖ The carrier may be a hard plastic, metal, or soft-sided one.
- ❖ There must be adequate ventilation on three sides.
- ❖ It must be leakproof.
- ❖ It must fit under the airline seat and be no larger than 17 inches in length, 16 inches in width, and 10½ inches high.
- ❖ If you will be taking a prop plane or small jet, your carrier can be no larger than 15 inches in length, 16 inches wide, and 10½ inches high. The difference in the 2 inches in length is because the space between seats on the smaller planes means that a larger carrier will not fit under your seat.

Be warned that there will be a charge for bringing your dog or cat with you—depending on the airline, anywhere from $50 to $150, whether in cargo or in coach. There is also a limit as to how many dogs can be on a flight. When you book your flight, inquire if any other animals are already boarding. This may well keep you from being bumped off last minute.

Similar rules apply for larger dogs. You provide the hard plastic or metal container or crate for travel in the cargo hold, and it must have at least three well-ventilated sides. Most airlines will only allow two large dogs to ride in cargo on a flight, so confirm with the airline that your dog will be traveling with you on the same airplane when you book. It

is a good idea to label the crate with identification and contact information. Add a number to call if for some reason you can't be reached. Attach this identification so that it cannot be lost during travel. You can also put in feeding instructions and any medical requirements—just in case there is a delay in the two of you getting back together.

Either way, before you're allowed to board, you will need to show certification of your pet's health from a veterinarian. This is required for public transportation, interstate shipment, and foreign travel. I do not advise taking your pet if your destination is a country that has a lengthy required quarantine time or any special health hazards. Check on the destination country's requirements before making your plans.

Generally, try to use nonstop flights and avoid layovers, which require unloading and loading again. It is scary enough to be on a flight, much less the hustle and bustle of being cargo. Realize too that there won't be the same temperature control in the cargo section, so there will be further stress for your pet. Because of possible temperature extremes, some airlines will not fly pets in cargo in certain months. Check ahead. It is also very helpful to have water available to give as soon as you arrive.

AUTO TRAVEL

Respect motel and campground properties. You and your pet, as well as those that come later, are much more apt to be welcome if you assure the management that you will:

❖ Never leave a dog alone in a motel room while you go out for an extended period (which may lead to barking and chewing).

❖ Have a bag and scooper with you and clean up any messes, inside or out.

❖ Only bring a neutered or spayed pet. This discourages wandering and territory-marking.

❖ Keep the pet on a leash at all times, so it doesn't charge through tender flowerbeds or bother other guests.

These guidelines help make you welcome with your pet when visiting people's homes, too.

PETS ON THE MOVE

Besides our round-trip vacations, every year many Americans make a significant one-way trip: moving to a new residence. This means an awful lot of animals have to pull up their roots, dealing once more with the stress of getting used to and claiming a new territory, as well as adjusting to new neighborhood challenges.

These relocations can easily disorient animals, so they run off, get lost, and can't find their way back. So make sure your pet is under your control at all times while the move is in progress. During the hustle and bustle of packing and unpacking, confine the animal to a quiet room, perhaps the bathroom, laundry room, or (for dogs only) a securely fenced yard. During this time, provide your pet with some familiar items for re-assurance, such as its bed, some toys, or a favorite rug. Why the excessive precautions? Because this is a time when pets get lost—people coming and going, leaving doors open, scaring the animals with noise. Cats will try to hide and end up inside a crate or furniture in the moving truck. One cat I know about spent two months inside a sofa bed before being found. It was skinny, but it lived.

Some unlucky pets are simply left behind when people move. This usually means slow and painful starvation, illness, bewilderment, or (if they're lucky) a quicker death by euthanasia in an animal shelter. Others may be foisted off onto a reluctant new caretaker. For example, one of my friends bought a house from a woman that moved back to France. When they moved in to their new house there were two abandoned cats waiting for them and a note saying they would be cursed if they did not take care of them. I suppose this was her way of transferring responsibility!

Pets forced to switch allegiances too many times can develop insecure personalities and behavior problems that make them undesirable to anyone. For the same psychological reasons, a high turnover of family members (through such events as divorce, marriage, birth, death, and children leaving home) can also be stressful to an animal's sense of security. Try to give your pet as much attention as possible during times of change or upheaval.

Unfortunately, even the most loving people sometimes find they cannot keep a pet because of housing problems, allergies, animal incompatibility, or other situations that make dealing with animal care an impossibility. If so, follow the Humane Society guidelines (below) to help find your pet a good home. These guidelines also apply to placing a litter of puppies or kittens.

FINDING A NEW HOME

Begin your search for a good adoptive home by advertising through the local paper and posting notices. Run newspaper ads several times to ensure wide coverage. List the animal's qualities (such as "Loves kids, healthy, quiet, house-trained and affectionate") and state simply that it needs a home. Post photocopied notices (preferably with an appealing picture of the animal) where responsible people might see them—in community centers, health food stores, doctors' and veterinarians' offices, churches, senior citizen centers, and employee lunchrooms.

Many local rescue groups now have Web sites that post pictures of animals needing homes. They might help you out. There are also breed-specific rescue groups that find new home matches across state lines. E-mail is a great tool as well.

Be aware that if you advertise that you're giving away a pet "for free," you might attract people who would neglect or mistreat it or sell it to a lab. Unfortunately, such things do happen to pets given away indiscriminately.

When someone calls to express interest, take your pet to *their* home so you can check it out for yourself. This may ease the transi-

tion for your pet also. Ask yourself the following questions.

❖ Does the house have a safe, fenced yard of adequate size?

❖ Is there a dangerous highway nearby?

❖ Will the pet be left alone too much?

❖ Does the interested party appreciate the basics of responsible pet care?

❖ Does anyone in the family oppose the adoption?

❖ Is anyone in the family allergic to animals?

❖ Is the potential caretaker apt to move around a lot?

❖ What happened to any former pets? (Beware of people who have gone through a series of pets that were lost, hit by cars, or given away; this will likely be the fate of yours as well.)

If you find it difficult to ask these kinds of questions, remember that a responsible pet care person-to-be will appreciate your concern for your animal.

Though it may be difficult and even sad to place your old friend in a new home, you will feel best in the long run if you take the time and care to do the job well. Some time later you may return to find everyone pleased with the new relationship.

LOST PETS

The danger of losing a pet is not limited to moves and vacations. The possibility is ever present. By tagging your pet with proper I.D.

and licenses and keeping it under your supervision, you greatly reduce its chances of being lost or stolen. Despite the most thoughtful precautions, however, animals sometimes still get lost. Here's what to do if your pet is missing.

Visit your local animal shelter. Go in person every day for a week or more after the disappearance. Most such organizations try to find you, but if a pet is unlicensed or not carrying identification, connecting that animal to you is almost impossible. In any case, the burden of responsibility is really yours. Visit all appropriate kennels, asking to see any quarantine, isolation, holding, and receiving rooms. Call out your pet's name as you go. Giving kennels or shelters a brief description over the phone is inadequate, since only you know your pet for sure. Many shelters are busy places and it is not unusual for the staff to be overworked and unable to remember all the animals there.

While at the shelters, be sure to fill out a lost pet report, providing photos, if possible, as well as noting any unique markings. Also, check out reports of found pets. To prevent possible euthanasia, people who find lost pets often keep them at their homes and just file reports with the local shelter or humane society. I once reunited

LOST

DATE: _____

THIS AREA: _____

HAVE YOU SEEN OUR PET?

PHOTO

(DOG OR CAT) _____ (BREED) _____ (COLORS) _____

(SEX) _____ (AGE) _____ (COLLAR) _____

(SPECIAL I.D. OR COMMENTS) _____

DON'T WAIT—WE MISS OUR PET

PLEASE CALL: (NAME AND ADDRESS) _____

_____

(PHONE)

a dog with a grateful person this way. Frightened by fireworks, the dog had jumped into the wrong pickup truck during a Fourth of July celebration. When this same truck accidentally rear-ended me on the way home, the driver was astonished to find a dog in the back of his pickup. I filed a "found pet" report and, fortunately, was able to make contact with the dog's person, who never would have traced this same path with his own inquiries.

Check with local police. This is particularly important if you have reason to suspect your animal was stolen.

Place an ad in a local daily paper. Put it in the lost-and-found section. Give a description of the animal, note the area where you last saw it and, if possible, offer a reward.

Post notices in the area where the pet was lost. The form shown opposite is a good model. Adding the word "reward" doesn't hurt. People are more likely to look at your flyer.

Most photos will reproduce adequately on a good copier. Post the notices on telephone poles, at laundromats, and on grocery store bulletin boards. Ask around. Ask the mailperson and neighbors that work at home in the area if they have seen your animal. Ask parents to ask their children. They are the ones who are often most aware of strays. Cats will get into garages and sheds surprisingly often. Our cat would do that occasionally, and one time it took repeated requests before a neighbor would check out his garage—but there our cat was!

REMODELING

A common problem time is remodeling the home. It is enough upset for you, living there, but it is also disorientating and confusing for your dog or cat. They can escape due to workers leaving the doors open or get trapped inside the construction. Patti Howard, a sometimes pet-sitter in Washington, D.C., tells me of the family that went to Hawaii for three weeks while construction was going on in their house (an attractive idea). Unfortunately, they did not arrange a comparable vacation for their pets. The sitter came in to feed the cats and could not find one because the bathroom contractors had walled her into the newly tiled bathroom. One of the cat's lives was saved by the diligent sitter searching and searching until he heard the muffled "meow" behind the wall. It took a hammer and screwdriver to break through the tile and rescue the cat. Another cat ended up stranded on the rooftop, having reached it through a temporary hole during the remodeling.

The most famous case was when Bill and Hillary Clinton's home was being renovated and the First Dog, Buddy, ran out and was hit by a car.

Remodeling time takes some thought. Invite your critters in for the planning.

HAZARDS IN THE HOME

Often, animals are unable to understand and avoid certain dangers unique to their human environment. It's hard to anticipate all the unexpected things a pet can get into, and we needn't worry excessively about them, but here are a few basic concerns.

Cats can sometimes die from the complications of swallowing yarn, string, or rubber bands. Because their barbed tongues make it difficult to spit objects out, they may be unable to stop the process once it starts. So offer them a ball of yarn for play only when you're there to supervise.

Though the signs are not specific, cats having this problem will stop eating and may have vomiting. A thread caught up around the tongue is very difficult to see. Just opening the mouth may not show it; a needle caught somewhere in the throat or esophagus will show up on an x-ray, as will bunching of the intestine.

Be on the lookout for ways your pet could ingest the many poisonous materials found in most homes. This ingestion could occur unintentionally (through skin or paws) or out of curiosity (through chewing or swallowing). Most homes contain numerous poisonous substances, from toxic houseplants, antifreeze, insecticides, and drugs to caustic cleansers and mothballs (beware of letting a cat sleep in a closet or drawer full of these little buggers—rather, debuggers). The challenge for you is like the one parents of toddlers face. See chapter 8 for more detailed coverage of dangerous substances.

Make a habit of glancing in your car, tool shed, garage, oven, refrigerator, dryer, or any drawer, cabinet, or closet before closing it. Your curious cat may have jumped inside

when you weren't looking. Such oversights can be fatal.

Take care that your animal does not chew on electric cords. Don't confine a puppy or kitten in a room with an exposed cord. Reprimand it firmly if you catch the animal chewing on or playing with one.

Also make sure that your pet doesn't chew up and swallow inedible objects like newspapers, books, plastic toys, or bags and other such things. A rawhide bone makes a good substitute chewing toy.

If you have toddlers, make sure they don't handle a small animal too roughly, because that endangers both parties. Also, the child may unintentionally cause a great stress for an animal by making a loud noise near its sensitive ears.

If a child is responsible for taking care of a pet, make sure the job gets done the same way you would do it, every day. Don't let the animal become the victim of a learning experience in "natural consequences." Teach your child the necessity of sticking to any responsibility he or she has assumed for an animal.

If you live in an upper-floor apartment (second floor and up), screen your windows. Despite their agility, cats can and do fall out of windows and off balconies. Many of my clients in New York City lost cats this way.

By taking these precautions and by adopting an overall attitude of watchfulness and consideration, modern life need not hold undue peril or stress for your animal or for you; instead, it can provide unique opportunities for adventure and enjoyment.

CHAPTER 13

SAYING GOOD-BYE: COPING WITH A PET'S DEATH

The evening wore on, the music from the radio drifting out and enveloping us all. And with each moment, my wife and I could see that the small black kitten she held in her lap was edging even closer to death. Only a week before, we had adopted her from the animal shelter clinic where I had twice saved her life—first from the ravages of parasites, and then from the institutional procedures that required unadopted strays to be put to sleep after a certain period.

But now further postponing seemed impossible. I had done what I knew how to do and yet Miracle, as we'd dubbed her on account of her heroic, though brief, rebound, was surely on her way out.

The signs were clear. Her small body grew steadily weaker and limper and her legs began to stiffen. Her eyes stared, dilated and motionless, fixed upon some awesome eternity. Occasionally she waved her head in small convulsions and feebly licked the inside of her mouth.

We had already discussed the possibilities. We could have struggled to save her all the way up to the end, violating her dignity with needles, tubes, and drugs. Or, to spare her—or maybe ourselves—the drawn-out process of dying, we could have injected her with the standard euthanasia solution, a painless passport to a quick end. Yet somehow, in that situation and with that animal, it just seemed right to let her go in her own way.

Without having to talk about it, we both knew it would be best this way. Looking at her, we realized how little we knew about the mystery of death or of life. We didn't know who or what a cat was, really.

We didn't know from where she had come or to where she would go. Yet we knew that beneath our surface differences there is a oneness, a bond uniting all living creatures.

We knew that soon this graceful, highly evolved body with its tiny, perfect eyes would return to the earth, never to fulfill its promises. We thought of how we would miss her innocence, her playful grace, her courage—and a wave of sadness swept over us. Yet, what must be must be. And it was all right to be as it was.

We placed her into her sleeping box atop some warm bottles covered with cloth and settled into bed. Gently and slowly, the darkness began to lower us into that unknown into which we all go each night. Through the growing silence there came a few indescribable sounds—long, low half-groans, half-meows. We reached over and felt Miracle's temperature. It was dropping.

Once, in the middle of the night, we awoke to hear another of the strange sounds, this one deeper, longer, with an air of finality.

The sunlight was streaming through the window when we awoke that morning, full of a fresh appreciation for the gift of living. We got up and looked in Miracle's box, knowing what we would find. She was indeed gone now. Her body was rigid and cold. Her eyes and mouth were open, frozen as if in surrender to some great force that had passed through her.

We found the right place to bury her, beneath a towering redwood on the edge of a nearby forest. We dug a small hole at the foot of the tree and then simply sat, silently.

The redwood was magnificent, sparkling and waving in the morning light, surging up from the earth to the sky. Into this great tree something of our small friend would pass. From form to form, life would go on. We laid her body in the soil, covering it over with the tree's roots and the sweet-smelling forest loam. As we tamped down the last of it we heard a small rustling in the bushes. We turned to see.

It was a cat, watching.

THE CHALLENGE OF DEATH

Often we think of death as something to fear, to put out of mind and avoid at all costs. Yet in the end it comes to all organisms. It will come to your animal, and one day it will surely come to you and me.

But as the passing of Miracle and of others we have known has taught us, death need not be feared. In fact, to be fully present with it and let its significance speak to you, you can make such an experience a thing of beauty. It can remind us, if we have forgotten to notice, just how mysterious and wondrous life truly is.

That is why it saddens me when I see and hear from so many people who are deeply burdened and upset at the anticipation or the memory of a pet's death. Their grief is real—often as great as or greater than that felt at the loss of a human friend or relative.

For others, however, the temptation is to just "stuff" their feelings inside and not really experience them, an understandable response. But because they are unwilling or unable to face their feelings and thus learn from them, people shut themselves off not only from the pain of death but also from its beauty and meaning. But facing our emotions can provide real opportunities for learning and flowering.

A pet's death can be a complex thing. All sorts of emotions can arise, including sadness, anger, depression, disappointment, and fear. With people for whom the relationship is especially important—such as a single person, a childless couple, or an only child for whom the animal has been a best friend—the grief may be that much greater. And, too, if the death was sudden and unexpected, or if it seemed preventable (as in an accident), the feelings of loss and disappointment can be particularly intense.

In addition to those psychological hurts common to losing either a human or an animal companion, a pet's death brings it own unique challenges. For one thing, the euthanasia option can burden the owner with a difficult decision. Another problem is that it is not socially acceptable to mourn openly over an animal, although the grief may be just as real as if you had lost any other family member. It might be hard to find a sympathetic listener to help you work through the experience. And even sympathetic employers are unlikely to allow absence from work for mourning a faithful cat or dog.

In fact, it *is* socially acceptable to replace the lost pet with a new one immediately after death. If a woman were to remarry the day after her husband's funeral, however, eyebrows would be raised. Simply replacing your last pet with a new one will not heal the grief you feel. Only time and insight can do that. And parents who rush out to buy a new pet for their bereaved child before she has really said goodbye to one just lost should realize that the unspoken message can be: "Life is cheap; relationships are disposable and interchangeable."

HANDLING GRIEF

Above all else, you need to know how to cope with the grief and other emotions that may surface before, during, or after death. If you can do that, any choices or actions required of you will come much more easily.

Lynne De Spelder, a friend who teaches, counsels, and writes on the subject of death and dying, emphasizes that coping with an animal's death is much the same as coping with the loss of a human friend: "It's really important to *handle* the grief. Research has shown the costs of mismanaged grief can be great, [such as] illness among survivors, for example. Hiding from grief makes it worse."

How can you handle it? Start with the most important thing: Give yourself *permission* to grieve. Lynne observed, "Women often deal with grief better than men simply because they are allowed to cry. Also, it's good to find someone who'll listen. If your spouse won't, find someone who will. If someone makes light of your grief, it's probably his own fear of emotion."

Suppose your crying and sadness seems to go on too long? That's a signal that you are dwelling too much in your thoughts and memories. Lynne and other grief counselors encourage people suffering from loss to discover and engage in nurturing activities—such as yoga, hiking, music, or sports—that help people to lovingly let go of the past and to open themselves to the goodness of the present.

From my experience of loss, I think there can be a certain resistance to letting go of these thoughts, even though we may agree it would be the healthiest thing to do. If the relationship has been close it can almost feel like a betrayal of that closeness to stop thinking about it. It becomes sort of an expression of loyalty that we hold onto the feelings and memories. To get beyond this, we have to realize that our lives would just come to a stop if we never got over the losses that life will undoubtedly bring us. I can still know that I loved the person or animal in my life; that will never change. It isn't a betrayal of them to carry on with what it is we have to do and with our own lives.

HELPING THE YOUNG CHILD

When you must help a child cope with the loss you all feel, it's important to first understand your own feelings. You must be honest and open about what happened. But don't try to console the child with an instant replacement or with explanations that can be misinterpreted or taken too literally, such as "he went away" or "she was taken to Doggie Heaven." If the child wants to see the dead body before burial, understand that it is a natural curiosity and should be allowed, provided you are emotionally stable about it yourself.

Talk with the child and make sure he is not harboring misunderstandings. Don't let him blame himself or even you for the death. If you had the animal put to sleep because it was clear that a painful death was inevitable, say so, and give the child a chance to understand. It helps to communicate your own dilemma, that you "did not know what else to do." It is a common human situation to have to act in the face of uncertainty and there is no shame in doing so.

THE ISSUE OF GUILT

I have been on the listening end for many, many people who have lost animals. Sometimes, with someone I know well, I have asked them more about their feelings. "What are you feeling the most about losing them?" or "How do you feel about how things went?" referring to their choice to use alternative forms of medicine instead of the usual conventional approach.

I am really surprised at the answers I get. The most common response I hear is that "I should have done more." Now of course this is always possible, that one could have done more, but I will hear this statement even from the *most devoted people you can imagine*. It can be someone that cared for a dog that could not walk or control their bowels, and for months they have been carrying them in and out, cleaning up after them all that time. These are people that *have spared nothing* in their nursing care. So I wondered, "How could they feel they had not done enough?"

I think this reveals something in the human-animal relationship that has not been understood—at least I didn't understand it. For some people, caring for an an-

imal is of immense importance; it represents something very basic about who they are. When that caring is not seen to succeed, the *sense of personal responsibility* is so great that it dominates everything else.

I don't know the answer to this pain, but my thoughts about the situation run like this: It is a noble human feeling to be responsible for another; it is appropriate and we need more of it in the world. Nonetheless, we must realize our limitations as humans. It is simply the way things are that, in spite of our best efforts, all beings will die, many from diseases that are unfortunate. So one thing to realize is that if you have tried your best, then that is all you can do. Yes, theoretically there may have been something missed or a path not taken, but it is always that way. Hindsight is wonderful—just not available when we need it. So it may help to first reflect on that: You did your best at that time.

Let me ask you: What if you had not been there? What would have happened if you were not in the picture? I think questions like this can help to put things in perspective. That you were there has meaning. Sure, you can always think of things you could have done differently, but the fact is you were the one who was there. What you were able to do for your friend could not have been done by anyone else. It was a gift.

MAKING A CHOICE

If your pet is suffering and you are forced to consider euthanasia, familiarity with the procedure and its alternatives may help you know what to expect.

Euthanasia: The idea of "putting an animal out of its misery" has long been accepted as a humane option, even though we rarely accept it as a choice for ourselves.

Veterinarians perform euthanasia in their office or sometimes as a house call by injecting an overdose of a barbiturate anesthetic into a vein or the heart. The animal loses consciousness within a few seconds, slumps over, and the vital functions cease soon thereafter. It is considered painless. However, if the animal is agitated (perhaps by its upset human companion), that can make it harder for the doctor to do the job properly. It can be very helpful, especially in a situation where there is anxiety or pain, to use a tranquilizer before giving the final injection. There is then a period of relaxation first.

Personally, I've always found the whole process rather uncomfortable, and I think most veterinarians feel the same. Mercy killing can make sense, however, in cases where the animal is in great and prolonged pain and the death is slow but inevitable.

It's unwise to make a hasty decision for euthanasia in a moment of anguish, before you clearly and rationally understand the animal's chances of survival and any other alternative possibilities. Otherwise, you may be burdened with doubts and regrets, forever wondering if your pet would have survived. I have found this depends to a great extent on what the "diagnosis" is. The animal with itchy skin may go through much discomfort but

one would never think of euthanasia because of this. If your pet has the diagnosis of cancer, however, then slight symptoms can be interpreted as the reason to make that decision—perhaps prematurely. I have overseen cases of cancer in pets that are doing quite well with minimal discomfort, even getting better; to have them "put down" because they did not feel well one day would have been rash.

It is really best to look past the diagnosis and directly at the situation of your animal. Are they relatively free of pain? Are they able to function? If so, then don't come to a hasty decision. Consider one of the alternatives we will discuss in chapter 14. I have been blessed to be able to help many "dying" animals recover enough to live normal lives for some time.

Hospital care: When your animal is so ill that you are considering hospitalizing it, ask the veterinarian for a realistic opinion of your pet's chances of recovery. Special care often pulls an animal through a serious crisis and enables it to live a few more years. Some conditions, however, allow for little hope for recovery. Heroic efforts to prolong a pet's life might involve extensive care and expense, as well as drawn-out suffering for the animal, only to prove futile in the end. I know it's a tough call, but here are some thoughts to consider in making the decision.

The cost of emergency treatment for an animal in a crisis can very considerably. Typically, the cost can be several hundreds of dollars after just a few days of intensive care.

Compared with human care, it's a real bargain. Still, the cost is a consideration, especially if extraordinary care is not going to make a significant difference.

Certainly there is a place for this kind of care in some situations. It may be obvious, however, that the animal can't survive and that heroic measures are not really appropriate. This can be difficult for you to judge yourself, so don't be afraid to ask your veterinarian for an assessment. Ask her to be frank with you. If it is clear that your pet can't be saved, he can still be made comfortable without having to go through all the procedures involved in trying to "rescue" him. For example, a veterinarian can administer fluids and drugs that will allow the animal to rest quietly. As soon as it becomes apparent that death is near, most doctors then put the animal "to sleep" (with your prior permission).

Home care: In the scenario in which death is expected and a decision is made not to continue the attempts to cure them, it is an option to allow your pet to die at home—like a hospice situation.

Many conditions that are terminal are *relatively* painless. The animal is not completely free of discomfort, but not suffering greatly. As a general guideline, if the animal seems reasonably comfortable and peaceful, you may wish to allow the process to unfold naturally. Later in this chapter I will describe some homeopathic treatments that can be used to ease the dying process.

There are some ways of dying that are *not* easy, however, and my recommendation is avoid putting pets through the suffering. Some examples of this are cats that have fluid accumulating in their chests (pleural effusion or hydrothorax), resulting in suffocation, or dogs having continual seizures. Use this guideline: If your animal is very agitated, crying in pain, restless, or struggling to breathe, then consider euthanasia rather than letting the process continue.

Why would one consider taking this path? A chief reason is that home is familiar and comfortable, whereas being taken in a car to a strange place with strange sounds and smells creates anxiety. It seems a better thing for the dying animal not to go through this anxiety in the last hours of life. There are veterinarians that make house calls for the purpose of euthanasia, and this is better in terms of reducing anxiety.

The other reason for allowing an animal to die at home is the chance to be with them in the last hours, to take care of them at this time, and to ensure that the suffering is minimal.

If it is better to take your pet to the hospital for this, you can still comfort them at the last. Ask your veterinarian if you can be there, to hold them, when the injections are given. Many veterinarians allow, even encourage, this. Talk it over with your veterinarian. In some places I have worked, the doctor would perform the euthanasia procedure, then leave the room and allow the person to be alone with their friend for final good-byes.

WHAT CARE SHOULD BE GIVEN IN THE LAST HOURS?

In terms of physical care, don't feed a dying animal; just give it water or vegetable juices. Provide a warm, comfortable, quiet place to rest. Occasionally your pet may need your help to go outside or to the litter box to eliminate. The dying animal may welcome the gentle and calm presence of those it loves, but do protect your pet from too much noise, activity, or disturbance.

When the end is very near, the animal will grow quite weak. The body temperature will drop below normal (for dogs and cats, below 100°F), and breathing may be faster than usual. At the moment of death there is often spasmodic or gasping breathing. The pupils may dilate and the animal may stretch out or perhaps pass urine. This final dying process usually lasts for only about a minute or less.

HOMEOPATHIC HELP FOR THE DYING ANIMAL

As I discuss in chapter 14, homeopathy is a method of treatment with the expectation that health will be restored. It also can be used to help the dying animal. In this instance, we do not expect recovery, and the treatment is intended to relieve pain, anxiety, restlessness and make the process as smooth as possible. I have considerable experience using remedies in this way, because many clients have asked for help in allowing their pets to die at home. (I would have used homeopathic treatment to help Miracle with the transition if I had known of it at the time.)

To forestall confusion later I will explain here that these medicines are also used in the *treatment* of other diseases and *they are not drugs that cause death.* In fact, homeopathic remedies are not instruments of euthanasia in the usual sense, e.g., drugs that cause quick death. They are euthanasia in the *original* sense of the Greek word, which meant "an easy or happy death." The difference, however, is that homeopathic remedies will not cause an animal to die if it is not already doing so. They can *ease* the transition, but they do not cause death. In a sense, we are treating the "condition" of dying to relieve pain and suffering. If the animal is close to death, it will come—perhaps not now, but in a couple of weeks. If they are not ready to go, then the remedy will have no effect and may actually improve them temporarily.

Here are the most useful remedies and their indications (to understand more about the use of homeopathy, see chapter 14.) Each one is accompanied by a brief description as to how the animal will look or act. Use this description as a guide for which remedy to use. It can happen that one state is relieved and another occurs, in which case you change to another remedy. What you are expecting to see is relief of the suffering, and if this happens after the treatment, then give nothing more. It is usual for just one remedy and one treatment to be sufficient. How long before relief can be expected? Very quickly, in just a few minutes. If a half-hour goes by without any effect, then the remedy was not effective and another one can be chosen.

1. *Arsenicum album* 30C is the one most useful and most often indicated (90 percent of patients). The animal will be restless, have extreme weakness (such as inability to stand), increased thirst, and a cold body. If you check the temperature it will be below normal (below 100°F). Not all of these elements need to be present at the same time for this remedy to be appropriate. It often happens, however, that you will notice restlessness or weakness coupled with a low body temperature. Give one dose of 1 to 2 pellets.

2. *Tarentula hispanica* 30C is a remedy for similar symptoms as *Arsenicum album*, in that there is just as much discomfort and restlessness. What is different is the patient will roll back and forth, from side to side. There may be nervous-like movements of the right front and rear legs. Typically, they keep in constant motion; curiously, soothing music will sometimes relieve this discomfort. I tend to use this remedy when *Arsenicum album* has no effect.

3. *Tarentula cubensis* 30C is a remedy that will not often be used at home. It is suitable for the animal dying from a severe infection. They will be very weak, perhaps not completely conscious, with a condition such as an overwhelming virus infection (like parvo-virus in dogs) or a bacterial infection such as blood poisoning. Another condition can be gangrene, where part of the body is dying, as may happen in some cancers. The affected areas tend to turn a purplish color. This remedy is particularly helpful in the very last stages of dying. In the homeopathic *Materia Medica*, the indication is that it "soothes the last struggles," which is as good a description as any. Give one dose.

4. *Pulsatilla* 30C is appropriate for the animal that is whimpering, complaining, or wanting to be held or carried about. It is also useful for the stage right before death when breathing becomes loud and labored (usually unconscious at this point). Give one dose.

CONCLUDING THOUGHTS

During the span of years you spent together, there were ups and probably there were downs. Through it all you each learned, loved, and did the best you knew how. When you think of the past, let it be with gratitude for the beautiful times you had together. When you think of the future, let it be with faith that Life is always bringing such beauty your way.

But *now* is the only place life ever is, always new and full of marvelous things. And what more could we ask for?

CHAPTER 14

HOLISTIC AND ALTERNATIVE THERAPIES

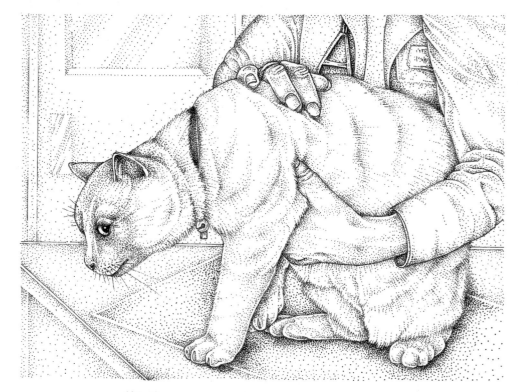

"My dog has arthritis. Can you tell me what vitamin or mineral will help him?"

Here is a very common question. The meaning behind it is understandable. This person is asking is if there is a nutrient that will act much like a miracle drug—not quite realizing the answer is not that simple. If it were, then these problems would not plague us.

The truth is that a health problem is rarely caused by just one factor. Even when it seems that it is, like an infection from a bacteria or virus, we come to realize that the hidden factor of the animal's level of health is as important as how virulent the bug is. In a group of animals that are exposed to an infectious disease, there are always some that do not become ill—and that is the key to understanding how to protect your animal. It comes down to how much resistance they have to becoming ill. This is the critical factor. It is never just the one thing—the bad bug, the nasty virus—there are always two factors involved, the other one being the health of the animal or person that is threatened. If they provide a good environment to grow in, then the germ will take advantage of that. If the "soil" is not suitable, then they can't grow there, no matter how much they want to. Let's focus on this question of natural resistance.

There are many reasons why our resistance can be low, and they usually fall into one of these categories.

❖ Being run down from an accumulation of toxins in the body.

❖ Being emotionally stressed.

❖ Having an underlying chronic illness that interferes with normal function.

❖ Missing some vital nutrients.

Let's look at these in turn.

TOXINS

This can be a scary topic and I don't mean to frighten you by focusing on it. We do, however, have to realize that today's world is not as clean as it was 100 years ago. Along with the tremendous technological advances we all enjoy have come side effects never anticipated. No one could have foreseen that the early automobiles, which seemed like a joke to most people and moved so slowly that someone needed to walk in front of them with a lantern so as not to frighten the horses, would one day result in millions of fast-moving vehicles, the extensive highway system, and, most important, the spewing of toxic substances all over our land.

A similar unintended effect has happened with many new chemical substances created for what seemed like useful purposes. It certainly seems a useful thing, for example, to make a chemical that kills mosquitoes or fleas, or one of a hundred other pests. Yet what we failed to fully realize is that these chemicals are poisonous not just to the intended victims, but also to many forms of life, including human beings and their pets. Sure, they are not as toxic to us as to these insects, but that *doesn't mean they are completely harmless.* It is a question of degree.

Well, doesn't government regulation control this? Aren't these chemicals checked to make sure they won't harm others? The short answer is "No." I will give you an example. Some years ago a new flea product came out (and is still in use) that you apply to the skin on the back of your dog. It then spreads all over the animal's body by itself. It is made to do this, to become a thin layer of pesticide that resists being washed off so that it can remain on the body for a long time. The idea is that, as fleas jump on, they contact this chemical and are killed before they can bite. A great idea, but here's the rub. My colleagues and I tried to determine how safe it was, not only for the dogs and cats it was being used on, but also for the human beings that were using it. This was a concern because there have been many stories out there of people being poisoned from using flea products. So, we perused the literature on this new product and could find no mention of its effect on human beings. We called the company. The spokesman and I talked, and it went something like this:

Me: "We are concerned about what this product might do to the people using it. Won't it also get on the hands from touching or petting the animal?"

Spokesman: "Well, it is completely safe for people to use if they follow the directions."

Me: "But the product is designed to spread easily all over the skin. What is to keep it from getting on the hands of a child hugging their dog? The chemical doesn't know the difference."

Spokesman: "Well it might, but that is not a problem."

Me: "How do we know it is not a problem? There were tests done to see if it was toxic to dogs. What tests have been done to see what it does to human beings?"

Spokesman: "It didn't have to be tested on people. It is only intended to be used on animals."

It has been some years since the conversation, but the essence of what was discussed is as I have described it. The basic message was that *it was not necessary to test it on people because its intended use was for animals.* You see the problem? There are many, many products out there that have never been tested fully to see what effects they will have on other species. Products for dogs are not tested on cats. Products for use on your lawn are not tested on dogs. And so on.

According to Helen Caldicott, M.D., co-founder of the Physicians for Social Responsibility, of about 80,000 chemicals now in common use, almost all of which are toxic (which is generally why they are used), a complete toxicology profile—that is, their complete effects on human beings—has been prepared for only 1,600 of them.

The problem is that no matter how much we try, toxic chemicals still end up in our bodies and in those of our animals. Marc Lappé, in his book *Chemical Deception*, tells us that assays of human tissues have detected residues of over a hundred different foreign chemicals and metals in our tissues.

Enough said on this. We discussed the presence of toxins and offered some coping strategies in chapter 8. The relevance here is that we have to assume that *some* amount of toxins are accumulating in our companion animals. As to their effects, as I explained above, we do not know exactly. But I can say this: Anything toxic is not good. The word "toxin" comes from the Greek for "poison." Usually it is used to refer to a poison from an animal or plant, but we are using here in the basic meaning—something poisonous that accumulates in the body.

One of the tasks of this book is to explain how to avoid exposure to these poisons, to the degree that we can. Relative success depends on many factors, like where you live and for how long, what food choices are available to you, even what your neighbors are doing in their yards. It comes down to these three simple rules:

1. Avoid chemical use.
2. Avoid adulterated foods.
3. Encourage elimination of poisons from the body.

We avoid chemical use by finding other ways of controlling fleas and parasites—not just on our pets but also in our environment, homes, lawns, and landscapes. We avoid adulterated foods for our animals by not using commercially prepared pet foods. We encourage elimination from the body by grooming, bathing, exercise, and the use of nutritional supplements that scavenge these contaminants and help the body expel them.

EMOTIONAL STRESS

Think how it has been for you when you are not well. Is a headache better when someone is giving you a hard time? How about having a tummy ache while being chased by the local bully? Animals feel emotional stress just like we do. What may differ from us is what causes them to be upset. We may be worrying about losing a job, or our child not doing well in school. The cat is worried because he can't use the litter box—the other cat in the house attacks him every time he tries to get to it. Your dog feels threatened by all the noise next door (the neighbor is remodeling) and thinks there is an angry pack out there getting ready to invade. You get the idea? The causes are different but the effect is the same.

Our bodies deal with stress by producing a variety of chemicals, one of the most important being a type of natural cortisone. This is necessary to how we cope with stress. Without it, we cannot live. But during *ongoing* stress, the balance is tilted towards constant production of these "calming" substances in the blood. Though they are part of what allows us to adapt to stress, there are other effects, one of which is a decrease in the efficiency of the immune system. Therefore, the stressed animal is more susceptible to infections and injuries and more affected by the toxins that have accumulated in the body.

One more thing to emphasize is that your animal will also be afraid or angry if *you* are afraid or angry first (see chapter 10). The relationship between you and your pet is like that between a child and parent. In this complicated world, as far as your animal is concerned, you are the one that understands what is going on. When you start to feel afraid, all your dog or cat can do is try to see where the danger is coming from. Which do you think is the more stressful, to be anxious about something you know about or to be afraid of something you can't perceive?

Of course it is natural for any of us to be

upset at times, and we may even need to express emotions to work through it. So what can we do to protect our pets? Be aware of this emotional component, of the effect of our upset on those around us. Perhaps take it to a different room. Better yet, resolve it. Maybe this is the good that comes out of having a pet in your life—you have to handle your problems quickly and maturely. For them.

AN UNDERLYING ILLNESS

There is nothing that saps our energy more than suffering from the pain and discomfort of illness. If there is already something wrong—arthritis, stomach pain, back pain—then this weakened area will more easily break down with time. Many, many of the difficult, long-term problems that plague our animals are of this type. Though antibiotics and vaccines have made infectious diseases much less frequent, the teeter-totter has dipped down on the side of chronic diseases. The common problems of today—the hyperthyroid cats, the dogs with hip dysplasia, the cats with inflammatory bowel disease or chronic bladder inflammation, the dogs with diabetes—these kinds of conditions were *extremely rare* when I first entered practice. It was not because I was not able to recognize them. *They did not exist then.* By far the majority of today's common and chronic problems have appeared in the last 20 years or so, and most of them are caused by the immune

system going haywire. By this I mean the illnesses that are termed "auto-immune diseases," which mean some part of the body is being attacked by the very system of defense that was meant to protect it from outer danger.

Why does this happen? I don't understand all the details. No one does at this point. But we can say this: In some way, the immune system is fooled into thinking normal body tissues are the enemy.

The immune system knows what is *supposed* to be present in the body and gets very excited and *fights* against anything it does not recognize. But it not only defends the body, *it also remembers prior battles.*

So the next question is, "Why does it go wrong?" As I said before, I cannot know for certain, but I have an opinion. Well, more than an opinion, in the sense I have observed and thought about this for a long time and studied the immune system during my PhD program. I think something is being done to the immune system to confuse it. We are exceeding its capacity to cope. What could have such an effect on the immune system? Well, is there anything we are doing today that was not done a century ago that interferes with how our bodies defend themselves against disease?

Three things come to my mind.

* The extensive use of antibiotics.
* The commonplace use of anti-inflammatory drugs like cortisone.
* The frequent use of vaccines.

These things were simply not done before. The antibiotic era began in 1928 with Alexander Fleming's discovery of penicillin. During the last few decades, however, so many more antibiotics have been developed and used.

In 1948, Edward C. Kendall and Philip S. Hench tried out cortisone on patients suffering from rheumatoid arthritis. This is a hormone secreted by the adrenal gland. By harvesting it and trying it out on patients, they found that it reduced inflammation in the body. This marked the beginning of a new practice of medicine, one based on suppression of symptoms as a routine approach. As time went on, a family of powerful synthetic forms of cortisone were created, drugs acting 10 or 20 times more powerfully than the version the body produces. This group of drugs, called cortico-steroids, is very commonly used in medicine today.

Vaccines started with Edward Jenner, who initiated smallpox vaccination in the 18th century. But this did not really develop into the multiplicity of vaccinations used today until the 20th century.

From these humble beginnings, we have the origin of the modern system of medicine that is based on the tripod of antibiotics, anti-inflammatory drugs, and vaccines. All of these have effects on the immune system and, at least to my mind, are the culprits in what has gone wrong with the immune system. I believe it is simply too much.

Based on these ideas, I advise my clients to avoid these treatments as much as possible.

Certainly there is a place for antibiotics and other drugs. I even agree that some vaccines are appropriate. My objection is *the indiscriminate use of them.* I don't think I exaggerate in saying that almost any time your animal is sick, he or she will likely be put on antibiotics and steroids. This is the "standard of practice" for veterinary medicine today. In this chapter and the latter part of this book, I will introduce some equally effective *alternatives* to this, other ways of treating illness that do not have this harmful impact on the immune system.

MISSING NUTRIENTS

Our last category has to do with a lack of necessary vitamins, minerals, proteins, and other food nutrients that are necessary for the immune system to work and for body tissues to be able to regenerate themselves. The human body contains a total of 100 trillion cells, the blood cells alone numbering 25 trillion. These numbers are so large that I can't grasp them myself, but here is a comparison that helps a little. The Milky Way galaxy is estimated to contain one hundred billion stars, *only one percent of the number of cells found in our bodies.* Yet this immense number of cells is constantly being regenerated, as old ones die and new ones take their place. Over a number of months or years, depending on the part of the body, everything is replaced, even the DNA that makes up our genetic code.

Realizing this, we can see how dynamic our biological structures are—going through continual repair and renewal. Therefore, there is a *constant* need for new material to keep the body intact and healthy. Much of what we are made up of can be created from food, by reorganizing and combining molecules that are already in the food. There are, however, certain substances—vitamins, minerals, and the amino acids that make up protein—that cannot be made in the body and must be obtained from food. So here we arrive at the crux of the problem: to stay entirely healthy, we must have food that provides these *essential nutrients*. The first part of this book, chapters 2 through 6, focuses on this most important aspect of health. To summarize, here are the chief points to understand:

❖ Use of artificial fertilizers forces rapid growth of food plants, which do not have time to take up the minerals from the soil that our bodies need.

❖ Harvesting plants while they are still unripe, to make shipping easier, prevents full development of the nutritional quality found in nature.

❖ Processing and packaging food destroys some very fragile components, especially certain vitamins, proteins, and enzymes. Often heating and cooking food does this.

❖ Shipping and storage of foods so that they have a long shelf life lets the fragile nutrients, like essential fatty acids, break down from being at room temperature and exposed to oxygen.

The very process of harvesting, shipping, and processing food compromises the fragile components in the food that we rely on to keep us in optimum health. Though measures can be taken to minimize these effects, it still behooves us to use food that is as fresh and natural as possible.

THE LIMITATIONS OF A PARTIAL APPROACH

Like all veterinarians, I learned the conventional approach of diagnosis and treatment in school and practiced it for years. And it has certainly had some remarkable successes, particularly with acute infections and trauma. Yet when we approach health problems from a symptom-centered perspective, our thinking tends to get so specialized and materialistic that we lose sight of the larger biological patterns and processes. Instead, we tend to rely heavily on the use of drugs and surgery, often to the exclusion of a broader program of health building and prevention.

As a result, contemporary medicine generally is geared toward *controlling* and *counteracting* symptoms and disturbances. It virtually ignores the body's innate ability to heal itself, given the right supports. Instead of strengthening the patient, the methods largely just compensate for the body's weaknesses.

Understandably, we are so eager for quick and easy solutions that we turn rather indiscriminately to some drug or vitamin, like the questioner at the beginning of this chapter. As a result, we may once again cover up symptoms without addressing underlying causes. Unfortunately, some modern drugs are especially good at such suppression. Some, like the various forms of synthetic cortisone, are so powerful that they can stop a great many widely varying symptoms in their tracks, *but the disturbance continues in the body, hidden from view.*

Time and again, when my associates and I take medical histories, we observe that animals vigorously treated with such drugs (apparently successfully) have gone on to develop another condition a few weeks or months down the line. Usually, it is more serious. For instance, a dog with a skin problem that is continually suppressed with a cortisone-like drug may later develop calcification of the spine, pancreatitis, or kidney failure. Or a cat with a chronically inflamed bladder that is treated with drugs will often later show a deeper problem like kidney failure, diabetes, or hyperthyroidism.

Though we tend to regard the new conditions as being unrelated to the prior ones, I suggest they are not. The suppressed disorder has simply made a more serious inroad into the body, now involving internal and more critical organs.

PROBLEMS CAUSED BY DRUGS

A related problem associated with such dependence on powerful drugs is the production of side effects or even iatrogenic ("doctor-caused") diseases. Although iatrogenic disturbances are considered to be a serious problem in human medicine, veterinary researchers have made little study of them. In my own opinion and experience, however, they are common in animal medicine as well. I have seen many pets improve considerably when prolonged drug treatment is simply stopped.

Some examples of common drug-related complications are loss of appetite or diarrhea (from the use of oral antibiotics), as well as skin rashes, convulsions, hearing loss (from the use of tranquilizers or antibiotics), severe life-threatening anemia (lack of red blood cells), and behavioral changes—usually towards irritability and aggressiveness, but sometimes appearing as anxiety manifesting as fear of noise, thunder, strangers, and even unusual objects.

If symptoms like this appear soon after therapy begins, they are probably related to the drug. It may not be the drug that is directly toxic so much as the overall energy-depleting effect of using such suppressive medicines. We must remember that symptoms are there for a reason, that they are part of the body's defense mechanism, and that to suppress them over and over again will only weaken the animal. The most common effect of long-term drug use is the animal becoming sluggish and inactive.

In many situations, drugs are not even called for, yet they are used to "appease the client" and to justify the expense of the office call. As an example, antibiotics are often prescribed to treat viral diseases. Yet, antibiotics are only effective against bacteria, not viruses. It is not just the veterinarian (or M.D.) who is to blame. Many people insist on a "shot" or some pills to take home, and if the doctor doesn't comply, they will go to another who will. Unfortunately, we have all been sold on the necessity for these drugs. I question that assumption, both on the basis of my own success and that of many other people who use more natural methods that work *with* the body's healing forces. Is it so difficult to think there may be other ways of healing disease besides using drugs? Why have we come to rely so heavily on drugs, as well as surgery and other compensatory methods?

The historical development of Western medicine is a complex subject, but I think a lot of it boils down to several culturally shared ways of thinking that most of us hold, whether doctor or client. One of these is that we want a "quick fix." We don't want to change our lives or habits that much. It's easier to just continue on the main pathway of our culture, even if it is limited by certain assumptions.

Even if we are willing to undertake a change of habits or lifestyle, we often settle for just adapting ourselves to live with a problem that we assume we can't change. For example, we learn to avoid certain foods that cause allergic reactions. Yet if we took the time and care to work a little harder at understanding and treating the disorder, we might be able to

do away with the allergic state altogether. And, in fact, I expect my patients to actually recover from food allergies during nutritional and homeopathic treatment.

DIVERGENT VIEWS IN MEDICINE

An even more fundamental stumbling block comes from the materialistic view that has long dominated Western science, with profound effect on modern thought and culture. Because scientists cannot see or measure such slippery phenomena as consciousness, thoughts, feelings, life energies, or whole systems, most of them have only studied the physical, material aspects of life. Accordingly, our current science, medicine, and culture regard the body as though it were a mere physical object, much like a machine, a collection of chemical and mechanical processes.

As a result, while virtually all cultures and systems of healing in the history of the world, including ours, have alluded to the presence of a unifying life force, our scientists no longer do. The Chinese call this life force *chi*. The Polynesians knew it as *mana*. The Sioux referred to it as *wakonda*. To the Egyptians, it was *ka* and to the Hindus it is still *prana*. In the Middle East, the word is *baraka*. In Africa, the Bushmen speak of *n/um*. The Aborigines, the most ancient culture on earth, call it *arungquiltha*.

In our own history of Western medicine and philosophy, it was called the *vital force*.

What do we mean when we use a term like this? The words themselves are not important. We could use chi or "the energy that makes us live;" it doesn't matter as long as we understand what it is pointing to. The concept is that a controlling, directing field of energy (an information field) is behind our physical and psychological manifestation. It is this which grows the body in its perfect order, which keeps it regenerating, and, especially important for our purposes, repairs anything that is broken or damaged. I would love to explore this with you in more detail, but entire books could be (and have been) written about this. Let me give you just one small example of the amazing organizational ability of the force of life.

Ocean sponges are relatively simple creatures, in that there are a limited number of cells that live on top of a supporting skeleton that gives the sponge shape (similar to how our bones give our bodies shape). The sponge creatures, of which there are many types, are consistent enough in their form and characteristics that we can recognize them under different names, as different species. You can take one of these sponges, cut it up into little pieces and squeeze them through a silk cloth so that all the little cells are separated from each other. It results in this "porridge" that has no recognizable shape or resemblance to what you started with. Here is the interesting part: If you let this gruel stand for a while *it gathers and reorganizes itself*, resulting in a completely normal sponge identical to the one that was sepa-

rated, a sponge that goes on living like nothing has happened.

As if this is not amazing enough, in one experiment, two different types of sponges—a red one and a yellow species, not related to each other—were put through this process and mixed together. Nonetheless, over the next 24 hours the red and yellow cells managed to separate themselves and reorganize back into the original sponges that they were at the beginning. As Lyall Watson puts it in his remarkable book, *Supernature*, that describes these experiments, "This ability to instill order is the most vital and peculiar characteristic of living beings."

But as modern science was taking shape, a philosophical split occurred between the *vitalists*, who asserted the existence of such a force that animated and governed physical organisms, and the *materialists*, who denied it and said that all life could be explained in terms of chemical and physical processes. The materialists predominated, and their views became the underpinning of our contemporary science, medicine, and culture. Because this perspective mostly discounts the organism's guiding intelligence, it is not surprising that mainstream medicine generally treats symptoms like an enemy that must be controlled and suppressed.

Understandably, this turning point in the history of science explains why most of us today look almost exclusively to physical explanations for disease. We look first for germs, parasites, genetic defects, or just plain wear and tear from old age. In addition, our bias is to focus our research money on those physical factors that best tie in with marketable solutions, such as a new drug, rather than those that would require a change of diet or lifestyle or a cleanup of the environment.

So, although doctors may pay some lip service to avoiding emotional stress or may notice how often patients get sick after suffering a psychological upset, the usual "fix" for a health problem involves drugs or surgery. While we may personally acknowledge the importance of thoughts and feelings and perhaps even a unifying intelligence responsible for our living form, as a society we do not seriously take this perspective into account in the prevention and treatment of most diseases.

THE RE-EMERGENCE OF HOLISTIC THERAPIES

In recent times, however, many practitioners and lay people alike have felt constrained by the limits of this approach and have begun to explore and revitalize a number of holistic therapies, both for humans and for animals. What do we mean by the word "holistic"? I have to laugh at some of the definitions I have come across. For example, one person told me, "My veterinarian uses holistic medicine. He gave me some vitamin C!" She really thought that using a vitamin was holistic medicine. So let me try to explain.

Considering what we have been talking about in this chapter so far, it will not be a surprise for me to say that "holistic" implies a different perspective on health. Let's start with what is familiar to us—the usual—and then contrast it with what we are calling the holistic view.

Shall we call the medicine of our common experience *contemporary medicine*? Such contemporary medicine is also called *allopathic* medicine, the word allopathic meaning that treatments are intended to control, stop, or inhibit the expressions of disease. This is the approach most of us are used to: the doctor and the veterinarian who offer antibiotics, shots for allergies, vaccinations, surgery, and so on. The basic principle with a drug or surgery is to *control* or to *block* what is seen to be the symptoms of illness. For example, an anti-inflammatory drug (aspirin, steroids) is used in allopathic approaches to stop the expression of inflammation. Another example is a drug that stops epileptic seizures by inhibiting some brain functions. Yes, I know—it seems self-evident, common sense. Yet we do have to acknowledge that if contemporary medicine was *completely* successful, I wouldn't be writing about this and you wouldn't be interested in reading it.

My path in searching for other ways of healing started, and continued, precisely because I came to see the limitations of this approach. Yes, the drug could stop the symptoms—for a while. But it often did not seem to really cure the patient. They would still not feel really well or would have fewer, but chronic, symptoms, sometimes later developing other problems as bad or worse than the first ones.

Another characteristic of allopathic medicine is the technique of looking at the patient "in pieces." Take Benny, for example. Benny was a cute little fox terrier with an excitable nature. When he had his first seizure, it was thought he may have been poisoned. When they recurred, he was put on an anti-epileptic drug. This did make the seizures go away, but Benny spent more time lying about and sleeping. As the months went by, he began losing hair in patches and getting an oily feel to his coat. Another diagnosis was made, of "hypothyroidism," meaning that his thyroid gland was underactive. He began to take a drug that replaced what was not being produced, and Benny did become perkier and his coat got somewhat better. But now he was on two drugs—the anti-epileptic drug and the thyroid hormone—and he was expected to stay on these the rest of his life.

Things went along fairly well for a couple of years, until he started having trouble with the stairs. Instead of a bouncy little guy, he had to come up the stairs slowly and carefully. He was clearly stiff. Further evaluation with x-rays resulted in the diagnosis of "spondylitis," meaning, basically, an arthritis-like condition of the spinal vertebrae. So he went on an anti-inflammatory drug and a painkiller. Now he was on four drugs, and though Nancy, Benny's person, did not exactly ask her veterinarian about the expected outcome, it was assumed he would be on these four drugs the rest of his life.

This little story brings out two points. One is that these health problems were being dealt with one by one, as if they were not connected to each other. After all, how could a problem with his brain (seizures) have anything to do with the thyroid gland? How could being hypothyroid make him have arthritis of his spine? I think it fair to say that most veterinarians would tell their client that these were "unrelated problems."

This is an example of seeing the patient in fragments. It is part of allopathic medicine to have this view. It makes dealing with things easier if you can just handle them one at a time.

THE HOLISTIC PERSPECTIVE

The holistic view differs with both these assumptions. It is understood that a succession of health problems are connected to each other. Why? Because only *one* individual is affected by these symptoms. The assumption is made that the animal is one individual intimately connected at all levels and, as with any complicated process, if one aspect is out of balance, this can throw off another area that is seemingly unrelated. So in Benny's case here's how I see it: The health problem that began as a seizure was an expression of a deeper disorder that was not cured by using a sleepy drug that made his brain run slower. With time, another expression of this disorder showed itself—the thyroid problem—which was also not cured by using a replacement drug. It did not fix the thyroid, just provided a synthetic form of the natural hormone. That he developed arthritis in some form was a further development of this same trouble.

The seizures, the underactive thyroid, the patchy hair loss and greasy coat, and the arthritis of the spine *are all the same disease from beginning to end.* The holistic perspective will not divide these up into different diagnostic categories separate from each other. This becomes even clearer if instead of "holistic" we spell it "wholistic."

"So," you say, "my vet is holistic, yet gives me a diagnosis for each health problem, just like you describe." Yes, this is common. Many veterinarians who are holistic in their perspective will still talk this way because they think you, as the client, are expecting this kind of language. Nonetheless, the holistic practitioner will understand the connection between these conditions in the linked way we are discussing here. That this is significant will be made clearer when we talk about holistic therapies.

Earlier we talked about how in the allopathic perspective, symptoms were to be *countered* with treatment. Holistic medicine is different here as well. Most practitioners with a holistic perspective, including myself, take the view that *symptoms represent the action of the individual's life force.* In creating symptoms, the life force is doing its best to throw off the disturbance through, say, diarrhea, vomiting, coughing, sneezing, pus formation, and the like. Accordingly, we as practitioners try to work *with* the action of the symptoms, gently helping the body in its attempt to restore harmony. In other words, we do not attempt to suppress the symptom, but rather to help the body complete what it

is trying to do. We also consider emotional and mental factors in health, carefully observing fluctuations at these levels and often advising changes that will promote greater internal harmony.

We are not denying the importance of physical factors. Certainly there are virulent microorganisms and environmental assaults of all kinds to consider. But it is important to realize that individuals who are exposed equally to these factors *vary tremendously in their resistance.* Have you ever noticed, for example, how there can be several animals in the same household, all on the same diet and exposed to the same environment, yet one of them seems to have all the fleas or to always pick up every infectious disease that comes along? What we are acknowledging with the holistic perspective is that the strength of the defense mechanism is the most important factor in susceptibility to disease of any sort. By defense mechanism, I mean not just the physical responses described by immunologists, but also the state of the total individual, encompassing mental and emotional qualities, as well as the subtle fields of energy of the life force.

Let me recap it like this: The individual animal is a whole organism, not parts patched together. When healthy and balanced, everything moves along smoothly and there are no symptoms. However, when injured or exposed to an infectious organism, the *whole patient* responds, and this response includes the production of symptoms. These symptoms (even inflammation or pain) are expressions of the healing process the body is going through.

A Contrasting Example

Let's use an example that will make the difference between the two medical perspectives more clear. Imagine, if you will, that you cut your arm and it bled for a while. Don't you fully expect the wound to heal? Don't you also know that the healing will take a while? The usual stages are 1) bleeding, 2) clotting, 3) the wound contracting, 4) a scab forming, 5) new skin growing in under the scab, 6) the scab coming off, 7) fresh, more fragile, healed skin underneath, and 8) the new skin becoming tougher, until it is like your other skin. Typically, this whole process will take a number of days, possibly a couple of weeks. Isn't it obvious that all of these stages are necessary for healing to occur?

Now consider this alternative. You start with the same cut but now take a drug that in a few short hours results in the wound becoming completely healed just like new. Possible? No, of course not. Yes, there are drugs that stop bleeding, take away pain, and prevent infection, but to truly heal, the tissues still have to go through all the healing stages. If the wound is interfered with very much, like using antibiotic ointments, picking off the scab, taking pain killers—it will actually take longer to heal, as these interventions work against the natural healing process.

Realize that we are talking about the healing of a fresh wound in a (presumably) healthy individual. Compare this now to a more chronic condition. Let's say your dog has arthritis in his rear legs, and he is given a prescription that reduces inflammation and pain. Amazingly, *in just a few hours*, he is markedly improved—running around like a puppy again. Wouldn't most people tell their friends about the wonderful cure? But think about it. Arthritis is a much slower and more gradual process than a wound. It comes on over months, maybe years, and there is considerable change in the body—thickening of tissues around joints, change in the joint fluid, even distortion of the cartilage and bones. Is it even possible for something like this to heal in a few hours? Or even in the two weeks it takes a wound to heal? Of course not. It takes considerably longer for arthritis like this to naturally heal to as close to normal as possible—literally months, maybe a year.

So what is happening with this fast response brought on by the drug that seems so miraculous? The drug is suppressing the symptoms that the body is producing in its attempts to heal the condition. It is an artificial effect. By blocking the process, it looks like everything is better, *but nothing has been healed.* We have come to expect this kind of rapid response as one of the miracles of modern allopathic medicine, and it does seem a miracle. The problem is that by blocking symptoms, yet not providing a way for the condition to be healed, the result is a superficial effect that allows the deeper disease to progress over time. This is why you may have had the experience of your pet getting sicker over time rather than better.

Does this perspective seem novel to you? You may be wondering, "Did you just make all this up?" Actually, science has come up with many ideas that now support this approach.

SUPPORT FROM MODERN PHYSICS

Interestingly, developments in modern physics have offered support for the holistic and vitalist perspectives. When the materialist doctrine became the prevailing view, physicists held the now outdated Newtonian idea that the world is ultimately composed of minute particles, discrete "basic building blocks" of matter, such as electrons, photons, and neutrons. Yet, as modern physicists have searched for increasingly smaller particles in hopes of finding The One Basic Building Block from which the rest are formed, they have not found it. Instead, they arrived at a wholly different view. Matter is not really so solid. In fact, according to Fritjof Capra in *The Tao of Physics*, "Particles are merely local condensations of the field; concentrations of energy which come and go, thereby losing their individual character and dissolving into the underlying field." To put it differently, it is an illusion to try to analyze things as though they were separate entities or parts, for all phenomena are manifestations of a whole field of energy that underlies its manifestation.

One of the important implications of this fundamental breakthrough of understanding in physics is that the fragmented, specialized, particulate approach to knowledge that typifies most of science (including medicine) is erroneous at its very root. We must learn to see problems in relation to the whole and not become lost in the divisions of our artificial labels and definitions.

Evolving into this new way of perceiving is not easy. It has taken me years to get where I am now. And I still feel like a beginner in many ways. But I do think a holistic approach is essential if we really want to aim for optimal health and well-being for both ourselves and our animal companions, and I do believe that it is the movement toward holistic therapies that will provide the answer for our most troublesome diseases.

HOW TO PUT THIS INTO PRACTICE

Let's say that this theory makes good sense to you. But your next thought may be, "How can this help my sick pet?"

With many simple conditions, all that is really needed to help an animal get well is to provide a supportive environment, some commonsense care, and a little time. Nature does the job, either with us or in spite of us. But if recurrent or chronic disease or weakness afflicts your animal, a return to health will most likely require major lifestyle changes, as well as specific therapeutic measures, alternative methods to the usual approach. In this approach we will consider the whole animal.

Start with the diet. Is it fresh and natural, or is it highly processed and of inferior quality? Will it support health? Next, consider the environment. Is it peaceful and wholesome or stressful and polluted? Is there adequate sunlight, fresh air, and uncontaminated water? Does the animal have a comfortable, secure, and quiet place to rest? Is the sanitation good? Does the animal receive regular and proper grooming and exercise, or is it unkempt and sedentary?

Now take a look at relationships. Does the animal have plenty of friendly and happy companionship, either with people or with other animals? Or is it often neglected, bored, and frustrated? Are your mental attitudes toward its problem supportive and positive? Or do you broadcast anxiety, worry, and fear? How is it expected to behave? Is it made to be a guard dog, for instance, when its personality rebels at this task? Is there any animal or person in its environment who threatens its well-being or wishes it harm? Did the animal lose someone or something dear to it when the problem began?

Granted, it's not always easy to unravel the problem or to change some circumstances. Still, it helps if you begin to think this way. Rather than focusing your thinking on just physical causes, consider *all* the influences— physical, psychological, environmental—that impact your animal.

If in doubt, start with the natural feeding program outlined earlier, make sure your pet gets regular affection, exercise, and grooming, and then see what problems, if any, remain. If a wholesome physical and emotional environment is not enough to restore it to health, then the problem may be more entrenched, involving an imbalance at a deep level. In that case there are several drugless, holistic therapies that can help to rebalance the body's energies and effectively stimulate healing. Remember, this is the approach we want to use.

It would require many volumes to thoroughly describe all of the possible therapies that could help your animal. However, let's look at the general philosophy and methods of some of the more common holistic therapies that veterinarians and others have used to heal animals. Then I'll describe in greater detail the approach that I favor, homeopathic medicine.

Bear in mind that these therapies are not as separate as they may appear. Most of them share the basic philosophy that I've been talking about here, and many include more than one alternative therapy. For instance, herbal medicine and dietary changes are often used along with acupuncture. As we discuss these treatments, I will suggest which methods will work best together.

NATUROPATHY

Defined by a medical dictionary as a "drugless system of therapy by the use of physical forces, such as air, light, water, heat, massage, etc.," naturopathy entails a comprehensive approach that emphasizes supporting the whole body's physical attempts to eliminate disease; that is, it assists the discharge of disease products. Naturopaths consider the major physical cause of disease to be an excessive buildup of toxic materials, often due to improper eating and lack of exercise. They say these clog the usual avenues of waste disposal.

Naturopaths employ a number of techniques to clean out the body, including some used by various cultures throughout recorded history. One is fasting, a way to rest the digestive system and allow the body to do some internal housecleaning. Patients who are fasting are often advised to drink a lot of pure water or juices to flush out the kidneys, and to take enemas or colonic irrigations to clean out the lower intestines.

Hot and cold treatments may be used to stimulate the circulation or encourage sweating. They may include baths, saunas, packs, compresses, fomentations, steaming, and the like. Other naturopathic methods include exercise, sunbathing, good hygiene, and various massage and brushing techniques. Besides the cleansing processes, patients are put on supportive programs of good nutrition (often emphasizing raw, organic foods and juices), proper food combining (to aid digestion), and judicious use of specific food supplements, vitamins, minerals, and herbs.

Some of these methods are rather difficult or awkward to apply to animals, but others lend themselves easily—particularly fasting,

exercise, good nutrition, sunbathing, and grooming (a form of massage). I encourage their use in many cases.

Donald Ogden, DVM, who made extensive and successful use of naturopathic methods for years in animal medicine, reported that nine out of ten of his skin irritation cases would improve within only two weeks. He has attributed his success to thoroughly bathing the animal, then fasting it for seven days on vegetable broths and then for seven additional days on vegetable solids and soups. He has advised breaking the fast with raw meat and raw or steamed leafy vegetables, followed by a balanced natural foods diet.

Dr. Ogden has also found that quiet rest and fasts of three to ten days (until the pet's temperature is normal and symptoms disappear) are very beneficial for many conditions, including obesity, rheumatism and arthritis, constipation, chronic cardiac insufficiency, bronchial diseases, heart worm, kidney and bladder stones, gastritis, kidney disease, pyorrhea, diabetes, liver disorders (unless cirrhosis has developed), open sores, and the fever stage of distemper.

However, he has advised against fasting an animal with a wasting disease such as cancer, advanced uremia, tuberculosis, prolonged malnutrition, hookworm disease, or distemper.

Naturopathic medicine works well in combination with other holistic approaches, including herbal medicine, chiropractic and other manual therapies, acupuncture, Chinese medicine, and homeopathic medicine. In my practice, I use fasting and enemas occasionally but rely more on the nutritional and hygiene aspects of naturopathic medicine to supplement my treatments.

HERBAL MEDICINE

Herbalists utilize many of the same methods as naturopaths. Their main emphasis, however, is upon the specific use of herbal leaves, roots, and flowers to stimulate healing. Basic to folk medicine in every culture since ancient times, herb use is probably the most fundamental system of applying specific remedies. When ill, wild animals have used herbs instinctively for eons.

In fact, many of our modern pharmaceutical drugs are actually compounds originally isolated from herbs and considered to be their active elements. For instance, digitalis derives from foxglove, atropine from belladonna (deadly nightshade), caffeine from coffee, theophylline from tea, arecoline from the areca (betel) nut, and reserpine (used for high blood pressure) from *Rauwolfia serpentina.*

Herbalists contend that the pharmaceutical derivatives and the whole plants from which they come are not the same, however, and I agree with this from my experience. The strength of herbs is in the unique and complex properties of the original natural substance. Again, the whole is more than the sum of its parts.

As compared to their pharmaceutical counterparts, herbs generally exhibit a slower and deeper action. They assist the healing process by helping the body to eliminate and detoxify, thus taking care of the problem the symptoms are expressing. For instance, they may stimulate physiological processes like emptying of the bowels or urination. In addition, they can serve as tonics and builders that resonate with and strengthen tissues in specific parts of the body (or the whole body, depending on the herb in question). They can also be highly nutritious, containing large amounts of various vitamins and minerals and other nutrients. And there are some herbal practitioners who believe that plant medicines, particularly those found locally, bring the healing energy of the environment to the user.

Herbal remedies have been successfully used to treat many illnesses in animals throughout the centuries. In recent years Juliette de Bairacli-Levy has popularized their use for this purpose through her detailed writings (which also emphasize the importance of natural diet and fasting). She's reported good results in using herbs to treat dogs with worms, fleas, skin problems, mange, distemper, kidney and bladder trouble, arthritis, anemia, diabetes, leptospirosis, obesity, wounds and fractures, constipation, diarrhea, jaundice, heart disorders, warts, and cataracts. De Bairacli-Levy recommends using the freshly gathered herb whenever possible and replacing dried herbs yearly. I concur with this advice. In chapter 15, I will describe the standard methods of preparing infusions, decoctions, and tinctures from herbs. In the "Quick Reference" section, I suggest specific herbs for various illnesses.

Besides the difficulty of finding fresh herbs, one disadvantage of using internal herbal therapy for companion animals is that the remedies are usually administered in sizable quantities at frequent intervals over long periods of time (weeks to months). Since they rarely taste appealing, you need to give them to a pet in capsules or else disguised in food (and that can be tough to do—they have really good taste buds). As every animal lover knows, it's not easy to force medication down a pet's throat, much less over a long period.

For that reason and others, I prefer to emphasize homeopathic medications, which taste good and are given less often. Many of these are derived from plants. Another related system I have used with animals are the 38 flower essences discovered by Dr. Edward Bach. (Both systems are described later in this chapter.)

I have, however, seen the power of well-chosen herbs as well and recognize their value. I find them most useful for *external* treatments on animals (as in flea powders and rinses, mite control, skin problems, and wounds) or for *minor* upsets (such as diarrhea, indigestion, and the like) that do not require prolonged treatment.

In summary, herbal medicines will act physically by providing nutrients and substances that promote more normal func-

tioning. They also can stimulate the natural healing processes of the body. In this way they serve as a sort of bridge between drug use and the more subtle effects of homeopathy and Bach Flower Essences.

Herbal medicine works well with naturopathy, chiropractic and other manual therapies, acupuncture and Chinese medicine, and, *when restricted to the milder herbs*, homeopathic medicine.

CHIROPRACTIC AND OTHER MANUAL THERAPIES

Since the time of Hippocrates, manipulative therapies have been in use throughout the world. Some of these, like chiropractic and osteopathy, both founded in the 19th century, view disease conditions as the result of misaligned or abnormal bodily structures (especially in the spine) that interfere with the normal flow of life force, nerve impulses, and blood circulation.

Of these, chiropractic has become the largest drugless healing profession in the U.S. I first became interested in the potential this therapy holds for animals when I talked with a local chiropractor who told me that many different conditions in pets have been helped by chiropractic, including epilepsy.

The original theory of chiropractic holds that subtle vertebral misalignments can block the essential flow of nerve energy passing through the spinal column. This irregularity, known as a subluxation, puts excessive pressure on the spinal nerves, thus interfering with various body functions. Treatment consists of careful manipulation of the vertebrae to restore correct alignment and full working order. To achieve this specialized skill, practitioners usually undergo at least four years of medical training.

A broader way to understand how manipulative therapies may work is to view the body and mind as one whole. Each part of the body both reflects and affects the whole system. Disturbances in one local part are felt throughout the entire system and may cause "resonant" problems in a generalized way. There are a number of advocates of diagnostic and manipulative therapy who focus on certain parts of the body from the understanding that they reflect or represent the whole organism. For instance, an iridologist "reads" disturbances in various organs by a careful examination of the iris of the eye. Practitioners of reflexology pinpoint and treat disturbances elsewhere in the body by manual pressure on certain points of the feet and hands. Some acupuncturists diagnose and treat problems solely at points on the ear, which is said to reflect the whole body. I have met one veterinary acupuncturist who now uses only the ear to successfully treat health problems in horses—even lameness! Polarity therapy, which involves the placing of hands on different parts of the body to channel energy flows, has also been used on pets and relies upon a method of reading and treating disturbances by a similarly holistic approach.

In the same way, it may be that body and mind disturbances are reflected in the spinal column, associated with irregular muscular tensions and vertebral displacements. If so, they should respond to corrective spinal manipulation.

Regardless of how and why it works, chiropractic manipulation has proved to be a real boon for many animal patients. For example, a *Prevention* magazine reader wrote me to describe the amazing response of her 18-year-old cat to chiropractic therapy. Twelve years prior, her cat began developing severe attacks of vomiting, loss of appetite, and intense itching of the face and shoulders. The poor cat licked and scratched until its skin was bloody. The owner consulted several different veterinarians, but their drug therapy offered only temporary help, at best.

By chance, this woman mentioned the situation to her chiropractor and he offered to try to help. Just one adjustment brought startling results: The cat stopped vomiting and began to eat well. Four adjustments were done and the condition has not reappeared in the two years since.

Another case that was reported in a veterinary publication concerned a silky terrier diagnosed by his veterinarian as having a "protruding disc," with pain and loss of function. X-rays revealed calcium deposits in the area and a misaligned vertebral joint. Surgery was rejected because of the high cost. After two weeks of unproductive drug therapy and confinement, chiropractic treatment was suggested. Though the dog had to be carried into the office, within a couple of minutes after the adjustment, he walked out painlessly. The improvement was lasting.

The use of chiropractic manipulation by veterinarians has developed rapidly in the last decade, and it is more common now to find a veterinarian who can offer this treatment. The American Veterinary Chiropractic Association trains veterinarians and can give you a referral (see www.drpitcairn.com for contact information).

Chiropractic works well in conjunction with herbal medicine, naturopathic medicine, acupuncture and Oriental medicine, and homeopathic medicine.

ACUPUNCTURE AND ORIENTAL MEDICINE

One traditional holistic approach that has made fairly significant inroads into the modern veterinary profession is acupuncture and other aspects of Oriental medicine. There are texts on the subject, as well as organizations for the training of veterinarians—the International Veterinary Acupuncture Society (IVAS) and the American Academy of Veterinary Acupuncture (see www.drpitcairn.com for both). In response to growing interest among students, some veterinary schools are also offering an elective course in acupuncture and Chinese medicine.

The basic theory behind this ancient and comprehensive system is that the fundamental energy fields (*chi*) that comprise the body (as well as all aspects of the universe)

manifest as two poles, *yin* and *yang*. They are reminiscent of the positive and negative electrical charges described by physics.

Yin is described as disruptive, distributing, expanded, and negative. Yang is said to be constructive, focusing, contracted, and positive. Your state of health depends on the proper balance between these two two sides of the same coin. A skilled therapist can correct excesses or deficiencies by manipulating certain critical acupoints along the body's meridians, the channels through which energy flows. The flow of energy must be redirected. This may be done with needles (acupuncture), finger pressure (acupressure or shiatsu), burning the herb mugwort near the point (moxibustion), or, in modern times, electrical stimulation (electroacupuncture), injection of various solutions (aquapuncture), the use of ultrasound (sonapuncture), lasers, and the implantation of small gold beads.

The American Veterinary Medical Association has taken an interest in acupuncture and has encouraged scientific documentation of its results. According to Allen Schoen, DVM, of Ridgefield, Connecticut, one of the pioneers in the field of holistic medicine and the one who introduced acupuncture to the well-known Animal Medical Center of New York City, the kinds of conditions that acupuncture can best help include:

❖ Musculoskeletal problems, such as arthritis, slipped disk, and hip dysplasia (malformed and dislocated hip joint)

- Skin diseases and allergic dermatitis
- Chronic gastrointestinal diseases, such as chronic diarrhea or vomiting, equine colic, and prolapsed rectum
- A variety of other problems such as chronic pain syndrome, breeding problems, respiratory arrest, and coma

Dr. Schoen notes that acupuncture, like other alternative healing methods, may take time and repetition to produce results. He asks new clients to commit themselves to at least eight treatments in chronic cases. "If someone has six treatments without seeing any results, and then stops, it doesn't mean that acupuncture doesn't work. It can take a while to stimulate the body to heal itself," he emphasizes. I have found the same thing in working with homeopathy—that it takes more time to observe the healing process happening than we expect from our experience with suppressive drugs.

Like any system of medicine, however, acupuncture has its "miracles." Sheldon Altman, DVM of Burbank, California, an active teacher, writer, and practitioner of veterinary acupuncture, tells of a Doberman suffering from panosteitis (a painful bone disease). With only one treatment, he walked out pain-free after six months of limping. The pain did not return. Don't we all wish such results for our own animals?

One of the most wonderful things about a holistic system like this is how apparently hopeless cases can be so helped. Dr. Schoen recalls the case of a golden retriever with a paralyzed esophagus who had vomited about 16 times a day for the previous year and a half. All conventional therapies had failed, and the owners had to use special feeding techniques to keep the food down. After four acupuncture treatments, her vomiting finally ceased. Treatments were tapered off and she has remained well since.

As you might guess, such an approach can also be used to *prevent* disease, much like getting a "tune-up" for the body. In fact, the ancient Chinese, who developed acupuncture over thousands of years of practice and observation, emphasized prevention above all else. They resorted to acupuncture or herbs only when the preferred methods (meditation, exercise, massage) were insufficient. Most contemporary acupuncturists emphasize a total approach to health and include advice on the use of food, herbs, and lifestyle recommendations, as well.

Acupuncture and Chinese medicine, like homeopathy, is a complete system that stands on its own. For that reason, it is best not to combine it with homeopathy, because, in my experience, the two can interfere with each other. Some practitioners use it along with naturopathic and manipulative therapies, and an experienced practitioner can best determine the suitability of this.

HOMEOPATHY

We now come to my own particular love, the science of homeopathy. In my search for effective holistic therapies, I started out using nutrition and herbs. I still do, along with naturopathic methods. But, by themselves, they didn't always address every circumstance. Excellent as the nutritional approach is, there are instances when the animal simply will not eat or will reject all but the most specific foods, a limiting factor. Also, some severe illnesses, like bacterial or viral infections, simply progress too fast for nutrition to make a difference. One wants a treatment method that will act decisively in these situations, restoring appetite, enhancing resistance against the infection, yet work with the body's healing process.

So I kept my eyes and ears open for a more effective system. I kept hearing praise for homeopathy. Finally, I decided to examine it for myself. That decision was a turning point that expanded my horizons to embrace a medical approach of unique elegance, order, and effectiveness.

Homeopathy is practiced on both people and animals in most of the world. Because it is so powerfully effective, it deserves far more attention than it presently receives in the U.S. The contributions of homeopathy to our general understanding of health and disease have been enormous. Because of its many virtues, I hope it will become a prominent medical art of the future.

To further this goal, in 1992 I began a post-graduate course for veterinarians, and it has continued every year since. In 1995, some of us who were practicing veterinary homeopathy started a professional organization, the Academy of Veterinary Homeopa-

thy, which accredits training programs, holds an annual conference, publishes a journal, and certifies veterinarians as qualified to practice. As of 2004, over 400 veterinarians have participated in this training and incorporated homeopathy in their practices.

The real beauty of the homeopathic system lies in the simplicity of its basic principles, combined with richly researched detail to guide the practitioner in choosing the most suitable remedy. *The Science of Homeopathy*, by George Vithoulkas, is an important modern discussion of the principles involved and is invaluable for a person interested in *any* form of holistic therapy.

Homeopathy was founded on one basic unifying principle, "Like is cured by like" (*Similia similibus curentur*), known as the Law of Similars and recognized by Hippocrates and many others. This principle has remained the foundation of homeopathy ever since the early 1800s when the German physician Samuel Hahnemann originated the system.

What does this phrase "like is cured by like" mean? Remember that earlier in this chapter we talked about the allopathic method of countering symptoms? Homeopathy is just the opposite in its approach. Medicines are used that stimulate similar symptoms in the body. "Whoa," you may think, "this doesn't make any sense. My cat is already sick; he doesn't need more of this." Allow me to explain.

Dr. Hahnemann noted that some herbs that were really, really helpful in curing some diseases would produce similar but milder symptoms of the illness if given to a healthy person. In other words, it is one thing to treat a sick person, but what does this herb really do in the body? He tested this theory by using herbs in healthy people to see what changes would occur. What he found is that an herb (or other substance—we will get to that) that could produce mild but similar symptoms to the disease condition being treated *acted to stimulate the body's healing mechanism.* He had actually found a way to enhance recovery from disease by using the body's own natural processes.

How does it act? Let me give you an example. Before I go into this I want to make clear that *very small doses* of homeopathic medicines are used. One of the fortuitous discoveries that Dr. Hahnemann made was that it took quite tiny amounts of this similar medicine to do the trick. Keep this in mind when we look at my example.

Let's say that you have an allergy—certain foods will set off a painful skin eruption of raised red welts, bumps that itch and sting. These bumps appear all over your body, along with a bad headache and feeling sleepy and sluggish. The only thing that gives relief (short of powerful painkillers) is to put a cold cloth over the worst places. The headache is slightly better from pressing on the head with the hands. What a terrible condition to have!

To treat this homeopathically we can use a *different* substance (it is important that it be different than the food that set it off) that will result in symptoms like this. Is there such a homeopathic medicine? Yes, made from honeybee venom. It was discovered by carefully studying the effects of this venom that it can result (in people stung, for example) in a skin eruption just like this—raised welts like nettle rash, relieved only by cold applications. Not only that, but some people will get a headache that is relieved by pressure and also feel sleepy and out of sorts. A good match, wouldn't you say?

To treat this, the person will be given a tiny dose of bee venom by mouth. How small? Much smaller than a drop—perhaps a millionth of a drop. This is when the miracle occurs. No sooner than the homeopathic pills are put in their mouth than symptoms start to clear up, often in just a few minutes. It is like a miracle—indeed, it is one when you are the one suffering.

So this is the basic principle: the medicine used is known to cause similar symptoms to what the patient has, and when given in very small doses, it will trigger a reaction that allows the body to heal itself.

A good practitioner can read a whole set of signals flashed by a disease. Rather than prescribing one medication for a headache, another for an upset stomach, and a third for depression, the homeopathic doctor will offer a *single* remedy for the whole set of symptoms that are present in the patient. She will choose the one medication that would produce all three symptoms if given repeatedly to a healthy person.

The specially prepared remedies used in homeopathy contain minute doses of botan-

Most homeopathic preparations can be purchased in a specific strength. For example, if treatment for nausea requires *Ipecac* 3X, you simply purchase the medicine at that strength.

The number following the name of the remedy indicates how many times the original substance has been diluted.

For example, 1X indicates that one drop of medication has been added to nine drops of alcohol and subjected to energetic shaking. The medication is now at 1/10 of its original concentration. If you add one drop of this 1X mixture to nine drops of alcohol, the solution would be labeled 2X, at 1/100th of its original strength.

Thus: 1X = 1/10 concentration; 2X = 1/100; 3X = 1/1,000 and so on. These same numerical indications of remedy potency also apply to powders, which are diluted with powdered milk sugar.

The same process applies to the making of the "C" preparations. Most of the prescriptions I suggest in this book use medicines as "30C," as in *Belladonna* 30C. Making this series of homeopathic remedies differs only in that each dilution is 1/100 instead of 1/10 (as above). Thus a 30C potency has been diluted 1/100 thirty times.

In rare instances, the "Quick Reference" section directs you to dilute certain medications on your own. For example, you may be asked to dilute *Echinacea* by adding ten drops of the tincture to one cup of water. Simply follow the directions in the "Quick Reference" section as you would a recipe.

icals, minerals, or animal products, such as bee venom and cuttlefish ink. These substances are diluted and repeatedly agitated many times, so that only minuscule amounts actually remain. Sometimes dilution is so extreme that it goes far beyond the point where the substance could act on a molecular level. While there is much debate about how such diluted materials can work, many homeopaths (myself included) believe what Dr. Hahnemann originally said about it— that the specially prepared medicine carries a healing energy derived from the original material, what he referred to as "potency."

I can testify from my own experience of more than 25 years of use that homeopathic remedies do work—and very, very well. When I am able to recognize the unique symptom picture—taking into account the mental, emotional, and physical levels—and match it to the right remedy, I can be certain the patient will respond.

The essential requirement is a very close similarity between the remedy and the pattern of the disease. Think of it like this: the remedy has the ability to *stimulate* the healing process of the patient because its pattern is so similar to the illness itself that the body cannot tell it apart. As a result, the patient's life energy will "try harder" than before to restore the body to normal healthy balance. It does this through all the normal mechanisms of healing—fever, inflammation, discharge (sweating, diarrhea, vomiting, drainage from a wound), production of interferon, production of antibodies, etc. And because it is given in such dilute form, it does not cause unwanted physical side effects. So we have the advantage of a treatment method that stimulates and accelerates natural healing forces without causing side effects. You can see why I was excited to learn about homeopathy!

To identify what conditions a remedy can cure, it is first tested by a group of human volunteers who take the substance in a diluted form for several days or weeks. Each day they note their changes—mental, emotional, and physical—in a diary. Combining this detailed information with that of the cases it has cured and the poisonings it has accidentally caused, homeopaths develop a characteristic "symptom picture" of each substance, known as proving. Eventually, it is added to a *Materia Medica,* a reference that catalogs the effects of hundreds of medicines. The chief reference work I use for this purpose is a ten-volume set of books called *Hering's Guiding Symptoms of our Materia Medica* that contains information on hundreds of homeopathic medicines.

SOME EXAMPLE CASES

Let me tell you about a few animal cases that demonstrate homeopathic treatment.

When I was first learning homeopathy, I encountered Misty, a cat suffering with septicemia, a rare, post-surgical reaction following a routine spay. It involves bacterial spread in the bloodstream and a general breakdown of the blood-clotting mechanism. She was in pitiable condition, with a high fever and vomiting. Dark blood leaked from her back, stomach, legs, feet, mouth, and vagina. I also detected bleeding under the skin (dark blue swellings under the eyelids and ears). Though antibiotics might help, I was not sure they would act quickly enough in this crisis situation—it often does not. She seemed to get worse even while I was examining her!

As a temporary measure I decided to administer fluids under her skin, to help counter her moderate dehydration. While doing so, I immediately noticed that she was very hypersensitive to pain, far more than I would expect. She could not bear being touched at all. At this point, I recognized the similarity between Misty's condition and the provings of the remedy *Arnica montana* (from the herb Leopard's Bane). Among the characteristics of *Arnica* are fever, hemorrhage, black and blue spots under the skin from bleeding, septic conditions, hypersensitivity to pain, and an aversion to touch.

So I immediately gave Misty a tablet of *Arnica* and repeated it every few hours. Later in the day she was much improved. By the next morning, her temperature had dropped and she was no longer bleeding. She was obviously calmer—eating for the first time since becoming ill. Within 48 hours, the only remaining evidence of what had so recently been a life-threatening condition were a few dry scabs where the hemorrhages had been, and she was discharged. She remained in good health. I was quite impressed that such results had occurred *without any necessity to use antibiotics or other drugs.*

I'm often amazed to see how *rapidly* homeopathic medications can work. I usually find that in acute problems, they restore health much more quickly than drugs, and I have used them to treat a gamut of acute problems from severe infections like parvovirus or distemper to gunshot wounds, bites, punctures, and abscesses. But they also excel in chronic conditions, which are the bulk of my practice—allergies, auto-immune diseases, hyperthyroidism, urinary disorders, appetite problems, behavioral abnormalities, paralysis, skin problems, gum disease, and so on. In short, the whole gamut of animal disease.

A recent example of a more advanced chronic condition is a dog I treated with se-vere advanced spinal arthritis. Wilkie is an old Lab cross with arthritis of the spinal bones, weakness of the rear legs, and gradual wasting away of his muscles. As often happens with this condition, he exerted himself too much on an adventure and was unable to rise to his feet the next morning. The weakened spine will be easily injured or there will be a small break in the calcium deposits around the bones. In any case, he couldn't use his legs anymore because of the paralysis and extreme pain. With homeopathic treatment, he has improved to where he can take fairly long walks—even running along at times. The difference in these chronic, advanced cases is that progress is slower, in this case taking several weeks to achieve this much recovery.

Homeopathy works very well with nutritional therapy. An example case that comes to mind is Toby, an older cat whose lab tests had confirmed that he had feline infectious peritonitis—a terminal condition not curable with drugs. His symptoms included repeated vomiting, diarrhea, loss of appetite, and swelling of the abdomen. Over a period of several days, my client and I gradually changed his diet to a home-prepared one (as outlined in this book) and increased his vitality through the use of vitamins and thymus gland nutritional supplements. I then recognized an appropriate homeopathic remedy, which for this particular fellow was *Arsenicum album* (white oxide of arsenic). (Lest this alarm you, let me assure you that, once again, the amount of arsenic in a homeopathic remedy is less than is found in the food you eat, where it is present as a trace mineral.)

So I gave him one dose, which was followed by a short aggravation of symptoms for a couple of days and then a continued improvement for a long period. Two months later the vomiting began to recur and I gave one more dose. He quickly returned to normal health and has remained stable ever since. On top of it all, his personality improved, so that he is now considerably calmer and steadier, and his weight increased from 6 to 11 pounds!

Favorable personality changes often accompany successful physical treatment. Indeed, homeopathic remedies *can* be used to treat personality problems. For instance, one client's cat had spontaneously developed a drastic personality change for the worse. Where she had once been friendly, she was now irritable, resistant to being held, and generally standoffish. Homeopathic treatment with *Nux vomica* (poison nut) restored her normal affectionate self.

This improvement of emotional or personality disorders is one of the most exciting aspects of working with homeopathy. Before I was knowledgeable about homeopathy, behavior problems in animals were frustrating and hopeless to deal with. Usually, the best advice available was using drugs like tranquilizers or elaborate training that was time-consuming and not very effective. With homeopathy, that whole picture has changed.

Another example is that of a dog who underwent a Jekyll-Hyde transformation not long after getting a rabies shot. Formerly happy and friendly, he became suspicious, aggressive, and "barky." Worse yet, he began biting people—hard! Fortunately, I was able to restore this dog to his normal, happy self with one dose of a remedy called *Stramonium* (Thorn Apple). This remedy is used for disturbances of the brain with the above symptoms of suspicion, aggressive behavior, and biting. (It's used in people that are mentally disturbed and who, believe it or not, exhibit this same behavior.) Unfortunately, we see these behavior disorders coming on after rabies vaccination much too often. Apparently, it causes a low-grade inflammation of the brain in some animals.

What about combining homeopathic therapy with other natural approaches? It should not be combined with acupuncture or Chinese medicine as it is too similar in action, and the two methods interfere with each other. It is compatible with naturopathic and nutritional therapies—as mentioned above in the case with Toby—as well as chiropractic and other manipulative therapies. Some mild herbs can be used with homeopathy, but tinctures of herbs, especially large doses and herbs that affect the nervous system, should be avoided.

RESEARCH IN HOMEOPATHY

Even though homeopathy has been successfully used for over 200 years, people will still ask what research supports its use. So it is good to know that considerable research into the efficacy of homeopathy has been done in modern times.

In a double-blind study of 46 human patients with rheumatoid arthritis, half were given homeopathic treatment and half were given placebos (unmedicated tablets of the same appearance). To rule out the effect of suggestion, neither the attending doctors nor the patients knew whether a remedy or a placebo was being taken. When the results were unveiled, they clearly showed that the treated group had significant improvement in subjective pain, joint tenderness, grip strength, and morning stiffness. All of this was accomplished without any toxic reactions or side effects (*British Journal of Clinical Pharmacology*, May 1980).

Another interesting aspect about homeopathic research is that the remedies are tested on *people*, not animals. Because important mental and emotional symptoms must be studied before the action of a substance is fully grasped, only astute human observers can note and report these internal events. They are volunteers, and any unpleasant symptoms they develop during the provings go away after they cease taking the substance.

This is a world apart from conventional laboratory studies, where we try to recreate our diseases in animals. From a holistic viewpoint, such research will never solve the problem of human disease. We can and must do that ourselves, by using this tremendous opportunity to study disease processes as they naturally occur in human beings. Although the suffering of laboratory animals is routinely justified as necessary for developing better treatments for humans, the success of homeopathic medicine underscores the fallacy of this assumption. And homeopathy has the capability to treat successfully any of the illnesses that are usually treated by allopathic (Western medicine) drug therapy.

FLOWER ESSENCES

In addition to homeopathic remedies, a similar system to homeopathy is Bach flower essences. Developed in England by Dr. Edward Bach, these essences are used to treat emotional states. Though these dilute infusions of flowers and tree buds are said to act primarily upon the mental state, a psychological improvement often brings a physical one as well. These extracts are given orally several times a day, often for several weeks. They are not the same as homeopathy, however, and act in a different way.

One case in which I used a flower essence involved a dog, Jamie, with a host of distressing symptoms. These included a loss of appetite, lack of energy, unusual behavior, vomiting, collapse, fever, a moist coat, a tense abdomen, and enlarged spleen. In addition, laboratory tests showed that she was anemic, with abnormally shaped red blood cells, an above-normal number of white blood cells, elevated liver enzymes (indicating liver damage), elevated cholesterol and bile pigments, high blood sugar, and so on. The x-rays taken were normal.

Because I knew the family was under stress, I suspected that emotional disturbance was playing an important role. Accordingly, I prescribed one of the Bach flower essences, *Larch*, to be given four times a day for a week. For the first few hours after starting the treatment, Jamie's symptoms became exaggerated, but she was markedly better by the next day. A week later, her symptoms were gone and have not returned for over a year. In addition, her personality changed. For the first time, she became more playful and outgoing with the other animals in the family. This change has persisted even though the original treatment was for only a week.

I've also found the Bach flowers useful in some conditions that developed shortly after a traumatic or upsetting experience. For instance, a woman brought in a cat a couple of weeks after it had been violently shaken by a large dog. He was uncomfortable, irritable, and constipated, with a fever, weight loss, fluid accumulation in the lungs, and a painful abdomen. The most severe injury was a displaced vertebra in the lower back, which I could feel was out of place. It hurt the cat very much when I touched it.

I prescribed the Bach flower *Star of Bethlehem* (indicated for fright after trauma), two drops every two hours. Three days later, the cat's owner called to say that her cat was quite recovered. The drops had noticeably relaxed her. After a couple of days of treatment, she began stretching by hooking her claws in a piece of firewood and pulling from side to side. Apparently the stretching corrected the back problem. Soon it was difficult to medicate the cat—she was too busy leaping tall fences in a single bound!

The 38 flower preparations discovered by Dr. Bach are compatible with any other system of treatment. They are mild in their effect and cannot cause problems even when "overused." I generally do not use them with homeopathy, preferring one method at a time. They are quite useful for emotional upsets, after injuries, and where there is a great fear.

THE HOLISTIC ALTERNATIVE

As you can see, some pretty remarkable things can happen when we adopt a new view of the wholeness of the body and mind and treat from there. The success of the holistic therapies described in this chapter depends on the skill of the practitioner, the strength and will of the patient, the degree of support in the environment, the appropriateness of the selected method, and the cooperation of you, your animal's friend and companion.

This brief survey was meant to introduce you to the many exciting approaches that can help to relieve the suffering of animals. And if we are but willing to extend our mental horizons, how much more is possible?

CHAPTER 15

HOW TO CARE
FOR A SICK ANIMAL

If your animal gets sick, there are several advantages to caring for it at home, if your family situation allows for seeing to the animal's needs. First, home is familiar and safe, free of the stress a pet is likely to feel trying to recuperate in a busy veterinary hospital filled with unfamiliar animals and people. Second, if you have the time, you can provide some really useful nursing care at home. Fasting, special nutrition, or meticulous cleaning might not be provided in a hospital, either because these things take too much time or because the philosophy of disease treatment is different. Third, at home you are in charge; alternative or natural forms of treatment can be used without conflict.

On the other hand, a veterinarian is a skilled professional. Years of training and experience enable him or her to assess the seriousness of a condition and use the proper diagnostic techniques. For conditions that are either very messy to take care of (like severe vomiting and diarrhea) or life-threatening (such as a car accident or severe infection), the veterinary hospital offers support that is impossible to provide at home, including such treatments as anti-shock therapy, intravenous fluids, and surgery.

Both at home and in the hospital, your pet can recover faster and more completely if you utilize the general health care principles in this book and some of the nursing care methods outlined in this chapter. If, however, you are giving your animal a prescription drug recommended by your veterinarian, do *not* use the homeopathic remedies suggested in the Quick Reference section of alphabetical entries at the end of this book, since they tend to work against each other. You can, however, use some of the herbal recommendations, particularly those that are suggested for external use or those whose primary purpose is to help rebuild the tissues.

A seriously ill animal has certain basic needs. When wild animals are sick or injured, they go off by themselves to rest in a secure, peaceful place and to allow nature to heal the condition. We need to provide our pets with a comparable opportunity. Most sick animals want to be quiet, safe, and warm and to have access to fresh air and sunlight. Also, they often will fast instinctively. The loss of appetite seen in many diseases, especially acute infectious ones, is part of the healing response, rather than a symptom to be forcibly overridden.

So provide comfortable bedding in a cozy spot that is free of drafts, disturbances, and loud noise, where your dog or cat can rest peacefully and feel protected. Keep the area clean, changing the blankets or towels as necessary. If your pet desires it, allow some access to fresh air and sunlight (but don't impose it).

FASTING

Generally, it's good to encourage fasting the first day or two of an illness, especially if there is a fever. A good rule of thumb is to fast your pet until its temperature returns to normal—one to two days, or as long as four to five, if necessary, provided that the animal is in reasonably healthy condition to start with. Remember that a normal body temperature is less than 101.5°F.

Fasting is one of the oldest and most natural methods of healing. Normally, the body constantly eliminates waste products, along with any tainted or toxic materials that were consumed. Fasting greatly reduces the body's usual assimilation and elimination load, allowing it to break down and expel older wastes that may have accumulated in the liver and fatty tissues. The body also gets a chance to unload the products of inflammation, tumors, and abscesses. Once the body has cleansed itself, the overworked glands, organs, and cells have a chance to repair and restore themselves.

Of course, you should not attempt a long fast without professional guidance. See the section on naturopathy in chapter 14 for conditions that generally benefit from fasting, as well as for those for which fasting should not be used.

The following program is a good basic guideline for fasting your animal. It can be used during illnesses, but it also can help your pet switch from its old eating habits to a new natural foods diet.

THE BREAK-IN PERIOD

Begin by easing the animal into the fast for one to two days. Feed it a lighter, simpler diet that includes a moderate or small amount of lean meat or tofu, along with some vegetables and cooked oatmeal. (Of course, if your animal is suddenly ill and loses its appetite, this step is not necessary or appropriate.)

Use vegetables considered beneficial to the kidneys and the liver—organs that will play major roles during the fast. They include broccoli, kale, cauliflower, cabbage, beets and turnips (with tops), dandelion greens, squash, spinach, corn, potatoes, cucumbers, parsley, carrots, and tomatoes. Serve these foods either raw and finely grated (which is preferable), or lightly steamed.

THE LIQUID FAST

Next, proceed with the main part of the fast, a liquid diet. In acute problems, continue the fast until the temperature is normal and the animal is well on its way to recovery. In more chronic or degenerative conditions, the length of the fast may vary from about three to seven days—until there is substantial improvement and a hearty appetite returns. If you begin reintroducing solids and your animal doesn't seem hungry for them, stay with the liquid fast a little longer.

During this period, offer plenty of the following:

❖ Water: Use a pure source, such as bottled, spring, filtered, or distilled water. Do not use tap water, which may contain unwholesome chemicals.

❖ Vegetable juices: Use fresh juices only. Don't use juice more than 48 hours old. If you can't give your pet fresh juice, offer chopped or grated raw vegetables (especially greens and juicy ones) blended with pure water and strained through a sieve. If you can't come up with either of these alternatives, feed water and the broth recipe that follows.

❖ Vegetable broth: Using the vegetables listed for the break-in period, make a soup stock by chopping and then simmering them for 20 to 30 minutes. You may add a small amount of meat or a bone to flavor the stock, but no spices or salt. Pour off the liquid for the animal and save the solids for a soup or casserole for yourself.

If your animal is young or run-down and seems to need a little extra energy, you can occasionally offer it a teaspoon or so of honey.

If you notice your pet having strained or constipated bowel movements early in the liquid fast stage, you can help get things going by slowly (over one to two minutes) administering an enema (see the instructions under "Special Care" in this chapter). Though an enema is seldom needed during a short fast if your pet is in fairly good shape, the animal with a chronic disease or an acute infection will benefit from several enemas during the longer fast.

BREAKING THE FAST

When it's time to end the fast, give your pet a simple diet for several days. This transition diet should last two to three days for every seven days the animal was on liquids. Offer water, juice, broth, and a moderate amount of raw or steamed vegetables (from the same group used before), plus a little unpasteurized milk, if available, or plain yogurt. After this period, begin adding other natural foods, starting with oatmeal or flaked barley cereal (cooked), milk, honey, and figs or prunes. Then, after a day or two, offer some raw lean meat (or tofu or cottage cheese), some other grains or dairy products, and some nutritional yeast, until you have worked into the standard natural diet with supplements.

It is very important that you break the animal out of the fast gradually and that you avoid any temptation to feed commercial foods or highly processed tidbits at this point, or else you may undo the beneficial ef-

fects of the fast and cause serious digestive upsets by overtaxing the system before it has fully reestablished peristalsis, the contractions that aid in digestion.

Carried out properly, a fast of this sort can be a great boon for your animal's health. I hope that you understand the spirit of the fasting instructions and do not misinterpret them. I am *not* saying that you can just put a sick dog on the back porch with no food and a little water to drink! I am not suggesting neglect by any means, but rather an attitude of support, which includes doing the right things at the right time. Though outwardly the two approaches may appear similar, your inner intent and concern is the decisive factor that makes the difference. If you are not sure what to do or how long to keep the fast going, then consult with a holistically oriented veterinarian before proceeding.

IF YOUR PET WON'T EAT

Sometimes an animal (usually a cat) starts fasting on its own but does not regain its appetite at the end of the fast. This can happen as a result of stomach upset, inflammation of the digestive organs, or as a reaction to toxic chemicals in the body or the environment (from pollution or kidney failure, for example). In cats, it is a very common symptom of chronic disease.

Fasting becomes a problem if there is rapid weight loss and developing weakness that robs the body of the energy to heal. So it may be necessary to force-feed (put food in the animal's mouth) to keep a pet alive or to get it started eating again. Before you do this, however, you may want to try tempting the animal into eating on its own by offering a tasty food that has a strong aroma, such as freshly broiled chicken or turkey.

If you must force-feed, try this healthful mixture.

PET PUREE

²/₃	cup raw chicken or turkey (may contain giblets)
¹/₃	cup half-and-half or whole milk
¹/₂	teaspoon bone meal (using Group I brands—see page 67—or ¹/₂ teaspoon eggshell powder)
	Cat or dog vitamins, as recommended on the label for one day

Puree all the ingredients in a food processor. Adjust the liquid as needed to make a thick, smooth paste. If you only have a blender, thin the food down and prevent strain on the motor by using short bursts rather than a long run. Refrigerate extras up to three days; throw it out if it begins to smell sour.

Feed ½ to 1 cup a day to a small animal, proportionately more to larger ones. The easiest method is finger-feeding. Using one hand, pry the mouth open (as described on page 281 in the directions for giving medications). Scoop up a gob of this food paste on a finger and wipe it on the roof of your animal's mouth, behind the front teeth. Most pets will swallow it rather than spit it out. Allow plenty of time for swallowing before of-

fering the next bit. If this doesn't work, you can thin the mix further and use a turkey baster, a plastic syringe without the needle, or an oral syringe (ask your veterinarian for one) to administer it. Give small amounts every few hours, rather than forcing the whole daily feeding in one or two doses.

Caution: You may need to wrap your pet (especially cats) in a towel before the feeding to avoid getting scratched in the process.

SPECIAL CARE

Depending on the animal's condition and symptoms, you may also need to provide other kinds of nursing care.

Enemas: Animals can benefit from the use of enemas in some conditions, particularly in fasting, constipation, bowel irritation caused by bone fragments or the presence of toxic material (like garbage or spoiled food in the digestive tract), dehydration, or excessive vomiting.

Use pure water that is warm but not hot (test it on your wrist)—only about two tablespoons for a cat and up to a pint for a large dog. (Even a small amount of fluid will stimulate the bowel to empty itself.) Add a few drops of freshly squeezed lemon juice to the water and administer the solution with a plastic or rubber syringe (or enema bag and nozzle with larger animals) over a two- to three-minute period.

Here's how: First, lubricate the end of the syringe with vegetable oil and, while someone else calmly and gently holds the animal while it stands on the ground or in a tub, insert the nozzle carefully into the rectum. With gentle, consistent pressure against the anus (so the fluid does not leak out), slowly fill the colon. If the solution does not flow in readily, it's probably because the syringe is up against a fecal mass, in which case you'll need to pull back on the nozzle or syringe and adjust the angle a bit. A bowel movement is usually stimulated within just a few minutes.

Administer an enema in this fashion once or twice a day for a couple of days. That's usually enough.

Dehydrated animals may simply retain the fluid. I have seen this many times. What happens is that the colon absorbs the fluid, which the body desperately needs. Thus, enemas are an excellent way to administer fluid therapy at home! Give them about every four hours under these circumstances, or until fluid is no longer retained.

If your animal has been vomiting a lot and can't keep water in its stomach, an enema can introduce fluid as well as salts needed to replace those lost through vomiting. Add a pinch of sea salt to the enema water, plus a pinch of potassium chloride (KCl, a salt substitute for people on low-sodium diets that is sold in supermarkets). This same salt-replacement fluid therapy will help a dog or cat with prolonged diarrhea. Again, administer every four hours or until fluid is no longer retained.

Bathing and cleaning: In some cases an animal is so fouled by vomiting, diarrhea, or skin discharges that a bath is definitely in order. You should, however, take on this task only at the end of an illness, when the animal is well on the way to recovery and its temperature is normal. Otherwise, rely upon the cleaning methods described below. Even then, be sure the animal does not become chilled. Dry him quickly by giving him a good toweling, followed by a warm sunbath or blow-dry, with the dryer set on low and held not too close to the fur. The only exception to the rule of waiting until toward the end of an illness is when the dog or cat, particularly a young one, is so heavily parasitized with fleas and lice that its strength is being sapped. Then a soapy bath that will remove and drown these parasites is in order.

Care of the body openings: Very often, a disease will cause discharges from various body orifices, especially the nose, eyes, ears, and anus. Sick animals, particularly cats, are made miserable by accumulations they cannot remove and that can irritate underlying tissues. Here are a few simple cleansing techniques that offer great relief.

The nose: If plugs and secretions have formed, carefully clean the nose with a soft cloth or gauze saturated with warm water. Sometimes patience is needed in trying to soften the material so you can gradually remove it. Two or three short sessions may be better than a single long one.

Once the nose is clean and dry, smear the area with almond oil, almond oil mixed with vitamin E oil from a capsule, or calendulated oil (which can be purchased from homeopathic pharmacies). Apply two or three times a day.

The eyes: To clean crusts and secretions from the eyes and eyelids, make up a soothing, non-irritating salt solution by mixing ¼ teaspoon of sea salt into a cup of distilled or filtered water. Stir well and use this mixture to clean the eyes the same way described above for the nose. After the eyes are clean, put one drop of one of the following soothing treatments in each eye: almond oil (for mild irritation), castor oil (for more irritated and inflamed eyes), or cod-liver oil (for eyes that are dry or ulcerated).

Or, instead of the above treatment, bathe the eyes frequently with one of the following two herbal infusions.

An infusion of eyebright (*Euphrasia officinalis*) is useful where there are injuries or irritation of the eyes. To make it, bring 1 cup of pure water to a boil; pour over 1 teaspoon of the herb. Let it steep, covered, for 15 minutes. Then pour off the liquid through a sieve or through cheesecloth, leaving the solid herb pieces behind. For every cup of the infusion, add ¼ teaspoon of sea salt. This makes the solution mild and soothing (like natural tears).

Goldenseal root is helpful when the eyes are infected or discharging thick, yellow material. To make a treatment solution, pour 1 cup of boiling water over ¼ teaspoon of goldenseal powder. Let it steep for 15 minutes; then filter off the liquid part. To this liquid, add ¼ teaspoon sea salt.

When the solution you are preparing has cooled down, gently clean and treat the eyes three times a day, or as needed. You can keep these solutions (covered) at room temperature on your countertop for two days. To avoid contamination of the whole preparation, always pour off a little into a dish or cup to use for treatment, and then put the cover back on the main batch. Discard this treatment fluid rather than return it to the stock you made.

The ears: If the ears contain much oily or waxy secretion, trickle about ½ teaspoon of almond oil into the ear hole, preferably using a dropper or squeeze bottle. To start, pre-warm the oil in a cup or glass that is partly immersed in a sink or bowl of hot water. Firmly lift the ear flap or tip. You may need someone to help you hold the animal's head in place, because if you let go or the animal pulls away before you finish the job, he will shake oil all over you. Let the almond oil run down into the ear for a few seconds.

Then, while still holding the ear flap, reach down with your other hand and massage the ear canal from the outside at the bottom of the ear opening. It feels like a firm plastic tube that you can compress as you massage. If you do it right, you'll hear a squishy sound. This treatment loosens up and dissolves the lodged wax. Use a tissue to remove any excess oil and materials that work their way out. Don't use a cotton swab except around the opening.

If the ear is very red and inflamed, use calendula oil or aloe vera juice. This can be obtained from health food stores or as fresh juice from a plant. It's usually adequate to treat the ear this way once every day or two.

Another treatment that can be used in irritated ears is green tea. Put two tea bags in a mug and fill with boiling water. Let it steep for 10 minutes and take the bags out. When cooled down, use to flush out the ears.

On the other hand, if the ear is painful when touched at the massage point but shows no discharge, some foreign body, such as plant material or a tick, may be inside the ear canal. It is best to have your veterinarian examine the ear and determine the cause of pain. If there is no obvious cause for the ear pain, a good treatment to use is Arnica oil (available at a homeopathic pharmacy or a health food store). Gently treat the ear (as described previously) once a day until the discomfort is gone.

The anus: Often the anus will get very inflamed as a result of excessive diarrhea, causing the surrounding tissue to get irritated and sometimes infected with bacteria. To keep this area clean during the diarrhea stage of an illness, sponge it gently with a damp cloth (rubbing can further irritate it). Pat (don't rub) it dry and then apply some calendula ointment. Apply two or three times a day or as needed.

USING HERBAL PREPARATIONS

In the description of the specific diseases that follows in the Quick Reference section starting on page 287, I have noted many instances when you may use various herbs and/or homeopathic preparations. For those who are not familiar with these remedies, I will describe some of the basic methods for making or obtaining them. Let's start with herbs. Three basic forms of herbs can be used in preparing treatments: fresh, dried, or tinctures.

Fresh herbs: When possible, use an herb that has been freshly harvested right before use. In some areas of the country, useful medicinal herbs can be located easily in vacant lots, along roadsides (avoid heavily traveled areas because of car exhaust contamination), in country fields or woods, or perhaps in your own herb garden. Those able to identify herbs in the field can collect them as needed.

For optimal effectiveness, pick an herb when its essential oils are at their peak. In general, that means you should collect any aboveground parts in the morning, after the dew has dried but before the hot sun has evaporated some of the oils. Ideally, leaves should be harvested just before the plant is about to begin its flowering stage. Gather flowers just before they reach full bloom (they have much less value after that).

If you're going for the *whole* aboveground part (leaves, stems, and all), pick it just before the flowering stage. Roots and rhizomes are best collected in the fall, when the sap returns to the ground, the leaves are just beginning to change their color, and the berries or seeds are mature.

Because many people are unfamiliar with using fresh herbs, the instructions in this book usually refer to dried herbs. But if the fresh plant is available, use about three times the volume indicated for dried herbs in the listings.

Dried herbs: In most cases you will probably just buy the herb dried, either loosely cut or powdered and perhaps packaged in gelatin capsules. Dried herbs can be administered either in these capsules or mixed with water in an infusion, decoction, or slurry. You can save some money on capsuled herbs by buying empty capsules from a pharmacy and packing your own. One "00" capsule holds about ½ teaspoon of powdered herb. If you need to powder the herb, use a coffee grinder or mortar and pestle to grind it to a fine dust.

If you gather or grow your own herbs, you can dry them for later use. Collect them after the morning dew on the leaves has dried. Tie the herbs in bunches and hang them upside down in a well-ventilated, dry, shaded area. Enclosed attics can be good for this. If you gather roots and barks, scrub them well, then chop them up and dry them on screening in direct sunlight. Once they are thoroughly dried, store them in opaque or capped brown jars in a cool, dark place. Properly cured and stored, herbs retain most of their medicinal qualities for some time. Since these properties are destroyed by heat, sunlight, and exposure to air, however, it is best to keep the herbs no longer than a year.

Herbal tinctures: Another way to obtain and use herbs is in the tincture form. The easiest way to get tinctures is to buy them from herbal supply houses or homeopathic pharmacies. But if you have access to the fresh plant, the best form of tincture is one made from freshly collected, organically grown material.

To make your own tincture, macerate and grind the fresh herb (or use a blender). Add 1 rounded tablespoon of herb to ½-cup vodka or brandy (at least 80 proof). Store the mixture out of the sunlight in a clean, tightly capped jar and shake it once or twice a day over two weeks. Then strain off the solids through a fine cloth or paper filter, collecting the liquid, which is your tincture. Store it in tightly capped glass bottles in a cool, dark area. (If you used dried herbs instead of fresh, figure 1 rounded teaspoon of the cut or powdered herb for each ½ cup of alcohol.)

Herbal tinctures are a very potent form of medicine and must be used carefully at low dosages, as the specific instructions in the Quick Reference section on page 439 will indicate. Tightly capped, they will keep for three years.

Preparing Herbal Medicines

The fresh or dried forms of herbs can both be used to make infusions, in which boiling water is added to the herb and steeped (like making tea). To make a less strong tasting, more palatable version of an infusion, double the amount of herb used and just soak it in cold water overnight. This is called a cold extract. If the herb comes as a root or a bark, simmer it in boiling water for 15 to 20 minutes (called a decoction).

Infusions or cold extracts should be prepared in a covered, nonmetallic container such as pottery or glass (to retain the volatile substances). Decoctions should be simmered in an open, nonmetallic pan (to concentrate the product). Be sure to always use purified water (distilled or filtered) for these preparations. Specific amounts to use in preparation are given in the Quick Reference section on page 438.

Tinctures should always be diluted, three drops per teaspoon of water, just before administering.

How to Give Liquid Medication

There are two techniques I recommend for getting any form of liquid medication (conventional medicine or a diluted tincture, decoction, infusion, or cold extract) down an animal's throat.

Pry the mouth open. Lightly grasp the animal's upper jaw with one hand and insert your thumb and fingers in the gaps just behind the fangs. (For a cat or tiny dog, just one finger is needed in addition to the thumb.) Most animals will then relax their mouths slightly so that you can pour the liquid with a spoon or dropper between the front teeth. Tilt the head back when you do this so that the liquid will run down to the throat.

Alternatively, you can make a pouch out of the animal's lip. Use one hand to pull out the corner of the animal's lower lip to make a little pouch and, keeping the head tilted

back, pour the liquid into it with the other hand.

In either instance, if the liquid doesn't go in, it's because the teeth are clenched too tightly. If so, pry them open slightly with your fingers. If your animal backs away, put its rear end in a corner so it can't move away from you during the process, or get someone to help hold your pet. Another way to do this is to sit on the floor or a bed with your pet between your legs. With her rear end toward you and the head facing away, you can keep her positioned more easily for the administration.

For a cat, you may need someone to help

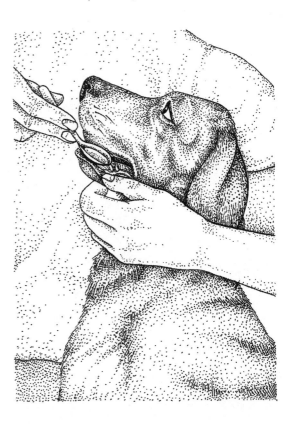

by gently but firmly holding its front feet, or you can do the job alone by wrapping the cat quickly and snugly in a towel. Be gentle and positive so your animal doesn't have reason to feel afraid and put up a struggle. You don't have to make a big prying effort. Just firmly and persistently work at putting your fingers between the teeth to open the mouth until the teeth separate a little.

After the medicine is in, induce swallowing by gently holding the mouth almost closed and massaging the throat. Swallowing is signaled by the tongue's emerging briefly from between the front teeth. Alternatively,

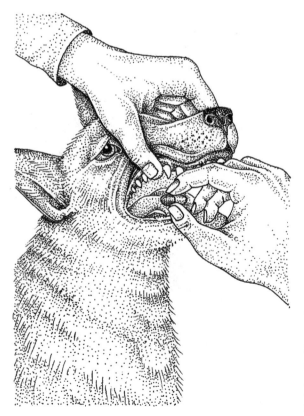

you can briefly put your thumb over the nostrils to achieve the same purpose.

How to Give Pills and Capsules

To give most solid medications like herbal capsules or vitamin pills, open the animal's mouth by grasping around the upper jaw, as described for liquids. Hold the capsule or pill between your thumb and the first finger or else between the first and second fingers. Use the remaining fingers to press down the lower front teeth and thus pry the jaw open.

Insert the medication into the throat, pushing it as far back as you can. Then induce swallowing as described above. At first this will seem difficult and awkward. After a few tries, however, you will become more experienced and find it much easier.

USING HOMEOPATHIC MEDICATIONS

To give a homeopathic or tissue salt tablet, use one of two methods.

Give the tablets or pellets whole. Administer them from the cap of the vial or from a clean spoon (it's best not to touch them).

Crush pellets to a powder (use three pellets). To do the crushing, make a crisp fold in a heavy paper. (A small file card is very good for this.) Pour the tablets from the bottle into the open fold. Fold the paper flat, with the pellets inside against the crease, and put the folded paper on a hard countertop. Tap against the pellets (in the paper) with a heavy glass to gradually crush them to a powder. The pellets from some pharmacies and other suppliers can be very hard, so don't try to do this on your antique wooden table.

With a word of encouragement, invite your animal to lick the powder off the paper (it tastes sweet). If he is not interested, use the same holding and prying technique described for other pills to get the medicine in. Prepare by pushing the powder down to the edge of the paper with your fingernail, then open the mouth and flick the powder from the paper onto the animal's tongue.

This method both eliminates the possibility of your pet spitting the medicine out and also keeps it from being contaminated.

There are distinct advantages to using homeopathic pellets or tablets. Because only a small number are given, they are easy to administer. Also, in many instances only one or just a few doses are needed during the entire course of treatment.

The homeopathic remedies mentioned in the Quick Reference section can be either ordered by mail (see the list on www. drpitcairn.com) or, in many cases, purchased in health food stores.

HOW TO PREPARE FLOWER ESSENCES

Dr. Bach's flower essences are available in 38 individual "stock" bottles. The specific preparations are made by combining them and diluting them into a formula. Here is how it is

done: If you wanted to make a formula of Chicory, Heather, and Clematis (three of the flowers out of the available 38), for example, you would first put two drops from the stock bottle for each of these flowers into a clean, 1-ounce dropper bottle. Then you would fill the bottle with spring water (not distilled) to make the dilution. This is your "treatment" bottle; a standard dosage is to give two drops four times a day. The drops can be put on the tongue, inside the lips, or added to food or water. Usually, this treatment is done for several days or weeks, depending on need.

YOUR HOME REMEDY KIT

Don't wait until your animal needs treatment to track down basic supplies. Like a Boy Scout, be prepared. Some preparations will have to be ordered by mail from the suppliers listed on www.drpitcairn.com. Others can be obtained at your local health food store, herb shop, or even grocery store. And, of course, you can grow or collect many herbs yourself. But in all cases, it's best to have a group of commonly used substances on hand. Most are really quite inexpensive. See chapter 17 for more suggestions for your first-aid kit.

You can also gather together a kit of the basic homeopathic remedies most often mentioned in the Quick Reference section or obtain a kit ready-made. That way, when the need is immediate, you will already have what you need.

PART TWO

QUICK REFERENCE

HOW TO USE THE QUICK REFERENCE SECTION

The very best medicine is prevention. Good diet, exercise, and a healthy environment are all essential for excellent health. But sometimes, regardless of what we do or don't do for them, animals get sick. If that happens, what can you do to help care for your pet and optimize its chances for full recovery?

In this section I describe many health problems common to dogs and cats and suggest specific treatments. Some of these treatments can be used in conjunction with conventional veterinary treatment, if necessary. Others, particularly homeopathic medicines, should not be used with drugs or other treatment methods like acupuncture. If possible, work with a cooperative, holistically oriented veterinarian or at least one who is sympathetic to your viewpoint. A list of veterinarians I have trained in homeopathic practice is available on my Web site, www.drpitcairn.com.

You may recall from the first part of the book that I believe total health requires a total approach. At the start it's important to consider and address any causative or contributing factors in the lifestyle, environment, or diet so that there are no external obstacles to your animal's recovery. Then, as much as possible, select from the treatment choices the one that best fits your pet's particular situation and most accurately corresponds to what you see as the problem. This will require careful observation on your part.

For treatment you can use herbs or homeopathic remedies that you obtained at local herb suppliers or natural food stores, if you have these in your area. Some of the medicines I advise using can be ordered from a homeopathic pharmacy. I believe in keeping a ready-to-use kit of common remedies on hand as an aid to timely treatment. Homeopathic remedy kits are available at a savings and are wonderful to have on hand. One that I put together is listed on my Web site.

HOW TO LOOK UP A PARTICULAR DISEASE

To find an elusive topic, check under a larger grouping. For example, canine distemper, chorea (a common aftereffect of distemper), and feline panleukopenia (often called feline distemper) are all listed under "Distemper." Many conditions are grouped according to the body part or organ they affect:"Stomach Problems," "Skin Problems," or "Ear Problems," for example. The cross references should help to lead you to the right category with a minimum of difficulty.

WHAT YOU CAN EXPECT

Except in some acute conditions that may clear up rapidly, healing generally takes time. It took a while for the body to get out of balance, and it takes time to restore it. Of course, if we give a painkiller or a suppressive drug such as cortisone, we may see some rapid relief, but this is not a true cure. Take away the drug and the symptoms are likely to return eventually, often worse than before.

Since our aim is to address the underlying weakness and restore health permanently, it's important to recognize the progressive stages and understand the gradually changing picture of symptoms in healing. That way we can tell if our treatment is really helping or whether another approach should be tried.

When a treatment is working, in the sense of health being recovered, an acute illness (sudden, self-limited) generally responds quickly (within a few minutes, a few hours or, at the longest, a day or two). Chronic illness, on the other hand, changes slowly. It often takes a couple of weeks or more to see a change for the better, and months, or even a year or two, for *complete* recovery.

The chance of complete recovery depends on several significant factors, including the age, level of vitality, and extent of illness in your pet. Though a disease that has progressed far enough to do extensive damage to the body cannot be completely reversed, it can be alleviated, sometimes very significantly. Of course, it isn't reasonable to expect organs or tissues to return to their previous undamaged state, but we may be able to stop the progression of the chronic disease permanently and enhance healing to the limit of the body's abilities.

For example, an old cat with kidney failure can be brought from a state of debilitating illness to one of relative normality. The treatment, however, may have to continue for the rest of his life, with occasional use of homeopathic medicines, a restricted protein diet, and fluid therapy as needed. Internally, our treatment may only have improved the kidneys' functioning from a level of 25 percent to 30 percent effective use. That 5 percent, however, can make all the difference.

On the other hand, if your animal is younger and has been ill only a relatively short time (not years), with little physical damage in the organs or tissues, there is a real chance of restoring the animal to its original healthy state.

Another consideration is the extent of previous drug treatment or surgery. The long-term action of drugs such as cortisone, for example, can damage the glands and organs of an animal so that a healing response cannot be aroused.

Surgery is the most irreversible of all treatments. Obviously, if an organ is removed (a common example is the removal of thyroid glands in cats with hyperthyroidism), it cannot be healed. If a client brings such an animal to me, I know at the outset that a cure is not possible. This is because we have to restore the thyroid glands to normal functioning to return this animal to true health. But if there are no thyroid glands . . .

I can say that in general, however, improved nutrition and use of healing methods like homeopathy, herbal medicine, and nutrition will surely improve the quality of your animal's life—often dramatically.

SIGNS OF PROGRESS

Many natural therapies include the notion of the "aggravation," a brief increase of symptoms that occurs just before the patient really starts to recover. You need to understand the significance of this favorable sign. Otherwise, you might jump to the conclusion that things are getting worse and load the animal down with a host of heavy-duty drugs that could actually interfere with the cure.

How can you tell whether your pet is going through a healing process or is actually getting worse? Here is a good general rule: If your animal has an increase of (usually) one symptom (diarrhea, for example) but, at the same time, seems to feel better overall, then the change is favorable. Equally important, a temporary healing increase in a symptom is almost always over quickly. Typically, in my work with homeopathy, this reaction to effective treatment will be gone in 12 to 24 hours.

In other words, although with a healing therapy some of the symptoms may temporarily worsen, *this is brief and followed by definite improvement.* If your pet goes through a period of increased symptoms that lasts for days and she still seems sick, it is probably not a healing crisis and the situation should be reevaluated.

It is important here to understand that the animal that is getting worse in general, or with several symptoms, is *not* being healed—the disease is getting worse. What is different with a healing process is that one or two symptoms may be mildly increased for a brief period, during which time your pet feels better and acts more normal.

Many physicians and healers have noticed certain patterns that the body expresses in its attempt to cope with health imbalances. Homeopaths have formalized these patterns as "Hering's Law of Cure," named after a famous American homeopathic physician, Constantine Hering. Here is the way I understand the process.

There is an underlying intelligence in the body (in homeopathy it's called the vital force) that is in charge of maintenance and repair. To do this, the body utilizes a few basic strategies to limit the problem and protect its most vital and important functions. Specifically, it attempts to:

❖ Prevent disturbances from spreading (for example, creating a local abscess instead of allowing the infection to spread throughout the body).

❖ Keep the disease on the surface of the body rather than let it get to the vital organs.

❖ Focus disease around the limbs, rather than on the trunk.

❖ Confine disease to the lower end of the body, away from the head, and therefore away from the brain and sensory organs.

❖ Maintain the problem at the physical level rather than the emotional or mental level, which would interfere more seriously with the overall functioning of the individual.

Therefore, a patient's health is taking a wrong turn if symptoms start to spread or begin to involve deep-seated organs. Common sense tells us that the more the condition disturbs the functioning of parts of the body that are most crucial to its survival and governing capacities, the worse it is.

Hering's Law can also help you to recognize a turn in the right direction, toward greater health, which can initially require a careful reading of more subtle indications. It is a favorable sign, for instance, if an animal with a chronic degenerative disease affecting vital organs begins to develop a skin rash or discharge, thus shifting symptoms away from organs toward the surface. Overall improvement will take place during this process, and, gradually, the surface problem will lessen as the internal disorder is healed. The vital force of the body focuses on this surface lesion as a way to rid itself of the disturbance.

Some cases can be more difficult to interpret, especially those in which the animal begins to re-experience old symptoms that were previously treated in a process that did not really cure them, but simply suppressed them for a time. In such situations it is best to work with a skilled holistic veterinarian.

If you study the principles outlined above, however, you will have an excellent guide for determining whether, as a whole individual, your animal is actually getting better or worse.

Let's look at some examples. Suppose your dog tends to get fungus infections around the feet and lower legs. After months of strenuous drug treatment, the feet have cleared up. Recently, however, little bald patches and irritation have begun to appear on the skin of the abdomen, chest, and near the head. Though this new problem may be diagnosed differently, it is really just another expression of the original problem that was suppressed but not really cured. *It is the same disease*, but it has changed form and location. And it has progressed from a less important, peripheral location (the feet) closer to a more important area (the head).

Here's a more subtle example of a condition getting worse. After repeated treatments and even surgery, your dog's chronically inflamed ears have finally cleared up. But now, several weeks later, you notice that he isn't as friendly as he used to be. He prefers to go off by himself and may even growl or bite. The seat of the disturbance has moved inward, from the physical to the emotional level. Though various drugs may be tried in an effort to control the personality changes, the overall problem will only get worse. Tranquilizers may make him easier to live with, more subdued and passive. But over time, he may weaken at the mental level, perhaps acting sluggish and disoriented. He may have spells of confusion. At this point the disturbance will interfere with the basic mental processes that help him process information and orient himself. (I have observed many dogs treated in this way develop seizures.)

Though this may sound like a farfetched example, I assure you it is not. Cases like this happen all too often. If this same dog were treated in a curative way at the point when his problem became emotional, you would see a return of the earlier physical symptoms after his moods improved. Most likely, it would be a re-emergence of the ear inflammation.

Then the ear or any other surface problem could be treated with the methods we discuss in this book. Once you have stimulated the body to move in a curative direction, it is also possible that the ear condition will go away on its own, without further treatment.

As another example, let's say you have a cat with an abscess. She also has been showing emotional signs of trouble—depression and lethargy. After treatment, however, she has begun to run around and act frisky. Even though there may still be a discharge from the abscess, the psychological improvement is a very favorable sign, and it will be followed by physical healing. It is indeed the first sign that healing is under way.

In general, these signs during therapy also indicate good progress.

- An increase in energy and overall playfulness
- Return of a calm, good-natured manner
- Self-grooming (especially true of cats)
- A return of normal appetite
- Re-establishment of normal bowel movements and urination
- Ability to have sound and restful sleep

HEALING DISCHARGES

Let's also look carefully at some of the methods the body uses to heal itself. Generally, when a disease is being eliminated, you will see signs of discharge. It signals that buildups of toxic materials are leaving the body. The most common ways this elimination occurs are through:

❖ Formation of a pus-pocket and drainage out of the body

❖ Development of skin eruptions (a very common route)

❖ A strong body odor ("doggy odor"), which is temporary

❖ The urine, which may become dark or strong-smelling

❖ The colon, in the form of dark, smelly feces or diarrhea

❖ Vomiting (especially during acute conditions)

❖ Shedding of the nails or of skin from the bottoms of the paws.

When using the holistic methods discussed in this book, you may see one or more of these forms of discharge, to a mild degree. This will particularly happen if the problem has been well-established in the body.

Sometimes the discharge can be fairly dramatic. For example, I'm reminded of a dog whose owner used herbs and fasting to successfully help her pet recover from a severe attack of distemper. Soon afterwards, however, the animal was covered with red, itchy skin that oozed sticky fluid—clearly a discharge phenomenon. A few more days of supportive treatments were followed by full recovery. Once such a recovery is complete, an animal will be much stronger and better able to withstand future diseases.

Let's summarize the ways to evaluate progress. Supportive, non-suppressive therapies exhibit two processes: 1) movement of symptoms in a favorable direction (away from the head toward the feet; away from vital organs to surface tissue; from mental and emotional to physical) and 2) some form of discharge. If you see these signs, chances are very strong that the animal is getting better, regardless of which form of therapy you are using.

I should add as a cautionary note, however, that treatment with some drugs, particularly with cortisone, can create a *false* sense of well-being that disappears when the drug is discontinued. So keep in mind that you are looking for a response that *comes from the natural processes of the animal*, assisted by the treatment. Such a response will lead to recovery and permanent healing, not a dependence on a drug.

In this Quick Reference section there are several references to small, medium, and large dogs, related to diet and kinds of treatments. Here are the criteria for sizes of dogs.

❖ Toy dogs—up to 15 pounds

❖ Small dogs—15 to 30 pounds

❖ Medium-size dogs—30 to 60 pounds

❖ Large dogs—60 to 90 pounds

❖ Giant dogs—over 90 pounds

COMMON PET AILMENTS AND THEIR TREATMENTS

ABSCESSES

Abscesses are a common complication of puncture wounds from fights. They plague cats much more than dogs, because cats' needlelike teeth and sharp, penetrating claws inflict narrow but deep wounds. Feline skin seals over very quickly, trapping bacteria, hair, or other contaminated material inside. Sometimes, even a broken-off claw or tooth is retained under the skin.

Cat abscesses usually occur around the head and front legs or at the base of the tail. Wounds around the head indicate that your cat was either the aggressor or bravely facing the enemy. Wounds at the tail area or on the rear legs mean that your cat was trying to get away.

In dogs, abscesses are usually caused by foxtails or plant awns that get trapped in the hair and work their way through the skin (especially between the toes, around or in the ears, and between the hind legs). An abscess that keeps draining and does not heal (called a fistula) usually indicates the presence of a foreign object somewhere in the tissue, sometimes several inches from the place of drainage.

TREATMENT

CATS

I have had several very healthy, well-fed cats that seldom, if ever, developed abscesses after injuries. My experience is that excellent nutrition is the best preventive.

Neutering also greatly reduces the problem. When several intact male cats live in close proximity, there will be frequent warfare as each tries to establish a territory and compete for females. In such circumstances, abscesses are a continuous problem.

Often, you can prevent an infection or abscess by giving the homeopathic remedy Ledum 30c within a few hours of the fight. Use Homeopathic Schedule 2, page 442.

If you can't treat it quickly, however, or an infection (or abscess) is already established, further symptoms will usually occur, such as swelling, pain, and fever (locally or of the whole body). In this case, the cat should fast for 24 hours, taking only liquids—meat and vegetable broth and spring water. Give 250 milligrams of vitamin C three times a day for at least three days to promote the activity of your cat's immune system.

In addition, use one remedy from the following list, whichever best fits the situation.

Homeopathic—*Hepar Sulph Calcareum* 30C: Use Homeopathic Schedule 2, page 442. The abscess has formed but not yet opened and drained. It will be extremely painful when touched. The cat will often become angry and try to bite or scratch. (It is normal that cats don't like to be touched where it hurts, but this reaction is excessive.) Using this remedy will open the abscess so it drains out and begins to heal.

Homeopathic—*Silicea* 30C: Use Homeopathic Schedule 2, page 442. Best for a developed abscess that has opened and is already draining pus.

Homeopathic—*Lachesis muta* 30C: Use Homeopathic Schedule 2, page 442. If the tissues near the abscess are turning bluish or the skin is dying (becomes very hard and starts to come off) and the pus smells just terrible. This will be a later stage, usually a few days after the bite.

Herbal—Purple cone flower (Echinacea angustifolia): Use Herbal Schedule 1, page 438. This remedy is indicated for the animal that is in poor condition, thin, very weak, and develops recurrent abscesses. It functions primarily to purify the system, especially the blood, and also restores health to the skin.

If an abscess has actually opened and drained, prevent the drainage hole from closing prematurely by cleaning away any discharge or scab once or twice a day either with hydrogen peroxide or with the herb Echinacea used according to Herbal Schedule 4 or 6 on page 439 or 440.

Later, when the abscess is healing and there is no longer any drainage, use the herb Calendula for external treatment, according to the same method as described for Echinacea above.

If the abscess has been present for a long time and has been draining pus for several weeks, administer the homeopathic remedy *Silicea* 30C, using Homeopathic Schedule 3, page 442. If there is no improvement after one week then give *Sulphur* 30C with the same schedule.

Dogs

If the abscess is the result of an animal bite, treat it the same way you would for a cat (above). Adjust the amount of vitamin C to the size of the dog. Three times a day, give about 250 milligrams (small dog), 500 milligrams (medium dog), or 1,000 milligrams (large dog).

However, if the abscess has been caused by plant material, porcupine quills, splinters, or other embedded foreign matter, the discharge will not stop until the object is eliminated. Since the tissues cannot "digest" the object, it must either be expelled or removed surgically.

The natural expelling process can be aided by using the homeopathic remedy *Silicea* 30C according to Homeopathic Schedule 5, page 442. A beneficial adjunct, though not absolutely necessary, is to apply hot compresses of a solution made up of Oat Straw (Avena sativa). Use Herbal Schedule 1 on page 438. If the affected area is a paw, soak the whole foot in a jar of the hot solution. Use Herbal Schedule 6 on page 440.

In natural healing, the tendency is for pus or fluid to drain out at a point lower than the site of the foreign body, allowing gravity to assist. Therefore, apply the poultice not only at the opening, but also several inches higher, so you cover the probable location of the foreign body. The hot solution will promote the flow of blood into the affected area and keep the process moving. When enough pus has formed around the foreign body to loosen it, it may flow out, right along with the pus. At that point, drainage will stop.

Note: Because of their structure, foxtails and plant awns tend to migrate deeply into the tissues. If you don't get results within a short time, you may have to resort to surgery. It is worth trying these methods first, as surgery is very often not effective in locating these little intruders. (See "Foxtails" for more information.)

ACCIDENTS

See "Handling Emergencies and Giving First Aid" on page 429.

ADDISON'S DISEASE

This is a disorder of the adrenal glands, which secrete natural cortisone, as well as hormones that regulate the different salts of the body. This condition is seen more often in dogs than cats and is not common. With this disease, the problem is that the glands no longer produce the needed hormones. An animal that does not have working glands cannot live, so they are critically important. One cause is thought to be a type of auto-immune disorder, in which the body attacks the glands and damages them—though just as often this results from prolonged use of cortisone-like drugs to control symptoms of other illnesses, like skin allergies. Because the synthetic drugs are so powerful, the adrenal glands get the message they don't have to work any more and just shut down.

How do you recognize it? Signs are vague and even veterinarians may have trouble figuring it out. It is certainly a clue if your pet has been on steroids for a long time and then becomes ill, but to confirm diagnosis requires some testing. Most commonly, the affected animals (usually dogs) have recurrent periods of appetite loss, vomiting, diarrhea, and weakness. In serious situations, vomiting and diarrhea can be accompanied by a life-threatening weakness and low body temperature. The Addison cases I have worked with have come to me already on drug treatment—usually replacement adrenal hormones, including cortisone-type drugs, as well as others that help regulate sodium and potassium. It is possible to cure these animals, if the condition has not existed for too long a time, but it is not something you can do yourself.

The feeding of a natural diet is really important as part of the treatment. Part of the problem is the inability to conserve sodium, while potassium levels become excessively high. Adding salt will help to balance this. In addition, careful homeopathic treatment can bring back adrenal function.

These animals need frequent monitoring of their blood levels to determine what their needs are, so after using a natural diet for a few weeks with added sprinkles of salt, have the blood test done again and see if adjustments need to be made.

Don't try to treat this yourself. Work with an experienced veterinarian to wean off drugs while doing other treatments.

AGGRESSION

See "Behavior Problems."

ALLERGIES

An allergy is an abnormally intense reaction to something that is usually harmless to the body—wheat, house dust, or plant pollen, for example. A reaction against some part of the body itself—like the skin, pancreas, or thyroid—is called an auto-immune disease.

The incidence of allergies and immune disorders has greatly increased since I first entered practice 40 years ago. Now these are among the most common conditions we are asked to treat.

Allergies present themselves differently in dogs than they do in cats. Dogs typically have itchy skin and eruptions, especially on the lower back near the base of the tail. However, these eruptions can occur anywhere and everywhere on the body. Other commonly associated symptoms are inflamed ears, excessive licking of the front feet, digestive upsets (gurgling, gas, and a tendency toward diarrhea), inflammation of the toes, and an irritated rear end (anus, genitals), with licking and dragging of the rear on the floor. Though other symptoms can also occur, this is a typical picture.

Like dogs, cats can also have skin eruptions, often called miliary dermatitis. Cats are more prone, however, to cystitis (bladder inflammation) and digestive problems. Oftentimes, there is no visible eruption on the skin, but cats will be greatly annoyed by stinging or biting sensations of the skin so that they are always jumping around, frantically licking themselves and pulling hair out in clumps. They act as though fleas were causing it (which of course can sometimes be the case).

Two similar immune disorders that occur—hyperthyroidism and inflammatory bowel disease—are chronic and serious conditions that require careful treatment. In my opinion, the major causes of these immune disorders are the frequent use of combination vaccinations, feeding pets commercial food diets, and overuse of cortisone drugs to suppress symptoms—all of which together have greatly weakened the immune system of animals over several generations.

Whatever the causes, once established, the problem is very difficult to eliminate. Successful treatment can be accomplished with the approach outlined in this book, but it takes a long time, usually a year or more.

In mild cases, actions you can take yourself may be sufficient. For instance, some research suggests that about a third of all allergies are caused by substances in foods. You can identify the immediate trigger by switching to a simplified diet for a while. If the symptoms subside but return when you go back to the original diet, you can assume that your pet is allergic to one or more of the ingredients in the daily diet.

Try the following diets as a test. They omit the most common food allergens: beef, wheat, milk, cheese, eggs, nuts, fruits, tomatoes, carrots, yeast, and various spices and additives. When given in sufficient doses, vitamin C acts like a natural antihistamine to control allergies. The B-complex found in the pet supplements is also very useful to that end.

CAT ALLERGY DIET

2	cups brown rice
2	pounds (4 cups) raw lamb or mutton (lamb preferred)
1	tablespoon Group I bone meal*
2	tablespoons vegetable oil
1	teaspoon cod liver oil (or equivalent)
10	days' dose of a complete vitamin-mineral supplement formulated for cats, made without yeast.

Vitamin C in the form of sodium ascorbate powder (500 milligrams daily)

* See chapter 4 for information on the bone meal groups.

Bring 4 cups of filtered or spring water to a boil. Add the rice, cover, and simmer for 40 minutes. Meanwhile chop or grind the meat. When the rice is done, thoroughly mix all ingredients except the vitamin C. Give the C fresh each day. (I recommend sodium ascorbate powder because it isn't very tart.) If you use one of the Group II bone meals, double the amount of that ingredient in the recipe. (Total amount of calcium in the recipe added by bone meal = 4,300 mg.) I specify vegetable oil in the recipe, but you can use a variety of oils, even animal fats. There has to be a source of essential fatty acids in the diet, and this is provided by the cod liver oil (or another source of fish oil) and vegetable oils such as corn oil (especially liked by cats), safflower, sunflower, evening primrose, or borage oils. Animal fats, such as poultry and pork, contain essential fatty acids. Beef and butter do not provide sufficient quantities (unfortunate, as cats do prefer the taste of beef).

The recipe is approximately 30 percent protein, 30 percent fat, and 40 percent carbohydrates.

Yield: Feeds an average adult cat for 8 to 10 days. Freeze about ⅔ of it to prevent spoilage.

Substitutes: Instead of rice, you may use 2 cups of millet (cooked for 20 to 30 minutes with 6 cups of water until soft) or 4 cups of dry oats (cooked for 10 minutes with 8 cups of water until thick and soft). You can also use other meats like turkey or chicken. Turkey is not very fat, so an extra source, like lard or beef fat, is appropriate to add in.

DOG ALLERGY DIET 1

4	cups brown rice
3	pounds (6 cups) raw lamb or mutton
2½	tablespoons Group I bone meal*
2	tablespoons vegetable oil (such as corn, safflower, sunflower, evening primrose, borage oil)

Complete daily vitamin-mineral supplement formulated for dogs, made without yeast

Vitamin C in the form of sodium ascorbate powder (give 500 milligrams daily, less for the very small dog).

* See chapter 4 for information on the bone meal groups. Group II bone meals should be doubled in amount.

Bring 8 cups of filtered or spring water to a boil. Add the rice, cover and simmer for 40 minutes. Meanwhile, trim any excess fat off the lamb or mutton (if you wish to have a lower fat diet); chop or grind the meat. When the rice is done (indicated by tender, firm grains), thoroughly mix all ingredients except the daily supplement and the vitamin C. Add these at the time of feeding.

Recipe is approximately 27 percent protein, 24 percent fat, and 47 percent carbohydrates. The amount of calcium provided by the bone meal = just over 1 gram (1100 mg).

Substitutes: Instead of rice, you may use 4 cups of millet (cooked for 20 to 30 minutes with 12 cups water) or 8 cups of dry oats (cooked for 10 minutes with 14 to 16 cups water). Cooked grains should be soft and mushy. For an even higher protein feed, you may reduce the amount of grain to 3 cups dry rice or millet (or 6 cups oats).

Yield: Produces 5,600 calories, enough to feed a small dog for 7 to 9 days, a medium dog for 3 to 4 days or a large dog for a couple of days. Freeze any of this food that can't be eaten in 3 days.

DOG ALLERGY DIET 2

6	cups millet
3	pounds (6 cups) raw turkey
2½	tablespoons Group I bone meal*
¼	cup vegetable oil

Complete daily vitamin-mineral supplement formulated for dogs, made without yeast

Vitamin C (give 500 milligrams daily, less for a very small dog)

* See chapter 4 for information on the bone meal groups. Group II bone meals should be doubled in amount.

Bring 9 cups of filtered or spring water to a boil. Add the millet, cover, and simmer for 20 to 30 minutes or until soft and fluffy. Thoroughly mix millet with all ingredients except the vitamin C and daily supplement. Feed these supplements fresh each day, as in the prior recipe. As specified in Allergy Diet 1, use vegetable oils that provide essential fatty acids. Recipe is approximately 23 percent protein, 18 percent fat, and 57 percent carbohydrates. The amount of calcium provided by the bone meal = just over 1 gram (1100 mg).

Substitutes: Instead of millet you may use 5 cups of brown rice (cooked with 10 cups of water for 40 minutes or until grains are tender, firm and separate) or 10 cups of dry oats (cooked with 18 to 20 cups of water for 10 minutes or until grains are soft and mushy).

Yield: Makes about 5,900 calories, enough to feed a small dog for 7 to 9 days, a medium dog for 3 to 4 days, or a large dog for a couple of days. Freeze any of the batch that can't be eaten in 3 days.

Be sure to use filtered, spring, or other non-chlorinated water. To give this diet an adequate chance, keep your animal on it for at least two months—and be strict about it. If the problem clears up or improves, slowly reintroduce the omitted foods one at a time to find out which one or ones are causing the problem. By determining which ingredients are causing a reaction, you may be able to switch to a quality kibble that excludes the problem food. This is especially helpful with a large dog, where cooking in such quantities can be challenging. Your best bet would be one of the lamb-rice kibbles formulated for dogs with skin problems. Read the label carefully.

If your pet's condition has not improved after a couple of months on a restricted diet, the cause of its problem may not be a food allergy. Bear in mind that allergies can be triggered by a variety of environmental factors, such as chlorine and other contaminants in water, household cleaning chemicals, release of gasses of formaldehyde and other chemicals from furniture and buildings, synthetic carpets and upholstery, plastic food bowls, certain plants or grasses, regularly administered drugs like heartworm preventive medicine or flea chemicals, and, of course, flea bites. Also, while many people have heard that they can be allergic to their pets, few realize that their pets can be allergic to them!

Determining exactly what substances are causing an allergic reaction can be difficult. Certain diagnostic procedures can be used, but I haven't found them very helpful. They do not always correlate with the clinical situation. Also, if you do find some offending substances, it may not be possible to eliminate them completely anyway.

The approach that works best for me is to put the animal on an organic natural diet (which by itself clears up a lot of problems) and to use homeopathic treatment to remove the underlying allergic tendency. In many cases that I handle, allergic tendencies can be greatly mitigated or eliminated completely.

The things you can do that will be most helpful are to use a strictly home-prepared, raw-meat diet (raw meat does not cause the same allergic reaction that cooked meat does). Several of my clients have also found that organic meat is tolerated just fine, but feeding meat from the usual supermarket sources sets off their symptoms.

Also stop vaccinating (or greatly reduce frequency). Animals with allergies do not respond well to vaccination, and I find that it accelerates the intensity and frequency of allergy symptoms (see "Vaccinations" for further advice on this). See "Skin Problems" for specific advice on dealing with that aspect of allergy disease.

ANAL GLAND PROBLEMS

Difficulties with the anal glands are primarily canine problems. Dogs have a pair of small scent glands on either side of the anus, under the tail. Similar in structure to the scent gland of the skunk, they contain a strong-smelling material that is apparently used to mark territory or to express extreme fear.

Problems manifest either as abscesses that form within the glands themselves or as what is called impaction, in which the glands become inactive and overfilled with secretion. In the latter case, the dog will often "scoot" along the floor or ground in an attempt to empty these glands, which have exceeded their normal capacity. Some of the factors that may play a role in the development of these problems are:

❖ Frustration in trying to establish a territory, perhaps from being crowded with other animals or from having inadequate space for exercise and exploration.

❖ Constipation or infrequent bowel movement, especially as a result of not being allowed outside frequently. Many an indoor animal will hold its urine or feces to the very limit rather than soil the house and displease its people.

❖ Toxicity because of poor food and inadequate exercise. In such a case a disorder of the skin or ears frequently occurs as well (also see "Allergies").

PREVENTION

Make sure your animal has adequate exercise, the opportunity to go outside and have frequent bowel movements, and psychological "space." Good nutrition is important also, as it is in most conditions. Especially useful are those nutrients that help promote healthy skin: zinc, the B complex, vitamin A, lecithin, and unsaturated vegetable oil.

Olive oil is a good source of unsaturated fatty acids and, by promoting muscular contraction of the bowels, has the advantage of being a slight laxative. Flax oil (fresh, refrigerated) is an even better source.

TREATMENT

Anal Gland Abscess

Homeopathic—First use the remedy *Belladonna* 6C, using Homeopathic Schedule 2, page 442. See if it looks better the next day. If not clearly healing, then give *Silicea* 30C using Homeopathic Schedule 3 on page 442. Belladonna helps with the initial inflammation and Silicea promotes the discharge of pus and encourages healing. Also apply warm or hot calendula solution (see "Abscesses") twice a day for at least five minutes each time. Continue the calendula treatment about three days, though a longer period is fine, if necessary.

Impacted Anal Glands

Since this condition is associated with sluggishness of the tissues and often with toxicity and obesity as well (see "Weight Problems"), regular vigorous exercise is an important part of the treatment. If you add vegetables and a little bran mixed with olive oil to the food, it will help to regulate the intestines and encourage bulky bowel movements. Copious evacuation will stimulate the natural emptying of the glands.

In addition, a hot fomentation of either marigold flower (*Calendula officinalis*) solution or red clover (*Trifolium pratense*) blossoms will stimulate the glands and soften their contents. Make a "tea" with these herbs, adding boiling water to the herb. A good ratio is a heaping tablespoon of the herb over which you pour a quart of boiling water. Let sit for 15 minutes or so, until cool enough to handle. Then pour off the liquid into a bowl and immerse a washcloth or small towel into the warm solution. Wring it out and apply to the body. As necessary, warm up the compress every couple of minutes by putting it back in the bowl and wringing it out again. The idea is to warm the affected area, increasing blood flow and softening the tissues. You can also make up this solution by using herbal tinctures—add 1 teaspoon of the tincture to 1 quart of warm water.

Immediately after the application, use gentle pressure with a "milking" action to help to empty the glands manually. Consider the manual emptying as a temporary measure, not something to do regularly. It's much better (I'm sure you would agree!) if the glands empty naturally.

A useful adjunct to the above measures is to give one dose of the remedy *Sulphur* 30C.

ANEMIA

Anemia is often caused by blood loss from wounds, or parasites such as fleas and worms, especially hookworm. The problem is characterized by white (or pale) gums, weakness, and a fast pulse. Occasionally, it indicates more serious diseases like feline leukemia or a toxicity resulting from drug exposure. Here, however, we'll consider only the more common and simple anemia caused by blood loss, with an emphasis toward promoting the growth of new red blood cells.

TREATMENT

A diet rich in iron, protein, and vitamin B_{12} is important. That's why the following foods are particularly helpful.

❖ Beef liver (for protein, B-complex, B_{12}, and iron)

❖ Nutritional yeast, supplemented with added B_{12} (same benefits as liver)

❖ Green vegetables (for iron and other minerals)

❖ Kelp powder (for iodine and other trace minerals)

❖ Vitamin C, 500 to 2,000 milligrams a day, depending on the animal's size (promotes the absorption of iron from the intestinal tract)

In addition to the nutritional supports, give one of these remedies (whichever seems best indicated) for ten days.

Homeopathic—*China officinalis* 6C, using Homeopathic Schedule 6(a) on page 442. This is strongly indicated following blood loss that has resulted in marked weakness and loss of strength.

Homeopathic—*Nux vomica* 6C, using Homeopathic Schedule 6(a) on page 442. Try this remedy when your pet has become withdrawn and irritable after the blood loss.

If anemia is caused by parasites, these must be controlled (see "Skin Parasites" or "Worms"). In such a case, use the nutritional advice given for anemia, but instead of using the anemia remedies suggested, follow the treatment guidelines under the appropriate section. (For an anemic animal, however, do not use the fasting program.)

Flea infestations are most safely controlled by a combination of frequent bathing with a nontoxic soap (there are several types available, some with herbal constituents; some contain d-limonene from citrus, which can be used on dogs but not cats), controlling fleas in the environment, and using the lemon skin tonic described in chapter 7. When the animal is stronger, you can use more strenuous flea-control methods if required, but I do discourage the use of poisonous chemicals, because they are not really effective in a long-term way and are very toxic to both humans and animals.

Sometimes very young kittens or puppies are so besieged by fleas that they are almost drained of their blood. In such cases, it is essential not to use flea powders or sprays, even though the temptation is great. The young animals are much too small and weak to handle such an assault. Instead, bathe them often and use the lemon tonic rinse. To prevent them from getting chilled, dry them thoroughly afterward. Towel them off and then use a hair dryer set on low or place them in a warm, sunny spot. Keep them warm and quiet in general and, if the weather allows, give them some fresh air and sunlight. Also use a flea comb to remove fleas not killed by the baths. Feed only natural foods—no commercial fare—and follow the treatment program suggested for anemia. You will be amazed at how quickly these little creatures can respond.

APPETITE PROBLEMS

Changes in normal appetite often show up as an aspect of an illness. This is a problem more common in cats than in dogs, probably because cats have such stringent nutritional requirements. The thing to understand about this is how gradually an inadequate appetite can creep up with a cat. Usually the first indication is what most people would call a finicky cat, one who rejects many different foods and prefers just one or two brands. Most people just give in to this demand and don't think much about it. However, especially if it is coupled with regular water drinking, you have the beginnings of a more serious condition.

The next stage is a fluctuation in preferences. Maybe your cat no longer relishes what it once did. Or perhaps you find it necessary to open a different brand of food at each meal. Even this variation is not always totally acceptable, and your cat may pester you frequently for more food, only to reject what you offer. It is no wonder that some people end up feeding their cat tuna or liver exclusively.

If this deterioration continues, the next stage is inadequate eating with a gradual loss of weight. You may see a skeleton cat that eats just barely enough (with coaxing and indulgence) to maintain life. Cats like this do not eat enthusiastically. They just lick at their food or eat around the edges, leaving the less desirable parts in the bowl. Over time, these cats will waste away until they are finally diagnosed with some disease that is the end product of this long decline.

How will you know if your cat has started into this pattern? Ask yourself some questions: Is your cat addicted to a particular brand of food? Will she eat only dry food? Must you open a new can at every feeding (can't use any leftovers)? Do you find yourself adding irresistible foods like tuna or liver to get your cat to eat? Are you required to sit there with your cat while he eats (perhaps petting him the whole time) lest he will leave his food?

If the answer to any of these questions is yes, you probably have a problem. Another test is to hold back on the food your cat always wants. Instead, offer a home-prepared diet or another good brand of canned food. If your cat does not accept the new food within five days, then you definitely have a problem.

Resolving this situation usually requires a specific homeopathic treatment (called constitutional therapy) or an equivalent method of alternative treatment best undertaken by a well-trained professional. Sometimes, however, appetite problems are just one symptom of a specific disease for which you will find treatment suggestions in this section. For example, a loss of appetite can be the main symptom of conditions as diverse as inflammation of the bowels, or failure of the kidneys. You will need some help from your veterinarian to figure out what the underlying problem is.

ARTHRITIS

Arthritis and bone disease are much more common in dogs than in cats and usually take one of several forms.

Hip dysplasia: a malformation of the hip sockets that allows excessive movement in the joint, causing chronic inflammation, calcium deposits, and further breakdown. This was first seen in the larger breeds of dogs, but now is seen in any breed. Larger dogs, however, have more trouble with it because they weigh more (see "Hip Dysplasia").

Dislocation of the kneecap: a malformation of the leg bones that causes the kneecap to repeatedly pull out of position, slip back and forth and set up a continuous low-grade inflammation. Mostly seen in small breeds, it is fostered by poor breeding practices and low-quality food.

Degeneration of the shoulder joint: the breakdown of cartilage in the shoulder, leading to inflammation and pain on movement. Mostly found in medium to large breeds, it is always an aspect of an overall chronic disease condition that affects other parts of the body as well.

Arthritis of the elbow: a condition that is caused by improper bone formation and is considered to be hereditary. It is generally seen in German shepherds. Like shoulder joint problems, it is part of a larger chronic disease condition.

Swelling and pain in the leg bones: seen in young dogs (a few months of age) of the large breeds. It is apparently partly caused by inadequate production of vitamin C and is the result of poor nutrition and heredity.

PREVENTION

Most of these conditions could be prevented if the female were properly fed throughout her pregnancy. The time of growth in the uterus is critical in terms of the formation of essential structural tissues. Inadequate nutrition is most detrimental at this time (see "Pregnancy, Birth, and Care of Newborns"). Avoiding commercial foods and feeding a natural, wholesome diet is an important part of a preventive program. Homeopathic treatment during pregnancy is also an excellent means of minimizing the likelihood of this problem in the next generation. Of course, the mother should not be vaccinated while she is pregnant (see "Vaccinations").

After birth, the regular use of vitamin C minimizes or prevents some of these problems. Depending on the size of the animal and its age, give 250 to 2,000 milligrams a day. For instance, a small puppy (like a Pekinese) would get 250 milligrams, a large puppy (like a German shepherd) 500 milligrams. After the dog matures, give 500 to 1,000 milligrams daily for most sizes and perhaps up to 2,000 milligrams for a giant breed like the Great Dane or Saint Bernard.

Prevention is very important in arthritic conditions, because once the joints are distorted, the damage has been done.

TREATMENT

Even in the face of an already-established condition, there are several things you can do to minimize your animal's arthritic discomfort. The first step is to feed the natural diet, as described in chapters 4 and 5.

Add vitamin C to the diet, 500 to 2,000 milligrams a day, depending on the animal's size. It's best to divide the daily amount and give it twice a day. Other vitamins and supplements that are especially important are vitamin E and a vitamin A and D combination. Increase the amounts in the recipes by an additional 50 to 100 IU of vitamin E. Double the vitamin A and E supplement (or cod-liver oil). Supplements containing glucosamine can also be very helpful with some animals, primarily where the joints are involved. It does not help every animal, but is worth a trial. For a large dog, add 500 mg to food once a day and adjust proportionately for other sizes. Results will be apparent within 3 weeks, often within 1 week, if this supplement will be beneficial to your dog.

Be sure to include raw, grated vegetables in the diet, particularly carrots, beets, and celery.

In addition to these nutritional guidelines, one of the following remedies may help. Choose the one which best fits your situation.

Herbal—Alfalfa (*Medicago sativa*): Indicated for the thin, nervous animal with a tendency toward digestive problems as well as arthritis. Depending on its size, add 1 teaspoon to 3 tablespoons of ground or dry blended alfalfa to the daily ration. Or you can administer alfalfa as an infusion using Herbal Schedule 3, page 439. A third choice is to give your pet 2 to 6 alfalfa tablets a day.

Herbal—Garlic (*Allium sativum*): Garlic is suited for the overweight animal with hip pain, especially a pet that has been on a high-meat diet. Include freshly grated garlic with each meal, using ½ to 3 cloves, depending on the body size.

Homeopathic—*Rhus toxicodendron* 6C (poison ivy): Do not use the herbal form, of course, but the safe homeopathic preparation, which you can order by mail in tablet or pellet form. Rhus tox. is indicated for a dog or cat with chronic arthritis, pain, or stiffness that is most apparent when the animal gets up after a long rest (for example, overnight). When it first starts to move, the animal shows discomfort or stiffness, but after a few minutes it seems to loosen up and feel better. If the pet also has a tendency toward red, swollen, itchy skin, Rhus tox. will work on both problems (see "Skin Problems"). Use Homeopathic Schedule 6(a), page 442.

Homeopathic—*Silicea* 30C: This medicine fits many dogs that have inherited joint and bone disease problems. Typically, the symptoms become more severe as the dog gets older, with stiffness, pain, and even distortion of the joints and legs in severe cases. I use this medicine for hip dysplasia, elbow dysplasia, joint arthritis, and arthritis of the spine (spondylitis). Use Homeopathic Schedule 4, page 442. Do not give this medicine more than once. If it is not effective, then work with a skilled veterinarian.

A disease that affects young dogs, hypertrophic osteodystrophy causes pain and inflammation of the bones of the legs. Here are a couple of remedies that can be useful.

Homeopathic—*Belladonna* 30C: When the condition has come on suddenly, is very painful and associated with a fever (temperature over 101.5 degrees F. or 38.6 degrees C.) Use Homeopathic Schedule 2, page 442.

Homeopathic—*Eupatorium perfoliatum* 30C: Try this remedy if Belladonna (above) was not sufficient to resolve the problem or if your dog does not fit the picture described for Belladonna. Use Homeopathic Schedule 2, page 442.

BEHAVIOR PROBLEMS

Behavioral abnormalities can be complex and difficult to change, but often you can help considerably. Poor breeding practices, especially in purebred dogs, have fostered the development of many such disturbances, including viciousness, epilepsy, repetitive habits, and other signs of nervous system imbalances. It is also my impression that many behavior problems have their roots in one or more of the following: poor nutrition and associated toxicity, chronic encephalitis (brain inflammation) following vaccination, inadequate exercise, insufficient psychological stimulation and attention, and the influence of the owner's personality patterns, expectations, or conditioning. For instance, family conflict, excessive attachment to a pet as an attempt to escape loneliness, or the desire to have an aggressive animal to feel safer from other people can all have a strong adverse influence on an animal's personality.

TREATMENT

In this brief discussion we'll focus on general measures that can be very helpful and, in some cases, may be sufficient to treat the disturbance, provided that the contributing environmental factors are understood and eliminated. Start with nutrition.

Take your pet off commercial food, if you have not already done so. Any food that contains artificial preservatives, coloring agents, or other additives contains chemicals that can irritate the brain tissue and cause abnormal responses. Feed our fresh foods diet.

Provide a complete vitamin supplement that is especially rich in B complex. I would use a multi-vitamin tablet, with the major B vitamins at the 5- to 20-milligram level, for a trial period of at least two months.

Use supplements to help eliminate and counteract the effect of substances that may be irritating the brain cells. If you suspect a buildup of toxic material, give your pet the following: zinc (2 to 20 milligrams a day, depending on the animal's size); vitamin C (250 to 2,000 milligrams a day); lecithin (½ teaspoon to 1 tablespoon of granules in the food daily); and bone meal (an extra ⅛ teaspoon to one teaspoon daily).

Algin (from seaweed) is also useful. It's a natural substance that works to remove heavy metals such as lead (which can be a contributing factor) from the body. Use Nori seaweed. Depending on the animal's size, use from ½-sheet to 1 full sheet of Nori per day, mixed with the food (chopped up) or, if liked, given straight as a treat.

The zinc and the vitamin C work as a team to eliminate toxic heavy metals, while lecithin protects the nerve cells against irritation. With the addition of bone meal, this group as a whole helps to detoxify the body and to protect the nerves.

Minimize exposure to toxic substances. Make sure your animal is protected from accidental poisoning by various household chemicals. Just as important, minimize its exposure to such pollutants as cigarette smoke, car exhaust, and anti-flea chemicals (which affect the nervous system).

In addition to these measures, one or more of the following treatments may be useful.

Homeopathic—*Belladonna* 30C: Indicated for a hyperactive, excitable animal, especially if there is a tendency to bite. They may be prone to spasms and convulsions or see things that "are not there," like flies in the air or bugs crawling on the carpet (hallucinations). Use Homeopathic Schedule 5, page

442. If this remedy is effective, then work with a homeopathic veterinarian for continued treatment with other medicines.

Herbal—Common oat (*Avena sativa*): Oats are well suited as a general nerve tonic and are particularly useful where nerve weakness or irritability may have appeared after other stressful diseases. This herb is good for animals that have received a lot of drugs, are old, or have a tendency to epilepsy. It is also helpful for the animal with weak legs, muscle twitching, or a trembling associated with weakness. All of this, of course, will be in addition to any particular behavior problems exhibited (this applies to all of the herbs to be described).

Though feeding rolled oats as a cooked grain in the diet is helpful, a more potent preparation is the tincture. Use Herbal Schedule 1, page 438.

Herbal—Blue vervain (Verbena): Vervain is suited for animals that are depressed and have weak nervous systems. It's also for those with irritated nerves and muscle spasms and is especially appropriate for those whose abnormal behavior is associated with epilepsy; in such cases it will strengthen the brain function. Use Herbal Schedule 1, page 438.

Herbal—Skullcap (*Scutellaria lateriflora*): This herb is useful for behavior disturbances that center around nervous fear. The animal may also show one or more of the following signs: intestinal gas, colic, diarrhea, muscle twitching, and restless sleep. Use Herbal Schedule 1, page 438.

Herbal—Valerian (*Valeriana officinalis*): Valerian suits the animal that tends to get hysterical, associated with a hypersensitivity. The animal shows a changeable mental disposition and an irritable temperament. Like skullcap, valerian may be most successfully used for animals that have digestive disturbances like gas and diarrhea when the nerves supplying the abdominal organs are overactive and those that may also have a history of leg pains or joint inflammation.

Since valerian is one of those herbs that can cause a toxic reaction if given in large doses over a long period of time, I advise that you try Herbal Schedule 1 on page 438 for no more than a week. If you don't see beneficial results by then, discontinue use and try one of the other suggested remedies, such as the oat tincture.

Herbal—German chamomile (*Matricaria*): Animals that will benefit from this herb are noisy, whining, moaning, and complaining. They will let you know about their pains or discomforts. They are sensitive, irritable, and thirsty and may snap or try to bite. Such animals don't like to be hot and are often mollified or quiet only when being carried or constantly petted. Use Herbal Schedule 1, page 438.

Use the suggested schedule for the herb you have chosen for two to three weeks (except for valerian, which should not be used for more than a week). If you see an improvement in that time, even a slight one, continue the treatment as long as the improvement goes on, up to a maximum of six

weeks. Then discontinue the regular use of the herb, but give a few more doses of it whenever symptoms return or worsen.

Also, the herb can be used preventively. Give it to your pet before an event you know will trigger the problem behavior, for example, before leaving him alone for long periods. In this way it can be used occasionally, as needed, over several weeks or months.

What if you don't see a good response over the trial period? Then discontinue the selected herb and either try it again after a few weeks on a better diet or use one of the alternative herbs suggested.

I would like to suggest one additional alternative for those who are willing to go a little further. In my own work I find that the best herbal system for behavior problems with psychological roots is the use of the 38 flower preparations, known as flower remedies, discovered by Dr. Edward Bach. These were originally developed for human use by Dr. Bach in England in the 1930s. I have found them effective for animals. They are dilute extracts of selected flowers given orally over a long period (weeks to months), often with remarkable improvements (see chapter 14 for more information).

It is beyond the scope of this book to cover this extraordinary system in depth, but for those interested readers who want to explore the system or who are already acquainted with it, I want to call special attention to the following flower essences (but not to the exclusion of the others).

- Chicory: for the overly attached, possessive animal
- Holly: for the vicious, aggressive, suspicious, or jealous animal
- Impatiens: for the uptight, impatient, or irritable pet
- Mimulus: for the animal afraid of specific things, like the dog afraid of men or of thunder
- Rock rose: for use where attacks of terror or panic are part of the disturbance
- Star of Bethlehem: for use where physical or emotional shock seems to have initiated the imbalance
- Walnut: for the animal that is overly influenced by a strong personality (human or animal) or apparently under the influence of bad heredity

Select up to four (no more) of the best-suited essences. Add two drops from the stock bottle of each of these essences to a clean one-ounce dropper bottle. Then fill the bottle with spring (not distilled) water. Store it at room temperature. If the solution clouds up in a few days, make a fresh batch.

Regardless of the size of your animal, give two drops of this diluted medicine orally four times a day until the desired results are obtained. If you can, drop it directly in the mouth. If not, mix it with a little food or milk. There is no unfavorable side effect or possible toxicity with this system.

A final note: Behavior problems are complex, but that does not mean they cannot be solved. Sometimes other treatments are needed—for example, an antidote to rabies vaccine. That level of treatment can only be administered by a veterinarian trained in homeopathy. If the simple measures here are not sufficient, you are encouraged to pursue further homeopathic treatment with a trained homeopath. See my Web site, www.drpitcairn.com, for a list of qualified practitioners.

BIRTH

See "Pregnancy, Birth, and Care of Newborns."

BLADDER PROBLEMS

Inflammation of your pet's bladder lining and urethra or the formation of urinary mineral deposits and stones is not unusual, particularly for a cat (see "Allergies"). Symptoms show up as increased frequency of urination, the appearance of blood in the urine, and, in severe cases, extreme discomfort, with straining and partial or complete blockage of the bladder.

Though conventional veterinary treatment almost always includes antibiotics, research shows that bladder problems are not caused by bacteria. In my own practice I have not found it necessary to use antibiotics for this problem for over 25 years.

Another common but erroneous idea is that because gritty material accumulates in the bladder, ash (minerals) in the food is responsible for urinary tract trouble. Research shows that ash doesn't cause the problem; rather, grit forms because the urine becomes too alkaline. Some commercial foods now add extra acid to make the urine more acid to prevent this. There are side effects from use of these acid formulations—leaching calcium from the bones is one unpleasant effect. What these formulas do is keep the urine acid, but do not cure or eliminate the underlying problem, which often results in kidney failure as cats get older.

It is clear to me that much of this problem originates in feeding pets poor-quality food, with a resulting toxicity and excessive elimination load on the linings of the urinary system. Almost invariably, the first attack follows a history of feeding dry commercial foods over a long period. Sometimes I say (as a way to make a point) that if you want to increase the chance of a bladder problem, feed dry food and leave it out all the time.

I've found that, once through the crisis, the condition is very responsive to diet changes and natural therapies, resulting in a stable cure rather than a temporary relief.

TREATMENT

First, change your pet's diet. If it mostly centers on commercial foods, the condition is almost sure to recur. Fasting is especially useful here, as it has been observed that continued eating aggravates and prolongs the problem. Therefore, during the acute phase of the condition (below), put the animal on a liquid fast, offering a broth. For cats, use a broth made from meat or fish. For dogs, use vegetables and meat. You may add a small amount of natural tamari soy sauce to season it and to supply easily digested amino acids. In addition, provide your pet with pure water (without chlorine or fluorine) at all times.

After improvement or recovery, adopt the natural diet as advised in chapters 3 and 4. Feed your cat only twice a day—morning and evening. Don't leave the food out for more than 30 minutes. If she does not want to eat at these times, let a natural hunger develop until the next feeding time. This is very important. Frequent feeding alkalizes the urine, leading to formation of "sand" and "stones." Cats, as carnivores, are meant to eat infrequently and fast in between.

For one month, also use these measures.

Give vitamin C, 250 milligrams twice daily. This will help maintain an acidic urine while you are making the diet changes, which makes mineral salts more soluble and counters the formation of crystals.

Increase the amount of vitamin E to minimize or prevent scarring of tissues that are healing. Add an extra 25 to 50 IU daily to your cat's food.

Give vitamin A. Add four drops of cod-liver oil (to the food) once a day or 10,000 IU of vitamin A once a week.

Besides diet, here are some specific treatments. Let's start with cats, who are more prone to bladder trouble. There are three different phases of the problem.

Cats

Acute Cases

If the urethra has become thoroughly plugged up, the cat cannot pass urine, and the bladder will become enlarged and hard from urine accumulation. It feels like a large stone in the back part of the abdomen.

This is a special problem for male cats, because they tend to have long and narrow urethras. (A female cat may have bladder problems, but she isn't likely to get plugged.) The condition is quite serious, since urine and poisonous waste products are backing up into the bloodstream. Make an emergency run to your veterinarian to have a catheter put in, a plastic tube that relieves the obstruction and allows urine to pass. If you are too far from a veterinarian or can't reach one right away, however, try one of these treatments while you are waiting for help.

Homeopathic—*Belladonna* 30C: Give 1 pellet every 30 minutes for a total of 2 treatments. This is the first remedy I think of using and is suitable for the cases with severe symptoms, much pain, straining, and agitation. Especially indicated if there is much fresh blood in the urine. It is often sufficient for many cats.

Homeopathic—*Nux vomica* 30C: Give 1 pellet every 30 minutes for a total of 2 treatments. This remedy is best for the cat that,

before the bladder trouble came on, has become irritable, doesn't want to be touched, and withdraws from company, preferring to be by himself.

Homeopathic—*Pulsatilla* 30C: Give 1 pellet every 30 minutes for a total of 2 treatments. This remedy is best for the cat that becomes quiet and unusually affectionate, wanting to be held as the attack came on.

Homeopathic—*Cantharis* 30C: Give 1 pellet every 30 minutes for a total of 2 treatments. The cat that needs this medicine will be very upset, angry, and growl with almost constant and intense attempts to urinate. Often the anger and growling is directed against the inflamed penis as he licks it intensely.

Homeopathic—*Coccus cacti* 30C: Give 1 pellet every 30 minutes for a total of 2 treatments. Choose this remedy if one or more of the previous ones listed here are not effective and it appears there is complete blockage and no urine coming out (due to stones or mucus plugging the urethra).

With any of these treatments, improvement will mean a sudden passing of a large quantity of urine with considerable relief for your cat. Often the cat will now drink a large amount of water and begin to be more comfortable, even grooming himself for the first time. If this happens, you may be through the crisis and catheterization will be unnecessary. Watch closely for the next several days to make sure that urination continues unimpeded. Follow the crisis with the nutritional changes already discussed above.

If your cat needs to be catheterized, an additional treatment that will assist recovery from this procedure is:

Homeopathic—*Staphysagria* (stavesacre) 30C: Use Homeopathic Schedule 2, page 442.

Subacute Cases

Here, the problem is not obstruction but inflammation. The cat feels a frequent urge to urinate, but the flow is scanty or blood-tinged. This misery can go on for days, perhaps with temporary improvement (especially with antibiotics). However, the problem continues or recurs every few weeks. The remedies that follow are often useful for this stage of the problem. From the three remedies below, choose the one that best suits the condition. Don't mix them.

Homeopathic—*Belladonna* 30C: Use Homeopathic Schedule 2. The first remedy to try. Symptoms are intense pain, agitation, frequent urging, even some traces of blood in the urine. Pupils of the eyes will be very dilated even in good light. Cat very excitable and nervous.

Homeopathic—*Pulsatilla* 30C: This remedy is useful for the cat that does not like heat in any form. Here is how you can tell. Put out a hot water bottle or heating pad wrapped with a towel. If your cat is not interested in huddling next to it and prefers to lie on something cool like cement, tile, linoleum, or even the bathtub or sink, then you will know it prefers coolness to heat. Usually the urine

is passed in small amounts and contains blood. Use Homeopathic Schedule 2, page 442.

Homeopathic——*Cantharis* 30C: Same indications as given above, especially the anger and growling at the condition. Symptoms intense. Use Homeopathic Schedule 2, page 442.

Homeopathic—*Mercurius vivus* (or *solubilis*) 30C: The cat needing this remedy will act very annoyed with his rear end, doing a lot of licking after urinating, thrashing the tail around, and straining to produce small quantities of urine. Sometimes the straining is associated with passing stool, with continued efforts even after some has been passed. These cats will have prior mouth problems, with red inflamed gums and loose teeth. If the cat also has become unusually thirsty before the attack, this is probably the remedy to use. Use Homeopathic Schedule 2, page 442.

Note: If you do not see any improvement after 24 hours of using one of these homeopathic preparations, discontinue the treatment and reassess the situation. If antibiotics and other drugs were used at any time, they may have altered the symptom picture. Think back to the symptoms that were present before treatment was started. Use these as your guidelines in choosing a remedy.

Chronic Cases

If one of the treatments above has been successful or if your cat has needed catheterization and is now recovered, then it is time to think of giving a homeopathic treatment that will stop the tendency for formation of sand and sludge in the bladder. The most useful remedy for this is *Calcarea carbonica* 30C, given once only. It is very important not to repeat this treatment. It is possible that another medicine may be more specific for you particular cat, and this is where the advice of a homeopathically trained veterinarian is especially helpful. What is called "chronic treatment" takes more skill and experience to be successful.

The remedy mentioned above will correct the problem in many cats, but you do have to be watchful for the tendency for this to return. Further treatment can be needed, perhaps not right away but in a few months time. How will you know if there is mineral deposit in the urine? Easiest way is to feel it with your fingers. Yuck! I know, an unpleasant thought, but it is surprising how easy it is to detect that way. Prepare the litter pan like this: wash it out and when dry, instead of putting litter in it, just tear up some strips of paper about ½ inch wide and several inches long. Put these in the pan instead of litter. It sort of looks to the cat that there is something there and he will scratch around in it and urinate just the same as with litter. Where the urine has settled on the bottom, feel it for grittiness. It will feel like small sand grains.

If you don't want to do this (understandably), then collect the urine into a clean container and take it to your veterinarian, either right away or refrigerated until you can, to be analyzed under the microscope. They will let you know if there is a problem.

Note: If you take some urine in a jar to a veterinarian, she may say to you that it will do no good to analyze it because it is not sterile. The veterinarian is thinking of looking for bacteria. Ask them to do it anyway. What we want is not a bacterial evaluation (not the cause anyway), but a "microscopic examination" to see if crystals are being formed. Also ask for one other thing: pH (how acid or alkaline the urine is) measurement, which should be about 6 to 7. The range of 2 to 5 is too acid and from 8 to 10 too alkaline. This information helps you to know how if there is a problem with the urinary system.

Herbal—What if indications are too vague to fit any of the remedies listed above? Try the following herbal treatment, helpful for a cat that never has a severe bladder problem, just a weakness in that area, such as a tendency toward urinary frequency or urinating outside the litter box.

Herbal—Use shave grass, also known as horsetail grass or scouring rush (Equisetum). To use the medication, use Herbal Schedule 2, page 439, for 2 to 3 weeks.

DOGS

Though bladder problems are more common in cats, dogs do get them too. Their most common disturbances are either cystitis (as in cats) or stone formation.

If your dog has a case of cystitis resembling the symptoms described above for cats (increased frequency of urination, discomfort, blood in the urine), you can use the feline treatment program, adjusting nutritional supplements to your dog's body size. However, I usually start with *Pulsatilla* 30C, using Homeopathic Schedule 2 on page 442. It seems suitable for many dogs with this condition.

What if it's a stone problem? They occur in two forms—small, pellet-size stones that form in the bladder but move down and block the urethra, and very large stones that fill the bladder.

Small stones are most troublesome to the male dog. They pass down into the urethra and get caught at the point where it passes through the bone in the penis (a hard opening that cannot become larger). When this happens, the unfortunate fellow will attempt to urinate frequently, without success, or will give off little spurts of urine instead of a full flow. In such cases immediately use:

Homeopathy—*Nux vomica* 30C: Homeopathic Schedule 2. First one to try.

Homeopathic—*Coccus cacti* 30C: Homeopathic Schedule 2. This remedy is a treatment for obstruction of the urethra with a stone, associated with severe crampy pains in the bladder.

Homeopathic—*Pulsatilla* 30C: Homeopathic Schedule 2. This remedy will often relieve the spasms of the muscles of the urethra where the stone is caught, allowing it to move out.

Herbal—Shepherd's purse (*Thlaspi bursa pastoris* or *Capsella*): Use Herbal Schedule 1, page 438. Like *Coccus cacti*, this is a treatment for presence of stones.

Sometimes the stone will pass through when these treatments are used. The remedy will not make the stone dissolve, of course, but it may reduce the spasms and inflammation from the presence of the stone. If it is small enough, the stone may then pass through.

Large stones are another matter. Numerous large stones can grow to fill the bladder and eventually irritate the lining, causing bleeding and recurrent bacterial infection. This form of large stone formation is more common in dogs than in cats. Such stones will need to be surgically removed. They usually will recur at shorter and shorter intervals, however, which necessitates repeated surgery.

The causes for this condition are not really understood. There are various ideas about the role of calcium and other minerals and the relation with vitamin D and other nutrients, but nothing is (in my opinion) really clear about the etiology.

The animals I have worked with have done well on a natural diet program with appropriate homeopathic treatment. Considering the many kinds of stones that can form and the many clinical problems that they can be associated with, however, I can give only general advice that will be helpful regardless of the type of stone involved. More specific, individualized treatment will be needed for persistent and recurrent problems.

First improve the diet. This will help the animal by strengthening the urinary tract, normalizing liver function, and adjusting the animal's metabolism. A home-prepared diet with the following supplements will be of great help.

Cod-liver oil: The lining of the bladder and urinary tract is kept in top condition by adequate vitamin A in the diet. In addition, vitamin D, which is produced by the animal's body in the presence of sunlight, can be deficient in many animals that live indoors much of the time. Use cod-liver oil or another source of both vitamin A and vitamin D. Give 2,500 IU per day of vitamin A to small dogs, 5,000 to medium dogs, and 10,000 to large dogs (see page 118).

Vitamin C: Give this vitamin to aid in detoxification and to acidify the urine, which helps control bacterial infection and reduces the likelihood that stones will form. Twice daily, give 250 milligrams to small dogs and 500 milligrams to medium dogs. Large dogs get 500 milligrams, three times daily (see page 118).

B-complex: The most important B vitamins for this condition are B_2 (riboflavin) and B_6 (pyridoxine). However, don't give them alone. Always use a complete natural formula so no imbalances of the B complex occur. Give small dogs a daily tablet with the major B vitamins (including B_2 and B_6) at the 10-milligram level; for medium and large dogs use the 20-milligram level (you many need use part of a tablet or capsule to get these amounts).

Do not restrict calcium in the diet. Sometimes people are advised to follow a low-calcium diet with the idea that restricting calcium will reduce the formation of stones. However, there is no evidence that this is effective; in fact, insufficient calcium actually makes the problem worse by increasing the amount of oxalate (a common component of bladder and kidney stones) in the urine.

Magnesium: This mineral helps prevent reformation of stones. Magnesium chloride or other magnesium chelates are good supplements to use, given at levels of 50, 100, or 300 milligrams a day, depending on the animal's size (see page 118).

Avoid exposure to cadmium, which is known to increase the formation of stones. The most common source of cadmium exposure for pets is cigarette smoke (even more reason to quit).

In addition to these dietary measures, I would use one of the following treatment programs for the tendency to form stones, either small or large in size.

Homeopathic—The treatment most likely to be effective, in my experience, is this sequential homeopathic treatment: First give the remedy *Thuya* (or *Thuja*) *occidentalis* (arborvitae) 30C, using Homeopathic Schedule 4, page 442.

Wait for one month and then do the same treatment (Schedule 4) with *Silicea* 30C. This treatment program will not be effective in every case, but will with many and is worth trying. It is important not to give the remedies more than once.

Homeopathic—*Urtica urens* 30C: Very helpful when there are large stones in the bladder with subsequent bleeding from irritation of the bladder wall. Use until surgery can be done to remove them. Use Homeopathic Schedule 5.

Herbal—Barberry (*Berberis vulgaris*): This herb is good for an animal with arthritic or rheumatic (muscle and joint soreness) tendencies in addition to bladder or kidney stones. Use Herbal Schedule 1, page 438, for a month to give it an adequate try.

Herbal—Sarsaparilla (*Smilax officinalis*): Useful in cases where "gravel" and small stones are in the urine, accompanied by bladder inflammation and pain. Urination may be painful and blood may be passed. Often the animal suited to this herb will also have dry, itchy skin that flares up most in the springtime. Use Herbal Schedule 1, page 438, for a month to give it an adequate try.

If your dog does have surgery to remove bladder stones, here's a treatment to relieve pain and assist recovery afterwards. Start it the day *after* (not before) surgery, if possible.

Homeopathic—*Staphysagria* (stavesacre) 30C: Use Homeopathic Schedule 2, page 442.

BREAST TUMORS

Breast tumors are more likely in older females that have not been spayed. Spaying your pet while it's young not only helps to ease the pet population problem, it also helps to prevent breast tumors. Like any problem with growths or tumors, it is best to avoid vaccinations and to emphasize the purest foods. A pure diet is especially important because the hormones that stimulate cancer growth are more likely to be higher in meat by-products. By using organic meats (or even just human-grade meats from a market), you significantly reduce exposure.

TREATMENT

In many cases, breast tumors are malignant and radical surgery involving removal of associated lymph nodes is recommended. My experience, however, is that this is not always the best approach. Surgery will result in a weakened immune system and can result in a decline in health. I find that the animals that have had surgery or chemotherapy cannot usually be helped by the alternative methods I use. You can try a more natural approach first, however, and, if there is no progress, consult a veterinarian about the possibility of surgery or other treatment.

It is difficult to give you general advice because this is a serious problem that requires professional evaluation. If your dog develops such tumors, I suggest that you have her examined by your veterinarian. If the tumors are not thought to be malignant, you certainly could try one of the following treatments. If they are thought to be malignant, however, you should work with your veterinarian rather than go it on your own.

One of these treatments may be suitable.

Homeopathic—Use this sequential homeopathic treatment: First give the remedy *Thuya* (or *Thuja*) *occidentalis* 30C (arborvitae) using Homeopathic Schedule 5, page 442. Wait for 1 month and then give *Silicea* 30C, also using Schedule 4.

Homeopathic—*Lachesis muta* 30C (venom

of bushmaster snake): This is suitable for a tumor that is in a left breast when the skin over the tumor is dark, bluish, or blackish. Use Homeopathic Schedule 4, page 442.

Herbal—Poke root (*Phytolacca*) is a very important herb for treating inflammation, infection, and drainage from the breast. It is indicated for tumors or hardening of this tissue with discharge of pus or bad smelling fluid. Use Herbal Schedule 3 (internal) and 4 (external), page 439, for as long as is necessary.

Herbal—Goldenseal (*Hydrastis canadensis*) is generally useful in treating any kind of cancer, especially if it is associated with a loss of weight. Use Schedule 1, page 438, for as long as it seems helpful. When using this herb for long periods, supplement the diet with extra vitamin B complex, as goldenseal tends to deplete the body of these vitamins.

Note: Remember that nutrition is all-important. Besides the natural diet, offer large amounts of vitamin C (500 milligrams to 5 grams daily, depending on the size of your animal), as well as vitamin E (50 to 200 IU) and vitamin A (2,000 to 5,000 IU) each day. All three vitamins are useful for detoxification.

BRONCHITIS

See "Upper Respiratory Infections."

CANCER

The dreaded disease cancer is becoming increasingly common in our time. Research suggests that environmental pollutants and chemicals in food are major factors in the development and support of this group of diseases. The way I see it, there are many factors that seem to "cause" cancer, but they don't take effect unless the individual is in a weakened, susceptible condition.

The condition of the thymus gland and its associated lymphatic tissues and immunological functions is extremely important. If an animal can be kept in excellent health with good food, adequate exercise, access to fresh air and sunshine, and a stable emotional environment, the immune system will be strong. Whereas a weaker animal might succumb to the effects of carcinogens, the strong one will more likely resist and detoxify them. Prevention is really the most we can do, and it is very important. No drug or vaccine can ever take the place of good health.

PREVENTION

Certain influences in animals' lives increase their exposure to carcinogens, and you should help your pet avoid them as much as possible. They include: chronic exposure to cigarette smoke; riding in the back of a pickup truck (from inhaling exhaust); resting on or close to a color TV set; drinking water from street puddles (which can contain hydrocarbons and asbestos dust from brakes); frequent diagnostic work with x-rays (all radiation effects are cumulative in the body); use of strong toxic chemicals over long periods (as with flea and tick control); and consuming pet foods high in organ meats and meat meal (concentrators of pesticides and growth hormones used to fatten cattle, which can promote cancer growth), as well as preservatives and artificial colors, known to cause cancer in lab animals.

Unfortunately, for a pet that already has cancer, the time for prevention has passed. By avoiding these toxins, however, we will at least not be adding stress to an already burdened body.

In addition to these precautions, a fresh natural diet is imperative. (Cancer is difficult enough to deal with. Don't compromise when dealing with a disease of this seriousness.) Supplement the diet with vitamins C, A, and E, as well as yeast and fresh raw vegetables (particularly sprouts and grasses, notable for their B vitamin and trace mineral contents).

TREATMENT

What can we expect in treating cancer? Helpful treatments have three possibilities: maintaining good-quality life during the time remaining, extending life beyond what is usually expected, or curing the condition with diminution or disappearance of the tumors.

The majority of my cases fall into the first two groups, because most of the animals I work with are older and not particularly healthy to start with. But even then the animal's quality of life usually remains good, much better than expected, during nutritional and homeopathic treatment. However, the animal may not live much longer than was expected when diagnosed. This outcome is true of about a third of my cancer cases.

Another third of my patients live longer than expected, sometimes considerably longer, especially if they are younger and have not had prior surgery. Eventually, they do succumb to the disease. This is more likely to happen with some types of cancers than others, of course.

The remaining third do better than this, with the tumors no longer growing—perhaps even regressing and disappearing for a while. As you would expect, this improvement is more likely to occur in a younger animal with more vitality. It seems to be very important that there be no prior use of corticosteroids or surgery if I am to obtain results like this. The use of nutrition and homeopathy depends on a vigorous immuno-defense system, so this system must be kept in tip-top condition.

Though chemotherapy, radiation, and surgery can have dramatic and rapid results, the quality of life for the animals afterwards does not impress me. Life is more than just physical duration. To me it is not enough for the patient to be alive—there must also be some pleasure in that life. From the beginning of my career in veterinary medicine, I have been averse to the harsh treatments used for cancer. It just doesn't feel right to me.

Further, I don't think that conventional treatment is effective in prolonging life. Recent evaluations of research into cancer treatment methods show that, contrary to popular belief, the overall death rate from cancer has stayed the same over the last 35 years. (Because of earlier diagnosis, the survival rate only appears to be longer than it used to be.) Considering the discomfort entailed in conventional treatment, I don't think it is worth it.

So, let's say you have thought about this and still opt for the conventional program. Then, I suggest the following measures to help support the body during conventional cancer therapy.

❖ Avoid commercial foods completely. Feed only fresh, unprocessed foods, including as much raw fare as the animal is willing to accept (see the discussion about food under "Breast Tumors"). Use only organic meat, if you can get it.

❖ Give high levels of vitamin C (one gram daily for every 15 pounds of body weight). Give half of this in the morning and half in the evening.

❖ Give oat tincture as described under "Behavior Problems."

❖ Use only spring, distilled, or other pure water, not tap water.

❖ If your animal becomes ill from the drugs used during treatment, feed cooked oatmeal (with milk and honey) if possible and give the homeopathic remedy *Nux vomica* 6C, using Schedule 2, page 442.

❖ Avoid all vaccinations. Giving a vaccine to an animal with cancer is like pouring gasoline on a fire.

On the other hand, if you decide to forego conventional treatment, follow the instructions above and add the following treatments as well. Start with the goldenseal and the treatment with *Thuya* (or *Thuja*).

Herbal—Goldenseal (*Hydrastis canadensis*) is generally useful for treating any kind of cancer, especially if it is associated with a loss of weight. Use Herbal Schedule 1, page 438, for as long as it seems helpful. When you use this herb for long periods, you will need to supplement the diet with extra vitamin B-complex.

Homeopathic—*Thuya* (or *Thuja*) *occidentalis* 30C: Use Schedule 4, page 442. This treatment should be done at the outset of any cancer case, as it removes the influence of prior vaccinations that may stimulate the growth of tumors.

If there is not enough improvement after three or four weeks, then try one of these treatments, using Schedule 6(b), page 442.

Homeopathic—*Natrum muriaticum* (salt, sodium chloride) 6C: This is most helpful with cats that have solid tumors or lymphosarcoma, especially if associated with appetite problems.

Homeopathic—*Silicea* (silicon dioxide, quartz) 6C: This is most helpful with dogs that have solid tumors or lymphosarcoma, especially if associated with a ravenous appetite and weight loss.

Homeopathic—*Conium maculatum* (poison hemlock) 6C: This is indicated for the animal that has very hard tumors.

Homeopathic—*Phosphorus* 6C: Useful

where the tumors tend to hemorrhage or bleed persistently.

It is very worthwhile working with an experienced veterinarian who can offer other homeopathic treatments, as there are many, many, other homeopathic medicines that have a place in this treatment program. Success is greatest when medicines carefully selected for the individual case are used.

CATARACTS

See "Eye Problems."

CHOREA

See "Distemper, Chorea, and Feline Panleukopenia."

CONSTIPATION

Constipation sometimes occurs when animals don't get enough bulk in their diet or don't get enough exercise. If a dog or cat is not allowed to evacuate when the urge is there, the animal may develop the habit of holding its stool. A dog that is not let out often enough or a housebound cat with a dirty litter box is most likely to develop this habit. In relatively simple cases like this, the following treatments will generally suffice.

TREATMENT

Feed a natural diet that includes fresh vegetables for adequate bulk. Raw meat seems to be a natural laxative for dogs and cats. Milk sometimes is the same for cats.

If the animal's stools seem dry, add ½ teaspoon to 1 tablespoon of bran to each meal (depending on the animal's weight). It will help the stools retain additional moisture. A similar treatment is to use ¼ teaspoon to 2 teaspoons of powdered psyllium seed, which is available in health food stores.

Use mineral oil temporarily where there is a large buildup of hard stools. Depending on the animal's size, add ½ teaspoon to 2 teaspoons to the food once a day, until a bowel movement occurs, but for no more than a week. Continued use is inadvisable because the oil will draw reserves of vitamin A from the animal's body and may also create a dependency on its use for normal evacuation. We could use a vegetable oil like olive, for example, but mineral oil has the advantage of remaining undigested as it passes through, while the vegetable oil is usually absorbed into the body and never makes it to the rectum.

Give the animal plenty of opportunity to relieve itself. Make sure your cat has a clean, accessible litter box and let your dog out several times a day.

Make sure the animal gets plenty of exercise. This is very important for massaging the internal organs and increasing blood flow throughout the body, often stimulating a sluggish metabolism. Long walks or runs or a game of fetch are excellent. For a cat, try games involving pouncing, such as "thing-on-a-string."

Dogs

Chronic Cases

If your dog has chronic constipation, try one of these remedies in addition to the advice just given. Pick the one that most closely matches your pet's situation.

Homeopathic—*Nux vomica* (poison nut) 6C: This is an effective treatment for constipation caused by poor-quality food in the diet, eating too many bones, or emotional upset (frustration, grief, scolding). It is best suited to a dog that has repeated but ineffectual straining and may show irritability, pain, and a tendency to hide or be alone. Use Schedule 6(a), page 442.

Homeopathic—*Silicea* (silicon dioxide, quartz) 6C: Silicea is best for the constipated animal that seems to have a weak rectum. With this weakness, the stool, though partly expelled, slips back in again. It's also good for a dog that has trouble getting the whole bowel movement out and for the poorly nourished animal. Use Schedule 6(a), page 442.

Homeopathic—*Natrum muriaticum* (salt) 6C: Useful when constipation is a continuing problem but there is no desire to have a bowel movement (or little concern about it). Use Homeopathic Schedule 6(a).

Where the rectum is weak, you should also consider the possibility of aluminum poisoning. Signs include chronic constipation with straining, and stools that are sticky and messy rather than hard. Even though the stool is soft, weak rectal muscles make passage difficult. Consider the possibility of aluminum poisoning in all recurrent cases, even though the symptoms may be different from those given.

If you suspect this problem, stop using aluminum cooking pots or dishes for your animal's food. Avoid pet food sold in aluminum cans. Also, do not feed processed cheeses (which may contain sodium aluminum phosphate as an emulsifier), table salt (which often contains sodium silicoaluminate or aluminum calcium silicate to prevent caking), white flour (which may be bleached with an aluminum compound, potassium alum) and tap water (aluminum sulfate may be used as a precipitant to remove water impurities).

To help remove the aluminum from the body, use high levels of vitamin C (500 milligrams to 3 grams daily) along with a zinc supplement (5 milligrams for cats and small dogs, 10 milligrams for medium dogs and 20 milligrams for large dogs—see page 118 for dog sizes—you will likely have to cut down a tablet to smaller size to have the correct dose). A chelated form of zinc is best.

Please understand that not all animals are adversely affected by aluminum; however, there are some individuals that are very sensitive to it.

Cats

Chronic Cases

For the cat with chronic constipation, use the basic treatment described above. In addition, choose the one remedy below that best suits your cat's condition.

Homeopathic—*Nux vomica* (poison nut) 6C: Use for the cat that strains ineffectually or passes only small amounts without relief. It may act irritable, withdraw to be alone in another room, or avoid your touch. Constipation may follow emotional upset, stress or too much rich food. There may be a history of nausea and vomiting. Use Schedule 6(a), page 442.

Homeopathic—*Calcarea carbonica* 30C: This is indicated for the most severe and persistent forms of constipation in cats. When the case is this severe, it is often called obstipation. Some cats never empty their bowels adequately, going two or three days between inadequate bowel movements. Use Schedule 4, page 442. *Do not repeat the medicine.*

Herbal—Common garlic (*Allium sativum*): For the cat with a big appetite that likes a lot of meat and tends to constipation, add ½ to 1 clove of freshly grated raw garlic to the daily food. Many animals like the taste.

Herbal—Olive oil (*Olea europaea*): This oil serves as a tonic for the intestinal tract and stimulates the flow of liver bile and the contraction of intestinal muscles. Any excess oil will also lubricate the fecal mass and soothe the mucous membrane linings of the intestine and rectum. Give ½ to 1 teaspoon twice daily, mixed with food, until the movements are regular. (You also can give it once a week as a tonic or to prevent hair balls.)

Note: Also consider the possibility of aluminum sensitivity, as described for dogs.

CORNEAL ULCERS

See "Eye Problems."

CUSHING'S DISEASE

This disorder is a dysfunction of the adrenal glands, much like Addison's Disease (page 295). With Addison's, the adrenal glands are not producing enough hormone; with Cushing's the opposite is true—the glands are over-producing corticosteroids (principally hydrocortisone). Of course what we want is "just enough and not too much," so this over-production can be a real problem.

Why does this happen? It's not really understood very well, but we do know that many of the dogs and cats develop Cushing's because the pituitary gland (a hormonal "master gland" in the brain) is pushing the adrenal glands to do so. This accounts for about 85 to 90 percent of cases. The situation is further complicated because the pituitary gland is influenced, in turn, by the brain, and it's entirely possible that the whole cascade of problems occurs because of psychological or physical stress—at least as contributing factors. Chances are that if your pet has this diagnosis, it is a dysfunction of the pituitary (and thus adrenal) gland that is the problem.

The remaining 10–15 percent have tumors

in the adrenal glands themselves, which causes the excessive production (the pituitary gland not involved). These tumors are often benign (not malignant), though not always.

What happens as a result of this condition? The usual and most common symptoms are excessive drinking and urinating (that precede the condition by weeks or months); enlargement of the abdomen due to weakness of the muscles, production of excessive abdominal fat, and enlargement of the liver; loss of body hair (on both sides equally), which comes out very easily. This latter is associated with developing thinness of the skin and a color change to dark brown or black (most often on the undersides). Though these symptoms are common, there are many other changes that can occur—changes in reproductive cycles, symptoms of diabetes, excessive weight gain (obesity), and so on. It is a very complicated condition and mimics many other disorders, so it takes considerable skill to determine that this is the problem.

A further complication is that Cushing's Disease may occur along with other chronic problems, almost as if it's a further deterioration of health in a pattern of decline. For example, your dog may have had years of skin allergies, arthritis due to hip dysplasia or cruciate ligament breakdown (knee joint deterioration), and now Cushing's Disease pops up. It seems to me that it is a fundamental breakdown in the body's ability to regulate inflammation and repair of tissues (in which the adrenal glands are intimately involved).

Recognizing this problem and treatment of it requires the skill of a veterinarian. There are blood tests of various types that can be done—both for testing hormone levels and for testing the functions of the adrenal glands. I have treated many of these cases over the years and, though surgery or drugs are the conventional approach, I still prefer to use homeopathy and nutrition as my first tools in resolving it. Because there can be multiple problems, how to treat this is very individual. I suggest you work with a homeopathically trained veterinarian who can set up a treatment schedule to address all the problems your animal has. As you might anticipate, excellent nutrition and reduction of stress are necessary adjuncts.

CYSTITIS

See "Bladder Problems."

DEMODECTIC MANGE

See "Skin Parasites."

DENTAL PROBLEMS

The mouth and its associated structures are especially important to animals, not only for eating but also for grooming and manipulating things. This part of the body contains many nerves and is served by a plentiful blood supply, making dental problems more serious than you might expect. Mouth pain can keep an animal from eating enough or grooming properly.

Four problems are most common: accidents that damage the teeth or gums, congenital or developmental disorders, periodontitis (calculus on the teeth and associated gum disease), and tooth decay. Let's look at each in turn.

Accidents

If a pet is hit by a car, it's not unusual that teeth are broken off or knocked out. In most cases, after the initial inflammation has subsided, the animal feels no real discomfort. Generally, a broken tooth can be left in place (if still firmly attached), at least until a convenient occasion for removal occurs, such as another need for surgical anesthesia. Sometimes, however, the root will become abscessed and require removal.

As for injured gums, an excellent immediate treatment to stop bleeding and promote rapid healing is:

Herbal—Calendula tincture (*Calendula officinalis*): Apply it directly to the bleeding gum with a saturated cotton swab, or dilute the tincture with 10 parts water and use it as a flushing mouthwash, applied with a syringe or turkey baster.

An excellent treatment for mouth pain from injuries is:

Homeopathic—*Arnica* (Leopard's Bane) 30C, using Schedule 2, page 442. The next day, give *Hypericum* (St. John's wort) 30C, also using Schedule 2.

Congenital or Developmental Disorders

Problems of this sort are so common in some breeds of dogs that they seem to be standard equipment. Cats, however, have very few congenital mouth problems, probably because they've been less modified by intentional breeding.

Some dogs, especially toy breeds, have teeth that are simply too crowded, often overlapping in position. Sometimes the jaw is too long or too short. Worst of all is the fate of breeds like the bulldog and Boston bull terrier, who have very short jaws with teeth that are crammed together, turned sideways, and completely out of position. They really have a mouthful of problems.

What can you do about it? I recommend extracting some of the permanent teeth as they develop, preferably while the dog is still young. Left untreated, the crowding and poor fit may lead to gum disease and loose teeth.

Some dogs have relatively straight, uncrowded teeth, but one jaw is longer or shorter than the other. As a result the teeth don't meet properly, causing discomfort and premature breakdown of both teeth and gums. If the difference between the jaws is ¼ inch or less, removal of some of the deciduous (baby) teeth before the arrival of the permanent set may restore proper alignment. But if the difference is greater, little can be done preventively. The treatment with the greatest chance of restoring normal mouth anatomy is to give:

Homeopathic—*Calcarea carbonica* 30C, Schedule 5.

Other structural problems include supernumerary (extra) teeth, which should be removed to prevent accumulation of food and debris, and retained baby teeth, which force the permanent teeth to grow beside or in front of them (trapping debris and perhaps distorting the jaw formation). They, too, should be removed by a veterinarian.

Periodontal Disease

This is the most common tooth and gum problem. It results from a change in the normal saliva, which creates a buildup of calcium salts, food, hair, and bacteria on the animal's teeth. These deposits put pressure on the gums, causing inflammation, swelling, pulling away, and receding gums. A pocket opens up between the gums and teeth, which collects still more debris and further worsens the problem. Eventually, the process can loosen the teeth and cause them to fall out. A serious complication is the development of an abscess, which destroys the root of the tooth.

Of course, periodontal disease doesn't destroy teeth overnight. It may take months or years. If your pet has periodontal disease, it will show these symptoms: bleeding gums, foul breath, excessive salivation, painful chewing (dropping food while eating or turning its head to the side to chew only on one side), and possible loss of appetite or weight. You can see heavy brown deposits (calculus) on the teeth, particularly on the back ones. And the teeth may be loose.

The usual causes for the buildup of calculus are misaligned teeth, overfeeding, poor-quality food, lack of hard, chewable things to exercise the teeth and gums, and frequent nibbling. Once the deposits have formed, they are rock-hard and can only be removed adequately by your veterinarian (under anesthesia) using careful hand-scraping or an ultrasonic cleaner. Often the infected and loose teeth must also be extracted and hemorrhage controlled.

After any dental work at the hospital, you can do a lot with follow-up care to both promote rapid healing and prevent recurrence. The gums will be very sore and inflamed. Certain herbs will be very helpful. Pick one of the following that seems best suited (or, if indicated, you may use both the goldenseal and the myrrh, ½ teaspoon of each).

Herbal—Purple coneflower (*Echinacea angustifolia*): This is useful where teeth were found to be infected and the animal is thin and run down. Boil 1 teaspoon of fresh-smelling rootstock in 1 cup of water for 10 minutes. Cover, remove from heat, and let steep for an hour. Strain and apply this decoction directly to the gums with a swab or use it as a mouthwash. It promotes saliva flow, so don't worry if your pet begins to drool.

Herbal—Goldenseal (*Hydrastis canadensis*): This herb is antiseptic and helpful for new gum tissue growth. Steep 1 teaspoon of powdered rootstock in a pint of boiling-hot water until cool. Pour off the clear liquid and use it to flush out the mouth and gums.

Herbal—Myrrh (*Commiphora myrrha*):

Myrrh is indicated for loose teeth. Steep 1 teaspoon of the resin in a pint of boiling water for a few minutes. Strain it and paint the infusion on the gums, or flush them using a syringe or turkey baster.

Herbal—Plantain (*Plantago major*): This herb helps when the condition is not serious enough to require major cleaning but when you see minor deposits on the teeth and the gums are inflamed. Bring 1 cup of water to a boil. Turn off heat and add 1 tablespoon of the leaves. Steep for 5 minutes. Strain and use as a mouthwash.

General directions for herbs: Whichever herb you pick, use it twice a day for 10 to 14 days. Alternatively, use the herb in the morning and apply vitamin E (fresh out of the capsule) to the gums with your fingers at night. (This treatment is very soothing.)

Homeopathic treatment as an alternative to herbal:

Cats—A dose of *Calcarea carbonica* 30C given once a month for 3 months will greatly improve the condition of the mouth for many cats. Vaccinations generally make this condition worse in cats, so minimize these.

Dogs—The remedy *Silicea* 30C given once a month for 3 months will help many dogs to have a healthier mouth.

The Importance of Nutrition

Diet is also extremely important in the period *after* teeth cleaning. Without proper nutrition the gums can't repair themselves or maintain necessary resilience. Emphasize those vegetables rich in niacin, folate, and minerals—leafy greens, broccoli, asparagus, lima beans, potatoes, and lettuce. Also, serve fresh liver twice weekly for its folate, vitamin A, protein, and other richly supplied nutrients. Other good folate sources are eggs or plain peanuts (which can be given as unsalted peanut butter).

Also add ⅛ to ½ teaspoon (depending on size) of bone meal powder (for extra calcium and phosphorus), 100 to 1,000 milligrams of vitamin C twice daily, and a B-complex tablet or capsule with the major vitamins at the 5- to 10-milligram level (amounts depend on the animal's size). Use these extra supplements for the next three weeks.

Also give your pet its own natural "toothbrush"—either bones or a hard raw vegetable like a carrot. For dogs, I advise that one day a week you feed nothing but one large raw bone. There is no better natural cleaner for teeth. But avoid cooked bones (which splinter) and small or easily splintered bones from chickens and turkeys (with dogs). These can be dangerous. These small bones, however, are OK for cats.

Some dogs that have trouble digesting bone fragments get irritation and either diarrhea or constipation; this is usually a result of weak stomach acid from improper feeding. Good diet and a B-complex supplement will likely clear up the problem. For the first few weeks, limit bone chewing to 30 minutes a day and watch to make sure that large pieces are not swallowed.

Cats can be given small raw bones as well, but do not really pick up on this practice unless they are started quite young. Somewhat more accepted is to feed part of a raw game hen once a week instead of the regular meals. Unfortunately, having lost their natural instincts, many mature cats will not adapt to this. It is worth trying, however, because it will keep their mouths quite clean and healthy.

Tooth Decay

This is primarily a problem in cats that develop decay along the sides of the teeth (near the gums) or in the roots. This is an increasingly common problem and, in my opinion, is a direct outcome of generations of eating commercial foods. There is little that can be done to reverse this once it happens. Often, the affected teeth need to be removed. Prevention is essential and the advice given in this book about nutrition is most important.

Post-Dental Treatment

A very excellent treatment program to use after dentistry (don't give these before as it will increase the amount of anesthesia needed) is to give *Arnica* 30C on picking up the cat or dog from the veterinarian's office (or at home). This will reduce pain and swelling in the gums and pain where teeth have been removed. The next day give *Hypericum* 30C once, to remove any residual pain, especially from extraction of teeth.

One more thing: If you're about to select a new pet, look for one with properly formed teeth and jaws (and parents with the same). See chapter 9 for information on hereditary defects.

DERMATITIS

See "Skin Problems."

DIABETES

Seen in both dogs and cats, the type of diabetes animals get is similar in most ways to the diabetes seen in humans. It has now been determined that human diabetes is an immune disorder in which the body attacks the pancreatic cells that make insulin. It is likely this same process that destroys the insulin-producing ability of our pets. Most of these immune problems we see in animals are made worse by vaccination or can come on after being vaccinated, so be aware of this link and be cautious about vaccinating animals in this condition (see Vaccinations in this section).

This failure of the pancreas to secrete insulin does not allow proper use of blood sugar. Instead of reaching the body tissues, the increasing levels of blood sugar spill over into the urine and are lost from the body. Thus, despite adequate caloric intake, the tissues are in a condition of semi-starvation all the time.

Thus, the animal eats a lot, but still gets thinner and thinner. The continuous presence of sugar in the urine also causes fluid loss. That's because the sugar must be dissolved in water to be eliminated, so it carries the water out with it. As a result, the animal is abnormally thirsty and passes large volumes of urine.

There is apparently more to this condition than just lack of insulin, however, because even if insulin needs are carefully met with injections of this hormone, there are still progressive changes and weaknesses that may persist. These sometimes include recurrent pancreatic inflammation, formation of eye cataracts, and an increased susceptibility to infection (particularly of the urinary tract).

TREATMENT

The usual treatment consists of strictly regulating sugar intake and using daily injections of insulin (derived from the glands of other animals). Feeding is usually restricted to canned food fed once a day, about 12 hours after the insulin is given (when its activity is highest).

The diabetic dogs I have treated have generally done well on the basic fresh and raw natural food diet given as two or three meals during the day, rather than one large one. Their insulin needs seem to stabilize, rather than going through erratic ups and downs from day to day. You may need to experiment with your animal to find the best frequency of feeding, also taking into account the advice of your veterinarian.

Above all, avoid the soft, moist dog foods that come in cellophane bags and don't need refrigeration. These products are very high in carbohydrates like sugar that are used as preservatives, as well as artificial colors and other preservatives.

A supplement that is quite helpful is glu-cose tolerance factor, a natural chromium-containing substance found in yeast. It can assist the body in using blood glucose more effectively. I always recommend supplementing the natural food diet with this element. Give one teaspoon to one tablespoon of brewer's yeast with each meal.

Vitamin E is also important because it reduces the need for insulin. Give 25 IU to 200 IU of this vitamin each day.

In addition to the nutritional advice given here, see that your animal gets lots of exercise, which has the effect of decreasing insulin needs. Erratic exercise could destabilize the insulin needs, though, so a regular, sustained program of exercise is best. It is also important for your pet to maintain a normal weight. Obese animals have a much harder time with this disease.

Severe Diabetes

The more severe cases need stringent dietary regulation. If your animal is not responding to the above program or is already quite ill, and stabilizing its condition is difficult, then the following will be helpful.

Dietary guidelines: The main goal of a special diet to control diabetes is to reduce the stress placed on the pancreas. That means strict avoidance of foods that contain sugar as well as a low fat intake (because the pancreas produces a number of enzymes particularly involved in the breakdown of fat). Therefore, use the natural diets given in this book, but avoid fatty meats and give only half of the fat or oil called for in the recipe.

Certain foods are particularly beneficial for diabetes, so emphasize them in your selections—especially millet, rice, oats, cornmeal, and rye bread. Excellent vegetables are green beans (the pods of which contain certain hormonal substances closely related to insulin), winter squash, dandelion greens, alfalfa sprouts, corn, parsley, onion, Jerusalem artichoke, and garlic (which reduces blood sugar in diabetes). Garlic also stimulates the abdominal viscera and increases digestive organ function. Use it regularly in some form (fresh or in capsules).

Milk and milk products are helpful because they are alkalizing (as are vegetables and most fruits), which helps to counter overacidity. They are best fed raw, as are meat, eggs, fruits, and some vegetables, because uncooked foods are much more stimulating to the pancreas. Fruits in season are fine, if acceptable to your animal; the natural fruit sugar (fructose) can be used by the diabetic animal. Feed them separately from other foods.

Cats, being natural carnivores, will sometimes revert back to normal if they are fed large amounts of fresh meat and avoid significant amounts of grain or vegetables (small amounts OK). If you have a cat with this condition, just feeding mostly meat with a pinch of bone meal added to each meal for a few weeks may make a huge difference. After that you can use the natural recipes given in this book, but increase the amount of meat in the recipes above what is recommended to maintain the improvement.

Specific treatments for diabetes include:

Homeopathic—*Belladonna* 30c given once when first diagnosed. Then put on the diet program described above. Wait a week and then give:

Homeopathic—*Thuya* (or *Thuja*) (arborvitae) 30C, using Homeopathic Schedule 4. If after a month diabetes persists, then look at the treatments suggested next. If the problem is resolved, then no further homeopathic treatment is needed.

Homeopathic—*Natrum muriaticum* (salt, sodium chloride) 6C. Those it is suitable for usually have appetite problems (usually excessive) and a marked weight loss. Sugar will be detectable in the urine, and there will be a tendency to anxiety and fearfulness. These animals do not tolerate heat well. Use Schedule 6(b), page 442.

Homeopathic—*Phosphorus* 6C. These animals have always been thin, have outgoing personalities, love attention, have ravenous appetites though vomit easily, and a thirst for cold water. Often there is a history of pancreatitis (inflammation of the pancreas). Use Schedule 6(b), page 442.

DIARRHEA AND DYSENTERY

Diarrhea, though common, is not a very specific condition. That is, many things can cause diarrhea, and yet the clinical appearance (frequent, soft, or fluid bowel movements) is about the same. The gastrointestinal tract has one major defense against irritants of many sorts, which is moving its contents along more quickly than usual. The cause of the irritation may include worms, bacteria, viruses, spoiled or toxic food, food sensitivities (see "Allergies"), bone fragments, or indigestible material like hair, cloth, or plastic.

The body's primary response to these irritants is to increase bowel contraction (called peristalsis) in order to flush them out of the system. Because the intestinal contents move along so quickly, the colon does not absorb the amount of water it usually does. Thus, the bowel movement is abnormally fluid.

Depending on what part of the tract is irritated, you may see certain additional symptoms. If there is inflammation and bleeding in the upper part of the small intestine, near the stomach, then the bowel movement will be very dark or black from digested blood. You also may notice a buildup of excess gas that causes belching, a bloated stomach, or flatulence. The animal in this pattern usually shows no particular straining when passing a stool.

A different picture appears when the inflammation is lower down in the colon. Generally, there is no problem with gas buildup. The diarrhea tends to "shoot" out of the rectum with force and obvious straining. If there has been bleeding in the colon, the blood will appear as a fresh red color mixed with the stool. The bowel movements tend to be more frequent than when the disturbance centers in the small intestine. Often you may notice excessive mucus that looks like clear jelly.

Because diarrhea can be associated with so many causes and other disorders, we must be alert to the possibility of other conditions causing this symptom. Most of the time, however, diarrhea is caused by eating the wrong kind of food or spoiled food, overeating in general, parasites (in young animals especially), or viral infections.

The following guidelines are useful for treating simple or mild conditions that fall in the above categories. If they don't resolve it, or if conditions are severe or otherwise seem to warrant it, seek professional help—sooner rather than later.

TREATMENT

Most importantly, do not feed any solid food for the first 24 to 48 hours. A liquid fast will give the intestinal tract a chance to rest and do its job of flushing things out. Make sure that plenty of pure water is available at all times and encourage drinking. A danger of excessive diarrhea is dehydration from the loss of water, sodium, and potassium. So provide these in the form of a broth made from vegetables, rice, and some meat or a bone. You may also add a small amount of naturally brewed soy sauce to enhance flavor and provide easily assimilated amino acids and sodium. Offer only the liquid part of the soup, serving it at room temperature several times a day during the fast period.

If the condition is mild or is a sudden attack following consumption of spoiled food, this treatment alone may suffice. In more severe cases, however, it will be wise to use one of the following as well. The best treatment is. . . .

Slippery elm powder: Available in most health food stores, this material from the inner bark of the slippery elm tree is an excellent treatment for diarrhea from any cause, and I use it frequently with the animals I treat. To make it, thoroughly mix 1 slightly rounded teaspoon of slippery elm powder with 1 cup of cold water. Bring to a boil while stirring constantly. Then turn the heat down to simmer and continue to stir for another 2 to 3 minutes while the mixture thickens slightly. Remove from the heat, add 1 tablespoon of honey (for dogs only—cats don't like sweets, so leave it out), and stir well. Cool to room temperature and give ½ to 1 teaspoon to cats and small dogs, 2 teaspoons to 2 tablespoons for medium dogs, and 3 to 4 tablespoons for large dogs (see page 118 for dog sizes). Give this dose 4 times a day, or about every 4 hours. Cover the mixture and store at room temperature. It will keep for a couple of days. It is easiest to buy the herb in bulk as a loose powder. It's available in capsules, but it is both less efficient and more expensive that way. You can order it in bulk through natural food stores.

Activated charcoal: Sold in drugstores as a powder or in tablets, this type of charcoal prepared from plant matter has the ability to absorb toxins, drugs, poisons, and other irritating material. It's especially useful for treating diarrhea that was caused by eating spoiled food or toxic substances. Mix it with water and give it by mouth every 3 or 4 hours for a 24-hour period (except during sleep). Because overuse of charcoal could interfere with digestive enzymes, a short course is best. Depending on the animal's size, use ½ to 1 teaspoon of powder or 1 to 3 tablets.

Roasted carob powder: Available in health food stores, this plant substance is commonly used as a chocolate substitute. However, it is also a popular and soothing aid to diarrhea. Give ½ to 2 teaspoons 3 times a day for 3 days. Mix it with water and perhaps a little honey, giving it by mouth.

Here are some homeopathic treatments especially useful for diarrhea. For all of them use Homeopathic Schedule 2, page 442.

Homeopathic—*Podophyllum* (May apple) 6C: This remedy is often useful for the diarrhea with a forceful, gushing type of stool, especially if it smells unusually bad.

Homeopathic—*Mercurius vivus* (mercury) 6C: The severe diarrhea attack (frequent, bloody stools with much straining after passing the stool) is suited to this medicine. This type of diarrhea can come on after eating toxic substances or from a viral infection.

Homeopathic—*Arsenicum album* (arsenic trioxide) 6C: Use this remedy for diarrhea resulting from eating spoiled meat. Usually there are frequent bowel movements, rather small in quantity. Also there is weakness, thirst, and chilliness.

Homeopathic—*Pulsatilla* (windflower) 6C: This is a good remedy for dogs or cats that have overeaten or had food that is too rich or fatty. They will get diarrhea from an upset stomach, generally becoming subdued and timid. Typically, they do not have any thirst with the diarrhea (which is unusual).

Homeopathic—*Calcarea carbonica* 30C: This is appropriate for longer-lasting diarrhea in cats, while *Silicea* 30C is most helpful for chronic diarrhea in dogs. In both situations, give one dose only.

General advice: During the treatment it is important to be watchful for the possibility that some causative factor remains, such as an irritating chemical (for example, a new flea collar), the use of milk (which bothers some animals), polluted water, or access to spoiled food in somebody's garbage can or a compost pile. An animal's lack of response to treatment can sometimes be traced to the persistence of such a cause. Also, consider worms and infectious diseases and treat them at home or with your veterinarian's help, as is appropriate.

Once recovery seems to be underway, feed small amounts of plain yogurt or liquid acidophilus drink or capsules (available in natural food stores) to help replenish the intestinal tract with friendly bacteria.

When you are bringing your pet out of the fast after a couple of days, start with the broth, mixed with the solid vegetables used to make it. After 24 hours you can introduce the yogurt and begin to reestablish a regular diet, using white rice (just for a few days, then brown rice) as the grain, because it is generally good for slowing down diarrhea.

DISTEMPER, CHOREA, AND FELINE PANLEUKOPENIA

We will consider all three of these diseases together, since they are related. Chorea (uncontrollable twitching or jerking) is a possible result of distemper. Panleukopenia is commonly known as cat distemper. Let's discuss each in turn.

Canine Distemper

Distemper is so common that few dogs escape exposure to the virus, which is spread through the air (from exhaling or sneezing) or by contact with contaminated bowls, toys, bones, and such. Most, however, do escape development of the disease.

Distemper progresses in stages. After a six- to nine-day incubation (usually not noticeable), the dog contracts a brief initial fever and malaise. Afterward, the dog is apparently normal for a few days or a week, and then it will suddenly show the typical distemper symptoms: fever, loss of appetite and energy, and perhaps a clear discharge from the nose. Within a short time the condition advances and the dog develops one or more of the additional symptoms: severe conjunctivitis (eye inflammation) with a thick discharge that sticks the lids together, heavy mucus or yellow discharge from the nose, very bad-smelling diarrhea, and skin eruption on the belly or between the hind legs.

Though early in my career I treated many distemper cases with the orthodox approach of antibiotics, fluids, and other drugs, I did not seen it do much good. Indeed, sometimes it seems to increase the likelihood of encephalitis, a severe inflammation of the brain (or smaller areas in the spinal cord) that often arises after apparent improvement or recovery. At this point dogs are usually put to sleep because medical treatment is almost always ineffective. I am convinced that the use of drugs increases the likelihood of encephalitis, while natural methods make it less probable. I have witnessed many successful recoveries in distemper cases treated with homeopathy and nutritional therapy. The suggestions that follow are gleaned from this experience.

TREATMENT

In order to prevent complications like encephalitis, it is crucial to withhold solid food while the dog is in the acute phase of distemper with a fever. (The normal rectal temperature is 100.5 to 101.5°F. (38 to 38.6°C). It might be a little higher at a veterinarian's office because of excitement.) Fast the dog on vegetable broth and pure water as described in chapter 15, until at least a day after the temperature becomes normal. If the fever returns, fast again. Because fevers tend to rise in the evening, record temperatures both morning and night to get a better overview.

In case you are wondering how long dogs can go without solid food before starving, the normal healthy animal can get along all right for several weeks. A dog that is sick with

distemper can profitably fast for seven days, provided it is an adult of normal weight and general condition. However, few will need to fast this long. Make sure you have fresh, pure water available at all times.

Vitamin C is an important aid. Many distemper cases can recover without ill effects by using vitamin C along with fasting. (However, I always use homeopathic treatment as well in my practice.) Dose as follows: 250 milligrams every two hours for puppies and small dogs, 500 milligrams every two hours for medium dogs, 1,000 milligrams every three hours for large or giant dogs. Don't continue the dosing through the night, because rest is also important. Once the acute phase and fever have passed, double the interval between doses. Continue until recovery is complete.

Special eye care may be necessary, because the lids can get severely inflamed. Bathe the eyes in a saline solution (see chapter 15). Then put a drop of sweet almond oil (also simply called almond oil), cod-liver oil, or olive oil in each eye to help heal and provide protection. Cod liver oil is especially useful when there are ulcers.

During the early stages of distemper, use of one of the following remedies should help considerably.

Homeopathic—_Distemperinum_ 30C: Specially prepared from the distemper-diseased animal, this is the most effective remedy for the early stages. I've seen it produce recoveries in just a day or two. The dog needing this will have been ill just a short time with symptoms like a cold and a runny nose with fever. Give 1 pellet morning and evening until improvement is evident and the fever has returned to normal. Then give only if symptoms flare up again.

Note: Some pharmacies may restrict this remedy to veterinarians. Check with more than one.

Homeopathic—*Natrum muriaticum* 30C is for the early stage, with a lot of sneezing. Use Schedule 2, page 442.

Homeopathic—*Pulsatilla* (windflower) 30C: This remedy is suitable for the stage of conjunctivitis with thick, yellow, or greenish eye discharge. Use Schedule 2, page 442.

Homeopathic—*Arsenicum album* 30C: This remedy is indicated for the dog that is very ill, with rapid weight loss, loss of appetite, weakness, restlessness, frequent thirst, and a slight clear discharge from the eyes that causes irritation of the eyelids and surrounding areas. Use Schedule 2, page 442.

If none of these works, consult with a homeopathic veterinarian if you are able to—there are many other remedies worth trying.

During the later stages of distemper, with bronchitis and coughing, select one of the following treatments (in case you did not treat earlier or it has gotten worse despite treatment).

Homeopathic—*Hydrastis canadensis* (goldenseal) 6C: Indicated for advanced distemper, with a thick, yellow discharge of mucus from the nose or down the back of the throat. Often there will be loss of appetite and emaciation. Use Schedule 6(c), page 442.

Homeopathic—*Psorinum* 30C: This is most useful for the dog that has survived distemper but cannot completely recover. Often there is a poor appetite, skin eruptions or irritated skin, and a bad body smell. Use Schedule 4, page 442.

Recovery

With proper treatment, distemper is not too severe, and you can generally expect recovery in a few days to a week. The initial state of health of the animal and the degree of immunity acquired from the mother (in the case of puppies) seem to be important factors in the severity of individual cases.

If recovery is not easy or complete or leaves the animal in a weakened condition, the following measures should help. Feed a convalescence diet (see "Feeding Dogs with Extra Needs" on page 92) emphasizing oats (which strengthen the nervous system) and B vitamins (give a natural B-complex tablet in the 10 to 50 milligram range for a few weeks).

For the dog weakened with distemper, give a tincture of the common oat (*Avena sativa*), a beneficial nerve tonic available from herb stores, natural food stores, or homeopathic pharmacies. Twice daily, give 2 to 4 drops for small dogs or puppies, 4 to 8 drops for medium dogs or 8 to 12 drops for large ones.

If the animal is left with a weakened digestive system, residual diarrhea, or chest complications, give fresh grated garlic (*Allium sativum*) three times daily. Use ½ small clove for small dogs or puppies, ½ large clove for medium dogs, and 1 whole clove for large ones. Add the grated garlic to the food or mix it with honey and flour to make pills.

Chorea

Usually an after-effect of the distemper virus infection, chorea is a condition in which some muscle in the body (usually a leg, hip, or shoulder) twitches every few seconds, sometimes even during sleep. It results from damage to part of the spinal cord or brain. Most pets with chorea are put to sleep because it is not considered curable; however, once in a rare while a spontaneous recovery occurs. I think it is worth giving alternative therapy a try, as it will improve the odds. See relevant information about diet and herbs under "Behavior Problems." In addition, try this specific treatment plan. All of these are to be given according to Homeopathic Schedule 4, page 442.

Homeopathic—*Nux vomica* 30C: After this treatment, wait and observe for 2 weeks. If there is no change for the better, then use the next treatment.

Homeopathic—*Belladonna* 30C: Again dose, then watch and wait for a 2-week period. If this noticeably helps but does not completely eliminate it, then use. . .

Homeopathic—*Calcarea carbonica* 30C.

Another remedy to consider is *Silicea* 30C, especially if these other medicines have had no effect. Give one dose and allow it to act for several weeks.

If this has still not solved the problem, there are other medicines that can be used, but you will need guidance from a homeopathic veterinarian.

Feline Panleukopenia (Feline Distemper; Infectious Enteritis)

This disease of cats comes on suddenly and severely, without apparent warning, commonly killing young kittens within 24 to 48 hours. The associated virus is thought to be spread through urine, feces, saliva, or the vomit of an infected cat. Epidemics are prevalent.

After an incubation period of two to nine days (usually six), the first signs are a high fever (up to 105 degrees F.; 40.6 degrees C.), severe depression, and severe dehydration. Vomiting often follows soon afterward. Initially, it is a clear fluid; later, it's tinged yellow with bile. Typically, the cat will lie with its head hanging over the edge of its water dish, not moving except to lap water or vomit.

Apparently, it's not the panleukopenia virus itself that produces these severe symptoms, but a secondary infection that results from the destruction of various tissues, including the white cells (which protect the body against infections). In many cases they are almost eliminated, which opens the door to the growth of other bacteria or viruses. In many ways this disease is very similar to the parvovirus infection of dogs.

TREATMENT

The most crucial factor in successful treatment is to catch the disorder in its earliest stages. Since young animals can die very quickly, there often isn't enough time to get a home treatment under way. Clinical methods like whole-blood transfusion, fluid therapy, and antibiotics can be successful if started early, so get professional care if possible.

If you aren't able to get such care right away and you are prepared with supplies, here is a regimen I suggest: As long as there is fever or vomiting, fast the animal on liquids (chapter 15). Administer high doses of vitamin C, about 100 milligrams per hour to very small kittens and 250 milligrams per hour to young and adult cats. It's easier to give it as sodium ascorbate powder. Use a pinch to make a 100-milligram solution or ¹⁄₁₆ teaspoon for a 250-milligram solution. Mix the sodium ascorbate with water and give orally.

If vomiting causes both the loss of essential fluids and the vitamin C you have administered (characterized by a rough hair coat, dry-looking eyes, and skin that is stiff when pulled up), focus on using the following homeopathic treatment alone until symptoms are improved. Then go back to giving vitamin C along with the homeopathic treatment. Use Schedule 1, page 441, for both these remedies.

Homeopathic—*Veratrum album* (white hellebore) 6C: Use this if the cat is weak, depressed, and cold, with vomiting (aggravated by drinking water) and diarrhea. If there is improvement, gradually decrease how often you give it over the next couple of days.

Eventually, give 1 tablet at a time when there is any recurring nausea or lethargy.

Homeopathic—*Phosphorus* 6C: This is the best choice for a cat that is limp, with extreme lethargy and apathy. If you pick the cat up, it will hang over your hand like a damp rag. If alert enough, it will also be thirsty for cold water, yet vomit about 10 to 20 minutes after drinking. The cat that should be treated with phosphorus has less coldness but more listlessness than the cat treated with *Veratrum album.*

If you find that despite either treatment, the vomiting is very severe and life-threatening, then follow the advice under "Vomiting."

Herbal—If you have them in stock, consider this alternative herbal treatment: Mix 1 teaspoon of the tincture or decoction of purple cone flower (*Echinacea angustifolia*) with 1 teaspoon of the tincture or decoction of boneset (*Eupatorium perfoliatum*) in ½ cup pure water. Give 1 drop of the mixture every hour until you see improvement, then reduce to every 2 hours until recovery.

If the cat is already very ill and close to death, you'll need a different approach. Such a cat will lie in a comatose state, hardly moving. Its ears and feet will feel very cold to the touch. Its nose may have a bluish look. As an emergency measure, administer camphor. Use an ointment containing camphor, such as Tiger Balm. Hold a small dab in front of the cat's nose so that a few breaths will carry in the odor. Repeat every 15 minutes until there is a response.

Once you see improvement you can go to one of the other treatments outlined. Be sure to discontinue the camphor and remove it from the vicinity when homeopathic or herbal remedies are used, or it will counter their effects.

Recovery

Once the cat is obviously getting well and the fever is gone (a temperature less than 101.5°F. or 38.6°C.), give solid food once again. Follow the diet and supplement instructions for canine distemper. Offer raw beef liver for a few days, which is a good "tonic" for cats. Take care to minimize stress and avoid chilling for several days after the initial recovery, as a relapse is possible. Continue the vitamin C at reduced levels (250 to 500 milligrams twice daily) for two weeks to prevent complications or residual effects.

DYSENTERY

See "Diarrhea and Dysentery."

EAR MITES

See "Ear Problems."

EAR PROBLEMS

Inflammation, irritation, pain, and swelling of the ears are common problems for both dogs and cats, often reflecting allergy or skin problems that also manifest in other parts of the body. Such allergies express themselves periodically as a sudden redness or flushing of the skin, perhaps after a meal during specific times of the year, such as pollen season. A dog with ear problems is likely an allergy victim if it also chews its front feet excessively and scoots its rear end along the floor or ground.

Cats can develop a similar problem, with an accumulation of dark wax or oily material in the ears, causing itching and head shaking. Ear mites are another possible cause of cat ear trouble, but more often it's allergies.

"Allergy Ears"

It's important to understand that the larger issue of allergies usually underlies an ear problem. Otherwise, you might just focus on the ears and ignore the rest of the situation or even make the situation worse if the ear treatment is suppressive. For more information on the underlying problem, see "Allergies." Here we will look at helpful ways to care for the ears, whether or not they are part of that larger problem.

Keeping the ears clean of discharges and secretions is very helpful in reducing irritation. Choose one of these three alternatives.

Herbal—Calendula: If the discharge is watery, smelly, and thin, flush and massage the ear canal once or twice a day with a solution of 1 cup of pure water (distilled, spring, or filtered), 1 teaspoon of a tincture or glycerin extract of marigold flower buds (*Calendula officinalis*), and ¼ teaspoon sea salt (see chapter 15 for more information on treatment of the ears).

Herbal—Aloe vera: For ears that are painful, sensitive, and raw looking inside but have little discharge, treat in the same way as above, but use fresh juice or a liquid gel preparation made from the leaves of the aloe vera plant.

Herbal—Sweet almond oil (almond oil): To soften and dissolve dark, waxy, oily ear discharge, flush and massage the ear canal with sweet almond oil (*Prunus amydalus*), which is also soothing and healing to the skin. If the ear is painful as well, alternate with the aloe treatment on a different day (oil and water don't blend well).

Herbal—Green tea: For ears that are producing mostly dark, smelly material. First, clean them with the almond oil (above) then use this treatment starting the next day. Put 2 bags (or 2 teaspoons loose tea) in a mug, add boiling water, and steep for 15 minutes. Strain and use warm to flush the ears. You can do this twice a day.

Along with one of these cleaning methods, it's helpful to use:

Homeopathic—*Pulsatilla* (windflower) 6C: The ear will be very swollen, red, and painful. The dog or cat will be submissive and "pitiful" with the ear problem and want to be held or comforted. Use Schedule 1 on page 441. Continue only if it is helping.

Homeopathic—*Silicea* (silicon dioxide, quartz) 30C: If Pulsatilla noticeably helped but did not last or completely clear up the problem, then give this remedy to finish the treatment. Give one dose.

Homeopathic—*Belladonna* (deadly nightshade) 6C: Indicated if the ear has flared up suddenly, with much heat and redness in that area. Often there will be a slight fever. The pupils will be dilated even in a lighted room. The dog or cat will be agitated and excitable. Use Schedule 1, page 441.

Homeopathic—*Calcarea carbonica* (calcium carbonate) 30C: If treatment with Belladonna has been strikingly effective, then wait 2–3 days after finishing that treatment and give one dose of this remedy to prevent the problem from returning in the future.

Homeopathic—*Hepar sulphuris calcareum* (calcium sulphide) 30C: These ears are extremely painful. The animal will not allow them to be touched and will bite if you persist. Use Homeopathic Schedule 2.

Homeopathic—*Graphites* (black lead) 30C: If other treatments have failed and the problem persists as itchy, sensitive ears, then try this remedy. Use Homeopathic Schedule 4.

There are several other factors that can complicate and aggravate allergy-related ear problems or that may be problems in their own right. For many breeds of dogs, the major factor has to do with the shape of their ears. Other minor and associated causes are water in the ear canal, which predisposes the ear to infections, trapped foxtails or other plant awns, and ear mites (a parasite, more often found in cats). Let's examine each of these.

Anatomical Problems

In nature, canine ears evolved to stand upright from the head—the best design both for hearing and for ear health. An upright ear like that of a wolf or coyote works well to funnel sounds directly into the ear canal. It also allows a proper exchange of air and moisture between the ear canal and the outside. If water should get in the ear, head-shaking and free flow of air will soon reduce the humidity to the proper level. Throughout thousands of years of raising domestic dogs, however, people selected many with heavier, hairier ears that tended to fold over or hang down a bit (basically a puppy trait). Maybe they seemed cute, or perhaps they just happened to accompany some other feature the people desired.

In any case, floppy ears have caused a great deal of unnecessary suffering for dogs and expense for people. A hanging ear creates an effective trap. It closes off the ear canal from the free exchange of air and moisture and makes it easier for stickers and debris to get stuck inside. Some breeds, like poodles, even have hair growing inside the ear canal, making the problem worse. With this in mind, now let's look at three complicating factors in ear problems. While they may afflict any dog, all three are inevitably worse in dogs with floppy ears.

Water in the Ear Canal

Many dogs enjoy a good swim. Invariably, they get water (sometimes not so clean) down their ears. In excess, such moisture can lead to a condition much like swimmer's ear in people—a low-grade irritation that can occasionally develop into more serious infections.

If your dog has this tendency, flush out the ears after a swim with a slightly acidic solution of warm water and lemon juice (figure about half a small, fresh-squeezed lemon to a cup of water; alternatively, use about a tablespoon of white (or apple) vinegar to a cup of water). This will diminish the chance of bacterial or fungal infection and is also healing to the ear tissue. If either preparation seems to "burn," dilute the mixture further with warm water. With the help of a dropper or small cup, fill and then massage the ear canal from the outside (see ear care instructions, Chapter 15). Afterward, allow the animal to shake its head well (it's hard to keep them from it!). Blot off all the excess moisture from the inside ear with a tissue and gently swab out just inside the ear opening with a cotton swab. Remember, you are just absorbing moisture; do not rub against the skin.

As an additional precaution, you can clothespin or tie the ears up behind the head to allow them to dry out further. Do not pin or tie the ear itself, only the hair at the end. Also, if hair grows inside your dog's ears, ask your vet or groomer to show you how to pull it out every so often.

Trapped Foxtails

Floppy ears are much likelier to trap foxtails and other plant stickers. The flap is like a hinged trapdoor that directs the stickers right into the ear canal. Though you can do little to prevent stickers (other than cutting down your weeds and controlling where your animal runs), here is how to deal with them if they get trapped in your dog's ears.

After the dog has an excursion in a field, immediately check the ears (and between the toes as well). If you see foxtails, pull them out. If you can't see any but think there is one deep down in the ear, don't try to remove it yourself. The ear can easily be damaged or the foxtail pushed right through the eardrum. Try pressing gently on the ear canal, which feels like a small plastic tube under the ear. If the dog cries out in pain, there is a good chance a foxtail is trapped inside.

If you can't get immediate veterinary care, put some warm oil (almond or olive) into the ear to soften the sticker and make it less irritating. There's also a slight chance that your dog can shake the foxtail out after this procedure, but don't count on it. As soon as possible, take your dog to a veterinarian, who will remove the culprit with the proper instruments (sometimes under anesthesia). Otherwise, very severe damage can occur.

Ear Mites

These parasites are very common in cats, and when dogs get them it is usually from cats. If you have a cat with ear mites and your dog shows symptoms, there's a good chance he has them too.

Though the mites are not possible to see with the naked eye, the discharge that forms in the ear is. It looks much like deposits of dried coffee grounds down in the ear canals. An affected cat will scratch like mad whenever you rub its ears.

A dog will shake its head and scratch its ears frequently. Usually, there is no bad smell or any discharge like that seen in cats, but the ear canal looks quite red and inflamed (different than in cats, who have less irritation) when your veterinarian peers in with an otoscope.

Generally, low vitality invites infestation, so an improved diet will indirectly aid in both prevention and recovery (see chapters 3 and 4). Garlic and brewer's yeast are especially helpful.

A mixture of ½ ounce of almond or olive oil and 400 IU vitamin E (from a capsule) makes a mild healing treatment for either cats or dogs. Blend them in a dropper bottle and warm the mixture to body temperature by immersing it in hot water. Holding the ear flap up, put about ½ dropper-full in the ear. Massage the ear canal well so that you hear a fluid sound. After a minute of this, let the animal shake its head. Then gently clean out the opening (not deep into the ear) with cotton swabs to remove debris and excess oil. The oil mixture will smother many of the mites and start a healing process that will make the ear less hospitable for them. Apply the oil every other day for six days (three treatments in total). Between treatments, cap the mixture tightly and store at room temperature. After the last oil treatment, let the ear rest for three more days. Meanwhile, prepare the next medicine, an herbal extract that is used to directly inhibit or kill the mites.

Herbal—Once the ears are cleaned out, one of the simplest ways to kill mites is with the herb Yellow Dock (*Rumex crispus*). Prepare it as described in Herbal Schedule 1, page 438, and apply it in the same way as the oil, above. Treat the ears once every three days for three to four weeks. Usually, this is enough to clear up the problem. If you observe irritation or inflammation during the treatment process, then also use the treatment for allergy ears, above.

In a very stubborn case, you may need to thoroughly shampoo the head and ears as well. The mites can hang out around the outside of the ears and crawl back in later. Also shampoo the tip of the tail, which may harbor a few mites from when it is curled near the head. Use a tea infusion of yellow dock as a final rinse. Remember also that toning up the skin with a nutritious diet is absolutely necessary for the pet with a stubborn mite problem.

If there is no improvement, the problem may not be mites at all. It's just as likely to be an expression of an allergy. Here's how to tell the difference: Ears with mites have a dry, crumbly, "coffee ground" discharge observable (with a light) down in the ear canal only; allergy ears exude an oily, waxy, dark brown, fluid-like discharge that flows up out of the ear canal and is also seen around the outside of the ear.

ECLAMPSIA

See "Pregnancy, Birth, and Care of Newborns."

ECZEMA

See "Skin Problems."

EMERGENCIES

See "Handling Emergencies and Giving First Aid" on page 429.

ENCEPHALITIS

See "Distemper, Chorea and Feline Panleukopenia."

EPILEPSY

Epilepsy has become fairly common in dogs, though it is rather unusual in cats. Often it's difficult to find the cause. In some cases it seems to be an inherited tendency, probably tied to intensive inbreeding. I think the biggest factor, however, stems from yearly vaccinations. I have seen many dogs that first developed epilepsy within a few weeks after their annual shots. Apparently, it is triggered by allergic encephalitis, an ongoing, low-grade inflammation of the brain caused by a reaction to proteins and organisms in the vaccine. This condition was discovered many years ago and has been well documented in laboratory animals. Some have even pointed to it as a significant cause of human behavior and learning problems. Fortunately, now that we know that annual vaccinations are not necessary, it will be easier to avoid this possible cause (see "Vaccinations").

In general, the health of the nervous system and brain is influenced by heredity, nutrition during the mother's pregnancy, lifelong nutrition, and any toxic or irritating substances that reach the brain. Also, certain brain diseases (for example, distemper) or a severe head injury can result in epilepsy.

For most animals, however, it's hard to point to an obvious cause. The convulsions may start without warning and continue with increasing frequency. An epileptic animal may be either young or old at the time of the first attack. The diagnosis of epilepsy is usually made only after other possibilities—like worms, hypoglycemia (low blood sugar), tumors, and poisons—have been eliminated. Thus, it is a sort of diagnosis by default, and the epilepsy may actually be caused by a mixed bag of things.

TREATMENT

My own approach is to use a natural diet to promote nutrition for the brain tissues and to detoxify or eliminate possible toxins in the environment and to use homeopathic remedies to control the seizures.

Nutrition should be geared toward preventing the intake of substances that may irritate the brain tissue. Work with hyperactive children indicated that food additives, for instance, may affect the brain this way. Thus I recommend that you put your animal on a strict regimen that excludes all commercial foods, snacks, or foods containing additives or coloring agents. Use the basic diet described in chapters 3 and 4, with certain modifications.

❖ Limit organ meats (especially liver and kidney) to once a week or less. They are more likely to be contaminated by pesticides, antibiotics, heavy metals, and hormonal substances.

❖ Consider a vegetarian diet for a dog (or using low-meat recipes for cats, as in chapter 5). Many human epileptics are significantly helped by avoiding meat, and it may help pets as well. Give it a trial of at least three months to see if it helps.

❖ Use special supplements. Since the B vitamins are very important to nerve tissue, use a natural, complete B complex in the 10 to 50 milligram range, depending on your pet's size. Niacin or niacinamide should be a minimum of 5 to 25 milligrams. Also supplement with ¼ to 2 teaspoons of lecithin and 10 to 30 milligrams of zinc (the chelated form is best). Give about 250 to 1,000 milligrams of vitamin C daily to assist detoxification. Again, use the level best suited to your pet's size.

❖ Protect your animal's environment. Avoid exposing your epileptic pet to cigarette smoke, car exhaust (rides in the back of pickup trucks are particularly harmful), chemicals (especially flea sprays, dips, and collars, which affect the nervous system), and excessive stress or exertion (but moderate regular exercise is beneficial). Don't let your animal lie right near an operating color TV or close to an operating microwave oven.

❖ Use treatments that strengthen the nervous system. See the herbs suggested under "Behavior Problems," giving special attention to common oat, blue vervain, and skullcap.

As an alternative to herbal treatment, there are specific homeopathic remedies that are often quite useful in this condition.

Homeopathic—*Belladonna* (deadly nightshade) 30C: Use Schedule 4, page 442. Start with this treatment and observe for a month; if the problem is no better, go to the next remedy (if the animal is better, do not give further remedies, but continue with the nutrition and other supportive methods discussed above). If the seizures come back after another month or so, then give one more dose of *Belladonna* 30C to see if that once again improves the situation. If it does not this second time, then give one dose only of *Silicea* 30C. Hopefully, this will be all that is needed. If not, then consult with a homeopathic veterinarian.

Homeopathic—*Thuya* (or *Thuja*) (arborvitae) 30C: In many dogs, epilepsy comes on after being vaccinated, especially with Distemper or Rabies vaccines. If the treatment already suggested above has not eliminated the problem, then give Thuya, and allow sev-

eral weeks to see if the seizure frequency decreases. Be aware that if either *Thuya* or *Silicea* has solved the problem, the epilepsy is likely to return if your dog is vaccinated again.

Homeopathic—*Arnica montana* (mountain daisy) 30C: Use Schedule 5, page 442. This remedy is indicated for the animal that has developed seizures after a head injury. It is an alternative to the two remedies just discussed and is appropriate only if you know that the cause of the problem is an injury to the head. Give one dose and allow a week or so to assess if the seizures have stopped. If the problem continues, then give one dose of *Natrum sulphuricum* 30C. This treatment protocol will resolve many seizures from concussion to the head, but if the problem still persists, there are other medicines that can be used in this way. Consult a homeopathic veterinarian.

EYE PROBLEMS

Five major problems can affect animals' eyes: cataracts, corneal ulcers, injuries, inflammation (infection), and ingrowing eyelids (called entropion). We will consider each of these in turn.

Cataracts

This condition is just like what happens with people. The round, clear lens in the interior of the eye (behind the pupil) that transmits and focuses light becomes cloudy or white (milky). Sometimes this happens as a result of injury to the eye. This condition, however, is also a frequent accompaniment of chronic disease and immune disorders in dogs. Many of the dogs with chronic skin allergies, hip dysplasia, and ear problems will develop this as they get older. Cataracts are also more common in animals that have diabetes mellitus, even with insulin treatment.

Veterinarians sometimes remove the lens surgically, and this may help. Unless the underlying condition is satisfactorily addressed, however, the eye is never really healthy. Prevention, by treatment of the chronic illness, is really the only effective method.

TREATMENT

See "Allergies" and "Skin Problems" for treatment suggestions, even though these do not deal directly with the eyes. You must take the approach of healing from the inside out. If the cataract is the result of an injury of the eyes, however, use this treatment.

Homeopathic—*Conium maculatum* (poison hemlock) 6C: Use Schedule 6(a), page 442.

There are other remedies that can be used for eye problems that are the result of injury. If this one is not effective, contact a homeopathic veterinarian.

The cataract associated with allergies and immune diseases is more difficult to treat and needs the expertise of a veterinarian skilled in the use of homeopathic treatment.

Corneal Ulcers

Ulcers of the cornea are usually the result of an injury, such as a cat scratch. When the surface of the eye is broken, it hurts and tears will form. The injury itself can be so small it's invisible unless a light is shone upon it from the side or a special dye is used. Bacteria may infect the scratch, but in the healthy animal a rapid, uncomplicated recovery is common.

TREATMENT

If the injury is deep or there is debris or a splinter stuck there, it will need careful professional treatment under anesthesia. Superficial injuries do not bleed. If you see blood, suspect penetration into and damage of delicate internal structures. This kind of injury can be very serious. The following recommendations are for treating slight irritations, shallow ulcers, or noninfected scratches *only*.

Nutritional—Cod-liver oil: Add ¼ to 1 teaspoon, depending on size, of cod-liver oil to the diet. Also add vitamin E to the diet, 100 to 400 IU daily depending on size.

Every 4 hours, apply a drop of cod-liver oil directly onto the eye or into the lower lid. The oil has protective functions, and the vitamin A in it will stimulate healing. Instead of dropping the oil into the eye, you can use an infusion of the herb eyebright (as described next).

Herbal—Eyebright (*Euphrasia officinalis*): Use the extract (which is available as either tincture or glycerin), 5 drops to 1 cup pure water. To this mixture also add ¼ teaspoon of sea salt. Mix well and store at room temperature. Put 2 to 3 drops in the affected eye 3 times a day to stimulate healing.

An immediately useful homeopathic treatment for the pain and inflammation is:

Homeopathic—*Aconitum napellus* (monkshood) 30C: Use Schedule 2, page 442.

Injuries

Other eye injuries include scratches, abrasions, and bruising of the eyeball. In these cases, use one of the following homeopathic treatments.

Homeopathic—*Euphrasia officinalis* (eyebright) 30C: Use Schedule 2, page 442. This is especially useful for scratches and abrasions of areas other than the cornea (see "Corneal Ulcers," above).

Homeopathic—*Symphytum* (comfrey) 30C: Use Schedule 2, page 442. This remedy is indicated for blows or contusions to the eyeball (the whole eye, not just the cornea in front—for example, from being hit by a rock, a car, or a club).

Inflammation

This is often part of a viral or bacterial infection. Use the eye cleansing treatment methods discussed in chapter 15 (with saline washes).

Ingrowing Eyelids (Entropion)

In this condition, the lids turn in and press the eyelashes against the corneal surface. The constant rubbing of the hairs causes a large (sometimes white), long-lasting ulcer to appear. This problem is not as easy to observe as you might suppose. Gently pull the lids away from the eye and let them fall back. Repeat several times. If the animal has ingrowing eyelids, you should be able to see the cuffing in of the lids as they are released. Some dogs are born with this condition, so you can see it when they are quite young. Others develop it after a long period of low-grade conjunctivitis (inner eyelid inflammation). The repeated inflammation and contraction cause the lids to turn in. Ingrowing eyelids are more common in dogs than cats.

Treatment

The usual correction is surgery, which is quite easy to perform and usually successful. I have also had very good results in young animals with this condition using:

Homeopathic—*Silicea* (silicon dioxide, quartz) 30C: Use Schedule 5, page 442. If after a couple of weeks there is no change, then surgery is indicated. It will help, temporarily, to put a drop of almond oil in the affected eye 3 times a day.

Of course, if the underlying cause is chronic inflammation, then you must deal with that. A helpful treatment is:

Herbal—Goldenseal (*Hydrastis canadensis*): Use the extract (tincture or glycerin) and add 5 drops to 1 cup of pure water. To this mixture also add ¼ teaspoon of sea salt. Mix well and store at room temperature. Put 2 to 3 drops in the affected eye 3 times a day to stimulate healing.

If the lids have become hardened through scarring, use:

Homeopathic—*Silicea* (silicon dioxide) 6C: Use Schedule 6(a), page 442.

FELINE IMMUNODEFICIENCY VIRUS (FIV)

This recently recognized disease of cats is also called Feline AIDS, because it causes a depression of the immune system just like AIDS (acquired immunodeficiency syndrome) in human beings. The virus is in the same family as human HIV (retroviruses), but fortunately it's different enough that it doesn't affect people. Since its discovery in a California cattery in 1986, the virus has been found in every part of the United States, and in other countries as well.

The incidence of infection is surprisingly high—14 percent of sick cats brought to veterinarians in the United States are positive for the virus; 44 percent is the rate among sick cats in Japan. As far as is known, FIV is spread only through bite wounds—from fighting—not from close physical or sexual contact. So it is not surprising that the disease is more common in unneutered males and in cats that roam outdoors. Reports indicate a wide range of ages affected—from two months to 18 years.

If the virus is not resisted by the immune system, the disease is very serious, usually causing severe, chronic illness with a wide range of symptoms. Typically, four to six weeks after becoming infected from a bite, the cat develops fever and swollen lymph glands (for example, those under the jaw), along with suppressive effects on the immune system. Often this will clear up, and the cat can seem normal for months or years, until excess stress or some other factor depresses the immune system. Then the disease is reactivated and the chronic phase begins—a process that ends in death six months to three years later (without alternative treatment).

Because a major effect of the virus is to depress the immune response, it is difficult to fully describe all the different ways in which symptoms can manifest. As is the case with human AIDS, many other infections get established and persist—infections that ordinarily would be brief and insignificant. For example, colds can lead to permanent upper respiratory symptoms, with runny eyes and a plugged up nose (or discharge).

One common symptom is an inflamed mouth, with periodontal disease and loose teeth. Examples of other problems include: blood disorders, anemia, bacterial infections, skin eruptions and infection, persistent mange (skin parasites), chronic diarrhea (and wasting away), inflammation of the interior of the eye, fevers, lymph gland enlargements, chronic abscesses, recurrent urinary tract infections (cystitis), and loss of appetite and weight. In addition, there can be other persistent infections, like fungal diseases or toxoplasmosis (see "Toxoplasmosis"). One of the most alarming expressions of the disease affects the brain. Cats will act demented, have convulsions, or attack people or other animals.

PREVENTION

Prevention is the most important way to approach this disease because, once established, it is very difficult to eliminate. If you can keep your cat healthy by using a raw, fresh diet—along with the rest of the general program in this book—its chance of resisting the disease is very high. Of course, preventing your cat from roaming and fighting significantly reduces the chance of infection.

If a new cat is coming into your home, isolate him or her from the other cats for at least three weeks. During this time, have a test done for FIV (and Feline Leukemia at the same time). This involves taking a blood sample at the veterinarian's office and is quite useful in determining if this new cat is carrying either virus. (Of course, if the test is positive, the cat will have to be kept isolated from the others to prevent transmission of the disease.)

Another important point is that any cat suspected of having FIV (or feline leukemia or other chronic viruses) should never be vaccinated. That's because the vaccine viruses stress the body (possibly triggering the latent state) and depress the immune system in many cats (again allowing the virus to get started). The principle is to avoid anything that will disturb or weaken the immune system. I know this advice runs counter to that of many veterinarians, who encourage vaccination as a way to protect a weakened cat. My clinical experience and background in immunology, however, convince me that this is the worst thing to do.

TREATMENT

It is possible to greatly help cats with this problem. Success depends on how much damage has already occurred and the age of the cat. Some will need treatment the rest of their lives and never regain their health. Others, younger and less advanced in the disease, may recover—at least in the sense that the disease goes into remission and they lead normal, healthy lives.

Because of the tremendous variability of symptoms, I will not offer specific treatments here. You can apply the different treatments described in other parts of this Quick Reference section as appropriate to the symptoms your cat has. It will be best, however, if you can work with an alternative veterinarian.

FELINE INFECTIOUS PERITONITIS (FIP)

This serious infection can be fatal for almost all cats that develop symptoms. It seems to come on after something depresses the immune system. For example, I have seen many cases occur within a few weeks of the cat receiving a vaccine against feline leukemia—probably from a temporary immunosuppressive action of the vaccine (an effect known to occur with several vaccines). It is not that the vaccine causes the disease directly, but rather that the cat was already carrying the FIP virus and the vaccine gave it an opportunity.

FIP is caused by a coronavirus, a group of

viruses that also cause disease in pigs, dogs, and humans. As far as is known, however, the FIP virus does not spread to humans or other animals.

It is thought that cats become infected through the mouth and throat, the upper respiratory tract, or, perhaps, the intestinal tract. People often don't realize when their cats begin to get FIP because they may show no particular symptoms or may run just a mild fever and seem like they're not feeling well for a few days. During this period (one to ten days after initial infection), the virus can be shed from the throat, lungs, stomach, and intestines and spread to other cats. After this the virus incubates anywhere from a few weeks to several years before symptoms appear.

Once symptoms appear and the disease progresses, the cat gradually loses its appetite (and weight), develops a persistent fever, and becomes depressed (inactive, subdued). Meanwhile, the virus spreads throughout the body tissues, especially affecting blood vessels. It is interesting to note that by this time (when symptoms are so evident) the cat is no longer shedding the virus and is not contagious.

This points up one of the real problems in control. When the cat is the most contagious, you don't realize anything is wrong, but once symptoms appear it does no good to isolate the cat. However, sanitation can be very helpful in limiting the spread of disease from one cat to another, because the virus can per-

sist in the environment (soiled floors, food or water bowls) for a long time—up to three weeks in home conditions. It is no surprise that this disease primarily impacts multiple-cat households or catteries and is not likely with cats isolated from others.

The most common symptoms are fever, loss of appetite, weight loss, rough hair coat, and, possibly, accumulation of fluid in the chest or abdomen. Early symptoms can also resemble a common cold, with sneezing and watery discharges from the eyes and nose. (Some of the chronic upper respiratory problems in multiple-cat households can be caused by this virus.) In other cats, the first symptoms may involve the gastrointestinal tract (vomiting, diarrhea); this is a serious form that can rapidly become fatal.

FIP can also affect the eyes, causing one pupil to be larger than the other or causing fluid or blood to accumulate in the eyeball. Like the other serious cat virus diseases in this section, FIP can sometimes affect the brain or interfere with reproduction.

PREVENTION

See the prevention advice for Feline Immunodeficiency Virus (FIV), above.

Unfortunately, the diagnostic test to see if a cat is carrying the virus is extremely inaccurate. There are too many other mild and insignificant related viruses that will give false positives on the test, indicating a problem where there is none. Many veterinarians no longer even test for this virus.

TREATMENT

Since FIP takes many forms, I can give only some general guidelines for its most common manifestations. The more severe forms require very careful and persistent treatment under the guidance of a veterinarian. I strongly suggest not using antibiotics or corticosteroids, however, as these drugs do not help at all and only further weaken the cat, almost certainly leading to eventual decline and death from the disease.

As severe as the disease can be, I have had very satisfying results in the majority of cases I have treated with homeopathy and nutrition. Inevitably, I will be asked if the cat is completely cured and free of the virus. Clinically and by their appearance, many cats can become normal. Because there is no way to be sure that the body is free of the virus (by testing or other means), however, this aspect of the question cannot be answered. But most people are satisfied when their cat begins to act normally and look well.

Here are some guidelines for treatment.

❖ In the early stages of FIP (which are characterized by fever and loss of appetite), try the treatments for feline leukemia (below).

❖ If the symptoms are primarily upper respiratory symptoms, then refer to the section "Upper Respiratory Infections."

❖ In the intestinal form with vomiting and diarrhea, use the treatments under the corresponding sections.

❖ If your cat has the very unfortunate form of FIP with accumulation of fluid in the chest and abdomen (hydrothorax or pleural effusion in the chest, ascites in the abdomen), the following treatments may help. However, this form is usually eventually fatal.

Homeopathic—*Arsenicum album* (arsenic trioxide) 6C: Indicated for the anxious, chilly, thirsty, and restless cat. This is the most likely remedy to help. Use Schedule 6(a), page 442.

Homeopathic—*Mercurius sulphuricus* (yellow sulphate of mercury) 6C: Tremendous difficulty with breathing. The cat has to sit up all the time because of the fluid in the chest. Use Schedule 6(a), page 442.

Homeopathic—*Apis mellifica* (honeybee venom) 6C: Very difficult breathing (as described above), but there is an aversion to heat and the cat seeks out the coolest places to sit (tile floor, bathtub, next to the toilet). The cat will also cry out occasionally, sometimes even while asleep. Use Schedule 6(a), page 442.

These remedies all have usefulness in treatment of this condition. Try one, and if it doesn't help after a few days, try one of the others.

VACCINATION

There is a vaccine for this disease, but research has shown it to be useless or even harmful if the cat is already has the virus in its body. Not recommended.

FELINE LEUKEMIA
(FeLV)

This serious disease of cats is caused by a retrovirus similar to the ones that cause Feline Immunodeficiency Disease (see above) or human AIDS. About 21 percent of sick cats that are brought to veterinarians are ill from feline leukemia, which is the greatest killer of cats except for accidents. FeLV occurs mostly in cats aged one to five years. It affects males and females equally, but occurs more often in neutered animals (no one knows why).

The virus is spread from one cat to another through body fluids (saliva, urine, blood, feces). For the same reason, mother cats can give it to their young during pregnancy or nursing. Fortunately, it takes close or prolonged contact between cats for the virus to spread. Most contagion occurs from bites, grooming, or sharing water and food bowls. It is not transmitted through the air or via human handlers.

About 70 percent of all cats are exposed to FeLV, and nearly all of them recover spontaneously—most showing little or no illness. Those that are weak, however, are affected more severely. The incidence of serious illness is also much higher in multi-cat households.

There are several types of feline leukemia virus, which cause slightly different symptoms. The most common signs of illness, especially early on, are weight loss, fever, and dehydration (lack of water in the tissues).

Other possible symptoms include anemia, immune suppression (like FIV, see above), bleeding disorders, kidney inflammation (and deterioration), arthritis, ulcers forming at body openings (mouth, anus, vagina, eyes), immune diseases like inflammatory bowel disease or eosinophilic granuloma complex, and persistent bladder inflammation (cystitis).

Other peculiar, less common symptoms are skin growths (like "horns"), deposits of cartilage, skin disease (with oily coats), and nerve damage (paralysis, urinary incontinence). With some cats, an odd symptom is that one pupil is smaller or larger than the other. Another odd symptom is the desire to eat clay litter or lick cement or mortar.

Many affected cats cannot reproduce properly, having spontaneous abortions, stillbirths, or what is known as fading kittens—kittens that waste away in spite of the best care.

As if this were not enough, many affected cats develop tumors or cancer. It is estimated that 30 percent of all cat tumors are a result of this virus.

Infection with FeLV progresses through six recognized stages.

❖ Stage 1—Infection of the mouth tissues. (The disease stops here in healthy cats.)

❖ Stage 2—The virus is spread from the mouth by certain blood cells.

❖ Stage 3—The virus infects lymph glands (such as the tonsils and glands under the throat or in other parts of the body—like when we get colds). Even if it reaches this point, most healthy cats can still block the infection from going further.

❖ Stage 4—Infection of the bone marrow. Once infection is established here, the cat will be infected the rest of its life, though the disease may still be controllable with proper treatment.

❖ Stage 5—The infection spreads again into the blood, through circulating cells.

❖ Stage 6—Various tissues in the body are persistently infected, especially the tear glands, salivary glands, and urinary bladder. These cats are now shedding the virus and are infectious to other cats.

PREVENTION

Follow the same preventive guidelines given for Feline Immunodeficiency Virus (FIV) on page 347, including testing and isolation of new cats coming into the home.

TREATMENT

Nutrition: This is a serious illness with many possible forms of expression, which means that complete guidelines for treatment could fill a whole book. Since the symptoms usually include loss of appetite, nutritional treatment is very difficult. You can force-feed your cat, however. It's not pleasant, but it can be life-saving in a crisis (see "Appetite Problems" for guidelines). If your cat is still eating, then it is essential that you feed a raw-meat, home-prepared diet. I realize that your cat may not accept such a diet, so you will have to do what is possible. But this is the very best strategy.

Vitamin C can be very helpful to cats with this disease; give 250 milligrams twice a day. Often sodium ascorbate, the salt form of vitamin C (ascorbic acid), is best tolerated. Add the powder to food or, if necessary, dissolve it in water or broth and give it with a syringe. Pureed raw liver is often accepted by these cats and provides some very useful nutrition. Give several tablespoons a day if possible.

Other useful treatments include:

Homeopathic—*Nux vomica* (poison nut) 30C: Use Schedule 3, page 442. This is especially indicated for the cat that becomes irritable and withdraws to a quiet part of the house or apartment.

Homeopathic—*Pulsatilla* 30C: Use Schedule 3, page 442. Most useful for the cat that becomes "clingy," wanting a lot of attention and to be held. She will act sleepy and sluggish and perhaps vomit easily if the food is too rich. There may be a tendency to lie in the bathtub or other cool places.

Homeopathic—*Phosphorus* (phosphorus) 30C: Use Schedule 3, page 442. This remedy is indicated for the cat that is extremely lethargic, like a wet washrag, or vomits about 10 to 20 minutes after drinking water (but not after eating food).

Homeopathic—*Arsenicum album* (arsenic trioxide) 30C: This cat will be very chilly, restless, and thirsty. What is most noticeable is how weak the cat is, barely able to walk, but weaving as he does so. The body temperature may be low, below 100°F. (37.8°C.) and the coat very dry and sticking up.

Homeopathic—*Nitricum acidum* (nitric acid, aqua fortis) 30C: This medicine is a good choice for a cat with a very painful, inflamed mouth. If she is also very irritable or angry when ill, then this medicine may be especially helpful. It is also suitable for lesions on the lips, anus, or eyelids. (The lesions look like ulcers or painful, raw areas.) Use Schedule 4, page 442.

Homeopathic—*Belladonna* (deadly nightshade) 30C: Use this if the mouth becomes extremely painful, the cat almost hysterical with the pain, the pupils dilated, perhaps even some fever. Use Homeopathic Schedule 2. If this helps, wait about 5 days and give one dose of *Calcarea carbonica* 30C (one dose only).

There are many other remedies that can be used. Consult a trained homeopathic veterinarian. (See my Web site, www.drpitcairn.com, for a list).

VACCINATION

Only partially effective. In my experience, vaccination makes cats more likely to become ill with other diseases such as FIP (see above). Not recommended.

FELINE PANLEUKOPENIA

See "Distemper, Chorea and Feline Panleukopenia."

FELINE UROLOGIC SYNDROME

See "Bladder Problems."

FLEAS

See "Skin Parasites."

FOXTAILS

See also "Ear Problems."

The number-one enemy of dogs and cats could well be the numerous foxtails, plant awns, and wild oat seeds (or any other local name for these prickly plants) that get caught in the hair and crevices of their bodies. Because of the way these stickers are constructed, they will not easily dislodge. Instead, they tend to migrate through the skin or into body openings (eyes, ears, nose, mouth, anus, vagina, sheath), where they cause tremendous problems. If a foxtail works through the skin, the body cannot digest it; even years later it will look fresh on removal.

Thus, although the body makes every effort to eliminate the sticker, it clings tenaciously to the tissue. The result is a constantly inflamed tract that drains pus and never heals completely. The plant material can migrate a foot or more into the body, making it difficult, if not impossible, to find. Toes are a favorite lodging place, as are the ears (see "Ear Problems") and eyes, where they can get behind the "third eyelid" and cause a lot of irritation.

PREVENTION

Always check over your animal after it has run in fields, vacant lots, or other weedy places. Check all the body openings, and run a comb or brush through the hair. Be sure to check between the toes, too. If you clip the hair between the toes during foxtail season, your job will be much easier and your animal's life much more comfortable. Also, have the hair coat trimmed to a short length, an inch or less, and trim away any hair growing around the ear hole or inside the ear flap. Stickers are much likelier to get into the ears of dogs with hanging ears. See "Ear Problems" for treating foxtails in the ears. Also, see "Abscesses."

TREATMENT

If your animal already has a foxtail under the skin, with chronic discharge from a small opening, and your veterinarian is not able to find and remove it, the following treatment may help as a last resort, only if surgery fails.

Homeopathic—*Silicea* (silicon dioxide) 6C: Use Schedule 6(b), page 442. This treatment can result in the body rejecting the foxtail through an opening in the skin. If you see that, you will know the problem is solved. It also helps to use hot compresses above the draining hole. The increased warmth will bring more blood into the area and more cells to participate in the healing process.

If the sticker does not work its way out, your veterinarian must keep trying to remove it surgically. Remember, in the case of foxtails, an ounce of prevention is worth at least a pound of cure.

HAIR LOSS

See also "Skin Problems."

Hair loss is often the result of skin allergies and excessive licking and chewing. Sometimes, however, the hair falls out without any sign of skin irritation. This can signal inadequate protein intake, as in cats that eat poorly, or it can mean that the protein is not very digestible even when appetite is good. Other deficiencies, particularly of trace minerals, will slow hair growth.

There are two remedies that are especially useful for simple hair loss unaccompanied by other symptoms.

Homeopathic—*Selenium* (selenium) 30C: Use Schedule 4, page 442. If this treatment is successful, you will see signs of hair growth within a month. Do not repeat this remedy without supervision.

Homeopathic—*Sepia* (ink from the cuttlefish) 30C: Use Schedule 4, page 442. This remedy suits a female that loses hair after giving birth and nursing the young. This is not necessarily a nutritional problem; it's more likely a hormonal imbalance, which can be corrected by this remedy.

HEART PROBLEMS

Disorders of the heart are relatively common in aging pets, both dogs and cats. They do not have atherosclerosis and the type of heart attacks that afflict humans, however. Rather, the problem is usually a weak heart muscle, with enlargement of one or both sides of the heart. Sometimes there is inadequate heart valve action or a rhythm that is too quick or too slow. Cholesterol is not a factor in this condition.

Typical signs of a heart problem include one or more of the following: becoming easily tired by exercise, bluish discoloration of the tongue and gums upon exercise, sudden collapse or prostration, difficult breathing or wheezing, a persistent dry cough that produces little expectoration, and an accumulation of fluid in the legs or abdomen (a potbellied look).

TREATMENT

Conventional veterinary treatment includes the use of a digitalis-type drug, a diuretic, and a low-sodium diet. The assumption is that the condition is progressive, and so treatment aims to control symptoms rather than to cure.

I prefer an alternative approach, emphasizing nutrition and homeopathic or herbal remedies. Though complete recovery may not be possible, these measures do more than just counteract symptoms; they can actually strengthen the affected tissues. Of course, the chance of help from any treatment depends upon the degree of tissue damage and the age of the animal.

The best route of all is prevention, in the form of a healthy lifestyle, with nutritious food and regular exercise. If symptoms have

already developed, however, here is what I suggest.

Nutrition should emphasize the basic natural foods diet (chapters 3 and 4). Feed the meat raw, rather than cooked, for its superior nutrition. Do not add any salt, soy sauce, bacon, or other salty foods or flavorings to the food. Use spring water or other water that is nonchlorinated and not fluoridated. If the animal is overweight, slim it down with the diet under "Weight Problems." Weight reduction is important, because more heart energy is required to pump blood through all that fat.

Supplement with a complete B-complex tablet with all the B vitamins, but especially niacin and pyridoxine. Major B-vitamin components should be at the 10, 25, or 50-milligram level (depending on animal size). It's also helpful to give a trace mineral supplement containing chromium and selenium (scale the recommended human dose on the label to your animal's size) and chelated zinc (5, 10, or 20 milligrams daily, depending on size).

Cats need to have adequate amounts of the amino acid taurine, found almost entirely in animal tissue (meat). You can get taurine as an extra supplement for cats, though it is often easier to feed larger amounts of raw meat (cooking inactivates taurine).

Other important measures are regular, daily exercise that is not too strenuous or exciting (a walk is ideal) and the avoidance of cigarette smoke. In the sensitive animal, many of the symptoms of heart disease can be caused by exposure to secondary cigarette smoke—including irregular pulse, pain in the heart region, difficult breathing, cough, dizziness, and prostration.

Specific remedies may be helpful. If the condition is not very advanced and has been recently diagnosed, try these remedies:

Homeopathic—*Calcarea carbonica* (calcium carbonate) 30C: Helps to restore strength to the heart muscle, especially if dilated and the action is weak. Cats needing this have had ravenous appetites in the past (though they may be changed since the heart problem), tend to be overweight, and prefer to be where it is warm, like on top of a radiator, heat vent, or equivalent. Use Schedule 4, page 442. Do not repeat this remedy without supervision.

Homeopathic—*Natrum muriaticum* (sodium chloride, table salt) 30C: Helpful for the animal that in the past has had a strong appetite but kept losing weight anyway. Tends to have a strong thirst and an aversion to heat, avoiding warm rooms and disliking warm weather. Pulse tends to be irregular. When ill, they do not want much attention and get irritated if you try to hold them or make them feel better. Use Schedule 4, page 442.

Homeopathic—*Phosphorus* (the element) 30C: Those needing this remedy vomit easily, crave very cold water (like from a faucet), which may be vomited up 10-20 minutes after drinking. Very sensitive to noise and odors. Easily frightened, especially by loud noises, like from thunderstorms or fireworks. Use Homeopathic Schedule 4, page 442.

For more severe or persistent symptoms in advanced illness if not controlled by nutrition and other measures (above), pick one of the following treatments, whichever seems best indicated. (Don't skip the other measures and expect good results, however!)

Homeopathic—*Crataegus oxycantha* (hawthorn berries) 3C: Indicated for the animal with a dilated heart, weak heart muscle, difficult breathing, fluid retention, and (often) a nervous or irritable temperament. Use Schedule 6(c), page 442.

Homeopathic—*Strophanthus hispidus* (Kombe seed) 3C: For the weak heart with valvular problems. The pulse is weak, frequent, and irregular, and breathing is difficult. There may also be fluid retention, loss of appetite, and vomiting. Obesity and chronic itching of the skin also point to this medicine. Use Schedule 6(c), page 442.

Homeopathic—*Digitalis purpurea* (foxglove) 6C: Give one pellet after each attack in which the animal collapses or faints after exertion, with the tongue turning blue. Often the pulse or heart rate is abnormally slow. There may be heart dilation and fluid retention. Liver disturbances may be evidenced by a white, pasty stool. If this treatment is helping, the attacks will become less frequent.

Homeopathic—*Spongia tosta* (roasted sponge) 6C: For the animal whose crises are characterized by a rapid pulse, difficult breathing, and fearfulness. It may have difficulty lying down and may breathe easier sitting up. A dry, persistent cough is an indication for this medicine. Use Schedule 6(b), page 442.

General directions for the homeopathic remedies are to use the medicine that seems best suited to the situation. If it helps for a while, use it as long as it does. If it stops helping or the symptoms change, then reevaluate and use another of the medicines listed. Many animals with this problem need ongoing treatment, especially if they are quite old. Some will gradually get better, however, and you will be able to discontinue treatment. It is strongly recommended that you get professional help for this condition, even in using the remedies listed here. It is a complex illness and needs frequent evaluation. (See my Web site for veterinarians trained in the use of homeopathic medicine, www.drpitcairn.com).

HEARTWORMS

The heartworm parasite actually lives in the heart of a dog (and rarely a cat), where it can grow as long as 11 inches and, in a minority of infestations, cause persistent coughing, difficulty breathing, weakness, fainting, and sometimes even heart failure. Adult heartworms produce young ones (called microfilaria), which circulate through the dog's bloodstream in greatest numbers when hungry mosquitoes are most likely to come a-biting (especially summer evenings). When a mosquito bites the dog, it can ingest these microfilaria and later infect another dog.

When a mosquito carries them to a new dog, the microfilaria progress through two more developmental stages under the skin, after which they enter the bloodstream via nearby veins. After reaching the heart, they settle into their new home, where they mature and reproduce, renewing the cycle about six months after the original mosquito bite.

A heartworm diagnosis is made when a veterinarian finds microfilaria (baby worms) in the blood, but not necessarily any symptoms of illness. Only a small percentage of dogs in an area may become noticeably sick from heartworm, which usually requires infestation with a considerable number of worms. Just a few worms are insignificant and may not require treatment.

Once a dog does show clinical symptoms, treatment can be very involved and almost always requires hospitalization. The drugs used in treatment are very toxic and hard on the animal (they involve the use of arsenic compounds). Thus, the preferred route is prevention, for which veterinarians prescribe drugs that kill the baby worms before they mature. Most often used is ivermectin, given once a month. There are various brands, some of which contain other anti-parasite chemicals. They kill baby worms that are under the skin, those which have been picked up in the month or so before the dose. Usually the drug is started before mosquito season and continued until a month or two after mosquito season is over. In some areas this means all year.

Are there side effects? Sure, and what has been reported are vomiting, diarrhea, seizures, paralysis, jaundice, and other liver problems, coughing, nosebleeds, high fevers, weakness, dizziness, nerve damage, bleeding disorders, loss of appetite, breathing difficulty, pneumonia, depression, lethargy, sudden aggressive behavior, skin eruptions, tremors, and sudden death.

Though a minority of dogs experiences these reactions, they are seen in many breeds. Veterinarians also report that many dogs get stomach and intestinal upsets, irritability, stiffness, and seem to just feel "rotten" for the first one or two weeks after each monthly dose of heartworm protection. An American Veterinary Medical Association report on adverse drug reactions showed that 65 percent of all drug reactions reported and 48 percent of all reported deaths caused by drug reactions were from heartworm preventive medicine.

I am reluctant, however, to tell people to stop the use of heartworm preventives, particularly in highly infested areas, partly because I cannot guarantee that their dogs will not get heartworm. I dislike the use of these drugs, and I think they cause much more illness than we realize.

What other choice do we have? Unfortunately, almost all heartworm research is directed toward finding new drugs to kill the microfilaria. Very little attention goes to enhancing the dog's natural resistance to the parasite. However, we do know of several facts that make that a promising direction to pursue: One is that wild animals are quite resistant to the parasite. That is, they get very light infestations and then become immune. Another factor is that an estimated 25 to 50 percent of dogs in high-heartworm areas become immune to the microfilaria after being infested and cannot pass heartworms to other dogs via mosquitoes. Finally, after being infested by a few heartworms, most dogs do not get more of them, even though they are continually bitten by mosquitoes carrying the parasite. In other words, they are able to limit the extent of infestation.

All this points to the importance of the health and resistance mounted by the dog itself. That takes us back to the central thesis of this book: If we care for our pets so as to maximize their health, their resistance to parasites (and disease) will be much higher. Isn't this a much more attractive way to go than to continually poison them with drugs? Clearly, we need serious research in this direction.

Another overlooked factor arises when we ask why there has been such an extensive spread of heartworm in dogs all over the United States in the last 30 years. I agree with the authorities who say that the incidence of heartworm increases whenever we upset the natural balance in a way that increases the mosquito population. For example, this happens when we expand irrigation acreage in farming areas. It is happening more now because global warming is opening up new areas to mosquito reproduction that were too cold before.

Wild animals like coyotes, however, thrive in the very same conditions, even without preventive drugs. The major difference is lifestyle——fresh, raw foods, plenty of exercise, no drugs, and no toxic flea products.

So it is likely the combination of environmental upset coupled with a deteriorating level of health through several dozen generations of dogs fed on commercial foods and poisoned with drugs and insecticides that has created this unnatural explosion of parasitism. It is particularly frustrating that recent research shows the incidence of heartworm infestation in dogs in any particular geographic area is the same now as it was in 1982, even after all these years of preventive treatment. It doesn't take too much contemplation to realize that the path of continued drug use is a dead-end road.

Some veterinarians who practice holistic medicine, myself included, have been experimenting with a homeopathic preventive made from microfilaria-infected blood, called a heartworm nosode. Though we have only been able to do small clinical studies, early results are very encouraging. This may eventually provide a true alternative to drug use.

The problem is that drug companies are not interested in such research, as the cost of such a preventive approach would not be profitable to them (homeopathic remedies costs pennies a day compared to dollars for drugs), so the research motivation (profit) and money is not there. I also said that more research was needed in the 1995 edition of this book, but nothing more has been achieved in this direction. If anyone is interested in funding such research, please contact me directly through the publisher.

PREVENTION

For those committed to a natural, non-chemical approach, here are some suggestions to help prevent heartworm. Use a completely natural (preferably organic) raw food diet fortified with raw garlic and liberal amounts of yeast. These foods may help to repel mosquitoes from the skin of some animals. To further minimize exposure to mosquitoes, you can keep your dog indoors in the evenings and night. Use a natural insect repellent when she does go outside: Rub one drop of eucalyptus oil, diluted in one cup of warm water, over the muzzle and the area between the anus and genitals (favorite mosquito-biting areas). Be careful to avoid rubbing the oil on the sensitive tissues of the eyes and mucous membranes.

TREATMENT

Remember that the presence of one or two heartworms is not serious in itself. But the dog that has a large number of worms and has also developed heart problems is in trouble. The treatment of such a condition requires experienced supervision, because the dog could undergo heart failure or embolisms (internal blood clots). So follow your veterinarian's treatment program. If you can, find one who uses herbal treatment, acupuncture, or homeopathic medicine. In addition, use the diet under "Heart Problems."

I do not like the conventional treatment for this condition, because strong poisons such as arsenic compounds are injected intramuscularly, and sometimes the treatment is worse than the disease. I have been called in to treat dogs whose health was permanently ruined by these drugs. Fortunately, these are in the minority and most dogs will do well. Still, the whole way of handling the problem is unappealing. But it is difficult to recommend gentler alternatives without supportive scientific data. While I have treated a few dogs ill from heartworms that were too sick or too old to undertake conventional treatment, I do not yet have a body of experience sufficient to establish a true alternative. We hope for this to happen.

HEPATITIS

See "Liver Problems."

HIP DYSPLASIA

This term describes a poorly formed hip joint. The veterinary profession generally regards hip dysplasia as a genetic problem complicated by a variety of environmental influences. The cause, however, is not really explained satisfactorily. Unfortunately, it is common among dogs.

Hip dysplasia is not present at birth. It develops during puppyhood, as the hip joint forms in a loose or "sloppy" way that allows too much movement of the leg bone in the hip socket. Irritation and scarring occur because the weak ligaments and surrounding joint tissues aren't able to stabilize the joint adequately. In addition, there tends to be a rheumatic tendency—inflammation and pain in the muscles and connective tissue of the legs and hips. Untreated, gradual loss of function will result. Some older dogs actually lose use of their rear legs.

PREVENTION AND TREATMENT

Orthodox treatment centers on a number of surgical procedures that involve cutting certain muscles, repositioning the joint, removing the head of the leg bone or completely replacing the hip joint with an artificial device. But there are other avenues of greater promise.

Prevention is the best place to start. Generations of poor feeding practices have contributed greatly to the development of hip dysplasia, the effects magnifying with each generation. If possible, you should avoid selecting an affected dog in the first place (see chapter 9). Apart from that, good prevention means feeding the pregnant female or newly acquired puppy a wholesome, fresh, well-supplemented diet as outlined in this book (see chapter 5). Be sure to include plenty of bone meal. Don't succumb to the fallacy that too much calcium in the diet causes this problem.

Another foolish idea is that hip dysplasia is caused by dogs growing too fast. Some people actually advocate restricting food or protein to prevent the puppy from developing normally. They think that keeping it small will somehow prevent the problem. It does not.

There is, however, a good preventive: Give lots of vitamin C (ascorbic acid), particularly if either parent had the condition or the pup is of a commonly affected breed, such as a German shepherd or other large purebreds. Indeed, there is some good evidence that hip dysplasia is in part caused by chronic subclinical scurvy (a lack of adequate vitamin C). In this view, the hip forms incorrectly as a result of weak ligaments and muscles around the joints. Vitamin C is essential to these tissues.

Wendell Belfield, DVM, reported in Veterinary Medicine/Small Animal Clinician that high amounts of vitamin C provided 100 percent prevention of hip dysplasia in eight litters of German shepherd pups coming from parents that either had the condition themselves or had previously produced offspring with it. He used the following program.

> ❖ The pregnant female is given two to four grams of sodium ascorbate crystals in the daily ration (½ to 1 teaspoon of the pure powder; ascorbic acid could also be used).
>
> ❖ At birth the puppies are given 50 to 100 milligrams of vitamin C orally each day (using a liquid form).
>
> ❖ At three weeks of age, the dose is increased to 500 milligrams daily of sodium ascorbate (given in the feed) until the puppies are four months old.

> ❖ At four months the dose is increased to one to two grams a day and maintained there until the puppies are 18 months to two years of age.

VACCINATION

The other important factor in prevention is that of vaccination. Looseness of the hips is one of the possible outcomes of vaccination of young developing animals, so an important part of a preventive program is to minimize these effects by using the smallest number of vaccines possible (see the discussion of vaccines in this section) and using them as infrequently as you can. Many breeders very much overvaccinate puppies, a practice not necessary for or conducive to good health. If you are obtaining a puppy from a breeder, work out an arrangement with him or her beforehand to use a modified schedule such as I recommend. This is very important as the hip dysplasia problem does not appear right away, and by the time it does it is too late to take preventive measures.

If vaccination cannot be avoided in spite of your best efforts, then give one dose of the homeopathic remedy *Silicea* (silicon dioxide) 30C. It will counteract this effect of vaccines in a significant proportion of puppies. Coupled with use of vitamin C, as recommended above and started as soon as you can, it is very likely to sidestep this whole problem.

For older animals that already have the problem, feed our natural diet (see chapters 3 and 4), including ample amounts of vitamin C, 500 milligrams to two grams a day. In arthritic cases, see if there is a suitable remedy among those described under "Arthritis." If you have access to acupuncture or chiropractic treatment, you may find your dog will experience marked improvement. See chapter 14 for more information.

INFECTIOUS PERITONITIS

See "Feline Infectious Peritonitis."

INJURIES

See "Handling Emergencies and Giving First Aid" on page 429.

INTERVERTEBRAL DISK DISEASE

See "Paralysis."

JAUNDICE

Jaundice, which can be caused by many factors, creates a visible yellowing of the tissues. We usually think of it as a liver disease, but it occurs for other reasons. If there is a rapid breakdown of red blood cells (due to, for instance, blood parasites, certain chemicals or drugs, various infections, or poisonous snakebites), the liver can't process all the released hemoglobin quickly enough. The result is a release of yellow pigment (which makes up part of hemoglobin), which backs up and stains the tissues yellow.

Your veterinarian will have to distinguish between jaundice caused by such factors and the type associated with liver disease. If the liver is ailing, the stool often looks pale in color. If the jaundice is from red blood cell breakdown, however, the stool is typically very dark from extra bile flow.

The type of jaundice caused by a sudden loss of intact red blood cells also leads to a form of anemia, even if no blood was visibly lost. To help the body form new red blood cells, follow the advice under "Anemia." Apart from dealing with any of those underlying causes of red blood cell breakdown, you can treat this type of noninflammatory jaundice simply by exposing your animal to direct sunlight (or indirect if it's too hot) for several hours daily for a few days. Sunlight stimulates the elimination of the pigments responsible for the jaundice. In addition, it may help to use:

Homeopathic—*Nux vomica* (poison nut) 30C: to enhance flow of liver bile and assist elimination of toxic material accumulated in the liver. Use Homeopathic Schedule 5, page 442.

KENNEL COUGH

See "Upper Respiratory Infections."

KIDNEY FAILURE

See also "Bladder Problems" for a discussion of kidney stones.

Deterioration of the kidneys is a common problem of old age for both dogs and cats (more so in cats). It is the second leading cause of death in cats (after feline leukemia), not counting accidents. It starts in most cats with increased thirst and recurrent cystitis (bladder problems). After many years, usually past middle age, it becomes apparent something is wrong with the kidneys. In other words, cats that will have kidney failure will, when young, have bladder trouble first. This process is more difficult to notice in dogs. Often, these cats will be put on special diets with acid added (to prevent the cystitis symptoms), but they simply cover up what is happening while the kidneys are deteriorating "behind the scenes." Many of the kidney failure cases that come to me are on antibiotic treatment, but since this is not a bacterial infection, they do not help and, if anything, make the cat more sick.

It is very difficult even to be aware that it is happening because of the tremendous capacity of the kidneys to compensate for loss of tissue. As long as one-third of the kidney tissue is functional, there are no obvious signs of sickness. Past this point, however, illness gradually develops. When only 15 to 20 percent of the kidney tissue is still functional, death comes.

The early signs of kidney failure typically are increased thirst, frequent urination with large quantities of pale urine, inability to hold urine all night, and occasional periods of low energy, lack of appetite, and nausea or vomiting that last for a few days at a time.

How much thirst is too much thirst? For dogs, use your common sense and notice any increases not attributable to hot weather or exercise. For cats, drinking water every day (or even less often) is suspicious, even if it's a young cat of two or three years. Because they evolved in dry regions, healthy cats drink little or no water by nature. The only exception to this rule is if your cat is eating only dry food (which I don't recommend). Dry food is so low in water (about 10 percent compared to 80 to 85 percent of a natural diet) that some cats are forced to drink even though it is not natural to them. If your cat is on a canned food or home-prepared diet (or you switch over to that) and is still drinking, however, you have a problem.

If you are observant, you can detect these signs of kidney failure early. That way you stand a much better chance of prolonging your animal's life with a special diet and other natural treatments than if you wait until an emergency.

TREATMENT

Once a kidney problem appears, the strategy is to avoid further deterioration, if possible, and to assist the function of what is left of the kidneys. We do the former with homeopathic, herbal, and nutritional treatment and the latter by reducing or eliminating the toxic load on the kidneys.

Let's consider the question of toxicity first.

Anything in the food or in the environment that is not usable by the body must be eliminated. This includes food preservatives, coloring agents, insecticides, pollutants, and the like. This elimination is primarily accomplished through the kidneys.

The cleansing function of the kidneys is related to that of the skin, which is another important eliminative organ. Skin irritations and eruptions often precede eventual kidney failure in old age. This process is accelerated if the skin discharge is repeatedly suppressed with corticosteroids.

Early symptoms of kidney disease progress into uremia (blood poisoning) characterized by low energy, frequent vomiting, dehydration, complete loss of appetite, foul breath, and, perhaps, an inflammation of the mouth or presence of mouth ulcers. At this point the animal needs an emergency intravenous infusion of large quantities of fluids to save its life. Afterwards, things return to normal, but it's a fragile normality, for in many cases 60 to 70 percent of the kidney tissue has been destroyed and cannot be regained. The kidneys can cope with this for a while by moving everything along faster. The fluids are pushed through much more rapidly (up to 20 times faster), resulting in a loss of essential salts, water, and other nutrients. Think of it like this: If a major freeway were blocked and everyone had to drive on surface streets to get around it, one way to keep traffic moving would be for the police to stand at intersections waving everyone on at higher than normal speeds. Imagine them yelling "Let's go! Move it along. We've got to get the job done!" This is what the kidneys do to compensate. Here's what we can do to help.

Nutrition: Our main dietary goal is to reduce the load of metabolic wastes on the kidneys; this waste results primarily from digestion of protein (producing urea) and the buildup of phosphorus and sodium. You can reduce the amount of this by using less protein, basically feeding a minimal level of protein of maximally usable quality. We do not want to feed too little protein, as this is harmful. Rather we give enough good quality protein to suffice and not a lot of extra. Also, it is vital to replace water-soluble vitamins that get flushed out of the body easily, especially vitamins B and C, and to supply plenty of vitamin A, which is good for the kidneys.

The following recipes meet these needs. They provide high quality protein and other supplements that are more likely to be lost from the body. We use enriched white rice because it is better digested than brown rice and also contains higher levels of iron and major B vitamins, which are hard to supply in a low-meat diet.

We will use calcium supplements that do not contain much phosphorus to avoid high blood levels (the kidneys have trouble regulating minerals when they get weak). The vitamins ensure adequate amounts of essential nutrients, which could become low in this diet. *Note:* It is important to avoid feeding special acid-forming diets to cats with kidney disease. These are the commercial foods formulated to prevent cystitis and are advertised as such. Chemicals have been added to these diets to force the urine to be acid; one side effect is that the body becomes too acid, and kidney function is reduced.

CANINE DIET FOR KIDNEY PROBLEMS

1/4	pound (1/2 cup) regular-fat hamburger
2³/4	cups cooked white rice, enriched
2	eggs (large, whole, raw)
1/4	cup cooked carrots
2	tablespoons cold-pressed safflower, soy, or corn oil
2	teaspoons Animal Essentials Calcium (or a slightly rounded teaspoon of eggshell powder)*
1/8	teaspoon iodized salt
2	tablespoons parsley (a natural diuretic, optional)
1/2–1	clove garlic, minced (for flavor, if appreciated—optional)
20	milligram-level of a complete B complex
1,000	milligrams vitamin C (1/4 teaspoon sodium ascorbate)

* These supplements are from Group III calcium supplements. See chapter 4 for more information.

Mix all ingredients together and serve raw if the dog will accept it. Otherwise, mix all but the vitamins together, bake about 20 minutes in a moderate oven and then wait until it cools to mix in the vitamins. Occasionally, substitute 1 to 3 teaspoons of liver for part of the meat. Be sure to provide plenty of fresh, pure water (filtered or bottled) at all times.

The recipe provides 17 percent good quality protein, 25 percent fat, and 55 percent carbohydrates. Overall, it is lower than the usual recipes in phosphorus (which tends to build up in this condition), but the calcium provided is adequate (a total of 2,400 mg).

Yield: Generally, feed as much as your dog will eat; as a guideline, this recipe should feed a 10-pound toy dog for three days or a 40-pound dog for a day. By tripling it you can feed a 60-pound dog for two days. Multiply the recipe as needed for convenience.

Note: *If your dog isn't eating well, force-feed vitamins separately, using these daily levels: toy and small dogs—10 milligrams B-complex and 250 milligrams vitamin C; medium-size dogs—as indicated in recipe; large and giant dogs—50 milligrams B-complex and 2,000 milligrams vitamin C.*

If your dog is eating well enough but losing weight, then increase the meat and fat in the recipe to compensate. The weight should be held steady.

FELINE DIET FOR KIDNEY PROBLEMS

$^{3}/_{4}$ pound ($1^{1}/_{2}$ cups) ground chicken (with skin) or turkey

4 cups cooked white rice, enriched

4 eggs

2 tablespoons cold-pressed safflower, soy, or corn oil

3 teaspoons Animal Essentials Calcium (or a scant 2 teaspoons of eggshell powder)*

$^{1}/_{4}$ teaspoon iodized salt

1 teaspoon parsley (a natural diuretic, optional)

5,000 IU vitamin A

2,000 milligrams vitamin C ($^{1}/_{2}$ teaspoon sodium ascorbate)

Taurine and other cat vitamins (about 5 days' worth—we want to add at least 250 mg taurine to this recipe amount)

50-milligram level B-complex (or 5–10 milligrams per day)

* These supplements are from Group III calcium supplements. See chapter 4 for more information.

Mix everything together in a large bowl. Serve raw if the cat will accept it. Otherwise, mix all but the vitamins together, bake about 20 minutes in a moderate oven, and then wait until it cools to mix in the vitamins. Your cat may have a poor appetite, so to some extent you will need to cater to him to keep him alive. Occasionally, substitute 1 to 3 teaspoons of liver for part of the meat. Be sure to provide plenty of fresh, pure water (filtered or bottled) at all times. Also encourage drinking by providing meat or fish broth (warm) once or twice a day.

Yield: Feed as much as your cat will eat. This makes about 5 to 6 days' food for the average cat.

Note: *If your cat isn't eating well, force-feed the vitamins separately. Follow the label directions for the cat vitamins and give 5 to 10 milligrams B-complex per day and 250 milligrams vitamin C ($^{1}/_{16}$ teaspoon sodium ascorbate) twice daily.*

Many cats with kidney disease will develop a state of low potassium levels in the body, which further complicates the situation and creates symptoms in its own right. If your cat does not respond adequately to the treatments suggested here (and below), consult your veterinarian about adding a potassium gluconate supplement to this diet.

Other therapeutic measures are to avoid cigarette smoke; chemicalized or chlorinated water (use filtered or bottled); highly processed, overcooked, spoiled, or commercial foods; stress; excessive heat, and unnecessary exposure to chemical products, car fumes, and polluted environments in general.

Vigorously brush the coat and skin regularly and give a weekly bath with a natural, mild, nondrying shampoo. Provide regular, mild outdoor exercise and exposure to fresh air and sun. Always allow easy access to a place for urination and defecation. Make lots of pure water available for drinking at all times and feed the daily rations as two meals instead of one (if that has been your practice).

Herbs and remedies that may strengthen your animal's kidney tissue are listed below. Pick one of them to try.

Herbal—Alfalfa (*Medicago sativa*): Using the tincture, 3 times daily give 1 or 2 drops to cats or small dogs (it can be diluted), 2 to 4 drops to medium dogs, and 4 to 6 drops to large dogs (see page 118). Continue until you see an improvement, then reduce to once a day or as needed. Alternatively, you may use alfalfa tablets, giving 1 to 4 twice a day (depending on the animal's size). Crush and mix with the food.

Herbal—Marsh mallow (*Althaea officinalis*): Prepare an infusion by adding 2 tablespoons of the flowers or leaves to 1 cup of boiling water. Let steep 5 minutes. Or make a decoction (which is more potent) by simmering 1 teaspoon of the root in a cup of boiling water for 20 to 30 minutes. Twice a day give ½ teaspoon to cats or small dogs, 1 teaspoon to medium dogs and 1 tablespoon to large dogs (see page 118). Try mixing it in the food. Continue for several weeks and then taper off to twice a week.

Homeopathic—*Nux vomica* (poison nut) 30C: Use Schedule 4, page 442. This remedy is useful as an occasional treatment for uremia. Often, it will help with the symptoms of toxicity, especially nausea, vomiting, and feeling generally ill.

Homeopathic—*Natrum muriaticum* (sodium chloride) 6C: This treatment will help with the body's use of water. It is indicated for the cat or dog that is very thirsty and prefers cool surfaces to lie on. Use Schedule 6(a), page 442.

Homeopathic—*Phosphorus* (the element) 6C: This is helpful to the cat or dog that has strong thirst for cold water and frequent vomiting after drinking or eating. Usually there is a decreased appetite with weight loss. Use Schedule 6(a), page 442.

Homeopathic—*Mercurius vivus* (quicksilver) 6C: The indicative condition is the development of ulcers in the mouth or on the tongue. Breath very foul, saliva increased, often sticky. These are symptoms of uremia and can be helped by using this remedy. To maintain improvement, the diet must be adjusted to reduce protein or it will recur. Use Homeopathic Schedule 4, page 442.

CRISIS THERAPY

A severe crisis in an animal with weak or failed kidneys is best handled by your veterinarian. Often the technique of intravenous fluid administration is critical to survival because anything given by mouth is immediately vomited. Your veterinarian may show you how to give daily fluid injections under the skin, which can help many cats to survive for additional months or years—often much longer than dogs survive with similar treatment.

An additional supportive treatment is that adapted from herbalist Juliette de Bairacli-Levy, who advises that you withhold all solid food until the crisis passes. Instead, give:

Cool parsley tea: Steep a tablespoon of fresh parsley in a cup of hot water for 20 minutes. Give 1 teaspoon to 2 tablespoons, 3 times a day.

Barley water: To make this, pour 3 cups of boiling water over a cup of whole barley. Cover and let steep overnight. In the morning strain and squeeze out the liquid through muslin or cloth. Add 2 teaspoons each of honey and pure lemon juice. Feed your animal ¼ to 2 cups of this liquid twice a day. (Make a bigger batch if necessary.)

Parsnip balls: Combine raw, grated parsnips (which help to detoxify the kidneys) with thick honey (an energy source). Roll into balls and give as desired. This combination is more likely to be accepted by dogs than cats—which are notoriously difficult to give anything unusual to by mouth.

Enemas: Make pure water available at all times. If your pet has trouble keeping fluids down, however, give 1 to 3 enemas per day until vomiting stops. For every 20 pounds of weight, make a solution combining ½ teaspoon sea salt, ½ teaspoon potassium chloride (a salt substitute available in many groceries), 1 teaspoon lemon juice, and 500 milligrams vitamin C, well-dissolved in a pint of lukewarm water. (See instructions for administration in chapter 15.) When an animal is dehydrated, it will retain the enema solution rather than discharging it, and this will help replenish the blood.

After the crisis stage, you can slowly return to using the usual food utilizing the maintenance program already described. Remember, the single most important thing is to give large volumes of fluids to rehydrate the tissues and to flush the kidneys. Without adequate fluid, treatment will not be successful. If vomiting is severe and continuous, use the suggestions under "Vomiting." Particularly, try the homeopathic remedy *Ipecac*, as described in that section.

LIVER PROBLEMS

The liver may be the most important organ of the body. It is involved in innumerable processes, including: the manufacture of blood proteins, fats, and the proteins responsible for blood clotting; storage of energy (as glycogen) for production of blood sugar as needed by the body; storage of the fat-soluble vitamins and iron; the detoxification of drugs, chemicals, and other unusable substances; the inactivation of hormones no longer needed, and the secretion of bile and other factors necessary for proper digestion. As if these tasks were not enough to keep it busy, the liver also must filter blood coming from the digestive tract to keep potentially harmful bacteria from reaching other parts of the body. It is the organ that prepares toxic material and waste products for subsequent elimination by the kidneys.

Therefore, as you can imagine, inflammation of the liver (hepatitis) and other disturbances of this vital organ are very serious conditions. Symptoms of liver trouble include nausea, vomiting, loss of appetite, jaundice (yellowing of the tissues, best observed in the whites of the eyes or inside the ears in animals), perhaps the passing of light-colored or "fatty"-looking bowel movements (from insufficient bile and poor digestion), and the swelling of the abdomen from fluid accumulation.

Liver malfunction is caused by many conditions. Viral infections or the swallowing of poisonous substances are factors, but in most cases, it's hard to tell just what initiated the problem.

TREATMENT

Because the liver is so central to the whole process of breaking down and using food,

treatment includes minimizing the work it must do by fasting or feeding small, frequent, easily digested meals. In the early, acute stage of liver inflammation, fasting is best, especially if a fever is present. Follow the directions for fasting given in chapter 15. Keep your dog or cat on a liquid diet for a few days until his or her temperature returns to normal or there is some improvement. During this period, give the following treatments.

Vitamin C: 500 to 2,000 milligrams four times a day, depending on size. This is most easily given as sodium ascorbate powder dissolved in a small amount of water. (¼ teaspoon is about 1,000 milligrams.)

One of the following remedies can also be helpful.

Homeopathic—*Belladonna* (deadly nightshade) 30C: This is most useful for the stage of fever, restless agitation, hot head, and dilated pupils, and is often the first remedy to use. Schedule 2, page 442.

Homeopathic—*Nux vomica* (poison nut) 6C: Use Schedule 6(a), page 442. If this does not help within a few days, try this next remedy:

Homeopathic—*Phosphorus* (the element) 6C: Use Schedule 6(a), page 442. These animals are usually thirsty, vomit easily, have diarrhea, or very narrow, hard stools.

As the animal improves and the symptoms subside, ease it onto a diet similar to that for kidney failure. You should, however, reduce the fat content by using lean meat and eliminating the added oil. Eggs are usually well-tolerated by the liver patient, as are grains. Feed small amounts at a time, dividing the day's ration into four servings, and warm the food to room temperature. Hold back on fats until the condition is normal. Then reintroduce them, starting in small amounts.

After a month or two of recovery, you can gradually and carefully move back to the basic recipes as outlined in chapter 4. During this time of healing, emphasize raw foods as much as possible (cottage cheese, eggs, meat, and finely grated vegetables). Some foods, of course, must be well-cooked for digestion (like grains and beans). Combine the foods only after the cooked ingredients have cooled. This precaution will provide optimal amounts of unaltered nutrients needed for the quickest possible recovery. If these foods are accepted, try including raw grated beets (about one to three tablespoons) every day as a liver stimulant. One to two tablespoons of fresh minced parsley is also useful.

During recovery, also continue the vitamin C. If, after some improvement, there is a relapse, go back to using the last remedy that was most beneficial. Usually the vitamin C can be discontinued after all symptoms are gone.

LYME DISEASE

This disease was first recognized (in people) in Europe in the early 1900s and has since been reported throughout Europe, Australia, Russia, China, Japan, and Africa. It has been called Lyme disease in this country since 1975, when it was first found to cause arthritis in children in Old Lyme, Connecticut. Considerable research revealed that the condition was caused by a spirochete (a microbe related to syphilis, though not spread by sexual contact) and transmitted by tick bites.

In people, Lyme disease causes a skin rash, tiredness, fever and chills, headache, backache, arthritis, and other symptoms. The situation is very different for animals, however. What I am going to say here you won't hear anywhere else (unless you have access to veterinary journals).

The short explanation is that this is not really a defined disease in dogs, like other infectious diseases (e.g., distemper or parvo). The long explanation will take some patience on your part. Let's start with some background.

How do we know that a germ causes a disease? Let's say that people start becoming sick with something new and we don't know what it is. If we check carefully and find some sort of bug in the blood—maybe that is what is causing it. So how do we know if that is right? After all, there are hundreds of bacteria, viruses, and fungi that normally live in and on our bodies and don't cause any disease at all. The obvious test is that we give the "new" bug to someone and see if they get sick—not only sick but with the same symptoms as seen before. Logical, right? This has always been the method of determining if a micro-organism is the cause of a disease. You will have to take my word for it that medical history is littered with supposed causes of disease that turned out to be quite harmless.

So, here is the story with Lyme disease in dogs. Though scientists have put the organism into dogs many, many times, they cannot reproduce the disease—they cannot cause Lyme disease by injecting the bug into dogs. Well, one way they can make dogs sick with some mild symptoms is to give them cortisone first (which suppresses the immune system) Not convincing? Not to scientists. The general conclusion is that dogs are indeed exposed via ticks, but they are naturally resistant to it and only those very few animals that have disturbed immune systems may show some mild symptoms. It seems that a fraction of dogs will have an excessive reaction, more like an allergy.

OK, I know this is not what your veterinarian told you and that there are all these dire warnings about Lyme disease and the need for antibiotics and how you should use the vaccine, right? So how do we reconcile this? I have treated many dogs over the years that have been diagnosed as having this disease and my experience also is that it is an insignificant disease. "Wait", you say, "Dogs actually do get symptoms and veterinarians say this is what it is. How can this be?"

What veterinarians are calling Lyme is dogs that develop signs of arthritis, painful joints, and lameness (usually). Sometimes there is a fever but just as often there is not. Because dogs in some parts of the country are frequently bitten by ticks that can leave red areas on the skin, the thinking goes like this: This dog is lame, there is evidence of a tick bite, so it must be Lyme disease. Usually antibiotics are prescribed and most dogs get better. What is not understood is these dogs will get better anyway. Studies of dogs with these symptoms indicate that 85 percent of them recover without any antibiotic treatment at all. The other 15 percent will continue to have symptoms whether or not antibiotics are used.

How often will tick-exposed dogs have any signs of illness? According to Dr. Meryl Littman of the University of Pennsylvania, even in areas of the country where the disease is most common and 90 percent of the dogs are exposed to the organism, only 4 percent show symptoms of lameness, decreased appetite, or fever. They appear to have a natural immunity.

So, what are we to make of all this? I think some insight is given by the observation of Dr. Shelly Epstein of Wilmington, Delaware. Since she greatly decreased the use of vaccines in her practice (to 3–4 total, using single, not combined vaccines), her practice sees only 1–2 dogs a year that have symptoms of Lyme disease. This is in contrast to her prior experience and that of the other practitioners in her area (who give 30–40 vaccinations to dogs) that are seeing a case of Lyme disease every week. It is likely that the overuse of vaccines is causing a disturbed immune reaction to the Lyme organism in animals that otherwise would have been resistant.

If you think your dog (or cat, though this

is rare) is showing these symptoms, it can be treated with homeopathy very easily. Here is what you can do.

TREATMENT

Homeopathic—*Aconitum napellus* (monkshood) 30C: This remedy is often suitable for the very earliest stage of illness with high fever, especially if it is accompanied by a restless anxiety. Use Schedule 1, page 441. This is the first treatment, in an early case. The remedies that follow are suitable for any remaining symptoms not cleared by this treatment.

Homeopathic—*Bryonia alba* (wild hops) 30C: Often dogs will lie very quietly, crying out at the slightest motion. Give this medicine to the dog that is reluctant to move because of the pain. Use Schedule 1, page 441.

Homeopathic—*Rhus toxicodendron* (poison ivy and poison oak) 30C: This is indicated for the dog that is stiff and sore, especially on first moving after lying for a while. As she moves around, however, the joints seem to limber up and the stiffness is not so noticeable. Use Schedule 1, page 441.

Homeopathic—*Pulsatilla* (windflower) 30C: Give this medicine to the dog that becomes submissive when ill and does not want to drink water. Use Schedule 1, page 441.

Homeopathic—*Mercurius vivus* (or *solubilis*) (the element mercury) 30C is helpful to the sick dog that has, along with the other symptoms, red and inflamed gums, bad breath, and a tendency to drool or salivate. Use Schedule 1, page 441.

Remember that any time there is an acute illness with fever, it is also helpful to fast your dog for several days (see chapter 15).

If the above treatments are not effective, it is very likely that what you are dealing with requires the skill of a homeopathically trained veterinarian.

VACCINATION

There are several vaccines on the market, and they are aggressively pushed by many veterinarians. Dr. Littman says that the dogs susceptible (the 4 percent that may show some symptoms) may not be protected by the vaccines that are available. In fact, there is concern that the vaccines may actually make the susceptible dog have a more severe disease if they are ever infected by a tick. My advice? Save your money.

MAD COW DISEASE

See the discussion in chapter 3. There is no way to detect it in dogs and cats and no treatment available at this time.

MANGE

See "Skin Parasites."

MITES

See "Ear Problems" and "Skin Parasites."

NEUTERING

See "Spaying and Neutering."

NOSE PROBLEMS

See "Foxtails" and "Upper Respiratory Infections."

OBESITY

See "Weight Problems."

PANCREATITIS

This condition, usually seen in overweight, middle-aged dogs, often first appears as a sudden, severe illness. Symptoms can include a complete loss of appetite, severe and frequent vomiting, diarrhea that may contain blood, reluctance to walk, weakness, and abdominal pain (crying and restlessness). The severity of the attack can vary from a mild, almost unnoticeable condition to a severe shock-like collapse that can end in death.

The problem centers in the digestive tract, with a focus in the pancreas. The underlying cause is not known, but I think it will soon be apparent that pancreatitis is another of the immune diseases (like hyperthyroidism in cats). As an immediate trigger, attacks can come on after overindulgence in rich or fatty foods, especially after a raid on a garbage can or compost pile. Frequent attacks of pancreatitis can finally result in a lack of insulin, leading to diabetes (see "Diabetes").

PREVENTION

Prevention consists partly of a properly balanced natural diet coupled with regular and adequate exercise. Exercise is important because it improves digestion and peristaltic movements of the intestinal tract, thus regularizing the bowels and keeping this part of the body preventively more healthy. It also keeps weight under control.

Do not overfeed your dog, because obesity is a predisposing factor to pancreatitis (no one knows why). Many people end up with fat dogs because they enjoy watching the animal eat heartily. For more information, see "Weight Problems."

Realize that this condition can also be chronic in nature, persisting in a low-grade form for months or years unless corrected. If you have a dog with a tendency toward pancreatitis, be especially careful about setting off an attack through a change of diet. I also advise using vaccines minimally in these animals because the immune system becomes much more active after vaccination, possibly precipitating an immune-mediated crisis.

TREATMENT

Treatment usually requires hospitalization, with fluid replacement therapy in the case of extreme vomiting and diarrhea. If the condition is mild but recurrent, the following measures should help to restore a balance of health.

Feed the basic natural diet and supplements (chapters 3 and 4), except minimize vegetable oils or butter, as well as other fatty foods that may irritate the pancreas. It's okay to use cod-liver oil for the vitamin A, but keep the amounts low or switch to vitamin A capsules. Be sure to use vitamin E to help prevent pancreatic scarring (100 to 400 IU, depending on size). For vegetables, emphasize corn (preferably raw) and raw grated cabbage, but include a variety of others as well. Avoid fruits.

Feed small, frequent meals instead of one large one. Offer all food at room temperature for best digestive action. Sometimes adding pancreatic enzymes to each meal will help as well, assisting the digestive process. They can be obtained in health food stores. Use the human products, giving ½ capsule to small dogs, up to 2 capsules for the larger dogs.

Use vitamin C and bioflavonoids regularly. Depending on the dog's size, give 250 to 1,000 milligrams of vitamin C three times a day, if possible. Sodium ascorbate powder may be better tolerated than ascorbic acid. (A teaspoon of sodium ascorbate powder has about 4,000 milligrams of C.) Give 25 to 50 milligrams of bioflavonoids (vitamin P) to enhance the action of the ascorbate.

Eliminate any food or supplement that seems to upset the digestive tract or aggravate the symptoms. Find a substitute form for any supplement you need to discontinue, for instance, a B complex instead of nutritional yeast.

In addition to these nutritional steps, try one of the following as a supportive treatment. To start treatment, work with one of these two remedies:

Homeopathic—*Nux vomica* (poison nut) 30C: Indicated for the dog that becomes very irritable, withdraws to another room (away from company), and is chilly. Use Homeopathic Schedule 2, page 442.

Homeopathic—*Belladonna* (deadly nightshade) 30C: Use when the problem has come on very suddenly, there is considerable fever, and the body feels hot to touch, and, the dog is very sensitive to sound and touch, with pupils dilated and evident excitability and agitation. Use Homeopathic Schedule 2, page 442.

If neither of these remedies proves satisfactory, then work with these that follow:

Homeopathic—*Iris versicolor* (blue flag) 6C: This remedy is particularly suited to the pancreas. It is very useful when the dog vomits repeatedly, with much drooling of saliva. Use Homeopathic Schedule 1, page 441.

Homeopathic—*Spongia tosta* (roasted sponge) 6C: Indicated if the pancreatitis is associated with coughing or breathing difficulties. Use Homeopathic Schedule 1, page 441.

Homeopathic—*Pulsatilla* (windflower) 30C: Very helpful if the dog shows no sign of thirst, seeks cool surfaces to lie on, and becomes clingy (wanting to be close all the time) and whiny. Use Homeopathic Schedule 2, page 442.

Herbal—Yarrow (*Achillea millefolium*): Use Herbal Schedule 1, page 441. Yarrow strengthens the pancreas and helps to control internal hemorrhages. It is indicated if there is dark, chocolate-colored, or black diarrhea (perhaps containing blood) that is foul-smelling.

Realize that after an attack is over, there is still susceptibility to further episodes. Be especially careful in this regard:

* Keep the diet simple and low in fat.
* Don't allow indulgences in junk food.
* Avoid vaccinations as much as possible.
* Keep the weight within normal limits.

PANLEUKOPENIA

See "Distemper, Chorea, and Feline Panleukopenia."

PARALYSIS

Causes of paralysis can range from accidents that damage the spine, to blood clots that form in brain arteries, to intervertebral disk disease ("slipped disk"), as well as many others. Here we will consider the two most common causes, which are intervertebral disk disease and spondylitis (a buildup of calcium on the spine from arthritis). To some extent we can regard these two conditions similarly because both are degenerative processes involving the spine.

In intervertebral disk disease, the fibrous capsule that holds the soft gelatinous material between the vertebrae in place breaks down, and the gel leaks out The apparent cause is a breakdown of the ligaments that keep this material in place. This puts pressure on the spinal cord. The condition is worst in breeds that have long backs in relation to their legs, such as dachshunds.

Spondylitis appears more often in large dogs like German shepherds. It involves a long-term inflammation of the vertebrae, which the body attempts to alleviate by immobilizing spinal movements with calcium deposits. Eventually, these deposits encroach on the nerves that branch out from the spinal cord, interfering with their functions. Symptoms are not obvious to the untrained eye. Be on the lookout for some rigidity of the back and some difficulty or pain on getting up. As it advances, a wasting away of the rear legs becomes evident, as well as difficulty using them on steps or slippery floors. Usually a diagnosis is made only after an x-ray is taken. Spondylitis is often associated with hip dysplasia, so also read about that topic.

PREVENTION

My opinion is that both intervertebral disk disease and spondylitis are expressions of the same problem—a deterioration of the spine brought on after years of poor nutrition, inadequate exercise, and stress. They are better prevented than treated. Your best insurance is to follow the natural diet recommendations in chapters 3 and 4 and the general care advice in chapter 7. Also, avoid selecting a breed that is prone to intervertebral disk disease (long-backed dogs) and breeds that are prone to hip dysplasia (such as German shepherds).

TREATMENT

Intervertebral disk problems, once they have developed, may be alleviated by this program.

Nutrition should be emphasized. Avoid commercial foods and treats, using only the natural diet and supplements advised in this book. Be sure to add 100 to 400 IU vitamin E (depending on your pet's size) and ¼ to 1 teaspoon lecithin granules to the daily ration. In addition, give 500 to 1,000 milligrams of vitamin C twice a day to strengthen the connective tissue involved and to counteract stress.

For specific treatment use:

Homeopathic—*Nux vomica* (poison nut) 30C: This is most effective for animals with recent pain in the back, muscle tightness or spasms along the lower back, and weakness or paralysis of the rear legs. Use Homeopathic Schedule 2, page 442. This remedy is appropriate for the more acute phase of the problem, but other medicines are needed for the underlying arthritis. This necessitates what is called constitutional treatment in homeopathy and is based on understanding the pattern of weakness over the lifetime of your animal. Work with a homeopathic veterinarian for this.

A paralyzed animal will benefit from massage of the back and legs and passive movement of the limbs to keep the muscles from shrinking away. If there is slight voluntary movement of the legs, exercise the animal by helping it to "swim" in a bathtub or pool. Support most of its weight with a towel or harness. Acupuncture and chiropractic have also been helpful for intervertebral disk problems.

Spondylitis, on the other hand, can be more difficult to treat once it has developed. The chance of improvement is much less for a dog already paralyzed than for one that is only weakened. A short fast (see chapter 15) may be appropriate in an early case, followed by the basic natural diet given in this book. The further instructions given under "Arthritis" will be very helpful.

Besides exercise and massage, use this remedy:

Homeopathic—*Belladonna* (deadly nightshade) 30C: Use Homeopathic Schedule 2 and note how much improvement follows. If there is a clear benefit from its use, wait one week and give one dose of *Calcarea carbonica* 30C remedy. Use this remedy only once, and do not use it unless Belladonna has helped. If it has not helped, give one dose of *Silicea* 30C instead, and allow it to work undisturbed at least a month before anything else is given.

For other treatment choices or to continue beyond this point, consult a homeopathic veterinarian for constitutional treatment. Acupuncture is also notably helpful for this condition.

POISONING

See "Handling Emergencies and Giving First Aid" on page 429.

PREGNANCY, BIRTH, AND CARE OF NEWBORNS

Also see "Reproductive Organ Problems."

The key to a successful and easy pregnancy and delivery is good nutrition. During gestation (63 to 65 days for cats, 58 to 63 days for dogs), tremendous demands are made on the mother's tissues to supply all the nutrients needed to build several new bodies. The general rule is that kittens or puppies come first. That is, they get whatever is available nutritionally, and the mother gets what's left. If she doesn't consume enough food to supply complete nutrition, her body provides whatever is lacking.

A female that is not adequately fed, or that is bred again and again, accumulates a nutritional deficiency that becomes greater with each pregnancy. Eventually, the mother will become diseased or the young will be weak and susceptible to disease—perhaps during their entire lives. The special recipes in chapter 5 for pregnant and nursing females and for young animals are designed to meet their special needs and prevent this nutritional depletion. Let's look at the two most common problems—eclampsia and dystocia (difficult delivery).

Eclampsia

Eclampsia is a severe disturbance that appears most often at the end of a pregnancy, right after birth, or during nursing. That's because it stems from calcium depletion. As new skeletons are formed or milk is produced, the calcium demand from the mother's body is great. Symptoms include loss of appetite, a high fever (sometimes dangerously so), rapid panting, and convulsions. During convulsions the muscles become

rigid, and the animal falls over with its head back. More typically, you may see a series of rapid contractions and relaxations of the muscles that looks like uncontrollable shaking.

Strenuous treatment is necessary, including intravenous injections of calcium by your veterinarian and ice baths (to bring down the temperature). Such treatment is usually successful, but the condition can recur if the young continue to nurse.

It is much better to prevent this problem in the first place with proper and bountiful nutrition, rather than to try to patch up the animal once it has occurred. In the event that your female already suffers from eclampsia, however, put her on the diet in chapter 5 that is appropriate for her state of pregnancy or lactation. Be sure to include all the ingredients, especially bone meal.

The treatment most likely to help during the crisis is:

Homeopathic—*Belladonna* (deadly nightshade) 30C: Give one pellet every 15 minutes until the symptoms are alleviated. Then use Schedule 1, page 441, until all is well. This treatment can be used whenever symptoms reappear.

Dystocia (Difficult Delivery)

Cats and dogs with normal anatomy rarely have problems giving birth, particularly if they are adequately fed during pregnancy. Lack of certain essential nutrients like calcium, however, may weaken the uterine muscles and cause weak or short contractions, a somewhat uncommon problem that has been increasing in incidence. In addition, certain fetal deformities can cause obstruction of the birth canal during labor.

The most severe birthing problems occur in dogs with an abnormal anatomy, usually from breeding trends in which the pelvis becomes too small for the size of the puppies. Other than the use of caesarean sections, little can be done about this problem except the obvious: Avoid breeding such animals and don't select them as pets (which creates a market for them).

Let's first review how delivery usually goes when all is normal. Two or three days before delivery, the mother may lose her appetite and show nesting behavior (carrying toys or other things to a particular area, tearing up paper to make a nest). There will be swelling of the vulva and a slight discharge. Twenty-four to 48 hours before birth, there will be a sudden drop in body temperature to below normal (usually below 101°F.; 38.3°C.), but this varies according to the individual and is best determined by checking the temperature twice a day for several days before.

The next thing is for labor to begin. Stage One is characterized by restlessness, panting, and shivering (perhaps also vomiting food once). This lasts 6 to 12 hours (but can be longer with the first birth). Stage Two is visible contractions, with delivery of the puppy. Some mothers will start this stage by wanting to go outside to urinate. They will lie on the side as contractions become stronger,

straining and licking the genitals. Some dogs will groan or even scream. Between contractions there is rapid panting. This stage lasts from 15 minutes to an hour.

Stage Three is the passing of the afterbirth(s), usually promptly eaten. It is important that all the afterbirths be passed, so each (one to a puppy) must be accounted for.

Problems can begin to occur at Stage Two, when contractions are not producing results. You will know that this is happening because straining goes on too long. If the mother labors more than four or five hours with the first puppy or three hours with subsequent puppies, then it has indeed been too long. In this case, use:

Homeopathic—*Pulsatilla* (windflower) 30C: Give one pellet and repeat in 30 minutes. As soon as labor proceeds, stop using the remedy, even if you've only given one or two doses. Remember that the mother will often naturally rest between deliveries, even napping for an hour or two. So don't rush things too much. If there is no delivery after two doses (one hour), then the remedy will not help. In which case, switch to:

Homeopathic—*Caulophyllum* (blue cohosh) 30C: Use same schedule as given above. One of these remedies is usually effective.

If a puppy or kitten is part way out and seems stuck (not immediately slipping out), pulling on it very gently may help. Hold the body, not the legs or head; note that any pressure more vigorous than an extremely gentle touch can cause damage to either the mother or the unborn. Get professional help if the baby has been trapped in the birth canal for more than a half hour (it will be dead by then). A caesarean section will probably be needed. This is a good time for your dog to be spayed, which will prevent this from happening again. Check with your veterinarian about this option.

If all goes well at home and the delivery is complete, use:

Homeopathic—*Arnica montana* (mountain daisy) 30C: Use Homeopathic Schedule 2, page 442. This is most helpful to strengthen the mother and prevent infection.

If an afterbirth remains inside, serious problems can result. If one is retained and there is fever or infection, use the following treatment along with what your veterinarian prescribes.

Homeopathic—*Secale cornutum* (ergot) 30C: Use Homeopathic Schedule 2, page 442. This remedy will often prevent or successfully treat infection following a retained afterbirth and result in the afterbirth being discharged.

CARE OF THE NEWBORN

Fortunately for you, the mother will generally do everything needed to care for the newborn, and it's best not to interfere unless there's a problem. Right after birth she will clean the little ones, and, as long as necessary, she will also lick up all the urine and feces voided by her growing young. This is nature's way of keeping a clean nest. It's convenient for you, but if the infants should develop diarrhea, you may miss the evidence.

Diarrhea is one of the more common problems at this stage of life, and it's usually caused by consuming too much milk (sometimes a problem with hand-raised puppies or kittens), infection in the mother's uterus or mammary glands (check if her temperature is above 102°F.; 38.9°C.), or giving antibiotics to the mother (they can get into the milk).

A puppy or kitten with diarrhea will get cold and dehydrated (the skin will be wrinkled and look too big for the body). It may crawl away from the nest and usually cries, even when returned to the mother.

If the problem is with the mother's milk, you'll need to feed the babies by hand with a pet nurser bottle sold at pet stores. Use the nursing formulas in chapter 5 or a commercial kitten or puppy formula. Dilute the formula half and half with pure water until the diarrhea is under control. The problem should correct itself after a few feedings. If not, try one of these two methods.

1. Use a mixture consisting of half formula (regular strength) and half warm chamomile tea (one teaspoon herb to a cup of boiling water). Feed on a regular schedule until the problem is controlled, usually by two or three feedings.

2. Use the half formula/half water mixture, but add to it a crushed pellet of the homeopathic preparation *Podophyllum* (May apple) 6C. Mix well. One such therapeutic feeding should be enough, but

repeat this formula every four hours if necessary.

Examine the mother's breasts to see if there are hard lumps, hot areas, or painful places (on pressure). If so, there may be an infection (mastitis) that will need treatment before the milk is safe for the puppies (see "Reproductive Organ Problems").

After the diarrhea is under control and if there is no problem with the mother, you can return the puppy or kitten to the nest, but be watchful in case the diarrhea returns.

If, as sometimes happens, the mother does not care for the young—letting them cry and avoiding contact and not nursing— you have a potentially serious problem, as the young ones cannot go long without eating. It is possible that there is something physically wrong with the mother, like an infection or retained puppy or kitten, so you will need to have your veterinarian check out this possibility. If the problem is emotional, however, then here is a treatment that is quite helpful.

Homeopathic—*Sepia* (cuttlefish ink) 30C: Use Homeopathic Schedule 2, page 442. If the mother does not accept the young within a few hours, then the puppies or kittens will have to be raised with a bottle. See chapter 5 for guidance on this.

RABIES

Rabies is a serious disease that affects many different types of animals, including human beings. Once the clinical signs develop, it is usually fatal. These symptoms often include very aggressive behavior and biting, which is how the disease gets spread (via saliva). Even if untreated, however, many people or pets bitten by a rabid animal do not develop the disease. The hitch is that once the condition develops, there is no orthodox treatment to save the patient. (Just yesterday I heard of the amazing case of a young girl with rabies saved by giving her an anesthetic that saved her brain until the immune system could catch up. I have also heard occasional reports of recovery by a variety of alternative methods, including homeopathy—fortunately, I have never treated it myself.)

One of the most exciting and promising new treatments is the use of vitamin C. It sounds unbelievable, but as far back as 20 years ago research studies were finding that vitamin C injections into guinea pigs infected with rabies decreased the death rate by 50 percent. Considering how few treatments are available for rabies, this is a dramatic finding. One can only hope that such research continues.

Because of its well-known fatality rate, however, the public is justly very afraid of this disease. For that reason, local governments have adopted precautions, including a legal requirement for a periodic rabies vaccination for dogs (cats are still optional in most states, but not all).

Most of the danger to humans is not actually from dogs and cats, but from wild animals such as skunks and raccoons that are captured for sale and/or adopted as pets.

Unfortunately, rabies vaccines developed for dogs and cats may not be completely safe or effective in these species. (For example, it is not recommended that wolf hybrids be vaccinated with rabies vaccine because of the risk of infection.) Since the chance of getting rabies from wild animals is so high—in addition to the ethical and ecological considerations of wild-animal adoption—it is not wise to keep them as pets. (See chapter 11 for ways to protect yourself from the bite of a dog and what to do if you have been bitten.)

RADIATION TOXICITY

The most common sources of radiation exposure for the average animal are diagnostic x-rays and radiation therapy (I do not recommend the latter). Other possibilities are less obvious—such as leakage from a nuclear power plant or storage area. Sometimes it is the water. Strange to say, there are some parts of the country where drinking water is contaminated with radiation leaking out of storage containers. (Hanford Nuclear Site in Washington near where I live has had several reported leaks over the years, and since it is next to the Columbia River, these leaks end up in the drinking water for Portland, Oregon.)

In any case, the body must repair a lot of cellular damage using cell functions that also may be affected by the exposure. Fortunately, there are ways to enhance this healing process. Use them after any known or suspected radiation exposure. (If there is leakage from a power plant or other atmospheric leakage, it would be best to keep your animal and yourself indoors for a while.)

Nutrition is the main aid. Emphasize rolled oats as your choice of grains for several weeks. It helps counteract nausea and other side effects. Be sure to include the normal supplements of nutritional yeast, cold-pressed unsaturated vegetable oil (for vitamin F), and kelp (contains alginate, which helps to remove strontium 90 from the body and to block absorption of radioactive iodine). In addition, give rutin (bioflavonoids), which has reduced the death rate in irradiated animals by 800 percent; vitamin C, which works with rutin to strengthen the circulatory system and counteract stress; and pantothenic acid, which helps to prevent radiation injuries and has increased the survival rate in irradiated animals by 200 percent. Depending on size, give daily: 100 to 400 milligrams rutin, 250 to 2,000 milligrams vitamin C, and 5 to 20 milligrams pantothenic acid.

If your animal is more than mildly affected by radiation and needs extensive treatment, a trained homeopath can provide an individualized prescription that may be of great help.

REPRODUCTIVE ORGAN PROBLEMS

The two most common reproductive problems affect female animals—pyometra and metritis. In both cases the uterus (womb) is the seat of the disorder, and prompt treatment is needed before the condition progresses too far. We'll look at each of these, and then at mastitis (mammary gland infection).

Pyometra

Coming on slowly over weeks or months, pyometra first appears as irregular heat periods and a discharge of reddish mucus from the vagina between heats. If unrecognized and untreated, it progresses to the point of severe depression, loss of appetite, vomiting, diarrhea, discolored vaginal discharge (not always present), excessive water consumption, and excessive urination. The large water intake mimics kidney failure, but the other symptoms help you tell the difference, particularly if there is a vaginal discharge and the animal is an unspayed dog or cat several years old that had many heats without being bred. A probable secondary cause is a high-hormone diet (from glandular meats or meat containing hormones used to fatten cattle). Concentrated in meat meal and other commercial pet food, hormones may predispose the uterus to malfunction.

Prevention, therefore, is simple—the spay operation for the young female.

Treatment

Dogs (and sometimes cats) with pyometra can suddenly develop a crisis that may require surgical removal of the uterus, which often has become quite large and distended with fluid. The process is much more serious and difficult yet basically the same as the spay operation.

Those animals not so severely affected may be helped by:

Homeopathic—*Pulsatilla* (windflower) 30C: Use Homeopathic Schedule 2, page 442. This remedy is best for the animal that is not very thirsty (which is unusual) and wants to be comforted (petted or held). If there is a vaginal discharge, it is usually thick and yellowish or greenish.

Homeopathic—*Sepia* (cuttlefish ink) 30C: Use Homeopathic Schedule 2, page 442. If there has been no improvement within 5 days of completing the *Pulsatilla* treatment above, then use this remedy. It is often sufficient.

Metritis

Right after giving birth and occasionally right after breeding, the uterus is susceptible to bacterial infection. Should infection occur, symptoms can be severe. They include fever, depression, not caring for the young, and a foul-smelling vaginal discharge.

Normal vaginal discharge following an uncomplicated delivery is dark green to brown and odorless. If all the young and all the afterbirths have come out properly, within 12 hours it becomes more like clear mucus (though possibly tinged with blood). But if a dark green to reddish-brown, thick and unusually foul-smelling discharge continues for 12 to 24 hours after the delivery, the uterus is probably infected.

TREATMENT

Once metritis has developed, it can become severe, so you should seek professional help. However, these remedies may also help.

Homeopathic—*Aconitum napellus* (monkshood) 30C: Use Homeopathic Schedule 2, page 442. This remedy is indicated for the animal that has a fever and is acting very frightened or anxious. It will startle easily and be very agitated.

Homeopathic—*Belladonna* (deadly nightshade) 30C: Use Homeopathic Schedule 2, page 442. This remedy is an alternative to Aconitum and is needed by the animal that has a fever and feels hot (especially the head) and has dilated pupils. Sometimes there is also an excitability similar to delirium, with a tendency to bite or act aggressively.

See the section on "Pregnancy, Birth, and Care of Newborns" for information on infection from retained afterbirths.

Mastitis

The mammary glands are most susceptible to infection when they are actively secreting milk. An infected breast will be hard, sensitive, painful, and discolored (reddish-purple). There may be abscesses and drainage as well. Your veterinarian will usually prescribe antibiotics. Here are some of the successful homeopathic treatments I have used. Use Homeopathic Schedule 2, page 442, for all of these.

Homeopathic—*Aconitum napellus* (monkshood) 30C: For the very first signs of infection, with fever, restlessness, and anxiety.

Homeopathic—*Belladonna* (deadly nightshade) 30C: For the dog with fever, dilated pupils, and excitability.

Homeopathic—*Phytolacca* (poke root) 30C: For mastitis where the breast is very hard to the touch and extremely painful.

Homeopathic—*Lachesis muta* (bushmaster snake venom) 30C: Use when a left breast is affected, especially if the skin over the area has turned bluish or black.

Homeopathic—*Pulsatilla* (windflower) 30C: For the dog that is whining, shows no sign of thirst, and wants comfort.

RINGWORM

See "Skin Parasites."

SINUSITIS

See "Upper Respiratory Infections."

SKIN PARASITES

See "Ear Problems" for a discussion of ear mites.

External parasites (such as ticks and fleas) seem to be most attracted to animals in poor health. I have seen many pets with fleas on the outside, worms on the inside, and some other problem like a chronic skin disease. I've also observed that when an animal is placed on my natural diet and my other recommended lifestyle changes are made, the number of fleas and other parasites often decrease markedly. They don't completely disappear, but they no longer constitute a problem. Other measures of control, if needed, are then much easier and more effective.

When I'm trying to evaluate an animal's overall health, I find it useful to judge the seriousness of any skin parasites that may be present. From least serious to most serious, I rank them in this order: ticks, fleas, lice, and, finally, mange mites or ringworm. By this scale I consider a cat with lice to be more seriously ill than one with fleas and a dog with mange worse off than one with ticks, and so on.

Let's discuss each of these parasites in turn and consider ways to control them without poisonous chemicals. You must realize, however, that by themselves, neither these suggested measures nor chemical insecticides are effective in the long run. The best results occur when an animal is on a natural diet, lives in a good environment, gets enough sunlight, and is exercised and groomed regularly, as discussed elsewhere in the book.

Ticks

Ticks are not permanent residents. Rather, they attach themselves, suck some blood, and later fall off to lay eggs. The young ticks that hatch out crawl up to the ends of branches and grasses and patiently wait (for weeks, if necessary) for something warm-blooded and good tasting to come along and brush against the vegetation. Then they drop on and find a nice, cozy place to attach.

PREVENTION

Groom your pet thoroughly before you let it run in an area likely to contain ticks, such as woods or fields. Remove loose hair and mats so access to the skin is easier, and dust the coat with an herbal flea repellent. (Commercial formulas containing eucalyptus powder are particularly useful.) Work the repellent through the hair and into the skin.

TREATMENT

When you return home after the adventure, check for any stalwart ticks that may have made it aboard your pet despite precautions. A fine-toothed flea comb may help to locate them or even capture any that are not yet attached. This also is a good time to remove foxtails (see "Foxtails"). Look especially closely around the neck and head and under the ears.

If you find a tick already attached, remove it like this: With the nails of your thumb and forefinger (or a pair of tweezers—some are now available just for this purpose), reach around the tick and grasp it as close to the skin as possible; don't worry, it won't bite! You want to remove the whole thing, not just pull off the tick's body and leave the head still embedded. Use a slow, steady pull (10 to 20 seconds) and, with a slight twist, pull out the little bugger—head, body, and all. You will have to pull strongly but not quickly. Look closely to see if you got the tick's tiny head; it will probably have a little shred of tissue still attached to it. Wash your hands when you are done with removal.

If the head is left behind despite your care, the area may fester for a while, much like a splinter under the skin. But this is minor and can be treated with the herbs echinacea or calendula as described under "Abscesses."

Sometimes small ticks crawl down inside the ear. If your dog is shaking its head a lot after a trip through tick land, have your veterinarian look down the ear canal with an instrument to check for this or for a possible foxtail.

What if all natural methods fail? At this time I have no other options to offer. Minor tick infestations can be handled with the methods I describe, but horrendous attacks are overwhelming. My clients and I have tried numerous methods that have not worked. So if you are dealing with hundreds or thousands of ticks (I am not exaggerating), you will have to turn to chemical treatment to control them.

Fleas

Ah! The bane of dog and cat alike. Once again, I have found that a healthy lifestyle is the best defense. Following are some additional specific measures that can also help.

❖ Add plenty of nutritional yeast and garlic to the daily ration. Use anywhere from one teaspoon to two tablespoons of yeast (depending on your pet's size) to each meal.

❖ Mix fresh garlic, ¼ to 1 raw clove, grated or minced, into each feeding.

❖ Wash the skin daily, if necessary, with a lemon rinse (see chapter 7). This makes it less attractive to fleas.

❖ Have your carpets treated with a borax-like powder that dramatically reduces flea populations (see chapter 7).

If in spite of all this commendable effort, your animal still has a serious problem with fleas (not just a few but dozens), check for roundworms and tapeworms (which can be carried by fleas) that may be sapping your pet of energy (see "Worms"). Also, try a specific homeopathic remedy to help strengthen the body so that it isn't so attractive to fleas. One that usually works best is:

Homeopathic—*Sulphur* (the element) 30C: Use Homeopathic Schedule 4, page 442. This is the treatment to try first; however, you must still continue all the flea-control measures suggested above. The remedy will only make your pet better able to resist flea infestation; it will not kill fleas directly. If after a month this has not improved the situation, give next:

Homeopathic—*Calcarea carbonica* 30C (for cats) and *Silicea* 30C (for dogs): Use Homeopathic Schedule 4, page 442.

A note about flea collars: They don't work. They are toxic. Some cats even hang themselves on them or get the collars caught between their jaws, causing serious damage. Others get permanent hair loss around the neck from allergic reactions, particularly when the collar is too tight.

Chemical insecticides in shampoos, soaps, powders, and sprays are also dangerous, as discussed in chapter 7. Notice the label warnings about wearing gloves or avoiding contact with your skin and so forth. How can it be so dangerous for you and yet safe for your pet? Think about it.

Lice

These little varmints are rather uncommon, but occasionally infest a run-down dog or cat. You have to look very carefully to see them on the skin or to see their eggs, which are attached to the animal hairs. Lice are slightly smaller than fleas and a lighter color—more tan or beige, rather than dark brown. Also, they don't jump like fleas. Fortunately, dog and cat lice do not infest people.

Treatment starts with frequent, preferably daily, use of a good shampoo containing d-limonene (for dogs only—a natural insecticide extracted from citrus). Leave the lather on for ten minutes before rinsing. Then follow with the lemon rinse described in chapter 7. The eggs are not killed by this, only the adults. The eggs continue to hatch out over a period of time, so continued baths are necessary until all the eggs are gone.

If you prefer not to use an insecticide, the lemon rinse recipe in chapter 7 might work (though I have no experience using it this way).

The most difficult part of lice control is getting the nits (the eggs attached to the hairs) off. They are glued to individual hairs and, short of cutting all the hairs off, you have to in some way remove them. The least toxic, though messy, way to do it is to apply mayonnaise and work it carefully into the hairs, then wash it out. Whew!

What else to do? Without delay, build up the animal's health with a natural diet. Start right off with some home-prepared food and emphasize nutritional yeast and garlic as previously prescribed for fleas.

Use the same basic steps outlined in the flea program (including grooming) to eliminate the young lice as they hatch. Building up your pet's health will make its skin less desirable to lice.

Homeopathic—*Sulphur* (the element) 30C: Usually helps raise resistance in general and parasites in particular. Use Homeopathic Schedule 4, page 442.

Note: We are used to quick results like those we get with chemicals that kill the lice almost immediately. They will not do anything for the animal's run-down health, however, which engendered the problem in the first place. Indeed, the toxic effect may weaken the animal even further. To work with nature is to be patient.

Mange

The most common form of mange is demodectic mange, which is caused by a microscopic mite that lives in hair follicles. The other type is called sarcoptic mange, caused by a scabies mite that burrows into the skin, making pets and people itch (see chapter 11).

Demodectic mange occurs most often in dogs (though it is also seen in rare instances in cats). It usually appears first as a small, hairless patch near the eye or chin. It doesn't itch much and may pass unnoticed. The mite associated with it is very widespread and is actually found on most healthy dogs and also on peoples' faces (around the eyebrows and nose) without any sign of its presence.

Demodectic mange causes a minor problem for some young dogs, but usually clears up spontaneously without treatment by the age of 12 to 14 months. In a small percentage of those affected, however, the mite continues to spread. Eventually, it can cover much of the body and result in hair loss and skin irritation and thickening. Bacteria (staph) can also get established, causing further complications such as "pimples" and a pustular discharge, particularly around the feet. This form of the disease is called generalized demodectic mange.

Animals that have generalized mange are susceptible to other serious illnesses and must be treated very carefully for their health to be restored. It is also very important that they not be vaccinated, as their immune system cannot react properly to the vaccine and only becomes more disordered.

TREATMENT

It is helpful to understand that problems with this parasite depend on a weak immune system, and this is what must be addressed. Unfortunately what is almost always done is the worst possible thing. The orthodox treatment is harsh, poisonous, and generally futile. (Mild cases clear up on their own anyway.) The hair is clipped off the whole animal. Then strong insecticides are "painted" on the skin or the dog is completely immersed in them. They are sometimes so toxic that only a part of the body can be done at a time. Unfortunately, antitoxic nutrition or vitamin supplements are seldom recommended, so the dog's underlying health goes from bad to worse. Even those dogs that apparently recover after weeks or months of treatment can have recurrences, or another, more serious, "unrelated" problem will develop. Cortisone-type drugs should not be used under any circumstances. They depress the immune system further and, therefore, just about guarantee nonrecovery (in the true sense) by any method.

Instead, I have had good results using just nutrition and homeopathic remedies, though treatment must be individualized and requires close attention to progress. Here are some general guidelines for a natural approach.

Fast the dog (if its weight and health are good) for five to seven days, as outlined in chapter 15. Afterwards, use the natural diet described in Chapters 3 and 4. Also add zinc (feed ground pumpkin seeds or give a tablet of chelated zinc—10 to 30 milligrams, depending on size), vitamin C (250 to 1,000 milligrams of ascorbate twice a day), and lecithin (½ to 3 teaspoons a day). Vitamin E is especially helpful in restoring immune capacity. Use larger doses twice a day, giving 400 IU to small dogs, 800 IU to medium-sized dogs, up to 1,600 IU for larger dogs. All of these supplements are very helpful to the functions of the immune system.

Rub fresh lemon juice on the affected spot every day, or use the lemon rinse recipe in chapter 7.

A homeopathic preparation that suits many cases of mange (either demodectic or sarcoptic) is:

Homeopathic—*Sulphur* (the element) 6C: Use Homeopathic Schedule 6(b), page 442. When the condition is obviously clearing, use the sulphur less frequently on a tapering-off program.

The dog with a staph infection of the skin occurring along with the mange will benefit from the use of:

Herbal—Purple cone flower (*Echinacea angustifolia*): Use Herbal Schedule 1, page 438, for internal treatment and Herbal Schedule 4, page 439, for treatment of the skin (both at the same time). You can use both this and the homeopathic *Sulphur* treatment if necessary, giving the *Sulphur* about 10 minutes before the echinacea dose.

The dog or cat with sarcoptic mange (more irritating than other kinds of mange) responds best to this treatment.

Herbal—Lavender (*Lavendula vera* or *L. officinalis*): Paint on oil of lavender (the pure oil diluted 1:10 with almond oil, or an already prepared formula that contains oil of lavender) once a day until the hair begins to grow back.

Ringworm

Though this disease sounds like it's caused by some kind of curly worm, it is actually the result of a fungus that's similar to athlete's foot. The growth starts at a central point and spreads out in a ring shape, much like an expanding ripple forms around a stone tossed in a pond. As the fungus grows in the skin cells and hair, the skin may become irritated, thickened, and reddened, and the hairs may break off and leave a coarse stubble behind.

In cats, which are more commonly affected, the condition often looks like circular gray patches of broken, short, thin hair, without much evidence of itching or irritation. Ringworm is contagious to people (especially children) and other animals; see the precautions in chapter 11. Like mange, widespread ringworm indicates the animal's health is not up to snuff, as it usually is the stressed, sick, or weakened ones that get severe infestations. Like generalized mange, ringworm that covers most of the body is a very serious problem indicating a severely compromised immune system.

TREATMENT

Nutrition: Start with a fast of two or three days (see chapter 15); then follow with the basic natural diet program in this book. Also add 5 to 20 milligrams of zinc chelate and ½ to 2 teaspoons of granular lecithin to the food (depending on body size). Essential fatty acids are very important for the health of skin and hair. If possible, add ¼ to 1 teaspoon of cod-liver oil (depending on the animal's size) to the food once a day.

Direct treatment: First, clip the hair around the bare spot and about ½ inch beyond it, being careful not to injure the skin. If you clip the hair, ringworm is less likely to spread and the topical treatment is easier to apply. Burn or carefully dispose of the infected hair that you remove, as it is contagious on contact. (In order to catch loose hairs, always be sure to vacuum carefully and frequently if you have a pet with ringworm. Also wash bedding and utensils often with hot water and soap.) Be sure to wash your hands.

Treating the sore spot will speed healing and help protect others from getting ringworm. Choose one of the following two herbs plus the homeopathic remedy.

Herbal—Plantain (*Plantago major*): Make a decoction of the whole plant by putting about ¼ cup of the plant (a common weed) per every cup of spring or distilled water into a glass or enameled pot. Boil about 5 minutes, then let the brew steep 3 minutes, covered. Strain and cool. Massage onto the skin once or twice a day until the condition clears.

Herbal—Goldenseal (*Hydrastis canadensis*): Make a strong infusion by adding 1 rounded teaspoon of the powdered rootstock to a cup of boiling water. Let stand till cold. Then carefully pour off the clear fluid and massage it onto the skin once or twice a day.

Homeopathic—*Sulphur* 6C: Use Homeopathic Schedule 6(a) on page 442.

SKIN PROBLEMS

Mange and ringworm are discussed under "Skin Parasites."

The skin gets dumped on from two sides. The rest of the body uses it to eliminate toxic material, especially if the kidneys aren't able to handle the job; at the same time, environmental pollutants or applied chemical products assault it from the outside. One thing is for sure—skin troubles are the number one problem in dogs and cats.

On the positive side, if your animal's only health problem is a skin disorder, consider yourself lucky. It's much worse if a surface condition (such as a skin problem) has been suppressed with repeated drug use; a more serious condition would be likelier to arise in that case. If a skin condition is the only problem your pet has, you can help prevent deeper problems by addressing it in a more curative manner. (The problem of suppression is discussed in chapter 14.)

The symptoms of skin disorder are among the easiest to detect. They usually include one or more of the following: very dry skin; flakiness or white scales resembling dandruff; large brown flakes, redness and irritation; itching (ranging from slight to so severe that blood is drawn); greasy hair and a foul odor to the skin and its secretions (which many people mistake as normal, or even as a pleasant "doggy odor"); pimples and blisters that form between the toes and discharge blood and pus; brown, black, or gray skin discoloration; formation of scabs or crusts, and hair loss. I also include chronic inflammation inside the ear canal (and under the ear flap), anal gland problems, and underactive (hypoactive) thyroid glands as related to skin disease.

Modern medicine tends to divide these many symptoms and regard them as separate diseases. I think this only confuses the picture, so that we don't perceive the problem as a whole. From a wider view, these symptoms appear as one basic problem that manifests a little differently in individual animals depending on heredity, environment, nutrition, parasites, and so on. Thus, one dog may have severely inflamed, moist, itchy areas ("hot spots") near the base of its tail, while another may have thick, itchy skin along its back, with greasy, smelly secretions—but they are really the same health problem.

What are the causes of this overall disorder?

❖ Toxicity—probably most of it from poor-quality food and some of it from other sources, like environmental pollutants and deliberately applied pest control chemicals.

❖ Vaccinations—inducing immune disorders in susceptible animals.

❖ Suppressed disease—remains of an inadequately treated condition that never was cured and that may periodically discharge through the skin.

❖ Psychological factors—boredom, frustration, anger, and irritability. As I see it, however, these are nearly always secondary issues that simply aggravate an already-existing problem.

It is possible to alleviate or even eliminate skin problems simply through fasting, proper nutrition, and the total health plan suggested in this book. It is surprising how much improvement can occur by these measures alone.

The homeopathic remedies listed below can also provide a real boost to healing. However, severe cases often require individualized treatment beyond the scope of this discussion; seek out a veterinarian who is skillful in the use of homeopathy, acupuncture, or other alternative therapies. You can find veterinarians trained in the use of homeopathy on my Web site, www.drpitcairn.com.

The most difficult conditions to treat are those previously dosed with lots of cortisone or its synthetic forms (azium, depo, flucort, prednisone, or prednisolone). Corticosteroids effectively suppress symptoms like inflammation and itching, but are in no sense curative. You may not know if your animal has received cortisone, because your veterinarian may have used terms like anti-itch shots or flea allergy pills. They usually look like clear or milky-white injections or little pink or white tablets. If you have good communication with your veterinarian, ask if he or she is giving your pet steroids. Generally, a natural approach will not work well if you also continue cortisone therapy.

Another typical treatment is a series of allergy desensitization injections with solutions made from the common flea or other suspected allergens. Sometimes they help, but often as not the relief is partial and not as satisfactory as eliminating the problem entirely.

TREATMENT

For an animal with acutely inflamed, irritated skin ("hot spots") that is otherwise in good condition, start with a fast. Use the directions in Chapter 15, breaking the fast after five to seven days for a dog and after three to five days for a cat. This fast mimics natural conditions in which wild predators' bodies have a chance to clean out between hunts. It also removes the demand on the system to both digest food and deal with the disorder at the same time.

Afterward, carefully introduce natural foods, as described in chapters 3 and 4. This healthier diet will supply needed nutrients and help to rebuild damaged tissue. Be sure all your ingredients are fresh and of high quality. Emphasize raw foods as much as possible.

The standard supplements in our diet are all helpful for skin problems, but the following will be especially useful. Be sure to include nutritional yeast and granular lecithin (both found in the Healthy Powder, page 53), cod-liver oil, cold-pressed unsaturated vegetable oil (or oil derived from fish, especially for cats), and vitamin E (or wheat-germ capsules). It would also be wise to include 5 to 20 milligrams daily of chelated zinc. In addition, vitamin C is very helpful—give 500 to 2,000 milligrams a day, depending on your dog's size (see page 118).

It helps to clip away the hair on severely inflamed areas and give a bath with nonirritating soap (not a medicated flea soap; use a natural organic soap as described in chapter 7). After drying the skin, apply a poultice or wash the area frequently with a preparation of black or green tea. It supplies tannic acid, which helps to dry up the moist places. Two to three times a day, or as needed, you also can smear on some vitamin E oil or fresh aloe vera gel (from the living plant or in a liquid preparation found in health food stores).

These homeopathic remedies are helpful for the time when symptoms flare up. (Other medicines are required to completely cure the tendency.)

Homeopathic—*Rhus toxicodendron* (poison ivy, poison oak) 6C: Use Homeopathic Schedule 2 on page 442. Suitable as a temporary medicine when itching flares up and is very intense. There tends to be swelling of the skin and relief from applying warm compresses.

Homeopathic—*Graphites* (a form of carbon) 6C: Use Homeopathic Schedule 2 on page 442. This remedy is indicated when the "hot spots" ooze a sticky, thick discharge, about the consistency of honey.

Homeopathic—*Mercurius vivus* (or *solubilis*) (mercury, quicksilver) 6C: Use Homeopathic Schedule 2 on page 442. Use this one if there's a pus-like yellowish or greenish discharge. Also, the hair will tend to fall out around the eruptions, leaving raw, bleeding areas. The condition is usually worse in hot weather or in very warm living quarters. Frequently these animals will have red gums, problems with the teeth, and very bad smelling breath.

Homeopathic—*Arsenicum album* 6C: This remedy suits dogs with skin eruptions that cause a great deal of restlessness and discomfort. They seem to be driven almost insane—constantly chewing, licking, and scratching. The skin lesions are very red and dry with loss of hair and an "eating away" of the skin, leaving angry red sores. Especially indicated if the dog becomes very thirsty and chilly as well. Use Homeopathic Schedule 2 on page 442.

For the animal with a long-term, low-grade condition of itchy, greasy, or dry and scaly skin (who may also have an underactive thyroid), start by fasting it one day every week, offering only broth (see chapter 15). The rest of the time feed only natural foods and supplements. It's important that you don't give any commercial foods or supplements with questionable ingredients (see chapter 2), because part of your pet's problem may be a hypersensitivity or allergy to artificial additives or processed ingredients. For example, many animals will have allergic reactions to cooked, but not raw, meat.

If the skin is greasy and foul-smelling, bathe your pet as often as once a week, as described in chapter 7. If the skin is dry, bathe less often. Also, be sure to control fleas (see "Skin Parasites"), using the lemon rinse described in chapter 7.

Constipation or sluggish bowels may also be contributing to the problem. If they are, address that first. Use one of the following two remedies.

Herbal—Garlic (*Allium sativum*): Give daily ¼ to 1 whole clove (fresh grated or minced) or 1 to 3 small garlic capsules. You can continue giving garlic indefinitely, as it also discourages fleas.

Homeopathic—*Nux vomica* 6C: Give 1 pellet before each meal, as needed, until bowels are regular (see also "Constipation"). If it is going to help, you will notice improvement within a few days.

If constipation or "hot spots" are not the present problem, then try working with one of these treatments.

Homeopathic—*Sulphur* (the element) 6C: Use Homeopathic Schedule 6(a) on page 442. This remedy is very helpful for the average case of dry, itchy skin, especially if your dog tends to be thin, "lazy," and not very clean, with red-looking eyes, nose, or lips. These animals generally don't like a lot of heat, but sometimes will seek out a warm stove in cooler weather.

Homeopathic—*Pulsatilla* 6C: Use Homeopathic Schedule 6(a) on page 442. Those animals needing this medicine will be easy-going, good natured, and affectionate. Their symptoms tend to be worse when eating rich or fatty food, and it is noticed that they rarely drink water. Often there is a preference for lying on cool surfaces as well.

Homeopathic—*Graphites* (a form of carbon) 6C: Use Homeopathic Schedule 6(a) on page 442. These dogs tend to be overweight, constipated, and easily overheated. Eruptions ooze sticky fluid. The skin is easily inflamed, even by slight injuries like scratches, and it does not heal easily. The ears can be plagued with irritation, a bad smell, and waxy discharge.

Homeopathic—*Thuya* (or *Thuja*) *occidentalis* (arborvitae) 30C: Use Homeopathic Schedule 4 on page 442. This remedy is an antidote to illness following vaccinations. Many of the animals I treat developed their skin problems within a few weeks after being vaccinated. I find that giving this remedy occasionally during treatment really helps such dogs recover. Another time to consider Thuya (or Thuja) is when other medicines have not done much good. If so, giving Thuya and then going back to one of the above remedies will sometimes result in progress.

Homeopathic—*Silicea* (silicon dioxide, quartz) 30C: If the problem persists in spite of the advice given so far, especially if there is an excessive appetite, stealing food, scavenging—even leading to being overweight—then this medicine will be of use. Use Homeopathic Schedule 4, page 442. Do not repeat this medicine.

Note: In general, these deeply ingrained skin conditions require patience and persistence. You will usually see clear, beneficial effects from the program within six to eight weeks.

Because vaccines tend to aggravate the condition, it is very important to avoid them during the treatment period. Sometimes medicines like those used for heartworm prevention will set off an attack. In this case it is best to use the monthly type of heartworm medication and give it only every six weeks (or stop using it altogether in severe cases).

Some obstinate cases will not completely recover no matter how long you treat them (though they will generally improve). These need more individualized treatment with other homeopathic remedies or one of the holistic approaches described in chapter 14. If you can, find a skilled professional to help.

For the animal suffering hair loss, try a slightly different program. Sometimes a pet will just begin to lose hair without any other apparent problem. Or the hair loss could be the result of poisoning—not necessarily the intentional kind, but rather the accumulation of toxic substances that may affect sensitive individuals. Common agents to consider include fluoride (in some drinking water and commercial pet foods; see chapter 8) and aluminum (from use of aluminum bowls or cooking utensils). Sensitivity to aluminum seems to vary, and not all animals show this reaction. Those that are poisoned by aluminum tend to have constipation problems as well.

It is also possible for hair loss to reflect a disturbance in the endocrine glands (especially hypothyroidism) or a deficiency of a certain nutrient. If your veterinarian has diagnosed either of these problems, then feed only the natural diet with added kelp powder. This is particularly important, because the powder's iodine content will help to stimulate the thyroid. Give ½ to 2 teaspoons of kelp powder daily (amounts depend on your animal's size). In addition, give 250 to 1,000 milligrams of vitamin C twice a day to aid detoxification and 5 to 20 milligrams of chelated zinc once a day to enhance the elimination of heavy metals. Discontinue use of aluminum utensils and fluoridated water (call your water company to find out if your tap water is so treated; if it is, use bottled or spring water).

If you have addressed all these things—nutrition, toxicity, water pollution—and your animal still has hair loss (not caused by scratching or chewing), then try these homeopathic remedies. Use Homeopathic Schedule 4, page 442, for all these remedies.

Homeopathic—*Thuya* (or *Thuja*) *occidentalis* (arborvitae) 30C: Try *Thuya* first because it is an antidote to the effects of vaccination, which is the primary reason for a persistently poor hair coat or for poor hair growth. (Sometimes hair loss is at a normal rate, but the issue is that no new hair grows in to replace it; in such a case this remedy is especially suitable.)

Homeopathic—*Selenium* (the element) 30C: Indicated for excessive hair loss with no new growth, especially if there are no other symptoms of illness. Use it after trying *Thuya* (or *Thuja*—see above), if that remedy has not been sufficient to resolve the problem.

If an animal develops the hair loss soon after giving birth, then use:

Homeopathic—*Sepia* (cuttlefish ink) 30C. Give one dose.

SPAYING AND NEUTERING

Spaying is a surgery to remove a female's ovaries and uterus to prevent pregnancy and to eliminate her heats (periods of sexual receptivity). Neutering, or castration, removes a male's testes (leaving the scrotum, or sac) to prevent reproduction and to reduce aggression, wandering, and territorial behaviors. Both operations are performed painlessly under anesthesia, and recovery is usually rapid and uneventful. Natural treatments can help ease the process.

If your pet is slow to wake up, groggy, or nauseous after surgery, give:

Homeopathic—*Phosphorus* (the element) 30C: Use Homeopathic Schedule 2, page 442. Response is usually fast—from a few minutes to an hour. Stop treatment as soon as there is apparent improvement.

If your pet has discomfort, pain, or restless behavior on returning home, try:

Homeopathic—*Arnica* (mountain daisy) 30C: Use Homeopathic Schedule 2, page 442. In addition to *Arnica*, I often use Dr. Bach's rescue formula (see page 270), 2 drops 4 times a day for 2 to 3 days.

For any red irritation or a discharge of fluid or pus around the skin sutures give:

Homeopathic—*Apis mellifica* (honeybee venom) 6C: Use Homeopathic Schedule 1, page 441. Also bathe the incision site in a mixture of 10 drops of *Calendula* tincture, ¼ teaspoon sea salt, and 1 cup of pure water. Dip a warm washcloth in the solution and hold it against the incision for a few minutes 3 or 4 times a day.

Extra vitamins A, E, and C are also useful after any surgery to help detoxify anesthetics and drugs. My standard regimen, regardless of animal size, is 10,000 IU of A, 100 IU of E, and 250 milligrams of C, all given once a day for three days both before and after surgery.

Does This Surgery Do Harm?

Some people are concerned about the health effects of such a major surgical alteration. Although it is surely a major intervention, the best I can say at this point in time is that neutering does not seem to cause major health problems or increase incidence of such common problems as skin allergies or cystitis. Most neutered dogs and cats live long and healthy lives. Some do tend to become less active, to act less aggressively (a benefit), and perhaps to gain weight. Obesity often follows indulgent feeding and lack of regular exercise.

On the other hand, I have seen more obvious harmful effects when neutering is used as a medical treatment for prolonged heats, cystic ovaries, infertility problems, spontaneous abortions, vaginitis, infections, and the like. These reproductive problems are the result of chronic ill health. Simply removing the affected organs will not really cure the underlying state. So the animal later develops other symptoms—really the same disease with a different focus.

When pets have reproductive health problems, I first recommend nutritional therapy and homeopathy, assuming that it's not an emergency and we still have some time. If this is not effective, surgery is still an option. However, if we are successful, as we often are, the chronic disease is cured. Then the animal can be neutered for the usual reasons without any long-term problem.

What are the reasons to neuter a healthy animal? A female dog or cat comes into heat two or more times a year. Preventing her from breeding is demanding, frustrating to your animal, and a potential source of health problems (see "Pyometra," page 381). Allowing her to breed adds to the tremendous animal overpopulation problem. Repeated breeding can also drain her health (see pages 375–79). Spaying also reduces her risk for breast cancer.

Neutering reduces the havoc wreaked by intact males—property damage, fights, the smell and stain of territorial marking, accidents caused when they wander onto public roadways, and packs that attack or threaten other animals or even people. By contrast, a neutered male is typically more affectionate and gentle, making a better companion.

The best time for surgery is after a pet reaches sexual maturity, which ensures the least effect on the neuro-endocrine system and allows full development of a normal adult body shape. Most females reach this point at age 6 to 8 months, most males at 9 to 12 months.

Some animals mature later, however, so you may want to wait until the signs are clear. For a female this means after her first heat (keep her carefully confined to prevent pregnancy).

A male cat matures when his urine develops an odor and he begins to show signs of territorial spraying of urine. The male dog will begin to lift one leg to urinate (and mark territory), mount other dogs, fight, roam, and become more aggressive. The risk of waiting, however, is that through inadvertent pregnancy we contribute to the overwhelming surplus of puppies and kittens. In most cases, plan to neuter females at 6 to 7 months and males at 9 to 10 months.

There are really no safe alternatives to surgical neutering. Over the years, various hormones and drugs have been used to prevent females from coming into heat or to stimulate abortion if necessary. These drugs always cause some problems, however, and they are soon pulled off the market. Perhaps a safe alternative to neutering will be found someday, but there is nothing out there now that I can recommend.

So if you are vacillating over having your animal altered, my advice is to wait no longer. If you're worried about money, contact a nearby low-cost spay/neuter clinic or call your local humane society for information about special reduced-fee programs arranged with area veterinarians.

STOMACH PROBLEMS

The stomach has its share of upsets, usually from eating the wrong kind of food (spoiled, tainted, indigestible) or too much food. (Beware the greedy eater!) However, stomach problems can also indicate a wide variety of other disorders—such as infectious diseases, kidney failure, hepatitis, pancreatitis, colitis (inflammation of the lower bowel), a foreign substance that doesn't belong in the stomach (swallowed toys, string, hair), and parasites, like worms.

Be aware that problems in other areas of the body can also cause symptoms like vomiting, nausea, and lack of appetite, fooling you into thinking that only the stomach is involved. Especially if vomiting is persistent or severe, which may indicate a serious, even life-threatening, problem. Have your veterinarian make a diagnosis.

Here we will discuss three common problems that are centered in the stomach itself: acute gastritis (sudden upset), chronic gastritis (low-grade, persistent upset), and gastric dilation (swelling with gas, sometimes causing the stomach to twist shut). The suggestions offered are alternative treatments for those animals newly diagnosed with these problems or animals that have them repeatedly so that ways to deal with this other than the usual drugs are needed.

Acute Gastritis

Gastritis is a term that means inflammation (not infection) of the stomach. Acute signifies that the attack is sudden, appearing in a few minutes or hours. The most common sufferer is the dog that likes to raid garbage cans or to eat dead animals found on roads or in the woods (cats, being more finicky, rarely have this as a cause). Compost piles are another common source of spoiled treasures. As partial scavengers, dogs often scrounge about in garbage cans and consume an extraordinary mixture of foods (often spoiled) that just don't sit well in the stomach.

The vomiting (and usually diarrhea) that follows is the body's attempt to right the wrong by getting rid of the noxious material. Some dogs instinctively try to remedy things by eating grass, which stimulates vomiting. This behavior also occurs in animals with low-grade stomach irritation.

Another cause of acute gastritis is consuming indigestible material, like large bone fragments. This is mostly a problem for dogs not used to eating bones. It's also the likely result of their consuming cooked bones (which are more apt to splinter) or inedible materials such as cloth, plastic, metal, rubber toys, golf balls, and the like. If bones are causing the problem, give your pet only large raw bones and give extra B vitamins to dogs to ensure adequate stomach acid. Supervise carefully. If your dog keeps trying to swallow large pieces, it's best not to trust him with bones.

Indigestible foreign objects in the stomach often require surgical removal, though sometimes they can be retrieved by passing a tube into the stomach. Cats may swallow sewing thread or yarn; if there is a needle attached, it can get caught up in the mouth or tongue while the thread passes down into the intestine. The unpleasant re-sult can be a "crawling" of the intestine up along the thread, which is often fatal unless corrected quickly.

Though the signs are not specific, cats having this problem will stop eating and may have vomiting. A thread caught up around the tongue is very difficult to see. Just opening the mouth may not show it; a needle caught somewhere in the throat or esophagus will show up on an x-ray, as will bunching of the intestine.

To help prevent your pet from swallowing such objects, don't let them play by themselves with any toy or object that could cause problems.

TREATMENT

If you suspect that your animal has swallowed something dangerous, get professional help within a few hours, or serious complications can arise. If you aren't sure what was swallowed, do not encourage vomiting. It would be too traumatic and dangerous for the object to come up if it is sharp, pointed, or very large. Such objects must be removed surgically. Meanwhile, use the treatment below to discourage vomiting.

If you know, however, that the swallowed material is small and not sharp or irregular, vomiting may expel the object, so you can allow the vomiting to proceed while you are waiting to see the vet.

The remedy that is useful for discouraging vomiting because of objects in the stomach is:

Homeopathic—*Phosphorus* (the element)

30C: Use Homeopathic Schedule 2, page 442. The vomiting is often associated with taking in water, occurring about 10 to 15 minutes after drinking. This remedy will relieve the vomiting for a while, but the foreign material will need to be removed (see above).

The following treatments will help for a simple, acute gastritis not caused by foreign bodies. The symptoms are: pain in the abdomen (it hurts the animal when you press its stomach, the animal doubles up with cramps, sits hunched, and acts depressed), vomiting or attempts to vomit, vomiting after eating or drinking, salivation, excessive drinking of water, and eating grass.

First, withhold all food for at least 24 hours and then reintroduce it slowly in small quantities. See the fasting instructions in chapter 15. Make fresh, pure water available at all times or, if vomiting is part of the problem, offer one or more ice cubes to lick every couple of hours. (You don't want to aggravate vomiting and stomach irritation by encouraging too much drinking.)

Many dogs and cats will also eat grass to make themselves vomit when the stomach is upset. This is a natural response and is appropriate behavior at the beginning of a stomach upset. If the problem is not quickly resolved, however, eating grass only makes the situation worse.

As a supplementary treatment, make chamomile tea. This treatment will suffice for mild upsets. Pour a cup of boiling water over a tablespoon of the flowers, steep 15 minutes, strain, and dilute with an equal quantity of water. If the tea isn't accepted, just make the ice available.

For more serious upsets, one of the following is useful:

Herbal—Peppermint (*Mentha piperira*): Use Herbal Schedule 1 on page 438. This is a good herbal treatment for dogs (cats don't like mint) and is often readily available.

Herbal—Goldenseal (*hydrastis canadensis*): Use Herbal Schedule 1 on page 438. This very useful herb is indicated when what is vomited up is thick, yellowish, and "ropy" (for example, thick strands).

Homeopathic—*Nux vomica* (poison nut) 6C: Use Homeopathic Schedule 1, page 441. Especially indicated for the dog or cat that acts ill with the vomiting and wants to go off by itself rather than seek company. This remedy also suits the animal that is sick from overeating.

Homeopathic—*Pulsatilla* (windflower) 6C: Use Homeopathic Schedule 1, page 441. Indicated for the dog or cat that wants attention and comfort, especially if it is not interested in drinking. Often animals requiring this remedy are made ill by eating food that is rich or fatty.

Homeopathic—*Ipecac* (ipecac root) 6C: Use Homeopathic Schedule 1, page 441. Useful where there is almost constant nausea and vomiting, especially if the problem was brought on by indigestible food or if there is blood in the vomit.

Homeopathic—*Arsenicum album* (arsenic trioxide) 6C: Use Homeopathic Schedule 2, page 442. This remedy is *par excellence* for gastritis brought on by spoiled meat, or spoiled food in general.

Homeopathic—*Belladonna* (deadly nightshade) 6C: Use Homeopathic Schedule 1, page 441. This is good for the animal that is primarily feverish, with dilated pupils and excitability.

Chronic Gastritis

Some animals develop a long-term tendency for digestive upsets, often after eating and sometimes once every few days. This can follow inadequate recovery from a previous severe attack of acute gastritis or may result from emotional stress, poor quality or disagreeable food, drug toxicity, or infections like feline infectious peritonitis or hepatitis. It can also be a part of an allergy problem, and many dogs and cats with skin eruptions will also have inflammation of the stomach and intestines. Sometimes there is no apparent cause.

Symptoms are poor digestion, a tendency to vomit, pain, depression or hiding (either immediately after eating or an hour or so later), loss of appetite, and gas. Many animals with chronic gastritis eat grass in an attempt to stimulate vomiting and cleansing of the stomach.

TREATMENT

The first and foremost treatment I recommend is to put the animal on a natural diet. I can't overemphasize the importance of a good diet, because the illness may be the result of the very food your pet has been eating. Also, be sure to read the discussion under "Allergies" to understand this possible underlying cause and to see recipes that you could use.

A further treatment might include one of the following, as indicated.

Herbal—Goldenseal (*Hydrastis canadensis*): Good for weak digestion, poor appetite, and weight loss. Use Herbal Schedule 2 on page 439.

Herbal—Garlic (*Allium sativum*): Especially useful for an animal that has a good appetite but gets upset with changes in the diet or is prone to gas and constipation. Make a cold extract by soaking 4 to 6 chopped cloves in ½ cup of cold water for 8 hours. Strain. Give ½ teaspoon to 1 tablespoon 3 times a day until the problem is relieved.

Homeopathic—There are several homeopathic medicines that are helpful for acute gastritis (discussed above) that are also helpful for the chronic condition. Sometimes the acute episode is the beginning of an illness that will turn out to be long lasting, though, of course, you can't know that at the beginning. Look over the remedies for acute gastritis, as any of them can be useful when the animal has the same indications as given there.

The main difference to understand is that with the chronic form of illness, the symptoms are often not as marked or as intense as in the acute stage, though the indications for the remedy are still there. For example, *Pulsatilla* is a frequently needed medicine. As with the acute condition, you may notice that your pet has become more "clingy," wanting attention. In addition, he may drink a lesser amount of water, but still some. None of these symptoms, however, will stand out as strongly as when they are seen in the acute form.

Consider, in particular, the remedies *Arsenicum album, Nux vomica, Pulsatilla*, and *Silicea*.

An additional remedy that was not mentioned before is:

Homeopathic—*Natrum muriaticum* (sodium chloride) 30C: Useful for the cat that has excessive hunger, is thirsty, and has discomfort after eating. Also good for stomach problems associated with worms. Use Homeopathic Schedule 4, page 442.

Gastric Dilation (Bloat)

This serious problem is seen mostly in the larger dog breeds (especially the Great Dane, St. Bernard, and Borzoi). Its cause is unknown, though veterinarians have found it to be linked with the feeding of commercial foods (especially large meals of concentrated dry forms of food). It occurs most often in dogs between the ages of 2 and 10 years, and most often at night.

The symptoms of the condition are that approximately two to six hours after eating, the stomach (upper abdominal area) gets enlarged with liquid and gas and sometimes feels like a tight drum. Most often, you will see excessive salivation, drooling, unsuccessful attempts to vomit, extreme restlessness and discomfort, desperate attempts to eat grass, and, eventually, weakness and collapse.

This is an emergency situation because the increased pressure on the walls of the stomach causes fluids to leak in from the blood, with consequent dehydration, shock, and possible death in a few hours. Another complication is that the stomach can rotate on itself—a condition called volvulus—and the twisting can completely block entry into or exit from the organ. Immediate surgery is required in this instance.

PREVENTION

Feeding a natural, home-prepared diet seems to be the best way to avert such problems. Feed two or three small meals a day instead of a single one.

Especially avoid feeding dry food or concentrated foods that will absorb water after they are eaten. The dog will eat more than its capacity, and when the food becomes distended with water, the total weight of the food is greatly increased. This can prevent the stomach from its natural emptying and also increase the chance of the stomach twisting around and blocking the movement of food out of it.

Regular exercise, which strengthens the muscles and "massages" the stomach and bowels, is extremely helpful.

TREATMENT

When gastric dilation first occurs, it is rather sudden and can be shocking. Sometimes the only thing noticed is that the dog is restless and desperately eating grass. If you look closely, you may see that the animal's belly is larger than normal, distended with gas.

Get to your veterinarian as soon as possible. If the condition is one of simple stomach dilation, it can be temporarily relieved at the hospital by passing a tube into the stomach. However, the condition tends to recur. Each time, the attack comes on sooner and with more severity. Eventually, the animal is put to sleep because of the apparent hopelessness of the situation and the high cost of repeated medical measures.

If there is also volvulus (twisting of the stomach), then surgery must be done to straighten out the twisted stomach and allow open passages in and out. The stomach wall is also "tacked down" by suturing it to the inside of the abdominal wall to prevent it from twisting in the future.

Even though you must see your veterinarian immediately, it is still appropriate for me to give you some treatment suggestions, because there will be times when you cannot get veterinary service immediately; further, the condition tends to recur, and you will become aware of the early signs. If you can intervene with treatment soon enough, it is possible to head off an attack. But it's important to remember that these treatments should never be considered a substitute for veterinary attention, especially if they persist.

One of the easiest and most available herbal treatments is one discovered by one of my clients, Betty Lewis of Amherst, New Hampshire. She breeds Great Danes and has found that freshly made raw cabbage juice is an effective treatment at the beginning of bloat and has used it successfully many times.

Herbal—Cabbage (*Brassica oleracea*): This plant is a member of the mustard family. Reduce fresh cabbage leaves to a liquid (with a juicer); do not add water. Give 1 to 2 ounces of this as a dose (to large breeds, less to smaller animals), repeating the treatment if symptoms return later.

Because of vomiting and the pressure closing off the opening to the stomach, I primarily use homeopathic preparations. The pellets or tablets will act especially quickly, even if not swallowed, if they are first crushed to a powder (between folded heavy paper) and placed on the tongue.

Of course, you will need to plan ahead and order these in advance since you will need them immediately.

Homeopathic—*Pulsatilla* (windflower) 30C: This is the first remedy I use in these cases. It resolves the majority of them. Give a dose of 3 crushed pellets every 30 minutes for a total of 3 treatments.

Homeopathic—*Belladonna* (deadly nightshade) 30C: This remedy is indicated when the problem has come on very suddenly, with severe and intense symptoms. There is agitation, desperate attempts to eat anything: grass, rags, even carpet. Pupils are dilated and the head may be hot. Give a dose of 3 crushed pellets every 30 minutes for a total of 3 treatments.

Homeopathic—*Nux vomica* (poison nut) 30C: Best for the dog that becomes withdrawn, irritable, and chilly. This is the best treatment when the stomach has become twisted. Give a dose of 3 crushed pellets every 30 minutes for a total of 3 treatments.

Homeopathic—*Carbo vegetabilis* (charcoal) 30C: Dogs needing this remedy will be greatly distended with gas and look very ill, with cold legs and ears and bluish color to the tongue and gums. It is suitable for the state of shock that accompanies this condition. Give a dose of 3 crushed pellets every 15 minutes for a total of 3 treatments.

If this treatment improves the general condition, one of the other remedies may be needed to complete the treatment. Wait a bit and see if recovery ensues. If not, then try one of those already discussed.

Dogs that have had this problem before, perhaps one serious episode from which they have not fully recovered, may benefit from homeopathic treatment to resolve this and prevent future attacks. What you will see in these dogs is a pattern of recurring indigestion and gas, with periodic swelling of the animal's stomach, which causes breathing difficulty. This state of chronic ill health will produce progressive weakening, low energy, and a cold body. Use Homeopathic Schedule 4, page 442, and, for this chronic condition, give the treatment at a time when there is no crisis.

Homeopathic—*Hepar sulph* (calcium sulphide) 30C: Use Homeopathic Schedule 4 on page 442. This is another treatment to use between crises, with the idea of pre-

venting further attacks. It is indicated for the dog that has a history of skin or ear eruptions with itching and discomfort. Sometimes this history is vague; the original skin problem may have been suppressed in the past and no longer be remembered. If this treatment is successful, the stomach will improve and the skin eruption will come back for a while. Further treatment may then be necessary to resolve this condition. (See "Skin Problems.")

Homeopathic—*Graphites* (carbon compound) 30C: Dogs needing this will have also have had skin and ear problems in the past. Typically the eruptions tend to be worse at the base of the tail. They will be overweight, tend to be chilly (and like warmth), and be constipated. Use Homeopathic Schedule 4, page 442.

Homeopathic—*Silicea* (silicon dioxide, quartz) 30C: Stomach problems are recurrent as indigestion or discomfort after eating. This can lead to frequent vomiting of food and nausea. These dogs often have accompanying rear leg trouble—stiffness, weakness, pain—that will be diagnosed as hip dysplasia, spondylitis, spondylosis, or degenerative myelopathy (all different manifestations of the same disorder). Use Homeopathic Schedule 4, page 442.

Note: If you achieve favorable results with one of these treatments, bear in mind that using drugs like tranquilizers, antibiotics, stimulants, or depressants immediately after a positive homeopathic response will very likely cancel out the favorable response and lead to a return of the original condition. For this reason, minimize or eliminate such treatment if the homeopathic remedies are doing the job.

STONES

See "Bladder Problems."

TEETH

See "Dental Problems."

THYROID DISORDERS

The thyroid is an extremely important gland that regulates the use of food, body weight, body temperature, heart rate, hair growth, one's activity level (low thyroid individuals tend to be sluggish), and other more subtle functions. The thyroid is an *endocrine* gland, one of the members of body-regulating glands that include the pituitary (linked directly to the brain, the "master gland" which regulates the other glands, controls total body size, milk production after birth, skin color, and several other functions), the pancreas (certain cells involved in insulin production), the adrenals (see "Addison's Disease" and "Cushing's Disease"), the parathyroid glands (regulating calcium), and the reproductive glands (testicles and ovaries). The endocrine glands are what control most of the functions of the body. When they have problems it almost always has to do with either overaction or underaction.

Hypothyroid

Hypothyroid (under-function) conditions affect dogs (not cats, except very rarely) and are actually quite commonly diagnosed. In the majority of dogs this disorder is part of an immune problem. In the same way that there will be allergies affecting the skin, the thyroid will be underactive because the immune system is affecting it, blocking normal function. In fact, these animals with immune problems will have several areas of the body affected at the same time—skin, thyroid, and bowels being the most frequent.

Reduced thyroid function can also happen (rarely) due to inadequate iodine, but more commonly from use of certain drugs. For example, a common treatment of skin allergies is to use corticosteroids (anti-inflammatory drugs), and these will interfere with thyroid hormone production. So, the young dog may start out with a skin problem but because of drug treatment for it, develops thyroid dysfunction secondarily. Phenobarbital, used to control epilepsy in dogs, also will block thyroid hormone production.

The signs of this problem are variable and often mimic the symptoms of other diseases. Most often one will see lethargy, mental dullness, slow heart rate, weight gain leading to obesity, recurrent infections, and intolerance of cold (seeking out warm places or the sun).

Changes in the skin are usually what alert people that something is wrong. There is a dry, dull hair coat and the hair comes out very easily. The outer coat comes off leaving a very thick wooly undercoat (from failure of the hair to be replaced properly so it sort of "piles up"). There may be patches of hair loss (equally on both sides, which distinguishes it from scratching hair out from itchy spots, which tend not to be symmetrical), the skin will be dry yet the hair greasy feeling that leaves a "doggy smell" on your fingers. As with Cushing's Disease (an adrenal gland dysfunction,) the skin can become darker than normal and be prone to infections and subsequent itchiness.

The conventional, allopathic, treatment is giving an artificial hormone every day for the life of the dog. The disadvantage of this is that the underlying cause (the immune-mediated disease or the drugs being used) is not addressed. As an additional side-effect, the artificial thyroid hormone causes the thyroid gland to shrink and produce even less natural hormone than before. If this is done long enough, the poor glands will never work again.

My cases have done very well with homeopathic and nutritional therapy, and I always advise trying alternative treatments before considering complicating the problem with a replacement hormone. If the dog is young enough and has not been on hormone treatment very long, he can be brought back to normal thyroid function and have his health restored. The dogs already on hormones for long periods may not be completely curable (because of the drug effect), but usually their health can be significantly improved and the hormone dosage considerably lowered.

PREVENTION

In my practice I see dogs with this problem after some suppressive treatment for other conditions. A common instance is use of corticosteroids for skin allergies. It really means a worsening of chronic disease—the same disease that was there before but now developing more internally. The only effective prevention I know is at the first sign of chronic illness (including allergies) in a young dog, seriously improve nutrition and seek alternative (drugless) treatment at that time.

TREATMENT

All the endocrine disorders are very deep and serious problems and much more difficult to manage than many of those we are discussing in this section. Improved nutrition can be very helpful, but in my practice I have usually included homeopathic treatment as well. The situation is complex, and changes during treatment are difficult to interpret. It needs individualized treatment by an experienced veterinarian.

Hyperthyroidism

Hyperthyroidism (over-function) is the bane of cats. It is the opposite of what happens with dogs (as explained above). Here the thyroid gland *overproduces* hormone. Again, there is considerable evidence that it is caused by the immune system attacking the gland (and therefore part of a larger problem) but, in the case of cats, it causes the gland to become too active instead of less so, as in dogs. It is encountered in mature cats, more frequently as they get older. When I first was in practice (1965 on) we did not see this disease. Now it is extremely common, so something is responsible for this dramatic increase in incidence, and I suspect frequent vaccinations to be an important factor. When I started practice, cats were vaccinated for one disease (Panleukopenia) and given one or two injections when they were young. That is all they received in their lifetime. Now they are given multiple vaccinations and repeatedly (yearly). Since, in this condition, the immune system becomes disturbed in such a way as to attack the thyroid glands it seems likely that vaccines, which directly stimulate the immune system, could be the trigger.

Because of the excessive hormone released, we get the opposite signs seen in dogs, so rather than becoming overweight cats become thin, wasting away gradually in spite of a good, or even excessive, appetite. Some cats, however, lose their appetite and stop eating. Often they will have larger formed stools, yet some will have diarrhea. These contradictions are confusing but it is typical of these complicated endocrine disorders that there can be a variety of manifestations.

The most common signs are excessive appetite, hyperactivity, fast and more forceful heart rate (sometimes visible at the chest), excessive thirst (with subsequent increased urine output), voluminous stools or diarrhea, panting, and fever.

It is not unusual for the thyroid gland to swell up or develop bumps on it. Some veterinarians will conclude that these are malignant tumors, but they are almost never so, rather just from the overactivity of the gland.

PREVENTION

Avoid excessive vaccinations (see "Vaccinations"), provide wholesome foods, and reduce toxic exposure (cats are very sensitive to chemicals).

TREATMENT

The conventional treatment plan is to basically eliminate the thyroid function. This is done in one of three ways: use of a drug to blocks thyroid activity; use of (injectable) radioactive iodine to destroy the thyroid tissues; surgical removal of the thyroids. While these measures will eliminate symptoms, there can be serious side effects and has the further disadvantage that it in no way cures the underlying problem. The thyroid is acting the way it is because the immune system is not right. Removing the thyroid does not address that and often there are other symptoms, part of the disease, that continue on after the conventional treatment.

I have treated these cases with considerable success using nutrition and homeopathy alone. Though it can take many months to restore health it is possible to do so with the added advantage that the overall health is much better than before. I always advise my clients to try this approach first. Once the thyroid glands have been destroyed or removed, you can't go back and expect to restore their function with other methods.

Successful treatment of this complex condition requires the skill of an experienced homeopathic veterinarian. (See what is written above for treatment of dogs.)

TICKS

See "Skin Parasites."

TOXOPLASMOSIS

This disease deserves to be discussed in some detail, not so much because of its importance to cats (which usually recover from it without treatment, very often without any symptoms), but because of its importance to unborn children. If a woman is infected for the first time during pregnancy, the fetus may be born prematurely, born with serious damage to the brain, eyes, or other parts of the body, or stillborn. Such problems are estimated to occur in 2 to 6 out of every 1,000 births in the United States.

Before we consider this disease further, first let's put things in perspective. The toxoplasma protozoa infest almost all species of mammals and birds in the world. Infection ranges from 20 to 80 percent of all domestic animals, depending on geographical area. In the United States, about 50 percent of the human population is also infected. But,

despite the widespread occurrence of this little parasite, few infected individuals actually get sick from it. People who do get clinically ill are those whose immune systems have been suppressed as a response to drugs used with organ grafts or by cancer chemotherapy or x-ray therapy. People who have an immuno-suppressive disease like AIDS may also become clinically ill with toxoplasmosis.

Cats are unique in that they are natural hosts for the parasite—toxoplasmosis grows better in cats than in any other animal. Those who do show symptoms will have mucus- or blood-tinged diarrhea, fever, hepatitis (liver inflammation), or pneumonia (difficult breathing). They usually get over it on their own, developing a strong immunity that protects against further infection.

Commonly, both cat and human can acquire the parasite and have no symptoms whatsoever. Here is where the danger lies: About one to three weeks after infection, the cat will often start passing oocysts, egg-like structures that can infect other individuals after a day or so of further development in the warm feces or soil. The cat passes these oocysts until it develops immunity—in about two weeks. (If its immune system is depressed with cortisone-like drugs, however, the process can start up again.) These eggs can then be picked up by a pregnant woman who has not already had a chance to develop her own immunity. Thus, the disease spreads to the fetus, where it can cause the serious problems already mentioned.

Here are the ways this organism can infect pregnant women (and other people):

❖ A bit of cat feces is accidentally ingested during the two weeks of oocyst shedding.

❖ By some mischance, soil used as a bathroom by an infected cat within the previous year is consumed.

❖ Infected raw or undercooked meat is prepared or eaten. This is actually the most common route of entry for both people and cats. And though you may deny your cat raw meat as a protective measure, remember that freshly caught mice and birds ain't cooked!

If you think about it, the possibilities for the spreading of the disease are pretty great. For instance, while changing a litter box, digging in the garden, or cleaning a sandbox, you might wipe your mouth. After doing one of these tasks, you might eat something before you've washed your hands. Does your cat walk from the litter box to your kitchen counter, table, or your pillow? Do you fix salad on the same board used to trim raw meat? You can see why such a large proportion of the population is infected.

This information is not meant to scare you. If you are among the 25 to 45 percent of women in the United States aged 20 to 39 who are already exposed and therefore immune to problems from this organism, you needn't worry about it at all; you won't pass it on to your unborn child even if you are exposed again while you are pregnant. Your doctor can perform a serum test to find out if you're in this group. Your cat can also be tested to see if it has developed an immunity from previous infection. If so, he won't pass oocysts in his stool any more, and the danger to you is much less.

If neither you nor your mate has developed an immunity by the time you conceive, take special precautions for the next nine months. Don't feed your cat raw meat. If you eat meat yourself, be careful to prepare it separately from foods to be eaten raw, like salads. Wash your hands well after meat preparation, cat-petting, gardening, and the like.

Unless you know that your cat is already immune, use gloves when you clean the litter box and wash up afterward. Better yet, have someone else clean the litter box. Dispose of the contents in a sealed container (not on the ground). If you want to disinfect the pan, rinse it with boiling water. Also control flies and cockroaches, because they can carry oocysts from the cat's feces onto food.

If you wanted to keep your cat from getting toxoplasmosis in the first place (assuming he hasn't already had it), you would have to make some serious compromises. Raw meat, for example, is nutritionally superior to cooked, but to prevent toxoplasmosis, you'd always have to cook it. You also would have to keep your cat from hunting and keep him away from any soil possibly contaminated by other cats. Obviously, the only way you can manage these restrictions is by keeping him inside all the time, which is not such a healthy solution. The choice is yours, of course, but with reasonable precautions you will have a much better idea what risks you really face.

If your cat is diagnosed with this problem, in addition to what your veterinarian prescribes, you can use the advice given here. Go to the section of this Quick Reference guide that discusses the symptoms you see (for example, diarrhea), and follow those instructions.

UPPER RESPIRATORY INFECTIONS ("COLDS")

The upper respiratory tract, which includes the nose, throat, larynx (voice box), and trachea (windpipe), is one of the favorite highways for germs traveling inside the body. Many microorganisms and viruses dry out and masquerade as dust. Others are embedded in dried secretions and scabs, which break into small particles and get stirred up into inhaled air.

In animals, these cold-like illnesses often start and remain in the upper respiratory tract, causing such symptoms as a runny nose or eyes, sneezing, a sore throat, coughing, and, sometimes, inflammation of the mouth. These infections resemble the human cold in many ways but have some unique aspects for pets. The three most common upper respiratory diseases found in companion animals are canine infectious tracheobronchitis (often called kennel cough), feline viral rhinotracheitis (FVR—a viral attack on the cat's eyes and upper respiratory tract), and feline calici virus (similar to FVR, but generally less involved with the eyes and nose). (Distemper is covered as a separate entry in this Quick Reference guide.)

Canine Infectious Tracheobronchitis

Also known as kennel cough or canine respiratory disease complex, canine infectious tracheobronchitis is thought to be caused by a variety of viruses, sometimes complicated by bacterial infection as well. It's common where many stressed dogs, especially young ones, are in close contact. It crops up in boarding kennels, animal shelters, grooming establishments, veterinary hospitals, dog shows, and pet shops.

Symptoms, which usually appear about eight to ten days after exposure, are typically a dry, hacking, awful-sounding cough that ends with gagging or retching, and perhaps a clear, watery discharge from the eyes and nose or a partial loss of appetite. Though it sounds awful, it's not a serious condition. A minimal number of dogs may have complications because of their weak immune systems.

TREATMENT

Antibiotics are not recommended in most cases, because the disease is viral. Often cough suppressants are used, but they do not help much and can have unpleasant side effects. The most effective thing to do is to place the affected dog in a steam-filled room (such as a bathroom with a tub full of hot water or after running a hot shower) or in a room with a cold-mist vaporizer. Veterinarians recognize this as a disease that just has to "run its course" (two or three weeks) before recovery. If possible, isolate your dog, since some of these viruses may also affect cats and people.

You can assist the healing process by putting your pet on a fast, giving vitamins, and using an herbal cough treatment.

A liquid fast can be useful when the symptoms first appear and should be continued for three days. Follow the directions for fasting in chapter 15, taking care to reintroduce solid foods carefully and slowly.

Vitamins help in several ways. Vitamin C is a good antiviral agent. Depending on the size of your dog, you can give 500 to 1,000 milligrams three times a day. Vitamin E stimulates the immune response. Give 50 to 100 IU of fresh d-alpha tocopherol from a capsule three times a day. Puncture the capsule and squeeze the oil right into the dog's mouth. Taper off frequency at recovery. Vitamin A also boosts immunity, helps counteract stress, and strengthens the mucous membranes of the respiratory tract. Use ¼ to 1 teaspoon of fresh cod-liver oil three times a day (depending on the animal's size) or give a 10,000 IU capsule of vitamin A once a day. Treat for a total of five days with vitamin A.

Herbal treatment can consist of an herbal cough syrup available at health food stores; adjust the recommended dose to your animal's size. Such preparations typically contain several of the following: wild cherry bark, licorice, comfrey root, coltsfoot, mullein, slippery elm, and horehound.

Alternatively, you can make your own herbal treatments.

Herbal—Peppermint (*Mentha piperita*): This is best suited for the dog with a hoarse "voice" and with coughing made worse by barking. Touching his throat is irritating and may bring on the cough. Use Herbal Schedule 1 on page 438.

Herbal—Mullein (*Verbascum thapsus*): Especially indicated when the cough is deep and hoarse and worse at night. It's also useful when the throat seems sore to the touch or there is trouble swallowing. Use Herbal Schedule 1 on page 438.

A couple of homeopathic remedies useful for this are:

Homeopathic—*Lachesis* (bushmaster snake venom) 30C: When the cough is brought on by touching the throat or by the pressure of a leash. Use Homeopathic Schedule 2, page 442.

Homeopathic—*Pulsatilla* (windflower) 30C: Dog wants attention, to be held, seeks out cool areas, no desire to drink water. Use Homeopathic Schedule 2, page 442.

After recovery, your dog should be relatively immune for some time, perhaps a year or two. However, a different but similar virus could re-create the "same" condition. Remember, stress seems to be the necessary factor to allow the virus to get established.

Feline Viral Rhinotracheitis (FVR)

This viral disease primarily affects the eyes and upper respiratory tract of cats. Symptoms include sneezing attacks, coughing, drooling of thick saliva, fever, and a watery discharge from the eyes. The condition ranges from mild and barely noticeable to severe and persistent. In the latter, the nose becomes plugged up with a thick discharge, ulcers form on the eye surface (cornea), and the eyelids stick together with heavy discharges. The cat becomes thoroughly miserable, refusing to eat and unable to care for itself.

There is no allopathic treatment which shortens the duration of the disease, but usually antibiotics, fluid therapy, forced feeding, eye ointments, and other measures are used to provide the best possible support for the ailing body. These cats are so out of sorts, however, that they often resist handling and treatments. It can be a real challenge to provide adequate care.

TREATMENT

If you catch the condition early, this regimen may avert the more serious stage: Give no solid food the first two to three days, or until the temperature is back to normal (less than 101.5°F). The cat usually will not eat anyway. Instead, provide liquids as described in the section on fasting in chapter 15. Give vitamin C (⅛ teaspoon sodium ascorbate powder dissolved in pure water, every four hours), vitamin E (50 IU twice a day), and vi-

tamin A (¼ teaspoon cod-liver oil or 2,000 to 2,500 IU vitamin A from fish-liver oil sources, once a day). Treat with vitamin A for a total of five days only (too much vitamin A can be a problem).

Homeopathic—*Aconitum napellus* (monkshood) 30C: This remedy corresponds to the early stages of illness, which are marked by fever and a general sense of not feeling well. If given when these symptoms first appear, it may avert any further development of the illness. Use Homeopathic Schedule 2, page 442.

If the cold condition is already established, one of these remedies may help.

Homeopathic—*Nux vomica* (poison nut) 30C: A remedy commonly suited to this condition, *Nux vomica* is a good choice for the cat that is grouchy and averse to being held or touched. Often it will retire to a quiet room so as not to be disturbed. Use Homeopathic Schedule 2, page 442.

Homeopathic—*Natrum muriaticum* 6C: This remedy is most helpful when the cold starts with much sneezing. As it develops, there may be thirstiness and a white discharge from the nose. Use Homeopathic Schedule 1, page 441.

Homeopathic—*Pulsatilla* (windflower) 30C: Cats needing this medicine are sleepy, sluggish, and have a thick discharge from the nose or eyes. Often the discharge is greenish in color. Such a cat may want to be held or comforted. Use Homeopathic Schedule 2, page 442.

Generally, at this stage it helps to clean the eyes and nose with a saline solution, which is similar to natural tears. Stir ¼ teaspoon of sea salt into one cup of pure water (without chlorine). Warm this to body temperature. Using a cotton ball, drip several drops into each nostril to stimulate sneezing and flushing of the nose. Also put some into each eye and carefully clean the discharge away with a tissue.

If the condition is very advanced when you start treatment, you'll need to take a different approach. Blend raw beef liver with enough water to make a soupy mix. Add two teaspoons of sodium ascorbate powder to every cup of this blend. Feed one teaspoon of this mixture every hour to provide health-boosting nutrients, including B vitamins (from the liver) and about 150 milligrams of vitamin C with each dose.

Clean the eyes and nose with a warm saline solution (as described above). If necessary, saturate a cloth with the solution and hold it against the nostrils briefly to soften and loosen the dried nasal discharge. Then carefully remove the discharge and continue with the saline nose flush. Put a drop of castor oil, almond oil, or cod-liver oil (especially if there are ulcers in the eye) in each eye; apply some to the nose, too (twice a day).

If your cat is not eating at this stage, you may need to force-feed it. Use the force-feeding recipe in chapter 15.

Useful treatments are:

Homeopathic—*Pulsatilla* (windflower) 6C: This is useful for the cat with thick greenish or yellow discharge, an obstructed nose, loss of appetite, bad breath, and a sleepy, sluggish demeanor. Often these cats will be attacked by other cats in the family when they are ill. Somehow the other cats sense a weakness. Use Homeopathic Schedule 6(c), page 442.

Homeopathic—*Silicea* (silicon dioxide, quartz) 30C: This remedy often follows *Pulsatilla* to complete a treatment. These cats will by chilly (seeking out warm places) and lose their appetites (but may drink more water than usual). The eyes will be very inflamed, the lids stuck together with discharge and even ulcers of the cornea (surface of the eye). Use Homeopathic Schedule 2, page 442.

Homeopathic—*Thuya* (or *Thuja*) (arborvitae) 30C: This remedy is sometimes needed if there is no response to other treatments or if the cold symptoms have come on within 3 to 4 weeks after receiving a vaccination. The nasal discharge can look very much like that described for *Pulsatilla* (above). Use Homeopathic Schedule 3, page 442.

Homeopathic—*Sulphur* (the element) 30C: If nothing else has helped, give this remedy. Use Homeopathic Schedule 3, page 442.

Herbal—Goldenseal (*Hydrastis canadensis*): This herb is very helpful if the nasal discharge (or discharge at the back of the throat) is very yellow and stringy. There may also be considerable loss of weight, even if the cat is still eating sufficiently. Use Herbal Schedule 2 on page 439.

Once the cat is eating, encourage a variety of fresh and raw foods, especially meats, grated vegetables, and brewer's yeast. Continue the vitamin C and eye treatment until recovery is complete.

Feline Calicivirus (FCV)

Sometimes FCV cannot be distinguished from FVR (above), but generally the nose and the eyes are not as involved. Typical signs include pneumonia and ulcers of the tongue, the roof of the mouth, and the end of the nose (above the lip). This condition is very difficult to treat because the mouth is so sore that the cat resists having anything put in it. You may need to wrap the cat up in a towel during treatment to keep from getting scratched (see chapter 15).

TREATMENT

Use the same early treatment as described above for FVR. In practical terms, at this stage you may not really know which of these viruses your cat has, so don't worry about making any distinction; the treatments we are discussing are suitable for either disease.

If it is clear from the presence of the pneumonia or ulcers that you are dealing with feline calicivirus, there are a couple of other remedies that may be more suitable for this problem.

Homeopathic—*Phosphorus* (the element) 30C: Use this remedy if there is pneumonia (fever, rapid breathing, gasping, perhaps coughing). It's especially indicated if your cat desires cold water and vomits about 15 minutes after drinking or, with the pneumonia, prefers to lie on her right side. Use Homeopathic Schedule 3, page 442.

Homeopathic—*Nitricum acidum* (nitric acid) 30C: This remedy is indicated if the focus of the illness is ulcers in the mouth. The mouth odor is very bad, the saliva blood-tinged, and the tongue red and "clean" looking (instead of heavily coated). These cats usually become very cranky and are difficult to handle or medicate. Use Homeopathic Schedule 3, page 442.

Homeopathic—*Mercurius solubilis* (or *vivus*) (quicksilver) 30C: Cats needing this medicine are very similar to those described above for *Nitricum acidum*. The difference is that they are not so irritable, they produce more saliva, and their tongues are coated with a yellow film and are often swollen, so that you can see indentations of the teeth on the edges. Use Homeopathic Schedule 3, page 442.

Your cat is recovering from this illness once her appetite returns and she is eating well. This is the major turning point.

UREMIA

See "Kidney Failure."

VACCINATIONS

The prevention of communicable diseases by administering "weakened" forms of the germs that cause them is a very popular and strongly supported method of disease prevention. If a "live" vaccine is injected into the body, the organism will grow in the tissues and produce a sort of mini-disease that stimulates the immune response. This response is intended to protect the body against the real thing for a variable period of time—months or years. Sounds wonderful, doesn't it?

I must point out, however, that there are some problems with vaccinations that should be understood by anyone interested in a holistic health approach. Vaccines are not always effective, and they may cause long-lasting health disturbances.

Vaccine Ineffectiveness

Many people assume that vaccines are 100 percent effective. This belief can be so strong that even a veterinarian may tell you, "Your dog can't have distemper (or parvovirus, hepatitis, or whatever, et cetera) because he was vaccinated for that disease. It must be something else." But one thing I learned from my doctoral studies in immunology is that vaccines are far from 100 percent effective. It is not just the injection of the vaccine that confers immunity; the response of the individual animal is the critical and necessary factor.

Several things can interfere with an ideal response (production of antibodies and immunity). These include vaccinating when the animal is too young; vaccinating when it is sick, weak, or malnourished; using the wrong route or schedule of administration, or, most importantly, giving the vaccine to an animal whose immune system has been depressed because of genetics, a previous disease, or drug therapy.

For example, the routine practice of giving vaccinations at the same time a pet is undergoing anesthesia or surgery (for example, a spay operation) can introduce the vaccine organism at a time when the immune system is depressed for several weeks. It is equally unwise to use corticosteroids (to control skin itching, for instance) at the time of vaccination. The steroid acts to depress the immune response and disease resistance, at the same time the vaccine challenges the body to respond vigorously to an introduced organism.

Even if your animal does have a good vaccine response and develops antibodies, there is no guarantee the disease will not occur. The immunity may be more against the vaccine organism than the natural disease. Or it may be that a mutant germ comes along that will not be susceptible to the antibodies formed. Or if something weakens the animal's immune system later, that system may lack the ability to respond fully, and the natural disease may be able to get a foothold. Such weakening factors include the kinds of things we've been discussing throughout this book—stress, malnutrition, lack of vitamins, toxicity, drug effects, and so on.

So we see that the effectiveness of vaccination is a complex phenomenon depending on many factors, not the least of which is the overall level of health as determined by the total lifestyle.

It is interesting that retrospective studies of human vaccination practices now show that the actual protective effect falls far below previous estimates. At the same time, there is emerging evidence of much harm done—especially to children.

Harmful Effects of Vaccination

Besides the possibility that they may not work, vaccines might also cause an acute disease or a chronic health problem. I have often noticed certain animals getting ill a few days to a few weeks after receiving vaccinations. Often the explanation given is that the dog or cat was already incubating the disease and was going to get it anyway. Granted that this may occasionally happen, in my opinion most of these instances are illness from the vaccine itself.

It is likely that the animal was in a weakened state and the vaccine virus therefore caused a more severe reaction than the "mini-disease" intended. Whatever the reason, I have seen this problem occur most often after canine distemper, canine parvovirus, feline rhinotracheitis, or feline calicivirus vaccines were given (sometimes these latter two also cause a low-grade nose or eye inflammation in cats, which may last for months). Other vaccines, like the feline leukemia vaccine, do not seem to induce the illness they are supposed to prevent, but instead create conditions for another equally serious illness. The most frequent example of this, in my experience, is the occurrence of feline infectious peritonitis (FIP) a few weeks after administration of the feline leukemia vaccine. Sometimes the second

virus was already in the cat, but the immune system was strong enough to withstand it until weakened by the vaccine disease (that is, the immune system was not able to cope with both diseases at the same time).

Long-term effects are the more serious possibility. Over the years, doctors practicing homeopathic medicine have accumulated information on the more subtle but stubborn problems of vaccination. To quote a contemporary writer on the subject, George Vithoulkas, "The experience of astute homeopathic observers has shown conclusively that in a high percentage of cases, vaccination has a profoundly disturbing effect on the health of an individual, particularly in relation to chronic disease."

This disorder "engrafted" onto an individual by injection of a foreign disease is called vaccinosis and can be associated with a wide range of conditions. In many cases homeopaths have found it necessary to address the effects of vaccinations before full health can be restored. For example, Vithoulkas describes the case of a woman with terrible anxieties that were the result of a rabies vaccination she received as a child. She had experienced this condition for almost 40 years until cured by a method of homeopathic treatment chosen to antidote the ill effects of this vaccine.

Do these chronic effects occur in vaccinated animals? Very definitely. They are among the most common problems that I face in my practice. I believe this because I have learned that it's usually necessary to use a homeopathic remedy that removes the effects of prior vaccinations before I am able to make significant progress in the difficult, chronic cases often brought to me. I have had a number of cases in which the individual dog or cat invariably took a turn for the worse whenever it was vaccinated.

Based on the experience of over 25 years of homeopathic practice, it is my opinion that most animal skin allergies (and similar skin diseases) are the result of repeated annual vaccinations. I also suspect that the widespread increase in diseases caused by immune system disorders (such as hyperthyroidism, inflammatory bowel disease, lupus, and pemphigus) is a result of increased use of vaccinations, especially of combination formulas. These vaccinations are highly unnatural to the body. Under natural conditions an animal is exposed to pathogens, but its body has ways to defend itself at the normal points of entry (the nose, mouth, or other mucous membranes). When a combination vaccine is given, a massive invasion of several potent pathogens charges quickly into the bloodstream, bypassing the frontline defenses. Is it any wonder that the immune system gets confused, "panics," and begins attacking the body itself?

Fortunately, many other veterinarians are now recognizing this problem. Reports have appeared in journals over the last few years describing diseases that follow routine vaccinations—bleeding disorders, bone and joint inflammation, even tumors and cancers in some cats. At this point the attitude of most veterinarians is that these happenings are an anomaly. I think it will take many more years for the realization to dawn that some degree of adverse health effects occur in the majority of those vaccinated.

What to Do?

What you can do depends on your access to a qualified holistic veterinarian. As an example, we have not used vaccinations (other than legally required rabies) in our practice for 25 years. In their place we give homeopathic remedies called nosodes, which are made from natural disease products. Distemperinum, for example, is made from the secretions of a dog ill from canine distemper. It is sterilized, diluted, and carefully prepared in accredited pharmacies. When properly used, this medicine can protect a dog from distemper even better than the vaccine can. In fact, this method of disease protection, first developed by a veterinarian in the 1920s, showed impressive results even before vaccines were developed.

Nosodes are also available for kennel cough, parvovirus, feline leukemia, feline infectious peritonitis, and other common dog and cat diseases. We have been using this method of protection for a long time with very satisfactory results and without the side effects and illness associated with vaccine use.

Are homeopathic nosodes simply a replacement for vaccines? No. They are not the same. They are used only temporarily and during times of likely exposure. For example, I was able to stop an epidemic of parvovirus in a dog breeding colony by using the nosode for parvovirus for the week (only) when the disease was likely to occur in the puppies. Once through that "window," they were alright and remained healthy. You will need guidance from a homeopathic veterinarian to use them properly.

What if you cannot find this service or you are afraid to not vaccinate? Let me suggest a modified plan that will at least minimize the chance of vaccine problems.

❖ Use single or simple vaccines instead of complex vaccines. Ideally, this means vaccinating for one disease at a time. Most practitioners will balk at such a request, however, because they will have to buy each single-disease vaccine in quantity (an entire box) to serve only one client, suffering financial loss and wasting the unused vaccine. So you are generally offered the choice of getting a "simpler" combined vaccine, that is, fewer individual vaccines contained in a single shot. For dogs this will be a "DH" (distemper-hepatitis) and for cats a "3-in-1" (Panleukopenia, Rhinotracheitis, and Calici virus).

Though not perfect, these are far better than getting mega-mixes that might include Distemper, Hepatitis, Leptospirosis, Parvovirus, Parainfluenza, Bordetella, Rabies, Lyme Disease, Brucellosis, and more (which may be given all at the same time to dogs), or Pan-

leukopenia, Rhinotracheitis, Calici, Feline Leukemia, Rabies, Chlamydia, Feline Infectious Peritonitis, et cetera (often given simultaneously to cats).

It is becoming more difficult to find single or simpler vaccines as time goes by. Sometimes only one manufacturer offers them. It may be that you will have to track it down yourself. It shouldn't be this way, but unfortunately it is.

❖ Where possible, use only "killed" or "inactivated" vaccines (as opposed to "modified live"). These "killed" vaccines cannot grow in the body and are generally safer to use (though more likely to cause hypersensitivity reactions——however, using vaccines less frequently often minimizes this problem).

❖ Use a reduced vaccination schedule for young animals. You do not have to give a lot of vaccinations to have as much protection as is possible. In most instances, immunization of puppies or kittens is enough for several years or a lifetime of protection.

❖ Don't vaccinate an animal too early. Avoid the temptation to vaccinate before 16 weeks of age. Remember that the earlier your animal begins vaccinations, the more harm may be done to the immune system, and also the more vaccines received, the greater the chance for vaccine-induced illness.

❖ Avoid annual boosters. There has never been scientific justification for the yearly booster shots recommended by veterinarians, even though they have become a popular practice. I advise against any further vaccinations after the initial series, as they are not necessary. Also, the latest official veterinary opinion states that annual revaccinations are neither required nor effective. Your veterinarian may not know of this or even agree with it. Rest assured, however, that experts in the field of veterinary immunology have taken this position and support your decision not to have your animal vaccinated every year. This is not new information, just ignored information.

DOGS

If you really want to play it safe, keep your new puppy isolated from contact with other dogs and just vaccinate once—at age 22 weeks or older. In my opinion, the only essential vaccines are distemper and parvo. Get the distemper vaccine at 22 weeks of age and the parvo a month later. (As I noted above, however, you might have to get distemper and hepatitis together.)

This should be very safe if your puppy is not exposed to other sick animals, but if it seems too risky to you, I suggest getting two vaccinations (for each disease), starting at 16 weeks, using this schedule.

- First distemper (hepatitis): 16 weeks
- First parvo: 20 weeks
- Second distemper (hepatitis): 24 weeks
- Second parvo: 28 weeks

CATS

The distemper (feline panleukopenia) vaccine can be given once at age 16 weeks and is sufficient for the life of the cat. I do not recommend the rhinotracheitis and calici virus vaccines. Further, it has been my experience that the feline leukemia vaccines are the most harmful of all the cat vaccines available.

It is with cats that the danger is greatest of activating a latent virus infection by repeated administration of vaccines. Be careful of this.

The Rabies Problem

What about rabies vaccination? This is a difficult problem for many people to face. From my own experience I am convinced that some animals are made ill by this vaccine. Yet rabies is the only vaccine required by law for dogs (and for cats in some states). This requirement is really for the protection of human beings, regardless of its benefit or harm to pets, so few exemptions are allowed.

DOGS

The most common disturbances following rabies vaccination are aggressiveness, suspicion, unfriendly behavior, hysteria, destructiveness (of blankets, towels), fear of being alone, and howling or barking at imaginary objects. These can be treated with homeopathic medicine, but sometimes with difficulty. One of the saddest things in our practice is to restore a dog's health (sometimes after prolonged and careful work), only to have the animal suffer a relapse and go into a decline after we acquiesce to a required rabies vaccine. It would be far better if we didn't have to vaccinate these animals again, but our present legal situation requires it. We find that the best we can do is to have clients administer an appropriate homeopathic medicine to the dog within two hours of getting the vaccine. This seems to help in preventing subsequent problems.

Sometimes a letter from your veterinarian that an animal is not healthy enough to receive a rabies vaccine will be accepted, especially if the animal is older and previously vaccinated.

Another possibility is that blood can be taken from your animal and tested for protection (antibodies) against rabies. This is called determining the "rabies titer." Some counties, here and there, are accepting this in place of a booster vaccine (not for the first one). Check out this option with your veterinarian. It may be necessary for you to find out yourself by contacting your local Department of Health and persisting with questions about this option.

At this point you have no other legal alternatives to getting rabies vaccinations for your dog. Many states require that you vaccinate your puppy at age 4 months (check your specific state requirements). How can we fit this into our recommended schedule? The best scenario is to have the rabies vaccine last, at least a month after completing all the others. However, this means waiting until your dog is 6 to 7½ months old (depending on the schedule you use). If this is not possible (legal), then get the rabies vaccination first at age 4 months (16 weeks), wait until age 22 weeks and then carry on with the schedule I gave you above.

CATS

If the law requires that your cat be vaccinated for rabies, the best timing is one month after the distemper vaccine is received (age five months).

VOMITING

Vomiting is one of those symptoms of underlying illness that rarely occurs by itself. Most often it is associated with an upset stomach, but it also can occur in response to poisoning, failed kidneys, side effects of drugs, pain or inflammation in some other area (like the peritoneum, pancreas, or brain), surgery, severe constipation, and many other conditions. Therefore, it's always necessary to look beyond the vomiting to understand what the underlying situation is and to treat that. So any time there is prolonged vomiting, seek the help of your veterinarian to determine the underlying cause.

There are times, however, when nothing else seems to be wrong or when vomiting is by far the major problem. If not controlled, prolonged vomiting can lead to severe dehydration and the loss of certain vital salts, particularly sodium chloride and potassium chloride.

Treatment

The problem in treatment is that nothing given by mouth will remain in the stomach long enough to act, so the best way to administer medicine is to use crushed homeopathic pellets, which will act almost immediately through absorption in the mouth, even if vomiting occurs right after.

The best choice is:

Homeopathic—*Ipecac* (ipecac root) 6C: Useful for persistent nausea and constant vomiting where much saliva is generated because of the nausea. Use Schedule 1, page 441.

In addition, withhold all food and water during the vomiting period, allowing the animal to lick ice cubes occasionally. To replace fluids and salts (if there is dehydration), give a small enema every couple of hours as described in chapter 15. To each pint of enema water, add ¼ teaspoon of sea salt (or table salt as a second choice) and ¼ teaspoon potassium chloride (sold as a salt substitute in many markets). Given as an enema, this fluid will be retained and absorbed in a dehydrated animal.

WARTS

Dogs and older animals are the pets most likely to develop troublesome warts, which sometimes itch and bleed. Most often, these warts (and similar growths) are an expression of vaccinosis (see "Vaccinations"). Such animals may also tend to develop more serious types of growths in the future if not corrected at this point.

There is no simple formula for treating warts, as it is most necessary to address the underlying tendency with individualized treatment (called constitutional prescribing in homeopathy). There are, however, some general things to be done that may be quite helpful.

Homeopathic—*Thuya* (or *Thuja*) (arborvitae) 30C: This is appropriate for the tendency towards wart formation. Give *Thuya* first, using Schedule 4, page 442. Let the stimulus of this medicine act for a month (though you may also be doing the local treatment described below). If the warts are not gone (or diminishing), then use one of the next two remedies.

Homeopathic—*Causticum* (a mineral remedy) 30C: This remedy is indicated for warts that tend to bleed easily. Use Homeopathic Schedule 4, page 442.

Homeopathic—*Silicea* (silicon dioxide, quartz) 30C: Useful when the wart is very large, especially if it occurs over the site of a prior vaccination. Use Homeopathic Schedule 4, page 442.

During the time that these remedies are being used, you may do one of these local skin treatments.

Nutrition—Vitamin E: Regular application of vitamin E from a punctured capsule can sometimes greatly reduce the size of a wart. It must be continued for several weeks to be effective.

Herbal—Castor oil: This oil is quite helpful when applied directly to warts and growths to soften them and to reduce irritation. Apply it when the wart is itchy or in some way troublesome. Castor oil can be obtained at most pharmacies.

WEIGHT PROBLEMS

Obesity

Like people, a significant number of pets become overweight, especially if they are inactive and are fed fatty or sweet snacks by well-meaning owners. Such foods contain inadequate amounts of protein, vitamins, enzymes, and other essential nutrients. Because of a lack in the nutrients it needs, the animal develops excessive cravings. The same thing can happen as a result of feeding poor quality commercial diets.

In some animals, the problem can result from a disturbance in the metabolism that causes an excessive and almost uncontrollable hunger that is very difficult to manage. In addition to the weight-loss program outlined below, such animals may need specific treatment (beyond the scope of this book) to correct the underlying imbalance.

In either case it's important to get excess fat off your pet because it can strain the heart, make the circulation sluggish, seriously complicate other disorders, and probably shorten life span.

My basic weight-loss program for pets involves three principles.

1. Increase activity levels. Take your dog for daily walks and runs. Encourage your cat to play. Increased activity raises the metabolic rate and burns calories faster.

2. Resist the temptation to feed extra snacks and treats. If your pet is really begging, you may feed modest amounts of the following: lean meat, carrots or other vegetables, apples, unsalted popcorn (without oil), and raw bones.

3. Feed a highly nutritious, low-fat, high-bulk diet that provides about two-thirds of the calories needed to maintain your animal's ideal weight. While they are low in fat, the following diets are high in protein, enzymes, vitamins, and minerals. They also include plenty of bran or vegetables to help fill your animal's stomach and minimize begging. This helps your animal to lose weight gradually and safely, while insuring sufficient basic nutrients.

Be sure to include the daily vitamin-mineral pet supplements noted, which are available in pet supply outlets, in natural food stores, or from many veterinarians.

DOG WEIGHT LOSS DIET 1

4	cups cooked vegetables (carrots, peas, green beans, corn and so on; use frozen or canned if you must for convenience)
1	cup oat or wheat bran
2	cups rolled oats
1	cup uncreamed (low fat) cottage cheese
½	pound (1 cup) ground or chunked turkey, chicken (without skin), lean beef, heart, liver, or lean hamburger

2½	teaspoons Animal Essentials calcium (or a scant 1½ teaspoons of eggshell powder)*
1	teaspoon vegetable oil
2	tablespoons nutritional yeast
	Balanced dog vitamins

* These supplements are from Group III calcium supplements. See chapter 4 for more information.

Cook the vegetables, using 3 to 4 cups water. When they are soft, add the bran and oats. Cover and let it sit for 10 minutes or until the oats are soft. Add the remaining ingredients, except the vitamins. Refrigerate extras. When serving a meal portion, add a balanced dog vitamin that supplies the minimum daily standards, as recommended on the label. (You may also add a bit of Healthy Powder, as described in chapter 3.) This recipe provides about 30 percent protein, 12 percent fat, and 53 percent carbohydrates. Calcium added by Animal Essentials supplement is 2,500 mg.

The low-fat content of this diet will aid in weight loss. However, it's also best to restrict the quantities you feed. Decide what your dog's ideal weight should be and feed two meals a day, together totaling approximately the amount shown below—a little less if your dog is inactive, a little more if it's active. Make sure there is no access to other food, except low-calorie snacks like carrot sticks. Averages 140 kilocalories per cup.

IDEAL WEIGHT (LB.)	FEED (CUPS)
10	1½
25	4
40	5
60	7
85	9

Variations: Instead of the oats, you may substitute 2½ cups cooked brown rice (1 cup dry + 2 cups water) or 3+ cups cooked bulgur (1¼ cups dry + 2½ cups water). Instead of cooking the grains with the vegetables (as with the oats), cook them separately.

DOG WEIGHT LOSS DIET 2

This recipe is simpler and more palatable—but best suited for a smaller dog because it uses relatively higher amounts of meat.

2	cups (1 pound) ground or chunked turkey, chicken, lean beef heart, liver or lean hamburger
5	cups boiled or baked potatoes (or 3½ cups cooked bulgur or rice)
2	cups oat or wheat bran (or vegetables, such as peas, green beans, carrots, or corn)
1	teaspoon vegetable oil
2½	teaspoons Animal Essentials calcium (or a scant 1½ teaspoons of eggshell powder)*

Balanced dog vitamins

* These supplements are from Group III calcium supplements. See chapter 4 for more information.

Combine all ingredients except the vitamins. When serving, add a balanced dog vitamin, supplying the minimum daily standards. (You may also add a bit of Healthy Powder, as described in chapter 3.) Feed about the same amounts as for diet #1. Immediately refrigerate extras.

This recipe provides 26 percent protein, 15 percent fat, and 56 percent carbohydrates. The calcium added by Animal Essentials calcium is 2,500 mg.

CAT WEIGHT LOSS DIET

2	cups (1 pound) ground or chunked turkey, chicken, lean beef heart, liver, or lean hamburger
1½	cups boiled or baked potatoes, with skin (or 1½ cups cooked bulgur or rice)
½	cup oat or wheat bran (or vegetables, such as peas, green beans, carrots, or corn)
1	teaspoon vegetable oil
1	teaspoon Group I bone meal*

Balanced cat vitamins that includes vitamin A. (Use enough of the vitamin formula to add 10,000 IU of vitamin A to this recipe.)

* See chapter 4 for information on types of bone meal. If you use Group II bone meals, double the amount.

Combine all ingredients except the vitamins. When serving, add a balanced cat vitamin supplying the minimum daily standards, as recommended on the bottle label. (You may also add a bit of Healthy Powder, as described in chapter 3.) Averages 250 kilocalories per cup. Feed as follows:

IDEAL WEIGHT (LB.)	FEED (CUPS)
6	²/₃
8	³/₄
10	a little less than 1
12	1

UNDERWEIGHT

If your animal has the opposite problem and is underweight, obviously a different approach is needed. If the weight loss is sudden, it may be from an infection or some other problem that needs to be taken care of first. Have your veterinarian check out this possibility.

To help bring up the weight, use the basic natural foods diets in chapters 4 or 5 and also treat with:

Herbal—Alfalfa (*Medicago sativa*): Use Herbal Schedule 3 on page 439. Continue treatment until the desired effect is achieved—increased hunger and weight gain.

Another treatment suitable for older, run-down animals is:

Homeopathic—*Calcarea phosphorica* (calcium phosphate) 6C: Especially good where there apparently is poor digestion or poor utilization of nutrients, as evidenced by lack of weight gain in spite of good nutrition and adequate appetite. Use Homeopathic Schedule 6(a), page 442.

WEST NILE VIRUS

This disease is transmitted by mosquitoes and primarily affects people and horses. In human beings, only about 1 in 5 become ill with mild symptoms, much like the flu. Occasionally some people (less than 1 percent bitten by infected mosquitoes) develop encephalitis (inflammation of the brain) with severe symptoms, convulsions, even death. It is known that other animals can be infected, most noticeably horses, which can also become seriously ill on occasion. There is no evidence that the virus is passed from one person to another or from horses to people. It seems to require the bite of an infected mosquito.

What about dogs and cats? Research has shown that they can become infected, but are unlikely to have symptoms, so it appears to be basically a "non-disease" in these animals. A few cats that were deliberately infected with the virus showed some mild symptoms—slight decrease in appetite, lethargy (more quiet or sleepy), and some fever for a time—but likely not anything that would be noticed by most people.

If you want to prevent exposure to the virus for your pets, use a mosquito repellent if they go outside when mosquitoes are likely to be out. There are some safe herbal repellants you can use.

WORMS

Worms are internal parasites that live in the intestines of animals. They are commonly found in most animals (especially when the animals are young) and are usually not a serious problem.

We can consider worm-infested animals in three categories.

❖ Very young animals that acquired them from the mother before or after birth (roundworms)

❖ Young or mature animals infested with fleas, or those that eat gophers or other wild creatures (tapeworms—carried by fleas and gophers, usually the latter)

❖ Mature but run-down animals that are in a toxic state and are susceptible to parasites, both inside (roundworms, hookworms, whipworms, tapeworms) and outside (fleas, lice, ticks)

The last category is beyond the scope of this discussion, since treatments can vary considerably. I suggest that you work closely with your veterinarian for such problems. Here we will consider the first two categories, which are more common and less severe. First of all, let's talk a little about the worms themselves.

How to Identify Worms

Tapeworms grow in the small intestine. Each worm has a "head" that stays attached to the intestine, as well as dozens of egg-filled segments that break off and pass out with the feces when ripe. These passed segments look like cream-colored maggots, about ¼ to ½ inch long, that are visible in the fresh stool or around the anus. They do not crawl quickly, but move by forming a sort of "point" on one end. After drying out, they look a lot like a piece of white rice stuck to a hair near the anus.

Though chemical worming treatment can kill the worm, sometimes it just causes the sudden loss of most of the segments, leaving the head still attached. Unfortunately, the head that remains behind soon grows a new body that begins passing segments again. Another problem is that animals get re-infested through eating wild creatures (and occasionally from swallowing fleas).

Roundworms infest most young puppies and kittens and are acquired from their mother, both before and after birth. Usually the infestation is not apparent and must be diagnosed by a veterinarian through a microscopic exam of the feces. Be sure to ask if the infestation is light, medium, or heavy and what kind of worms were found.

If the infestation is heavy, you can usually spot outer signs such as an enlarged belly, poor weight gain, and, perhaps, diarrhea or vomiting. Sometimes whole worms are actually vomited or passed with the feces. They resemble white spaghetti several inches long and will often wiggle when first voided. Usually, only young animals a few weeks old to a few months of age will vomit roundworms.

Hookworms are generally less common than tapeworms and roundworms in this country; but they are still significant. They are more of a problem in the southern parts of the United States or in areas where crowded and unsanitary conditions prevail. Severe hookworm infestation is serious be- cause the worms suck the animal's blood and cause severe anemia. In this kind of situation, it may be best to seek professional help. In young animals with severe infestation, the loss of blood into the intestine causes the stool to look black and tar-like. It may also become fluid and foul smelling. The gums will become pale, reflecting the developing anemia, and the youngster will appear weak and thin.

Whipworms are in a category of their own. They are quite common but usually cause no symptoms, often lying dormant for long periods. If there are symptoms—usually persistent, watery diarrhea—I believe it means something is wrong with the animal's immune system. If so, individualized treatment is required.

TREATMENT, CATEGORY 1

Early roundworm problems in young animals can be mild and insignificant or severe and life-threatening, depending on the health of the puppy or kitten at birth. At a certain stage of pregnancy, worms that have been sleeping dormant in the mother become active and migrate to the developing young in the uterus, infesting them even before birth. This can happen even if the mother tests negative.

It sounds awful, but it is seldom a serious problem because there are usually just a few of these worms. If the mother is not healthy, however, these worms take advantage of the situation and migrate in larger numbers than usual. Puppies or kittens born from these weak mothers can be heavily parasitized and never thrive.

It's important to understand that if the young animals are otherwise healthy and if they are fed a very good diet that's high in protein, the roundworm numbers will gradually decrease to almost nothing over the first few months of life without any treatment at all. After the age of six months, dogs are seldom infested with this worm (as detectable with stool exams). Cats, once they get over their initial worms, become immune for life and are never again re-infested. In both dogs and cats, a few of the original worms may persist in a dormant state until pregnancy occurs (thus spreading to the next generation), but they do not cause any problem and are not detectable in stool tests.

One important factor in the continued resistance of mature animals to roundworms is that they receive sufficient vitamin A. A long-term deficiency of vitamin A will allow worms to re-infest and grow in otherwise resistant animals.

My experience with the care of young animals is that they do not need worm treatment unless they have large numbers of worms or show visible signs of their effects (failure to thrive, pot-belly, diarrhea, or soft stools). Usually, it is enough to see that they have good nutrition. Therefore, I do not support the practice of routinely worming puppies and kittens without even checking to see if they do have a significant worm problem. Why give them these toxic chemicals needlessly? I have seen problems from routine worming treatments, such as poor growth, diarrhea, and loss of appetite—ironically, these are just the problems you want to avoid. Have your veterinarian check the stool for these parasites before having any treatment.

What if you do need to treat young animals? I suggest the following measures (use all of them, if possible).

Homeopathic—*Cina* (Wormseed) 3C: Give 1 tablet 3 times a day for at least 3 weeks. Have the stool checked again in a microscopic evaluation at a lab to make sure the worms are gone.

Nutrition—Add ½ to 2 teaspoons (depending on the animal's size) of wheat or oat bran to the daily fare. This roughage will help to carry out the worms. Also, feed the same quantity of one of these vegetables—grated raw carrots, turnips, or beets.

Herbal—Garlic (*Allium sativum*): Depending on the pet's size, mix ½ to 2 cloves of fresh, chopped, or grated garlic into the daily ration.

Mineral—Diatomaceous earth (skeletal remains of diatoms, a very small sea creature): Can be purchased at natural food stores and some pet stores. This substance, which is sometimes used for the control of fleas, is also effective against roundworms. The action is the same—the shell remnants of the diatoms are irritating to the outside of worms (as they are to the fleas) and cause them to loosen their hold and be flushed out. Add ¼ to 1 teaspoon of natural diatomaceous earth to each meal. Don't use the kind made for swimming pool filters—just the natural unrefined product available (usually) through herbal or garden suppliers.

Alternatively, there are several herbal wormers available now that are quite useful in treatment. If you purchase one at a health food store, follow the directions on the label.

I suggest that you give this nontoxic treatment a three-week trial and then check again for worms. If the worms are still there, then it is best for your pet to get the conventional drug treatment. If a young animal has gone through this program, even if the program was not completely effective, I find that it seems to withstand the drug treatment better.

Other Worm Problems

If your puppy or kitten has been diagnosed with hookworms (a problem in some southern states), go ahead with conventional treatment first. Hookworms can be a more serious problem, and I would rather you treat this parasite under supervision. You can, however, do my treatment after the usual worming as a way to "mop up" any remnants and to prevent further infestations.

Tapeworms are not usually a problem in young animals. They're more likely to appear after the animal is old enough to go hunting (see below).

TREATMENT, CATEGORY 2

After the animal equivalent of childhood, the most common problem is tapeworms. (If you do have a roundworm problem, however, use the treatment outlined for Category 1.) Tapeworms are always picked up from eating another creature (such as fleas, rodents, or, usually, gophers). They are not directly passed from one dog or cat to another, even if the stool is eaten. The tapeworm must go through a developmental cycle inside another animal before it can grow into the infectious form. What this means is that parasites will recur as long as your animal continues to hunt and eat wild creatures.

Tapeworm parasites do not usually cause any detectable health problems and are not serious (though they are disgusting to see). There's no reason to panic, thinking they must be eradicated immediately. If you follow the natural health program in this book, particularly the fresh diet, you will find that parasite problems lessen as your pet's general health improves. As your animal detoxifies and builds up strength, many parasites will be sloughed off.

The idea in treating tapeworms is to use substances that annoy or irritate the worms and to use them over a long period of time. Eventually, the worms will give up and loosen their hold, passing on out.

Herbal—Pumpkin seeds (*Cucurbita pepo*): These seeds are a wonderfully safe treatment against tapeworms. Obtain the whole, raw seeds and keep them in a sealed container at room temperature. Grind them to a fine meal and give them to your pet to consume immediately. If, for some reason, you must grind the seeds ahead of time, store the ground seeds in a sealed container in your freezer. Take out the needed portion quickly each day and reseal the container before much moisture enters it. It's best, however, to grind the seeds fresh before use. An electric seed grinder (sold in health food stores) or a food processor can do the job. Add ¼ to 1 teaspoon (depending on the size of your animal) to each meal.

Nutritional—Wheat-germ oil: Buy a very good quality wheat-germ oil at a health food store, and you have an excellent natural tapeworm discourager as well as a good adjunct to other treatments. Add ¼ to 1 teaspoon, depending on the animal's size, to each meal. Feed a small amount of food so the enzymes work better.

Nutritional—Vegetable enzymes: The enzymes of many plant foods, especially those from figs and papaya, eat away at the outer coating of the worm. Dried figs can be chopped or ground and added to food (more accepted by dogs than cats). Use ¼ to 1 teaspoon, depending on your animal's size, to each meal. Feed a small amount of food so the enzymes work better.

Papaya is an excellent enzyme source, but it's not readily available everywhere. You can use enzyme supplements that contain papain (the papaya enzyme) and other digestive enzymes. Follow the instructions on the label.

Homeopathic—*Filix mass* (male fern) 3C: A time-honored herb used against tapeworms, this remedy can be given as 1 tablet 3 times a day for 2 to 3 weeks, shorter if the segments go away sooner. (The remedy discussed under roundworm treatment, *Cina* 3C, can also be used if *Filix mas* is not available.)

Fasting once a week, allowing just a raw bone and water or broth, is an excellent practice generally. It's especially useful, however, if worms are a problem, because it weakens them and makes them more vulnerable to the treatments being used. Since the worms get their food from the animal's food, they don't get to eat either.

If your pet has a stubborn problem in getting rid of any type of intestinal worm, also try an occasional dose of castor oil. Giving this after a day of fasting will flush out all the weakened worms. Use ½ teaspoon for puppies less than three months old and for all young cats; 1 teaspoon for puppies three to six months old and adult cats; 1½ tablespoons for medium-size dogs, and 2 tablespoons for large dogs.

A Last Segment

In the above discussion I suggest some relatively simple things to do for worm problems. If they don't work, then I recommend using conventional drug treatment. However, I know some of you will not want to give up on a natural approach to this problem. So I am including this more complicated naturopathic approach as a backup. Though more involved, this is a highly effective method (adapted from the suggestions of herbalist Juliette de Bairacli-Levy).

The same program can be used for either tapeworms or roundworms. Basically, it consists of fasting and the use of repellent herbs, along with castor oil (to flush out the intestinal tract).

1. Start by feeding a special diet for three to four days that will help weaken the worms by eliminating foods they prefer (fats, sugars, eggs, whole milk). Give two small meals a day, consisting of rolled oats (softened with water or skim milk), lightly boiled fish, and a liberal sprinkling of nutritional yeast.

2. Next, fast the animal for two days, primarily on water. If the animal is younger than six months, fast it for just a day on water, with a bit of honey added for energy. On the first night of this fast, give some castor oil to act as a purgative to help clear the bowels. Use ½ teaspoon for puppies less than three months old and for all young cats; 1 teaspoon for puppies three to six months old and adult cats; 1½ tablespoons for medium-size dogs, and 2 tablespoons for large dogs (see page 118).

On the second day of the fast, give herbal deworming tablets (available at many health food stores or by mail; see www.drpitcairn.com). Alternatively, make your own formula by combining equal parts of fresh grated garlic with powdered rue and wormwood (herbs) in No. 2 gelatin capsules (sold at drugstores). Make this fresh each day or refrigerate it because of the garlic. Dose according to product instructions or as follows for the homemade mix: three to five capsules for small or young animals; six to eight capsules for medium or large dogs.

About 30 minutes after giving the herbs, administer another dose of castor oil (same amount as before). Then wait another 30 minutes and feed a small amount (about a cup for a medium dog) of a warm, laxative, semi-liquid mixture of raw milk thickened with slippery elm powder, honey, and rolled oats. If this is vomited, try again in 30 minutes. The slippery elm forms a smoothing jelly that helps to remove the worms and eggs from the intestines.

3. For the next three days continue feeding this same mixture of milk, elm, honey, and oats in three small meals a day. Each morning, at least 30 minutes before feeding, give the herbs again, but cut the dose in half. Each evening it helps to give a mild, cleansing laxative, such as ⅛ to ½ teaspoon (depending on body size) of powdered senna with a pinch of ginger. Give it in a capsule or mix into water or food.

4. Slowly return to a normal natural foods diet over the next few days. Stop giving the evening laxative once the animal is eating solid food and having bowel movements. For some time afterward, include in the daily diet the foods recommended earlier (carrots, pumpkin seeds, beets, and so on).

During this period and for about three weeks after the fast, use fresh garlic regularly on the food or give it in gelatin capsules at about half the dose used in the worming capsules. Also, feed an occasional charcoal tablet (once every two or three days, but for no more than a month afterward) to absorb and remove any remaining impurities in the intestines.

With careful application of either of these programs, you should meet with success in nearly all cases. Just to be certain all the worms are gone, have your veterinarian check the stool about six to eight weeks after treatment and periodically thereafter until you are sure the problem is resolved.

Note: Your parasitized animal can be a source of health problems for other animals or for children. Especially with roundworms and hookworms, people can become exposed by contact with contaminated soil. Though these parasites do not really grow well in people and do not usually cause serious problems, they can be troublesome and annoying (primarily causing skin irritation). Until the problem is cleared up, it makes sense to take special care to prevent contamination of the environment. Collect all fecal material to bury (deeply) in one place, flush down the toilet, or package carefully to dispose of through your sanitary service.

HANDLING EMERGENCIES AND GIVING FIRST AID

Important. Read this first! The care you give an animal in the first few minutes of an emergency can make the difference between life and death. The first-aid remedies I suggest definitely work and will be tremendously helpful in that time between the beginning of the emergency and arrival at your veterinarian's office. But they are meant as temporary lifesaving procedures to use while you contact the doctor and ready transportation. Do not use these methods as a way of delaying needed professional help. Instructions for more prolonged treatment apply only if you *cannot* reach medical care.

For this information to serve you, plan ahead and have supplies on hand in a convenient place. An emergency is not the time to begin assembling these tools and remedies or to start reading "how to do it." The information that follows is provided in brief outline form, alphabetically, for ready reference when needed. But please study all the categories ahead of time so you can find the right heading in a hurry during a time of crisis.

Here is a list of supplies you should have on hand in order to make full use of my suggestions. See www.drpitcairn.com for suppliers of the homeopathic remedies. Dr. Bach's stress-relieving rescue formula is available at natural foods stores, and the other supplies are found in drug stores.

Homeopathic Remedies

For each, order 2 drams of the remedy as #10 pellets (little tiny ones, like grains of sand, which are easiest to give), approximately 10 or so as a dose given from the cap of the vial.

- *Aconitum* 30C
- *Arnica montana* 30C
- *Arsenicum album* 30C
- *Calendula* 30C
- Calendula tincture—one-ounce dropper bottle
- Calendula ointment—can be purchased from homeopathic pharmacies
- *Carbo vegetabilis* 30C
- *Glonoine* 30C
- *Hypericum* 30C
- *Ledum* 30C
- *Nux vomica* 30C
- *Phosphorus* 30C
- *Symphytum*30C
- *Urtica urens* tincture—one-ounce dropper bottle

Other Remedies

- Activated charcoal granules
- Ammonia water
- Fresh warm coffee (caffeinated)
- Raw onion
- Dr. Bach's stress-relieving rescue formula—10½-milliliter dropper bottle of the stock. Prepare a solution from purchased stock in this manner: Add four drops of stock to a one-ounce dropper bottle filled a third of the way with brandy, as a preservative. Add enough spring water to fill the bottle and shake well. Make this diluted solution in advance and use it as recommended for treatment. It will keep for at least a year if kept out of the sun and away from heat.

Materials

- (2) blankets—thick and strong
- Adhesive tape—one-inch-wide roll
- Elastic bandage—three inches wide
- Enema bag
- Gauze pads—one package
- Natural soap—like Dr. Bronner's natural soap
- Plastic bowl—for preparing dilutions
- Sea salt—for making saline (¼ tsp. per cup of water)
- Water—for dilution (spring or distilled water is best; tap water is okay)
- Empty plastic syringe—for administering remedies
- Empty dropper bottle(s)—for preparing remedies

WHAT TO DO IN EMERGENCIES

BREATHING STOPPED

Follow these steps to apply Artificial Respiration Technique.

1. Open the mouth, pull out the tongue, check back into the throat to make sure no obstructions are present. Clear away mucus and blood if necessary. Replace the tongue.

2. Give one dose of *Carbo vegetabilis* 30C. Place a few pellets on the tongue. Drip water on the tongue to dissolve the pellets.

3. Close the mouth and place your mouth over the nostrils. Exhale as you fill the animal's lungs, allowing it to exhale after. Do this 6 times a minute for dogs, 12 times a minute for cats. Inflate the chest until you can see it rise.

4. Administer Dr. Bach's rescue formula, starting after 5 minutes. Place two drops on the gums or tongue and continue every 5 minutes until breathing is restored. Then every 30 minutes (if you can't reach help) for four treatments.

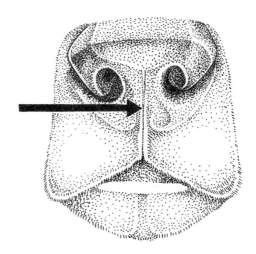

BREATHING AND HEART BOTH STOPPED

(Listen at chest.)

Follow these steps.

1. Use the Artificial Respiration Technique including use of one dose of *Carbo*

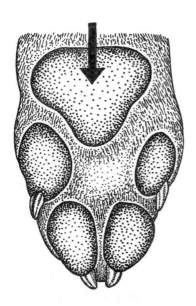

vegetabilis 30C (see "Breathing Stopped") and the External Heart Massage Technique (see "Heart Stopped," page 434), step one, at the same time. This is easiest for two people.

2. Apply acupressure. Use the edge of your thumbnail or the pointed cap of a pen to put strong pressure over the center of the large pad of each rear foot. If there's no response at first, try reaching the same point by coming in from under the back edge of the pad. After a few seconds, release and apply pressure to the point on the nose shown in the diagram. Alternate between acupressure and cardiopulmonary resuscitation. If two people are working, have each one apply one of the techniques continuously.

3. After five minutes, give one dose of *Arnica montana* 30C. Place a few pellets on the tongue.

4. After 5 more minutes, administer Dr. Bach's rescue formula. Place two drops on the gums or tongue and continue every 5 minutes until breathing is restored. Repeat every 30 minutes (if you can't reach help) for four treatments.

BURNS

("White" skin or scorched hair)
   Use one technique.

   1. Apply *Urtica urens* tincture. Add six drops of the tincture to one ounce (two full tablespoons) water. Saturate gauze with the solution and place over the burn. Do not remove the gauze, but keep it moistened by adding more of the solution. If necessary, hold in place with a bandage.

   2. Give one dose of *Arsenicum album* 30C.

   3. After 5 more minutes, administer Dr. Bach's rescue formula. Place two drops on the tongue every 30 minutes for a total of three treatments. Repeat every four hours until relief is evident.

CAR ACCIDENTS

(Obvious injury; greasy or very dirty coat)
   Follow these steps.

   1. Move the animal to a safe place. If the animal is found on the road, without bending its spine or changing its position, slide it onto a board or taut blanket and transport it to a safer location. You may need to tie a strip of cloth or wrap a pressure bandage around the mouth temporarily (as a muzzle) or put a blanket over the animal's head, to keep it from biting someone.

   2. Give a dose of *Arnica montana* 30C. Place a few pellets on the tongue every 15 minutes, for a total of three doses. Do this only if it is safe to do so. An injured animal will bite without restraint and can cause very serious injury. If it seems unsafe to administer a medicine, dissolve two pellets in some water or milk and drip it onto the lips from a safe distance above. If you happen to have a syringe with a needle on it, you can squirt the diluted medicine fairly accurately between the lips and into the mouth.

   3. Keep the animal warm and watch for shock (see "Shock," page 437).

CARDIOPULMONARY RESUSCITATION

(See "Breathing and Heart Both Stopped," page 431.)

CONVULSIONS

(Stiffening or alternate rapid contraction/ relaxation of muscles; thrashing about; frothing at the mouth)

   1. Do not interfere with or try to restrain the animal during the convulsion. It is too dangerous to you and does not help the animal.

   2. If breathing stops after the convulsion, use artificial respiration (see "Breathing Stopped," page 430). If the heart stops

too, use cardiopulmonary resuscitation (see "Breathing and Heart Both Stopped," page 431).

3. Give *Aconitum* 30C. If possible, put a few pellets on the tongue (see warning about being bitten in "Car Accidents," opposite).

4. If convulsions continue, after 5 minutes give *Belladonna* 30C.

5. After 5 more minutes, administer Dr. Bach's rescue formula, two drops every 15 minutes, if the animal is frightened or disoriented, up to three doses or until relief is evident.

6. Consider poisoning as a possible cause (see "Poisoning," page 435).

CUTS

(Lacerations, tears)

Follow these steps.

1. Flush out the cut with clean water. Remove obvious debris like sticks, hair, and gravel.

2. Apply calendula lotion. Add six drops calendula tincture to one ounce (two full tablespoons) water; saturate gauze pads, and tape them in place. If this is irritating, flush with saline and bandage with dry pads.

3. Wash minor wounds that do not need professional care with soap and water and dry carefully. Clip hair from the edges of the wound. Apply calendula ointment twice a day until healed. Leave unbandaged if possible.

Also give one dose of *Calendula* 30C.

FRACTURES

(Leg "bends" at sharp angle; animal won't use leg)

❖ *If the lower leg is obviously broken,* very carefully wrap a roll of clean newspaper or magazine around it and tape it to prevent unrolling. Do not try to set the leg yourself; just keep the lower end from swinging back and forth.

❖ *If a wound is present at the fracture site,* cover it with clean gauze before applying a temporary splint, as above.

❖ *If the fracture is not apparent or is high up,* do not attempt to splint. Let the animal assume the most comfortable posture . A padded box may be best for transporting small animals to the veterinarian. Walking on three legs may be best for a larger dog.

1. Give *Arnica* 30C. One dose is usually enough, but repeat again in 4 hours if there is still much pain.

2. Next day give *Ruta* 30C, which will remove residual pain from having torn the membrane that covers the bones (or give after surgery to reduce pain).

3. Wait another 3 days and give *Symphytum* 30C to accelerate healing of the bones.

GUNSHOT WOUNDS

(Look for two holes opposite each other on the body, great pain and anxiety.)

1. Give *Arnica* 30C, a few pellets every 15 minutes, for a total of three doses.

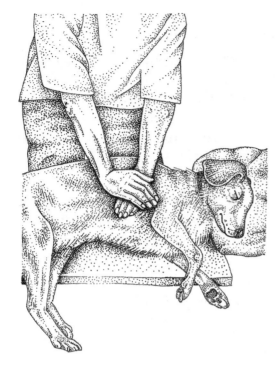

Heart Massage: Using both hands, press firmly and release 60 times a minute.

2. Apply hand pressure with dry gauze over the wound, if necessary, until bleeding stops. Or temporarily use the Pressure Bandage Technique (see "Pressure Bandage Technique," page 436).

3. Give *Hypericum* 30C if there is no relief from the three doses of *Arnica*. Give a few pellets every 15 minutes for a total of three doses.

4. Continue treatment with *Arnica* 30C or *Hypericum* 30C, whichever was most useful. Give a dose every 4 hours, as long as it seems needed to control pain. Typically, 3 doses will do all the good

that can be accomplished with this medicine.

5. If there is still apparent pain, give *Calendula* 30C, one dose.

HEART STOPPED

(No heartbeat felt or heard at chest)
Follow these steps:

1. Apply External Heart Massage Technique. Place the animal with its right side down on a firm surface. Place one or both hands (depending on animal's size) over the lower chest directly behind the elbow. Press firmly and release at the rate of once every second (see the illustration, left). *Caution:* Excessive pressure can fracture ribs.

2. Give one dose of *Carbo vegetabilis* 30C. As soon as you can, place a few pellets on the tongue, then drop some water on the pellets to dissolve them in the mouth.

3. Administer Dr. Bach's rescue formula. Put two drops in the side of the mouth, repeating every 5 minutes until there is a response. Then every 30 minutes (if no help is available) for four doses.

4. Apply artificial respiration if the heart does not start within a minute (see "Breathing Stopped," page 430).

5. Successful heart massage (and respiration) can be recognized by the return of normal "pink" color to the gums.

HEAT STROKE

(Animal found unconscious in hot car)

Follow these steps.

1. Remove the animal immediately to a cool, shady area. Use the car's shadow if necessary.

2. Wet the animal with water. Apply continuously to cool the body as much as possible. Place ice packs or cold, wet towels around the body and head during transport to the veterinarian.

3. Give one dose of *Belladonna* 30C.

4. If no improvement within 30 minutes, give one dose of *Glonoine* 30C.

5. Administer Dr. Bach's rescue formula. Put two drops in the mouth every ten minutes until you arrive at the veterinarian's.

6. If breathing has stopped, follow instructions for "Breathing Stopped," page 430.

HEMORRHAGE

(Bleeding from a wound or body opening)
For skin wounds, use these treatments.

1. Give one dose *Arnica* 30C. Wait for 30 minutes. If bleeding has not stopped, give the next remedy.

2. Give one dose *Phosphorus* 30C.

3. Locally apply a calendula "lotion" (six drops tincture in one ounce of water).

4. If necessary, use the Pressure Bandage (as described on page 436).

For internal bleeding, (pale tongue, gums, and inside of eyelids, with weakness) use these treatments.

1. Give one dose *Arnica* 30C and repeat it every 30 minutes for three treatments.

2. Give *Phosphorus* 30C in three 3 doses (as above), if *Arnica* 30C is not sufficient.

3. Keep the animal calm. If hysteria is a problem, begin treatment by placing two drops of Dr. Bach's rescue formula in the mouth every five minutes for three treatments. Then follow with *Arnica.*

INSECT BITES

(Bee, hornet, and wasp stings; centipede, scorpion, and spider bites; red, painful swellings)

For local use: For bee, hornet, or wasp stings, apply a freshly sliced onion. Alternatively, rub in one drop of ammonia water (can be purchased for cleaning floors and windows—in a pinch, you can use ammonia detergent or an ammonia-based window cleaner).

An effective herbal treatment is to rub in a drop of nettle extract (*Urtica urens* tincture or glycerine extract) directly on the sting.

Hold a dull knife perpendicular to the skin and scrape across the area of the sting a few times. This will grab the stinger and pull it out without pain. Do not try to grab a stinger with your fingers or with tweezers, as it will squeeze more poison into the wound.

Internally, for all insect bites give *Ledum* 30C, a few pellets every 15 minutes for a total of 3 treatments.

POISONING

(Symptoms appear in three major forms: excess salivation, tears, and frequent urination and defecation; muscle twitching, trembling, and convulsions; severe vomiting.)

Follow these steps.

1. Give granular activated charcoal. Mix five heaping teaspoons of granules in 1 cup of water. Depending on the animal's size, give about ¼ to 1 cup by spoonfuls in the cheek pouch. If this causes excess struggle or worsens symptoms, discontinue. Your veterinarian will be able to apply treatment under sedation or anesthesia.

2. Give *Nux vomica* 30C, a few pellets on the tongue every 15 minutes for a total of 3 doses. Do not continue treatment if the symptoms worsen.

3. Keep the animal warm and as quiet as possible. Stress has a very negative influence.

4. Call the National Animal Poison Control Center if you know where the poison came from. Call 800-548-2423 ($30 credit card charge per case) for specific advice on treatment or antidotes.

Otherwise, bring the suspected poisons and container (if known), as well as any vomited material, to the doctor for possible identification of the poison.

PRESSURE BANDAGE TECHNIQUE

(To control hemorrhage, excessive bleeding; to keep gauze and medication in place)

Follow these steps.

1. Place dry or medicated gauze (calendula ointment is a good choice) over the wound and wrap an overlapping elastic

To control bleeding: Place medicated gauze over the wound. Wrap an elastic bandage around the wound.

bandage around it. Apply only slight tension to the wrap because excessive pressure (especially on a leg) can cut off blood flow like a tourniquet. If the wound is on the lower half of the leg, wrap all the way to and including the foot (to prevent swelling).

2. Secure the end of the bandage with adhesive tape to prevent unwinding.

3. Remove the bandage at once if swelling occurs below the wrap (as on a leg). If you can reach the foot pads, periodically check that they remain warm; if they're cold, then the bandage is too tight. Remember, bandaging is a tempo-

rary measure; use it until bleeding stops or you can reach the veterinarian.

PUNCTURES

(From teeth, claws, sharp objects)
Follow these steps.

1. Wash wound with soap and water. Use a natural soap, not a strong detergent.

2. Extract any embedded hair you see in the hole.

3. Apply direct pressure over the wound with gauze only if bleeding is excessive (see "Pressure Bandage Technique," above). Moderate bleeding is appropriate to flush out the wound.

4. Give *Ledum* 30C, a few pellets every two hours, for 3 doses.

SHOCK

(Accompanies serious injuries. Symptoms are white gums, rapid breathing, unconsciousness.)

❖ *If much bruising or trauma is evident or internal hemorrhage is suspected,* use *Arnica* 30C, one dose every ten minutes until a response is seen. Then treat every two hours until the gums are once again pink and your pet seems to be normally alert.

❖ *If the animal is unconscious,* give *Aconitum* 30C, one dose every ten minutes until consciousness returns. If there is no response within four doses, switch over to *Arnica* 30C and use the same schedule as you would for *Aconitum.*

❖ *If the animal appears to be dying (cold,*
blue, lifeless), give *Carbo vegetabilis* 30C, one dose every five minutes for three treatments. If he rallies, follow with *Arnica* 30C as described in the first step of this section.

Note: Keep the animal warm with a blanket in a horizontal position.

SUDDEN COLLAPSE

(Sudden unconsciousness without warning; fainting)
Follow these steps.

1. First check to see if breathing or the heart has stopped. If so, use the treatment described under "Breathing Stopped" (page 430) or "Breathing and Heart Both Stopped" (page 431).

2. Use Dr. Bach's rescue formula, two drops every 5 minutes until a response, and then every 30 minutes.

3. Give a warm coffee enema (for caffeine). Use ¼ cup for small dogs, ½ cup for medium dogs, and 1 cup for large dogs. Press gauze against the anus for 15 minutes to prevent the fluid from coming out.

4. Count out the heart rate for a minute, if possible, by listening to the lower left chest (near where left elbow touches the chest). This will be useful information for your veterinarian, as an abnormal heart rate (too fast or too slow) is a frequent cause of fainting.

5. If none of this has helped then, give one dose of *Arsenicum album* 30C.

SCHEDULE FOR HERBAL TREATMENT

General Directions: Use freshly harvested and dried herbs if possible, preferably this year's crop. After a few years, herbs lose potency from exposure to air. Alcoholic extracts of herbs, called tinctures, are an especially useful form because they are more stable, maintaining potency for at least two years and sometimes longer. Available in one-ounce dropper bottles, they are easily added to water for dilution. Gelatin capsules are also useful for preserving powdered herbs. They help the herbs stay fresh by excluding the oxygen, which degrades them.

SCHEDULE 1: INTERNAL

In this schedule, give the herbs *three times a day* until there are no more symptoms, or for a maximum of seven days. Depending on the form of herb you use, they're prepared a little differently (see chapter 15 for more information on herbs and on techniques for giving medications to pets). Here are the options.

(a) *Infusions.* Make an infusion by first bringing one cup of pure water (filtered or distilled) to a boil. Pour it over one rounded teaspoon of dried herb or one rounded tablespoon of fresh herb. Cover and steep for 15 minutes. Then extract the liquid by straining it through a cheesecloth or sieve.

Here's how much to give your pet three times a day (morning, mid-afternoon, and at night before bed): ½ teaspoon for cats or small dogs (less than 30 pounds); 1 teaspoon for medium dogs (30 to 60 pounds); or one tablespoon for large dogs (60 pounds and over).

(b) *Cold extracts.* Add two rounded teaspoons of dried herb or two rounded tablespoons of fresh herb to one cup of cold, pure water. Cover and let it sit for 12 hours. Strain out the solids and administer the liquid extract three times a day, in the same quantities listed for infusions (a).

(c) *Decoctions.* In some cases the instructions specify that you should prepare a decoction, the method to prepare certain dried roots, rhizomes, and barks. To do so, add one rounded teaspoon of the herb to one cup of pure water. Bring to a boil and simmer uncovered for 15 to 20 minutes. Strain out the solids and administer the liquid three times a day, in the same quantities listed for infusions (a).

(d) *Tinctures.* If you have the tincture form of the herb (see chapter 15, page 280, for preparation instructions or they can be purchased in natural food stores), dilute it, three drops to one teaspoon (nine drops to one tablespoon) of pure water. Administer this solution three times a day in the same quantities listed for infusions (a).

(e) *Gelatin capsules.* Herb capsules that are prepared for human consumption can also be given to animals, but in smaller doses. Small dogs and cats will get half of a capsule as a dose; medium dogs will get one as a dose; large dogs will receive two capsules each dose. Remember that one dose is given three times a day with this schedule.

SCHEDULE 2: INTERNAL

On this schedule, give the herbs *twice* a day, on approximately a 12-hour schedule. Use the same procedures and quantities as de-

scribed in Schedule 1. Likewise, continue treating until symptoms are gone or a week has passed.

SCHEDULE 3: INTERNAL

With this program, you'll give the herbs *only once a day* (every 24 hours). Again, follow the same procedures and quantities outlined in Schedule 1, treating until the symptoms are gone, or for a maximum of one week.

SCHEDULE 4: EXTERNAL

This program calls for an herbal compress. First make a hot infusion, decoction, or tincture dilution of the herb (or herbs), as in Schedule 1. Let it cool a bit so that it's hot, but not so hot that it will burn or cause discomfort. If you can stand it, then it's likely your pet can also. Next, immerse a washcloth or small hand towel in the solution, wring it out, and apply it to the affected area on your pet's body. Put a dry towel over this moist compress to keep the heat in. After five minutes, refresh the compress: dip it back in the hot solution, wring it out again, and re-apply.

If you can, treat for 15 minutes, though your pet may only allow you 5 minutes or so. You can use this compress twice a day for up to two weeks.

SCHEDULE 5: EXTERNAL

Prepare a hot compress, as in Schedule 4, but alternate it a couple of times with a cold compress (a second cloth dipped in tap water). This method is more stimulating, encouraging a strong blood supply to the area. First use the hot herbal compress for 5 minutes, and then follow it with 2 minutes of the cold water compress. Repeat one more time, using the same sequence. The whole treatment lasts about 15 minutes. This can be performed twice daily for a period up to two weeks.

SCHEDULE 6: EXTERNAL

In this approach, you make a warm-to-hot infusion, decoction, or tincture dilution of the herb (or herbs), as in Schedule 1. When the temperature is acceptable, immerse your animal's foot, leg, or tail (the affected part) directly into the solution. If your pet will put up with it, soak the area for at least five minutes and then towel dry. Soak twice a day, as needed, for up to two weeks.

SCHEDULE FOR HOMEOPATHIC TREATMENT

General Directions: Give the remedy by first dispensing one or two pellets into the vial cap or a clean spoon, or by crushing three of them in a small, folded paper. (Pellets come in different sizes; we are assuming the standard size, which is round pellets ⅛ inch in diameter. If the pellets are smaller, use more of them, as in the First Aid section. The idea is for our patient to taste them and swallow at least one.) Then pour them directly into your pet's mouth or throat—do not touch them yourself (see chapter 15).

Homeopathic remedies do not work as effectively if they are added to food. Each of the schedules below indicates how long you should withhold food before and after giving the remedy.

Water is less of a problem, but it is a good practice to prevent your pet from drinking for 5 minutes before and after giving the medicine.

SCHEDULE 1: ACUTE DISEASE TREATMENT

Give one pellet or tablet every 4 hours until the symptoms are gone. Provide no food for ten minutes before and after treatment.

If your animal shows signs of improvement, you can stop using the medicine. If there is a fever, however, then continue treatment until the temperature is below 101.5°F.

If you do not see improvement within 24 hours, however, you should try one of the other suggested remedies.

SCHEDULE 2: ACUTE DISEASE TREATMENT

Give one or two pellets every 4 hours for a total of three treatments. Provide no food for ten minutes before and after treatment. No further homeopathic treatment will be needed for the next 24 hours. If your animal is not noticeably improved by then, try another remedy or go to one of the other treatment choices.

SCHEDULE 3: ACUTE DISEASE TREATMENT

In this method you give only one treatment. Provide no food for one hour before and after treatment. If there is no improvement within 24 hours, then choose another remedy to use. If a definite improvement has occurred, then no further homeopathic treatment will be needed.

SCHEDULE 4: CHRONIC DISEASE TREATMENT

In this method you give only one treatment. Give two whole pellets or three pellets crushed to a powder. Place on the tongue. Give no food for one hour before and after the treatment. Wait for a full month before any further treatment; it would be a mistake to repeat the remedy in a few days. If at the end of that month no improvement is evi-dent, then you will need to choose a new medicine.

SCHEDULE 5: CHRONIC DISEASE TREATMENT

Here you will give just three doses, 24 hours apart, and then wait for a month. For each of the three treatments, give two whole pellets or three pellets crushed to a powder. Place on the tongue. Provide no food for 30 minutes before and after each treatment. Do not give any further treatment for a month. If you have not seen any improvement by then, choose a new treatment.

SCHEDULE 6: CHRONIC DISEASE TREATMENT

Here you will repeat doses over a longer period. Depending on the recommended option, you will give it (a) once every day (b) twice a day—approximately every 12 hours, (c) three times a day—morning, mid-day, and evening before bed. Provide no food for five minutes before and after giving the medicine.

The treatment period is usually a week or 10 days. If it has helped some but not enough, this can be an indication that either a better medicine should be used or there is something else slowing down the recovery. It is best to get advice from a holistic veterinarian at this point.

Evaluating

Response to medication: Deciding whether a given treatment has helped so far is an important part of your overall success with homeopathic medicines. It determines your next move: whether to continue, stop, or try another treatment.

The first and best sign that a treatment is helping is that your animal appears to feel better overall, with improved energy, spirits, activity level, and moods. Secondarily, you will see specific improvements in its physical condition, though these will occur more slowly.

Another good sign, one that you could easily misinterpret, is that the body may produce a temporary discharge as part of the healing process. Depending on the illness, this may take the form of brief diarrhea (one day), vomiting (once), or eruption and discharge from the skin. Or in the case of a virus infection, for instance, the body may produce a fever for a few days as it mobilizes its defenses. None of these reactions, however, should be severe or long-lasting. And, again, if the program is working, your animal will be feeling better in an overall sense.

Many health problems are complex and difficult to treat, and you will greatly benefit if you can work with a skilled veterinary homeopathic practitioner. If you are in doubt or your animal is getting worse, it is best to consult such a veterinarian. You can find a list of veterinarians trained by Dr. Pitcairn in the use of homeopathy on his Web site, www.drpitcairn.com.

ADDITIONAL RECIPES— SNACKS AND TREATS

WHEAT OR RYE CRISPS FOR DOGS

Here's one of Joan Harper's (*The Healthy Cat and Dog Cookbook*) simplest recipes for dog biscuits. (Commercial products often include meat meal, with all its disadvantages.) They're good for occasional treats or rewards and to exercise teeth and gums, but too low in protein and other nutrients for regular chow. This recipe contains 15 percent protein, 28 percent fat, and 56 percent carbohydrates.

1	cup whole-wheat or rye flour
1/4	cup soy flour
3	tablespoons lard, bacon, fat, or oil
1	teaspoon Group I bone meal (double this if using Group II, or about 1,400 mg of calcium from another source)*
1	clove garlic, grated, or 1/4 teaspoon garlic powder (optional)
1/3	cup water or broth
1 to 2	teaspoons nutritional yeast (optional)

*See information on calcium supplements in "Table of Calcium Supplementation Products" on page 67.

Combine the dry ingredients. Add the water or broth and mix well. Roll out on a cookie sheet and bake at 350°F until golden brown. Break into bite-size chunks. Sprinkle with nutritional yeast if your dog is fond of it.

KITTY OR DOGGIE CRUNCHIES

This recipe, an adaptation of a tried-and-true kibble created by Joan Harper, is nice for an occasional treat or to help a confirmed kibble-eater make the transition to home cooking. It is nutritionally complete for both cats and dogs, with 36 percent protein, about 17 percent fat, and a calcium/phosphorus ratio of 1.3 to 1.

1	pound chicken necks and gizzards or other poultry, ground
1	(16-ounce) can of mackerel, chopped
2	cups full-fat soy flour
1	cup wheat germ
1	cup powdered skim milk
1	cup cornmeal (dry)
2	cups whole-wheat flour
1	cup rye flour (or another cup of wheat flour)
2	tablespoons Animal Essentials calcium (or the equivalent of 6,000 mg of calcium from a Group III source)*
1/2	teaspoon iodized salt or 3 tablespoons kelp
4	tablespoons vegetable oil (half can be meat drippings, or butter)
1/2	tablespoon (1 1/2 tsp) cod-liver oil (or up to 20,000 IU vitamin A)
1/4	cup alfalfa powder or trace mineral powder
3	cloves garlic, minced
400	IU vitamin E
1	quart water
1/2	cup brewer's yeast

*See information on calcium supplements in "Table of Calcium Supplementation Products" on page 67.

Mix all the ingredients except the yeast and knead into a firm dough. Roll it out on a cookie sheet about ½ to ¼ inch thick. (Use a pastry scraper to divide it into strips.) Bake at 350°F for 30 to 45 minutes. Cool and break into bite-size chunks. Sprinkle with the yeast and store in airtight containers. Refrigerate whatever amount will not be consumed in 3 days.

Note: I could not find exact nutritional information for chicken necks, so the recipe is calculated assuming half chicken gizzards and half chicken (roaster) meat. If some chicken neck or backs or wings—inexpensive sources—are used, then additional calcium will come from the included bones. You might reduce the calcium supplement part of the recipe by 1 teaspoon in that instance. If you use boneless chicken, the recipe will contain less calcium. The nutritional profile for alfalfa powder (a wonderful source of trace minerals) was not available to me, so is not included in the calculation. I do not expect this to alter the values significantly.

DOG BISCUITS DELUXE

2	cups whole-wheat flour
$1/2$	cup soy flour
$1/4$	cup cornmeal
1	teaspoon Group I bone meal (or double that for Group II)*
1	tablespoon Animal Essentials calcium (or 3,000 mg calcium from a Group III source)*
$1/2$	cup sunflower or pumpkin seeds
1–2	cloves garlic, minced, or $1/2$ teaspoon garlic powder (optional)
1	tablespoon brewer's yeast (optional)
2	tablespoons butter (melted), fat, or oil
$1/4$	cup unsulfured molasses
1	teaspoon salt
2	eggs mixed with $1/4$ cup milk

*See information on calcium supplements in "Table of Calcium Supplementation Products" on page 67.

Mix the flours, cornmeal, bone meal, and seeds together. Add the garlic and yeast, if desired. Combine the butter, fat, or oil, molasses, salt, and egg mixture; set aside 1 tablespoon of this liquid mixture and combine the rest with the dry ingredients. Add more milk, if necessary, to make a firm dough. Knead together for a few minutes and let the dough rest ½ hour or more. Roll out to ½ inch thick. Cut into crescents, rounds, or sticks and brush with the remainder of the egg mixture. Bake at 350°F for 30 minutes or until lightly toasted. To make harder biscuits, leave them in the oven with the heat turned off for an hour or more. Biscuits keep longer if you use oil instead of butter. These treats provide 20 percent protein, 18 percent fat, and 57 percent carbohydrates.

KITTY CATNIP COOKIES

1	cup whole-wheat flour
2	tablespoons wheat germ
$1/4$	cup soy flour
$1/3$	cup powdered milk
1	tablespoon kelp
$1/2$	teaspoon Group I bone meal (or double this for Group II or add about 700 mg from Group III sources)*
1	teaspoon crushed dried catnip leaves
1	tablespoon unsulfured molasses
1	egg
2	tablespoons oil, butter, or fat
$1/3$	cup milk or water

*See information on calcium supplements in "Table of Calcium Supplementation Products" on page 67.

Mix the dry ingredients together. Add the oil, butter, or fat, molasses, egg, and milk or water. Knead together until it forms a dough. Roll out flat on an oiled cookie sheet and cut into narrow strips or ribbons. Bake at 350°F for 20 minutes or until lightly toasted. Break into pea-size pieces, suitable for cats. Good for treats, exercising gums, and cleaning teeth.

LIVER BROWNIES (DOGS OR CATS)

This wonderful recipe was developed by Kathy Gibson-Anklam of Rockwood Hospital for Pets in Merrill, Wisconsin. The brownies have been extremely popular with their clients, and all the pets love them. The recipe provides 30 percent protein, 21 percent fat, and 45 percent carbohydrates.

6	large eggs
$1/3$	cup vegetable oil
800	IU Vitamin E
1	tablespoon fresh, chopped garlic
2	pounds raw liver (beef or chicken)
3	cups whole-wheat flour
1	cup corn meal
1	cup rolled oats
$1/2$	cup lecithin granules
$1/4$	cup kelp powder
8	teaspoons Animal Essentials calcium (or 8,000 mg calcium from another Group III source)*
1	tablespoon brewer's yeast
$1/2$	cups water (enough to make a batter)

*See information on calcium supplements in "Table of Calcium Supplementation Products" on page 67.

Beat eggs and oil. Squeeze contents of vitamin E capsules into egg mixture and add garlic.

Process the liver to a paste in a blender or food processor. Add to the egg mixture.

Add the dry ingredients to the liver mixture, plus enough water to be able to stir well. You want to have a thick batter when you are done.

Spread the batter in a greased 17" × 11" jelly roll pan. Bake at 350°F for 35 to 45 minutes until nicely browned and firm to the touch.

Cool completely. Cut into bite size pieces. Refrigerate or freeze. Use refrigerated brownies within 4 to 5 days.

Note: This treat will be very enticing to dogs and cats because of the high liver content. It is, however, very high in vitamin A, which comes primarily from liver. So use this as an occasional treat; *not* for daily use.

FAT CONTENT OF MEATS

MEAT	FAT (GRAMS/ 100 GRAMS)

Beef

Heart, lean	3.6
Liver	3.8
Kidney	6.7
Brain	8.6
Ground beef, lean	10.0
Ground round	12.3
Tongue	15.0
Chuck roast	19.6
Heart, fatty	20.7
Ground beef, regular	21.2
Sirloin steak	26.7

Chicken

Liver	3.8
Whole, fryer	4.9
Fryer, neck, back, wings	8.8
Whole, roaster	17.9

Fish

Haddock	.1
Cod	.3
Abalone	.5
Sole	.8
Tuna, canned in water	.8
Squid	.9
Pollock	.9
Red Snapper	.9
Perch, yellow	.9
Halibut	1.2
Smelt	2.1
Bass	2.4
Herring, Pacific	2.6
Catfish	3.1
Perch, white	4.0
Carp	4.2
Mackerel, Pacific	7.3
Sardines, raw	8.6
Shad	10.0
Sardines, canned in oil and drained	11.1
Herring, Atlantic	11.3
Mackerel, Atlantic	12.2
Salmon, Atlantic	13.4
Salmon, Chinook	15.6
Tuna, canned in oil	20.5

Lamb

Choice grade	21.3

Pork

Loin, raw	28.0
Loin, cooked	31.8

Rabbit, whole	8.0
Snail	1.4

Turkey

White meat	1.2
Whole	14.7

Low fat = 0–10 grams fat per 100 grams of food.

Medium fat = 10.1–20 grams fat per 100 grams of food.

High fat = 20.1–40 grams fat per 100 grams of food.

NUTRITIONAL COMPOSITION OF RECIPES FOR TREATS AND SNACKS

RECIPE	TOTAL KCAL.	DRY WEIGHT (G.)	PROTEIN (%)	FAT (%)	CARB (%)
Wheat or Rye Crisps	870	171	15	28	56
Kittie or Doggy Crunchies	5,213	1,145	36	17	43
Dog Biscuits Deluxe	3,121	650	19	25	52
Kitty Catnip Cookies	1,113	244	20	18	57
Liver Brownies	4,632	973	30	21	45
Standard Recommendations (cats)†	~ 350	–	≥26	≥9	–
Standard Recommendations (dogs)†	See chart on page 87	–	≥18	≥5	≥67
Wild Diets (cats)††	–	–	46	33	16
Wild Diets (dogs)††	–	–	54	42	1

*The high amount of vitamin A comes almost entirely from the liver. See the note at the end of the recipe about not overfeeding this treat.

**The 5,000 IU of vitamin A per kilogram of food is a minimum standard. The recipes are designed to have considerably greater amounts of vitamin A for the maintenance of good health.

† Standard Recommendations are based on the guidelines for producing commercial foods. The amounts in our recipes are meant to exceed these minimums in most categories.

†† The percentages found in the natural, wild diet are included for comparison purposes. Not all categories are known and therefore, some are left empty.

Note: Except where noted for wild dogs or cats, standard recommendations are percentage total dry weight and are for maintenance of adult dogs and cats under normal conditions. Sources: AAFCO Nutrient Profiles—Report of the Canine Nutrition Expert Subcommittee, 1992; Report of the Feline Nutrition Expert Subcommittee, 1992; the Merck Veterinary Manual, 6th Edition, 1986; the Committee on Animal Nutrition, Board on Agriculture, National Research Council revised 1986 edition of Nutrient Requirements of Cats; and the Committee on Animal Nutrition, Board on Agriculture, National Research Council revised 1985 edition of Nutrient Requirements of Dogs.

Note: The symbol "≥" is to read as "equal to or greater than amount listed." Thus, the notation "≥5,000 IU" reads "the amount should be equal to or greater than 5,000 IU." The symbol "≤" reads the opposite, meaning "equal to, or less than."

FIBER (%)	ASH (%)	CALCIUM (%)	PHOSPH. (%)	CALC:PHOS RATIO	VIT. A ($^{IU}/_{KG}$)
2	2	.89	.81	1.1:1	~ 10,000
2	5	.88	.67	1.3:1	~ 17,000
2	5	.86	.66	1.3:1	~ 10,000
2	5	.72	.67	1.1:1	~ 3,000
1	4	.98	.79	1.2:1	~ 400,000*
–	–	≥.80	≥.60	1:1**	≥5,000 **
–	–	≥.60	≥.50	1:1–2:1	5,000–50,000
–	3	–	–	–	–
–	–	–	–	–	–

NORMAL VITAL SIGN VALUES

DOGS

Body temperature: 100.5 to 101.5°F (if taken at home when at rest, slightly higher in a veterinarian's office, but not above 101.8°). This range for normal temperature is more restricted than most veterinarians use, but is a more accurate guide based on considerable experience with "fever" cases.

Pulse: 70 to 120 beats per minute (at rest, higher after physical exertion or if excited or frightened). The lower rate is normal in large dogs; higher rate in small dogs.

Respiratory rate: 10 to 30 breaths per minute (at rest, higher after physical exertion or if excited or frightened). Generally faster in smaller animals.

CATS

Body temperature: 100.5 to 101.5°F (see qualifications as given for dog values, above).

Pulse: 110 to 130 beats per minute (same qualifications as for dogs, above).

Respiratory rate: 20 to 30 breaths per minute.

PARTS OF A DOG AND CAT

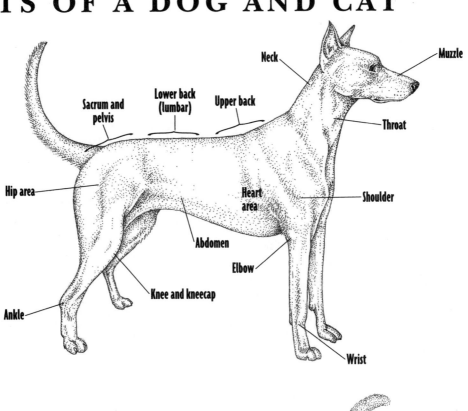

Neck
Muzzle
Lower back (lumbar)
Upper back
Sacrum and pelvis
Throat
Hip area
Heart area
Shoulder
Abdomen
Elbow
Knee and kneecap
Ankle
Wrist

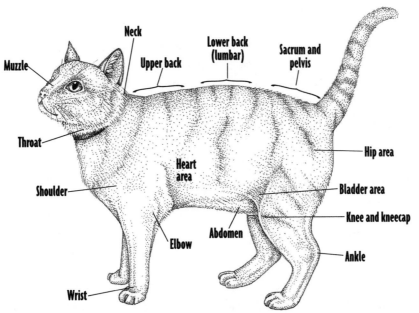

Neck
Muzzle
Upper back
Lower back (lumbar)
Sacrum and pelvis
Throat
Hip area
Heart area
Shoulder
Bladder area
Abdomen
Knee and kneecap
Elbow
Ankle
Wrist

ENDNOTES

CHAPTER 2

R. L. Wysong, DVM. *DVM Magazine,* June 1987, p. 50.

Robert Abady. *The State of Animal Nutrition.* 1988, p. 3.

Ann N. Martin. *Food Pets Die For* (Oregon: New Sage Press, 1997), pp. 63–68.

David A. Dzanis, DVM, PhD, Dipl. ACVN. "Understanding Nutritional Requirements of Dogs, Cats." *DVM Best Practices,* April 2002, p. 4.

Orville Schell. "The Meat Inspector." *Alicia Patterson Foundation Reporter,* February 1981, vol. 4, no. 1, p. 10.

In Town, vol. 3, no. 4, April 1993, p. 9.

Earth Island Journal, Summer 1996, vol. 11, no. 3, pp. 27–31.

Francis M. Pottenger. "Pottenger's Cats: A Study in Nutrition." *DVM Magazine,* March 1985, p. 73.

Duff Wilson. *Fateful Harvest* (Harper Publishers, 2001).

Marc Lappé. *Chemical Deception: The Toxic Threat to Health and the Environment* (San Francisco: Sierra Club Books, 1991), p. 7.

CHAPTER 3

The Reuter European Business Report (London). April 28, 2000.

Tom Buddig. "Mad Cows, Mad Dogs, and Canadians." *PHXnews* (Phoenix). December 28, 2003.

Denise Grady. "Mad Cow Quandary: Making Animal Feed." *New York Times,* February 6, 2004.

Michael Greger, M.D. "American Beef Supply at Risk." Report on the Canadian mad cow crisis by for the Organic Consumers Association, as found at www.organicconsumers.org/madcow03.htm. May 21, 2003.

William R. Quesnell. *Minerals, the Essential Link to Health* (La Mesa, California: Skills Unlimited Press, 2000), p. 57.

CHAPTER 7

Information from "Are Spot-On Flea Killers Safe?" by Kathleen Dudley. *Whole Dog Journal,* February 2002, pp. 18–22.

CHAPTER 14

Helen Caldicott, MD. *If You Love This Planet: A Plan to Heal the Earth* (W. W. Norton & Company, 2002).

Marc Lappé. *Chemical Deception: The Toxic Threat to Health and the Environment* (San Francisco: Sierra Club Books, 1991).

Paul Devereaux et al. *Earthmind: Communicating with the Living World of Gaia* (Rochester, Vermont: Destiny Books, 1989), p. 20.

Lyall Watson. *Beyond Supernature* (New York: Bantam Books, 1988), p. 39. For a discussion of the experiments see pp. 37–38.

INDEX

Underscored page references indicate boxed text and tables.

Boldface references indicate illustrations.

needs of, 207
nutrients needed by, 21–22, 54, 55, 56, 58–59,
59, 101
oils for, 117
outdoor vs. indoor, 205–7
recipes for (*see* Recipes)
vegetarian diet for, 100, 101
Cat scratch fever, 217
Cat Weight Loss Diet, 421
Checkup
for choosing pet, 161–62
how to perform, <u>114</u>
Chemical contamination
of commercial pet foods
effects of, 26–28
sources of, 24–26
of meats, 34
Children
helping, after death of pet, 236–37
pet care and, 232
Chiropractic, 260–62
Choosing a pet. *See* Pet selection
Chorea, 335
Chronic encephalitis, causing aggression in dogs, 203
Cleaning products, safe, 142–43
Cleaning techniques
bathing, 124–25
for removing discharges, 277–79
Cleanliness
for flea control, 127–28
for housebreaking, 212–13
for preventing disease transmission, 215
for removal of toxins, 122–23
Cleft palate, in cats, 159
Cod liver oil, vitamin A in, 57
Cold extracts, herbal, 438–39
Colds. *See* Upper respiratory infections
Collapse, first aid for, 437
Collars, cat, 207
Commands for dogs, teaching, 198–99, 202
Commercial pet foods
additives in, 22–24
alternative to (*see* Natural diet)
health effects from, 18–19, 310
inadvertent chemical contamination of
effects of, 26–28
sources of, 24–26
ingredients in
carbohydrates, 11
fats, 12
fiber, 12
protein, 10–11

life energy missing from, 19–20
for maintenance of health, 88
misleading labels on, 10–13
objections to, 16
story illustrating, 14–15
poor quality of, 16–18
reason for odor of, 19
toxins in, 145
vitamins and minerals in, 13–14
Compresses, herbal, 439–40
Conditioner, rosemary, 125
Congenital defects. *See* Birth defects
Constipation
enema for, 275
in kittens and puppies, 96
in traveling pets, 225
treatment of, 320–22, 324–25
Contemporary medicine, vs. holistic therapies,
252–53, 255–56
Convulsions, first aid for, 432–33
Corneal ulcers, 344–45
Cortisone
origin of, 247
problems with, 249, 288, 289, 292, 389
Cottage Cheese Supplement for Dog Kibble, 64
Crates. *See* Carriers
Crude protein, in commercial pet foods, 11
Cryptorchidism, in cats, 159
Cushing's Disease, 322–23
Cuts, first aid for, 433
Cysteine, for cats, 59
Cystitis. *See* Bladder problems

D

Dairy products in natural diet, 38, 39
Deafness, in cats, 159
Death of pet
author's experience with, 233–34
care before
home, 239
homeopathic, 240–41
hospital, 238–39
physical, 240
challenges of, 235
from euthanasia, 237–38
guilt over, 237
handling grief from, 236
helping children after, 236–37
Declawing, of cats, 210
Decoctions, herbal, 439

Dehydration, enema for, 277
Demodectic mange, 216, 385–87
Dental problems, 323–24
    from accidents, 324
    congenital or developmental, 324–25
    periodontal disease, 325–27
    tooth decay, 327
Dermatitis. *See also* Skin problems
    in cats, 296
Diabetes, 327–29
Diarrhea
    causes of, 330
    clinical features of, 329–30
    in newborns, 96, 378–79
    treatment of, 330–32
Di-calcium phosphate, calcium in, 52
Diet(s). *See also* Natural diet; Special diets
    for allergies, 297–99, 300
    avoiding toxic chemicals in, 145–46
    after dental treatment, 326–27
    for epilepsy, 342
    for kidney problems, 364, 365
    for weight loss, 419–21
Digestibility of protein, 10
Discharges
    cleaning, in sick animals, 277–79
    from healing progress, 291–92, 443
Diseases. *See specific diseases*
Disease susceptibility, factors
                contributing to
    emotional stress, 245–46
    missing nutrients, 247–48
    toxins, 242–45
    underlying illness, 246–47
Disease transmission
    from bites and scratches, 217–18
    preventing, 213–14
    from skin and hair contact, 215–17
    from wastes, 214–15
Dislocation of kneecap, 304
Distemper
    canine, 332–35
    feline, 335
Distemper vaccines, 416
Dog allergy diets, 298–99
Dog Biscuits Deluxe, 446, <u>450–51</u>
Dog bites, 192, 203–5
Doggie Oats, 65–66
Dog Loaf, 70
Dogs. *See also* Puppies
    anatomy of, **453**
    behavioral patterns in, <u>164–77</u>

behavior problems in
    aggression, 203–5
    barking, 201–3
birth defects in, 157–58, <u>164–77</u>
caloric needs of, <u>87</u>
confining, to property, 193–95
emotional needs of, 195–96
feeding schedule for, 113
housebreaking, 212–13
ideal food for, 85–87
identification for, 195, 225
illnesses and diseases in (*see specific conditions*)
as omnivores, 98
recipes for (*see* Recipes)
separation anxiety in, 196
sizes of (*see* Dog sizes)
social needs of, 196
special diets for, 90, <u>92</u>, 93, 100
training (*see* Dog training)
walking, 194–95, 225
Dog sizes
    criteria for, 292
    herb use based on, <u>118</u>
Dog training
    assuming leadership role in, 196–98
    general guidelines for, 199–201
    teaching commands in, 198–99, 202
Dog Weight Loss Diet 1, 419–20
Dog Weight Loss Diet 2, 420–21
Drugs. *See* Medications
Dust, toxins in, 136–37
Dying pet, care for
    at home, 239
    homeopathic, 240–41
    in hospital, 238–39
    physical, 240
Dysentery. *See* Diarrhea
Dystocia (difficult delivery), 376–78

E

Ear discharges, cleaning, 278–79
Ear mites, 340–41
Ear problems, 337
    "allergy ears," 337–38, 341
    relating to anatomy, 339
        ear mites, 340–41
        trapped foxtails, 339–40
        water in the ear canal, 339
Eclampsia, 376
Eczema. *See* Skin problems

Egg(s)
  and Grain, Easy, 105
  in natural diet, 38–39
  Quick Canine Oats and, 72
  Quick Feline Eggfest, 83
  Supplement for Dog Kibble, Fresh, 64
Eggshell powder, calcium in, 52
Elbow, arthritis of, 304
Electric cords, as pet hazard, 232
Electromagnetic effects on health, 147–48
Emergencies
  breathing and heart both stopped, 431–32, **431**
  breathing stopped, 430–31
  burns, 432
  car accidents, 432
  convulsions, 432–33
  cuts, 433
  fractures, 433
  gunshot wounds, 433–34
  heart stopped, 434, **434**
  heat stroke, 434–35
  hemorrhage, 435
    pressure bandage technique for, 436–37, **436**
  insect bites, 435
  poisoning, 435–36
  preparing for, 429
  puncture, 437
  shock, 437
  sudden collapse, 437
  supplies for, 429–30
Emotional factors in pet illnesses
  example of, 184–85
  human emotions, 187–89
  loss or change, 186–87
  patterns in, 185–86
Emotional needs of dogs, 195–96
Emotional stress
  lowering natural resistance, 245–46
  supplements for, 224
Encephalitis, chronic, causing aggression in dogs, 203
Enemas, 275, 276–77
Entropion, 345
Environmental hazards
  electromagnetic energies, 147–48
  preventing birth defects from, 156–57, 160
  protection against, 148–49, <u>150–51</u>
  toxins as (*see* Toxins)
Epilepsy, 341–43
Essential fatty acids, 54–57
Estrogen, contaminating meat, 34

Euthanasia
  considerations for, 237–38
  homeopathy and, 240
  of unwanted animals, 193, 220
Exercise, 120–21, 225
External Heart Massage Technique, 431, 434, **434**
Eye discharges, cleaning, 278
Eye problems
  cataracts, 343–44
  congenital, 158, 159
  corneal ulcers, 344–45
  inflammation, 345
  ingrowing eyelids, 345
  injuries, 345
  irritation, from travel, 226

F

Falls, preventing, 232
Fasts
  bone, 45
  for introducing new foods, 111–12
  for sick animals
    break-in period, 274
    force-feeding for breaking, 275–76
    with liquid diet, 274–75
    transition diet for breaking, 275
Fats
  in commercial pet foods, 12
  in ideal pet foods, 85–87
  in meats, <u>449</u>
Fatty Feline Fare, 82
Feeding amounts, guidelines for, 62, 87, 90, 93
Feeding schedule
  for dogs and cats, 113
  for kittens, <u>95</u>
Feline calicivirus, 411
Feline Feast, 78–79
Feline immunodeficiency virus (FIV), 346–47
Feline infectious peritonitis (FIP), 347–49, 413
Feline leukemia (FELV), 347, 350–52
Feline leukemia vaccine, 413, 416
Feline panleukopenia, 335–37
Feline panleukopenia vaccine, 416
Feline urologic syndrome. *See* Bladder problems
Feline viral rhinotracheitis, 409–11
FELV, 347, 350–52
Fencing, for confining dogs, 194
Fever, fasting for, 273
Fiber, in commercial pet foods, 12
Finicky eaters, 110

FIP, 347–49, 413
First aid. *See* Emergencies
Fish
    essential fatty acids in, 56
    taurine in, 59
FIV, 346–47
Flavorings in natural diet, 49–50
Flea-control products
    ingredients in, 125–27, 130–33
    safety concerns about, 243–44
Fleas, 124, 215, 384–85
    anemia from, 302–3
    safe control of, 124, 125, 127–29, 134
Flower essences, 270–71, 283
Fluoride, as toxic, 145, 146
Food allergies, 50, 116–17, 250, 297
    diets for identifying, 297–99
Force-feeding
    for appetite loss, 275–76
    with Pet Puree, 276
Formaldehyde, 138–39
Formulas, for orphaned kittens and puppies, 93–96
    nutritional composition of, 106–7
Foxtails, 124, 153, 339–40, 352–53
Fractures, first aid for, 433
Free-roaming pets, hazards to, 192–93
Fresh Egg Supplement for Dog Kibble, 64
Fresh Meat Supplement for Dog Kibble, 63
Fruit, as snack, 48

G

Garlic
    for easing switch to natural diet, 117–18
    as flavoring, 49
Gastric dilation (bloat), 399–402
Gastritis
    acute, 395–98
    chronic, 398–99
Gelatin capsules, herbal, 439
Grains in natural diet, 39–40, 40
Grief, from death of pet, 235, 236
Grooming, 123–25
Guilt, over death of pet, 237
Gunshot wounds, first aid for, 433–34

H

Hair abnormalities, in cats, 159
Hair balls, in cats, 159

Hair contact, diseases from, 215–17
Hair loss, 353
Hash, Quick Canine, 74
Hazards
    environmental (*see* Environmental hazards)
    in home, 231–32
Healing crisis, 110, 115–16
Healing discharges, 291–92, 443
Health problems. *See also specific health problems*
    causes of, 242–43
    expectations of recovery from, 288–89
    guide to treatments for, 287–88
    healing discharges when treating, 291–92, 443
    how to locate, in Quick Reference Section, 288
    signs of progress in treating, 289–91, 292, 443
    underlying, lowering natural resistance, 246–47
Healthy Powder
    ingredients in, 52–53
        analysis of, 54–55
    recipe for, 53–54
Heart Massage Technique, External, 431, 434, **434**
Heart problems, 353–56
Heart stopped
    with breathing stopped, first aid for, 431–32, **431**
    first aid for, 434, **434**
Heartworms, 356–59
Heat stroke, 225, 434–35
Heavy metals, contaminating pet foods, 25–26
Hemorrhage
    first aid for, 435
    pressure bandage technique for, 436–37, **436**
Hepatitis, 368–69
Herbal medicines, 7–8, 259–60. *See also* Herbs
    administering, 281–83
    for illnesses and diseases (*see specific conditions*)
    preparing, 280–81
    schedules for, 438–40
Herbs. *See also* Herbal medicines
    added to pet food, 43–44
    dried, 280
    for easing switch to natural diet, 117–18, 118
    fresh, 279–80
    obtaining, 284, 287–88
    in tinctures, 280
Hering's Law of Cure, 290–91
Hernias
    in cats, 159
    in dogs, 158
Hip dysplasia, 158, 304, 359–61
Holistic therapies
    author's introduction to, 6–8
    vs. contemporary medicine, 252–53, 255–56

determinants of success with, 271
healing perspective in, 253–55
how to practice, 256–57
modern physics supporting, 256
specific
    acupuncture and Oriental medicine,
      262–63
    chiropractic and other manual therapies,
      260–62
    flower essences, 270–71
    herbal medicine, 259–60
    homeopathy, 263–70, 266
    naturopathy, 257–59
Home care
for dying pet, 239
for sick pet, 272–73
Homeopathic treatment
administering, 283
author's involvement in, 263–64
avoiding, with prescription drugs, 273
cases treated with, 267–69
for dying animal, 240–41
for emergencies, 429–30
evaluating response to, 443
for illnesses and diseases (see specific conditions)
obtaining, 283, 284, 287–88
preparation of medicines in, 265–66, 266
principles of, 264–67
research on, 269–70
schedule for
    for acute disease, 441–42
    for chronic disease, 442
used alone, 287
Home remedy kit, 283–84, 288
Hookworms, 214, 423, 425, 428
Hospital care
for dying pet, 238–39
for sick pet, 273
Hot spots, 390
Housebreaking issues, 212–13
Hyperthyroidism, 297, 403–5
Hypothyroid conditions, 402–3

I

Iatrogenic diseases, 249
Identification for pets, 195, 207, 225
Illnesses. See also Health problems;
    specific conditions
underlying, lowering natural resistance, 246–47
Immune system, factors weakening, 8, 246–47

Inbreeding, 155, 160
Infectious enteritis, 335–37
Infectious peritonitis, 347–49
Inflammatory bowel disease, 297
Infusions, herbal, 438
Ingrowing eyelids, 345
Insect bites, first aid for, 435
Intervertebral disk disease, 374–75
Invisible electric fences, for confining dogs, 194

J

Jaundice, 361
Juices, in liquid fasts, 274

K

Kennel cough, 222, 407–8
Kennel stays, 222–23
Kibble booster mixes, 62–63
    Cottage Cheese Supplement for Dog Kibble, 64
    Fresh Egg Supplement for Dog Kibble, 64
    Fresh Meat Supplement for Dog Kibble, 63
Kidnappings, 193
Kidney failure, 361–62
canine diet for, 364
crisis therapy for, 367
feline diet for, 365
symptoms of, 362
treating, 362, 366–67
Kidney missing, in cats, 159
Kitten Formula, 94–95
Kittens
feeding schedule for, 95
flea treatment in, 302–3
orphaned
    diarrhea and constipation in, 96
    feeding, 93–95
Kitty Catnip Cookies, 447, 450–51
Kitty or Doggie Crunchies, 445, 450–51
Kneecap dislocation, 304

L

Labels, on commercial pet foods, 10–13
Lead exposure, 25–26, 34, 137
Legumes in natural diet, 40–41, 41
Leptospirosis, 214–15
Leukemia, feline, 347, 350–52
vaccine for, 413, 416

Lice, 385
Licenses, dog, 195
Lifestyle of modern pets vs. wild ancestors, 120
Limb defects, in cats, 159
Linoleic acid, 54–55, 56
Linolenic acid, 56
Liquid diet, for fasting, 111, 274–75
Liquid medications, how to give, 281–82
Liquid vitamin A and D, 57
Litter box, for car travel, 225
Litter box problems, 207–8
Liver Brownies, 448, 450–51
Liver problems, 367–69
Lost pets
    euthanized, 193
    finding, 195, 229–31
    from moving, 228
Lyme disease, 369–71

M

Mackerel Loaf, 81
Mad Cow Disease, 36–37, 371
Mammary gland abnormalities, in cats, 159
Mange, 216, 385–87
Meats
    increased consumption of, 97
    in natural diet
        advantages and disadvantages of, 33–35
        fat content of, 449
        Mad Cow Disease and, 36–37, 371
        protein, fat, and carbohydrate content of, 86
        selecting and preparing, 35–36
        storing, 37–38
    production of, 99–100
Meat Supplement for Dog Kibble, Fresh, 63
Medications
    avoiding homeopathic treatment with, 273
    herbal treatments with, 273
    liquid, how to give, 281–82
    side effects of, 249–50
    solid, how to give, 282–83
    superficial effects of, 255–56
Metritis, 381–82
Mexi-Dog Casserole, 104
Micro-chip, for identification, 195
Milk, mother's, formulas replacing, 93–96
Milk products in natural diet, 38, 39
Millet, Beans 'n', 108
Minerals
    in commercial pet foods, 13–14
    for pollution protection, 146

Mini Doggie Oats, 66
Mites, ear, 340–41
Mosquitoes, West Nile virus from, 422
Motion sickness, 225–26
Mouth problems, congenital, 324–25
Moving, preparing pet for, 228–29

N

Nail trimming, in cats, 210–11
Natural diet, 28
    basic food groups in
        eggs and dairy products, 38–39
        grains, 39–40
        legumes, 40–41
        meats, 33–38
        vegetables, 42–44
    best ingredient choices for, 44, 46–47
    of European pets, 15
    flavorings in, 48
        garlic, 48
        yeast sprinkle, 48–49
    how to use, 31–32
        principles for, 32–33
    introducing
        animals' resistance to, 109–10
        cleansing reactions from, 110, 113–14
        feeding schedule for, 113
        healing crisis from, 110, 115–16
        herbs for help with, 117–18, 118
        interpreting reactions to, 116–17
        methods of, 110–13
    recipes for (see Recipes)
    snacks in
        biscuits, 48
        bones, 44–45
        fruit, 48
        nuts and seeds, 48
        veggie burgers, 48–49
    success stories about, 29–30
    supplements with (see Supplements)
Naturopathy, 257–59
Nausea, from travel, 225–26
Neighbor relations, pets affecting, 190–92
Nervousness, during travel, 226
Nervous system disorders, in dogs, 157–58
Neutering. See Spaying and neutering
Newborn care, 378–79. See also Kittens; Puppies
Nose, cleaning discharges from, 277
Nosodes, homeopathic, 414–15
Nutrient deficiencies, lowering natural resistance,
    247–48

Nutrition. *See also* Diet(s); Natural diet; Special
    diets
  animals' quick response to, 10
  author's interest in, 3–4, 5, 6
  importance of, 8
Nutritional standards, in recipes, 85–87
Nuts, as snack, 48

O

Oats
  Beefy, 75
  Doggie, 65–66
  for easing switch to natural diet, 118
  and Eggs, Quick Canine, 72
  Mini Doggie, 66
  Quick Canine Oatmeal, 73
Obesity, 419–21
Oils
  for cats, 117
  as supplement, 54–57
Omega-3 fatty acids, 56
Omega-6 fatty acids, 54–55, 56
One-on-One recipe for dogs, 71–72
Oriental medicine, 262–63
Orphaned kittens and puppies, feeding, 93–96
Overpopulation problem, 193, 218–20

P

Pancreatitis, 372–74
Panleukopenia, feline, 335–37
Paralysis, 374–75
Parasites
  ear mites, 340–41
  skin (*see* Skin parasites)
  worms (*see* Worms)
Parvo vaccine, 416
Periodontal disease, 325–27
Pesticides
  contaminating pet foods, 25
  exposure to, 140
  on produce, 43
  safer alternatives to, 141, 143–44
Pet foods. *See* Commercial pet foods; Natural diet
Pet Puree, for force-feeding, 276
Pet selection
  based on behavioral patterns and birth defects
      in cats, 178–83
  based on behavioral patterns and birth defects
      in dogs, 164–77

considerations for
    genetic characteristics, 152–53
    health assessment, 161–62
    lifestyle and preferences of owner, 162–63
Pet-sitting, 223–24
Pills and capsules, how to give, 282–83
Poisoning. *See also* Toxins
  causes of, 144–45, 232
  first aid for, 435–36
  of free-roaming pets, 193
Polenta for Cats, 192
Polenta for Dogs, 103
Pollution
  in food, 145–46
  indoor air, 138–39
  precautions against, 141–42, 146, 150–51
  water, 146–47
Pottenger Cat Studies, 21
Poultry Delight, 80
Pregnancy, 375–76
Pressure-treated wood, toxins in, 139–40
Protein
  in commercial pet foods, 10–11
  in ideal pet foods, 85–87
Pulse, normal values for, 452
Punctures, first aid for, 437
Puppies
  orphaned
      diarrhea and constipation in, 96
      feeding, 93–94, 95–96
  predicting adult size of, 91
Puppy Formula, 95–96
Pyometra, 381

Q

Quick Canine Hash, 74
Quick Canine Oatmeal, 73
Quick Canine Oats and Eggs, 72
Quick Feline Eggfest, 83
Quick Feline Meatfest, 84
Quick Reference Section, how to use, 287–92

R

Rabies, 217, 218, 379–80
Rabies vaccine, 203–4, 416–17
Radiation toxicity, 380
  protection against, 146
Radon, 139
Raw foods, 20–21

Toys, 121
Training cats, 209–10
Training dogs. *See* Dog training
Transporting pets, in carrier, <u>211</u>, 212, 225, 226–27
Travel
    with pets
        on airplane, 226–27
        basic guidelines for, 224–26
        motel and campground stays during, 227–28
    without pet
        kennel stays during, 222–23
        pet-sitting during, 223–24
Treats. *See* Snacks and treats
Tumors, breast, 316–17

U

Udo's Choice, 56
Ulcers, corneal, 344–45
Unconsciousness, first aid for, 437
Underweight, 421
Upper respiratory infections
    canine infectious tracheobronchitis, 407–8
    feline calicivirus, 407, 411
    feline viral rhinotracheitis, 407, 409–11
Uremia. *See* Kidney failure

V

Vacations. *See* Travel
Vaccinations
    aggressive behavior after, 203–4
    allergies and, 297, 300
    alternatives to, 414–16
    avoiding, with feline immunodeficiency virus, 347
    distemper, 416
    feline leukemia, 413
    feline panleukopenia, 416
    harmful effects of, 413–14
    hip dysplasia and, 360–61
    ineffectiveness of, 412–13
    kennel requirements for, 222–23
    Lyme disease, 371
    origin of, 247
    parvo, 416
    purpose of, 411–12
    rabies, 203–4, 416–17
Vegecat, taurine in, 59, 101
Vegetable broth, in liquid fasts, 274
Vegetable juices, in liquid fasts, 274
Vegetables in natural diet, 42–43
    home-grown, 43–44

Vegetarianism
    health benefits from, 97–98
    for pets, 96, 100–101
    reasons for practicing, 99–100
Vegetarian recipes. *See* Recipes, vegetarian
Veggie burgers, as snack, 48–49
Veterinarians, holistically oriented, 287
Veterinary medicine, conventional, limitations of, 5–6, 247, 248–49
Vital sign values, normal, 452
Vitamins
    in commercial pet foods, 13
    for pollution protection, 146
    recommended, 57–58
Vomiting, 417–18

W

Walks, for dogs, 194–95, 225
Warts, 418–19
Waste matter
    cleaning up, 213
    diseases transmitted in, 214–15
    hazards from, 193, 213
Water
    in ear canal, 339
    in liquid fasts, 274
    toxins in, 145, 146–47
Weight Loss Diet, for cats, 421
Weight Loss Diet 1, for dogs, 419–20
Weight Loss Diet 2, for dogs, 420–21
Weight problems
    obesity, 419–21
    underweight, 421
West Nile virus, 422
Wheat-germ oil, vitamin E in, 58
Wheat grass, growing, 43
Wheat or Rye Crisps for Dogs, 444, <u>450–51</u>
Whipworms, 423
Worms, 422–28
    heartworms, 356–59
    hookworms, 214, 423, 425, 428
    roundworms, 214, 423–25, 428
    tapeworms, 215, 422–23, 425–26
    whipworms, 423

Y

Yarn, as cat hazard, 232
Yeast sprinkle, 49–50